WITHDRAWN

LOWER GENITAL TRACT NEOPLASIA

RCOG Press

Since 1973 the Royal College of Obstetricians and Gynaecologists has regularly convened Study Groups to address important growth areas within obstetrics and gynaecology. An international group of eminent scientists and clinicians from various disciplines is invited to present the results of recent research and to take part in in-depth discussions. The resulting volume, containing the papers presented and also edited transcripts of the discussions, is published within a few months of the meeting and provides a summary of the subject that is both authoritative and up-to-date.

SUPER ARDUA

Some previous Study Group publications available

Infertility
Edited by A.A. Templeton and J.O. Drife

Intrapartum Fetal Surveillance
Edited by J.A.D. Spencer and R.H.T. Ward

Early Fetal Growth and Development
Edited by R.H.T. Ward, S.K. Smith and D. Donnai

Ethics in Obstetrics and Gynaecology
Edited by S. Bewley and R.H.T. Ward

The Biology of Gynaecological Cancer
Edited by R. Leake, M. Gore and R.H.T. Ward

Multiple Pregnancy
Edited by R.H.T. Ward and M. Whittle

The Prevention of Pelvic Infection
Edited by A.A. Templeton

Screening for Down Syndrome in the First Trimester
Edited by J.G. Grudzinskas and R.H.T. Ward

Problems in Early Pregnancy: Advances in Diagnosis and Management
Edited by J.G. Grudzinskas and P.M.S. O'Brien

Gene Identification, Manipulation and Treatment
Edited by S.K. Smith, E.J. Thomas and P.M.S. O'Brien

Evidence-based Fertility Treatment
Edited by A.A. Templeton, I.D. Cooke and P.M.S. O'Brien

Fetal Programming: Influences on Development and Disease in Later Life
Edited by P.M.S. O'Brien, T. Wheeler and D.J.P. Barker

Hormones and Cancer
Edited by P.M.S. O'Brien and A.B. MacLean

The Placenta: Basic Science and Clinical Practice
Edited by J.C.P. Kingdom, E.R.M. Jauniaux and P.M.S. O'Brien

Disorders of the Menstrual Cycle
Edited by P.M.S. O'Brien, I.T. Cameron and A.B. MacLean

Infection and Pregnancy
Edited by A.B. MacLean, L. Regan and D. Carrington

Pain in Obstetrics and Gynaecology
Edited by A.B. MacLean, R.W. Stones and S. Thornton

Incontinence in Women
Edited by A.B. MacLean and L. Cardozo

Maternal Morbidity and Mortality
Edited by A.B. MacLean and J. Neilson

Lower Genital Tract Neoplasia

Edited by

Allan B MacLean and Albert Singer and Hilary Critchley

RCOG Press

It was not possible to refer all the material back to the authors or discussants but it is hoped that the proceedings have been reported fairly and accurately.

Hilary OD Critchley MD FRANZCOG FRCOG
Professor of Reproductive Medicine, University of Edinburgh, Room SU304, Centre for Reproductive Biology, The Chancellor's Building, University of Edinburgh, 49 Little France Crescent, Edinburgh EH16 4SB

Allan B MacLean MD FRCOG
Professor of Obstetrics and Gynaecology, Royal Free & University College Medical School, Royal Free Campus, Rowland Hill Street, Hampstead, London NW3 2PT, UK

Albert Singer PhD(Syd) DPhil FRCOG
Professor of Gynaecological Research, University of London, Department of Women's Health, The Whittington Hospital NHS Trust, St Mary's Wing, Highgate Hill, London N19 5NF

Published by the **RCOG Press** at the
Royal College of Obstetricians and Gynaecologists
27 Sussex Place, Regent's Park
London
NW1 4RG

www.rcog.org.uk

Registered Charity No. 213280

First published 2003

ISBN 1 900364 81 6

DECLARATION OF INTEREST

All contributors to the Study Group were invited to make a specific Declaration of Interest in relation to the subject of the Study Group. This was undertaken and all contributors complied with this request. Dr Cusick is an occasional consultant and grant-holder for Digene Corp.; Professor Herrington provides a specialist clinical opinion to Pathlore; Dr Richart is a consultant to Molecular Diagnostics and on the speakers bureau for Digene Corp., Cytyc Corp. and 3M Pharmaceuticals; Professor Singer is a consultant for Polartechnics Ltd (Australia); Professor Stanley is a consultant for Xenova, 3M Pharmaceuticals, GlaxoSmithKline and Merck Vaccines Research; Dr Tidy holds a patent using electrical impedance in the detection of intraepithelial neoplasia and is a member of the Advisory board of Maxia Pharmaceuticals; Professor Wilkinson is a consultant for Spectra and Welch Allyn and is on the Speakers Bureau of Cytyc Corp.

RCOG Editor: Sophie Leighton and Jane Moody
Index: Liza Furnival
Typeset by Karl Harrington, FiSH Books, London
Printed by Antony Rowe Ltd, 2 Whittle Drive, Highfield Industrial Estate, Eastbourne, East Sussex BN23 6QT

Contents

Back row (from left to right): Christopher Perrett, Malcolm Adams, Peter Sasieni, Sun-Kuie Tay, C Simon Herrington, John Shepherd, John Monaghan, Ralph Richart, Edward J Wilkinson, Euphemia McGoogan, Alastair Deery, Walter Prendiville, John Tidy

Front row (from left to right): Margaret Stanley, Ron Jones, Margaret Cruickshank, Albert Singer, Allan MacLean, Hilary Critchley, Mahmood Shafi, Alison Fiander

Participants

Malcolm Adams
Medical Director and Consultant Clinical Oncologist, Velindre Cancer Centre, Velindre Hospital, Whitchurch, Cardiff CF14 2TL, UK

Hilary OD Critchley
Professor of Reproductive Medicine, University of Edinburgh, Room SU304, Centre for Reproductive Biology, The Chancellor's Building, University of Edinburgh, 49 Little France Crescent, Edinburgh EH16 4SB, UK and Convenor of Study Groups, Royal College of Obstetricians and Gynaecologists, UK

Margaret E Cruickshank
Consultant and Senior Lecturer in Gynaecological Oncology, University of Aberdeen, Department of Obstetrics and Gynaecology, Foresterhill, Aberdeen AB9 2ZD

Jack Cuzick
Head of Department of Mathematics, Statistics and Epidemiology, Cancer Research UK, PO Box 123, 61 Lincoln's Inn Fields, London WC2A 3PX, UK

Alistair Deery
Consultant and Honorary Senior Lecturer in Histo/cytopathology, Department of Cytopathology, Royal Free Hospital, Pond Street, Hampstead, London NW3 2QG, UK

Alison N Fiander
Professor and Head of Department of Obstetrics and Gynaecology, University of Wales College of Medicine, Heath Park, Cardiff CF14 4XN, UK

C Simon Herrington
Professor of Pathology, University of Liverpool, Department of Pathology, Duncen Building, Royal Liverpool University Hospital, Daulby Street, Liverpool L69 3GA, UK

Ronald W Jones
Honorary Professor, University of Auckland and Gynaecologist, National Women's Hospital, Private Bag 921189, Auckland 3, New Zealand

Euphemia McGoogan
Senior Lecturer in Pathology and Associate Medical Director, Lothian University Hospitals NHS Trust, Royal Infirmary of Edinburgh, 51 Little France Crescent, Edinburgh EH16 4SA, UK

Allan B MacLean
Professor of Obstetrics and Gynaecology, Royal Free and University College Medical School, Royal Free Campus, Hampstead, London NW3 2PT, UK and Convenor of Study Groups, Royal College of Obstetricians and Gynaecologists, UK

John M Monaghan
(Retired) Senior Lecturer in Gynaecological Oncology, Northern Gynaecological Oncology Centre, Queen Elizabeth Hospital, Sheriff Hill, Gateshead, Tyne & Wear NE9 6SX, UK

Chris W Perrett
Non-Clinical Lecturer, Department of Obstetrics and Gynaecology, Royal Free and University College Medical School, Royal Free Campus, Hampstead, London NW3 2PT, UK

Walter Prendiville
Associate Professor and Consultant Gynaecologist, RCSI Department of Gynaecology, Coombe Hospital, Dublin 8, Ireland

Ralph M Richart
Professor of Pathology in Obstetrics and Gynecology and Vice Chairman for Anatomic Pathology, Columbia University College of Physicians and Surgeons, Sloane Hospital for Women, 630 West 168th Street, New York, NY 10032, USA

Peter Sasieni
Professor, Department of Epidemiology, Mathematics and Statistics, Cancer Research UK, Wolfson Institute of Preventive Medicine, Charterhouse Square, London EC1M 6BQ, UK

Mahmood I Shafi
Consultant Gynaecological Surgeon and Oncologist, Birmingham Women's Health Care NHS Trust, Metchley Park Road, Edgbaston, Birmingham B15 2TG, UK

John H Shepherd
Professor of Surgical Gynaecology and Consultant Gynaecological Surgeon and Oncologist, Barts and The London NHS Trust, St Bartholomew's Hospital, West Smithfield, London EC1A 7BE, UK

Albert Singer
Professor of Gynaecological Research, University of London, and Consultant Gynaecologist, Whittington Hospital, London N19 5NF, UK

Pat Soutter
Reader in Gynaecological Oncology, Queen Charlotte's & Chelsea Hospital, Du Cane Road, London W12 0HS, UK

Margaret A Stanley
Professor of Pathology, Cambridge University, Department of Pathology, Tennis Court Road, Cambridge CB2 1QP, UK

Tay Sun-Kuie
Associate Professor and Senior Consultant, Department of Obstetrics and Gynaecology, Singapore General Hospital, Outram Road, Singapore 169608

John Tidy
Senior Lecturer in Gynaecological Oncology, Obstetrics and Gynaecology, Section of Reproductive and Developmental Medicine, Division of Clinical Sciences (South), University of Sheffield, The Jessop Wing, Sheffield Teaching Hospitals Trust, Tree Root Walk, Sheffield S10 2SF, UK

Edward J Wilkinson
Professor and Vice Chairman, Department of Pathology, University of Florida College of Medicine, Division of Anatomic Pathology, PO Box 100275, Gainesville, Florida 32610-0275, USA

Additional contributors

Nicholas Coleman
Group Leader, Medical Research Council, MRC Cell Unit, MRC/Hutchison Research Centre, Hills Road, Cambridge CB2 2XZ, UK

Carol Louise Hanna
Consultant Clinical Oncologist, Velindre Hospital, Velindre Road, Whitchurech, Cardiff CF14 2TL, UK

Hui Kim-Man
Director, Division of Cell and Molecular Research, National Cancer Centre, Hospital Drive, Singapore

Stephen Man
Department of Virology, Heath Hospital, Cardiff CF14 4XN, UK

Narendra Pisal
Clinical Research Fellow, Department of Women's Health, Whittington Hospital, London N19 5NF, UK

Cinzia G Scarpini
Research Associate, University of Cambridge, Department of Pathology, Tennis Court Road, Cambridge CB2 1QP, UK

Preface

The ninth Study Group of the Royal College of Obstetricians and Gynaecologists was held in October 1981 on the theme of 'Preclinical neoplasia of the cervix'. Twenty-one years later another Study Group (the 44th) on a similar theme was convened, to see what progress had been made on the understanding and management of cervical, vulval, vaginal and perianal neoplasia.

The Group comprised epidemiologists, molecular biologists, pathologists, gynaecologists and gynaecological oncologists and a clinical oncologist. Twenty-one years ago, one page was devoted to the 'wart virus' and it is encouraging to see just how far our understanding of aetiology and molecular pathology has developed and that, in the future, management may be less dependent upon surgery and more likely to use vaccination, gene therapy or chemoradiation.

The topical and perhaps controversial areas of liquid-based cytology and the role of human papillomavirus screening are addressed. Inclusion of the content of discussion sessions provides an insight into the breadth of views held by the participants and identifies the issues for which there are still more questions than answers.

Finally, it is rather sobering to realise that most of the women who develop cancers of the lower genital tract will live in the developing world, where diagnosis and appropriate management tools are less readily available.

Allan MacLean
Albert Singer
Hilary Critchley

SECTION 1

HUMAN PAPILLOMAVIRUS AND THE LOWER GENITAL TRACT

Chapter 1

Epidemiology of lower genital tract neoplasia

Peter Sasieni

Apart from some extremely rare tumours, lower genital tract neoplasia can occur in the cervix, the vulva or the vagina. At all three sites, there are both invasive cancers and non-invasive intraepithelial neoplasia, although the relationship between the two is quite different depending on the site. Neoplasia of the cervix is far more common than that of either the vulva or the vagina and it will be the focus of this chapter. Two issues dominate the epidemiology of cervical cancer: human papillomavirus (HPV) and cytological screening. A full account of screening is beyond the scope of this chapter, but it is important to appreciate the huge impact of screening in much of the developed world and the almost complete failure of screening in the developing world.

Descriptive epidemiology

Invasive cervical cancer rates have fallen in most countries over the last half-century.[1] Currently there are approximately half a million new cases each year.[2] The majority of cases are squamous cell carcinoma, but a significant and growing proportion are adeno- or adenosquamous carcinomas. Cervical cancer rates vary considerably between countries and even between different populations within a single country. Estimated rates in parts of Africa and Latin America are nine times higher than those in parts of the Middle East and in Singapore rates in Chinese women are twice those in Indian women (Table 1.1).[2] The age distribution of incident cervical cancer differs between countries and has also changed over time. Figure 1.1 shows the age-specific rates in England and Wales in 1972, 1985 and in 1997, as well as those for Shanghai (1978–82), Denmark (1983–87) and Cali, Colombia (1983–87). The reasons for these variations in pattern are the effects of changing sexual mores on the prevalence of HPV infection in different generations and the dramatic effect of cervical screening in some populations. In all populations, invasive cervical cancer is extremely rare in teenagers, and remains rare under the age of 30 years: rates in women over the age of 75 years are generally much higher than those of women in their twenties.

Incidence rates of vulval and vaginal cancer are much lower in all countries and the variation in rates between countries appears to be smaller (Table 1.1). In England and Wales, for instance, the cumulative risk of cervical cancer up to the age of 79 years was 1.4% in 1980–84, compared with 0.2% and 0.06% for vulval and vaginal cancers, respectively. Incidence rates for these rarer cancers rise exponentially with age and are extremely low under the age of 50 years (Figure 1.2).

Table 1.1. Age-standardised incidence rate of cancer of the cervix, vagina and vulva in different populations: 1988–1992[90]

Population	Age-standardised incidence rate per 100 000 women		
	Cervix	Vagina	Vulva
Los Angeles:			
Hispanic	17.9	0.5	1.0
Black	11.6	0.5	0.8
White (Non-Hispanic)	7.2	0.5	1.3
Harare:			
African	67.2	–	0.8[a]
European	10.4	–	0.9[a]
Israel:			
Jews	5.3	0.4	1.2
Non-Jews	3.0	0.4[a]	0.3[a]
Singapore:			
Chinese	16.3	0.5	0.5
Malay	11.1	0.3[a]	0.3[a]
Indian	8.6	0.3[a]	0.3[a]
Europe:			
Denmark	15.2	0.6	1.3
Finland	3.6	–	–
Eastern Germany	21.2	0.2	0.6
The Netherlands	7.1	0.4	1.3
Sweden	8.0	0.4	1.3
UK	12.5	0.4	1.5
Latin America:			
Colombia, Cali	34.4	1.2	0.8
Peru, Trujillo	53.5	0.9[a]	2.5

[a] rate based on fewer than ten cases

HPV and cervical cancer

Ever since Rigoni-Stern's groundbreaking observation of 1842[3] that whereas married women were more likely to die of cervical cancer than breast cancer, the reverse was true for nuns, it had been suspected that cervical cancer was caused by a sexually transmitted agent. It was another 150 years, however, before certain types of HPV were recognised as that causal agent.[4] The evidence linking HPV with cervical cancer is extremely strong and satisfies virtually all the epidemiological criteria for causality: strength, consistency and specificity of association, temporality of events, biological gradient, plausibility and experimental evidence. The ultimate test of causality will be whether vaccination against HPV can dramatically reduce the incidence of cervical neoplasia. Although such evidence does not yet exist, recent reports indicate that a prophylactic vaccine to HPV type 16 is able to prevent HPV infection in young women[5] and it must surely be only a matter of time before the effect of vaccination on cervical neoplasia is observed.

Strength of association

Numerous case–control and several cohort studies have demonstrated an extremely strong association between the presence of DNA from certain oncogenic types of HPV and cervical neoplasia. The relative risk of high-grade cervical neoplasia or cancer associated with testing positive for a high-risk HPV is typically between 20 and 200[6–11]

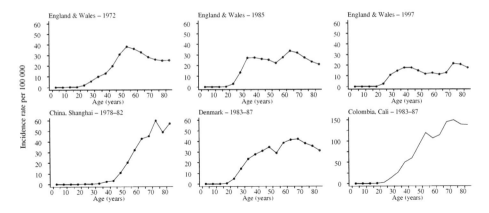

Figure 1.1 Cervical cancer incidence as a function of age in England and Wales (1972, 1985 and 1997), Denmark (1983–87), China (1978–82) and Colombia (1983–87); note the different vertical scale for Colombia

and even greater relative risks have been found in association with persistent HPV infection.[12] Studying a large international series of invasive squamous carcinomas of the cervix, Walboomers et al.[13] found HPV DNA in over 99% of biopsies, leading them to conclude that HPV was necessary for cervical cancer to develop. Other researchers have found HPV in over 95% of invasive cervical cancers and it is of only academic interest whether the negative findings in a small number of biopsies are due to failure to detect HPV DNA that is present, misclassification of the biopsy or the existence of a small number of cancers that are truly not associated with HPV infection.

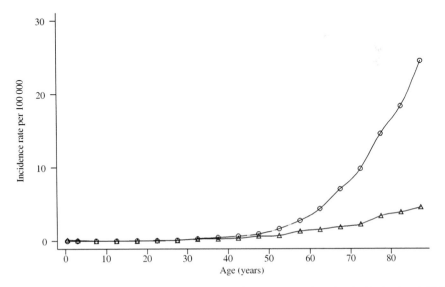

Figure 1.2 Age-specific incidence rates for cancer of the vulva and vagina in England and Wales (1980–1984) ———O——— Vulva ———△——— Vagina

Consistency of association

The strong association between high-risk HPV types and cervical cancer is seen in every population in which it has been studied. The International Agency for Research on Cancer (IARC) has carried out case–control studies in a number of countries in Latin America, Spain, Thailand, Philippines and Morocco, and has found an HPV prevalence of 78–98% in women with invasive cervical cancer and 6–22% in controls.[14]

HPV DNA is not found only in invasive cancer. In a systematic review of the literature, Cuzick et al.[15] reported HPV prevalence rates in high-grade pre-invasive cervical neoplasia (high-grade squamous intraepithelial lesions, HSILs, or cervical intraepithelial neoplasia, CIN, grade 2–3) of 70–90%. By comparison, prevalence rates in low-grade lesions were 20–50%, and 5–20% in women with normal cytology and no history of cervical neoplasia. Strong evidence of the association has been collected from North America, Central and South America, Northern Europe, Western Europe and China.

Specificity of association

Although many sexually transmitted diseases are associated with cervical cancer, the magnitude of the relationship is much less than for high-risk HPVs. Additionally, the low-risk anogenital HPVs (types 6 and 11) are associated with low-grade lesions (and warts) but not with high-grade CIN.[16] Thus it seems unlikely that the association is simply due to co-infection of HPV with some other agent that is the primary cause of the disease.

Temporality

One of the key elements for establishing causality is to demonstrate that the exposure precedes the disease. It is important, for instance, to show that HPV is not simply an opportunistic infection in women who have already developed early cervical neoplasia. Although the natural history of HPV infection and cervical neoplasia is not fully understood, several studies have elucidated the key stages. HPV is a sexually transmitted infection. In many countries, it is extremely common and infection within a few years of becoming sexually active is the norm.[17,18] Low-grade cervical disease can follow soon thereafter and high-grade disease is generally associated with persistent infection (Figure 1.3).

Rozendaal et al.[19] followed 1600 women, whose initial smear was either borderline or normal and found a relative risk of 71 for development of CIN2 or CIN3 associated with high-risk HPV on the initial smear. Case–control studies using stored sera from large cohorts have found HPV-16 antibodies present in sera taken a decade before the diagnosis of cervical cancer or high-grade CIN[20,21] with relative risks of between 4 and 13. Similarly, studies looking for HPV DNA in archival smears frequently find high-risk HPVs in smears taken five to ten years prior to diagnosis of CIN3 or invasive cervical cancer.[22,23]

Biological gradient

It is difficult to quantify a woman's exposure to high-risk HPVs, but one can quantify the viral load in an infected woman and the time over which HPV DNA is detectable. Kjaer et al.[12] tested over 10 000 women for high-risk HPV twice approximately two

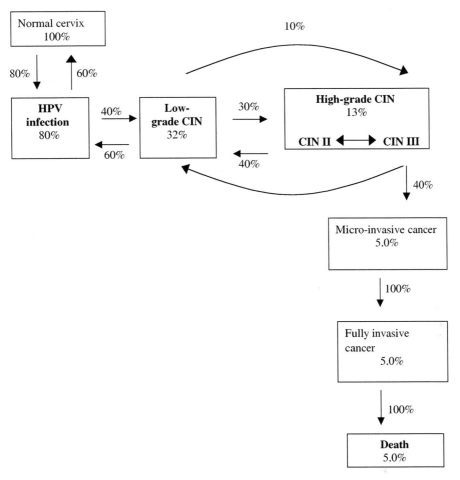

Figure 1.3 Flow chart of the natural history of cervical intraepithelial neoplasia (CIN); the percentages given are rough estimates of what might happen over the lifetime of women born in the UK during the second half of the 20th century in the absence of screening, vaccination and treatment; each box includes the percentage of the population who will reach that box; the percentages on the arrows between boxes refer to the proportion of women who reach a particular state (the starting box) who will either progress or regress (adapted from Sasieni, 2001[91] and reproduced with permission from Arnold); HPV = human papillomavirus

years apart. Although a single positive test was strongly associated with high-grade disease (OR 35), persistent infection with the same high-risk HPV type gave an odds ratio of 692 with a 95% confidence interval of 145 to 3000. Other studies[24,25] have suggested that viral load can be used as a surrogate for viral persistence, but extremely high viral loads do not seem to increase the risk of high-grade disease.[26]

Biological plausibility

The strong epidemiological evidence in favour of a causative role of HPV infection is supported by molecular studies, which have demonstrated that gene products from oncogenic HPV types block the action of tumour suppressor proteins. The HPV E6 protein binds the p53 gene product[27] and the E7 protein forms complexes with pRb.[28] Recent advances have led to a good understanding of the precise role of these two HPV gene products in the deregulation of cell cycle control as reviewed in other chapters of this book.

Although the evidence that HPV infection plays a critical role in cervical cancer development is overwhelming, definitive proof will come from HPV vaccines. Results reported in 2002 show conclusively that vaccines are able to prevent infection of young women with HPV-16 (see Chapter 20).[5] Time will tell whether this will be sufficient to reduce greatly the incidence of cervical cancer in vaccinated women.

Other risk factors

Although high-risk HPV infection seems to be necessary for development of cervical cancer, the vast majority of women infected will not develop cervical cancer. Figure 1.3 shows a flowchart with estimates of the proportions of the population who might be affected by the various stages of cervical neoplasia if the disease were allowed to take its natural course. Many of the proportions in the figure are approximate because of difficulties in observing the natural history. Nevertheless, it is clear that in the UK (and in many other countries) the majority of women will have been infected with a high-risk HPV by the age of 25 years,[17,18] but that at most 5% will develop invasive cervical cancer over the next 60 years (even in the absence of screening). The factors that determine who will develop invasive cancer and who will not are not fully understood, but they are clearly a mixture of genetic, environmental and random influences.

Genetics

The best epidemiological evidence of an inherited genetic influence in cervical cancer comes from a study of cervical cancer (mostly carcinoma *in situ*) in related individuals using Swedish national registries.[29] The relative risk for biological mothers of cases was 1.83 (95% CI 1.77–1.88) and for full sisters it was 1.93 (95% CI 1.85–2.01). By contrast, the relative risks for adoptive mothers and non-biological sisters were 1.10 (95% CI 0.76–1.54) and 1.15 (95% CI 0.82–1.57), respectively, and the relative risk for half-sisters was 1.45 (95% CI 1.31–1.60). Although the genes involved have not been identified, several groups have found associations between certain class II human leukocyte antigens (HLA), and the role of these genes should become clearer in the near future.

Immunosuppression

Although accounting for only a small proportion of cervical cancer in the population, immunosuppression is clearly responsible for a substantial increase in risk for affected women. Renal transplant patients on immunosuppressive therapy are at increased risk of cervical carcinoma[30] as are women who are HIV-seropositive.[31,32]

Smoking

Smoking and sexual behaviour are often correlated within populations, so that it is difficult to say whether the association found in most epidemiological studies between smoking and cervical cancer is causal or whether it is simply due to confounding.

However, smoking is still associated with cervical neoplasia (both CIN and invasive cancer) even after adjusting for standard measures of sexual behaviour, such as age at first sexual intercourse, number of sexual partners or even for HPV. Szarewski and Cuzick systematically review 11 cohort studies and 32 case–control studies that have addressed the association between cervical cancer and smoking.[33] The summary odds ratios for various groups of studies (defined by design and end-point) vary between 1.5 and 2.2 and are highly statistically significant. The International Agency for Research on Cancer (IARC) has carried out several case–control studies, primarily in developing countries, and analysed the results from the combined studies looking only at HPV-positive cases and controls.[34] This analysis (with far more cases than controls) yields a significant association (OR 2.0) and a dose–response effect, strongly suggesting that the relationship between smoking and cervical cancer is not simply due to confounding by HPV infection. A similar finding was obtained by Deacon et al.[35] in a nested case–control study in Manchester: the odds ratio for CIN3 in HPV-positive women was 2.6 (95% CI 1.5–4.5).

Epidemiological evidence of a different type comes from a study by Szarewski et al.[36] in which 81 smokers with an initial low-grade cervical lesion were encouraged to quit smoking and were followed closely for six months. After application of dilute acetic acid, the cervix was photographed at the beginning and end of the study in order to quantify any change in lesion size. The association between smoking cessation and change in lesion size was striking: 41% of those who stopped had no lesion at the end of the study, compared with 0% of those who continued to smoke; the lesion grew in 32% of those who did not cut back, compared with in 0% of those who stopped. Another prospective study[37] found that smoking was the only factor that influenced subsequent development of CIN3 ($n = 58$) or invasive cancer ($n = 10$) in a cohort of 1812 HPV-positive women who were followed for up to ten years.

Both cotinine and nicotine have been found in cervical mucus of smokers[38–40] and it is possible that this could have a direct carcinogenic effect on the cervix. Alternatively, smoking may play a role by suppressing the local immune response to HPV infection, although the details are as yet far from clear.

Oral contraceptives

It is extremely difficult to disentangle the confounding between oral contraceptives, sexual behaviour and barrier forms of contraception. IARC tried to remove the confounding by looking for the association only in HPV-positive women pooled from a number of case–control studies predominantly in developing countries.[14] Compared with never-users, women who had used oral contraceptives for less than five years did not have an increased risk of cervical neoplasia (OR 0.7; 95% CI 0.5–1.0). The odds ratio was 2.8 (95% CI 1.5–5.4) for five to nine years of use and 4.0 (2.1–8.0) for use for ten years or longer. Although this dose–response relationship is quite convincing, some caution is required in interpreting the results.[41] Most of the studies used hospital controls and it is therefore possible that the results could be confounded by any association between pill use and hospitalisation. Further, the questionnaire-based contraceptive history provided few details. There was, for instance, no distinction between oral and other types of hormonal contraception, nor between combined and progestogen-only preparations. It is also counterintuitive that there was no relationship between oral contraceptive use and HPV prevalence in the controls, particularly since others have found oral contraceptive use to be associated with HPV persistence in infected women.[42,43]

It should also be noted that the only cohort study to date following HPV-positive women found no relationship between oral contraceptive use and subsequent development of CIN3.[37]

Other factors

Other factors – reproductive, dietary and infectious – have been put forward as potential cofactors with HPV in the aetiology of cervical cancer, but the evidence is far from conclusive. IARC has found increasing parity[44] to be a significant risk factor in HPV-positive women. They also found that lack of circumcision in male partners of monogamous women was a significant risk factor for cervical cancer.[45] Fresh fruit and vegetables have sometimes been found to be associated with a decreased risk of cervical cancer,[46,47] but the results are not consistent.[48] Several groups have documented the association between *Chlamydia trachomatis* and cervical neoplasia.[49–53] The study by Wallin *et al.*[53] for instance, found evidence of *C. trachomatis* infection pre-dating HPV infection, but it is unclear whether chlamydia was simply a marker for greater exposure and/or vulnerability to HPV or whether infection *per se* makes future persistent HPV infection more likely.

Cervical screening

Dramatic decreases in cervical cancer rates following the introduction of screening have been seen in several industrialised countries. Age-standardised incidence of cervical cancer fell substantially between 1965 and 1980 in Denmark, Sweden and in Finland in particular, following the introduction of mass screening in the mid to late 1960s.[54] By contrast, rates in Norway, which was the only Nordic country without mass cervical screening, increased. UK rates have fallen by 50% in the last decade and this is primarily due to a well-organised screening programme with excellent population coverage.[55] Age-standardised mortality rates in England and Wales fell by between 1% and 2% per year from the mid-1950s until about 1986. Since then the decrease in mortality has accelerated[56] and is currently running at 4–5% per year (Figure 1.4). More sophisticated analyses suggest that the effect of organised screening has been to reduce cervical cancer mortality by about 50% in women aged 20–69 years.[57] The same analysis suggests that screening also has a substantial effect on adenocarcinoma of the cervix.[58] However, the conclusions are more dependent on the assumption that cohorts of women who have demonstrated extremely high rates of cervical cancer in their twenties and thirties would continue to have extremely high rates as they age.

Studies conducted in eight countries comparing the screening experience of women diagnosed with invasive cervical cancer with that of healthy controls demonstrated that cervical screening could be effective in identifying women at increased risk of developing cervical cancer.[59] Compared with women who had never been screened, women with two or more negative smears were 15 times less likely to develop cervical cancer within a year of having a negative test. The effect lasted several years but decreased with the time since the negative smear, so that after five to six years women were only three times less likely to develop cancer than those who had never been screened. A more recent study suggests a somewhat smaller effect and shorter duration of protection, suggesting that while screening was clearly hugely successful at a public health level, new developments would be required to eradicate the disease.[60] Other population-based case–control studies using medical records (rather than patient interviews) to obtain screening histories have obtained similar findings.[61–65]

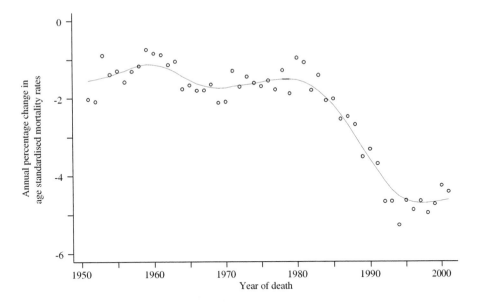

Figure 1.4 Annual percentage change in age-standardised mortality from cervical cancer, England and Wales 1950–2001; the data points are 11-year moving averages and the superimposed line is a moving average of the data points

Vulval and vaginal cancers

Cancers of the vulva and the vagina are uncommon malignancies in all parts of the world, with rates that increase almost exponentially with age (Figure 1.2). In 1998, there were 851 cases of vulval cancer and 165 cases of vaginal cancer in England, of which 55% and 41%, respectively, were in women over the age of 75 years. By contrast, there were 2594 cases of cervical cancer and 32 908 cases of breast cancer, only 16% of which were diagnosed at over 75 years of age. Over 80% of vulval cancers are squamous in origin, with 5–10% being melanomas. Age-standardised mortality rates from both cancers have fallen considerably in England and Wales since 1958: by 43% for vulval cancer (2.5–1.4/100 000) and by 66% for vaginal cancer (0.9–0.3/100 000). Analysis of age-specific trends shows that rates have declined by a similar percentage in all ages.[66] Trends in incidence rates for vulval and vaginal cancers show no clear patterns in England and Wales, but an increase in vulval cancer, predominantly in women under the age of 65 years, has been recorded in the USA.[67] Vulval intraepithelial neoplasia (VIN) is said to be more common than it was a generation ago,[68–71] but it is unclear to what extent this is due to more frequent biopsies and referrals to gynaecology departments in preference to dermatology departments, and to what extent it is a real increase mirroring that of HPV infection.

Little is known about the aetiology of these cancers because they are rare. Vulval cancer is more common in women of lower social class[72,73] and smoking appears to be a risk factor,[74–76] but the data are far from conclusive. Brinton *et al.*[74] found that 15% of 209 women with vulval cancer reported a history of genital warts, compared with 1.4% of 348 community controls. Using polymerase chain reaction, Hording *et al.*[77] detected HPV (types 16, 18 or 33) in 31% of 62 vulval cancers and none of 101 normal vulval specimens. Thus, although there is a significant association between HPV infection and vulval cancer, the relationship is less strong than it is with cervical cancer and the majority of vulval cancer cases are not caused by HPV infection. Another risk factor that has consistently been associated with vulval cancer is immunosuppression – invasive vulval cancer is significantly more common in women with renal transplants,[78] and both vulval cancer and VIN have increased incidence in HIV-seropositive women.[79–81]

It has been suggested that vulval cancer consists of two distinct diseases, with the HPV-related type primarily affecting women under the age of 65 years and a second type of unknown pathogenesis affecting older women.[82,83] In older women, keratinising squamous cell cancers arise in a background of non-neoplastic epithelial disorders such as lichen sclerosus and are not associated with HPV infection. Less commonly, invasive vulval cancer can arise from an area of HPV-related warty vulva or VIN, particularly in young women.[68]

Even less is known about the aetiology of vaginal cancer. It is more common in women with a previous positive cervical smear followed by negative histology[84] and there is one report of increased rates of vaginal cancer in alcoholics.[85] Vaginal cancer in adolescents is extremely rare and has been attributed to *in utero* exposure to diethylstilboestrol (DES), a synthetic oestrogen used to prevent spontaneous abortions between 1940 and 1970.[86–88] Teenage vaginal cancer is almost never diagnosed in cohorts who could not have been exposed to DES *in utero* (either because they were born prior to 1945 or because DES was never prescribed in that country). But even in those who were exposed, the risk of vaginal cancer is only about one in 1000 by the age of 30 years.[89]

References

1. Coleman MP, Esteve J, Damiecki P, Arslan A, Renard H, editors. *Trends in Cancer Incidence and Mortality.* IARC Scientific Publications No. 121. Lyons: International Agency for Research on Cancer; 1993.
2. Parkin DM. Global cancer statistics in the year 2000. *Lancet Oncol* 2001;2:533–43.
3. Stern R. Statistical facts about cancers on which doctor Rigoni-Stern based his contribution to the surgeon's subgroup of the IV Congress of the Italian scientists on 23 September 1842. *Giornale par service al Progressi della Terapeutica*, Series 2. 1842;2:507–17.
4. IARC Working Group. *IARC Monographs on the Evaluation of Carcinogenic Risks to Humans, Vol. 64, Human Papillomaviruses.* Lyons: International Agency for Research on Cancer; 1995. p. 88–9.
5. Koutsky LA, Ault KA, Wheeler CM, Brown DR, Barr E, Alvarez FB, *et al.* A controlled trial of a human papillomavirus type 16 vaccine. *N Engl J Med* 2002;347:1645–51.
6. Bosch FX, Munoz N, de Sanjose S, Navarro C, Moreo P, Ascunce N, *et al.* Human papillomavirus and cervical intraepithelial neoplasia grade III/carcinoma *in situ*: a case-control study in Spain and Colombia. *Cancer Epidemiol Biomarkers Prev* 1993;2:415–22.
7. Cuzick J, Szarewski A, Terry G, Ho L, Hanby A, Maddox P, *et al.* Human papilloma virus testing in primary cervical screening. *Lancet* 1995;345:1533–6.
8. Eluf-Neto J, Booth M, Munoz N, Bosch FX, Meijer CJ, Walboomers JM. Human papillomavirus and invasive cervical cancer in Brazil. *Br J Cancer* 1994;69:114–19.
9. Munoz N, Bosch FX, de Sanjose S, Tafur L, Izarzugaza I, Gili M, *et al.* The causal link between human papillomavirus and invasive cervical cancer: a population-based case-control study in Colombia and Spain. *Int J Cancer* 1992;52:743–9.
10. Schiffman MH, Bauer HM, Hoover RN, Glass AG, Cadell DM, Rush BB, *et al.* Epidemiologic evidence showing that human papillomavirus infection causes most cervical intraepithelial neoplasia. *J Natl Cancer Inst* 1993;85:958–64.
11. Van den Brule AJ, Walboomers JM, Du Maine M, Kenemans P, Meijer CJ. Difference in prevalence of human papillomavirus genotypes in cytomorphologically normal cervical smears is associated with a history of cervical intraepithelial neoplasia. *Int J Cancer* 1991;48:404–8.
12. Kjaer SK, Van den Brule AJ, Paull G, Svare EI, Sherman ME, Thomsen BL, *et al.* Type specific persistence of high risk human papillomavirus (HPV) as indicator of high grade cervical squamous

intraepithelial lesions in young women: population based prospective follow up study. *BMJ* 2002;325:572.

13.   Walboomers JM, Jacobs MV, Manos MM, Bosch FX, Kummer JA, Shah KV, *et al.* Human papillomavirus is a necessary cause of invasive cervical cancer worldwide. *J Pathol* 1999;189:12–19.

14.   Moreno V, Bosch FX, Munoz N, Meijer CJ, Shah KV, Walboomers JM, *et al.* Effect of oral contraceptives on risk of cervical cancer in women with human papillomavirus infection: the IARC multicentric case–control study. *Lancet* 2002;359:1085–92.

15.   Cuzick J, Sasieni P, Davies P, Adams J, Normand C, Frater A, *et al.* A systematic review of the role of human papillomavirus testing within a cervical screening programme. *Health Technol Assess* 1999;3:1–196.

16.   Lorincz AT, Reid R, Jenson AB, Greenberg MD, Lancaster W, Kurman RJ. Human papillomavirus infection of the cervix: relative risk associations of 15 common anogenital types. *Obstet Gynecol* 1992;79:328–37.

17.   Moscicki AB, Hills N, Shiboski S, Powell K, Jay N, Hanson E, *et al.* Risks for incident human papillomavirus infection and low-grade squamous intra-epithelial lesion development in young females. *JAMA* 2001;285:2995–3002.

18.   Woodman CB, Collins S, Winter H, Bailey A, Ellis J, Prior P, *et al.* Natural history of cervical human papillomavirus infection in young women: a longitudinal cohort study. *Lancet* 2001;357:1831–6.

19.   Rozendaal L, Walboomers JM, van der Linden JC, Voorhorst FJ, Kenemans P, Helmerhorst TJ, *et al.* PCR-based high-risk HPV test in cervical cancer screening gives objective risk assessment of women with cytomorphologically normal cervical smears. *Int J Cancer* 1996;68:766–9.

20.   Lehtinen M, Dillner J, Knekt P, Luostarinen T, Aromaa A, Kirnbauer R, *et al.* Serologically diagnosed infection with human papillomavirus type 16 and risk for subsequent development of cervical carcinoma: nested case-control study. *BMJ* 1996;312:537–9.

21.   Dillner J, Lehtinen M, Bjorge T, Luostarinen T, Youngman L, Jellum E, *et al.* Prospective seroepidemiologic study of human papillomavirus infection as a risk factor for invasive cervical cancer. *J Natl Cancer Inst* 1997;89:1293–9.

22.   Wallin KL, Wiklund F, Angstrom T, Bergman F, Stendahl U, Wadell G, *et al.* Type-specific persistence of human papillomavirus DNA before the development of invasive cervical cancer. *N Engl J Med* 1999;341:1633–8.

23.   Van der Graaf Y, Molijn A, Doornewaard H, Quint W, van Doorn LJ, van den Tweel J. Human papillomavirus and the long-term risk of cervical neoplasia. *Am J Epidemiol* 2002;156:158–64.

24.   Cuzick J. Viral load as a surrogate for persistence in cervical human papillomavirus infection. In: Franco ELF, Monsonego J, editors. *New Developments in Cervical Cancer Screening and Prevention.* Oxford: Blackwell Science; 1997.

25.   Ylitalo N, Sorensen P, Josefsson AM, Magnusson PK, Andersen PK, Ponten J, *et al.* Consistent high viral load of human papillomavirus 16 and risk of cervical carcinoma *in situ*: a nested case-control study. *Lancet* 2000;355:2194–8.

26.   Lorincz AT, Castle PE, Sherman ME, Scott DR, Glass AG, Wacholder S, *et al.* Viral load of human papillomavirus and risk of CIN3 or cervical cancer. *Lancet* 2002;360:228–9.

27.   Werness BA, Levine AJ, Howley PM. Association of human papillomavirus types 16 and 18 E6 proteins with p53. *Science* 1990;248:76–9.

28.   Dyson N, Howley PM, Munger K, Harlow E. The human papilloma virus-16 E7 oncoprotein is able to bind to the retinoblastoma gene product. *Science* 1989;243:934–7.

29.   Magnusson PK, Sparen P, Gyllensten UB. Genetic link to cervical tumours. *Nature* 1999;400:29–30.

30.   Birkeland SA, Storm HH, Lamm LU, Barlow L, Blohme I, Forsberg B, *et al.* Cancer risk after renal transplantation in the Nordic countries, 1964-1986. *Int J Cancer* 1995;60:183–9.

31.   Wright TC, Jr., Ellerbrock TV, Chiasson MA, Van Devanter N, Sun XW. Cervical intra-epithelial neoplasia in women infected with human immunodeficiency virus: prevalence, risk factors, and validity of Papanicolaou smears. New York Cervical Disease Study. *Obstet Gynecol* 1994;84:591–7.

32.   Fordyce EJ, Wang Z, Kahn AR, Gallagher BK, Merlos I, Ly S, *et al.* Risk of cancer among women with AIDS in New York City. *AIDS Public Policy J* 2000;15:95–104.

33.   Szarewski A, Cuzick J. Smoking and cervical neoplasia. In: Gray N, editor. *Tobacco, the Public Health Disaster of the Twentieth Century.*

34.   Plummer M, Herrero R, Franceschi S, Meijer CJLM, Snijders P, Bosch X, *et al.* Smoking and cervical cancer: pooled analysis of a multicentric case-control study (unpublished data submitted for publication).

35.   Deacon JM, Evans CD, Yule R, Desai M, Binns W, Taylor C, *et al.* Sexual behaviour and smoking as determinants of cervical HPV infection and of CIN3 among those infected: a case–control study nested within the Manchester cohort. *Br J Cancer* 2000;83:1565–72.

36.   Szarewski A, Jarvis MJ, Sasieni P, Anderson M, Edwards R, Steele SJ, *et al.* Effect of smoking cessation on cervical lesion size. *Lancet* 1996;347:941–3.

37.   Castle PE, Wacholder S, Lorincz AT, Scott DR, Sherman ME, Glass AG, *et al.* A prospective study

of high-grade cervical neoplasia risk among human papillomavirus-infected women. *J Natl Cancer Inst* 2002;94:1406–14.

38. Sasson IM, Haley NJ, Hoffmann D, Wynder EL, Hellberg D, Nilsson S. Cigarette smoking and neoplasia of the uterine cervix: smoke constituents in cervical mucus. *N Engl J Med* 1985;312:315–16.

39. Hellberg D, Nilsson S, Haley NJ, Hoffman D, Wynder E. Smoking and cervical intraepithelial neoplasia: nicotine and cotinine in serum and cervical mucus in smokers and nonsmokers. *Am J Obstet Gynecol* 1988;158:910–13.

40. Prokopczyk B, Cox JE, Hoffmann D, Waggoner SE. Identification of tobacco-specific carcinogen in the cervical mucus of smokers and nonsmokers. *J Natl Cancer Inst* 1997;89:868–873.

41. Skegg DC. Oral contraceptives, parity, and cervical cancer. *Lancet* 2002;359:1080–1.

42. Vandenvelde C, Van Beers D. Risk factors inducing the persistence of high-risk genital papillomaviruses in the normal cervix. *J Med Virol* 1992;38:226–32.

43. Brisson J, Bairati I, Morin C, Fortier M, Bouchard C, Christen A, *et al.* Determinants of persistent detection of human papillomavirus DNA in the uterine cervix. *J Infect Dis* 1996;173:794–9.

44. Munoz N, Franceschi S, Bosetti C, Moreno V, Herrero R, Smith JS, *et al.* Role of parity and human papillomavirus in cervical cancer: the IARC multicentric case–control study. *Lancet* 2002;359:1093–101.

45. Castellsague X, Bosch FX, Munoz N, Meijer CJ, Shah KV, de Sanjose S, *et al.* Male circumcision, penile human papillomavirus infection, and cervical cancer in female partners. *N Engl J Med* 2002;346:1105–12.

46. Cuzick J, Sasieni P, Singer A. Risk factors for invasive cervix cancer in young women. *Eur J Cancer* 1996;32A:836–41.

47. Schiff MA, Patterson RE, Baumgartner RN, Masuk M, van Asselt-King L, Wheeler CM, *et al.* Serum carotenoids and risk of cervical intraepithelial neoplasia in Southwestern American Indian women. *Cancer Epidemiol Biomarkers Prev* 2001;10:1219–22.

48. Kjellberg L, Hallmans G, Ahren AM, Johansson R, Bergman F, Wadell G, *et al.* Smoking, diet, pregnancy and oral contraceptive use as risk factors for cervical intra-epithelial neoplasia in relation to human papillomavirus infection. *Br J Cancer* 2000;82:1332–8.

49. Koutsky LA, Holmes KK, Critchlow CW, Stevens CE, Paavonen J, Beckmann AM, *et al.* A cohort study of the risk of cervical intraepithelial neoplasia grade 2 or 3 in relation to papillomavirus infection. *N Engl J Med* 1992;327:1272–8.

50. Munoz N, Bosch FX, de Sanjose S, Vergara A, del Moral A, Munoz MT, *et al.* Risk factors for cervical intraepithelial neoplasia grade III/carcinoma *in situ* in Spain and Colombia. *Cancer Epidemiol Biomarkers Prev* 1993;2:423–31.

51. Hakama M, Lehtinen M, Knekt P, Aromaa A, Leinikki P, Miettinen A, *et al.* Serum antibodies and subsequent cervical neoplasms: a prospective study with 12 years of follow-up. *Am J Epidemiol* 1993;137:166–70.

52. Koskela P, Anttila T, Bjorge T, Brunsvig A, Dillner J, Hakama M, *et al.* Chlamydia trachomatis infection as a risk factor for invasive cervical cancer. *Int J Cancer* 2000;85:35–9.

53. Wallin KL, Wiklund F, Luostarinen T, Angstrom T, Anttila T, Bergman F, *et al.* A population-based prospective study of *Chlamydia trachomatis* infection and cervical carcinoma. *Int J Cancer* 2002;101:371–4.

54. Hakama M, Hakulinen T, Pukkala E, Saxen E, Teppo L. Risk indicators of breast and cervical cancer on ecologic and individual levels. *Am J Epidemiol* 1982;116:990–1000.

55. Quinn M, Babb P, Jones J, Allen E. Effect of screening on incidence of and mortality from cancer of cervix in England: evaluation based on routinely collected statistics. *BMJ* 1999;318:904–8.

56. Sasieni P, Cuzick J, Farmery E. Accelerated decline in cervical cancer mortality in England and Wales. *Lancet* 1995;346:1566–7.

57. Sasieni P, Adams J. Effect of screening on cervical cancer mortality in England and Wales: analysis of trends with an age period cohort model. *BMJ* 1999;318:1244–5.

58. Sasieni P, Adams J. Changing rates of adenocarcinoma and adenosquamous carcinoma of the cervix in England. *Lancet* 2001;357:1490–3.

59. IARC Working Group on evaluation of cervical cancer screening programmes. Screening for squamous cervical cancer: duration of low risk after negative results of cervical cytology and its implication for screening policies. *BMJ* 1986;293:659–64.

60. Sasieni PD, Cuzick J, Lynch-Farmery E. Estimating the efficacy of screening by auditing smear histories of women with and without cervical cancer. The National Co-ordinating Network for Cervical Screening Working Group. *Br J Cancer* 1996;73:1001–5.

61. Cohen MM. Using administrative data for case-control studies: the case of the Papanicolaou smear. *Ann Epidemiol* 1993;3:93–8.

62. Macgregor JE, Campbell MK, Mann EM, Swanson KY. Screening for cervical intra-epithelial neoplasia in north east Scotland shows fall in incidence and mortality from invasive cancer with

concomitant rise in preinvasive disease. *BMJ* 1994;308:1407–11.

63. Herbert A, Breen C, Bryant TN, Hitchcock A, Macdonald H, Millward-Sadler GH, *et al.* Invasive cervical cancer in Southampton and South West Hampshire: effect of introducing a comprehensive screening programme. *J Med Screen* 1996;3:23–8.

64. Viikki M, Pukkala E, Hakama M. Risk of cervical cancer after a negative Pap smear. *J Med Screen* 1999;6:103–7.

65. Andersson-Ellstrom A, Seidal T, Grannas M, Hagmar B. The pap-smear history of women with invasive cervical squamous carcinoma. A case–control study from Sweden. *Acta Obstet Gynecol Scand* 2000;79:221–6.

66. Sasieni PD, Adams J, Cuzick J. Trends in gynaecological cancers in England and Wales. *J Epidemiol Biostat* 1997;2:187–95.

67. Howe HL, Wingo PA, Thun MJ, Ries LA, Rosenberg HM, Feigal EG, *et al.* Annual report to the nation on the status of cancer (1973 through 1998), featuring cancers with recent increasing trends. *J Natl Cancer Inst* 2001;93:824–42.

68. Jones RW, Baranyai J, Stables S. Trends in squamous cell carcinoma of the vulva: the influence of vulvar intraepithelial neoplasia. *Obstet Gynecol* 1997;90:448–52.

69. Iversen T, Tretli S. Intraepithelial and invasive squamous cell neoplasia of the vulva: trends in incidence, recurrence, and survival rate in Norway. *Obstet Gynecol* 1998;91:969–72.

70. Levi F, Randimbison L, La Vecchia C. Descriptive epidemiology of vulvar and vaginal cancers in Vaud, Switzerland, 1974-1994. *Ann Oncol* 1998;9:1229–32.

71. Joura EA, Losch A, Haider-Angeler MG, Breitenecker G, Leodolter S. Trends in vulvar neoplasia. Increasing incidence of vulvar intraepithelial neoplasia and squamous cell carcinoma of the vulva in young women. *J Reprod Med* 2000;45:613–15.

72. Berg JW, Lampe JG. High-risk factors in gynecologic cancer. *Cancer* 1981;48 Suppl 2:429–41.

73. Peters RK, Mack TM, Bernstein L. Parallels in the epidemiology of selected anogenital carcinomas. *J Natl Cancer Inst* 1984;72:609–15.

74. Brinton LA, Nasca PC, Mallin K, Baptiste MS, Wilbanks GD, Richart RM. Case–control study of cancer of the vulva. *Obstet Gynecol* 1990;75:859–66.

75. Daling JR, Sherman KJ, Hislop TG, Maden C, Mandelson MT, Beckmann AM, *et al.* Cigarette smoking and the risk of anogenital cancer. *Am J Epidemiol* 1992;135:180–9.

76. Madeleine MM, Daling JR, Carter JJ, Wipf GC, Schwartz SM, McKnight B, *et al.* Cofactors with human papillomavirus in a population-based study of vulvar cancer. *J Natl Cancer Inst* 1997;89:1516–23.

77. Hording U, Kringsholm B, Andreasson B, Visfeldt J, Daugaard S, Bock JE. Human papillomavirus in vulvar squamous-cell carcinoma and in normal vulvar tissues: a search for a possible impact of HPV on vulvar cancer prognosis. *Int J Cancer* 1993;55:394–6.

78. Blohme I, Brynger H. Malignant disease in renal transplant patients. *Transplantation* 1985;39:23–5.

79. Chiasson MA, Ellerbrock TV, Bush TJ, Sun XW, Wright TC, Jr. Increased prevalence of vulvovaginal condyloma and vulvar intraepithelial neoplasia in women infected with the human immunodeficiency virus. *Obstet Gynecol* 1997;89:690–4.

80. Frisch M, Biggar RJ, Goedert JJ. Human papillomavirus-associated cancers in patients with human immunodeficiency virus infection and acquired immunodeficiency syndrome. *J Natl Cancer Inst* 2000;92:1500–10.

81. Conley LJ, Ellerbrock TV, Bush TJ, Chiasson MA, Sawo D, Wright TC. HIV-1 infection and risk of vulvovaginal and perianal condylomata acuminata and intraepithelial neoplasia: a prospective cohort study. *Lancet* 2002;359:108–13.

82. Crum CP. Carcinoma of the vulva: epidemiology and pathogenesis. *Obstet Gynecol* 1992;79:448–54.

83. Lee YY, Wilczynski SP, Chumakov A, Chih D, Koeffler HP. Carcinoma of the vulva: HPV and p53 mutations. *Oncogene* 1994;9:1655–9.

84. Viikki M, Pukkala E, Hakama M. Risk of endometrial, ovarian, vulvar, and vaginal cancers after a positive cervical cytology followed by negative histology. *Obstet Gynecol* 1998;92:269–73.

85. Weiderpass E, Ye W, Tamimi R, Trichopolous D, Nyren O, Vainio H, *et al.* Alcoholism and risk for cancer of the cervix uteri, vagina, and vulva. *Cancer Epidemiol Biomarkers Prev* 2001;10:899–901.

86. Herbst AL, Ulfelder H, Poskanzer DC. Adenocarcinoma of the vagina. Association of maternal stilbestrol therapy with tumor appearance in young women. *N Engl J Med* 1971;284:878–81.

87. Greenwald P, Barlow JJ, Nasca PC, Burnett WS. Vaginal cancer after maternal treatment with synthetic estrogens. *N Engl J Med* 1971;285:390–2.

88. Bornstein J, Adam E, Adler-Storthz K, Kaufman RH. Development of cervical and vaginal squamous cell neoplasia as a late consequence of *in utero* exposure to diethylstilbestrol. *Obstet Gynecol Surv* 1988;43:15–21.

89. Melnick S, Cole P, Anderson D, Herbst A. Rates and risks of diethylstilbestrol-related clear-cell adenocarcinoma of the vagina and cervix. An update. *N Engl J Med* 1987;316:514–16.

90. *Cancer Incidence in Five Continents, Volume VII.* Parkin DM, Whelan SL, Ferlay J, Raymond L,

Young J, editors. IARC Scientific Publications No. 143. Lyons: International Agency for Research on Cancer; 1997. p. 862–3, 936–9.

91.   Sasieni PD. Use of routine data to monitor and evaluate cervical screening. In: Duffy SW, Hill C, Esteve J, editors. *Quantitative Methods for the Evaluation of Cancer Screening*. London: Arnold; 2001.

Chapter 2

Cell cycle control and the human papillomavirus

C Simon Herrington

Introduction

Human papillomaviruses (HPVs) have been identified as the major aetiological factor in cervical carcinogenesis.[1] Epidemiological evidence indicates that the majority of cervical neoplasia is attributable to HPV infection but, although certain HPV genes are capable of immortalisation and cooperation in the process of transformation, not all non-invasive lesions progress to the full malignant phenotype, indicating that other co-factors are required.[2] The biological rationale of HPV, when infecting squamous epithelium, is to replicate by subverting host DNA replication machinery. This is generally a symbiotic relationship, infection being associated merely with epithelial hyperplasia which, when exuberant, leads to the formation of clinically apparent warts. Neoplasia is an infrequent result of HPV infection[3] and is an unwanted event from the viewpoint of both the host and the virus. However, neoplastic transformation by HPV is clearly of clinical importance and study of the mechanisms continues to provide important insights into this process. In view of the viral requirement for cellular machinery for DNA synthesis, one of the main functions of the viral proteins is to interfere with normal cell cycle control. Hence, study of the means by which the virus interacts with cellular pathways is central to understanding both the viral life cycle and HPV-associated neoplastic transformation.

Human papillomaviruses

Before considering the cell cycle, it is important to review the basic molecular biology of HPVs and the pathology of HPV infection. Papillomaviruses are small DNA viruses approximately 55 nm in diameter. The viral genome is a double-stranded circular DNA approximately 7.9 kilobases in length and is contained within the viral capsid.[4] The molecular organisation of the genome is similar for all the HPV types identified to date, of which there are at least 100, with numerous less well-characterised partial sequences in addition. The genome can be divided into early and late regions (Figure 2.1) and contains seven early and two late open reading frames (ORFs). There is also a non-coding region, referred to as the upstream regulatory region (URR) or long control region. Early gene expression occurs at the onset of infection, and the products of these genes mediate specific functions controlling viral replication and, in the case of the oncogenic viruses, cellular transformation. The E1 gene product is involved in viral DNA replication and genome maintenance and, as a DNA helicase, is the only viral protein to possess enzyme activity.[5] The E2 gene product is involved with E1 in viral

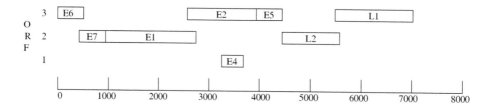

Figure 2.1 Example of molecular organisation of human papillomavirus; E represents early genes and L represents late genes; E1/E2: episomal DNA replication; E2: enhancer regulator, repressor: E6/E7: immortalisation/transformation; L1: minor capsid; L2: major capsid (reproduced with permission from Blackwell)[30]

DNA replication and it is also a negative transcriptional regulator.[5,6] The E4 gene products disrupt the cytoplasmic keratin network,[7] producing the koilocytic morphology characteristic of productive HPV infection. The E5 gene may play a role in cellular transformation through interaction with cell membrane growth factor receptors.[8] The E6 and E7 genes, which lie immediately downstream of the URR, encode the major transforming proteins, which under appropriate conditions are capable of inducing cell proliferation, immortalisation and transformation.[9] Finally, the L1 and L2 ORFs encode for the major and minor capsid proteins respectively and are expressed towards the final stages of the viral cycle and, hence, within superficial, terminally differentiated cells.[10]

The molecular classification of HPVs is phylogenetic, based on DNA and protein sequences,[11] but the HPVs can also be divided into low-, intermediate- and high-risk types according to their segregation with the different grades of intraepithelial and invasive disease. Low-risk HPV types (e.g. HPV 6, 11, 40, 42, 43, 44), also termed non-oncogenic HPVs, are usually associated with benign exophytic genital warts. They are also associated with wart virus change and cervical intraepithelial neoplasia (CIN) grade 1 (low-grade squamous intraepithelial lesions, LSILs) but are only rarely found in CIN2 and CIN3 high-grade squamous intraepithelial lesions (HSILs) and invasive carcinomas. By contrast, intermediate-risk (particularly HPV 31, 33, 39, 52 and 58) and high-risk (HPV 16, 18, 45 and 56) HPV types, also known collectively as oncogenic HPVs, are associated with 'flat' condylomas, all grades of CIN and invasive carcinoma.[12] The concept of oncogenic and non-oncogenic HPVs is supported by many epidemiological case–control studies, which have collectively shown a consistent association between oncogenic HPVs and high-grade cervical disease. Moreover, the risk of progression from LSIL to HSIL is greater in patients with persistent oncogenic HPV infection[13,14] and in those with high viral load,[13] suggesting that prolonged exposure to viral effects is important in the pathogenesis of cervical disease. Whether this is related to viral factors, such as sequence variation, or is a reflection of host factors, such as immune status, remains to be determined.

Pathology of human papillomavirus infection

HPVs are epitheliotrophic, possibly infecting squamous epithelia through small abrasions. The subsequent virus life cycle is then closely linked to keratinocyte differentiation. The viral genome is maintained as a low copy episome in the proliferating basal/parabasal epithelial cells that are thought to be the site of initial infection.[15] As the keratinocyte undergoes progressive differentiation, extrachromosomal viral genome amplification and gene expression increase until late 'L' gene expression and virion production occur in terminally differentiated superficial cells. This form of infection leads to koilocytosis, nuclear enlargement, dyskeratosis, multinucleation and, in some cases, LSILs. Such lesions may regress, persist or progress.

Under some circumstances, viral DNA gains entry into basal cells but productive infection does not occur. This may lead to latent HPV infection if viral DNA persists as an episome, but viral DNA may also integrate into host DNA either as a single copy or as multiple head-to-tail tandemly repeated copies. Early studies of cell lines suggested that HPV DNA integration occurred at chromosomal fragile sites.[16] However, the site of integration into the host genome does not appear to be consistent in naturally occurring lesions, either by fluorescence *in situ* hybridisation[17] or when fusion transcripts are analysed.[18] The viral breakpoint is more consistent, as integration often causes disruption of the viral E2 gene, resulting in loss of function.[19] Moreover, disruption of either the E1 or E2 gene can lead to enhanced immortalisation capacity.[20] The mechanisms of viral integration are not well understood, although it has been demonstrated that expression of E6 or E7 of HPV 16 increases integration of foreign DNA compared with HPV 6 or 11.[21] This is consistent with the observation that viral integration is rare in lesions infected with non-oncogenic HPVs. Viral integration also precludes late gene expression, even if the late genes are retained in the integrated viral genomes.[22] Therefore, integration of viral DNA prevents productive infection. Viral integration with associated disruption of the E2 gene leads to removal of transcriptional repression of early gene expression and is therefore one mechanism of upregulation of E6/E7 expression. However, the observation that episomal viral DNA is frequently present and amplified in cervical carcinomas[23,24] led to the suggestion that HPV amplification may provide an alternative mechanism for the upregulation of early gene expression in some tumours. The overall result of these processes is deregulation of E6/E7 gene expression, with failure of the switch to viral DNA replication and late gene expression. As the E6 and E7 proteins are the major cell cycle dysregulators, this step is likely to be important in neoplastic transformation. This concept is consistent with the association between these molecular changes and HSILs (CIN2, CIN3).[25]

Although HPV DNA, particularly the E6 and E7 genes, can immortalise primary cervical cells in culture,[26] full transformation of normal cells requires cooperation between HPV and other oncogenic sequences, such as activated *Ha-ras*,[27] in keeping with other factors being involved in the neoplastic process *in vivo*. Clearly, many such additional factors may be involved but time alone could be important, as persistent HPV infection is associated with lesion progression.[13,14] Thus, persistent interference with cell cycle control, as described below, may lead to secondary cellular genetic abnormalities and hence transformation. This does not, however, exclude the involvement of other factors such as, for example, smoking and immunosuppression, both of which are clearly linked epidemiologically to the development of cervical neoplasia.[28,29]

These observations lead to a model of HPV-associated squamous neoplasia, in which productive viral infection is associated with LSILs (HPV effect and CIN1). Deregulation of E6/E7 expression, with concomitant failure of the switch to late gene expression, occurs in HSILs (CIN2, CIN3) but further factors, possibly secondary to prolonged cell cycle dysregulation by viral proteins, are required for invasion, tumour development and metastasis. Other factors, such as smoking and immunosuppression, may, however, be involved at several points along the pathway.

HPV and the cell cycle

The cell cycle is central to the viral life cycle, as HPV uses cellular DNA replication machinery to replicate its genome.[30] The rationale of the virus is to force the cell into a synthetic state resembling the synthesis (S) phase of the cell cycle. However, this needs to be accompanied by squamous differentiation, so that viral replication is coupled to epithelial maturation, which is required for virion production.[10] Normally, squamous epithelial cells exit the cell cycle when they undergo differentiation. The virus therefore needs to force differentiating squamous cells to express the cell cycle associated proteins required to support viral replication. Viral proteins act at several different points in the cycle (Figure 2.2) in order to achieve this and the remainder of this chapter will deal with these effects.

Gap 1 and synthesis phases

Cyclins/cyclin-dependent kinases

Several different regulatory cyclins and their catalytic partners, the cyclin-dependent kinases (CDKs), are involved in controlling the cell's passage from the gap 1 (G1) phase into the S phase. Before committing to a further round of DNA replication, the cell must ensure not only that the preceding cell division has taken place correctly but also that no errors have been acquired since that division, for example as a result of the effects of external mutagenic stimuli. This cell cycle transition is therefore tightly controlled by a variety of proteins whose function is to detect abnormalities, arrest the cell cycle if appropriate and initiate cell death, usually through apoptosis, to delete the abnormal cell. Cyclins D, E and A are all involved at this point.[31,32] The main target of cyclin D, and its catalytic partners CDK 4 and 6, is the retinoblastoma protein (pRb). Phosphorylation of pRb prevents it from binding to, for example, the E2F transcription factor, thus releasing this factor and initiating transcription of S phase-associated genes. In HPV-infected cells, E7 binds to, and leads to the degradation of, pRb, obviating the cells' requirement for cyclin D/CDK activity.[33] Functionally, therefore, E7 binding has the same effect as phosphorylation. This is not necessarily absolute, as it is likely to depend upon, for example, the affinity of E7 binding to pRb, which is known to vary between HPV types, being lower for non-oncogenic HPVs than for oncogenic HPVs.[34] This is consistent with the observation that cyclin D1 expression is absent in the majority of LSILs infected with high-risk HPV types but that it can be detected in such lesions infected with low-risk HPV types.[35] Interference with pRb function is the main mechanism of action of the E7 protein at this point in the cell cycle, but E7 can also bind to the other pocket proteins p107 and p130, and directly to members of the E2F family, so can influence this pathway in a pRb-independent manner.[36–38]

Cyclin E is synthesised late in the G1 phase and, together with its binding partner CDK2, is involved until early in the S phase, when it is rapidly degraded. Like cyclin D/CDK, this complex catalyses phosphorylation of pRb and other pocket proteins with consequent release of E2F and initiation of DNA synthesis. The E7 protein binds to cyclin E and also enhances its transcription.[36] Cyclin A is the main S phase cyclin and also binds to CDK2. E7 binds to cyclin A and enhances its transcription,[36] consistent with the viral mechanism of upregulation of S phase-associated molecules. This maintains continuing DNA replication. Cyclin A also plays a role in mitosis, where it binds to CDK1 but it is less important at this point in the cycle than cyclin B (see below).

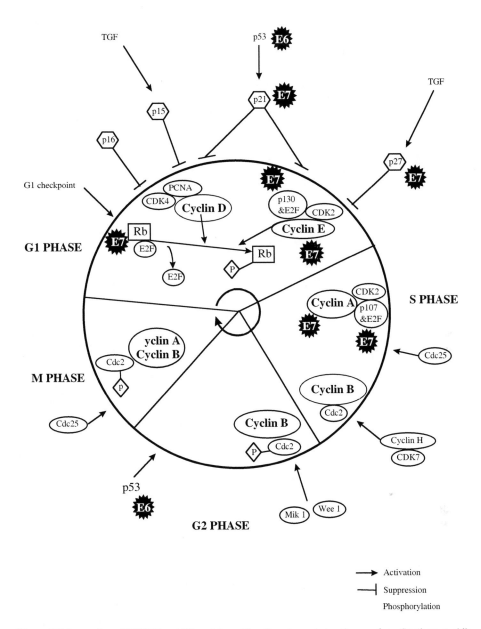

Figure 2.2 Interaction of HPV E6 and E7 proteins with cell cycle control pathways; from Southern et al.[30]; reproduced with permission from Blackwell

Overall, therefore, the major function of the HPV E7 protein is to disrupt the protein complexes involved in control of the G1/S phase transition. However, a study has shown that the HPV E6 protein can also induce S phase entry.[39] The site of action of E6 appears to be upstream of pRb, and both oncogenic (HPV16) and non-oncogenic (HPV1) proteins possessed this property.

Cyclin-dependent kinase inhibitors

A further group of proteins, the cyclin-dependent kinase inhibitors (CKIs) provides a counterbalance to the effects of cyclins/CDKs by inhibiting cell cycle progression. There are two main groups of CKIs, namely the p21 (WAF1, CIP1, SDI1) family and the INK family.[40] The former group, which includes p21, p27 and p57, interacts with a number of different CDKs, whereas the latter group, which includes p15, p16, p18 and p19, targets the cyclin D/CDK4 and 6 complexes (Figure 2.2). Therefore, the INK group is of limited mechanistic relevance to HPV infection, as cyclin D/CDK function is not required for S phase progression in the presence of high-affinity E7 binding (see above). However, this group of molecules may be important in non-oncogenic HPV infection. Moreover, the detection of p16 expression has been put forward as a potential diagnostic marker for the assessment of cervical smears and biopsies. In the presence of oncogenic HPV infection, E7 gene activity leads to marked upregulation of p16 expression, which can therefore be used as a marker of such infection, irrespective of HPV type.[41,42] It remains to be established whether this approach has sufficient sensitivity and specificity for routine clinical application.

The p21 family is, however, of mechanistic relevance, as it acts at several points at the G1/S transition; p21 expression causes cell cycle arrest at G1/S but this can be prevented by HPV E7 expression.[43] In particular, the HPV E7 protein can prevent p21-mediated inhibition of CDK2 in differentiating keratinocytes.[44] In normal keratinocytes, p21 is constitutively expressed but rapidly degraded. In cells expressing E7, reactivation of S phase genes occurs in post-mitotic, differentiating cells. In a subset of these cells, p21 forms a complex with both cyclin E and CDK2[45] and viral DNA synthesis is prevented. By contrast, a separate subset of cells does re-enter the S phase but, in these, neither cyclin E nor p21 is detectable.[46] These observations suggest that p21 can prevent post-mitotic, differentiated cells from re-entering the S phase in the presence of the E7 protein. However, transcription of p21 is p53-dependent, so that the binding of p53 by E6 (see below) leads to reduced p21 gene transcription; p21 levels are therefore influenced by a variety of positive and negative factors, the end result being determined by the prevailing environment. This is consistent with evidence that the expression of oncogenic E7 in differentiated keratinocytes results in either cell cycle arrest, with prevention of S phase re-entry, accompanied by expression of cyclin E, p27 and p21 proteins or endoreduplication.[47]

The p53 protein

The p53 protein is of central importance to the maintenance of genome integrity, particularly at the gap 2 (G2) phase to mitosis (M) phase transition (see below). However, it is also involved at the G1/S transition, partly through its effects on p21 levels.[48] Thus, the binding of p53 by HPV E6 protein is likely to have an effect on this part of the cell cycle. It has also been shown that the E2 protein can bind directly to p53[49] and can induce S phase arrest with re-replication of cellular DNA.[50] The effects of HPV on p53 function are therefore complex.

Gap 2 and mitosis phases

After DNA synthesis, the cell progresses through G2 phase and then M phase. The cell must check that chromosomes have been replicated accurately and have been distributed appropriately into daughter cells. This involves various checkpoints and close control of mitosis. The main regulatory complex involved in mitosis is that between cyclin B and CDK1, which together constitute mitosis-promoting factor (MPF). Cyclin B expression is restricted to basal/parabasal cells in productively infected squamous epithelium with low-grade morphology. Cyclin A and Ki67 are, however, expressed throughout the epithelium,[51] consistent with induction of S phase-associated genes, as described above. However, high-grade lesions (CIN 2 and CIN 3) express both cyclins A and B throughout the epithelium, suggesting that cell cycle progression occurs in the neoplastic cells in these lesions.[52] Moreover, numerical chromosome imbalance was identified in HSILs, but not in LSILs.[51,52] The mechanisms underlying these differences between low- and high-grade lesions are not clear. The HPV E7 protein has an effect on G2/M checkpoints.[53] It has also been shown that, although E7 binds to and stabilises p53, the bound p53 is functionally impaired in that it remains transcriptionally inert.[54] Moreover, E7 dysregulates CDK2 activity, which is involved in the initiation of centrosome duplication[55] and expression of E7 is associated with chromosome reduplication.[56] The E6 protein has greater effect, partly through its interaction with p53, and interferes with several mitotic checkpoints.[57] The ability of the E6 proteins of oncogenic HPVs to bind to, and degrade, p53 is significantly greater than that of the non-oncogenic HPVs, consistent with the association of oncogenic HPVs with neoplastic transformation.[34] However, the E6 and E7 proteins of HPV 16 have been shown to cooperate in the induction of abnormal centrosome numbers, multipolar mitoses and numerical chromosome imbalance[58] and these abnormalities are also seen in raft cultures expressing episomal whole HPV 16 genomes, demonstrating that these effects are seen in the context of homologous transcriptional control.[59]

Conclusion

HPV proteins interfere with cell cycle control mechanisms in a number of ways. The E6 and E7 proteins are particularly important and, from the viewpoint of productive viral infection, their main function is to force differentiating squamous epithelial cells to synthesise the components required for viral replication, namely S phase-associated genes. However, the E6 and E7 proteins of oncogenic and non-oncogenic HPVs interact with cellular proteins, particularly p53 and pRb respectively, in different ways, and these differences are likely to underlie their associations with different clinical lesions. Thus, non-oncogenic HPV infection is associated with expression of G1/S phase-associated cyclins, epithelial hyperplasia and productive infection. Oncogenic HPV infection, if persistent, is associated with failure of productive infection, with expression of G1/S and G2/M cyclins and with neoplastic transformation. Non-oncogenic HPVs succeed in directing the infected epithelium to replicate viral DNA and support virion production, whereas the oncogenic HPVs induce abnormalities in host DNA that can, eventually, lead to death of the host. Further investigation of the interaction between HPV proteins and cell cycle control proteins will give insight not only into HPV-related disease but also into the normal cell cycle. Moreover, improved understanding of the mechanisms involved will allow rational approaches to molecular diagnosis and treatment to be developed.

References

1. Walboomers JM, Jacobs MV, Manos MM, Bosch FX, Kummer JA, Shah KV, et al. Human papillomavirus is a necessary cause of invasive cervical cancer worldwide. *J Pathol* 1999;189:12–19.
2. Herrington CS. Human papillomaviruses and cervical neoplasia II: interaction with other factors. *J Clin Pathol* 1995;48:1–6.

3. Helmerhorst TJ, Meijer CJ. Cervical cancer should be considered as a rare complication of oncogenic HPV infection rather than a STD. *Int J Gynecol Cancer* 2002;12:235–6.

4. De Villiers EM. Taxonomic classification of papillomaviruses. *Papillomavirus Report* 2001;12:57–63.

5. Herrington CS. Control of HPV: implications for squamous neoplasia. *J Pathol* 1996;178:237–8.

6. Thierry F. Proteins involved in the control of HPV transcription. *Papillomavirus Report* 1993;4:27–32.

7. Doorbar J, Ely S, Sterling J, McLean C, Crawford L. Specific interaction between HPV-16 E1-E4 and cytokeratins results in collapse of the epithelial cell intermediate filament network. *Nature* 1991;352:824–7.

8. Banks L, Matlashewski G. Cell transformation and the HPV E5 gene. *Papillomavirus Rep* 1993;4:1–4.

9. Herrington CS. Human papillomaviruses and cervical neoplasia I: virology, classification, pathology and epidemiology. *J Clin Pathol* 1994;47:1066–72.

10. Doorbar J. Late stages of the papillomavirus life cycle. *Papillomavirus Report* 1998;9:119–26.

11. Southern SA, Herrington CS. Molecular events in uterine cervical cancer. *Sex Transm Inf* 1998;74:101–9.

12. Lorincz AT, Reid R, Jenson AB, Greenberg MD, Lancaster W, Kurman RJ. Human papillomavirus infection of the cervix: relative risk associations of 15 common anogenital types. *Obstet Gynecol* 1992;79:328–37.

13. Ho GYF, Burk RD, Klein S, Kadish AS, Chang CJ, Palan P *et al.* Persistent genital human papillomavirus infection as a risk factor for persistent cervical dysplasia. *J Natl Cancer Inst* 1995;87:1365–71.

14. Remmink AJ, Walboomers JMM, Helmerhorst TJM, Voorhorst FJ, Rozendaal L, Risse EK *et al.* The presence of persistent high-risk HPV genotypes in dysplastic cervical lesions is associated with progressive disease - natural history up to 36 months. *Int J Cancer* 1995;61:306–11.

15. Schneider A, Koutsky LA. Natural history and epidemiological features of genital HPV infection. *IARC Sci Publ* 1992;119:25–52.

16. Popescu NC, DiPaolo JA. Preferential sites for viral integration on mammalian genome. *Cancer Genet Cytogenet* 1989;42:157–71.

17. Kalantari M, Blennow E, Hagmar B, Johansson B. Physical state of HPV16 and chromosomal mapping of the integrated form in cervical carcinomas. *Diagn Mol Pathol* 2001;10:46–54.

18. Wentzensen N, Ridder R, Klaes R, Vinokurova S, Schaefer U, Doeberitz MK. Characterisation of viral-cellular fusion transcripts in a large series of HPV16 and 18 positive anogenital lesions. *Oncogene* 2002;21:419–26.

19. Choo KB, Pan CC, Han SH. Integration of human papillomavirus type 16 into cellular DNA of cervical carcinoma: preferential deletion of the E2 gene and invariable retention of the long control region and the E6/E7 open reading frames. *Virology* 1987;161:259–61.

20. Romanczuk H, Howley PM. Disruption of either the E1 or the E2 regulatory gene of human papillomavirus type 16 increases viral immortalization capacity. *Proc Natl Acad Sci U S A* 1992;89:3159–63.

21. Kessis TD, Connolly DC, Hedrick L, Cho KR. Expression of HPV 16 E6 or E7 increases integration of foreign DNA. *Oncogene* 1996;13:427–31.

22. Frattini MG, Lim HB, Laimins LA. *In vitro* synthesis of oncogenic human papillomaviruses requires episomal genomes for differentiation-dependent late expression. *Proc Natl Acad Sci USA* 1996;93:3062–7.

23. Berumen J, Casas L, Segura E, Amezcua JL, Garcia-Carranca A. Genome amplification of human papillomavirus types 16 and 18 in cervical carcinomas is related to retention of the E1/E2 genes. *Int J Cancer* 1994;56:640–5.

24. Berumen J, Unger E, Casas L, Figueroa P. Amplification of human papillomavirus types 16 and 18 in cervical cancer. *Hum Pathol* 1995;26:676–81.

25. Nilsson CH, Bakos E, Petry KU, Schneider A, Durst M. Promoter usage in the E7 ORF of HPV 16 correlates with epithelial differentiation and is largely confined to low-grade genital neoplasia. *Int J Cancer* 1996;65:6–12.

26. Hawley-Nelson P, Vousden KH, Hubbert NL, Lowy DR, Schiller JT. HPV16 E6 and E7 proteins cooperate to immortalize human foreskin keratinocytes. *EMBO J* 1989;8:3905–10.

27. Matlashewski G, Osborn K, Banks L, Stanley M, Crawford L. Transformation of primary human fibroblast cells with human papillomavirus type 16 DNA and EJ-ras. *Int J Cancer* 1988;42:232–8.

28. Winkelstein W. Jr. Smoking and cervical cancer – current status: a review. *Am J Epidemiol* 1990;131:945–57.

29. Schneider A, Kay S, Lee HM. Immunosuppression as a high risk factor in the development of condyloma acuminatum and squamous neoplasia of the cervix. *Acta Cytol* 1983;27:220–4.

30. Southern SA, Herrington CS. Disruption of cell cycle control by human papillomaviruses with special

reference to cervical carcinoma. *Int J Gynecol Cancer* 2000;10:263–74.

31. Hunter T, Pines J. Cyclins and cancer II: cyclin D and CDK inhibitors come of age. *Cell* 1994;79:573–82.

32. Sherr CJ. G1 phase progression: cycling on cue. *Cell* 1994;79:551–5.

33. Gonzalez SL, Stremlau M, He X, Basile JR, Munger K. Degradation of the retinoblastoma tumor suppressor by the human papillomavirus type 16 E7 oncoprotein is important for functional inactivation and is separable from proteasomal degradation of E7. *J Virol* 2001;75:7583–91.

34. Munger K, Scheffner M, Huibregtse JM, Howley PM. Interactions of HPV E6 and E7 oncoproteins with tumour suppressor gene products. *Cancer Surv* 1992;12:197–217.

35. Southern SA, Herrington CS. Differential cell cycle regulation by low and high risk human papillomaviruses in low grade cervical squamous intra-epithelial lesions. *Cancer Res* 1998;58:2941–2945.

36. Zerfass K, Schulze A, Spitkovsky D, Friedman V, Henglein B, Jansen-Durr P. Sequential activation of cyclin E and cyclin A gene expression by human papillomavirus type 16 E7 through sequences necessary for transformation. *J Virol* 1995;69:6389–99.

37. Smith-McCune K, Kalman D, Robbins C, Shivakumar S, Yuschenkoff L, Bishop JM. Intranuclear localization of human papillomavirus 16 E7 during transformation and preferential binding of E7 to the Rb family member p130. *Proc Natl Acad Sci* 1999;96:6999–7004.

38. Arroyo M, Bagchi S, Raychaudhuri P. Association of the human papillomavirus type 16 E7 protein with the S-phase-specific E2F-cyclin A complex. *Mol Cell Biol* 1993;13:6537–46.

39. Malanchi I, Caldeira S, Krutzfeldt M, Giarre M, Alunni-Fabbroni M, Tommasino M. Identification of a novel activity of human papillomavirus type 16 E6 protein in deregulating the G1/S transition. *Oncogene* 2002;21:5665–72.

40. Pavletich NP. Mechanisms of cyclin-dependent kinase regulation: structures of CDKs, their cyclin activators, and CIP and INK4 inhibitors. *J Mol Biol* 1999;287:821–8.

41. Keating JT, Cviko A, Riethdorf S, Riethdorf L, Quade BJ, Sun D, et al. Ki-67, cyclin E and p16INK4 are complementary surrogate biomarkers for human papillomavirus-related cervical neoplasia. *Am J Surg Pathol* 2001;25:884–91.

42. Klaes R, Friedrich T, Spitkovsky D, Ridder R, Rudy W, Petry U, et al. Overexpression of p16 (INK4A) as a specific marker for dysplastic and neoplastic epithelial cells of the cervix uteri. *Int J Cancer* 2001;92:276–84.

43. Morozov A, Shiyanov P, Barr E, Leiden JM, Raychaudhuri P. Accumulation of human papillomavirus type 16 E7 protein bypasses G1 arrest induced by serum deprivation and by the cell cycle inhibitor p21. *J Virol* 1997;71:3451–7.

44. Jones DL, Alani RM, Munger K. The human papillomavirus E7 oncoprotein can uncouple cellular differentiation and proliferation in human keratinocytes by abrogating p21Cip-1 mediated inhibition of cdk2. *Genes Dev* 1997;11:2101–11.

45. Jian Y, Schmidt-Grimminger D-C, Chien WM, Wu X, Broker TR, Chow LT. Post-transcriptional induction of p21cip1 protein by human papillomavirus E7 inhibits unscheduled DNA synthesis reactivated in differentiated keratinocytes. *Oncogene* 1998;17:2027–38.

46. Jian Y, Van Tine BA, Chien WM, Shaw GM, Broker TR, Chow LT. Concordant induction of cyclin E and p21cip1 in differentiated keratinocytes by the human papillomavirus E7 protein inhibits cellular and viral DNA synthesis. *Cell Growth Differ* 1999;10:101–11.

47. Chien WM, Noya F, Benedict-Hamilton HM, Broker TR, Chow LT. Alternative fates of keratinocytes transduced by human papillomavirus type 18 E7 during squamous differentiation. *J Virol* 2002;76:2964–72.

48. Kuerbitz SJ, Plunkett BS, Walsh WV, Kastan MB. Wild-type p53 is a cell cycle checkpoint determinant following irradiation. *Proc Natl Acad Sci USA* 1992;89:7491–5.

49. Massimi P, Pim D, Bertoli C, Bouvard V, Banks L. Interaction between the HPV-16 E2 transcriptional activator and p53. *Oncogene* 1999;18:7748–54.

50. Frattini MG, Hurst SD, Lim HB, Swaminathan S, Laimins LA. Abrogation of a mitotic checkpoint by E2 proteins from oncogenic human papillomaviruses correlates with increased turnover of the p53 tumor suppressor protein. *EMBO J* 1997;16:318–31.

51. Southern SA, Herrington CS. Differential cell cycle regulation by low- and high-risk human papillomaviruses in low-grade cervical squamous intraepithelial lesions of the cervix. *Cancer Res* 1998;58:2941–5.

52. Southern SA, McDicken IW, Herrington CS. Evidence for keratinocyte immortalization in high-grade squamous intraepithelial lesions of the cervix infected with high-risk human papillomaviruses. *Lab Invest* 2000;80:539–44.

53. Thomas JT, Laimins LA. Human papillomavirus oncoproteins E6 and E7 independently abrogate the mitotic spindle checkpoint. *J Virol* 1998;72:1131–7.

54. Eichten A, Westfall M, Pietenpol JA, Munger K. Stabilization and functional impairment of the tumor suppressor p53 by the human papillomavirus type 16 E7 oncoprotein. *Virology* 2002;295:74–85.

55.   Duensing S, Munger K. Human papillomaviruses and centrosome duplication errors: modelling the origins of genomic instability. *Oncogene* 2002;21:6241–8.

56.   Southern SA, Noya F, Meyers C, Broker T, Chow LT, Herrington CS. Tetrasomy is induced by human papillomavirus type 18 E7 gene expression in keratinocyte raft cultures. *Cancer Res* 2001;61:4858–63.

57.   Thompson DA, Belinsky G, Chang THT, Jones DL, Schlegel R, Munger K. The human papillomavirus-16 E6 oncoprotein decreases the vigilance of mitotic checkpoints. *Oncogene* 1997;15:3025–35.

58.   Duensing S, Lee LY, Duensing A, Basile J, Piboonniyom S, Gonzalez S, *et al*. The human papillomavirus type 16 E6 and E7 proteins cooperate to induce mitotic defects and genomic instability by uncoupling centrosome duplication from the cell division cycle. *Proc Natl Acad Sci USA* 2000;97:10002–7.

59.   Duensing S, Duensing A, Flores ER, Do A, Lambert PF, Munger K. Centrosome abnormalities and genomic instability by episomal expression of human papillomavirus type 16 in raft cultures of human keratinocytes. *J Virol* 2001;75:7712–6.

Chapter 3

Cell-mediated immunity and lower genital tract neoplasia

Margaret A Stanley, Nicholas Coleman and Cinzia Scarpini

Human papillomavirus infection and lower genital tract neoplasia

Papillomaviruses are small double-stranded DNA viruses that infect squamous epithelia. The viruses are highly species-specific; human papillomaviruses (HPVs) comprise a large family of about 130 distinct genotypes with a predilection for either cutaneous or mucosal epithelia. About 30 HPV types sporadically or regularly infect the genital tract and can be classified into two groups:

- low-risk HPV types that have little or no oncogenic potential, such as HPV-6, HPV-11 and their relatives
- high-risk or oncogenic HPV types, such as HPV-16, 18, 31, 33, 35, 45 and others.

HPV infection of the anogenital skin and mucosae results in lesions with two morphologies: anogenital warts (condyloma acuminata) and squamous intraepithelial lesions (SILs). Condylomas are polypoid growths that generate infectious virus and have a low to negligible risk of malignant progression. SILs are classified histologically and form a distinct spectrum of histological atypia. In the cervix, these are graded according to the degree to which they have lost cytoplasmic maturation and exhibit cytological atypia. In Europe, three grades of cervical intraepithelial neoplasia (CIN) are recognised: CIN1 (mild), CIN2 (moderate) and CIN3 (severe). The Bethesda classification used in the USA recognises two classes: low-grade squamous intraepithelial lesions or LSILs (CIN1) and high-grade squamous intraepithelial lesions HSILs (CIN2/3). In the vagina, vulva, anus and penis, a similar but not identical spectrum of changes can be identified – vaginal intraepithelial neoplasia, vulval intraepithelial neoplasia (VIN), anal intraepithelial neoplasia (AIN) and penile intraepithelial neoplasia – but the likelihood of progression of these lesions to malignancies is still unclear. It is probable, but not unequivocally proven, that the majority of these intraepithelial lesions are the result of HPV infection.

LSILs at any site can be associated with both high- and low-risk HPV types, although high-risk types predominate. The majority of LSILs maintain the virus as an episome and support a complete virus replication cycle, and viral gene expression is tightly regulated. Late genes are expressed and virus particles are generated. HSILs (at least in the cervix) are associated almost exclusively with high-risk types. In general, high-grade CIN do not support a complete viral infectious cycle. Late gene expression is either lost or significantly reduced, the viral DNA sequences may be integrated into the host genome and expression of the E6 and E7 oncogenes is deregulated with the expression of these oncoproteins throughout the epithelium. CIN3 lesions are characterised by chromosomal aneuploidy and genetic instability and can progress to malignancy. The evidence that HSILs at other sites also exhibit genetic instability is incomplete but, at least for VIN and AIN, this looks increasingly likely.[1]

HPV infectious cycle: implications for immune responses

The unique and complex replication cycle of the HPVs causes difficulties in studying the biology and pathogenesis of these viruses. They are exclusively intraepithelial pathogens with a replication cycle that is both time and differentiation dependent. The replication cycle is one in which viral infection is targeted to basal keratinocytes but high-level expression of viral proteins and viral assembly occurs only in differentiating keratinocytes in the strata spinosum and granulosum of squamous epithelium. *In vitro* systems that generate large amounts of infectious virus are not available. The viral genome is small (8 kb of double-stranded DNA) and encodes a maximum of eight genes, six of which encode non-structural or early proteins E1, E2, E4, E5, E6 and E7 and two of which encode structural or late proteins L1 and L2. Viral genes are differentially expressed, both temporally and spatially, throughout the infectious cycle (Figure 3.1).

This infectious cycle raises several important issues with respect to immune recognition. First, infection and vegetative viral growth are absolutely dependent upon

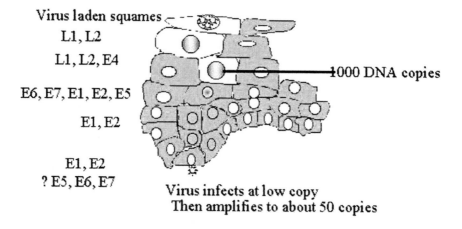

Figure 3.1 Infectious cycle of human papillomavirus: virus, at low copy number, infects cells in the basal layer of the epithelium; it is likely that there is amplification of viral copy number at this time to around 50–100 copies per cell; in the proliferating compartment of the epithelium, there is restricted viral gene expression and viral copy number is maintained at 50–100 copies/cell; viral DNA replication and amplification of copy number to thousands of copies per cell occur in non-dividing keratinocytes in the upper spinous layers; all viral genes are expressed; only in the superficial epithelial keratinocytes are viral capsid proteins synthesised and virus particles assembled

a complete programme of keratinocyte differentiation. Viral infection is targeted to the basal keratinocytes, but high-level viral expression of viral proteins and viral assembly occurs only in the upper layers of the strata spinosum and granulosum of squamous epithelia. Viral gene expression is confined to the keratinocyte and there is no evidence that viral genes are expressed in any cell other than keratinocytes, raising the issue of how non-structural viral proteins could be presented by professional antigen-presenting cells (APC), such as Langerhans cells, for the initiation of an immune response.

Second, the replication cycle takes a long time; even in the best scenario the timescale from infection to release of virus would be a minimum of three weeks, since this is the length of time it takes for the basal keratinocyte to undergo complete differentiation and desquamate. In reality, the period between infection and the appearance of lesions can vary from six weeks to months or even years,[2,3] indicating either that the virus has highly effective immune evasion strategies or that the immune system is ignorant of viral presence, or both.

Third, there is no cytolysis or cytopathic death as a consequence of viral replication and assembly; these key events for the virus occur far from sites of immune activity in the differentiating keratinocyte, a cell destined for death and desquamation. The virus actually delays nuclear condensation in differentiating keratinocytes, forming the koilocyte, the pathognomic cell of HPV infection. This may be the consequence of the combined effects of viral E6 and E7 proteins in halting apoptosis until viral replication is completed, but then the virus-laden keratinocyte proceeds to its inevitable death by natural causes.

As a consequence of this, HPV infection is not accompanied by inflammation and there is no obvious 'danger signal' to alert the immune system. This is a viral strategy that results in persistent, chronic infections, as the host remains ignorant of the pathogen for long periods. The central questions are therefore whether natural infection with HPV evokes a host response, what the nature of this response is and when and how it occurs.

Immune responses to virus infections

Before discussing HPV-specific immunity, it is helpful to review briefly the basic features of the immune response to viruses. Put simply, cell-mediated immune responses are essential for the clearance of virus-infected cells and the generation of immune memory and antibody-mediated humoral immunity clears free virus particles from body fluids and can prevent reinfection by virus.

T lymphocytes are the 'generals' of the immune system and the key players in cell-mediated immunity (CMI). T cells cannot recognise macromolecules but need antigen processed into short peptides that are then bound to the major histocompatibility complex (MHC) proteins and presented as a membrane bound receptor complex on the cell surface. Polymorphic MHC molecules fall into two groups: class II (human leucocyte antigen [HLA] -DP, DQ, DR) and class I (HLA-A, B, C). HLA class I is expressed to varying extents on all except red cells but class II is constitutively expressed only on APC, such as dendritic cells, Langerhans cells and B lymphocytes.

There are two major subsets of T cells identified by the surface markers CD4 or CD8. CD4+ T cells recognise antigen presented by class II MHC; CD8+ T cells recognise antigen presented by class I MHC. Antigen in the context of class I MHC is endogenous antigen that is usually derived from intracellular synthesis of proteins broken down in the proteasome into short peptides and presented on the cell surface as

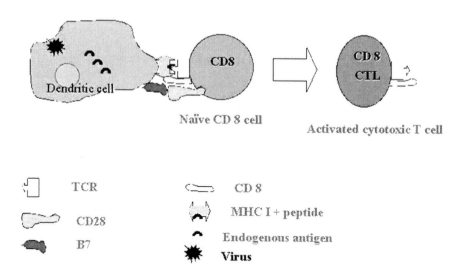

Figure 3.2 Antigen presentation to CD8+ cells: CD8+ T cells are activated by endogenously processed antigen presented as a complex with major histocompatibility complex class I; antigen-specific CD8+ cells are predominantly cytotoxic effector cells; from Sterling JC, Tyring SK. *Human Papillomaviruses Clinical and Scientific Advances.* London: Arnold; 2001 (reproduced with permission)

an MHC/peptide complex for recognition by the T cell receptor on the CD8+ lymphocyte (Figure 3.2). The geometry of the MHC/peptide complex is so precise that it can only be recognised and bound with the correct affinity by a T cell receptor that matches it precisely.

Usually antigen presented in the context of MHC class II is exogenous antigen taken up from the extracellular milieu and broken down in the endosome of the APC for association into the class II complex for presentation on the cell surface and recognition by the specific T-cell receptor on the CD4+ T cell. The interaction between the CD4+ T cell and the APC is complex and requires several other receptor–ligand interactions to occur in a regulated order before the T cell is activated and starts to proliferate (Figure 3.3). In particular, the T cell must receive a specific second signal from the CD80 molecule on the MHC. Failure to receive the second signal can render the T cell anergic or unresponsive to any subsequent encounter with the antigen. T cell activation results in the secretion of a repertoire of small proteins or cytokines that help and regulate other cells. The pattern of cytokine expression defines two subsets of CD4+ T cells known as Th2 or Th1 cells.

- Th2 cells secrete IL-4 and IL-10 (and other cytokines) and help antigen-primed B cells to differentiate into plasma cells and secrete antibody for humoral responses.

- Th1 cells secrete interferon-γ (IFN-γ) and help to activate macrophages, natural killer cells (NKC) and cytotoxic T lymphocytes (CTL) generating CMI.

Whether the T cell takes the Th2 or Th1 path is strongly influenced by the APC, as a consequence of the receptors that the APC expresses and the cytokines secreted. These

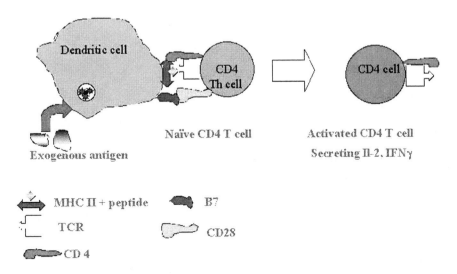

Figure 3.3 Antigen presentation to CD4+ cells: the dendritic cell processes exogenous antigen and presents it as a complex with major histocompatibility complex class II to the naïve T cell; the T cell receptor recognises this complex and the T cell is activated; in the appropriate cytokine environment the activated T cell differentiates along the Th1 pathway; from Sterling JC, Tyring SK. *Human Papillomaviruses Clinical and Scientific Advances.* London: Arnold; 2001 (reproduced with permission)

functions of the APC are in turn activated by signals received from the receptor–ligand interactions between the APC and the pathogen and also by the cytokines released by other cells in the immediate vicinity. The APC in effect 'tells' the T cell what sort of defence is needed and is central to the generation of an effective and appropriate immune response.

It seems that only APCs can initiate primary immune responses and activate virgin T cells but that HPV non-structural proteins (such as E6 and E7) are only expressed in keratinocytes, so how can cell-mediated immune responses be induced against them? The most likely explanation is that antigen released from dying HPV-infected cells is taken up by APC and enters both the class I and class II processing pathways. The APC first presents to the CD4+ T cell, which then signals back to the APC via CD4+/CD4+ ligand interactions. This activates or licenses the APC to present directly to naïve CD8+ T cells that can then differentiate into potent CTLs and kill HPV-infected cells that they detect (Figure 3.4).

Cell-mediated immunity in HPV infections

The increased incidence and progression of HPV infections in immunosuppressed individuals[4] illustrates the critical role of cell-mediated immune responses in the resolution and control of HPV infections. HIV-infected patients show multiple recurrences of cervical HPV infections.[5] The evidence from allograft recipients and HIV-infected individuals[6] indicates that it is the absolute deficit in CD4+ T cells that is the important risk factor for HPV-induced disease and associated neoplastic

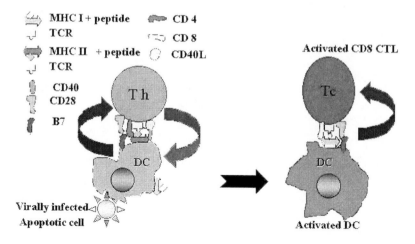

Figure 3.4 T cell help for killer T cells: antigens released from dying or dead cells (such as virally infected cells) can be taken up by dendritic cells and processed for presentation to Th cells via major histocompatibility complex (MHC) class II; the Th cell then signals back to the dendritic cell, stimulating it to present the antigen via MHC class I to activate cytotoxic CD8+ cells; from Sterling JC, Tyring SK. *Human Papillomaviruses Clinical and Scientific Advances.* London: Arnold; 2001 (reproduced with permission)

progression in the immunocompromised individual. This suggests that CD4+ T cells play a central role in the resolution and control of HPV infection.

Histological studies

Clues to the nature of the cellular immune response to HPV infection have come from immunohistological studies of spontaneously regressing genital warts. Non-regressing genital warts are characterised by a lack of immune cells; the few intraepithelial lymphocytes are principally CD8+ cells and mononuclear cells are present mainly in the stroma. Wart regression is characterised by a massive mononuclear cell infiltrate in both stroma and epithelium. The infiltrating lymphocytes are predominantly CD4+ cells but many CD8+ T cells are present and are concentrated in the epithelium. The lymphocytes are activated and express the IL-2 receptor: most are 'antigen-experienced', expressing the CD45 RO marker. The wart keratinocytes express HLA-DR and the intercellular adhesion molecule 1 (ICAM-1), implying that there has been local release of cytokines such as IFN-γ. There is upregulation of the adhesion molecules required for lymphocyte trafficking on the endothelium of the wart capillaries,[7] reinforcing the notion of local releases of pro-inflammatory cytokines and chemokines.

These appearances are characteristic of a Th1-biased lymphocyte response and this impression is reinforced by the analysis of cytokine expression in the regressing lesions. There is expression of mRNA for the proinflammatory cytokines IFNγ, tumour necrosis factor (TNFα) and the interleukin-12 (IL-12) p40 subunit. Interestingly, bioactive IL-12 is expressed not only by dendritic cells and macrophages in the regressing wart but also by the infected keratinocytes. No statistical differences in Langerhans cell numbers were seen between regressors and non-regressors,[7] although loss of dendritic arborisations was seen in Langerhans cells in non-regressing lesions, a phenomenon also reported in HPV-associated cervical lesions.[8] Cross-sectional studies, however, provide only a snapshot of a dynamic process and, in a longitudinal study examining the action of imiquimod, a topical preparation with immunomodulatory activities, a decrease in mRNA for the Langerhans cell marker CD1a was observed during wart regression post treatment.[9] This was reflected morphologically by a decrease in CD1a positive intraepithelial dendritic cells as warts regressed.

The response to genital warts represents host defence to HPV infection uncomplicated by the genetic instability that characterises neoplasia.[10] The situation in HPV-infected cervical epithelium is more complicated, since there are two biological processes: HPV infection and neoplasia. Immunohistochemical studies of cervical LSILs suggest that overall these lesions are immunologically quiescent with few infiltrating T cells and a decreased number of Langerhans cells compared with normal ectocervical epithelium.[11] It is possible that this decrease simply reflects the normal egress of antigen carrying Langerhans cells from the epidermis to the draining node for antigen presentation. However, virtually all cervical SILs arise in the transformation zone, often associated with squamous metaplasia, and there is evidence that Langerhans cell numbers are reduced in squamous metaplasia[12] and in the transformation zone, where these cells have an immature phenotype.[13] The reduced numbers of Langerhans cells in SILs may simply reflect the histogenesis.

HSILs also show a decreased number of Langerhans cells,[14] a phenomenon that may be related to neoplasia since there is *in vitro* evidence that immortalised HPV-infected cervical cells inhibit Langerhans cell recruitment.[15] T cell infiltrates in LSILs and HSILs have been documented in several studies but with differing results. A significant reduction in intraepithelial T cells, particularly in the CD4+ subset, was found by Tay *et al.*,[16] but others found an increase in the intraepithelial CD8 subset.[17] These discrepancies are not unexpected if the biology of HPV-associated cervical disease is considered. HSILs are aneuploid, genetically unstable lesions exhibiting heterogeneity in the expression of immunologically relevant molecules such as adhesion molecules and cytokines, which affects the recruitment of lymphocyte subsets to the epithelium. Furthermore, all published studies are cross-sectional and the stage in the natural history of the disease (regression, persistence or progression) cannot be known. Surveillance and defence against viral infection and tumours are mediated by a range of effector mechanisms. An important group of effectors have the morphology of large granular lymphocytes; these include the NKC subset. Large granular lymphocytes (LGLs) with the NKC phenotype CD56+, CD16+, CD3-, CD2^{variable}, CD57^{variable}, which are rarely found within either normal cervical epithelium or CIN but they are found in the stroma, particularly in the endocervix. A separate subset of LGLs with the phenotype CD56+, CD16-, CD3+, CD2+, is found within the ectocervical epithelium and this subset dominates the intraepithelial population in high-grade CIN,[18] a phenomenon related to neoplasia rather than HPV infection.

Cytokines

Both initiation and regulation of cell-mediated immune responses are strongly dependent on the local cytokine milieu. The production of these molecules is not restricted to immunocytes such as lymphocytes, dendritic cells and macrophages; keratinocytes themselves are important sources. Keratinocytes constitutively secrete low levels of several cytokines[19] and can be induced by various stimuli (injury, ultraviolet irradiation, infection) to produce significant amounts.[20] The expression of the cytokines IFN-α, TNF-α and IL-10 is of particular interest in cervical HPV-associated disease.

IFN-α has antiviral, antiproliferative and immunostimulatory properties; there is good evidence that expression of the high-risk HPV E6 and E7 proteins can inhibit the induction of IFN-α inducible genes[21,22] and it has been shown that HPV-16 E7 binds to the p48 component of the interferon-induced transcription complex.[23] High doses of IFN-α can partially overcome this effect and this is probably the basis for the therapeutic effect in HPV-induced genital warts of the immune response modulator imiquimod, a topical preparation that induces IFN-α and other proinflammatory cytokines.

Secreted TNF-α is a potent activator of Langerhans cells. The protein in its intracellular form is constitutively expressed by keratinocytes *in vivo* and *in vitro*.[24] In a small unpublished study, the authors examined, by immunohistochemistry, the expression of TNF and two of the cellular receptors for this molecule, p55 and p75, in normal cervix, LSILs and HSILs. In all samples, as would be expected, positive staining for TNF and both receptors was seen on stromal macrophages. Endothelial cells and the basal and parabasal cells of normal cervical epithelium stained positively for TNF and the p55 receptor but were negative for p75 (Figure 3.5). A similar distribution was seen in most cases of LSIL but in one case p55 receptor staining was lost by the abnormal epithelium. In HSILs (Figure 3.6), all cases showed a loss of epithelial TNF expression and three of five cases showed a loss of p55 staining. In another larger immunohistochemical study[25] in normal cervix and SIL examining TNF expression only, essentially similar findings were reported but with more variability in patterns of expression in both LSILs and HSILs.

It has been suggested that HPV E6/E7 expression in infected keratinocytes could have a direct influence on the release of TNF-α.[26] Exogenously added TNF inhibits the growth of HPV immortalised cells[27,28] and both TNF-α and IL-1α are able to downregulate transcriptionally the expression of E6 and E7 in HPV-16-transformed keratinocytes.[29] Important questions therefore are whether the TNF-α detected by immunohistochemistry is intracellular or is secreted and whether the downregulation of expression in HSILs is a consequence of enhanced expression of the early genes E6 and E7 of the oncogenic HPVs. These issues cannot be addressed easily using *in vivo* biopsies and this was examined in a study that determined TNF-α expression and secretion *in vitro* by normal cervical keratinocytes and five HPV-16 immortalised cervical keratinocyte cell lines for details of their origin.[30,31] Western blot analysis of protein extracts showed that all cell lines expressed TNF-α protein but enzyme-linked immunosorbent assay of culture supernatants revealed that only normal cervical keratinocytes released immunodetectable amounts of TNF-α, indicating that the TNF detected in HPV immortalised cells is in the intracellular form. Importantly, exogenously added IL-1α, a molecule that downregulates HPV-16 E6/E7 expression, had no effect on TNF expression or secretion (Figure 3.7). These observations strongly suggest that HPV-16 oncogene expression *per se* is not responsible for the inability of HPV immortalised cells to secrete TNF but that this phenomenon is more likely to be the consequence of events related to genetic instability and immortalisation.

IL-10 is a cytokine that inhibits Th1 responses, a property mediated via its effects on APC.[32] Keratinocytes can be induced to secrete IL-10[33] and it is likely that this plays a role in regulating the Langerhans cell phenotype and function in squamous epithelium. IL-10 expression at both mRNA and protein level in normal cervix and SIL was examined in a careful study by Mota *et al*.[25] No expression could be detected in

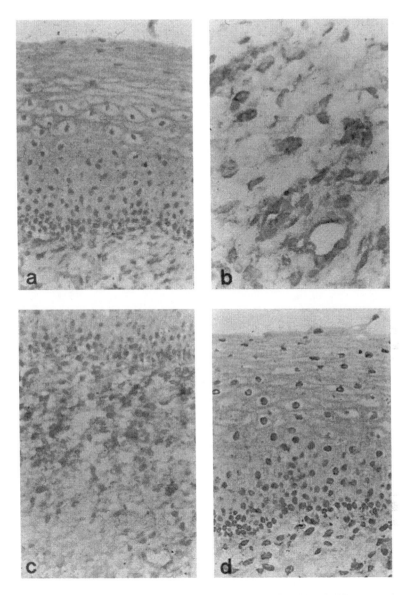

Figure 3.5 Expression of tumour necrosis factor alpha (TNF-α) and the p55 and p75 receptors in normal cervical tissue: weak expression of TNF-α (detected by indirect immunoperoxidase staining with MAb J1D9) can be seen in the basal epithelium (a) but is clearly present on mononuclear cells and endothelium in the stroma (b); p75 (detected with the MAb utr 1) was expressed by stromal cells only (c) but p55 (detected by the MAb htr 9) was expressed on the nucleus of both stromal and epithelial cells (d); magnification (a), (c), (d) = x 250; (b) = x 500

normal cervix but a proportion of both low-grade and high-grade lesions showed epithelial expression. Expression in LSILs was usually in basal cells but many HSILs exhibited full thickness expression. In unpublished studies by Scarpini, Stanley and Coleman, epithelial IL-10 expression could not be detected in either normal cervix or SIL but could be detected in infiltrating lymphocytes in high-grade lesions.

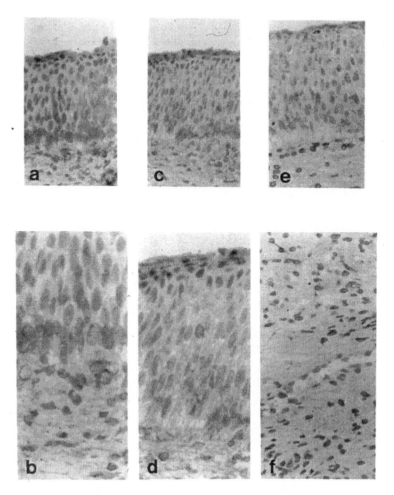

Figure 3.6 Expression of tumour necrosis factor alpha (TNF-α) and the p55 and p75 receptors in high-grade cervical lesions: although TNF-α staining can be detected on stromal cells, no epithelial expression is evident (a), (b); p75 staining can be detected on stromal and intraepithelial mononuclear cells (c), (d); p55 is expressed on stromal cells but its expression on epithelium is either diminished or lost (e), (f); magnification (a), (c), (e) = x 250; (b), (d), (f) = x 500

CD4 T cell responses

Immunohistological studies indicate clearly that regression of HPV-infected lesions is associated with a Th1 response but the viral antigens that provoke this response are not known. The evidence from both experimental models and human studies shows that viral proteins are immune targets. In a murine model in which viral antigen is expressed in keratinocytes and mimics the natural route of infection, delayed-type hypersensitivity (DTH) responses to E6 and E7 can be shown.[34,35] The ability to prime the immune system and elicit a DTH response in this system depends upon antigen dose. Low levels of antigen induce immune non-responsiveness,[36] a phenomenon associated with a switch in Th1–Th2 cytokine expression in the CD8+ T cell subset in the draining lymph node that suggests a suppressor effect.[37]

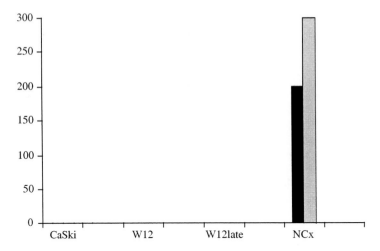

Figure 3.7 Tumour necrosis factor alpha (TNF-α) release by normal and the HPV-16 immortalised keratinocyte lines W12 (at early and late passage) CaSki; cells were grown in keratinocyte serum-free growth medium to logarithmic phase, the medium alone (black bar) or medium plus 400 ng/ml IL-1α (dashed bar) was added for 24 or 48 hours; supernatants were collected, cell debris removed and TNF-α measured by sandwich enzyme-linked immunosorbent assay using a commercially available kit with a sensitivity of 4.4 pg/ml (R&D Systems); the values shown are pg/ml/10^6 cells

Specific T cell responses to HPV-16 L1 and E7 have been identified in patients with all grades of SIL in cross-sectional studies. All patients with current HPV infection, including 92% of the HSIL group, had lymphoproliferative responses to one or more HPV-16 L1 peptides.[38] The majority of peptide-specific T cells were CD4+ lymphocytes. In a study examining lymphoproliferative responses to E7 peptides, 47% of normal controls responded to both 'N' and 'C' peptides but only 33% of the women with CIN showed a response to E7.[39] Those with high-grade lesions contained a higher proportion of responders than the CIN1 group. T cell proliferative responses to HPV-16 E7 were determined in a cohort study of women all initially presenting with mild to moderate dyskaryosis.[40] During follow-up, the cohort could be divided into those who cleared virus, those with fluctuating infection and those with persistent infection. Interestingly, the strongest T cell responses were observed in women with persisting HPV infection and progressing cervical lesions (99% reactive) compared with those with clearing or fluctuating infection (41% reactive). A different outcome was reported in a study by Kadish *et al.*,[41] who determined T cell proliferative responses to E6 and E7 peptides at three-month intervals over a 12-month period in a cohort of women with CIN1or 2. Cell-mediated immune responses in this group to an E7 peptide (37–54aa) correlated significantly with regression of disease and resolution of infection. Intriguingly, these responses were not HPV type-specific.

T cell responses to antigens other than E6 and E7 have not been well documented. However, there is increasing evidence that the E2 protein is an important immune target for effective viral clearance. In cottontail rabbit papillomavirus infection, which provides a good model for papilloma/carcinoma progression, the induction of T cell proliferative responses to E2 protein was the best predictor of lesion regression.[42] In a recent study, HPV-16 E2-specific T helper responses could be detected in 50% of healthy donors, suggesting that E2-specific CD4+ T cell memory is associated with a successful host response to HPV infection.[43]

Cell-mediated cytotoxicity

CD8 T cell responses

Cell-mediated cytotoxicity is the most important effector mechanism for the control and clearance of viral infections and is implemented by a range of cells, including cytotoxic T cells and NKCs. The role of these effectors, particularly CTLs, in HPV infection is a topic of intense contemporary interest. There is now good evidence that HPV-specific CTL can be detected in patients with previous[44] or continuing HPV infection.[45–47] Both CD4+ and CD8+ cytotoxic effectors have been shown to be involved in these responses.[48] CTL responses have been described in six of ten CIN3 patients in an assay in which peripheral-blood mononuclear cells (PMBCs) were restimulated with adenovirus recombinants expressing an HPV-16 and -18 E6/E7 fusion protein and lysed autologous targets infected with a recombinant vaccinia virus expressing the same fusion protein.[49] No CTL responses were identified in control subjects. However, the HPV status of controls and patients was not defined in this study. Recent studies show that high-affinity HPV E7-specific CTL are rare in patients with carcinoma or HSIL but can be detected with increased sensitivity using the technology of fluorescently labelled HLA peptide complexes (tetramers).[50]

Increased numbers of T cells are seen locally in squamous cell carcinoma of the cervix[51] with a dominance of CD8+ cells. In a more recent study, HPV-16 and -18 E6/E7-specific CTL were detected in PBMCs, draining lymph nodes and tumour of cervical cancer patients.[47] Limiting dilution analysis was used to determine the frequency of the HPV-specific CTL and these were present in significantly higher numbers in the tumours and lymph nodes than peripheral blood. The association between HPV-16 E6 and E7-specific CTL and HPV-16 persistence was examined in a longitudinal study of women with polymerase chain reaction-determined cervical HPV-16 infection. Lack of CTL response to E6 but not E7 correlated with persistent HPV infection, suggesting that a CTL response to HPV-16 E6 is important for viral clearance and, by implication, neoplastic progression.[52]

There is some support for the notion that the CTL response to E6 is important for viral persistence. A sequence variant of HPV-16 is over-represented in HLA-B7 cervical cancer patients. This variant exhibits a single amino acid change in the HPV-16 E6 protein in a putative HLA-B7 restricted CTL epitope,[53] a change that alters the affinity of binding of the T cell receptor/HLA-B7 peptide complex and could therefore compromise the CTL response. A recent study by Evans et al.[54] is highly relevant to this issue. This study addressed the question of whether cervical carcinoma cells can process and present HPV E6/E7 antigen for CTL recognition. HLA-A*0201 restricted CTL clones were generated against HPV-16 E6 CTL epitopes. The clones recognised E6 transfected lymphoblastoid cells but not HLA A*0201 HPV-16 E6+ carcinoma cells, even when the endogenous level of E6 in the latter was enhanced by transfection. This defect in recognition was due to class I downregulation on the tumour cells but even when class I was upregulated by IFNγ, unless E6 expression was concomitantly increased by transfection, CTL recognition failed, suggesting that both antigen processing and presentation of E6 are compromised in invasive carcinomas.

Natural killer cells

Cytotoxic effector mechanisms also include NKCs, a subset of lymphocytes that kill virally infected or tumour cells lacking surface expression of MHC class I molecules.

There is evidence for defective NKC function in HPV 16-associated disease. PBMCs from patients with active HPV-16 neoplastic disease display a reduced NKC activity against HPV 16-infected keratinocytes, although their response to K562 cells is not affected[55] and *in vitro* expression of the E7 protein of HPV-16/19 precludes the lysis of HPV-transformed cells by interferon-stimulated NKCs.[56] Target recognition by NKCs does not involve classical antigen receptors because these cells do not express T or B cell antigen receptors, nor do they rearrange their immunoglobulin or T cell receptor genes. NKCs express clonally distributed receptors specific for HLA I type molecules and, functionally, these receptors can be inhibitory or stimulatory. Inhibitory receptors block NKC-mediated cytotoxicity upon binding to HLA ligands. Stimulatory receptors also bind HLA class I motifs but trigger NKC-mediated cytotoxicity. NKC-mediated cytolysis of a virally infected or tumour cell depends upon the balance between the negative and positive signals received by the NKC. It is evident that MHC class I expression is critical for both CTL and NKC effector mechanisms and specific downregulation or loss of class I alleles would be a way of evading cytotoxic effector mechanisms and is indeed a well-recognised mechanism for evasion of host defences by viruses.

The inconsistencies between the various studies on the cell-mediated immune response in cervical HPV infection are not surprising. All studies use either recombinantly expressed proteins or synthetic peptides and there is no standardisation of either assay or reagents. Most reports describe cross-sectional studies with small numbers of patients and the actual stage in the natural history of the disease is unknown. Most importantly, all studies use circulating PBMCs and the frequency with which HPV antigen-reactive T cells are detected is so low that the sensitivity and specificity of these assays (except in the case of the tetramer studies) is at the absolute extreme. HPV infections are local mucosal infections; there is no viraemic phase and the probability is that the immune response is local and compartmentalised with relatively few antigen-specific T cells entering the systemic circulation. Until effective assays for local mucosal T cell responses are available, it seems inevitable that our understanding of the functional T cell response in HPV infections will remain fragmentary.

MHC class I expression

Loss or allele-specific downregulation of MHC class I expression occurs in more than 90% of cervical carcinomas.[57] This phenomenon is not confined to invasive disease and has been shown to occur in all grades of CIN. A recent longitudinal study examined HLA-B expression in a cohort of women with mild or moderate dyskaryosis on study entry.[58] During follow-up, the cohort divided into those who cleared the infection, those who had fluctuating infection and those who had persistent infection. In this cohort, it appears that allele-specific downregulation is associated with clinical progression and may be a comparatively early event in the CIN spectrum. In a proportion of cases, this downregulation of MHC class I is post transcriptionally regulated and due to a loss of transporter-associated protein.[59] It is unlikely that all class I loss is due to this one mechanism and the regulation of any one of several MHC gene products could be disturbed. Whatever the mechanism, functionally these changes may be crucial to HPV-related cancer progression since, as discussed above, loss or allele-specific downregulation of class I would interfere with both CTL and NKC recognition of their targets, disabling the major cytotoxic effector mechanisms.

MHC class II expression

The keratinocytes of the genital tract do not express class II proteins but can be induced to do so by cytokines such as IFNγ and TNF-α.[60] When anogenital warts regress, the keratinocytes express HLA-DR and this is thought to be due to the release of proinflammatory cytokines by infiltrating lymphocytes and macrophages.[7] In LSILs, a variable expression of class II is observed, ranging from none[61] to focal patchy expression[60] but in HSILs it is present predominantly as extensive diffuse staining.[60,62] At least 80% of cervical cancers express class II proteins on the malignant keratinocytes.[63] It is likely that expression of MHC class II on neoplastic keratinocytes is induced rather than constitutive; increased numbers of T cells occur in the stroma underneath class II positive CIN[60] and there is an increase in tumour-infiltrating lymphocytes in DR-positive regions of carcinomas.[64] A significant proportion of HSILs express ICAM-1 as well as HLA-DR, but the expression of these molecules is not coordinated[65] and ICAM-1 expression in HSILs is likely to be constitutive rather than induced and a reflection of neoplasia rather than viral infection.[66]

Evasion of cell-mediated immunity by HPV

Epidemiological studies show clearly that cervical HPV infection is extremely common but also that infection generally resolves within 6–24 months after HPV detection.[67] These studies[68,69] also show that viral persistence is a key factor in progressive cervical intraepithelial disease, suggesting that host defence to HPV has not been successful in these women.

The HLA haplotype can clearly influence the natural history of HPV infection in each individual since, for any one protein antigen, different alleles of the MHC will present different peptides to the immune system. Thus the HLA haplotype could be a major determinant of whether infection is cleared or persists, which, in the case of the oncogenic viruses, could influence the risk of neoplastic progression. If this thesis is correct, then it could be reflected in different HLA frequencies in patients with persistent or chronic HPV infections (including carcinoma) compared with the appropriate control populations. Immunogenetic studies suggest that there is a relationship between susceptibility to infection with specific HPV types and HLA-DQ haplotypes,[70,71] although its exact nature remains unclear.[72,73]

The data discussed previously on cytokine expression and the evidence that LCs in CIN are reduced in number and lack co-stimulation molecules do suggest that the epithelial microenvironment in many CIN, particularly CIN2/3, limits effective cell-mediated immune responses and may result in an inappropriate immune response. This notion is supported by the observation that in individuals with progressive cervical lesions the immune response is a Th2 type rather than Th1, leading to the concern that there may be partial tolerance to viral antigen.[74]

The genetic instability that is the hallmark of high-grade CIN gives these lesions the potential to evolve immune escape mechanisms rapidly. Modulation of the cytokine milieu and cytokine response is a common immune escape mechanism that occurs in high-grade lesions. Crucially, downregulation or loss of MHC class I occurs in almost all cervical carcinomas,[57] in a proportion of HPV-associated VIN[75] and in CIN,[58] where it is associated with progression.

We are beginning to gain a better understanding of what constitutes an effective host response to HPV infection, as well as of the deficiencies in that response that lead to persistence and development of intraepithelial neoplasia. The hope is that this understanding can be translated into effective immunotherapies.

References

1.   Haga T, Kim SH, Jensen RH, Darragh T, Palefsky JM. Detection of genetic changes in anal intra-epithelial neoplasia (AIN) of HIV-positive and HIV-negative men. *J Acquir Immune Defic Syndr* 2001;26:256–62.

2.   Oriel JD. Natural history of genital warts. *Br J Vener Dis* 1971;47:1–13.

3.   Koutsky LA, Holmes KK, Critchlow CW, Stevens CE, Paavonen J, Beckmann AM, *et al.* A cohort study of the risk of cervical intra-epithelial neoplasia grade 2 or 3 in relation to papillomavirus infection. *N Engl J Med* 1992;327:1272–8.

4.   Benton EC, Arends MJ. Human papillomavirus in the immunosuppressed. In Lacey C, editor. *Papillomavirus Reviews: Current Research on Papillomaviruses.* Leeds: Leeds University Press; 1996. p. 271–9.

5.   Fruchter RG, Maiman M, Sedlis A, Bartley L, Arrastia CD. Multiple recurrence of cervical intra-epithelial neoplasia in women with the human immunodeficiency virus. *Obstet Gynecol* 1996;87:338–44.

6.   Palefsky JM, Minkoff H, Kalish LA, Levine A, Sacks HS, Garcia P, *et al.* Cervicovaginal human papillomavirus infection in human immunodeficiency virus-1 (HIV)-positive and high-risk HIV-negative women. *J Natl Cancer Inst* 1999;91:226–36.

7.   Coleman N, Birley HD, Renton AM, Hanna NF, Ryait BK, Byrne M, *et al.* Immunological events in regressing genital warts. *Am J Clin Pathol* 1994;102:768–74.

8.   Morelli AE, Sananes C, Di Paola G, Paredes A, Fainboim L. Relationship between types of human papillomavirus and Langerhans' cells in cervical condyloma and intra-epithelial neoplasia. *Am J Clin Pathol* 1993;99:200–6.

9.   Tyring SK, Arany I, Stanley MA, Tomai MA, Miller RL, Smith MH, *et al.* A randomized, controlled, molecular study of condylomata acuminata clearance during treatment with imiquimod. *J Infect Dis* 1998;178:551–5.

10.   Stanley M, Coleman N, Chambers M. The host response to lesions induced by human papillomavirus. In: Mindel A, editor. *Genital Warts Human Papillomavirus Infections.* London: Edward Arnold; 1994. p. 21–44.

11.   Hawthorn RJ, Murdoch JB, MacLean AB, MacKie RM. Langerhans' cells and subtypes of human papillomavirus in cervical intra-epithelial neoplasia. *BMJ* 1988;297:643–6.

12.   Roncalli M, Sideri M, Gie P, Servida E. Immunophenotypic analysis of the transformation zone of human cervix. *Lab Invest* 1988;58:141–9.

13.   Giannini SL, Hubert P, Doyen J, Boniver J, Delvenne P. Influence of the mucosal epithelium microenvironment on Langerhans cells: implications for the development of squamous intra-epithelial lesions of the cervix. *Int J Cancer* 2002;97:654–9.

14.   Viac J, Guerin Reverchon I, Chardonnet Y, Bremond A. Langerhans cells and epithelial cell modifications in cervical intra-epithelial neoplasia: correlation with human papillomavirus infection. *Immunobiology* 1990;180:328–38.

15.   Hubert P, Van den Brule F, Giannini SL, Franzen Detrooz E, Boniver J, Delvenne P. Colonization of *in vitro*-formed cervical human papillomavirus-associated (pre)neoplastic lesions with dendritic cells: role of granulocyte/macrophage colony-stimulating factor. *Am J Pathol* 1999;154:775–84.

16.   Tay SK, Jenkins D, Maddox P, Singer A. Lymphocyte phenotypes in cervical intra-epithelial neoplasia and human papillomavirus infection. *Br J Obstet Gynaecol* 1987;94:16–21.

17.   Viac J, Chardonnet Y, Euvrard S, Schmitt D. Epidermotropism of T cells correlates with intercellular adhesion molecule (ICAM1) expression in human papillomavirus (HPV) induced lesions. *J Pathol* 1992;168:301–6.

18.   McKenzie J, King A, Hare J, Fulford T, Wilson B, Stanley M. Immunocytochemical characterization of large granular lymphocytes in normal cervix and HPV associated disease. *J Pathol* 1991;165:75–80.

19.   Wang B, Amerio P, Sauder DN. Role of cytokines in epidermal Langerhans cell migration. *J Leukoc Biol* 1999;66:33–9.

20.   Nozaki S, Feliciani C, Sauder DN. Keratinocyte cytokines. *Adv Dermatol* 1992;7:83–100.

21.   Chang YE, Laimins LA. Microarray analysis identifies interferon-inducible genes and Stat-1 as major transcriptional targets of human papillomavirus type 31. *J Virol* 2000;74:4174–82.

22.   Nees M, Geoghegan JM, Hyman T, Frank S, Miller L, Woodworth CD. Papillomavirus type 16 oncogenes downregulate expression of interferon-responsive genes and upregulate proliferation-associated and NF-kappaB-responsive genes in cervical keratinocytes. *J Virol* 2001;75:4283–96.

23.   Barnard P, McMillan NA. The human papillomavirus E7 oncoprotein abrogates signaling mediated by interferon-alpha. *Virology* 1999;259:305–13.

24.   Kock A, Schwarz T, Kirnbauer R, Urbanski A, Perry P, Ansel JC, *et al.* Human keratinocytes are a source of tumour necrosis factor: evidence for synthesis and release upon stimulation with endotoxin

or ultraviolet light. *J Exp Med* 1990;172:1609–14.

25.   Mota F, Rayment N, Chong S, Singer A, Chain B. The antigen-presenting environment in normal and human papillomavirus (HPV)-related premalignant cervical epithelium. *Clin Exp Immunol* 1999;116:33–40.

26.   Malejczyk J, Malejczyk M, Kock A, Urbanski A, Majewski S, Hunzelmann N, *et al.* Autocrine growth limitation of human papillomavirus type 16 harboring keratinocytes by constitutively released tumor necrosis factor alpha. *J Immunol* 1992;149:2702–8.

27.   Villa LL, Vieira KB, Pei XF, Schlegel R. Differential effect of tumor necrosis factor on proliferation of primary human keratinocytes and cell lines containing human papillomavirus types 16 and 18. *Mol Carcinog* 1992;6:5–9.

28.   Vieira KB, Goldstein DJ, Villa LL. Tumor necrosis factor alpha interferes with the cell cycle of normal and papillomavirus immortalized human keratinocytes. *Cancer Res* 1996;56:2452–7.

29.   Kyo S, Inoue M, Hayasaka N, Inoue T, Yutsudo M, Tanizawa O, *et al.* Regulation of early gene expression of human papillomavirus type 16 by inflammatory cytokines. *Virology* 1994;200:130–39.

30.   Stanley MA, Browne HM, Appleby M, Minson AC. Properties of a non tumorigenic human cervical keratinocyte cell line. *Int J Cancer* 1999;43:672–6.

31.   Cottage A, Dowen S, Roberts I, Pett M, Coleman N, Stanley M. Early genetic events in HPV immortalised keratinocytes. *Genes Chromosomes Cancer* 2001;30:72–9.

32.   Enk AH, Angeloni VL, Udey MC, Katz SI. Inhibition of LC-APC function by IL-10. A role for IL-10 in induction of tolerance. *J Immunol* 1993;151:2390–97.

33.   Enk AH, Katz SI. Identification and induction of keratinocyte-derived IL-10. *J Immunol* 1992;149:92–5.

34.   McLean CS, Sterling JS, Mowat J, Nash AA, Stanley MA. Delayed type hypersensitivity response to the human papillomavirus type 16 E7 protein in a mouse model. *J Gen Virol* 1993;74:239–45.

35.   Chambers MA, Stacey SN, Arrand JR, Stanley MA. Delayed type hypersensitivity response to human papillomavirus type 16 E6 protein in a mouse model. *J Gen Virol* 1994;75:165–9.

36.   Chambers MA, Wei Z, Coleman N, Nash AA, Stanley MA. 'Natural' presentation of human papillomavirus type 16 E7 protein to immunocompetent mice results in antigen specific sensitization or sustained unresponsiveness. *Eur J Immunol* 1994;24:738–45.

37.   Lopez MC, Stanley MA. Cytokine profile of draining lymph node lymphocytes in mice grafted with syngeneic keratinocytes expressing human papillomavirus type 16 E7 protein. *J Gen Virol* 2000;81:1175–82.

38.   Shepherd PS, Rowe AJ, Cridland JC, Coletart T, Wilson P, Luxton JC. Proliferative T cell responses to human papillomavirus type 16 L1 peptides in patients with cervical dysplasia. *J Gen Virol* 1996;77:593–602.

39.   Luxton JC, Rowe AJ, Cridland JC, Coletart T, Wilson P, Shepherd PS. Proliferative T cell responses to the human papillomavirus type 16 E7 protein in women with cervical dysplasia and cervical carcinoma and in healthy individuals. *J Gen Virol* 1996;77:1585–93.

40.   De Gruijl TD, Bontkes HJ, Stukart MJ, Walboomers JM, Remmink A, Verheijen R, *et al.* T cell proliferative responses against human papillomavirus type 16 E7 oncoprotein are most prominent in cervical intra-epithelial neoplasia patients with persistent viral infection. *J Gen Virol* 1996;77:2183–91.

41.   Kadish AS, Timmins P, Wang Y, Ho Gloria YF, Burk RD, Ketz J, *et al.* Regression of cervical intra-epithelial neoplasia and loss of human papillomavirus (HPV) infection is associated with cell-mediated immune responses to an HPV type 16 E7 peptide. *Cancer Epidemiol Biomarkers Prev* 2002;11:483–8.

42.   Selvakumar R, Ahmed R, Wettstein FO. Tumor regression is associated with a specific immune response to the E2 protein of cottontail rabbit papillomavirus. *Virology* 1995;208:298–302.

43.   de Jong A, Van der Burg Sjoerd H, Kwappenberg KMC, Van der Hulst JM, Franken Kees LMC, *et al.* Frequent detection of human papillomavirus 16 E2-specific T-helper immunity in healthy subjects. *Cancer Res* 2002;62:472–479.

44.   Nakagawa M, Stites DP, Farhat S, Sisler JR, Moss B, Kong F, *et al.* Cytotoxic T lymphocyte responses to E6 and E7 proteins of human papillomavirus type 16: relationship to cervical intra-epithelial neoplasia. *J Infect Dis* 1997;175:927–31.

45.   Evans CA, Bauer S, Grubert T, Brucker C, Baur S, Heeg K, *et al.* HLA-A2-restricted peripheral blood cytolytic T lymphocyte response to HPV type 16 proteins E6 and E7 from patients with neoplastic cervical lesions. *Cancer Immunol Immunother* 1996;42:151–60.

46.   Alexander M, Salgaller ML, Celis E, Sette A, Barnes WA, Rosenberg SA, *et al.* Generation of tumor-specific cytolytic T lymphocytes from peripheral blood of cervical cancer patients by *in vitro* stimulation with a synthetic human papillomavirus type 16 E7 epitope. *Am J Obstet Gynecol* 1996;175:1586–93.

47.   Evans EM, Man S, Evans AS, Borysiewicz LK. Infiltration of cervical cancer tissue with human papillomavirus- specific cytotoxic T-lymphocytes. *Cancer Res* 57:2943–50.

48. Nakagawa M, Stites DP, Palefsky JM, Kneass Z, Moscicki AB. CD4-positive and CD8-positive cytotoxic T lymphocytes contribute to human papillomavirus type 16 E6 and E7 responses. *Clin Diagn Lab Immunol* 1999;6:494–8.

49. Nimako M, Fiander AN, Wilkinson GWG, Borysiewicz LK, Man S. Human papillomavirus-specific cytotoxic T lymphocytes in patients with cervical intra-epithelial neoplasia grade III. *Cancer Res* 1997;57:4855–61.

50. Youde SJ, Dunbar PR, Evans EM, Fiander AN, Borysiewicz LK, Cerundolo V, *et al.* Use of fluorogenic histocompatibility leukocyte antigen-A*0201/ HPV 16 E7 peptide complexes to isolate rare human cytotoxic T-lymphocyte-recognizing endogenous human papillomavirus antigens. *Cancer Res* 2000;60:365–71.

51. Ghosh AK, Glenville S, Bartholomew J, Stern PL. Analysis of tumour-infiltrating lymphocytes in cervical carcinoma. In: Stanley MA, editor. *Immunology of Human Papillomaviruses*. New York: Plenum; 1994. p. 249–53.

52. Nakagawa M, Stites DP, Patel S, Farhat S, Scott M, Hills NK, *et al.* Persistence of human papillomavirus type 16 infection is associated with lack of cytotoxic T lymphocyte response to the E6 antigens. *J Infect Dis* 2000;182:595–8.

53. Ellis JR, Keating PJ, Baird J, Hounsell EF, Renouf DV, Rowe M, *et al.* The association of an HPV16 oncogene variant with HLA B7 has implications for vaccine design in cervical cancer. *Nat Med* 1995;1:464–70.

54. Evans M, Borysiewicz LK, Evans AS, Rowe M, Jones M, Gileadi U, *et al.* Antigen processing defects in cervical carcinomas limit the presentation of a CTL epitope from human papillomavirus 16 E6. *J Immunol* 2001;167:5420–8.

55. Malejczyk J, Malejczyk M, Majewski S, Orth G, Jablonska S. NK cell activity in patients with HPV16 associated anogenital tumors: defective recognition of HPV16 harboring keratinocytes and restricted unresponsiveness to immunostimulatory cytokines. *Int J Cancer* 1993;54:917–21.

56. Routes JM, Ryan S. Oncogenicity of human papillomavirus or adenovirus transformed cells correlates with resistance to lysis by natural killer cells. *J Virol* 1995;69:7639–47.

57. Garrido Guerrero E, Carrillo E, Guido M, Zamorano R, Garcia Carranca A, Gariglio P. Different arrangement of human papillomavirus E2 binding sites distinguishes cutaneous types from those associated with mucosal lesions. *Arch Med Res* 1996;27:389–94.

58. Bontkes HJ, Walboomers JM, Meijer CJ, Helmerhorst TJ, Stern PL. Specific HLA class I down-regulation is an early event in cervical dysplasia associated with clinical progression. *Lancet* 1998;351:187–8.

59. Cromme FV, Airey J, Heemels MT, Ploegh HL, Keating PJ, Stern PL, *et al.* Loss of transporter protein encoded by the TAP-1 gene, is highly correlated with loss of HLA expression in cervical carcinomas. *J Exp Med* 1994;179:335–40.

60. Coleman N, Stanley MA. Analysis of HLA DR expression on keratinocytes in cervical neoplasia. *Int J Cancer* 1994;56:314–19.

61. Warhol MJ, Gee B. The expression of histocompatibility antigen HLA DR in cervical squamous epithelium infected with human papilloma virus. *Mod Pathol* 1989;2:101–4.

62. Cromme FV, Meijer CJ, Snijders PJ, Uyterlinde A, Kenemans P, Helmerhorst T, *et al.* Analysis of MHC class I and II expression in relation to presence of HPV genotypes in premalignant and malignant cervical lesions. *Br J Cancer* 1993;67:1372–80.

63. Glew SS, Duggan-Keen M, Cabrera T, Stern PL. HLA class II antigen expression in human papillomavirus associated cervical cancer. *Cancer Res* 1992;52:4009–16.

64. Hilders CGJ, Houbiers JGA, Van Ravenswaay Claasen H, Veldhuizen RW, Fleuren GJ. Association between HLA-expression and infiltration of immune cells in cervical carcinoma. *Lab Invest* 1993;69:651–9.

65. Stanley M, Coleman N, Chambers M. The host response to lesions induced by human papillomavirus. *Ciba Found Symp* 1994;187:21–44.

66. Coleman N, Greenfield IM, Hare J, Kruger-Gray H, Chain BM, Stanley MA. Characterization and functional analysis of the expression of intercellular adhesion molecule 1 in human papillomavirus related disease of cervical keratinocytes. *Am J Pathol* 1993;143:355–67.

67. Schiffman MH. Epidemiology of cervical human papillomavirus infections. *Curr Top Microbiol Immunol* 1994;186:55–81.

68. Remmink AJ, Walboomers JM, Helmerhorst TJ, Voorhorst FJ, Rozendaal L, Risse EK, *et al.* The presence of persistent high risk HPV genotypes in dysplastic cervical lesions is associated with progressive disease: natural history up to 36 months. *Int J Cancer* 1995;61:306–11.

69. Londesborough P, Ho L, Terry G, Cuzick J, Wheeler C, Singer A. Human papillomavirus genotype as a predictor of persistence and development of high-grade lesions in women with minor cervical abnormalities. *Int J Cancer* 1996;69:364–8.

70. Apple RJ, Becker TM, Wheeler CM, Erlich HA. Comparison of human leukocyte antigen DR DQ disease associations found with cervical dysplasia and invasive cervical carcinoma. *J Natl Cancer*

Inst 1995;87:427–36.

71.   Ghaderi M, Wallin KL, Wiklund F, Zake L, Hallmans G, Lenner P, *et al*. Risk of invasive cervical cancer associated with polymorphic HLA DR/DQ haplotypes. *Int J Cancer* 2002;100:698–701.

72.   Glew SS, Duggan Keen M, Ghosh AK, Ivinson A, Sinnott P, Davidson J, *et al*. Lack of association of HLA polymorphisms with human papillomavirus related cervical cancer. *Hum Immunol* 1993;37:157–64.

73.   Cuzick J, Terry G, Ho L, Monaghan J, Lopes A, Clarkson P, *et al*. Association between high-risk HPV types, HLA DRB1* and DQB1* alleles and cervical cancer in British women. *Br J Cancer* 2000;82:1348–52.

74.   De Gruijl TD, Bontkes HJ, Walboomers JM, Stukart MJ, Robbesom AA, Von Blomberg BM, *et al*. Analysis of IgG reactivity against Human Papillomavirus type-16 E7 in patients with cervical intra-epithelial neoplasia indicates an association with clearance of viral infection: results of a prospective study. *Int J Cancer* 1996;68:731–8.

75.   Abdel Hady ES, Martin Hirsch P, Duggan Keen M, Stern PL, Moore JV, *et al*. Immunological and viral factors associated with the response of vulval intra-epithelial neoplasia to photodynamic therapy. *Cancer Res* 2001;61:192–6.

Chapter 4

Human papillomavirus and the lower genital tract

Discussion

Discussion following the papers by Dr Sasieni, Professor Herrington and Professor Stanley

Adams: Dr Sasieni, you alluded to nutrition in relation to susceptibility to human papillomavirus (HPV), but you raised several questions, suggesting that further research might be needed. Would you like to enlarge on that?

Sasieni: In general, the question of diet and cancer epidemiology is difficult to resolve; for example, with bowel cancer, what we thought we knew ten years ago is probably all wrong. I do not know what studies should be conducted in order to examine diet *per se*, but there are suggestions, particularly from studies in developing countries,[1-3] and even from one that we carried out ourselves in South-East England,[4] that diet has a role.

There is also some interesting information about indole-3 carbinol, found in cabbages or brassicas in general, and whether that can have an effect. There have been various molecular studies in the USA showing that it can induce apoptosis[5,6] and a small clinical study[7] that showed a rather dramatic regression of CIN3. It is being used to treat warts, and laryngeal warts in particular I believe, with some success – although this is not in a controlled fashion but open label in the USA. I do not know what the exact role of diet is.

Questionnaire-based case–control studies may not be the way forward. It is also very difficult to look for particular micronutrients in blood, so some kind of intervention study may therefore be the better way. It is actually fairly easy, given the large number of women who have early lesions, and possibilities for carrying out studies in those populations do therefore exist. However, influencing changes of diet, other than by adding food supplements, is notoriously difficult.

MacLean: There was a presentation at the RCOG/RANZCOG meeting in Sydney, Australia, October 2002, by Kim McFadden from the Department of Health in Wellington, New Zealand. The Department had been able to demonstrate that they could come down almost to the street block where people lived to define the amount of poverty in a particular area and correlate that with cervical cancer.

One of the difficulties in the UK is that people move around so much, and in cities it is certainly very difficult to know where they have grown up and how that correlates. However, in a country like New Zealand, and perhaps in Wales too, it may be easier to define what people's nutritional and environmental backgrounds would have been, because they do not move very much from where they were born.

Sasieni: Even in the Thames Cancer Registry in the Greater London area, cervical cancer has the greatest deprivation gradient of any cancers. Cervical cancer remains more common with a greater deprivation score. It may be that it is more common now because of the associated lack of screening. It becomes quite difficult to study the effects of poverty in the presence of screening. In all countries, people with greater levels of deprivation and lower social class take up screening less. Much of that relates to strange beliefs and fears that if you go for screening you are somehow tempting fate and you are more likely to develop the cancer. A number of psychosocial studies have found this to be a major barrier for the uptake of all forms of screening in certain populations.

Singer: The study you quoted of Ann Szarewski *et al.* also looked at folic acid supplementation, but she was not able to show much with it.[8]

Sasieni: She had to give up trying to recruit patients for that study.

Singer: Looking at it more broadly, with the enormous difference between the developed and the developing world, it would be naïve to think that nutrition did not play a part in this. Perhaps I could ask Professor Stanley whether there is any effect of nutrition on these highly complex immune systems? The factors are put down to male behaviour, but this is different in the developing world from the developed world, so there must be something else. I have always wondered whether nutrition had an effect on immune mechanisms here.

Stanley: That is a tough question to answer, because there is such a complex interplay. One of the key factors is parity. Every time you are pregnant, your Th1 responses go down, so you could quite easily argue that it is because these women are multiparous and therefore the major immune defence has gone. Vitamin A is interesting, with its alleged relationship to neoplasia, and I wonder whether vitamin A deficiency is a risk factor for the start of the whole process.

Sasieni: On the vitamin A issue, one of the mechanisms by which smoking may have an effect on the cervix is its effect on antioxidants. That would tie in.

In terms of these much higher rates of cervical cancer in developing countries than in the developed world, there is evidence that this is only the case now because of screening, and that rates of invasive cervical cancer in women in their twenties in England and Wales are as high as they are anywhere in the world in young women, at a stage before we are able to intervene with screening. That is not entirely true, because there are some small cancer registries from jungle areas of Brazil with even higher rates but, in terms of the main published rates, the rates in young women in this country and several others in the West are extremely high. There are even higher rates of cervical intraepithelial neoplasia grade 3 (CIN3). On the other hand, it might just be that these would not continue through into later life because of better diet, fewer pregnancies and a very different lifestyle in the West.

Stanley: Julian Peto, Professor of Epidemiology at the Institute of Cancer Research, argues that if we look at the CIN3 incidence, it is as high as the worst parts of the world. If you assume that there will be a progression rate of, say, 30%, that would produce cervical cancer rates comparable to Zimbabwe and North-East Brazil.

Sasieni: Yes, I completely agree with Julian Peto that if it were not for screening, we would be looking at an epidemic of cervical cancer, both squamous and adenocarcinoma, in 20–30 years' time in this country. However, I would question whether 30% of all high-grade disease would progress. We are finding far more small high-grade lesions because we are looking much harder. If we go to the New Zealand experience, the high-grade disease they had may not be the same as the high-grade disease we have today.

In Kieran Woodman's study,[9] three percent of women who were HPV-negative at the start had high-grade disease within about 18 months – and these were teenagers. This suggests that there is some form of high-grade disease, particularly in young women, that must be transient. The rates that they were finding were higher than would occur in 30-year-old women, and cancer had not developed by then.

Richart: On your point about what used to be followed as high-grade CIN, there is no doubt that the criteria have changed and that we have had a great deal of 'diagnosis creep'. What we used to call high-grade CIN, or carcinoma *in situ*, was really full-thickness, highly atypical cells. Both the Kolstad study[10] and Koss's[11] were classical carcinoma *in situ* prevalence cases, which had almost certainly been persistent for a long time before entering the studies.

Those of us who were performing colposcopy 30 years ago were mainly seeing prevalence cases with mostly large lesions. Virtually none of us ever saw one of those high-grade lesions remit spontaneously. Well-established lesions do not remit. Another factor influencing the natural history of CIN is whether there was intervention. We know that even a single punch biopsy is an interventional procedure, and the remission rate doubles when you take a biopsy, whether or not the lesion is removed.

The lesions that are now being called high-grade CIN are nearly all incidence cases because women are so heavily screened, at least in the USA and Europe. They are strikingly different from the prevalence cases we used to see.

Perrett: You mentioned the link between human leukocyte antigen (HLA) and cervical cancer. Are there any specific HLA types and does that tie in with chlamydia infection or any other type of infection?

Sasieni: I do not know of any tie-in with the chlamydia infection. A number of studies looking at HLA types have been able to tie it in with HPV infection, suggesting that the HLA type that they find is more strongly associated in HPV-16 associated lesions. In many studies there are problems with selection of controls. There seemed to be a fairly consistent story for DQ3.

Sasieni: There is now talk about HLA type DR15, which is actually from a very well-known study.[12] The problem is that there is not very much consistency between the studies. There was consistency about DQ3 and then the recent studies have not been finding it. I did not want to go into HLA types, because of the lack of consistency between studies.

There are also questions about different populations in the selection of controls. It was seen with the p53 story and cervical cancer that the selection of controls is extremely important for these genetic studies.[13,14] Sometimes, people are just using opportunistic controls from some other group of patients they have had. There are some large cohorts, which the Scandinavians in particular have collected retrospectively, looking at HLA-typing. Those are more likely to give reliable results.

Deery: Professor Herrington, do you notice any consistent or systematic differences, morphologically, between those lesions that are designated ultimately as HPV alone and those lesions that are designated as CIN1?

Herrington: Systematic differences, no. Subjectively, those that do not have identifiable basal abnormality are more likely to be HPV-6 or HPV-11-infected, but that is not an absolute rule. HPV6 or 11 infection is more often associated with basal cell hyperplasia, rather than basal cell atypia, but the difference between hyperplasia and atypia is highly subjective. This is what suggests that lumping together HPV-only with basal atypia of CIN1, call it what you will, is logical in that you are looking at productive infections.

Going back to what Professor Richart said about some high-grade lesions in fact just being productive infections, I would concur with that. It is not infrequently that we see biopsies that we would call HPV-only, for example, and perhaps CIN1 with a moderately dyskaryotic smear, for example. Or there may be the converse, where the smear may be low grade with mild dyskaryosis, but the biopsy has a highly atypical mitosis or something like that, and we are pushed into calling it high-grade. There is difficulty at these boundaries.

MacLean: Could you expand on that? I suspect that one of the debates we may have will be that histology is no longer able to distinguish between lesions or to demonstrate the way in which they behave. Using cell cycle proteins or other aspects demonstrated by immunohistochemistry, do you think there will be a comment in the future about the histopathological appearances, so that you will then give a profile based either on cell cycle proteins or perhaps on the presence or absence of immune response?

Herrington: That is possible, although we are certainly not there yet. To take the p16 example, this has been put forward as a good molecular marker but it is actually a marker of high-risk HPV infection and it does not actually grade the intraepithelial lesion. This is one of the problems that I have with the introduction of this marker.

It may help, for example, with the immature metaplasia versus high-grade SIL – the example that was given earlier, but if you have a thick lesion with clear-cut productive infection at the top and you want to grade the dysplasia, p16 will not give you the answer. Whether other markers will is another question, because it does not matter how many markers you throw at this – you will have to use something as your gold standard.

If progression is your gold standard, and identifying those lesions that will progress is your objective, it will be very difficult to do, for reasons of interference with natural history with biopsy, for example. It has always been the problem that the lesion is removed and therefore the natural history is interfered with: how can you test markers accurately against a true end-point? This is a problem that we will always face. As we stand, we test markers against the gold standard, which is histopathological diagnosis where, as has been said, the goalposts are shifting almost year on year. We face problems with regard to evaluating new molecular markers.

Richart: HPV typing does not correlate very well with morphology in the low-grade lesions and is not useful clinically in that group of lesions. As 80% of the low-grade lesions are caused by oncogenic-risk HPVs, HPV typing does not provide much additional information.

Finally, most pathologists have trouble defining the boundaries between metaplasia and the low-grade lesions. Ascertainment is critical to epidemiological studies. Many of the older studies did not show a significant correlation because the ascertainment was so poor. Until you have better ascertainment, all data that flow from the diagnosis are confounded.

I am persuaded that the markers will give us some value, because they will help with ascertainment. Although diagnoses are generally good in academic centres, small community hospital pathologists are generally less skilled. A substantial number of patients are most likely being treated for a disease that they do not have, because the boundary is so difficult to define. At least, in the USA, pathologists are afraid of missing a lesion, because of litigation, so over-diagnosis is common. Here, the markers may prove to be of some value.

Herrington: That is one area in which p16 could be of use, in identifying those lesions that do not actually mean anything. The studies in which I have been involved demonstrate very clearly when something is not potentially neoplastic. That may well be one of the benefits of doing that.

I have recently been involved in a very interesting experiment. I saw a poster by a pathologist from the North of England who is quite a mathematician. Rather heretically, he said that we should not be deconstructing from three grades of CIN, but we should actually be pushing it up to 100. He asked a group of people to say, on a grade of 1 to 100, where the lesion lay, and he found that there was much better agreement between observers if you did that, and then pulled it down into smaller categories.[15]

We did this in a study of cyclin expression in glandular lesions. We basically assessed positivity by percentage, which effectively uses a 100-point scale. Then, if you do a box-and-whiskers plot of that, it shows where you should put the cut-off in order to achieve the best discrimination between the various categories. You obviously need the diagnostic categories in the first place, which are used as the gold standard, but it was very convincing for p16, for example, in that you could set the cut-off at 25% and you would never get a tubo-endometrioid metaplasia confused with a high-grade cervical glandular intraepithelial neoplasia. There is therefore something to be said for doing things in a little more detail and not having preconceived ideas, and perhaps using expanded scales before moving back to the smaller number of points on the scale.

Richart: From a clinical point of view fine gradations are not terribly important because patients are treated as either low-grade or high-grade.

Adams: Following on from the work you have done on the Th1 response and its importance in HPV infection, how critical is it when going for vaccination strategies to identify adjuvants that stimulate Toll receptors and interleukin-12? Second, how do you explain the success of constructs that incorporate E7 and heat shock proteins?

Stanley: You have just answered the question! The Stressgen® vaccine (Stressgen Biotechnologies Corporation, Victoria, Canada) is in fact a brilliant example of an adjuvant that will drive a strong Th1 response. The results, which were presented recently, reinforce my view that the Stressgen vaccine is giving a short-term, effective innate immune response. There are not very good data that you have long-term E7-specific memory.

Also, imiquimod is used, which binds the Toll receptor, so that there is now a reasonable understanding of how it might actually work, and its effect is by generating large amounts of interferon, so that it also engenders a good innate immune response. However, imiquimod needs to be combined with a vaccine that gives you the right sort of antigen. In other words, yes, you do need adjuvants, particularly for immunotherapeutics, which will drive the right sort of immune response.

The question I did not address, mainly because I cannot show the data very clearly, is that one of the serious problems for cell-mediated immunity, and the reason why the studies on patients have been so equivocal, is that it is almost certain that the strong responses are local ones. There is actually not much memory out there in the systemic circulation, which means that, when you take the peripheral blood mononuclear cells, you are looking for a rare cell. What you need is the draining node or the lymphocytes from the region. We are right at the edge of our assay systems, and that is the serious and central problem with looking at cell-mediated immunity in HPV disease.

Deery: Is any credibility to be given to the idea of long-term latency of certain viral infections?

Stanley: Absolutely, and it is the animal work that persuades me of this. When there is spontaneous regression of animal papillomavirus infections, you can detect the viral DNA sequences in the dog at least, for 12–15 months thereafter – and 12–15 months represent about eight years in a dog's life. This has also been shown for the rabbit. When you use a prophylactic vaccine, and in our case this has been a DNA vaccine but I am sure others would have found it with VLPs, you achieve sterilising immunity, because you prevent infection so successfully. So, yes, once you have had these infections, you have them for life, and they are well controlled by immunosurveillance. If that immunosurveillance drops, as is seen in immunosuppressed individuals, there is a degree of recurrence.

Deery: The question follows what we see in the epidemiology of the prevalence of HPV infections, as detected by different molecular methods within populations, that there are low peaks around the perimenopausal period. Is that what this is about?

Stanley: It is hard to say; there is an argument that it may be a cohort effect. We would have to hold back on that. It is a plausible argument that, as you age, your immune control is not as effective, but it may also be that this relates to the particular cohort that we are looking at. I cannot answer that question, but my inclination is that this is a small blip in recrudescence of a latent infection.

One of the arguments is that HPV can never be found when smears are carried out but I have to remind people that it is latent, right down in the stem cells. We have just completed an experiment in dogs (unpublished), in which we smeared their mouths but could not find any virus; we had to strip the epithelium out and digest it before we could find the virus. You will not find it on smears or brushes, but you would have to cut out the relevant piece.

Critchley: Professor Stanley, I am an outsider to this field but I was interested in your local cytokine milieu being disturbed as a key factor in predisposing to HPV infection. What do we know about the regulators of this local Th1 and Th2? Elsewhere in the reproductive tract, this is strongly influenced by sex steroids. If you go back to what we heard earlier about the epidemiology and the link with hormonal contraception, it would be interesting to know whether it was the progestogen contraceptives in particular that were associated with the increased risk. This could be an opportunity when thinking about future research for interventions, because you may be able to have a mode of altering the hormonal influence on this cytokine milieu at a local level, rather than systemically.

Stanley: In all these surfaces there is a balance, which is about not eliciting a strong cell-mediated response to trivial injury and trivial infection. This is why it is so hard to drive Th1 responses. The default response at a surface is Th2, and that is where the immune system will go, because it is less destructive. Graft versus host disease is an excellent example of a powerful Th1 response. So this is rather a balance, but I certainly take the point that the information we have about the interaction between the hormone milieu and the steroid milieu, and the responses at these surfaces, not just from the immunocytes but from the keratinocytes. I do not know of any good studies that have been done, but I think they have a certain influence and I agree that this could be an area for investigation.

Prendiville: Does the seroconversion to capsid proteins that you mentioned as part of the successful clearance confer any kind of protection in relation to the future?

Stanley: The indication is that it should protect against new infections from the same virus type. There is no evidence that it will protect against infection from another virus type. It is very hard to say this in the human population, but in animal populations there is no question that, once you have that antibody, you can challenge the animals with huge amounts of virus and they do not develop a lesion, nor do they establish a detectable subclinical lesion. Once you have antibody, you are protected, which is why I think the vaccines will work.

Tidy: Do we have any explanation of how HPV enters the epithelium and the basal cells become infected? They are a long way from the entry-point of the virus.

Stanley: It is micro-trauma, they always say – sex is a violent act.

Tidy: But we have no idea what the receptor is for the HPV?

Stanley: No, there was some evidence that it was the alpha-6 beta-4 integrin, which was an attractive explanation, because that is an integrin on basal cells, and it is highly expressed on epidermal stem cells. There are some data to suggest that syndecans will bind HPV VLPs, but then those big polysaccharides do bind viruses. There are no good data on what the primary receptor is. The ligand for it is certainly in L1, but it is not clear what the primary receptor is. There may be several receptors and there is certainly something in L2 that has to bind cellular proteins for an effective infection; this is a combinatorial process.

References

1.   Potischman N, Brinton LA. Nutrition and cervical neoplasia. *Cancer Causes Control* 1996;7:113–26.
2.   Shannon J, Thomas DB, Ray RM, Kestin M, Koetsawang A, Koetsawang S, *et al*. Dietary risk factors for invasive and in situ cervical carcinomas in Bankok, Thailand. *Cancer Causes Control* 2002;13:691–9.
3.   Schiff MA, Patterson RE, Baumgartner RN, Masuk M, van Asselt-King L, Wheeler CM, *et al*. Serum carotenoids and risk of cervical intraepithelial neoplasia in Southwestern American Indian women. *Cancer Epidemiol Biomarkers Prev* 2001;10:1219–22.
4.   Cuzick J, Sasieni P, Singer A. Risk factors for invasive cervix cancer in young women. *Eur J Cancer* 1996;32A:836–41.
5.   Chen DZ, Qi M, Auborn KJ, Carter TH. Indole-3-carbinol and diindolylmethane induce apoptosis of human cervical cancer cells and in murine HPV16-transgenic preneoplastic cervical epithelium. *J Nutr* 2001;131:3294–302.
6.   Jin L, Qi M, Chen DZ, Anderson A, Yang GY, Arbeit JM, *et al*. Indole-3-carbinol prevents cervical cancer in human papillomavirus type 16 (HPV 16) transgenic mice. *Cancer Res* 1999;59:3991–7.
7.   Bell MC, Crowley-Nowick P, Bradlow HL, Sepkovic DW, Schmidt-Grimminger D, Howell P, *et al*. Placebo-controlled trial of indole-3-carbinol in the treatment of CIN. *Gynecol Oncol* 2000;78:123–9.
8.   Cuzick J, Szarewski A, Terry G, Ho L, Hanby A, Maddox P, *et al*. Human papilloma virus testing in primary cervical screening. *Lancet* 1995;345:1533–6.
9.   Woodman CB, Collins S, Winter H, Bailey A, Ellis J, Prior P, *et al*. Natural history of cervical human papillomavirus infection in young women: a longitudinal cohort study. *Lancet* 2001;357:1831–6.
10.   Kolstad P, Klem V. Long-term followup of 1121 cases of carcinoma *in situ*. *Obstet Gynecol* 1976;48:125–9.
11.   Koss LG, Stewart FW, Foote F, Jordan MJ, Bader GM, Day E. Some histological aspects of behavior of epidermoid carcinoma *in situ* and related lesions of the cervix. *Cancer* 1963;16:1160–211.
12.   Ghaderi M, Wallin KL, Wiklund F, Zake LN, Hallmans G, Lenner P, *et al*. Risk of invasive cervical cancer associated with polymorphic HLA DR/DQ haplotypes. *Int J Cancer* 2002;100:698–701.
13.   Storey A, Thomas M, Kalita A, Harwood C, Gardiol D, Mantovani F, *et al*. Role of a p53 polymorphism in the development of human papillomavirus-associated cancer. *Nature* 1998;393:229–34.
14.   Rosenthal AN, Ryan A, Al-Jehani RM, Storey A, Harwood CA, Jacobs IJ. p53 codon 72 polymorphism and risk of cervical cancer in UK. *Lancet* 1998;352:871–2.
15.   Klaes R, Benner A, Friedrich T, Ridder R, Herrington CS, Jenkins D, *et al*. p16INK4a immunohistochemistry improves interobserver agreement in the diagnosis of cervical intraepithelial neoplasia. *Am J Surg Pathol* 2002;11:1389–99.

SECTION 2

CYTOLOGY, HISTOLOGY AND THE NATURAL HISTORY OF LOWER GENITAL TRACT NEOPLASIA

Chapter 5

The current status of cervical smear cytology for the detection of cervical cancer precursors

Alastair Deery

Cytological sampling of the cervical transformation zone

The jilted heart-shaped, wooden 'Ayre spatula' was first described in 1948 by Ayre.[1] The emphasis was upon gathering an exfoliative sample of cells and mucus from the cervical os. The concept of using cervical exfoliative cytology for the detection of cervical cancer seems to be attributable to Papanicolaou in 1928.[2] The introduction of cervical screening on an opportunistic and non-systematic basis in parts of the USA and a five-grade classification of cell abnormalities (Table 5.1) culminated in an *Atlas of Exfoliative Cytology* by Papanicolaou in 1954.[3]

The consequence of mass screening, using this technique, was evidenced within a systematic cervical screening programme in British Columbia by Bryans *et al.* in 1964.[4] There was a 50% reduction in the incidence of invasive cancer and a 67% reduction in clinically evident cancer (FIGO stages Ib to IV).

The nature of the collection device received enthusiastic attention and 'development' throughout the 1970s and 1980s. There were changes in the material from which the device was made (plastic versus wood), its plasticity (rigid versus flexible), the form of its edges (sharp versus rounded) and the extent to which its leading finger pointed ever more accusingly into the endocervical canal (e.g. 'Aylesbury', 'Armovical', 'Multispatula' spatulas).[5-9] From such trials of one spatula against another (few with outcome histology) came early evidence that paired smear samples would inevitably reduce the false negative rate overall.[7] During the 1980s, with the increasing recognition and concern about the need to detect precursors of endocervical adenocarcinoma, several authors[10-12] were finding apparent evidence for a superiority of a combined spatula and cytobrush[10,11] or a cytobrush alone[12] in detecting both squamous and glandular (endocervical) cell numbers, atypias, abnormalities or dysplasias by comparison with a rigid Ayre or plastic spatula sample. Some of these studies evidenced their advantages by histological outcomes.[11,12] At the end of the 1980s,[13] it was clear enough that simple carpentry to extend the tip of the Ayre (hence the Aylesbury) produced more blood and more endocervical cells but no more 'dyskaryosis'. This was unfortunately shortly after the introduction of the NHS Cervical Screening Programme in 1988, which included a recommendation for the use of the Aylesbury wooden spatula.

In 1988, early trials of a new plastic flexible ectocervical broom sampler (Cervex", Rovers Medical Devices BV, Oss, The Netherlands) evidenced improvement in the false negative rate by comparison with the Ayre wooden sampler[14] or equivalence in detection of dyskaryosis by comparison with the combined Ayre/cytobrush method.[15] Neither study relied on histological outcome data. In 1991, Pretorius et al.[16] demonstrated an identical predicted rate of histopathological outcome of any disease grade or combination of disease grades, considering the combined Ayre/cytobrush technique versus a single endo/ectocervical plastic broom sampler, 'the Bayne brush'. The presence of endocervical cells in this last study was not found to correlate with the cytological detection of disease. Other comparative cytological studies[17-19] continued to demonstrate equivalence between the combined spatula/endocervical brush and single ecto/endocervical broom. A histopathologically based study in 1994[20] demonstrated the same conclusion. A meta-analysis of 29 cytological and histological based studies in 28 papers in 1996[21] revealed an equivalence between the extended-tip spatulas, the combination spatula/cytobrush and the Cervex broom sampler, as well as the clear superiority of all three techniques over a single cytobrush or rigid spatula or swab used alone. A laser cone biopsy-controlled study in 1997[22] revealed no significant difference in disease detection between a combined spatula/cytobrush and a broom sampler.

However, all of these studies, with the exception of Spurrett, Ayre and Pacey's,[12] either disregarded endocervical cell neoplastic precursors or had too few cases to allow comment on their detection. In 2000, Selvaggi and Guidos[23] revealed in the midst of a ThinPrep® (Cytyc Corporation, Boxborough MA, USA) Papanicolaou test trial that the endocervical cell component was absent in ThinPrep Papanicolaou test slides in 24% of samples procured by broom alone, as compared with 10% spatula/cytobrush and 13% with broom/cytobrush. While this was a significant difference within the study, in ThinPrep smears all these figures for the absence of endocervical cells are worse than those achieved in earlier conventional smear studies with the combined spatula/cytobrush or single Cervex broom.[16-20,22,24-26] None of the conventional smear studies has revealed a significant difference in endocervical cell yield with these techniques.

A meta-analysis and review by Martin-Hirsch et al.[27] of 34 trials of collection devices (to 1997) concluded with an impression that devices that effectively collect endocervical cells also appear to detect dyskaryosis more effectively. Again, no trial included in this analysis considered endocervical abnormalities separately or in significant numbers of cases.

The various classifications of cytology smears around the world identify apparent absences of certain cellular components of smears that allow a fraction of smears taken with any collection device to be characterised as: insufficient; inadequate; unsatisfactory; adequate but limited and so on. None of these systems or guidelines relies upon any rigorous evidence. The amount of squamous material that might be desirable in a conventional smear within a 50 x 22 mm cover slipped area varies from 10–50% within different screening programmes. There are no studies that evidence any figure in preference to any other against an acceptable standard.

It has usually been considered that confirmation of correct sampling of the cervical transformation zone may be obtained by identification of endocervical cells and/or metaplastic cells within cervical smears. But if we consider the cervical geography, the cervical transformation zone is a clinically relatively easily defined area that is visible colposcopically, witnessed on the vaginal face of the cervix, after speculum insertion. It lies between the discontinuous and sometimes sketchy line formed by the junction of the original (ectocervical) squamous epithelium and acquired metaplastic squamous epithelium and extending centripetally to the usually irregular junction of the metaplastic squamous epithelium and the columnar epithelium of the endocervical canal.

When a collection device is used in the presence of a speculum, in the majority of cervices most of the squamous cells resulting on the smear are metaplastic cells. This is a different clinical fact from the cytopathological observation of 'metaplastic squamous cells', often with 'pseudopodic' cytoplasmic processes identified traditionally by cytologists within Papanicolaou smears. These cytologically identified 'metaplastic squamous cells' are probably migrating immature metaplastic cells, which are commonly seen within incomplete and immature zones of squamous metaplasia. These represent a tiny fraction of the actual metaplastic squamous epithelium present within the smear. It follows that they are not relevant for assessments of smear adequacy.

Endocervical cells can be recognised by their morphologically cylindrical cell characteristics within smears, although this is with considerable variability even between experienced pathologists.[28] Outwith meta-analyses, however, there are no studies with acceptable standards that identify a correlation between endocervical cells within smear samples and detection of intraepithelial neoplasia. This is true for both squamous and glandular precursor lesions, which both reside predominantly within the transformation zone.

Endocervical cancer sampling has attracted much concern and attention in the literature over the past decade, along with an increasing clinical perception of need to detect cervical glandular intraepithelial neoplasia (CGIN) or adenocarcinoma *in situ* (AIS) and endocervical adenocarcinomas. The most important studies, admittedly with small numbers of AIS cases, suggest that endocervical brush samples are extremely sensitive but much less specific (few false negatives and many false positives) than endocervical curettage histological samples.[29–31] Unfortunately, there are no studies with sufficient case numbers to identify results with different samplers. It is unlikely that cytological evaluation and review of possible endocervical glandular lesions can or should lead discussion or selection of a cervical cytology sampling device for general screening.

A single device for mass screening should be preferred on clinical organisational and economic grounds and to date the device that fulfils these criteria is the plastic broom or ectocervical brush sampler. Within the papers cited within this review, there are no subgroups such as younger or older (postmenopausal) women or pregnant women, post-cone or post-irradiation groups where the evidence is different. General perceptions from practising cytopathologists are that cervical broom smears are more even and more easily interpretable than spatula or mixed spatula/brush smears. Liquid-based preparations have sometimes quietly assumed the benefits of a better cervical sample in comparison to historical conventional rigid spatula smears.

For endocervical canal sampling in referred populations, the results of various strategies to detect squamous and glandular disease do not advise a preferred alternative sampling strategy, based on the small number of publications and their results.

Conclusions

- There is clear agreement in studies and trials of conventional cervical smears of the equivalent effectiveness of combined spatula/endocervical brush or ectocervical broom spatulas.

- There is clear evidence that either of these techniques is superior to single spatula samples of wooden or plastic composition. Such devices should be taken out of use in cervical screening programmes.

- The use of a single sampler when there is equivalence of disease detection is economically and strategically preferable. This recommendation prefers the use of a single ectocervical broom sampler on these grounds within available data.

- For subcategories such as young women (aged under 40 years), peri- or postmenopausal women, pregnant women and post-conisation or post-irradiation patients, there is no preference between the use of a spatula/cytobrush combination or ectocervical broom sampler.

- There are no studies that evidence the value of an additional endocervical cytological sample to detect increased amounts of cervical precursors of glandular or squamous neoplasia beyond that procured by the ectocervical broom sampler.

- A reduced number of ThinPrep smears appear to contain an endocervical component by comparison with studies of conventional smears using the same sampling devices.

The terminology for describing and interpreting the contents of cervical smears

It is critical that the terminologies used for cytological and histological descriptions and interpretations are accurate, similar, consistent and clearly understood so that they can be correlated with the clinical colposcopic findings. These clinical findings have generally met with agreement around the world. Likewise, there has been considerable congruity between the pathological descriptions of broadly what is normal and abnormal. One of the principal hopes with the increased understanding of the aetiology of cervical neoplasia over the last 20 years is that the morphological nomenclature or descriptors would gradually integrate that information and become more unified.

Within the setting of a great flurry of scientific and conference activity at the start of the new millennium, there has been a real expectation and a will that nomenclature around the globe should draw together and reduce the difficulties of sharing scientific information about disease diagnosis and progression for the benefit of all. First came the 2001 Bethesda System update,[32] followed logically by the American Society for Colposcopy and Cervical Pathology management guidelines.[33] An Australian web-based conference soon followed in 2002 and agreed to adjust the relatively recent Australian terminology to follow approximately the Bethesda smear categories. Overlapping in time with this, a British Society for Clinical Cytology (BSCC) Conference was held in April 2002, which agreed to pursue broadly similar categories. The proposed revisions have been assembled in parallel array as far as possible in Table 5.1.

The striking change that has come over cervical cytology nomenclature in the last decade is the result of expectation of ever more discrete clinicopathological outcomes from particular smear categories. Unrealistic views of women are transmitted through clinicians and accompanied by medico-legal pressures from perceived and real cytological under-assessments of cervical neoplastic disease. Some common features of terminological changes throughout the nineties in all systems have been a steady erosion and loss of any narrative report, with its place being taken sometimes by an isolated code or else a 'stack' of coded histological predictions of disease outcome, such as 'dysplastic cells'.

There are ever-broadening and overlapped categories of smears with 'indeterminate', 'atypical', 'inconclusive', 'undetermined', 'minor atypia' or 'borderline changes', with few accompanying meaningful descriptions and no well-defined atypical, abnormal or dyskaryotic cellular changes. In all systems, this is now the largest category of 'abnormal' smear findings. The recent classifications seek to subcategorise these by eventual histological outcome without relation to the smear

Table 5.1. Comparison of nomenclatures for satisfactory smears

Papanicolaou	BSCC 1986/1995	BSCC 2002 (proposed)	Australia 2002 (draft)	Bethesda 2001
I. Negative	Negative	No dyskaryotic cells	Negative	Negative for intraepithelial lesion or malignancy
II. Atypical but not neoplastic cells	Borderline (including koilocytotic atypia after clarification in 1995 document)	Borderline NOS (low grade) No low-grade glandular category proposed Borderline?high-grade Borderline?glandular	Atypia – minor atypical changes (inc. koilocytotic changes, parakeratosis etc) Enatyp (endocervical atypia) Inconclusive atypical glandular cells suspicious of AIS	Atypical squamous cells: ASC-US 'undetermined significance' (90% of ASC) Atypical glandular cells NOS ASC-H 'cannot exclude high grade' (10% of ASC) Atypical glandular cells favour neoplasia
III. Suspicion of neoplastic cells	Mildly dyskaryotic cells (not including koilocytotic atypia after 1995)	Low-grade dyskaryosis including koilocytotic atypia	Low-grade squamous epithelial abnormality	Low-grade squamous intra-epithelial lesion (LSIL)
IV. Strong suggestion of neoplastic cells	Moderately dyskaryotic cells Severely dyskaryotic cells	High-grade dyskaryosis (option to predict CIN2 or CIN3 outcome)	High-grade squamous epithelial abnormality (option to specify CIN2/3) AIS	High-grade squamous intra-epithelial lesion (HSIL) AIS
V. Malignant cells	Severely dyskaryotic cells ?invasive ?glandular neoplasia	Invasive squamous carcinoma CGIN Adenocarcinoma – specify site Other malignancy	Carcinoma Adenocarcinoma	Squamous cell carcinoma Adenocarcinoma

AIS = adenocarcinoma *in situ*; ASC = atypical squamous cells; BSCC = British Society for Clinical Cytology; CGIN = cervical glandular intraepithelial neoplasia; CIN = cervical intraepithelial neoplasia; NOS = nitric oxide synthase appearances. In the huge majority of such smears, no cervical disease is present. The sizes of these categories are a measure of the increasing ineffectiveness of the Papanicolaou smear and its estrangement from the proper control of the nomenclature by screening pathologists.

Appearances of many subcategories of 'atypical glandular cells' of supposed specificity and gradation of severity of disease. In fact, there is little definition between categories by clinicopathological outcome. After biopsy those that have any neoplastic process are in fact found to have squamous precursor disease.

The clinical response, which induces and triages this increasingly diverse range of defensive cervical smear categorisations, has been to bundle nearly all of them subsequently in an identical clinical envelope for further and extensive diagnostic investigations.

Conclusions

Cytology terminology needs to be reclaimed by practising cytologists. One of the probable reasons for the retention of 'dyskaryosis' by the BSCC in 2002 was to maintain a descriptive or narrative cytological nomenclature separate from accompanying histopathological predictions.

The description of cells is essential for maintaining educational standards in the transfer of cytological knowledge. The ingredients of cellular changes, which allow cells to be placed in morphological categories, must be evidenced and there has been little advance in this area of study.

The word 'dyskaryotic' is certainly not itself important to retain and might be substituted by 'atypical', 'abnormal' or even 'dysplastic'. However, around the world currently 'atypia', for example, may mean 'minor but not neoplastic changes' (Australia); 'atypical squamous or glandular cells' with a mainly benign outcome (USA) or atypia not neoplastic (European – Papanicolaou system, grade II). This is an unsatisfactory and unnecessary situation and the conservative and often parochial arguments of those leading 'consensus processes' need to be adjusted.

Cytology sensitivity has probably not altered over the period of these terminology changes,[34] is in any event difficult to determine and seems unlikely to be adjusted by changes in preparatory method.[35,36]

New molecular methods of determining and categorising women at risk of developing cervical neoplasia have arrived and, although they are several strides away from implementation, they must soon take pole position in new cervical cancer screening programmes.

Cytology urgently needs to preserve its descriptive power in order eventually to adopt a reduced but more specific clinical role alongside other possible viral, molecular and antigenic assessments to direct effective colposcopic management, treatment and follow-up.

References

1.   Ayre JE. Cervical cytology in the diagnosis of early cancer. *JAMA* 1948;136:513.
2.   Papanicolaou GN. New cancer diagnosis. Proceedings – 3rd Race Betterment conference. Battle Creek, Michigan. Race Betterment Foundation; 1928.
3.   Papanicolaou GN. *Atlas of Exfoliative Cytology*. New York: The Commonwealth Fund; 1954.
4.   Bryans FE, Boyes DA, Fidler HK. The influence of a cytological screening programme upon the incidence of invasive squamous cell carcinoma of the cervix in British Columbia. *Am J Obstet Gynecol* 1964;88:898–906.

5. Rubio CA, Berglund K, Kock Y, Zetterberg A. Studies on the distribution of abnormal cells in cytologic preparations. III. Making the smear with a plastic spatula. *Am J Obstet Gynecol* 1980;137:843–6.
6. Colon VF, Linz LE. The extended tip spatula for cervical cytology. *J Fam Pract* 1981;13:37–41.
7. Beilby JO, Bourne R, Guillebaud J, Steele ST. Paired cervical smears: a method of reducing the false-negative rate in population screening. *Obstet Gynecol* 1982;60:46–8.
8. Kivlahan C, Ingram E. Improved yield of endocervical cells in Papanicolaou smears in a residency setting. *J Fam Pract* 1985;20:381–5.
9. Pistofides GA, Brown ER, Harris VG, Grainger JM, Spring JE, Carr JV, *et al.* Detection of abnormal cervical smears. A comparative study. *Acta Obstet Gynecol Scand* 1988;67:153–4.
10. Taylor PT Jr, Andersen WA, Barber SR, Covell JL, Smith EB, Underwood PB Jr. The screening Papanicolaou smear: contribution of the endocervical brush. *Obstet Gynecol* 1987;70:734–8.
11. Alons-van Kordelaar JJ, Boon ME. Diagnostic accuracy of squamous cervical lesions studied in spatula-cytobrush smears. *Acta Cytol* 1988;32:801–4.
12. Spurrett B, Ayre B, Pacey NF. The inadequacy of instruments used for cervical screening. *Aust N Z J Obstet Gynecol* 1989;29:44–6.
13. Goorney BP, Lacey CJ, Sutton J. Ayre v Aylesbury cervical spatulas. *Genitourin Med* 1989;65:402.
14. Waddell CA, Rollason TP, Amarilli JM, Cullimore J, McConkey CC. The cervix: an ectocervical brush sampler. *Cytopathology* 1990;1:171–81.
15. Szarewski A, Kuzick J, Nayagam M, Thin RN. A comparison of four cytological sampling techniques in a genito-urinary medicine clinic. *Genito Urin Med* 1990;66:439–43.
16. Pretorius RG, Sadeghi M, Fotheringham N, Semrad N, Watring WG. A randomized trial of three methods of obtaining Papanicolaou smears. *Obstet Gynecol* 1991;78:831–6.
17. Fokke HE, Salvatore CM, Schipper ME, Bleker OP. The quality of the Pap smear. *Eur J Gynaecol Oncol* 1992;13:445–8.
18. Szarewski A, Curran G, Edwards R, Cuzick J, Kocjan G, Bounds W, *et al.* Comparison of four cytologic sampling techniques in a large family planning center. *Acta Cytol* 1993;37:457–60.
19. Cannon JM, Blythe JG. Comparison of the Cytobrush plus plastic spatula with the cervex brush for obtaining endocervical cells. *Obstet Gynecol* 1993;82:569–72.
20. Germaine M, Heaton R, Erickson D. A comparison of the three most common Papanicoloau smear collection techniques. *Obstet Gynecol* 1994;84:168–73.
21. Buntinx F, Brouwers M. Relation between sampling device and detection of abnormality in cervical smears: a meta-analysis of randomised and quasi-randomised studies. *BMJ* 1996;313:1285–90.
22. Risberg B, Andersson A, Zetterberg C, Nordin B. Cervex brush vs spatula and cytobrush. A cytohistologic evaluation. *J Reprod Med* 1997;42:405–8.
23. Selvaggi SM, Guidos BJ. Specimen adequacy and the ThinPrep Pap test: the endocervical component. *Diagn Cytopathol* 2000;23:23–6.
24. Buntinx F, Boon ME, Beck S, Knottnerus JA, Essed GG. Comparison of Cytobrush sampling, spatula sampling and combined cytobrush/spatula sampling of the uterine cervix. *Acta Cytol* 1991;35:64–8.
25. Stillson T, Knight AL, Elswick RK Jr. The effectiveness and safety of two cervical cytologic techniques during pregnancy. *J Fam Pract* 1997;45:159–63.
26. Eisenberger D, Hernandez E, Tener T, Atkinson BF. Order of endocervical and ectocervical sampling and the quality of the Papanicolaou smear. *Obstet Gynecol* 1997;90:755–8.
27. Martin-Hirsch P, Jarvis G, Kitchener H, Lilford R. Collection devices for obtaining cervical cytology samples. *Cochrane Database Syst Rev* 2000;(3):CD001036.
28. O'Sullivan JP, Ismail SM, Barnes WS, Deery AR, Gradwell E, Harvey JA, *et al.* Inter- and intra-observer variation in the reporting of cervical smears: specialist cytopathologists versus histopathologists. *Cytopathology* 1996;7:78–89.
29. Andersen W, Frierson H, Barber S, Tabbarah S, Taylor P, Underwood P. Sensitivity and specificity of endocervical curettage and the endocervical brush for the evaluation of the endocervical canal. *Am J Obstet Gynecol* 1988;159:702–7.
30. Hoffman MS, Sterghos S, Gordy LW, Gunasekaran S, Cavanagh D. Evaluation of the endocervical canal with the endocervical brush. *Obstet Gynecol* 1993;82:573–7.
31. Mogensen ST, Bak M, Ducholm M, Frost L, Knoblauch NO, Praest J, *et al.* Cytobrush and endocervical curettage in the diagnosis of dysplasia and malignancy of the uterine cervix. *Acta Obstet Gynecol Scand* 1995;76:69–73.
32. Solomon D, Davey D, Kurman R, Moriarty A, O'Connor D, Prey M, *et al.* The 2001 Bethesda system: terminology for reporting results of cervical cytology. *JAMA* 2002;287:2114–19.
33. Wright TC Jr, Cox JT, Massad LS, Twiggs LB, Wilkinson EJ. 2001 Consensus guidelines for the management of women with cervical cytological abnormalities. *JAMA* 2002;287:2120–29.
34. Renshaw AA. Measuring sensitivity in gynaecologic cytology. *Cancer* 2002;96:210-17.
35. Hartmann KE, Nanda K, Hall S, Myers E. Technologic advances for evaluation of cervical cytology: is newer better? *Obstet Gynecol Surv* 2001;56:765–74.

36.   Sulik SM, Kroeger K, Schultz JK, Brown JL, Becker LA, Grant WD. Are fluid based cytologies superior to the conventional Papanicolaou test? A systematic review. *J Fam Pract* 2001;50:1040–46.

Chapter 6

Is intraepithelial neoplasia still a valid concept?

Ralph M Richart

Introduction

The concept of a precursor to invasive cancer of the uterine cervix dates back to 1886, when Williams[1] identified and commented upon the presence of abnormal epithelium adjacent to squamous cell cancer of the cervix and suggested that it might be a precursor. No other commentary appears to have taken place until 1900, when Cullen[2] also recognised intraepithelial lesions adjacent to squamous cell cancer but expanded on Williams' initial observations by commenting both on the histological appearance of these precursors and on their spatial relationships to the invasive cancer. The term 'carcinoma *in situ*' (CIS) was coined by Schottlander and Kermauner but was reintroduced by Broders in 1932.[3] These initial observations were made by pathologists who concluded that the epithelial changes that they recognised adjacent to invasive cancers were precursors because of both their distribution and their histological and cytological similarity to invasive cancer. The clinical observations that confirmed the pathologists' hypotheses were initially published by Galvin *et al*.[4] Both groups identified patients who had CIS in cervical biopsies preceding invasive cervical cancer. Koss *et al*.[5] also described CIS and detailed the relationship between this precursor and invasive cancer but it was not until Kolstad and Klem followed untreated patients with CIS and reported their subsequent development of invasive cancer, that CIS was widely accepted to be a precursor to invasive cancer.[6] Subsequently, McIndoe *et al*.[7] also reported a series of patients with untreated CIS who had been followed and who developed invasive cancer during the follow-up period.

After Papanicolaou and Traut[8] described the use of exfoliative cytology to detect cancers and precancers of the uterine cervix, large-scale screening programmes were initiated in most developed countries. As a result of the screening, presumed precursors of cervical cancer were detected and treated. The protection afforded to the screened population by detecting and treating presumed cervical cancer precursors and the comparison of the incidence of cervical cancer and deaths from cervical cancer in screened versus unscreened populations were the ultimate test of the concept of intraepithelial neoplasia, both validating the concept and leading to millions of lives being saved over the last 50 years.[9–12] All of these data taken together have led to the almost universally accepted conclusion that intraepithelial neoplasia is an entity that can be defined, that it is a precursor to invasive cancer and that its detection and eradication will protect a woman from developing invasive cancer.

Definitions

When the concept of CIS was established, pathologists defined the lesion as one in which the full thickness of the epithelium is replaced by undifferentiated cells. The term 'full thickness' means that isodiametric or 'third-type' cells must extend from the basal lamina to the surface. This definition was memorialised in 1961[13] at the first International Congress of Exfoliative Cytology when the Committee on Histological Terminology defined CIS as follows: 'Only those cases should be classified as CIS which, in the absence of invasion, show a surface lining epithelium in which, throughout its whole thickness, no differentiation takes place. The process may involve the lining of the cervical glands. It is recognized that the cells of uppermost layers may show some slight flattening. The very rare case of an otherwise characteristic CIS that shows a greater degree of differentiation belongs to the exceptions for which no classification can provide.'

Dysplasia, a term introduced by Reagan and colleagues[14] was defined as follows:

'All other (than carcinoma *in situ*) disturbances of differentiation of the squamous epithelial lining of surface and glands... They may be characterized as of high or low degree, terms which are preferable to suspicious and non-suspicious, as the proposed terms describe the histological appearance and do not express an opinion'.

At the time that the term 'carcinoma *in situ*' was introduced, there was serious concern that patients with CIS might have undetected invasion or even develop metastatic disease. Hence, for several decades the treatment of choice for patients with CIS (after invasion was ruled out using a cold knife conisation) was simple hysterectomy or, in some centres, extended hysterectomies with lymph node dissection. Patients with dysplasia were commonly followed without treatment or, if the dysplasia was 'severe', treated with cold knife conisation alone.

There were no rationale or data to support the practice of treating patients with full thickness undifferentiated cells with hysterectomy and treating those with a few layers of surface epithelium that was better differentiated with cold knife conisation or with follow-up alone. This practice was in place because it was the best guess of the morphologists and clinicians who had established the rules and because insufficient time had elapsed to accumulate enough clinical experience to know if the diagnostic and therapeutic construct then in use was rational.

Cervical intraepithelial neoplasia versus squamous intraepithelial lesions

After a series of experiments looking more objectively at the morphology and biological behaviour of the dysplasia or CIS spectrum of disease, the term 'cervical intraepithelial neoplasia' (CIN) was introduced[15] but still subdivided into CIN1, CIN2 and CIN3. There were two major implications of this new classification scheme. One was that there was no objective difference between severe dysplasia and CIS and the two should be treated similarly, and the second was that there was both a morphological and an experimental continuum from CIN1 through to CIN3 that could not be subdivided into discrete compartments by any method then available. It was explicitly stated that the concept of a continuum meant that cytological or histological subdivisions would necessarily be arbitrary, as would management schemes based on such arbitrary subdivision.

After it was discovered that human papillomavirus (HPV) was the aetiological agent for cancer and its precursors and that most low-grade CIN lesions were, in fact, simply a productive viral infection, the classification of presumed cervical cancer precursors had to be rethought. When it was also discovered that papillomaviruses could be divided into two groups – with and without oncogenic risk – and that cervical cancers and their precursors contained only oncogenic-risk HPV types, it was apparent that the morphological spectrum of presumed cervical cancer precursors would better be subdivided by their molecular and natural history attributes rather than purely morphologically. These new data led to the introduction of the term 'squamous intraepithelial lesion' (SIL)[16] and to a modification of the CIN terminology,[17] dropping one of the three subclassifications and including only 'low-grade CIN' and 'high-grade CIN'. Low-grade CIN was redefined as being a surrogate term for the lesion that is produced by HPV as a productive infection. CIN2 and CIN3 were combined as 'high-grade CIN' and redefined as a 'true cancer precursor'. The histological and clinical implications of the reclassification were discussed as follows:[17]

'Diagnostic surgical pathology and cytology terminology should not only provide the clinician with an understanding of the abnormality thought to be present, but should also rely on a classification system that is consistent with the current understanding of the science involved. Under these conditions, it appears to be most consistent with both goals to divide the HPV-related lesions of the cervix into low-grade CIN lesions, which have an uncertain potential, and high-grade CIN lesions, which are putative cancer precursors. There would not seem to be any clinical value in continuing to subdivide the presumed cervical cancer precursors into three categories – CIN 1, CIN 2, and CIN 3 – because their treatment is most rationally based principally on the lesion's size and distribution rather than its histological grade. It would also seem to be scientifically unsound to continue a tripartite approach to this terminology, for the reasons outlined previously. Both the patient and science would best be served by changing the terminology and replacing CIN 1, 2, and 3 by a slight modification in terms. The low-grade lesions could be diagnosed as "low-grade CIN with HPV-related changes" and the higher-grade lesions as "high-grade CIN" unencumbered by grades or other clinically valueless modifiers.

Lesions diagnosed by the pathologist as high-grade CIN would be understood by the clinician to be true cancer precursors; the patient would be evaluated appropriately using colposcopy, biopsy, and endocervical curettage to rule out invasion, and then treated based on well-established protocols. Lesions diagnosed by the pathologist as "low-grade CIN with HPV-related changes" would be understood by the clinician to have uncertain potential, and the patient could be treated or followed, after ruling out invasive cancer and performing HPV typing, as the clinician thought appropriate.

Although morphologic criteria would be used for making a diagnosis, an operational approach to that diagnosis would make the diagnostic categories much more useful clinically than are the present purely morphologic definitions. These definitions have become enmeshed in a web of descriptors, causing major differences in terminology and dooming the clinician to the unending task of trying to make clinical sense of a series of morphologic categories that mean something different to everyone.'

At this point both the two-stage CIN terminology and the two-stage SIL terminology defined low-grade as a productive infection and high-grade as a putative neoplasm. There are cogent arguments for the use of SIL and equally cogent arguments for the use of CIN as the preferred terminology. This has been well summarised by Wright et al:[18]

'In our opinion, using the term lesion rather than neoplasia better reflects the natural history of these histopathologic entities, because the majority of what were previously considered to be cervical cancer precursors are histologically low grade and represent self-limited HPV infections that spontaneously resolve in the absence of therapy. "Intraepithelial lesion" better describes these low-grade viral infections than does the term "intraepithelial neoplasia." Proponents of the CIN terminology contend that the use of the term lesion is imprecise when referring to what they consider to be high-grade neoplasia, which is frequently aneuploid and has the potential for progressing to invasive cancer.'

Despite the endorsement of the SIL terminology by the Bethesda system of nomenclature, recent usage seems to have coalesced around using the SIL terminology for cytology and the CIN terminology for histology so that it will immediately be clear whether cytological diagnoses or histological diagnoses are being referred to. Terms and usage evolve, however, and it seems certain that this usage will also evolve and become codified or supplanted by other terminology when more data are accumulated.

CIN as a continuum

Irrespective of the terminology and the definitions, there is still a debate as to whether CIN is a continuum. As has been stated previously, it is clear that most, if not all, cervical cancers start out as an HPV infection. It is still not clear whether HPV can transform a normal squamous cell in a 'single hit' without spending at least some time as a low-grade productive infection. As the endocervical epithelium appears not to support a productive infection, it seems likely that HPV can transform normal endocervical cells *ab initio* and it can be argued that if this occurs in the endocervix, it could reasonably be expected to occur in the squamous epithelium as well. If that is the case, the proportion of cancers that do arise directly from papillomavirus-transformed normal cells would appear to be small. This is confirmed by recent prospective follow-up studies[19] of patients screened by Papanicolaou smears and HPV DNA testing. Those patients who are double-negative have been followed prospectively and evaluated for the acquisition of HPV-related lesions, including cervical cancer. If invasive cancer was commonly initiated by the direct papillomavirus transformation of the normal cell, then some of the double-negative patients who are still exposed to the virus would be expected to develop invasive cancer during the follow-up period. This appears to be a rare event and argues against this mechanism of cancer production occurring with significant frequency.

It has been established that most HPV infections are with oncogenic-risk papillomaviruses and that only 15–20% occur with the no-oncogenic-risk HPV types. About 90% of cervical HPV infections remit spontaneously; the highest risk status is conferred upon those women who continue to shed oncogenic-risk HPV. It has also been established that the transit time of patients with high-grade CIN has a broad distribution, with some patients developing cancer early in the disease process and others maintaining their high-grade CIN lesions without invasion for decades. So, although it is not clinically useful, it is an interesting intellectual exercise to consider whether a continuum exists in the high-grade CIN (non-productive infection) category.

The data for the existence of a continuum from 'early' CIN2 to CIN3 are less morphological than they are molecular. Although it is possible to construct a morphological continuum, this may be a classical morphologist's artefact if it is not supported by evidence that the construction is correct.

If we make the assumption that (as seems likely) the key event that changes a low-grade HPV infection to an intraepithelial neoplasm is the integration of the HPV into the host genome (or an event with similar consequences – these will be treated as one entity and will be referred to as an 'integration event'), then it may be productive to examine post-integration event natural history in the monoclonal expansion of the cell in which the event took place.

It is established that, at the time of the integration event, the disruption of the E2 HPV open reading frame leads to de-control of the E6 and E7 oncogenes of HPV with the overproduction of their encoded proteins. It is also established that, although E6-encoded proteins may have transforming activities, the E7-encoded protein confers most of the risk but that the two operating together are synergistic and substantially increase the risk of either alone. The E7 oncoprotein binds to the product of the *Rb* gene as well as to the p130 and p107 *Rb*-related pocket proteins. All of these proteins are critical to the regulation of the cell cycle, and their removal and rapid degradation lead to cell cycle disruption and immortalisation. The E6 oncoprotein complexes with p53, increases its ubiquitin-dependent proteolysis and deprives the cell of the proofreading functions orchestrated by p53, eventually leading to the unmasking of mutations and to aneuploidy.

Because pRb and p53 are critically involved in regulating cell division, their inactivation is catastrophic for the cell and results in significant cell-cycle dysregulation. With pRb non-functional, there is a release of transcription factors that makes the cell independent of mitogenic stimuli, and the checkpoint for cell proliferation and transcription is lost. Both the G1-S and G2-M checkpoints become disrupted and, with the overexpression of cyclin E and loss of functional p53, chromosomal instability, unmasking of mutations and aneuploidy result.

Conclusion

It has not so far been possible to track the time sequence of these intracellular events, and there are virtually no data on either the usual sequence or the timing of such events in HPV-infected cells that have suffered an integration event. Recently, however, it was recognised that p16^{INK4A}. CDC6 and mini-chromosome maintenance (MCM) proteins may be useful as a marker for cell cycle disruption. Recent immunohistochemical studies[20] using antibodies to p16 have provided evidence that cell cycle disruption occurs in epithelia, which are morphologically classified as low-grade CIN lesions. If these observations are confirmed, it would lend support to the contention that there is, in fact, a morphological, molecular and functional continuum that begins with low-grade CIN and ends with high-grade CIN and invasion. Similar studies[20] with MCM antibodies, correlating the presence of these presumptive cell cycle disruption markers with both HPV type and ploidy levels will provide additional information on the time sequence of these events and whether the continuum concept can be supported. However, it is clear that other markers such as telomerase expression increase with the grade of CIN, again suggesting a molecular continuum, although one that is poorly defined.

References

1. Williams J. *On Cancer of the Uterus, Being the Harveian Lectures for 1886*. London: HK Lewis; 1988. p. 8–13.
2. Cullen TS. *Cancer of the Cervix*. London: Henry Kimpton; 1900.
3. Broders AC. Carcinoma *in situ* contrasted with benign penetrating epithelium. *JAMA* 1932;99:1670–4.
4. Galvin GA, Jones HW, Te Linde RW. Clinical relationship of carcinoma *in situ* and invasive carcinoma of the cervix. *JAMA* 1952;149:744.
5. Koss LG, Stewart FW, Foote FW, Jordan MJ, Bader GM, Day E. Some histological aspects of behaviour of epidermoid carcinoma *in situ* and related lesions of the uterine cervix. *Cancer* 1963;16:1160–211.
6. Kolstad P, Klem V. Long-term followup of 1121 cases of carcinoma in situ. *Obstet Gynecol* 1976;48:125–9.
7. McIndoe WA, McLean MR, Jones RW, Mullins PR. The invasive potential of carcinoma in situ of the cervix. *Obstet Gynecol* 1984;64:451–8.
8. Papanicolaou GN, Traut HF. The diagnostic value of vaginal smears in carcinoma of the uterus. 1941. *Arch Pathol Lab Med* 1997 121:211–24.

9.   Devesa SS, Young JL Jr, Brinton LA, Fraumeni JF Jr. Recent trends in cervix uteri cancer. *Cancer* 1989;64:2184–90.

10.   Hakama M. Screening for cervical cancer: Experience of the Nordic countries. In: Franco E, Monsonego J, editor. *New Developments in Cervical Cancer Screening and Prevention.* London: Blackwell; 1997. p. 190–9.

11.   American Cancer Society: Cervical cancer facts and figures [www.cancer.org/cancerinfo].

12.   Janerich DT, Hadjimichael O, Schwartz PE, Lowell DM, Meigs JW, Merino MJ, *et al.* The screening histories of women with invasive cervical cancer, Connecticut. *Am J Public Health* 1995;85:791–4.

13.   Weid GL. Proceedings of the First International Congress on Exfoliative Cytology. 1961.

14.   Reagan JW, Hamonic MJ. Dysplasia of the uterine cervix. *Ann N Y Acad Sci* 1956;63:662–82.

15.   Richart RM. Cervical intraepithelial neoplasia: a review. In: Sommers SC, editor. *Pathology Annual, 1973.* New York: Appleton Century-Crofts; 1973. p.301–28.

16.   Luff RD. The Bethesda System for reporting cervical/vaginal cytologic diagnoses: report of the 1991 Bethesda Workshop. *Hum Pathol* 1992;23:719–21.

17.   Richart RM. A modified terminology for cervical intraepithelial neoplasia. *Obstet Gynecol* 1990;75:131–3.

18.   Wright TC, Kurman RJ, and Ferenczy A. Precancerous Lesions of the Cervix. In: Kurman RJ, editor. *Blaustein's Pathology of the Female Genital Tract.* 5th ed. New York: Springer-Verlag; 2002. p. 253–324.

19.   Kjaer SK, van den Brule AJC, Paull G, Svare EI, Sherman ME, *et al.* Type specific persistence of high-risk human papillomavirus (HPV) as indicator of high-grade cervical squamous intraepithelial lesions in young women: Population-based prospective follow-up study. *BMJ* 2002; 325:6–10.

20.   Richart RM. The role of markers in the detection of human papillomavirus-related lesions. In: *Lower Genital Tract Neoplasia.* London RCOG Press; 2003. p.131–8.

Chapter 7

The natural history of lower genital tract precancers: an historical perspective

Ronald W Jones

Introduction

Our knowledge of the natural history of the precursor lesions of lower genital tract cancer – a subject that some would regard as having created more discussion and debate than any other in the field of gynaecology in the 20th century – remains at best sketchy and incomplete. While the knowledge accumulated over the past century has helped to reduce the morbidity and mortality from lower genital tract cancers, the general acceptance of the neoplastic potential of the precursor lesions and the interventions which have followed has limited progress in establishing a more detailed understanding of their natural history. From a clinician's perspective, how do we progress our understanding of the natural history of the precursor lesions of lower genital tract neoplasia? With the exception of a long-term study now being conducted in New Zealand, it is unlikely that further clinical studies of the type conducted in the second half of the 20th century will provide clinically relevant information on the natural history of cervical intraepithelial neoplasia (CIN). The knowledge gained from the past using clinical observation and light microscopy now needs to be seen as a foundation as we move forward to a new understanding of 'natural history' using molecular medicine. It may be an irony that by the time we fully understand the biological aspects of the natural history of many of the lower genital 'dysplasias', immunisation against the central aetiological agent, human papillomavirus (HPV), may make such knowledge superfluous. The recognition of the role of HPV has added an entirely new dimension to our understanding of the natural history of many of the lower genital tract precancers, and the natural course of this infection relates closely to the natural history of these. This chapter addresses aspects of the historical foundations of our knowledge, and not the role of HPV infection.

Cervix

An understanding of the natural history of cervical cancer precursors is necessary if we are to provide our patients with optimal management advice. While, on the one hand, we know that only a small proportion of women with dysplastic cervical lesions will ever develop cancer, our current practice is to treat all but the mildest abnormalities. This has two effects: first, it interrupts the natural history of the lesions, making it impossible to determine whether the lesion would progress or regress and, second, it creates a significant economic, social and personal burden resulting from the unnecessary investigation and treatment of many innocent lesions that are regarded as cancer precursors.

Historical background

In order to establish a foundation for our knowledge, it is useful to examine briefly the available historical evidence. To begin with, we should acknowledge the contribution of Dr John Williams, obstetric physician at University College Hospital, London, who in the Harveian Lecture of 1886 described for the first time the histological features of an intraepithelial cancer of the cervix, discovered by chance in an asymptomatic woman.[1] Williams stated: 'This is the earliest condition of undoubted cancer of the portio vaginalis which I have met with, and it is the earliest condition which is recognisable as cancer. It is superficial and remains superficial for a long time'. A decade later, a number of European authors began reporting their clinical and microscopic observations of cases of 'leukoplakia' of the cervix, some of which progressed to cancer.[2–5] Schauenstein in 1908 was the first to report a detailed histological analysis of atypical cervical epithelium, proposing that invasive cervical cancer derived from changes in the surface epithelium.[6] Similar findings were reported by others, including the association between atypical cervical epithelium and adjacent invasive cervical cancer.[7–9] Rubin's observations almost a century ago are worthy of consideration today: "What shall we regard as metaplastic non malignant epithelial changes and what shall we regard as typical carcinomatous epithelium, or an atypical epithelium that will sooner or later develop into a fully fledged carcinoma? Unless we can decide upon the determining features of the diagnosis of a cancerous epithelium, it is evident that we may never hope to improve our prophylactic therapy for carcinoma".[8]

It is worth noting this early concept of cervical cancer prevention. Pemberton and Smith were the first to report on the long latent phase of the disease.[10] The definition of carcinoma *in situ* (CIS) by Broders[11] in 1932 and the CIN classification by Richart[12] in 1968 followed. The varied descriptive terminology of lesions less than CIS caused confusion and in the early 1950s Reagan *et al.*[13] popularised the term 'dysplasia'. Further clinicopathology studies and the development of colposcopy prepared a foundation for the observations of Babes[14] and Papanicolaou[15] and the application of cervicovaginal cytology as a predictor of the precursors of cervical cancer.

The natural history of cervical dysplasia and CIS has been addressed in numerous studies in the latter half of the 20th century. Limitations of these studies include:

- method: for example, the limitations of cytology as a 'diagnostic' tool; interference with the natural history of the lesion by 'diagnostic' biopsies

- time: the natural history of cervical dysplasias and CIS, particularly from a population or screening perspective, is best measured in decades, not years, and few studies extend this long

- ethical issues: these are best illustrated by the 'unfortunate experiments' in New Zealand and India[16–18]

- cohort effects.

Reviews of the vast literature on 'natural history' have significant limitations; for instance, the oft-quoted 'critical review' of CIN by Östör[19] in 1993 has served to confuse rather than enlighten. In this paper, progression rates for CIN3 to invasion are quoted in the range 0–50% with an average of 'at least' 12% and regression rates from

Table 7.1. Development of invasive carcinoma in untreated carcinoma *in situ*; created by Kolstadt[17]

Author	Years observed (n)	Patients (n)	Cancer (%)	Incidence (%)
Funk-Bretano	9	124	41	30.2
Karlstedt	1–23	94	41	18.1
Kottmeier	3–10	40	9	22.4
Lange	1–10	100	24	24.0
Masterton	1–5	25	7	28.0
Petersen	8–22	127	39	30.7
Polahovsky	2–5	85	30	35.3
Total	1–23	595	167	28.3

0–100%. There are two broad approaches to the study of the natural history of cervical cancer precursors: either to follow patients with untreated lesions and observe the outcome or to use data obtained from population screening.

Carcinoma *in situ* (CIN 3)

Younge reported a prospective experiment into the natural history of CIS, which was terminated in 1938 on account of the number of women who were observed to progress to cervical cancer.[20] This was followed by Petersen's classic 1955 precytology study of 127 'untreated' Danish women with cervical precancerosis ('usually designated carcinoma *in situ*') in 1930–1950, which reported 34 (26%) women developing invasive cervical cancer during a 15-year follow-up.[21] The high regression rate noted in this study might be explained by the apparently innocuous 'treatments' received by some women. Lange (also from Denmark) reported that in a more representative population, 24 of 100 (24%), women with similar lesions progressed to invasive cancer.[22] The remarkable uniformity in the reported crude proportions of women with untreated CIS of the cervix who develop invasive carcinoma (20–30%) has also been observed by Kolstadt (Table 7.1).[17]

Examining the significance of cytologically diagnosed CIS, in 1962 Boyes *et al.* reported results from the British Columbia screening programme that demonstrated a significant reduction in cervical cancer incidence, and concluded that removal (i.e. treatment) of CIS by population screening 'is capable of virtually eliminating invasive carcinoma of the cervix'.[23] A further cohort screening study from British Columbia concluded that some degree of regression is part of the natural history of CIS and dysplasia and that the probability of progression to invasion is greater at older ages.[24]

Then, in 1963, Koss *et al.*[25] reached the following conclusions as a result of a long-term study of cervical dysplasia and CIS, which largely retain their validity to this day:

- CIS is a lesion of the cervical epithelium that beyond doubt is a precursor of cervical cancer

- CIS is very fragile and poorly established and may be readily eradicated by a variety of minor procedures

- spontaneous disappearance of CIS apparently does occur but it is an extraordinarily rare event

- histologically less advanced lesions classified as borderline atypias (dysplasias) behave similarly and may develop into CIS and even invasive cervical cancer

- CIS and lesser but related lesions have an extraordinarily slow evolution that continues over a period of many years

- the behaviour of CIS and related lesions of the cervix is at marked variance with invasive cervix cancer. This knowledge should not be used to minimise the importance of these lesions, but rather to establish new concepts of early cancer.

McIndoe *et al.*[16] reported in 1984 the outcome of a study into the natural history of CIS conducted by Associate Professor Green in the 1960s and 1970s in Auckland, New Zealand. This study provides the best modern evidence of the natural history of CIS of the cervix because it includes a large group of inadequately treated women in whom CIS persisted for long periods. The 948 women in the study were separated into two groups according to their cytology follow-up after histological diagnosis of CIS. Group 1 consisted of women with normal cytology follow-up and group 2 had persistent abnormal cytology follow-up. Of the 817 women with normal cytology follow-up (group 1), 12 (1.5%) developed invasive cervical or vaginal vault cancer, 4–19 (median 9) years later. CIS recurred in 6 (0.8%) 4–11 (median 6.5) years later.

The 131 women in group 2 continued to produce abnormal cytology consistent with cervical neoplasia. At final histological diagnosis, 29 (22%) had developed carcinoma, in 90 CIS persisted, in five dysplasia was present and in three no abnormality was detected. The relative risk for group 1 compared with group 2 was 24.8. The percentage probability of the occurrence of invasive carcinoma with increasing time is shown in Figure 7.1. Eighteen percent of women had developed invasive cervical or vaginal vault cancer by ten years and 36% by 20 years. The annual risk of progression to

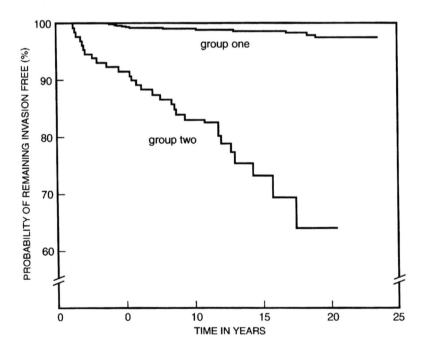

Figure 7.1 Probability of remaining invasion-free for group 1 and 2 patients at increasing intervals from diagnosis of carcinoma *in situ*; reprinted with permission from the American College of Obstetricians and Gynecologists[14]

invasion was approximately 2%. According to this study (and that of Koss[25]), spontaneous regression of CIS is an uncommon event, occurring in only 5% of group 2 women. Both groups had an identical frequency of high-risk HPV types.[26] A feature of this study was the persistence of the lesion (without invasion) for periods of up to 20 years. In some women, the lesion slowly extended over extensive areas of adjacent epithelium. Examples of CIS extending from the cervix down the vagina to the vulva and others where the disease has extended upwards through the uterine cavity, along the fallopian tubes to the peritoneum, were observed. Notably, none of the patients in the first 17 years had been lost to follow-up.

In this study, 25 women were managed by a small incomplete diagnostic biopsy alone. Of these, 15 cases (60%) had normal cytology after the biopsy; in one of these cases invasion occurred four years later. This dramatically illustrates the effect of small diagnostic biopsies on the course of CIN. However, eight of the ten women with continuing abnormal cytology developed invasive carcinoma. All of the material in this New Zealand study, including the original cytology and histology, is currently being reviewed and the minimum follow-up will be 26 years. These data will be available in late 2003.

'Invasive potential' relates to lesion size. Detailed histopathological examination of large numbers of cone biopsy specimens led Burghardt[27] to conclude that early stromal invasion originated centrally from atypical epithelium within endocervical glands in the majority of cases, that lesser 'dysplastic fields' were almost always located distal to a CIS lesion (centripetal structure of CIN) and that the likelihood of invasion was directly related to the size of the lesion. More recently, Tidbury et al.[28] have demonstrated that in women with microinvasive carcinoma there is usually a large area of CIN3 occupying most of the surface of the transformation zone and showing widespread glandular extension.

Mild and moderate dysplasia (CIN1 and CIN2)

Canadian groups, notably from British Columbia and Ontario, have used cytological records of historical cohorts to make a significant contribution to our understanding of the natural history of cervical dysplasia (CIN1 and CIN2). In spite of its limitations as a diagnostic tool, cytology has the advantage of not allowing the natural history to be disturbed by a diagnostic biopsy and it is therefore more suitable for examination of the natural history of CIN1 and CIN2.

The recent study by Holowaty et al.[29] demonstrated that both mild and moderate dysplasias are more likely to regress than progress. Sixty-two percent of women with a mildly dysplastic smear and 54% of women with a moderately dysplastic smear regressed to having two normal smears by ten years. The annual risk of progression from mild to severe dysplasia was a constant rate of 1% per year (the annual progression for CIN3 to invasion was 2%[16]). The risk of progression from moderate dysplasia was approximately 5% per year. Overall, moderate dysplasia was 2.5 times more likely to progress to CIS than was mild dysplasia. The Canadian studies support the theory of the CIN spectrum, with the risk of progression for moderate dysplasia as intermediate between the risks for mild and severe dysplasia.

The conclusions reached from these studies of the natural history of CIN confirm the inverse correlation of regression with histological grade and a direct correlation of progression with histological grade. They also support our current guidelines for practice: that women with CIN3 should be treated, while an initial observational policy is appropriate for CIN1. The above study suggests that a more cautious approach to the management of CIN2 may need to be considered. As noted earlier, our understanding of the natural history of CIN is inextricably related to the complexities of the natural history of HPV infection.[30]

Adenocarcinoma *in situ* and endocervical atypias

The presence of atypical glandular cells in smears many years preceding the presentation with an overt cervical adenocarcinoma and the finding of adenocarcinoma *in situ* (AIS) at the margin of cervical adenocarcinomas provides strong circumstantial evidence that AIS is a cancer precursor. However, the low prevalence of HPV DNA in low-grade endocervical atypias does not support the concept of a low-grade glandular precursor to AIS.[31] In addition, evidence suggests that the mechanism of HPV-mediated neoplastic transformation in glandular cells is different from that in squamous cells and there is no glandular counterpart to the low-grade squamous lesions.[32]

Vulva

Vulval intraepithelial neoplasia (HPV-related; warty/basaloid)

The natural history of squamous vulval intraepithelial neoplasia (VIN) continues to be the subject of considerable debate. While some consider the lesion to have a significant invasive potential, others consider that only symptomatic lesions require treatment.[33,34] A number of important points need to be addressed in relation to the natural history of VIN.

- A clear distinction needs to be made between HPV-related (warty/basaloid) VIN and non-HPV-related differentiated VIN.

- VIN1 is an uncommon histological diagnosis and usually represents HPV effect or reactive change alone. Most VIN lesions present as high-grade (VIN 3) histology.

- There is no evidence that the VIN1–3 histological spectrum represents a biological continuum.

- Clinical observations have been valuable in defining the natural history of this lesion, for example spontaneous regression.

- Discussions on the natural history of VIN have been confused by failure to differentiate clearly between the outcome of treated and untreated VIN.

The current (1986) classification of squamous VIN is similar to CIN.[35] The International Society for the Study of Vulvovaginal Disease (ISSVD) recommended a change to the current classification in 2003. VIN1 will no longer exist, as it refers only to reactive or HPV effect. VIN2 and VIN3 will be combined and termed VIN. VIN will be reclassified into VIN (HPV-positive, warty/basaloid) and differentiated VIN (HPV-negative) types.[36]

Background

By 1960, the body of clinical observations had firmly established that CIS of the vulva (VIN3) was a precursor of invasive vulval cancer.[37] Coinciding with the increasing frequency of the condition from the 1970s, there was a significant shift of opinion with respect to its invasive potential. This related to the reported 'low progression' rates to invasive cancer of 2–5%.[33] It was not generally appreciated that these 'low progression' rates reflected the outcome following treatment and not the natural history of the untreated condition. The nature of VIN was also questioned in a number of case reports of spontaneous regression of the lesion. Finally, it was considered that the 30-year interval between the mean ages at presentation of VIN and vulval cancer tended to exclude a causal association.

Morphological evidence of the neoplastic potential of vulval intraepithelial neoplasia

VIN3 can be demonstrated adjacent to approximately 30% of squamous cell carcinomas of the vulva. Nearly all stage 1A vulval cancers arise in a field of VIN3. These 'associations' provide circumstantial evidence that VIN3 is a cancer precursor. There is very little documented evidence of histological or clinical progression of VIN1 to VIN3. The VIN grading system should therefore be seen as a convenient histological description of a spectrum of intraepithelial changes and it should not be inferred that it is a biological continuum.

Clinical evidence

Progression

There are few reports of the outcome of untreated VIN3. One study reported progression in seven of eight cases to invasive cancer, including in three women in their thirties.[38] With treated VIN3, almost all large series report invasion to occur in 2–5% of cases during follow-up.[33] This is approximately ten times the rate of cervical cancer following treatment of CIN3. The reported transit time to invasion is less than ten years in more than 90% of cases.[33] However, when follow-up extends for long enough periods, 'new' vulval cancers are seen to arise many years after adequate treatment of VIN3 (unpublished data, see below). Small VIN lesions may progress rapidly to invasion, while others may slowly extend over large areas of adjacent skin before becoming invasive. Immunosuppressed women have a small increased risk of progression.

Two mechanisms exist for the development of vulval cancer in women with a history of VIN. First, cancer may arise as a consequence of the progression of persisting VIN and, second, by the *de novo* development of cancer in a field of risk. The latter possibility is supported by a large Norwegian study which reported that 8 of 16 (50%) women who later developed vulval cancer had negative resection margins at the time of primary surgery for VIN.[39]

A review of 370 women with VIN3 on the National Women's Hospital (New Zealand) dataset provides some insight into the nature of the condition. Twenty-one women in the cohort developed invasive vulval cancer. Ten of these were 'untreated', having received biopsy alone or grossly inadequate excisional surgery of significant lesions. In this group, the transit time to invasion was 1.2–6.4 years (mean 3.5). Eleven (3.2%) treated cases subsequently developed vulval cancer between 1.8 and 17.0 years (mean 7.7). On the basis of previously negative surgical margins and prolonged clinical observation, we estimate that at least half of the cancers arising in previously treated VIN represent 'new' disease and not progression from pre-existing disease. Only three of the 15 cases presenting with progression since 1980 have been patients over 50 years of age. The disease regressed without treatment in 32 women with specific clinical features (see below).

Two studies report that the increasing incidence of VIN over the past 20–30 years may now be responsible for a changing pattern of squamous cell carcinoma of the vulva.[40,41] In one study, two cohorts of women with squamous cell carcinoma of the vulva and separated by at least two decades were reviewed. In the earlier cohort, only 1 of 56 (1.8%) patients was aged under 50 years, whereas in the more recent cohort, 12 of 57 (21%) patients were aged under 50 years. Ten of the 13 (77%) women aged under 50 years compared with 13 of 100 (13%) women aged over 50 years had an HPV-related warty or basaloid VIN associated with the invasive vulval carcinoma.[40]

The behaviour of VIN1 and VIN2 lesions is poorly documented. VIN2 is a relatively uncommon histological diagnosis and, like its counterpart on the cervix, should at present be regarded for management purposes as a high-grade abnormality.

Up to 90% of the common warty/basaloid VIN lesions are HPV-positive. Such lesions should be considered to be part of contiguous field of risk. HPV-16 has been demonstrated serially in the vulva of women with VIN3 and in their subsequent VIN-related squamous cell carcinomas.[42] Up to 50% of all women with VIN have at some time had preinvasive or invasive disease of the cervix and vagina.[38] While recurrences of VIN or the development of invasive cancer may occur at the margins of incompletely resected disease, such events may occur anywhere in the field of HPV-infected (and previously normal) vulval, urethral, perianal and vaginal skin.

Regression

Spontaneous regression of high-grade VIN occurs in a well-defined clinical setting.[43] It is generally seen in non-white women under 30 years of age. The median transit time to complete regression is less than one year. The lesions are frequently asymptomatic and may be seen in association with pregnancy. The lesions are usually multifocal, pigmented and papular. The natural history of HPV-related VIN is shown in Figure 7.2.

Differentiated (HPV-negative) vulval intraepithelial neoplasia

This HPV-negative lesion is relatively uncommon and is seen mainly in older women with lichen sclerosus and/or squamous hyperplasia and has a strong association with keratinising carcinoma. It has subtle histological features that are largely limited to the basal epithelium and the VIN1 to VIN3 grading system is not applicable. Differentiated VIN appears to have a relatively brief intraepithelial phase before progressing to invasion.[44]

Vulval dermatoses

An association between abnormal vulval skin, usually white (leukoplakia) and cancer has been recognised for almost a century. Confusing clinical and pathological terminologies have prevented a better understanding of the natural history of potential precursor lesions. The ISSVD has done much to foster improved understanding and terminology in this area.

Histological examination of the epithelium adjacent to invasive squamous vulval carcinoma reveals lichen sclerosus in about 60% of cases and VIN (HPV-related) in about 30%.[45] Available evidence (see above) strongly points to VIN as a cancer precursor. However, the situation with respect to lichen sclerosus is much less clear. Most series report that approximately 5% of women with vulval lichen sclerosus develop cancer.[44] The influence of treatment on outcome is rarely discussed. Lichen sclerosus is by far the most common vulval dermatosis. Rarely, cancer can arise in the less common vulval dermatoses such as lichen planus[46] or, rarely, lichen simplex chronicus. It is therefore tempting to suggest that cancer may arise in any vulval

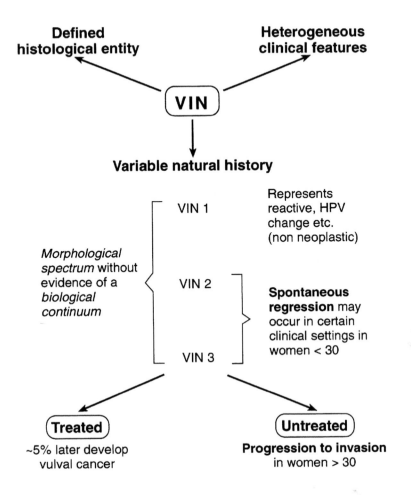

Figure 7.2 Vulval intraepithelial neoplasia (VIN): a disease of 'contradictions'; reproduced from *Eur J Gynaecol Oncol* 2001;22:393–402, with permission from IROG Canada Inc.

dermatosis where there is chronic irritation, increased epithelial proliferation and mitotic activity, and not specifically lichen sclerosus. Malignant change in lichen sclerosus is more likely to occur where there is additional squamous hyperplasia and/or differentiated VIN.

Paget's disease of the vulva and melanoma *in situ* of the vulva

These conditions are both included in the current (1986) ISSVD non-squamous VIN terminology.[35] Paget's disease of the vulva is associated with concurrent underlying cutaneous adnexal carcinoma in up to one-fifth of cases. Progression of intraepithelial Paget's disease of the vulva to invasion occurs rarely. Melanoma *in situ* of the vulva is rare and has more in common with the corresponding mucosal lesion than cutaneous *in situ* melanoma. Progression to invasive melanoma occurs, but the evolution appears to be slow.[48]

Vagina

Vaginal cancer is a rare condition and can follow pre-existing squamous or glandular abnormalities.

Squamous vaginal intraepithelial neoplasia

Vaginal intraepithelial neoplasia (VAIN) is a relatively uncommon condition with an estimated incidence of two in 1000. Only limited information is available on its natural history. Documented examples of progression of VAIN1 to VAIN3 are rare. The situation may be similar to the vulva where the VIN1 to VIN3 grading system represents a morphological spectrum of intraepithelial changes but does not represent a biological continuum. VAIN3 is unquestionably a cancer precursor.

VAIN is frequently seen as part of an HPV field effect. Benedet noted that two-thirds of the 136 cases of VAIN in his series had prior, concomitant or subsequent intraepithelial or invasive cancer in the vulva (including urethra) and cervix.[49] In a review of 132 cases of VAIN, Rome[50] noted that 55 (42.5%) women had previously undergone hysterectomy for CIN or invasive carcinoma. Occult invasion has been noted in 13–28% of surgically excised specimens.[50,51]

The majority of VAIN1 lesions represent HPV effect alone and should not be regarded as cancer precursors. In a rare 'no treatment' prospective natural history study of VAIN, Aho et al.[52] reported that 14 of 18 (78%) VAIN1–2 lesions regressed spontaneously. This fits with the known natural history of the HPV/CIN1 lesion. In this study, one VAIN1 lesion progressed to invasion in five years and one VAIN3 progressed to invasion in four years.

With the exception of the Aho et al.[52] study, there is little prospective information on the natural history of VAIN. In the natural history of CIN3 study of McIndoe et al.,[16] 29 women with evidence of persistent abnormal cytology developed invasive carcinoma, 20 in the cervix and nine in the vaginal vault. This study demonstrated that VAIN3 can slowly extend over wide areas of the vagina before progressing to invasion. Rome[50] reported that eight of 132 women with VAIN in his series developed invasive carcinoma over one to seven years, of whom five represented treatment failures, two progressed without treatment and one further case probably represented new disease (after 14 years). Four of 136 cases in the Benedet series progressed to cancer.[49]

Vaginal adenosis

Adenocarcinomas may arise in areas of vaginal adenosis. This is well documented in patients exposed to diethylstilboestrol (DES) in utero. While vaginal adenosis occurs in nearly half of patients exposed to DES in utero, the estimated risk of developing clear cell adenocarcinoma in the offspring is 1:1000 or less.

The future

Traditional methods for studying the natural history of the common precursor lesions of lower genital tract cancer may have only a limited role. Further progress requires the development of inexpensive and specific biomarkers for progression to invasive carcinoma.

References

1.   Williams J. Harveian Lectures on cancer of the uterus. *Lancet* Jan 1 1887, 6–9; and Jan 8 1887,59–62. [References 2 – 7 are cited in Petersen O. *Precancerous Changes of the Cervical Epithelium in Relation to Manifest Cervical Carcinoma*. Acta Radiologica Supplementum 127. Copenhagen: Danish Science Press Ltd; 1955.]

2.   d'Hotman de Villiers A, Thérèse A, Thérèse L. 1896. Cited in: Petersen O. *Precancerous Changes of the Cervical Epithelium in Relation to Manifest Cervical Carcinoma*. Acta Radiologica Supplementum 127. Copenhagen: Danish Science Press Ltd; 1955. p. 156.

3.   Verdalle. 1903. Cited in: Petersen O. *Precancerous Changes of the Cervical Epithelium in Relation to Manifest Cervical Carcinoma*. Acta Radiologica Supplementum 127. Copenhagen: Danish Science Press Ltd; 1955. p. 162.

4.   Jayle F, Bender X. 1905. Cited in: Petersen O. *Precancerous Changes of the Cervical Epithelium in Relation to Manifest Cervical Carcinoma*. Acta Radiologica Supplementum 127. Copenhagen: Danish Science Press Ltd; 1955. p. 156.

5.   v Franqué O. 1907. Cited in: Petersen O. *Precancerous Changes of the Cervical Epithelium in Relation to Manifest Cervical Carcinoma*. Acta Radiologica Supplementum 127. Copenhagen: Danish Science Press Ltd; 1955. p. 154.

6.   Schauenstein W. 1908. Cited in: Petersen O. *Precancerous Changes of the Cervical Epithelium in Relation to Manifest Cervical Carcinoma*. Acta Radiologica Supplementum 127. Copenhagen: Danish Science Press Ltd; 1955. p. 160.

7.   Pronai K. 1909. Cited in: Petersen O. *Precancerous Changes of the Cervical Epithelium in Relation to Manifest Cervical Carcinoma*. Acta Radiologica Supplementum 127. Copenhagen: Danish Science Press Ltd; 1955. p. 160.

8.   Rubin IC. The pathological diagnosis of incipient carcinoma of the uterus. *Am J Obstet Dis Women Child* 1910;62:668–76.

9.   Schottländer J, Kermauner F. 1912. Cited in: Peterson O. *Precancerous Changes of the Cervical Epithelium in Relation to Manifest Cervical Carcinoma*. Acta Radiologica Supplementum 127. Copenhagen: Danish Science Press; 1955. p.161.

10. Pemberton FA, Smith S. The early diagnosis and prevention of carcinoma of the cervix. *Am J Obstet Gynecol* 1929;17:165–76.

11. Broders AC. Carcinoma *in situ* contrasted with benign penetrating epithelium. *JAMA* 1932; 99:1670–4.

12. Richart RM. Natural history of cervical intraepithelial neoplasia. *Clin Obstet Gynecol* 1968;5:748–84.

13. Reagan JW, Seidemann IL, Saracusa Y. The cellular morphology of carcinoma *in situ* and dysplasia or atypical hyperplasia of the uterine cervix. *Cancer* 1953;6:224–35.

14. Tasca L, Östör AG, Babes V. History of gynecologic pathology. XII. Aurel Babes. *Int J Gynecol Pathol* 2002; 21: 198–202.

15. Papanicolaou GN, Traut HF. The diagnostic value of vaginal smears in carcinoma of the uterus. *Am J Obstet Gynecol* 1941;42:193–206.

16. McIndoe WA, McLean MR, Jones RW, Mullins PR. The invasive potential of carcinoma *in situ* of the cervix. *Obstet Gynecol* 1984;64:451–8.

17. *The Report of the Inquiry into Allegations Concerning the Treatment of Cervical Cancer at the National Women's Hospital*. Auckland: Government Printing Office; 1988.

18. Luthra UK, Prabhakar AK, Seth P, Agarwal SS, Murthy NS, Bhatnagar P, et al. The natural history of precancerous and early cancerous lesions of the uterine cervix. *Acta Cytol* 1987;31:226–33.

19. Östör AG. Natural history of cervical intraepithelial neoplasia: a critical review. *Int J Gynecol Pathol* 1993;12:186–92.

20. Younge PA, Hertig AT, Armstrong A. A study of 145 cases of carcinoma *in situ* of the cervix uteri at the Free Hospital for Women. *Am J Obstet Gynecol* 1949;53:867–99.

21. Petersen O. *Precancerous Changes of the Cervical Epithelium in Relation to Manifest Cervical Carcinoma*. Acta Radiologica Supplementum 127. Copenhagen: Danish Science Press Ltd; 1955.

22. Lange P. *Clinical and Histological Studies on Cervical Carcinoma*. Acta Pathologica et Microbiologica Scandinavica Supplementum 50. Copenhagen: Danish Science Press Ltd; 1960.

23. Boyes DA, Fidler HK, Lock DR. Significance of *in situ* carcinoma of the uterine cervix. *BMJ* 1962;5273:203–5.

24. Boyes DA, Morrison B, Knox EG, Draper GJ, Miller AB. A cohort study of cervical cancer screening in British Columbia. *Clin Invest Med* 1982;5:1–29.

25. Koss LG, Stewart FW, Foote FW, Jordan MJ, Bader GM, Day E. Some histological aspects of behavior of epidermoid carcinoma *in situ* and related lesions of the uterine cervix. *Cancer* 1963;16:1160–211.

26. Shah KV, Kessis TD, Shah F, Gupta JW, Shibata D, Jones RW. Human papillomavirus investigation of patients with CIN 3, some of whom progressed to cancer. *Int J Gynecol Pathol* 1996;15:127–30.

27. Burghardt E. *Colposcopy, Cervical Pathology, Textbook and Atlas.* Stuttgart: Georg Thiene Verlag; 1984.

28. Tidbury P, Singer A, Jenkins D. CIN3: the role of lesion size in invasion. *Br J Obstet Gynaecol* 1992;99:583–6.

29. Holowaty P, Miller AB, Rohan T, To T. Natural history of dysplasia of the uterine cervix. *J Natl Cancer Inst* 1999;91:252–8.

30. Woodman CB, Collins S, Winter H, Bailey A, Ellis J, Prior P, et al. Natural history of cervical human papillomavirus infection in young women: a longitudinal cohort study. *Lancet* 2001;357:1831–6.

31. Goldstein NS, Ahmad E, Hussain M, Hankin RC, Perez-Reyes N. Endocervical glandular atypia: does a preneoplastic lesion of adenocarcinoma in situ exist? *Am J Clin Pathol* 1998;110:200–9.

32. Stoler MH. Human papillomaviruses and cervical neoplasia: a model for carcinogenesis. *Int J Gynecol Pathol* 2000;19:16–28.

33. Jones RW. Is vulvar intraepithelial neoplasia a precursor of cancer? In: Luesley DM, editor. *Cancer and Precancer of the Vulva.* London: Arnold; 2000. p. 67–73.

34. Van Beurden M, Van Der Vange N, Ten Kate FJW, De Craen AJM, Schilthuis MS, Lammes FB. Restricted surgical management of vulvar intraepithelial neoplasia 3: focus on exclusion of invasion and on relief of symptoms. *Int J Gynecol Cancer* 1998; 8:73–7.

35. Report of the ISSVD Terminology Committee. *J Reprod Med* 1986; 31: 973-4.

36. Report of the ISSVD Oncology Committee. Modifications to the terminology of squamous vulvar intraepithelial neoplasia. *J Reprod Med* (in press)

37. Abell MR, Gosling JR. Intraepithelial and infiltrative carcinoma of the vulva: Bowen's type. *Cancer* 1961;14:318–29.

38. Jones RW, Rowan DM. Vulvar intraepithelial neoplasia III: a clinical study of the outcome in 113 cases with relation to the later development of invasive vulvar carcinoma. *Obstet Gynecol* 1994;84:741–5.

39. Iversen T, Tretli S. Intraepithelial and invasive squamous cell neoplasia of the vulva: trends in incidence, recurrence, and survival rate in Norway. *Obstet Gynecol* 1998;91:969–72.

40. Jones RW, Baranyai J, Stables S. Trends in squamous cell carcinoma of the vulva: the influence of vulvar intraepithelial neoplasia. *Obstet Gynecol* 1997;90:448–52.

41. Joura EA, Lösch A, Haider-Angeler M-G, Breitenecker G, Leodolter S. Trends in vulvar neoplasia. Increasing incidence of vulvar intraepithelial neoplasia and squamous cell carcinoma of the vulva in young women. *J Reprod Med* 2000;45:613–15.

42. Park JP, Jones RW, McLean MR, Currie JL, Woodruff JD, Shah KV, Kurman RJ. Possible etiologic heterogeneity of vulvar intraepithelial neoplasia. *Cancer* 1991;67:1599–1607.

43. Jones RW, Rowan DM. Spontaneous regression of vulvar intraepithelial neoplasia 2–3. *Obstet Gynecol* 2000;96:470–2.

44. Hart WR. Vulvar intraepithelial neoplasia: historical aspects and current status. *Int J Gynecol Pathol* 2001;20:16–30.

45. Leibowitch M, Neill S, Pelisse M, Moyal-Baracco M. The epithelial changes associated with squamous cell carcinoma of the vulva: a review of the clinical, histological and viral findings in 78 women. *Br J Obstet Gynaecol* 1990;97:1135–9.

46. Meffert JJ, Davis BM, Grimwood RE. Lichen sclerosus. *J Am Acad Dermatol* 1995;32:393–416.

47. Jones RW, Rowan DR, Kirker J, Wilkinson EJ. Vulval lichen planus: progression of pseudoepitheliomatous hyperplasia to invasive vulval carcinomas. *Br J Obstet Gynaecol* 2001;108:665–6.

48. Kingston N, Baranyai J, Jones RW. Recurrent primary vulvovaginal melanoma arising in melanoma in situ (unpublished data submitted for publication).

49. Benedet JL, Sanders BH. Carcinoma *in situ* of the vagina. *Am J Obstet Gynecol* 1984;148:695–70.

50. Rome RM, England PG. Management of vaginal intraepithelial neoplasia: a series of 132 cases with long-term follow-up. *Int J Gynecol Cancer* 2000;10:382–90.

51. Ireland D, Monaghan JM. The management of abnormal vaginal cytology following hysterectomy. *Br J Obstet Gynaecol* 1988;95:973–5.

52. Aho M, Vesterinen E, Meyer B, Purola E, Paavonen J. Natural history of vaginal intraepithelial neoplasia. *Cancer* 1991;68:195–7.

Chapter 8

Cytology, histology and the natural history of lower genital tract neoplasia

Discussion

Discussion following the papers by Dr Deery, Professor Richart and Mr Jones

Wilkinson: Dr Deery, one of the conclusions in the Martin-Hirsch[1] paper that you quoted was that the extended-tip spatula, rather than the conventional or Ayre spatula, was the preferred device. Their point was that this seemed to sample better than a regular spatula in the studies that they examined. Do you have any comments about that?

Deery: Yes, within meta-analyses there is a general trend for devices that improve the endocervical cell yield also to improve the detection of conditions such as dyskaryosis or atypia. However, individual studies do not allow that to be established significantly. It may be that if you had a large enough study, properly controlled and with decent outcomes, you might see a difference, but to date that is not evident. This is something that comes out in meta-analysis of many papers and it is a trend, but it does not actually reach significance.

Shepherd: I get very confused by some of these things such as brooms. I am of the generation that can remember chimney-sweeps and I tend to assume that a broom is a sort of conical thing that they used to use, rather than a kind of brush.

Deery: The brush terminology is quite distracting because when the brushes were originally introduced, they were endocervical brushes that were used to take material from the endocervical canal selectively. However, there have since been developments such as the Cervex brush® (Rovers Medical Devices BV, Oss, the Netherlands), as it is properly called, which looks more like a broom but has a raised central area and is a flexible, ectocervical brush.. I have deliberately distinguished it by calling it a broom, because I was talking about a range of endocervical brush cervical techniques. The only point I was making in relation to the NHS Cervical Screening Programme that began in 1988 is that we are still using wooden spatulas. These are cheap and there is good evidence from the last 10–12 years that this is not the device of choice.

We have one of the highest unsatisfactory rates in the world, with an average of 10–12%, which has been creeping up from eight or nine percent over the last few years. There is no other programme in the world with such unsatisfactory rates. This is partly an educational problem but, without doubt, it also has something to do with the spatula devices that we use, which produce rather thick, difficult smears with lots of obscurational artefact.

Some of us are now considering using liquid-based cytology to achieve a sharp reduction in our unsatisfactory rate. However, if we simply used the preferred spatula device, which involves a different method of transferring the material to slides, we could probably lower our unsatisfactory rates quite dramatically, at a much lower cost than a liquid-based technique. Nevertheless, I am not arguing against the liquid-based technique, because it has other advantages.

MacLean: What are the relative costs of the spatula versus these brooms?

Deery: This differs in various parts of the world. A plastic broom costs about 30 (UK) pence, whereas you can buy several hundred spatulas for the same money.

Shepherd: What you are implying here is extremely important. The thesis of your talk was detection of glandular lesions, but that is not something that we have been able to say before is the intention of screening programmes. You are now introducing an extremely important but different aspect of cervical cancer screening.

Deery: No, that was not the thesis at all. There is a discussion about which sampler to use when you are looking critically at colposcopy, to try to explore the endocervical canal in patients with abnormal smears who have been referred for investigation. There is still an issue when deciding which sampler to use.

What I was saying was that such arguments should not direct your choice of sampler. Among the best samplers for squamous lesions is undoubtedly, on balance, the ectocervical broom or brush. This is just as good as combined techniques that employ a rigid plastic spatula with an extended tip, plus an endocervical brush, in an attempt to obtain an endocervical canal specimen. The reality is that the broom performs as well as combined techniques. It is simpler, organisationally, to take that advantage. With the traditional wooden spatula used in the UK, it is a simple change that would not cost very much, but would dramatically achieve a number of substantial differences in reading smears in laboratories as well.

Tidy: It is accepted that in the meta-analysis it was shown that the extended tip could sample the endocervical canal better, but individual studies do not confirm that. Going on from one other statement – to return to the subject of liquid-based cytology – is there an inherent problem in the preparation method that reduces the capture of endocervical cells on to the final slide preparation, from what you stated?

Deery: There are very few studies. I do not really want to talk about liquid-based technology, but what exists is quite interesting because with both CytoRich® and ThinPrep® and their different techniques, there is a suggestion that if you conduct large numbers of repeat preparations on the same sample, produced within liquid specimens, you can recover a certain number of glandular diagnoses.

Internationally, where there have been opportunities over the last several years to examine liquid-based specimens alongside conventional specimens using broom or ectocervical brush specimens, there are generally very few pathologists or papers giving evidence that liquid-based cytology actually detects as many glandular lesions. This work has taken place largely in Australia and New Zealand, where they are very good at detecting glandular lesions. Much of the basic literature has been written there and, generally speaking, their cytology services are highly capable of detecting those kinds of lesions. There is also a concern about liquid-based samples and detectability of endocervical lesions, although we may have to concede in the end that this is not what mass screening programmes are actually for.

Sasieni: I have not looked at the literature for some time but, as I remember, there are actually more abnormalities with the broom in many of the early studies. Also, I did not think that any of these studies showed that the broom was significantly better than any device other than a brush on its own. From the Buntinx review,[2] there was nothing to indicate that the broom was better than the extended-tip spatula alone. I would be interested in your comments on that. Early on, at least, there seem to be more abnormalities because the broom caused more bleeding, but clearly this is not a problem with liquid-based cytology.

Deery: What I said was that they are equivalent. If you read this review, both individual studies and meta-analyses have shown this. They produce a more attractive specimen for cytologists and pathologists to look at, because of a different technique for spreading the material on the slide, but they are equivalent to the individual studies that are evidential.

Shafi: One of the problems is that, whichever sampling device you use, what matters is actually the visualisation of the cervix and the correct application of the device to obtain a good smear. That is where we have failed in many situations, particularly in our current screening strategy. Moving on to the comparison nomenclatures that you have listed here – the Bethesda system, the Australian system and the proposed British Society of Clinical Cytology system – we are using three different systems, which I suspect is causing a great deal of confusion. I predict that we will probably move away from the current high unsatisfactory rates to a continuing increase in the borderline, borderline-query-high-grade and borderline-query-glandular rates, and that will impact on UK colposcopy services. Why can these not all be brought together under one classification? I cannot see the logic of having three disparate nomenclature systems in the English-speaking world.

Deery: I am saying the same thing, essentially. There are consensus conferences, with international observers and visitors, but essentially within national boundaries, which are making sense of the different and divergent screening strategies that exist throughout the world. There is definitely a different focus in the UK, with its mass organised screening programme, from the USA, where the focus is on those women who are brought into an opportunistic programme and then assured, as much as possible, within that programme, by fairly intensive investigation and frequent screening, that they do not have a disease. There is a different emphasis placed on the establishment of an absolute negative.

There are very few organised programmes, and they have to approach mass screening on a risk basis. They try to reduce mortality and incidence, but they do not chase up every single lesion. It has been suggested that human papillomavirus (HPV) screening would be an effective way of detecting adenocarcinoma in patients referred with abnormal atypical glandular cells. However, there is some hand-wringing about the apparent lack of association between metanephroid and clear cell tumours and HPV, and these are a tiny fraction of the adenocarcinomas. Approximately 90% of adenocarcinomas of the endocervix, however, are mucinous adenocarcinomas that are associated with HPV and would therefore be detectable. There is also a different focus. We would be very happy with detecting 90% of adenocarcinomas. However, from the literature and by review at least, and from talking to people, I feel that they are not too happy with detecting anything less than 100%.

Critchley: I hope I am not just returning to this issue of sampling, but there is a point of clarification. You said that the best sampler for a squamous lesion was this ectocervical broom, the Cervex, which was equivalent to an extended tip and a brush. Is that then dependent upon technique? If you are using the former in liquid-based cytology, you take the smear in a very different way, rotating it five times as opposed to once when we rotate with a traditional wooden spatula and ectocervical brush. Could you clarify that? When you say it is the same, are you rotating it once or several times?

Deery: It is the same. The advice for the use of the ectocervical brush sampler is to rotate it five times in the cervix, whereas the advice that usually came with training in the use of the Ayre spatula, if it was available, was to rotate it through 360 degrees, and then to spread it in a circular fashion on the slide. That produces quite a thick, and quite variably thick, smear, which is quite difficult to look at. This is something that we have all accepted over the years but the reality is that the broom specimens, taken conventionally, and swept backwards and forwards across the slide, to produce horizontal trails of material, are much better samples to look at. They involve retraining individuals to take smears in a particular way. Many of these introductions of new technology involve retraining people, and there are of course benefits from that. So it is the same mechanism, whether you put it into a liquid-based sample or on to a conventional smear.

McGoogan: We should not lose sight of the fact that, with a cervical smear, we are trying to identify abnormal cells. I remain unconvinced that the presence of endocervical cells is a good measure of quality. I would reference Mitchell and Medley's paper in the early 1990s on that.[3]

Moving on, you are suggesting that we conduct a proper trial of the efficiency of the different sampling devices, but I would ask how you would go about that. We know that second and third samples from a cervix, taken at the same time, contain different complements of cells.

Deery: You have to involve yourself in a randomised study, and there are such examples in the literature. You accept that your second and third sample will have an increased amount of blood and so on, and will have a deficit by comparison with the first samples. However, provided the study is big enough, and you randomise all the samplers to first, second and third position, you can quite happily conduct one. We have just completed such a study, which has not yet been published, using broom samplers and liquid-based and conventional smears. It is very straightforward and it has been done in the past for up to seven collection devices.

McGoogan: What would be your measure of outcome or quality?

Deery: The problem in cervical cytology is always outcome measures. You have to include a fraction of those that are negative by your available techniques, which means that you have to carry out colposcopy on a proportion of the population that have no abnormal findings by cytology. Also, all of your patients who have abnormalities require colposcopy and a protocolled biopsy procedure. Over the years, there have been very few such studies in the literature, and this is one of the problems when making decisions about collection devices and so forth.

Prendiville: The question I wanted to ask comes back to the one that was raised earlier about the usefulness of public health messages in relation to HPV, given that there is now very clear evidence that oncogenic HPV causes cervical cancer and cervical intraepithelial neoplasia (CIN). There is also very clear evidence that transient infections are innocent. Is there a consensus among epidemiologists and public health physicians about the message that we should convey to women about HPV, given the potential for causing psychosexual morbidity if we tell half the population that they have a carcinogenic virus?

Richart: I have a question for Dr Deery. There was a recent paper by Laura Koutsky's group that I thought was particularly well designed, which showed no predictive value for the presence of endocervical or metaplastic cells in a Papanicolaou smear.[4]

Jones: Who makes the decision as to which sampling device is used? Do doctors or managers make that decision?

Deery: Within a screening programme, the decision is usually made by consensus within a central group, with or without consultation and advice from other disparate groups. It is not quite clear who makes the decision in the end and on what basis.

Sasieni: Professor Richart, there is the point about a double negative being a good indicator of zero risk of invasive cancer, generally, for seven to ten years and perhaps longer. That may be longer, which I do not think you said, but I am thinking about older women. What are your feelings about screening older women these days?

Richart: Very few of the studies are sufficiently age-stratified or contain large numbers of older women to be able to answer that question.

Sasieni: I am thinking about over 60-year-olds.

Richart: There are good data to suggest that HPV DNA testing is a good triage test for older women who have ASCUS. There are few data on HPV DNA screening in older women. I would anticipate, however, that HPV DNA testing would be equally effective in older women as in younger cohorts.

Sasieni: I was just thinking that in all places where there is an organised screening programme, it stops somewhere between the ages of 54 years and 65 years. In the USA, screening continues in older women in theory, but there are mixed answers as to how much screening there is of women in their seventies. There is also a very steep rise in the incidence of invasive cervical cancer over the age of 65 years in most countries, with Finland, where they stop screening earlier, being the most dramatic. What are your views about whether screening would work, if we continued to screen as long as women had a life expectancy of at least ten years, say?

Richart: I think it would work. Patients who are double negative are doubly reassured. The negative predictive values in virtually all the major well-conducted studies now are in the 99.5–100% range. Patients over 60 years old with cancers have HPV-related cancers like everyone else, and I see no reason why it should not work equally well in them. Having said that, however, if you have a 70-year-old woman who is double negative, I do not see that there is any good reason to screen her again in the short term.

Shepherd: You have accepted or implied that five to seven percent of your high-grade CIN lesions may have reached this category without first going through a low-grade CIN category. Why can you not extrapolate that to invasive cancers and really poorly differentiated anaplastic cancers?

Richart: First, those are descriptive data. The posit is still speculative but does serve as a basis for discussing *de novo* cancer.

More importantly, however, in the patients who are prospectively followed after being double negative, the number of invasive cancers that occur is very small. Irrespective of the theory, if you are a double negative patient, the chance of developing a high-grade CIN or invasive cancer over the next five years is extremely low.

Singer: There were three studies during the eighties with which we were involved, because we always felt that there were small-volume CIN3 lesions, the biological potential of which was pretty dubious. Michael Campion, worked on this in the early eighties – and his study is quoted as one of the first and classic papers, for which we followed the low-grade ones cytologically every four months, and followed them to CIN3.[5] Re-examining the videos and photographs at the time showed that there were large areas of low-grade disease, in the middle of which was a small volume of high-grade disease. Because it was deluged – the cells coming off were low-grade – the disease was said to be low-grade. If you looked closely, you could virtually see what were originally small areas of high-grade cells, growing just within the high-grade field. I am sure that they had been there from the beginning. So that was in one paper.

About two years later, Michael Jones published a paper in *The Lancet*. He followed up the women in Aylesbury, UK, who had been followed cytologically with mild dyskaryosis. We knew that after two negatives they were being discharged, so he colposcoped and smeared these women and found that 12% of them had CIN3, although they had been cytologically negative. These were all cases of small-volume disease and you can argue about whether it was of any consequence.

Then Mike Jarmulowicz, when he was with us in 1989, looked at a number of micro-invasions, and also a number of CINs, looking at volume. He measured the amount of CIN3 associated with micro-invasion. We showed that you needed a large volume to have micro-invasion. Indeed, those women who were picked up with mild smears and who had associated CIN3, who are presumably the ones we are picking up quite often now with positive HPVs, as Michael Jones found, were all small-volume. As Professor Richart said, it is probably one of the better parameters for a clinician; if you have a large volume of high-grade disease, you really have a very high risk of micro-invasion with it. It is very rare to have invasion from a small-volume CIN3 lesion.

Richart: Colposcopy has a higher sensitivity than specificity, but both are lower than we thought only a few years ago.

The other issue you addressed speaks basically to verification bias. There are several studies that looked at verification bias. The best may be that of Jerry Belinson and his colleagues from the PRC.[6] In that study, every patients in the series was examined colposcopically and biopsied with a small bronchial biopsy punch. There was no evidence of verification bias.

In a recent review of Hybrid Capture II®-based data, we reported on almost 45 000 patients who had been examined using Papanicolaou smears and HPV DNA.[7] The data are compelling that this combination provides a negative predictive value of more than 99% for CIN3 or more.

Jones: Ian Duncan convinced me that women who had regular smears that were all normal until the age of 50 years could stop having smears. Can anyone tell me what happened to Ian Duncan's Scottish review?[8]

McGoogan: It is not statistically significant, as yet, because they did not have enough women with a verified sequence of smears over their lifetime. There were some women who went on to have a high-grade lesion.

Monaghan: We have extended the Ian Duncan study. When Grainne Flannelly (Consultant, National Maternity Hospital, Dublin) was working with me, she went to five major centres with computerised records. We modified the study slightly by identifying patients as having an index smear shortly before the age of 50 years and then looking back from there to make sure that these women had a real negative smear history. We then looked forward from that index smear and ran into exactly the same problems as those Ian Duncan encountered with his smaller study. When that study was completed – now four and a half years ago – we just did not have enough longitudinal data. There was a trend, although there was no statistical significance. This was not a trial, simply an observational study. We had to put together slightly different data for Aberdeen from the other four centres, because their system of recording was slightly different but, essentially, it matched. It showed the same trend as Ian Duncan had shown.

We really need to do that work all over again with much more information. It really was quite remarkable, doing this ten years after the national screening programme had started, with a huge number of women having gone through the programme, and yet there were still not enough longitudinal data.

Stanley: Mr Jones, did you look for HPV in your warty basaloid vulval intraepithelial neoplasias (VINs)? What was the incidence?

Jones: Yes, we did, and the majority were HPV-16 positive. In those cases that progressed to invasive cancer, HPV-16 was also in the cancer.

Stanley: We do not have 400 cases of VIN, but we have a reasonable number. We have also been carrying out a comparative genomic hybridisation on them. The lesions that do not respond to immunotherapies are undoubtedly genetically unstable, with markers that are consistent with the progressive markers that have been found in the cervix. I am really asking whether this is an area of investigation in which we may need to do some of the sorting out that was done in the cervix, to try to obtain a more rational assessment of the biological problems associated with these lesions.

Jones: I would agree with you. We have known for a long while that VIN is a remarkably heterogeneous disorder in its colour and its focality. There are so many different features and each group needs to be broken down.

MacLean: Mr Jones, in terms of lesion size and some of the discussion that Professor Richart was conducting in relation to the risk of invasion, you showed an example of a woman whose VIN increased in size before it became invasive. Has it been your experience that patients with recurrent or residual VIN after treatment then develop invasion? My experience is that they do not always grow larger before the invasion is noted.

Jones: I would agree. There is of course an increased risk of invasion in unifocal lesions, which can often be quite small. By the same token, invasion can of course occur in multifocal lesions. However, this is such a heterogeneous disorder that multicentre studies are needed to address these issues.

Singer: You showed a photograph of a woman smoking, but that was about the only reference you made to it, although it is one of the major aetiological factors. Could you tell me where it fits in? Did many of these who regressed stop smoking? We have found that. I would also ask Professor Stanley why the vulva is so sensitive to smoking?

Stanley: I do not know why the vulva is so sensitive to smoking. There are some serious epidemiological investigations to be conducted here, because there has clearly been some kind of behavioural change over the last 50 years, if this increased incidence is real rather than just a reflection of improved detection. It is either because of the detergents we use when washing our underwear or, I seriously wonder, if it is related to a change in sexual behaviour, particularly oral sex. Children read magazines that tell them how to do it, which did not exist when I was young.

Jones: The first point of contact for HPV is in fact the vulva and not the cervix and so it is perhaps surprising that we are not seeing more in the vulva.

MacLean: But how exactly does smoking affect it? I can understand that there is cotinine in cervical mucus, but it is a little more difficult to understand.

Monaghan: Mr Jones, first of all you talked about what you felt, for which you did not have good evidence, about the increased incidence or prevalence of VIN in your population. Is this a reflection of a more centralised service, or of your own practice, rather than an increase? In our own practice, there has not been any significant change; it is common, but I have not seen what you have been reporting.

Second, many years ago various pathologists, and people doing research on the vulva in particular, used various morphometric techniques – microdensitometry and others – to look at the tissues alongside tumours. Without exception, they found alterations in these tissues. Is this a reflection of widespread HPV infection, which gives you the repetitive pattern of appearance of the tumour? Or is it the fundamental change in the epithelium?

Jones: It is the latter. This is certainly a field effect and that is why we are seeing new cancers developing in the same field of the vulva at some later period. Of course, the recurrence rate of VIN is in the order of 30%. To answer your question about the increasing incidence, there are at least three studies.[9–11] There is one I quoted from Norway, and the SEER study from the USA, and these have all reported a statistically increased incidence in VIN in the last two decades.

Monaghan: I ask because I know that there has been a shift during that time from care of these problems by dermatologists to care by gynaecological oncologists. I just wonder whether, in the past, many of these patients had been managed in another field, and it had simply not been recognised as a VIN problem.

Jones: I think that the increasing incidence of VIN is real.

Shepherd: Your group of Maori 15–20-year-olds had a remarkably high incidence of VIN. What did their cervical cytology show? Were there any other abnormalities in the vagina or on the cervix?

Jones: A small proportion had had abnormal smears, but this was not a striking feature. This was a reversible HPV effect and the most striking aspect was the racial factor, with only one European in the group.

Stanley: Were the HPV-16s in the Maori group too?

Jones: We did not type them.

Shafi: Vulval cancer remains a rare cancer and, even in your own series, there has been no change in the actual numbers over the cohorts that you have studied, although there is a change in the age profile of the patients. Yes, it may well be changing in regard to the VINs coming through, and to having these two different cancers, but what has happened with the older age groups? Is their incidence therefore falling?

Jones: I think you are right. We are treating lichen sclerosus and the chronic vulval dermatosis more effectively than we were. Women used to live with lichen sclerosus, except that they had to itch for life. Today, they come to the doctor and ask for treatment, and so we are probably reducing the number of vulval cancers in older women.

MacLean: In the UK, or in England at any rate, because I have recently looked at the data, the number of vulval cancers has risen from about 750 cases a year thirty years ago, to 850 cases a year currently, so although we do not have a breakdown as to whether they are associated with lichen sclerosus or VIN, they are on the increase. It is difficult to assess because the registration does not exclude melanomas and Paget's associated disease and so on, but it is certainly not decreasing in this country.

Monaghan: But surely that is due to a change in the profile of the population over that period of time? We have far more older people now than we had then.

MacLean: Looking at it per 100 000 age distribution, it is still increasing. Before we break, although it is not essential to have recommendations from every presentation, perhaps we could just think about one or two areas. Dr Sasieni, perhaps the Study Group should make some sort of comment about the fact that HPV is found in 80% of sexually active women, while less than two percent develop cervical cancer.

Sasieni: One has to be careful with that last figure.

MacLean: I know, but we probably need to make some epidemiological statement for educational purposes that clearly not everyone with HPV develops cervical cancer. That is one of the concerns within the population.

Professor Herrington, there is the question of whether you might include something about researching the role of molecular biological markers in both diagnostic and prognostic or predictive labelling of these lesions as a means of developing this in the future. Perhaps some of what Professor Richart said would include looking at that?

Perhaps we should ask Professor Stanley to flag something up for research purposes? There is no doubt that the host response is something that we do not understand, and this is an area in which we clearly need further research. I am not sure whether you can say anything at this stage, other than that these are research areas.

Stanley: There are some key research questions to address. One of the pleas is that it should be conducted properly. They have to be natural history studies. The key problem for cell-mediated immunity is the assays and their sensitivity. I would like people to be aware that this is no quick fix and will be quite difficult to carry out, unless and until the assay system is improved. There is very little doubt that the immune response is a local one, and the systemic circulation is just not a sufficiently sensitive indicator of it.

MacLean: Dr Deery, I know that you have given us recommendations, but perhaps you could bring them down to one or two sentences? I was not quite sure from your comment whether you already have a study that provides an answer, or whether you feel that other large studies are required to look at sampling devices.

Deery: There is room for a study, which is why I included it in this recommendation. There is room for a study that will probably be carried out several times, comparing the detection of both glandular and squamous disease with the available preferred samplers – the combination techniques as well as the broom sampler. There is a gap in the literature, and it would require quite a large study to reach significance, with good outcome data. I have no doubt that a study will be done in the next few years. We also already have enough evidence to suggest that our continued use of the wooden spatula in the cervical screening programme in this country is not the best advice.

MacLean: Mr Jones, would you like to comment? You have raised many important issues within the chapter. Do you want to say that the distinction between the over-treatment of cervical disease and the opinion that VIN is probably not a premalignant lesion is a mistake we have made in the past? Does it need to be stated as a recommendation for educational purposes that anyone managing this disease must recognise the real malignant potential of VIN?

Jones: I would agree with that. On public education, it seems to me that the more knowledge women have about these conditions, the better they are able to cope with them. We now have what is called an HPV project in New Zealand, so that every woman who has an abnormal smear and is then referred for colposcopy is given a small pamphlet with information about colposcopy and HPV infection. It describes the scenarios that you put to Dr Sasieni with regard to the ubiquitous nature of HPV infection and the rarity of cervical cancer. Women who then attend the colposcopy clinic will we hope have read this and assimilated some of the background, so that they can ask more intelligent questions at their consultation.

References

1. Martin-Hirsch P, Jarvis G, Kitchener H, Lilford R. Collection devices for obtaining cervical cytology samples. *Cochrane Database Syst Rev* 2000;(3):CD001036.
2. Buntinx F, Brouwers M. Relation between sampling device and detection of abnormality in cervical smears: a meta-analysis of randomised and quasi-randomised studies. *BMJ* 1996;313:1285–90.
3. Mitchell H, Medley G. Longitudinal study of women with negative cervical smears according to endocervical status. *Lancet* 1991; 337:265–7.
4. Baer A, Kiviat NB, Kulasingam S, Mao C, Kuypers J, Koutsky LA. Liquid-based Papanicolaou smears without a transformation zone component: should clinicians worry? *Obstet Gynecol* 2002;99:1053–9.
5. Campion MJ, Cuzick J, McCanced J, Singer A. Progressive potential of mild cervical atypia: prospective cytological colposcopic envirological study. *Lancet* 1986;ii:237–40.
6. Belinson J, Qiao YL, Pretorius R, Zhang WH, Elson P, Li L, *et al*. Shanxi Province Cervical Cancer Screening Study: a cross-sectional comparative trial of multiple techniques to detect cervical neoplasia. *Gynecol Oncol* 2001;83:439–44.
7. Lorincz A, Richart RM. HPV DNA testing as an adjunct to cytology in cervical cancer screening programs. *Arch Pathol Lab Med* 2003 in press.
8. van Wijngaarden WJ, Duncan ID. Rationale for stopping cervical screening in women over 50. *BMJ* 1993;306:967–71.
9. Iversen T, Tretli S. Intraepithelial and invasive squamous cell carcinoma of the vulva: trends in incidence, recurrence and survival rate in Norway. *Obstet Gynecol* 1998;91:969–72.
10. Sturgeon SR, Brinton LA, Devesa SS, Kurman RJ. In situ and invasive vulvar cancer incidence and trends 1973–1987. *Am J Obstet Gynecol* 1992;166:1482.
11. Joura EA, Losch A, Haider-Angeler MG, Breitenecker G, Leodolter S. Trends in vulvar neoplasia. Increasing incidence of vulvar intraepithelial neoplasia and squamous cell carcinoma of the vulva in younger women. *J Reprod Med* 2000;45:613–15.

SECTION 3

NEW APPROACHES TO DETECTING LOWER
GENITAL TRACT NEOPLASIA I

Chapter 9

Liquid-based preparations

Euphemia McGoogan

Introduction

The current cervical smear test uses technology that is over half a century old and beset by limitations. Unfortunately, little attention has been paid to the smear test because its inherent deficiencies have been incompletely understood. It is only as a consequence of the recurrent adverse publicity for cervical screening over the past ten years, with a main focus on laboratories, that these limitations have been widely recognised and accepted. Historically, the drive for the development of better slide preparations from cervical scrape samples came from the demands of the early automated scanning devices, which required a monolayer with as little cellular overlap as possible.

More recently, the drive towards better-quality samples and preparations has come from a desire to improve the quality of the routine screening test for cervical screening programmes. It is well established that regular screening of a high proportion of the population at risk results in a major decrease in the incidence and mortality from cervical cancer.[1,2] Screening programmes such as that in the UK have successfully reduced the incidence of cervical cancer by implementing regular screening for over 80% of the population at risk, backed up by quality-assurance programmes with standards for public health, smear-taking, laboratories and colposcopy, with coordinated teams working together in all areas of the programme.[3,4]

The smear test has remained essentially unchanged since its first description in the late 1930s by George Papanicolaou, a Greek gynaecologist who was researching into cervical cancer in the USA, where his name has been given to the smear test or 'Pap test'. Cells are scraped from the surface of the cervix with a wooden spatula and spread on to a glass slide. The cells are then 'fixed' with a preservative fluid or spray to prevent degeneration and the 'smear' is sent to the laboratory for analysis. In the laboratory, the smear is stained with a series of dyes to make them visible through the microscope. If the preservation is poor or the smear is too thick, the cells do not stain crisply and they are difficult to assess. The inherent limitations of the conventional cervical smear test mean that it lacks sensitivity, specificity, reliability and repeatability. Analyses of published articles in peer-reviewed literature[5-8] have repeatedly shown that a single smear test can only identify about half the women who have cervical intraepithelial neoplasia (CIN) in their cervix (sensitivity).

The inherent limitations can be considered under three headings:

- clinical factors, including the actual site, size and histological type of the lesion, as well as contamination of the sample by blood or inflammatory exudate

- factors influenced by the smear-taker, including incorrect or inadequate sampling of the cervix and suboptimal preparation and fixation
- laboratory factors, such as staining and microscopic assessment by cytotechnologists and pathologists.

However, the quality of the staining is limited by poor fixation, and poor-quality staining and preparation limit the quality of the microscopic slide assessment. In addition, abnormal cells are not collected evenly on the sampling device and only a selected (non-random) proportion of cells is placed on the glass slide, so that all or none or just some of the abnormal cells may be transferred to the slide. Some samplers have more of a trapping effect than others and the amount of cellular material transferred to the slide varies from about two-thirds at best to less than 10% at worst. Thus, no matter how skilled the smear-taker and depending on the sampler used, up to 90% of the cells removed from the cervix are discarded with the sampler. Furthermore, the cellular distribution on the glass slide is uneven. Sampling and preparation alone are assessed in the literature as responsible for 53–90% of false negative tests. Low sensitivity may not be the greatest problem in organised screening programmes. In order to decrease the false negative rate, many laboratories have increased their false positive rate, increasing their inadequate and equivocal result reporting rates. Thus, they have decreased their specificity and fewer normal women receive a normal smear test result.

Smear adequacy

In the UK, where the dyskaryosis terminology is used, the criteria for sample adequacy are more stringent than those of the Bethesda system in the USA, since the recall interval for normal women is at least three years. The inadequate reporting rate is therefore higher in the UK than in the USA. However, even within the UK, the inadequate rate has gradually increased over the last ten years to a current level of about 10%. Thus, up to one in ten women attending for screening must return for a repeat test simply because the first test was unsatisfactory for interpretation.

The National Audit Office Report (1998)[9] noted that only 53% of laboratories had an inadequate reporting rate within the national standard of 5–9%. In 1996, laboratories had reported a range of inadequate rates of 1.5–34.8%. Furthermore, only 51% of laboratories had a borderline/mild dyskaryosis combined rate within the national acceptable range (4–7%) and the range in 1996 was 2.7–25.1%.

Apart from the 'emotional harm' to the woman, there are economic costs associated with increased referral for repeat smear or further investigation. This adds an increasing cost to the NHS and an unnecessary burden to primary care teams, computerised recall systems and laboratories. Therefore, further improvements in the sensitivity and specificity of the routine screening test need to begin in the doctor's clinic with improved techniques of specimen collection to allow better-quality samples, better slide preparations for microscopic assessment and potential for ancillary tests.

The main deficiencies of the conventional smear result from the use of rigid (usually wooden) spatulas designed to remove cells from the surface of the cervix but not for spreading the cellular material on to the glass slide. Thus, the cells are unevenly spread and distributed on the glass slide and may be obscured by blood, inflammatory exudate, exogenous material or thick streaks of other cells. Various chemicals are used as fixatives and several different fixation methods are employed. However, many samples exhibit serious fixation artefact, with partial air-drying. These lead to suboptimal staining that compromises microscopic assessment. All of these problems can be addressed by liquid-based cytology technology.

For countries with organised screening programmes and stringent criteria for adequacy, the potential benefits from lowering the inadequate rate alone merit consideration of converting to liquid-based preparations.

Methodology

In the liquid-based cytology technique, a plastic broom or a combination of plastic spatula and endocervical brush is used to collect the sample. Instead of the cellular material being removed from the cervix and spread on to a glass slide, the samplers are rinsed or the head of the broom is detached into a vial of liquid transport medium, creating a cell suspension. Thus, the specimen sent to the laboratory is a cell suspension containing almost all of the cells removed from the cervix and these cells remain well preserved for several weeks at room temperature in the preservative fluid.

In the laboratory, the cell suspension can be processed to remove excess blood and inflammatory exudate and a small representative aliquot of epithelial cells can be deposited in a thin layer within a small area on a glass slide. The slide preparations therefore contain a proportional representation of all the epithelial cell types in the original sample.

The cell suspension may be prepared manually but this is extremely labour-intensive and it is difficult to ensure that a randomised (i.e. representative) sample of cells is placed on the glass slide. However, there are now several commercially available devices that can perform this task in either a semi- or a fully automated fashion. Three of these devices have been approved by the US Food and Drug Administration (FDA) as suitable for cervical screening: two ThinPrep® processors (Cytyc Corporation) and the SurePath® system (previously known as AutoCyte-Prep® or CytoRich®) manufactured by TriPath Imaging Inc.

With both the ThinPrep processors, cells are scraped from the cervix using either a Cervex® broom (Rovers Medical Devices BV) or a combination of plastic spatula and endocervical brush. The sampling devices are rinsed thoroughly into a vial containing a proprietary transport fluid (PreservCyt®, Cytyc Corporation) and the cell suspension is sent to the laboratory.

The ThinPrep® 2000 Processor (T2000) is a small bench-top instrument that processes one sample at a time. The basic component of the ThinPrep process is a disposable plastic tube with a filter bonded to one end. An electronically charged glass slide labelled with the sample number, the filter and the uncapped vial of cell suspension are loaded into the T2000. There are three key phases to the process:

- dispersion: the device inserts the filter tube into the vial of cell suspension, spins it round to disperse mucus or any clumps of cells that have settled at the bottom of the vial

- cell collection: a negative pressure pulse is produced in the filter tube that draws the fluid through the filter, trapping a layer of cellular material; some red cells, neutrophils and cell debris may pass through the pores of the filter; the flow of fluid through the filter is monitored and controlled to optimise cell collection

- cell transfer: when all the pores of the filter are blocked by cells, the filter tube is inverted and the filter is gently brought into contact with an electronically charged glass slide so that the cells transfer to the glass slide, which is immediately dropped into a jar of fixative.

Approximately 30 average samples can be prepared in one hour; a T2000 can process about 50 000 samples per annum. However, the process is labour-intensive and repetitive. The operator must take care to ensure that the slide is labelled with the correct sample number to avoid transposing cases. On the other hand, the process is fully automated and the operator cannot influence the quality of the slide preparation. Slide staining is not part of the process and slides may be stained by the routine staining method used by the laboratory.

The ThinPrep® 3000 Processor (T3000) is a floor-standing, fully automated version of the T2000. Batches of 80 capped vials are loaded into the device and the operator can walk away. The T3000 uses an automated process similar to that of the T2000 but the device labels each slide individually, copying the bar code on the vial, thus eliminating potential for mislabelling. A batch of 80 slides can be prepared in about two hours and takes about ten minutes of operator time. Since the device is fully automated, it can be set up to run after normal laboratory working hours or 24 hours per day if staff are available to load and unload samples. Thus, one T3000 can process between 80 000 and 150 000 samples per annum. Again, the operator cannot influence the quality of the final slide preparation and slides may be stained by the routine staining method used by the laboratory.

The SurePath system uses a different methodology. A sample must be collected from the cervix using a Cervex sampler, since the head of the broom is detached into a vial containing a proprietary transport fluid. In the laboratory, there are multiple preparation stages, some of which are automated and each of which can influence the quality of the final slide preparation. First, the vials are vortexed to detach the cells from the broom head and break up mucus and clumps of cells. Next, 7 ml of each cell suspension is aspirated from the vial and gently layered on to centrifuge tubes filled with a density reagent gel and previously labelled with each sample number. This step can be automated using the PrepMate™ device, which allows the processing of 12 samples at a time. The centrifuge tubes are then gently centrifuged at 200 g for two minutes and the operator aspirates the supernatant. The residual sample is centrifuged at 800 g for ten minutes to produce a cell pellet and the supernatant is decanted by inverting the rack of centrifuge tubes so as not to disturb the cell pellets. The density reagent centrifugation process removes red blood cells, inflammatory cells and debris, thereby 'enriching' the cell sample.

Glass slides are covered with a proprietary slide coat solution and allowed to dry. Individual settling chambers are then clamped to the glass slides that have previously been labelled with the slide number. These are placed in sequence on the PrepStain™ device. The cell pellets are vortexed again to resuspend the cells and batches of up to 48 centrifuge tubes are loaded on to the PrepStain for automated slide preparation and staining. A robotic arm using disposable pipette tips delivers deionised water to the pellet in the centrifuge tube and agitates it to ensure it is resuspended. It then transfers an aliquot of cell suspension to each settling chamber in turn. The cells are allowed to sediment under gravity to form a thin layer on the glass slide.

After 10–20 minutes, the excess fluid, including any cells that have not stuck to the glass slide, is removed from the staining well by the robotic arm. Thereafter, the robotic dispensers deliver the components of the Papanicolaou stain individually to each staining well in sequence. Thus each slide is stained *in situ*.

The overall laboratory process is labour-intensive and the quality of the final slide preparation is operator-dependent. Particular proficiency is required when loading and unloading at each stage. Care must be taken when labelling the centrifuge tubes and slides to avoid transposing cases. Adequate training in the operation of the system is therefore crucial.

There are qualitative differences between the ThinPrep and SurePath preparations that may influence the ease of screening and the method of assessment. The SurePath system produces slides with a 1.3 cm-diameter circle of deposition containing around 100 000 cells. ThinPrep slides have a 1.9 cm-diameter circle of deposition also containing about 100 000 cells. Both are thin-layer, not monolayer, preparations and, consequently, both have a certain depth of focus. The SurePath preparations, however, are rather thicker than ThinPrep, resulting in a greater depth of focus, and they require greater diligence on the part of the screener to ensure that all the layers of cells are examined to avoid false negatives.The FDA has licensed SurePath as 'equivalent' and the ThinPrep as 'superior' to the conventional smear.

The microscopic appearance of a liquid-based preparation is that of a circular deposit of evenly distributed cells. The margins of the deposit are usually well demarcated and all the cellular material is contained well within the area of the cover slip. In ThinPrep slides, the cellular deposit is of uniform thickness and thus the need for frequent focus changes is reduced. Individual cells and cell groups are more three-dimensional than those in conventional smears, since they have been preserved in a liquid medium. Cellular preservation is enhanced and the good fixation allows more consistent staining, resulting in improved microscopic detail. Well-preserved single cells are commonly seen. Some groups and sheets of cells are retained, but the cell aggregates are smaller than in conventional smears and, even within groups, nuclear morphology is easily visualised. Examples of the improved preservation and staining include the cilia that are more frequently seen on endocervical cells and the occasional flagellum seen on trichomonas organisms. Preparation artefacts such as partial air drying, 'cornflake' artefact and air bubbles in the mountant are markedly diminished. Background material such as menstrual or inflammatory exudate, cell debris, cytolysis, microorganisms and tumour diathesis can still be identified, although they do not obscure the epithelial cells. Residual neutrophil polymorphs in the processed sample from a heavily contaminated cell suspension tend to adhere to form microscopic balls, thus not obscuring epithelial cells on the slide. Similarly, although sperm are small enough individually to pass through the pores of the ThinPrep filter and to be pulled out in the density reagent Surepath step, they often aggregate in semen to form small masses. Blood is almost completely removed in the SurePath process, while it is usually still visible in ThinPrep slides as a red granular deposit in the background.

Any abnormal cells present are not obscured by thick clumps of normal cells or by blood or inflammatory exudate and the improved nuclear detail facilitates more accurate grading. However, since this is a representative aliquot from the original sample, the total number of abnormal cells on the slide may be fewer in number and the observer must therefore be prepared to make a confident diagnosis on a smaller number albeit of better-preserved dyskaryotic cells.

Whichever system is used to prepare the liquid-based cytology sample, the difference in slide quality compared with the conventional smear is obvious even to the naked eye. At present, liquid-based preparations appear to offer a real opportunity to enhance cervical screening programmes through improved collection and preparation techniques. Since all the cellular material removed from the cervix is sent to the laboratory preserved in an optimal state, sample adequacy is improved, resulting in a drop in the inadequate reporting rates while improving or at least maintaining sensitivity and specificity.

Although there is little available information in peer-reviewed literature, there are several other laboratory devices under development that will also prepare liquid-based cytology samples. These include Cytoscreen® (Biosource International) with its proprietary fluid CYTeasy® (Seroa) and collection device Cytoprep® (Cytoprep Inc.),

EasyPrep® (Labonord), CellPrint® (3t), Cyto-Tek® (Bayer), ThinSpin® (Shandon), InPath® system (Ampersand Medical Corporation), Alphagenetics (Menarini) and Cyprep® (Veracel). While these systems offer alternative and often cheaper methods of processing cell suspensions, evidence of their ability to deliver an appropriately preserved, representative cell sample on to the glass slide in a consistent manner is not yet available in peer-reviewed literature.

In the three FDA-approved systems described in detail above, a randomised aliquot of cells is placed on the glass slide, which means that the cell population on the slide is representative of the cells scraped from the cervical epithelium. Hutchinson et al.[8] and Bergeron et al.[10] showed that liquid-based preparations had greater specimen homogeneity than conventional smears and suggested that this accounted for increased diagnostic accuracy.

Use in cervical screening

Having achieved a major improvement in the coverage and quality of the NHS Cervical Screening Programme, attention has now turned to improving the screening test. In 1999, the newly formed National Institute for Clinical Excellence (NICE) commissioned a literature review and modelling of liquid-based cytology to look at its cost-effectiveness if used in UK cervical screening programmes. This was published in June 2000.[7] The authors stated that there were no published randomised control trials of liquid-based cytology using invasive cancer or mortality as outcome. Few studies before 1999 used histological outcome as a 'gold standard' and most comparisons were split-sample studies comparing cytology results for conventional and matched liquid-based cytology rather than direct-to-vial. Therefore, there were no published studies that could provide direct evidence regarding cost-effectiveness of liquid-based cytology for cervical screening in the UK. Economic modelling was used to estimate the cost implications of implementing liquid-based cytology, but this was considered to be too inaccurate. However, the report concluded that it was likely that liquid-based cytology would reduce the numbers of inadequate samples and false negative results, as well as the time required for examination of specimens by cytologists. They recommended a full cost-effectiveness study of liquid-based cytology on a trial of its introduction in a low-prevalence population for routine screening to obtain more accurate information than is possible using modelling. In June 2002, NICE decided to set up three regional pilots of direct-to-vial liquid-based cytology to confirm the cost-effectiveness. In addition, NICE requested that these pilots should be combined with an evaluation of reflex human papillomavirus (HPV) testing of cervical samples showing low-grade abnormalities using the Digene Hybrid Capture II® test (oncogenic types panel only).

Bids were invited from health authorities and three laboratories were chosen for these pilots. Two (Bristol and Norwich) laboratories fully converted to ThinPrep and one (Newcastle) to Surepath. The plan was to obtain a total of 100 000 routine screening tests (liquid-based cytology with reflex HPV) over a 12-month period starting in March 2001. It was July 2001 before all three laboratories fully converted and, because a 12-month period was required for the HPV arm of the pilots to allow follow-up information to be collected, the report is not expected before Autumn 2003.

The NHS in Scotland took a different approach. A subcommittee looking into automation in cervical screening had recommended to the Scottish Cervical Screening Programme National Advisory Group that demonstration sites should be established in Scotland to test the feasibility and cost-effectiveness of introducing liquid-based

Table 9.1. Results of Scottish pilot studies (ThinPrep®): weighted average; positive predictive value for high-grade lesions was maintained at 79.5–87.5% (total samples n = 30 228)

	Conventional (%)	ThinPrep (%)
Unsatisfactory	7.63	1.84
Borderline	3.98	3.67
Mild dyskaryosis	1.10	2.12
Moderate/severe dyskaryosis	1.10	2.03

cytology. In June 2000, the decision to set up these demonstration sites was announced. Scotland chose to involve four completely different laboratories, covering a wide range of service profiles (Airdrie, Dundee, Aberdeen and Inverness). Each laboratory would only half convert to direct-to-vial liquid-based cytology. It was proposed to obtain a total of 30 000 routine screening tests over a six-month period starting in March 2001. For this small study population, it was felt that all laboratories should use the same liquid-based cytology system. The ThinPrep system was chosen because Cytyc had a better-established infrastructure to support the laboratories at that time. The pilots did not include HPV testing and were completed on time in November 2001. The results were published by the Scottish Executive Health Department in April 2002.[11]

The results are summarised in Table 9.1. The inadequate rate was significantly reduced in each laboratory. The borderline rate was maintained but there was an increase in the identification of all grades of dyskaryosis and, in particular, the high-grade reporting rate was doubled. Since the positive predictive value of the cytology compared with the colposcopic biopsy remained high, this was viewed as a true increased detection and not as overcalling. This large increase was considered to be due to correct identification of women with high-grade disease who were currently on early recall for inadequate smears or borderline/mild dyskaryosis (i.e. prevalent disease) and it was expected that the high-grade reporting rate would decrease over the following 18 months and level off at a lower rate as incident disease was picked up. However, this lower rate is expected to remain above that achieved by conventional smears (i.e. increased sensitivity). This is exactly the experience of the Edinburgh laboratory, where a group of primary-care teams has been collaborating in a research project that required them to change the routine cervical screening test to ThinPrep direct-to-vial over a period of almost two years (Table 9.2).

Further evaluation of the Scottish liquid-based cytology pilot showed that smear-takers find liquid-based cytology simpler, convenient and easy to use and that overall workload was reduced. There was a sharp reduction in anxiety for women with fewer unsatisfactory smears. Liquid-based cytology reduced workload and increased productivity for laboratories. A more appropriate referral pattern was achieved for colposcopy due to improved detection rate of high-grade lesions of between three and

Table 9.2. Edinburgh ThinPrep® results January 2000 – January 2002

	Conventional smears[a] (%)	ThinPrep[b] (%)
Unsatisfactory	10.0	0.6
Negative	82.4	92.2
Borderline	4.0	2.7
Mild dyskaryosis	2.2	2.7
Moderate/severe dyskaryosis	1.4	1.8

[a] n = 8670 in 1999; [b] n = 17 880 in two years

nine women per 1000 tested. It was noted that liquid-based cytology allows scope for further developments in screening such as HPV and chlamydia testing from residual material in the vial and it would pave the way for introducing automated scanning devices in the future. The cost-effectiveness evaluation was complex since it was recognised that some data were more reliable than others and that it would be highly dependent on the final configuration of screening service in Scotland. After taking into account savings from fewer tests, it was estimated that the additional cost to the health service in Scotland would be up to £2120 per 1000 women tested.

On 2 April 2002, the Scottish Minister for Health announced that liquid-based cytology should be implemented as the routine screening test throughout Scotland by April 2004. He invested £2.75 million to assist with procuring the equipment and with training of laboratory and primary care staff for conversion to liquid-based cytology. The expectation is that liquid-based cytology will lower the inadequate result rate, increase the detection of significant disease, reduce the overall workload for laboratories and colposcopy clinics, facilitate improved turnaround times, reduce anxiety in women and provide a better-quality screening programme for women.

Many published studies have considered adequacy of liquid-based preparations compared with conventional smears. Unfortunately, the studies do not use consistent criteria for adequacy. Even where the Bethesda system was used, it is likely that it was interpreted in different ways, since the criteria applied are either not stated or are highly subjective and variable, making comparative evaluation difficult. Furthermore, most published studies prior to 1999 were 'split-sample' rather than direct-to-vial. In the split-sample studies, a conventional smear was prepared as normal from a single cervical scrape sample and then the liquid-based preparation was made by rinsing the residual material on the device into a vial of preservative fluid. Clearly this is not the intended use, since with split samples there is a substantial deficit of cellular material that would otherwise be included in the cell suspension for the liquid-based preparation. However, despite the fact that one might expect the liquid-based preparation to be poorly cellular and at higher risk of being inadequate, the majority of studies reported that liquid-based methods had a larger proportion of samples classed as totally satisfactory. According to the calculations of Payne et al.,[7] the split-sample liquid-based preparations appear to have half the unsatisfactory specimen rate of conventional smears (RR 0.54; 95% CI 0.51–0.56).

Critics of liquid-based cytology have expressed concern that inadequate samples are being reported as satisfactory slides, since it is not possible to discriminate between slides from highly cellular samples and those on to which all the cells from a scanty sample have been concentrated. Table 9.2 shows experience of a significant decrease in the inadequate rate using ThinPrep direct-to-vial drawn from routine smears collected from a small number of primary-care teams in Edinburgh, Scotland. These are compared with conventional smears from the same teams in the previous year to converting to liquid-based cytology. If those samples previously evaluated as inadequate were simply being called negative, one would expect the percentages of borderline and dyskaryotic smears to remain the same (Table 9.3). However, this is not the case and the additional adequate samples appear to be unevenly distributed among the reporting categories.

Sensitivity and specificity

It is difficult to draw clear conclusions as to sensitivity and specificity that are due to deficiencies in the study design of many published articles. Most studies use a selected population with a high incidence of disease. Many studies lack verification of the diagnosis, negative results are not verified and total study numbers are small.

Table 9.3. Expected versus actual ThinPrep® reporting rates if inadequate samples were simply called negative on the ThinPrep (total samples $n = 17\ 880$)

	GP conventional smears in 1999 (%)[a]	Expected ThinPrep (n)	(%)	Actual ThinPrep (n)	(%)	Difference
Unsatisfactory	10.0	107	0.6	107	0.6	
Negative	82.4	16324	91.4	16486	92.2	+162
Borderline	4.0	715	4.0	482	2.7	−233
Mild dyskaryosis	2.2	393	2.2	483	2.7	+90
Moderate/severe dyskaryosis	1.4	250	1.4	322	1.8	+72

[a] $n = 8670$

Nonetheless, a consistent finding is an increased detection of abnormal cells in liquid-based preparations using ThinPrep but closer to equivalence using SurePath.[12–24]

Table 9.4 has been extracted from the literature review of Payne et al.[7] and contains split-sample studies published in the last six years, where the study number was greater than 1000. Unfortunately, the prevalence of significant abnormality and hence the type of population studied varies considerably, as shown in column seven. Column five indicates the percentage of cases where the conventional smear contained abnormal cells that were not identified in the liquid-based preparation made from the residual material on the sampling device. Column six shows where the residual material on the sampling device contained abnormal cells that were not identified on the matched conventional smear. In almost all instances, the liquid-based preparation found abnormal cells more frequently than the matched conventional smear.

Table 9.4. Split-sample published studies of more than 1000 for both SurePath® (AutoCyte-Prep®) and ThinPrep®[7]

Study	Date	Country	No.	Conventional > LBC LSIL+ (%)[a]	LBC > Conventional LSIL+ (%)[b]	Both are LSIL+ (%)	LBC type
Awen et al.[12]	1994	USA	1000	0.0	0.5	1.3	ThinPrep
Laverty et al.[13]	1995	Australia	1872	2.4	3.3	7.5	ThinPrep
Wilbur et al.[14]	1994	USA	3218	0.8	3.1	17.0	ThinPrep
McGoogan et al.[15]	1996	Scotland	3091	1.0	0.3	3.6	Both Autocyte-prep and Thinprep
Sprenger et al.[16]	1996	Germany	2863	2.0	5.1	36.2	Autocyte-prep
Takahashi and Naito[17]	1997	Japan	2000	0.4	0.3	3.2	Autocyte-prep
Bishop[18]	1997	USA	2032	1.1	3.1	3.1	Autocyte-prep
Laverty et al.[19]	1997	Australia	2064	3.9	1.6	5.0	Autocyte-prep
Lee et al.[20]	1997	USA	6747	1.9	3.3	6.1	ThinPrep
Roberts et al.[21]	1997	Australia	35560	0.3	0.5	1.7	ThinPrep
Stevens et al.[22]	1998	Australia	1325	1.3	0.2	3.9	Autocyte-prep
Corkill et al.[23]	1998	USA	1583	0.8	3.7	1.9	ThinPrep
Hutchinson et al.[24]	1999	Costa Rica	8636	2.5	2.8	2.4	ThinPrep

[a] Signifies the proportion where the conventional smear result was LSIL+ but the liquid-based method result was negative or ASC-US; [b] signifies the proportion where the liquid-based method result was LSIL+ but the conventional smear result was negative or ASC-US; ASC-US = atypical squamous cell of undetermined significance; LBC = liquid-based cytology; LSIL = low-grade intraepithelial lesion

Table 9.5. ThinPrep® versus conventional smear for high-grade lesion detection (published in peer-reviewed, indexed literature subsequent to US Food and Drug Administration approval)

Study	ThinPrep (*n*)	Design	Adjudication	Sensitivity for high-grade lesion[a]
Cytyc Corp.	10226	DTV	Biopsy	Significant increase [↑59%] (p < 0.001)
Bernstein *et al.*[25]	Meta-analysis	DVT Split		Significant increase (OR 2.26; 95% CI 2.06–2.47)
Bolick and Hellman[26]	10694	DTV	Biopsy	Significant increase (*P* < 0.001)
Carpenter and Davey[27]	2727	DTV	Biopsy	Increase 26% (NS)
Diaz-Rosaria and Kabawat[28]	56339	DTV	Biopsy	Significant increase (*P* < 0.001)
Ferris *et al.*[29]	992	DTV`	Biopsy	Significant increase (*P* < 0.001)
Guidos and Selvaggi[30]	9583	DTV	Biopsy	Significant increase (*P* < 0.001)
Hutchinson *et al.*[24]	8636	Split	Biopsy	Significant increase (*P* < 0.001)
Obwegeser and Brack[31]	997	DTV	Biopsy	Equivalent to CP
Papillo *et al.*[32]	16314	DTV	Biopsy	Significant increase (*P* < 0.01)
Roberts *et al.*[21]	35560	Split	Biopsy	↑ Increase 16% (NS)
Scottish Health Executive[11]	30228	DTV	Biopsy	Significant increase (*P* < 0.001)
Wang *et al.*[33]	972	Split		Significant increase (*P* = 0.006)
Weintraub and Morabia[34]	39864	DTV	Biopsy	Significant increase (OR 1.68; *P* < 0.001)
Yeoh *et al.*[35]	16541	DTV	Biopsy	Significant increase (*P* < 0.01)

[a] significant if *P* value ≤ 0.05; DTV = direct-to-vial study; NS = not significant; split = split-sample study

In 1999, the FDA accepted Cytyc Corporation's claim that ThinPrep improves the sensitivity of the Papanicolaou test. The submitted data were from a multisite direct-to-vial clinical study evaluating T2000 ThinPrep slides prepared prospectively and compared with a historical control cohort of conventional smears. The results showed a detection rate of 511/20.917 for the conventional smear versus 399/10 226 for the ThinPrep slides. This indicated a 59.7% (*P* > 0.001) increase in the detection of high-grade lesions by ThinPrep. Table 9.5 lists ThinPrep studies published subsequent to FDA approval[21,24–35] that continue to confirm that use of ThinPrep results in an increase in the sensitivity for high-grade lesions. The more recent direct-to-vial published studies using SurePath[10,36–40] continue to confirm equivalence to the conventional smear but statistically significant evidence of increased sensitivity is lacking. In July 2001, the 'superiority' label was extended to the T3000 device. Factors other than sensitivity and adequacy must be taken into account when considering the clinical implications and cost-effectiveness of implementing liquid-based cytology.

Implementation

The shortage of trained cytotechnologists and cytopathologists in the UK has now reached crisis point, with many cytotechnologist and pathologist posts remaining permanently unfilled. There is much anecdotal evidence that liquid-based preparations are popular with cytotechnologists and this was the view of laboratory staff in the Scottish pilot studies. Certainly the initial response is favourable when viewing liquid-based preparations for the first time. The clarity of presentation, the improved cell preservation and lack of overlapping by other cells, blood or inflammatory exudate are much appreciated.

In addition, liquid-based cytology allows faster and more reliable assessment by laboratory staff. The cells are in a predetermined small area on the slide and, particularly in the ThinPrep slides, the cells are mainly in one focus plane when using the x10 screening objective. The need for continuous major adjustments in focus is therefore eliminated and this allows for significant time saving when screening the slide. Table 9.6 summarises the early experience in Edinburgh[15] with previous versions of ThinPrep and CytoRich (now SurePath). Three cytotechnologists of varying experience routinely assessed liquid-based cytology slides in approximately half the time taken for conventional smears. Checking the identity of the slide and writing the report take the same amount of time whether liquid-based preparations or conventional smears are used, but it is clear that the productivity of cytotechnologists can increase by at least 25% and a saving of up to 60% has been reported in other studies. Since the number of unnecessary early repeat smears for inadequate and borderline results will be reduced, overall laboratory workloads should decrease. Thus backlogs can be reduced and turnaround times enhanced even with current depleted staffing levels.

Since only an aliquot of cell suspension is used to prepare one slide, there is sufficient cellular material left in the sample to prepare multiple glass slides with an identical cell population that can be used for teaching slide libraries or for external quality-assurance schemes. The residual cell suspension can be used for additional investigations, such as reflex HPV testing, which may further improve the sensitivity and specificity of the screening test. Improved distinction between low- and high-grade lesions may be achieved on morphology alone using liquid-based cytology and thus overtreatment of lesions that would regress spontaneously could be avoided. Additional investigations for sexually transmitted infections such as chlamydia and gonorrhoea can also be carried out on the cell suspensions, as can molecular biological techniques and cytogenetic studies. This would prove invaluable should other more specific molecular tests become available in the future to identify women already harbouring or likely to progress to a high-grade lesion.

The nature of the evenly dispersed discreet cell deposit on the slide makes liquid-based preparations eminently suitable for immunocytochemical processes such as *in situ* hybridisation, and they are also ideal for automated scanning systems. There has been encouraging progress with automated scanners over the last few years. It is possible that these could be introduced within the next two years.

Before a laboratory converts a cervical screening service to liquid-based preparations, consideration must be given to appropriate smear-taker training to ensure

Table 9.6. Comparison of primary screening times for conventional smears, ThinPrep® and SurePath® (CytoRich); average time per slide (minutes)

Screener	Conventional smear	ThinPrep	CytoRich (SurePath)
A	5.45	2.89	2.33
B	6.32	3.06	3.18
C	8.15	4.18	3.94
Average	6.64	3.37	3.11

Table 9.7. SurePath® versus conventional smear for detection of high-grade lesions (published literature since US Food and Drug Administration approval)

Study	Study type	SurePath (*n*)	High-grade lesion detection[a]
Tripath	Split	8807	Similar to conventional Papanicolaou
Day et al.[36]	DTV	18819	Statistically equivalent (0.249% conventional smear versus 0.266% SurePath) +7%[a]
Hessling et al.[37]	Split	2438	Statistically equivalent (192 conventional smear versus 197 SurePath) +3%
Bergeron et al.[10]	Split (all biopsy)	500	Statistically equivalent (0.82% conventional smear versus 86 SurePath) +4%
Marino and Fremont-Smith[39]	DTV	15534	Significant increase (*P* = 0.0002)
Tench[38]	DTV	2231	Statistically equivalent
Minge et al.[40]	Split	2156	Comparable number of HSILs

[a] significant if *P* value ≤ 0.05; DTV = direct-to-vial study; HSIL = high-grade intraepithelial lesion; Split = split-sample study

correct sampling of the cervix using the Cervex sampler, which requires five turns of the broom to collect adequate numbers of cells. Care must be taken to transfer all the cellular material on the head of the broom, or the head of the broom itself if using SurePath, into the vial immediately.

The transport of cell suspensions rather than dry glass slides to the laboratory must also be considered. Transport of samples to the laboratory may need different arrangements depending on the transport method. Liquid-based cytology in appropriate packaging has now been approved for transport by the Royal Mail in the UK.

In the laboratory, an additional resource is required to produce the new slide preparations. Conventional cervical smears arrive in the laboratory already 'prepared' and only require to be stained and cover-slipped. Liquid-based cytology samples require preparation and this has an equipment, consumable and staffing resource attached to it, as well as accommodation, which may be significant if the SurePath system is used. Extra space is also needed for the storage of processing consumables, again greater for the SurePath system and for vials before and after preparation. The SurePath system requires that both the vial and the centrifuge tube are stored and, if HPV testing is carried out, the centrifuge tubes must be refrigerated. The ThinPrep vial does not need to be refrigerated for HPV testing. Eventually, disposal of the cell suspensions in vials and centrifuge tubes may require additional arrangements and resources.

More importantly, the microscopic appearances of liquid-based preparations differ from conventional smears, and staff must learn how to interpret these new appearances, as well as recognise new 'alarms' to replace the more familiar clues in conventional smears. There is a steep learning curve and both cytotechnologists and cytopathologists must undertake significant additional training in order to achieve the same sensitivity and specificity on liquid-based preparations as for conventional smears.

A UK-wide training programme involving the evaluation of over 600 preselected liquid-based cytology slides was developed for the laboratory staff in the pilot sites. This training was system-specific and undertaken by all laboratory staff (medical and technical) planning to evaluate cervical liquid-based cytology samples. An NHS Certificate of Liquid-Based Cytology Screening was presented to those who successfully completed the course. A short training course was also developed for primary care staff involved in collecting liquid-based cytology samples for the pilots throughout the UK.

The routine microscopic screening method must also be altered to ensure that fields of view are overlapped more than for conventional smears. An overlap of 30% is recommended by the author. The screener must use the high-power lens much more frequently to check clumps and single cells, since the nuclear detail will be visible and may indicate neoplasia. It must be fully understood that, since only an aliquot of the sample is used for the liquid-based preparation, the total number of abnormal cells on the slide may be considerably fewer than are seen in cellular conventional smears. Great care must be taken not to miss small numbers of small single severely dyskaryotic cells from a high-grade lesion, the so-called litigation cells.

Bethesda 2001 has attempted to provide a definition for adequacy for liquid-based preparations (5000 cells) that may be acceptable in the USA. However, in the UK dyskaryosis terminology, the criteria for adequacy are markedly different from Bethesda and a definition for use in the UK is required. This should be addressed by the review of the British terminology that has been undertaken by the British Society for Clinical Cytology (www.clinicalcytology.co.uk).

Cost is a major consideration within organised screening programmes and the additional cost of laboratory consumables for liquid-based cytology must be evaluated. It is acknowledged that this cost would decrease as liquid-based preparations reduce numbers of inadequate smears and thus reduce the need to recall women for a repeat smear. The initial capital costs of equipment and staffing efficiencies could be saved if preparation was centralised in a smaller number of processing laboratories. Prepared slides could then be distributed to peripheral laboratories for microscopic assessment. However, significant savings from liquid-based cytology will be made in primary care, with fewer women returning to have repeat samples for inadequate tests and borderline results and reductions in the administration for call and recall and fail-safe follow-up. There should also be savings in colposcopy clinics if fewer normal women with recurrent inadequate or borderline smears are referred for assessment. Some mechanism must be identified to transfer costs from these settings to laboratories.

The report to NICE by Payne et al.[7] indicated that their modelling studies suggested that the cost-effectiveness of liquid-based preparations might be in the ratio of under £10,000 per life saved (at a five-year screening interval) and under £20,000 per life saved (at an under three-year screening interval). The Scottish pilot data suggest that the overall cost to the NHS would be less than £2.12 per woman tested.

References

1. Day NE. Screening for cancer of the cervix. *J Epidemiol Community Health* 1989;43:103–6.
2. MacGregor JE, Moss S, Parkin DM, Day NE. Cervical cancer screening in north east Scotland. In: Hakama M, Miller AB, Day Ne, editors. *Screening for Cancer of the Uterine Cervix.* IARC Scientific Publications No. 76. Lyon: International Agency for Research on Cancer; 1986. p. 25–36.
3. NHS Cervical Screening Programme. *Review 1998.* Sheffield: NHSCSP; 1998.
4. Quinn M, Babb P, Jones J, Allen E. Effect of screening on incidence and mortality from cancer of the cervix in England: evaluation based on routinely collected statistics. *BMJ* 1999;318:904.
5. Fahey MT, Irwig L, Macaskill P. Meta-analysis of Pap test accuracy. *Am J Epidemiol* 1995;141:680–89.
6. ACOG Committee Opinion. New Pap test screening techniques. *Int J Gynecol Obstet* 1998;63:312–14.

7.   Payne N, Chilcott J, McGoogan E. Liquid based cytology in cervical screening: a rapid and systematic review. *Health Technol Assess* 2000;4:1–73.

8.   Hutchinson ML, Isenstein LM, Goodman A, Hurley AA, Douglass KL, Jui KK, *et al*. Homogenous sampling accounts for the increased diagnostic accuracy using the ThinPrep processor. *Am J Clin Pathol* 1994;101:215–19.

9.   National Audit Office. *The Performance of the Cervical Screening Programme in England*. HC 678 Session 1997–98. London: HMSO; 1998.

10. Bergeron C, Bishop J, Lemarie A, Cas F, Ayavi J, Huynh B, *et al*. Accuracy of thin-layer cytology in patients undergoing cervical cone biopsy. *Acta Cytol* 2001;45:519–24.

11. Scottish Cervical Screening Programme. Report of the Steering Group on the Feasibility Pilot for Introducing Liquid Based Cytology [www.show.scot.nhs.uk/sehd/publications/ScreeningLiquidCytologyv2.pdf].

12. Awen C, Hathway S, Eddy W, Voskuil R, Janes C. Efficacy of ThinPrep preparation of cervical smears: a 1,000-case, investigator-sponsored study. *Diagn Cytopathol* 1994;11:33–6.

13. Laverty CR, Thurloe JK, Redman NL, Farnsworth A. An Australian trial of ThinPrep: a new cytopreparatory technique. *Cytopathology* 1995;6:140–8.

14. Wilbur DC, Cibas ES, Merritt S, James P, Berger BM, Bonfiglio TA. ThinPrep Processor. Clinical trials demonstrate an increased detection rate of abnormal cervical cytologic specimens. *Am J Clin Pathol* 1994;101:209–14.

15. McGoogan E, Reith A. Would monolayers provide more representative samples and improved preparations for cervical screening? Overview and evaluation of systems available. *Acta Cytol* 1996;40:107–19.

16. Sprenger E, Schwarzmann P, Kirkpatrick M, Fox W, Heinzerling RH, Geyer JW, *et al*. The false negative rate in cervical cytology. Comparison of monolayers to conventional smears. *Acta Cytol* 1996;40:81–9.

17. Takahashi M, Naito M. Application of the CytoRich monolayer preparation system for cervical cytology. A prelude to automated primary screening. *Acta Cytol* 1997;41:1785–9.

18. Bishop J. Comparison of the CytoRich system with conventional cervical cytology. Preliminary data on 2,032 cases from a clinical trial site. *Acta Cytol* 1997;41:15–23.

19. Laverty CR, Farnsworth A, Thurloe JK, Grieves A, Bowditch R. Evaluation of the CytoRich Slide Preparation Process. *Anal Quant Cytol Histol* 1997;19:239–45.

20. Lee KR, Ashfaq R, Birdsong GG, Corkill ME, McIntosh KM, Inhorn SL. Comparison of conventional Papanicolaou smears and a fluid-based, thin-layer system for cervical cancer screening. *Obstet Gynecol* 1997;90:278–84.

21. Roberts JM, Gurley AM, Thurloe JK, Bowditch R, Laverty CRA. Evaluation of the ThinPrep Pap test as an adjunct to the conventional Pap smear. *Med J Aust* 1997;167:466–9.

22. Stevens MW, Nespolon WW, Milne AJ, Rowland R. Evaluation of the CytoRich technique for cervical smears. *Diagn Cytopathol* 1998;18:236–42.

23. Corkill M, Knapp D, Hutchinson ML. Improved accuracy for cervical cytology with the ThinPrep method and the endocervical brush-spatula collection procedure. *Journal of Lower Genital Tract Disease* 1998;2:12–16.

24. Hutchinson ML, Zahniser DJ, Sherman ME, Herrero R, Alfaro M, Bratti MC, *et al*. Utility of liquid based cytology for cervical carcinoma screening: results of a population-based study conducted in a region of Costa Rica with a high incidence of cervical carcinoma. *Cancer* 1999;87:48–55.

25. Bernstein SJ, Sanchez-Ramos L, Ndubisi B. Liquid-based cervical cytologic smear study and conventional Papanicolaou smears: a metaanalysis of prospective studies comparing cytologic diagnosis and sample adequacy. *Am J Obstet Gynecol* 2001;185:308–17.

26. Bolick DR, Hellman DJ. Laboratory implementation and efficacy assessment of ThinPrep cervical cancer screening system. *Acta Cytol* 1998;42:209–13.

27. Carpenter AB, Davey DD. ThinPrep Pap Test: performance and biopsy follow-up in a university hospital. *Cancer* 1999;87:105–12.

28. Diaz-Rosario LA, Kabawat SE. Performance of a fluid-based, thin-layer Papanicolaou smear method in the clinical setting of an independent laboratory and an outpatient screening population in New England. *Arch Pathol Lab Med* 1999;123:817–21.

29. Ferris DG, Heidemann NL, Litaker MS, Crosby JH, Macfee MS. The efficacy of liquid-based cervical cytology using direct-to-vial sample collection. *J Fam Pract* 2000;49:1005–11.

30. Guidos BJ, Selvaggi SM. Use of the ThinPrep Pap test in clinical practice. *Diagn Cytopathol* 1999;20:70–73.

31. Obwegeser JH, Brack S. Does liquid-based technology really improve detection of cervical neoplasia? A prospective, randomized trial comparing the ThinPrep Pap Test with the conventional Pap test, including follow-up of HSIL cases. *Acta Cytol* 2001;45:709–14.

32. Papillo J, Zarka MA, St. John TL. Evaluation of the ThinPrep Pap Test in clinical practice. A seven-month 16,314-case experience in northern Vermont. *Acta Cytol* 1998;42:203–8.

33. Wang TY, Chen HS, Yang YC, Tsou MC. Comparison of fluid-based, thin-layer processing and conventional Papanicolaou methods for uterine cervical cytology. *J Formos Med Assoc* 1999;98:500–5.

34. Weintraub J, Morabia A. Efficacy of a liquid-based thin layer method for cervical cancer screening in a population with a low incidence of cervical cancer. *Diagn Cytopathol* 2000;22:52–9.

35. Yeoh GPS, Chan KW, Lauder I, Lam MB. Evaluation of the ThinPrep Papanicolaou test in clinical practice: six-month study of 16, 541 cases with histological correlation in 220 cases. *Hong Kong Medical Journal* 1999;5:233–9.

36. Day SJ, Deszo EL, Freund GG. Dual sampling of the endocervix and its impact on AutoCyte-Prep endocervical adequacy. *Am J Clin Pathol* 2002;118:41–6.

37. Hessling JJ, Raso DS, Schiffer B, Callicott J Jr, Husain M, Taylor D. Effectiveness of thin layer preparations vs conventional Pap smears in a blinded, split-sample study extended cytologic evaluation. *J Reprod Med* 2001;46:880–6.

38. Tench W. Preliminary assessment of the AutoCyte PREP. Direct-to-vial performance. *J Reprod Med* 2000;45:912–16.

39. Marino JF, Fremont-Smith M. Direct-to-vial experience with AutoCyte PREP in a small New England regional cytology practice. *J Reprod Med* 2001;46:353–8.

40. Minge L, Fleming M, VanGeem T, Bishop JW. AutoCyte Prep system vs. conventional cervical cytology. Comparison based on 2,156 cases. *J Reprod Med* 2000;45:179–84.

Chapter 10

Human papillomavirus screening for lower genital tract neoplasia

Jack Cuzick

Professor Cuzick was unable to submit a chapter. This chapter has been produced from the transcription of Professor Cuzick's presentation and has been seen by him for editing.

Introduction

The arguments for human papillomavirus (HPV) screening are well known. There are three potential roles for HPV testing and cervical screening. First is the triage of borderline or mild smears, making use of its negative predictive value. Second, there is the issue of post-treatment surveillance. The current recommendations for women who have had treatment for cervical intraepithelial neoplasia grade 3 (CIN3) are for annual smear tests for at least five years. Some centres use cytology indefinitely but there is some evidence that this can be curtailed. Third, there is the issue of primary cervical screening.

Cytology has served us well and, we know now that organising a good programme can reduce mortality from cervical cancer by the order of 50–60%. A recent audit showed that over half the cases of cancer currently seen are women under the age of 70 years who have had completely normal screening histories but whose cancer has been missed by cytology. Thus, we are reaching the limit of where we can go with cytology. We need to think about moving forward. There are also issues of cost, as the burden of maintaining this huge industry of cytoscreeners to make cytology work is substantial.

Triage of smears with minor abnormality

There are two large studies in the USA looking at the role of HPV in the triage of borderline/mild smears: the ASCUS–LSIL Triage Study (ALTS) and the large Kaiser Permanente Borderline Pap Study. The hypothesis is that, when cytology is inconclusive, HPV helps to determine whether more rapid referral or reduced surveillance is appropriate. Exactly how this is done still needs to be worked out and it depends to some extent on the system being used. From data in our study, it appears that HPV-negative borderline smears should be treated as normal. The real question is how to react to HPV-positive borderline smears, and I shall discuss that in some more detail at the end of the chapter.

Follow-up after treatment

This is another area where studies now show that, when there is incomplete excision of a lesion, the subsequent smears remain HPV-positive. When there is complete excision, however, the positivity tends to disappear over a period of about six months. Thus, if an HPV test is carried out at one year and no HPV was found on the smear, then at that stage the woman could probably be returned to routine surveillance, with that test and cytology. However, if there is evidence of HPV after a year, this is fairly strong evidence that there is still disease present, and colposcopy is needed to establish the location of the residual disease.

Thus, there are two advantages: first, there is more rapid determination of incomplete excision and this is identified within a year. Cytology is particularly insensitive after treatment. Second, because the test is more accurate, smears do not need to be taken for five years, which avoids the anxiety of annual smears and worrying about whether the disease will recur.

There are a number of large studies going on to document this fully. Several studies that have been completed but most include only a small number of women. However, this is an area in which there is much research being undertaken.

Primary screening

The key area to focus on is primary screening. One of the major issues is whether HPV should be an adjunctive test to cytology. That is, is it sensible simply to add HPV testing to cytology, perhaps at every other test or some such stage, to improve the overall sensitivity? Or can we make it the sole primary test? That is the direction in which we are moving. At the moment, we are thinking about using HPV testing in triage of borderline cytology but, in fact, now that we are seeing the results, evidence is emerging that we should think about reversing the role of these tests by using HPV as the primary test because it is more sensitive, completely automated and there are no concerns in terms of subjective assessment. We should then carry out cytology on the HPV-positives, to determine whether it is necessary to refer immediately, or whether there should be further surveillance.

HPV testing is highly effective at reducing the inadequate rates, because the sample is almost always adequate for HPV. Of course, liquid-based cytology does that as well. These are two areas in which both of the new technologies are quite effective.

One of the key issues is that screening with a better should test allow the screening interval to be lengthened. The reason why cytology works is that, with a disease with a long natural history, a fairly insensitive test performed repeatedly will generally provide two or three chances to detect something before it progresses to invasive cancer. If there were a better test, we could seriously consider going back to the five-yearly intervals that we had originally used for cytology, and possibly even longer. There are enormous cost implications, and also simple convenience, if screening does not have to take place every two to three years.

The last issue is a little more speculative, but there is emerging evidence that self-sampling can be done for HPV testing. Generally, the self-sample is not as specific as that taken by a doctor or nurse, because it samples the whole vagina, so that if there is some positivity, it is not specific to the cervix. Nevertheless, the sensitivity is at least as good as conventional cytology and may offer an opportunity for introducing some kind of test for women who, even with our well-organised programme, refuse to attend for a cervical smear.

The general principle is that screening should be performed as infrequently as possible and should use the best available tests. In the long run, we waste many people's time and, ultimately, money by carrying out short-term, repeated tests. It is obvious that, unless the test is enormously expensive, it is generally better to conduct a superior test less frequently than to use a conventional test at short intervals. This has even been recognised in the USA now, where the American Cancer Society's new recommendations are that a conventional test has to be done every year. If you move to liquid-based cytology, they will allow you to go to two years, and if you use liquid-based cytology and HPV, the recommended interval is three-yearly. The Americans generally over-screen by most European standards, but it is apparent that they are already beginning to adopt the three-year interval.

These are the new data from HART, using an LSIL cut-off or mild dyskaryosis cytology. Sensitivity for cytology is 72%, versus 98% for HPV. However, that comes at a price, in that the specificity is generally less and there are more false positives. In fact, they are not really false positives; they are women who are HPV-positive but who do not have high-grade lesions. This is a particular problem in younger women because we know that many HPV infections will regress naturally over a period of 6–12 months. There is therefore an issue here of how to manage women who are HPV-positive but who do not show a cytological abnormality, or with the fact that the false-positive rate or specificity will generally be lower.

The HART study was designed to examine this and the information described here is taken from this study. It focused on women aged 30 years or more, and looked initially at the sensitivity and specificity of HPV testing compared with routine cytology in these women. This has been done in a range of studies, so this was a confirmatory study. The area in which new ground was broken was in a randomised option of the best management of women with borderline abnormal smears who were HPV-positive but cytology-negative.

The study ran in five centres around the UK: Birmingham, Manchester, Mansfield, Edinburgh and London. It was as routine as possible, with women attending their GPs for routine screening. Tests were conducted in two different laboratories that produced identical results, with a central review of the histology, to ensure that there was a consistent call on the lesions. Women were included who were up to the age of 60 years, with routine smears, no abnormalities in the last three years and who were never treated for CIN.

Over 11 000 women were entered in the study and just over 10 000 women within the age band gave complete samples and consented to the basic process. Of those, about two percent showed cytological abnormalities, which were mild dyskaryosis or worse. Those were all referred for immediate colposcopy, with good compliance.

At the other end of the spectrum, almost 90% were negative on both tests. For comparison to ensure that nothing was missed, a five percent sample of those samples was randomised to attend for colposcopy, while the remainder returned to routine screening. This was to check the sensitivity, in that both tests were double negatives. About 62% of selected women attended for colposcopy. When the cytology was reviewed, no high-grade disease was found in this group, although some low-grade disease was found. A small proportion of those women referred for colposcopy had two unsatisfactory smears and these were excluded from the main part of the study.

The novel area that was studied was those women who had borderline cytology or who were HPV-positive and cytology-negative. That group of over 800 women was randomised either to be referred immediately or to be followed up at six and 12 months. There was no action on the six-month sample, unless the cytology indicated that there was a high-grade lesion present. Follow-up was attempted to one year, with about 70% attendance in both arms.

It is extremely important to consider, in the screening context, that HPV-positivity is age-dependent. That is quite crucial in terms of thinking about how to use it in screening. Overall a clear age dependence is shown: after the age of about 40 years, the HPV-positivity rate is around five percent, but even between the ages of 30 and 34 years it is up at about 15%. Other studies have shown that, in the 20–29 year age-group, the level is generally around 20%, so there is a rapid fall here that is basically due to changes in sexual behaviour and the increased infection rate in younger women. Most of these infections are transient, and much of what is seen in older women are the HPV infections that are not transient.

Comparing HPV with cytology, and using a cut-off of mild dyskaryosis or worse, then cytology had a sensitivity of 72% generally – fairly high, compared with the literature – and a specificity of over 98.6%, with a strong positive predictive value. About one-third of those women with mild lesions actually had high-grade biopsies. Dropping cytology down to the borderline area, which probably provides a better comparison against HPV, the sensitivity improved up to about 80%. Specificity, of course, decreased to about 96%, and there was a positive predictive value of around 16%.

With HPV, there was extremely high sensitivity, at 98% for the standard cut-off of 1 pg, but the specificity dropped a little more, down to 93.4%. The positive predictive value was a little less than borderline cytology overall, running at about 13%. The positivity is therefore probably too low for screening, set at 1 pg/ml, and it probably should be at 2 pg/ml. At that point, hardly any disease was missed, but the specificity was increased, giving a positive predictive value that was a little higher. This was not a large effect, but a slight gain. Using both tests, no disease was found in those who were negative on both tests in a small sample, which points to 100% sensitivity and a specificity of about 94%.

One of the issues that the study focused on was the key randomisation of women with borderline smears which could have been HPV-positive or HPV-negative, or negative smears that were HPV-positive. The three groups were: borderline smears that were HPV-negative; borderline smears that were HPV-positive, a rather smaller proportion since most of the borderline smears were actually HPV-negative in the study; and the largest group is those in which the cytology was negative but HPV was positive. Those groups were randomised to either immediate colposcopy or surveillance at six and 12 months.

In terms of high-grade lesions, there was no difference in numbers between those in the immediate colposcopy and those in the surveillance groups, so there is really no evidence that high-grade lesions will disappear over this period of a year. However, about 60% of the low-grade lesions had regressed over the period of a year. So, simply by waiting for a year, you will have about the same yield of high-grade lesions, but only about 40% as many low-grade lesions.

Costs are crucial here, and will ultimately determine directly where HPV fits into the screening programme. The potential for lower costs is associated with longer screening intervals – performing fewer screens makes a huge difference when the time spent by the doctors and nurses who take them is taken into consideration. There are also fewer inadequate smears, with streamlined management of borderline smears and a shorter surveillance interval after treatment. On the other hand, there are increased laboratory costs, because the HPV test costs more. There will also be increased referral and surveillance rates per screen, because each screen will tend to lead to more positives, if you are going to react to the HPV-positives. The costs have been calculated at almost exactly what the Audit Office had estimated, about £131 million per year for the screening programme. With five-year testing, HPV and cytology, where HPV is used as an adjunctive test, routine costs are slightly lower, at £100 million per year, because fewer tests are being done. Many of those follow-ups due to inadequate or borderline results would be eliminated, so those costs would fall. Colposcopy costs would increase slightly, because there would be more referrals per screen, although there would be fewer screens overall. There would not be much difference here, but a slight increase in terms of colposcopy, biopsy and treatment. Overall, however, the net gain would be fewer costs for routine smear tests.

The details of these estimates could be disputed but the principle is clear: if you screen less often with a good test, you will not only do a better job, you can save money. Based on this example, costs would reduce from £131 million to about £100 million per year, a saving of about 25%.

Conclusions

HPV-positivity is highly age-dependent, and that really determines how it should be used in screening, particularly in primary screening. The Hybrid Capture® II screening test is highly sensitive. This has been well-documented in women over the age of 30 years, although there is less evidence in younger women. The specificity is lower than that of cytology but generally acceptable above the age of 35 years. There is an issue about specificity, particularly in younger age groups.

It is safe to return women with HPV-negative borderline lesions to routine follow-up. In the study described in this chapter, all of the women with borderline lesions that demonstrated high-grade disease were HPV-positive. One of the major advantages of HPV is that referral of about 50% of these borderline lesions can be eliminated. The 50% that are HPV-negative can be treated as negative and returned to routine follow-up.

HPV remains positive in high-grade lesions. In fact, all of those that were positive in the study who were followed by surveillance remained HPV-positive, demonstrating that it is safe to manage these cases conservatively. Even for borderline cytology, or negative cytology if it is HPV-positive, a key factor is not to overreact to that HPV-positivity. It is safe to repeat those tests after 6–12 months, by which stage half of them will become HPV-negative and can be advised to return to routine screening. It is possible to reduce the referral rate if this policy is followed and current HART data actually support this approach. Those who are HPV-positive, in the absence of mild dyskaryosis or worse, can simply be followed at 6–12 months because nothing will progress to cancer in that period of time. If at re-testing at that time there is a lesion present, HPV will still be a reliable test and nothing will be missed. Many unnecessary referrals can be eliminated. Lastly, it is safe to reduce the positivity threshold or to increase the productivity threshold, up to about twice the level currently used – 2 pg/ml or two relative light units is appropriate for clinical work.

Future proposals

For the future, it is hoped that a large-scale European trial can be undertaken. If there is a good test available, screening probably does not need to start any earlier than 25 years of age. There is no evidence that cytology has ever benefited any woman much under the age of 30 years. The HPV test is clearly a sensitive test that is not specific, so it therefore makes good sense to screen primarily with the HPV test. Patients whose results are normal can go on to five-yearly recall and cytology only needs to be performed on those who are HPV-positive, to determine whether the patient needs immediate referral or whether a follow-up at 6–12 months is appropriate.

HPV testing is a simple automated test that is completely objective in outcome. It would eliminate approximately 90% as being negative, allowing cytology to be reserved for women in whom there is some concern about disease. This removes much of the problem with use of cytoscreeners. If the cytology is mild or worse in the presence of HPV, going directly to colposcopy is probably advisable. If the results are normal or borderline and HPV-positive, the test should be repeated a year later. If both tests are negative, the patients can return to normal five-yearly recall. If they are still HPV-positive and cytology is not worse than mild, or if it is HPV-negative and borderline, some additional follow-up is probably needed.

The stage at which follow-up should stop is open to debate, but there should probably be one more test at a further 6–12 months. If results remain positive, the patient should be referred for colposcopy. This is potentially the direction in which screening should consider going, although there are a number of steps to get there, but it seems to make logical sense to use the sensitive, objective test first, even though it is not quite as specific. Cytology can then be used as triage to determine whether patients need immediate referral or short-term re-testing.

Further reading

Cuzick J. Time to consider HPV testing in cervical screening. *Ann Oncol* 2001;12:1511–14.

Cuzick J, Beverley E, Ho L, Sapper H, Mielzynska I, Lorincz A, *et al.* HPV testing in primary screening of older women. *Br J Cancer* 1999:81:554–8.

Cuzick J, Sasieni P, Davies P, Adams J, Normand C, Frater A, *et al.* A systematic review of the role of human papilloma virus (HPV) testing within a cervical screening programme: summary and conclusions. *Br J Cancer* 2000;83:561–5.

Manos MM. HPV testing for clarifying borderline cervical smear results. *BMJ* 2001;322:878–9.

Sasieni P, Cuzick J. Could HPV testing become the sole primary cervical screening test? *J Med Screen* 2002;9:49–51.

Chapter 11

Real-time screening techniques in the detection of cervical cancer

Albert Singer and Narendra Pisal

Introduction

Cervical cancer is a largely preventable disease because of its easily recognisable and treatable premalignant stage. In countries that have implemented regular screening programmes to detect these lesions, cervical exfoliative cytology has been a successful screening tool. In many Western countries that have adopted such programmes, the incidence and mortality of cervical cancer have dropped dramatically. Eighty percent of the 466 000 cases of cervical cancer occur annually in the developing countries, where only 5% of the female population has had a Papanicolaou smear within five years[1] and cervical cancer is the leading cause of cancer death.[2] By contrast, in the developed countries, where 85% have had at least one Papanicolaou smear in their lifetime, it is only the tenth leading cause of cancer death.[2] Despite similar populations, Finland has a lower incidence of cervical cancer than Norway, the former having a well-established cervical screening programme. Fifty percent of those women in the USA with newly diagnosed invasive cervical cancer have never had a Papanicolaou smear[3] and a further 10% have not had a smear in the five years before the diagnosis.[3] In the UK, since the introduction of computerised call and recall system, the incidence of cervical cancer has decreased from 16.4 per 100 000 to 9.3 per 100 000 between 1988 and 1997. In the same period, mortality from cervical cancer has decreased from 7.0 to 3.7 per 100 000. Therefore, the best way to improve cervical cancer detection and reduce its incidence is by regular population-based screening.

Despite its success, exfoliative cytology is associated with certain drawbacks, mainly in respect of the significant false negative rate.[4-6] An inherent disadvantage is the delay between the test being taken and results becoming available. Consequently, alternative methods have been developed in an attempt to address this delay. Real-time screening tests can reduce some of the anxiety associated with the cytological screening test by providing instantaneous results. Real-time tests such as visual inspection with acetic acid (VIA) and visual inspection with Lugol's iodine (VILI) have also been used in 'one-stop cervical cancer prevention clinics' in developing countries (see also Chapter 15).

Currently available real-time screening techniques

Currently available real-time screening techniques are:

- visual inspection acetic (VIA)

- visual inspection lugol's iodine (VILI)

- optico-electrical devices (i.e. Truscreen®)

- fluorescent devices (i.e. Cerviscan®).

The advantages of real-time screening are:

- reduced anxiety

- improved compliance

- possibility of repeating inadequate tests immediately

- 'one-stop' screening, counselling and treatment, avoiding repeated visits

- potential to be used for secondary screening as an adjunct or triage.

TruScreen®

The TruScreen®, previously known as Polarprobe (Johnson & Johnson), is an optoelectronic probe-shaped device that algorithmically classifies cervical tissue types and provides a final patient result for each case. The TruScreen employs a real-time approach to the detection of tissue abnormalities. Traditionally, screening and diagnostic tests rely on biochemical information or recognition of abnormalities based on cell morphology, such as cytology, or tissue structure, such as radiology. The TruScreen device is an *in vivo* system that uses the electrical and optical properties of cervical tissues to reach a diagnosis.

The main components of the device (Figure 11.1) include a pen-shaped handpiece that contains the tissue stimulation and sensor elements. The handpiece is connected by a cable to a console that contains a microprocessor control module and a digital signal processor. The instrument uses a software-implemented tissue classifier, which provides the operator with instant feedback in the form of a printed result.

The handpiece is a 17-cm pen-shaped instrument with a 5-mm diameter flat tip. The tip contains the tissue stimulator and sensor elements (Figure 11.2). These consist of three peripheral electrodes and four central light-emitting diodes (LEDs). The console contains a microprocessor module and a digital signal processor. The handpiece is covered by a single-use sheath that is discarded after use to prevent cross-infection. The microprocessor handles the data to and from the digital signal processor that implements the complex algorithmic calculations necessary for operation of the tissue classifier.

The cell membranes and varying internal structures of any tissue form a complex of capacitors and resistors. When an electrical voltage is applied to tissue and then turned off abruptly, the tissue behaves like a decaying battery, lasting a fraction of a second. Because both the decay time and the waveform will differ between different types of tissue, the voltage decay waveform can provide a dynamic signature of the tissue that assists in its classification.[7–10] Truscreen applies low-voltage pulses (0.8 V of 260 μs duration) to the cervix via a combination of its three electrodes and the resultant electrical decay curve is measured and analysed (Figure 11.3).

Analysis of electrical properties alone is unable to distinguish unambiguously between the different cervical tissue types because of the degree of overlap. Additional parameters are therefore required to provide complementary information. Optical properties are used for this purpose in the form of selective wavelength spectroscopy. Four LEDs transmit light at specific wavelengths within the electromagnetic spectrum

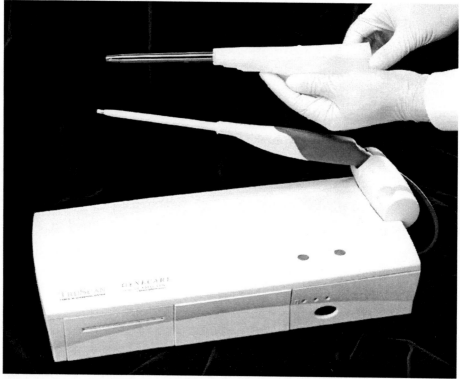

Figure 11.1 TruScreen® system showing the handpiece, microcomputer console and the single-use sheath

– two red diodes (600 nm), a green diode (525 nm) and an infrared diode (940 nm). These are activated in sequence and the tissue response is detected by a detector photodiode at the excitation, as well as at the off-excitation frequency, producing a relatively broadband spectrum for analysis.

By combining the electrical decay and spectroscopic information from a particular area on the cervix, TruScreen is able, by means of a classification algorithm, to categorise the tissue.[7,11] The system incorporates a handpiece with a tip designed to take

Figure 11.2 Tip of the TruScreen® handpiece showing electrical and optical sensors

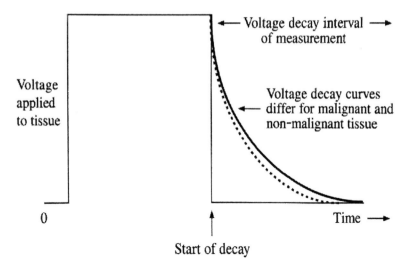

Figure 11.3 Electrical decay curve for tissues

measurements from 5-mm diameter areas of the cervical tissue. During the examination, 'stop/go' lights on the handpiece guide the operator to move the tip of the probe to a tissue spot, stop for the measurement to be performed and then move to the next tissue spot. This sequence is repeated until the area of the cervical transformation zone has been covered. After the operator has signalled the completion of the examination by pressing a button on the handpiece, the screening result is calculated and printed out from the console.

The TruScreen is capable of classifying approximately 17 different basic cervical tissue types, as well as junctions between different tissue types. The expert system has been 'trained' to recognise various normal and abnormal cervical tissue types using a previously obtained database of over 1500 patients collected from a geographically diverse range of centres. These specific tissue type classifications are grouped in a manner that is useful for cervical screening, and hence the 'worst case' tissue type seen on the cervix determines the final device output. The initial model of the TruScreen returns one of two possible final patient screening results: 'normal' – normal squamous epithelium, columnar epithelium, physiological metaplasia – or 'abnormal' – cervical intraepithelial neoplasia grades 1–3 (CIN1–CIN3), invasive cancer.

Sensitivity and specificity

Used as a primary screening test, TruScreen has been shown in a study[12] of 769 women either referred with an abnormal smear or attending for routine screening to have a sensitivity of 70% for CIN2 and above (Table 11.1). The specificity was 81%. In this study, a smear was obtained at the time of probing and the combined sensitivity increases to 95% without a further decline in specificity. These data suggest that using TruScreen solely as a primary screening tool will incur great public health costs due to low specificity. However, the high sensitivity means that it has the potential to be used as an adjunct to conventional cytology. It would also be valuable in the triage management of women presenting with minor cytological abnormalities.

Table 11.1. Sensitivity and specificity of Truscreen®[12]

	Truscreen alone (%)	Cytology alone (%)	Truscreen + cytology (%)
Specificity for normal	81	95	80
Sensitivity for CIN1	67	45	87
Sensitivity for CIN2 and CIN3	70	69	93

Cerviscan®

Cervical tissue fluoresces when excited at spectral regions in the ultraviolet and visible region. This fluorescence response for normal and abnormal cervical tissues varies in intensity and spectral contents. These optical properties are assessed by Cerviscan® (LifeSpex Inc.), which is a multispectral tissue fluorescence imaging system for detecting cervical intraepithelial lesions. The instrument is in its early stage of development and initial studies on a Papanicolaou-positive population suggest that it may be a useful adjunct to colposcopy. This light-based system can provide the colposcopist with an objective fluorescence map of the visible cervix and indicate areas of abnormality for directed biopsy.[13] Further population-based studies are needed before the device can be used as a primary screening tool.

Optical detection technology

Medispectra's optical detection technology (Medispectra, Lexington, MA) is a light-based system that uses a combination of laser-induced fluorescence, white light backscatter technology and a multivariate algorithm to classify normal and abnormal cervical tissues. Initial studies have shown this to be a useful adjunct to colposcopy.[14]

Visual inspection-based techniques

The difficulties in implementing cytology-based screening programmes in developing countries have led to the investigation of screening tests based on visual examination of the uterine cervix. Among these tests, visual inspection with 3–5% acetic acid (VIA) involves non-magnified visualisation of uterine cervix after application of 3–5% dilute acetic acid. Visual inspection with Lugol's iodine (VILI) involves naked eye examination of the cervix after application of Lugol's iodine solution (see also Chapter 15).

The results of test performance in cross-sectional study settings (Table 11.2) indicate that the sensitivity of VIA to detect high-grade precancerous lesions ranged from 66–96%; the specificity varied from 64–98%; the positive predictive value ranged from 10–20% and the negative predictive value ranged from 92–97%. Where cytology and VIA have been compared under the same study conditions, the sensitivity of VIA was found to be similar to that of cytology, whereas the specificity was consistently lower. Test characteristics of VIA suggest that it is a suitable test for early detection of cervical neoplasia. Results are summarised in Table 11.2.

A wide range of personnel, including doctors, nurses and other allied health workers, can administer and report the results of VIA. A positive test is based on well-defined, densely opaque acetowhite lesions in the transformation zone close to the

Table 11.2. Sensitivity and specificity of visual inspection with acetic acid (VIA)

Year	Study	Place	Cases (n)	VIA Sensitivity (%)	VIA Specificity (%)	Cytology Sensitivity (%)	Cytology Specificity (%)
2002	Denny,[15]	South Africa	2754	70.0	79.0		
2001	Singh,[16]	India	402	82.0	94.0	78.0	99.0
2001	Belinson,[17]	China	1997	71.0	74.0		
1999	JHPIEGO,[18]	Zimbabwe	10934	76.7	64.1	44.3	90.6
1998	Sankaranarayanan,[19]	WHO	3000	90.0	92.0	86.0	91.0

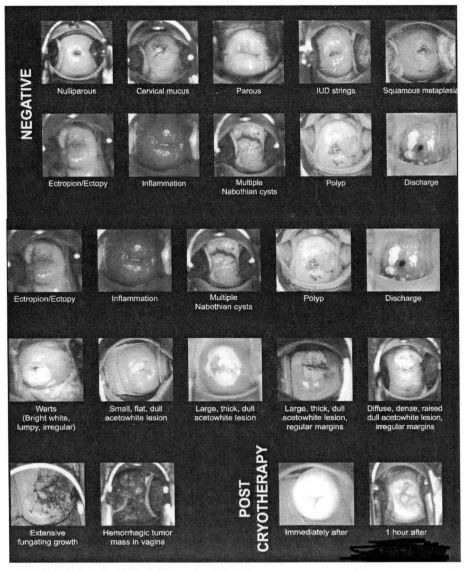

Figure 11.4. Picture chart for visual inspection with acetic acid

squamocolumnar junction. A picture chart (Figure 11.4) is used for pattern recognition after application of acetic acid.

The major limitations of VIA include low specificity, which can lead to over-investigation and overtreatment of screen-positive women, as well as lack of standardised methods of quality control, training and competency evaluation. Its capacity to detect endocervical disease is limited and the major strengths include its simplicity and low cost, real-time availability of results and potential for immediate linkage with investigations/treatment, good sensitivity and fast-track training of providers.

The efficacy and cost-effectiveness of VIA-based population-screening programmes in reducing the incidence of and mortality from cervical cancer is not known and remains to be established, as do the long-term complications and safety of over-treatment in the context of a VIA screening programme. Currently studies organised by the World Health Organization are continuing in several locations to evaluate further the accuracy of VIA in detecting cervical cancer precursors and to address its efficacy in reducing the incidence of cervical cancer.

Preliminary results from continuing cross-sectional studies in India and West Africa indicate that the sensitivity of VILI to detect high-grade cervical precursors ranges from 80–90% and the specificity ranges from 75–85%. The role of sequential testing of VILI following VIA is also being addressed.

Conclusion

Real-time screening tests offer the advantage of instant results, with reduced anxiety and improved compliance. However, these tests have not been used in the context of a population-based screening programme. Cervical cytological screening has significantly reduced the incidence and mortality of cervical cancer and there is no indication to change cytology-based screening in countries where this is established. However, in developing countries, cytology-based screening programmes are difficult to implement because of the cost and training implications. Real-time screening tests may have a role to play in these situations. The tests that offer most promise are the visual inspection methods, which are simple and use low technology. The World Health Organization has initiated population-based studies to address issues such as reduction in incidence and mortality and overall cost-effectiveness. Cervical cancer is a major health problem in these countries and efforts need to be targeted to challenge this. New technologies such as Truscan® (Johnson & Johnson, New Brunswick, NJ, USA) offer a great potential for improving the efficacy of the existing screening techniques. Initially, these technologies will be used as adjunctive or triage strategies in combination with cytology.

References

1.   Sherris ID, Wells ES, Tsu VD, Bishop A. *Cervical Cancer in Developing Countries: A Situation Analysis*. Working paper. Washington DC: World Bank; 1993.
2.   Parkin DM, Laara E, Muir CS. Estimates of the worldwide frequency of sixteen major cancers in 1980. *Int J Cancer* 1988;41:184–97.
3.   National Institutes of Health. Consensus Development Conference. Statement on cervical cancer. Apr 1–3 1996. *Gynecol Oncol* 1997;66:351–61.
4.   Gay JD, Donaldson LD, Goellner JR. False-negative results in cervical cytological studies. *Acta Cytol* 1985;29:1043–6.
5.   Shingleton HM, Patrick RL, Johnston WW, Smith RA. The current status of the Papanicolaou smear. *CA Cancer J Clin* 1995;45:305–20.

6. Koss LG. Accuracy of diagnosis. *Cancer* 1989;64 Suppl:249–52.
7. Coppleson M, Canfell K, Skladnev V. The Polarprobe – an instantaneous optoelectronic approach to cervical screening. *CME Journal of Gynecologic Oncology* 2000;5:31–8.
8. Coppleson M, Reid BL, Skladnev VN, Dalrymple JC. An electronic approach to the detection of pre-cancer and cancer of the uterine cervix: a preliminary evaluation of Polarprobe. *Int J Gynecol Cancer* 1994;4:79–83.
9. Quek SC, Mould T, Canfell K, Singer A, Skladnev V, Coppleson M. The Polarprobe – emerging technology for cervical cancer screening. *Ann Acad Med Singapore* 1998;27:717–21.
10. Spitzer M. Cervical screening adjuncts: recent advances. *Am J Obstet Gynecol* 1998;179:544–56.
11. Schneider A, Zahm DM. New adjunctive methods for cervical cancer screening. *Obstet Gynecol Clin North Am* 1996;23:657–73.
12. Singer A, Pisal N, Canfell K, Skladnev V. New technology in diagnosis. In: *Proceedings of the XIth International Congress of Cervical Pathology and Colposcopy, Barcelona, June 9–13, 2002.* Bologna, Italy: Moduzzi Editore;2002. p. 117–21.
13. Dattamajumdar A, Wells D, Parnell J, Lewis J, Ganguly D, Wright T. Preliminary experimental results from multi-center clinical trials for detection of cervical precancerous lesions using the Cerviscan system. Paper presented at 23rd annual meeting of IEEE – Engineering in Medicine and Biology, Istanbul, Turkey, October 25–28, 2001.
14. Burke L, Modell M, Niloff J, Kobelin M, Abu-Jawdeh G, Zelenchuk A. Identification of squamous intra-epithelial lesions: fluorescence of cervical tissue during colposcopy. *Journal of Lower Genital Tract Disease* 1999;3:159–62.
15. Denny L, Kuhn L, Pollack A, Wright TC Jr. Direct visual inspection for cervical cancer screening: an analysis of factors influencing test performance. *Cancer* 2002;94:1699–707.
16. Singh V, Sehgal A, Parashari A, Sodhani P, Satyanarayana L. Early detection of cervical cancer through acetic acid application – an aided visual inspection. *Singapore Med J* 2001;42:351–4.
17. Belinson J, Qiao YL, Pretorius R, Zhang WH, Elson P, Li L, *et al.* Shanxi Province Cervical Cancer Screening Study: a cross-sectional comparative trial of multiple techniques to detect cervical neoplasia. *Gynecol Oncol* 2001;83:439–44.
18. Visual inspection with acetic acid for cervical cancer screening: test qualities in a primary-care setting. University of Zimbabwe/JHPIEGO Cervical Cancer Project. *Lancet* 1999;353:869–73.
19. Sankaranarayanan R, Wesley R, Somanathan T, Dhakad N, Shyamalakumary B, Amma NS, *et al.* Visual inspection of the uterine cervix after the application of acetic acid in the detection of cervical carcinoma and its precursors. *Cancer* 1998;83:2150–6.

Chapter 12

New approaches to detecting lower genital tract neoplasia I

Discussion

Discussion following the papers by Dr McGoogan, Professor Cuzick and Professor Singer

Wilkinson: Dr McGoogan, I have a question regarding the thin-layer cytology studies. Many of those studies, some of which had commercial support, were compared with conventional cytology as being practised by optimised cytology, including the use of optimised collection device approaches, using spatula and brush or broom. Many of those studies are comparing apples and oranges.

Some studies using optimised collection techniques have shown little benefit with thin-layer cytology.[1] I am rather concerned about that as an overall strategy – the idea that thin-layer cytology will solve the problem when the collection technique is really the issue. If you have such a high unsatisfactory rate, I think one of the highest I have ever seen in cytology, there must be some significant problems with the collection methods that are currently being applied.

McGoogan: I do not agree that the high unsatisfactory rate indicates a problem with our collection method. I think the problem is with the criteria that the laboratories are using to call a smear adequate. For example, in Bethesda until 2001, you were looking for 10% of your slide to be covered with cells and 30% of the cells on the slide to be visible – those were the criteria for adequacy. In the UK, the criteria are for one-third of the slide to be covered by cells, and more than 50% to be visible, so different criteria are being used.

With litigation becoming more common in the UK, people are more conscientious about their acceptance of a slide as adequate. They are more likely to call a slide inadequate, either because of too few cells on the slide or because of obscuring factors such as blood and inflammatory exudates, which in the past they would probably have accepted as adequate. It is actually our criteria that are different, rather than the collection method or the skills of our smear-takers. In fact, in the UK, we have had a major change in the identities of our smear-takers over the last five or six years. Most of the smears are now taken in primary care by practice nurses who have been trained. Until 1990, most smears were taken by doctors who innately know how to take a cervical smear, do they not? It is therefore not the quality of the smear-taking but the criteria that the laboratories are using.

Critchley: Dr McGoogan, I was interested when you said that there was the potential to make about ten slides from a liquid-based preparation and that you could see future opportunities if new tests were to become available. How do you handle that if you are taking a smear from a patient? Is consent required for these additional smears to be made? If a new test were identified that detected a new problem, you would have to go back to that patient. With our current audits, we are becoming increasingly conscious about storing material and providing new information, but such consent will become part of the smear-taking process in future if you are going to keep these slides.

McGoogan: Of course, we would not make ten slides routinely – there is just the possibility of doing that. Routinely, you would make one slide, because one is as good as the next.

In practice, we are allowed to use the sample for training and educational purposes, and also for quality assurance – so we are allowed to make an additional slide for those purposes. If you have any intention of using it for a research project, albeit testing a new technology, then you must go back to the patient and obtain permission. By that time, however, we would have thrown out the sample, because we are not keeping them – they are disposed of as soon as we have the cytology result.

In the English pilot studies,[2] women were informed that if their cytology was low-grade, their sample would be used for human papillomavirus (HPV) testing, but their consent was not required for that. They were simply informed that this was how it was being done at the time.

This means that in future we will be able to use the sample for more tests, if we so choose. For example, you could use the liquid-based sample to do primary HPV testing and then cytology on the leftover material in the vial. Liquid-based cytology is a platform for so many different things and if we find there is a better way of testing them, we will not have to keep changing the way in which we collect the sample in primary care.

MacLean: Dr Deery discussed a trial on samplers (Chapter 8). In the light of what Dr McGoogan has said, it is probably just the National Institute for Clinical Excellence (NICE) that needs to be convinced for England to follow Scotland. Is there any place for considering such a trial on samplers, or are we inevitably heading towards liquid-based cytology? Could we have comments from Dr McGoogan and Dr Deery?

McGoogan: We are all reluctant to say anything that could be construed as anticipating NICE's decision. In England, for example, we are not allowed to start preparing people to train on liquid-based cytology. We do not know what NICE will say. If they are wise, they will follow Scotland, but we just do not know.

However, the writing is on the wall. Taking what Dr Deery said yesterday about plastic spatulas, and particularly the Cervex broom, they work with liquid-based cytology and with conventional smears. We just accept that and we do not need a trial to prove it.

Deery: I agree with Dr McGoogan that it is impossible at the moment to comment on liquid-based cytology and what the conclusions of the groups will be. There is still tremendous variability in the results coming back from liquid-based cytology and there are still very few trials that show a proper standard of colposcopy and biopsy to justify the results. Most of the studies are reviews of slides conducted by groups of people with variable expertise.

Many of the thin-layer studies, as has been suspected for a long time, show learning curves, simply because they involve the retraining of people to take smears, to examine smears and to interpret cytology. That does not evidence one way or the other in split samples, but there is a suspicion that, when all the noise has died down, as Dr McGoogan is suggesting, those amazing results, by comparison with conventional cytology, will actually return to normal and the cytology sensitivity will not have changed that much. However, there may be other advantages to using liquid-based cytology.

McGoogan: Could I just respond to that? I did not say that it would come back to normal as compared to conventional smears – I think it will always remain of greater sensitivity than the conventional smear, but depending on which system you use. Up till now, we have talked about liquid-based cytology as if every system is equal. Since Scotland is now involved in a tendering exercise for choosing which system each laboratory will use, I am particularly concerned that we should be aware that there are inevitably differences in the end result of the system. The systems that we are looking at have different technology, but we must be very cautious not to allow other systems to be used widely without clear evidence that they work and achieve what we want. For example, the EasyPrep® is used in some parts of Europe but there is no evidence in the literature that it actually works. We ought to be cautious about what we mean by liquid-based cytology and what the standards are that we expect it to achieve, rather than talking about it as something generic.

Richart: I would like to introduce the topic of automated screening. There are two devices at present, one manufactured by TriPath and one by Cytyc.

To use the Cytyc device the laboratory must use Cytyc's proprietary stain, which is almost stoichiometric for nuclear DNA but looks like a Papanicolaou stain, to enable the smear to be examined microscopically with no change in criteria.

The device has been approved by the US Food and Drug Administration (FDA) and is expected to be marketed in the second quarter of 2003. Using the automated device, cytotechnologists perform as well as or better than screening manually and their throughput is doubled. The data that Dr Cuzick presented are compelling. A Papanicolaou smear and adjunctive HPV DNA testing is likely to be state of the art in the immediate future but the Papanicolaou smear adds less than 10% to the sensitivity. I would expect to see this method evolve into one that uses HPV DNA testing as the primary screen with HPV DNA positive patients having the Papanicolaou smear screened using an automated screener.

Cuzick: I agree – that is what I said. Liquid-based cytology is clearly the platform; the only issue is cost. Once you have that, all these things are made possible. My view is also that we will have to target primary screening.

Richart: With respect to cost, at the moment these things are being bought in very small numbers, which means that they are expensive. If you go to any manufacturer and ask for 30 million of something a year, all of a sudden testing becomes much less expensive. In fact, most companies at present use 'market pricing' and the cost will vary from one country to another. You should not base the cost analysis on current retail prices, as is commonly done. You have to find out what the price would be if you ordered 30 million tests a year: that would give a totally different price.

Singer: In a way, this is thinking the unthinkable and getting rid of cytology, or downgrading it. I know that there are data on this but what percentage of the total study would be positive then? Would it be 20% or 25% of women who would be HPV-positive and on whom you would then just do cytology?

Cuzick: Yes. In our study, which started at the age of 30 years, it is under 10% who are positive. If you were to use it as the primary screen and start from the age of 25 years, it would go up a little, but you would never have more than 15% positive in any European population – anywhere except the developing world.

Cuzick: If 85% of them are negative, you do not need to see them for five years. You do cytology more frequently on that 15%.

Richart: If you assume Dr Cusick's 15% HPV DNA positive rate and use an automated screener, the number of cytotechnologists needed will decrease by 90% for smears in women over 30 years.

Tidy: Just to be controversial, when you set out to do a screening test, you are supposed to know the natural history of the condition and have some form of treatment available, and be able to impact on that. For cervical cytology and cervical intraepithelial neoplasia (CIN), we are pretty well there and the whole screening programme is based on that. What we are saying is that we are using HPV as a surrogate test. If you put HPV into a screening test then, yes, you can detect HPV, but we do not actually know a tremendous amount about its natural history – although Kieran Woodman's paper is extremely lucid.[3]

A by-product of being HPV-positive is that you might have high-grade CIN, and you need another way to detect it. You need the cytology because, if everyone goes to colposcopy, everyone will be treated, because colposcopic recognition of CIN is poor. You then have a fundamental public health issue because women are now being screened for a sexually transmissible virus that is known to cause cancer in some women. 'We have no way of curing you, and you might get rid of it one day. And, by the way, we might find some high-grade CIN, but that might help us manage the screening programme.'

There is no evidence that HPV testing reduces the incidence or mortality from cervical screening. The important point about HPV testing is that you may be able to manage patients within the screening programme more efficiently. This is a fundamental change in what women will expect from their cervical screening programme, but they have to be aware that they will be having a test for a sexually transmissible virus – a by-product of which is that you will recognise some women with high-grade disease who you would not otherwise have recognised with cervical cytology. That is a fundamental change.

Cuzick: Some fundamental education needs to take place. First of all, borderline cytology is not very different from HPV and it is a manifestation, in some cases, of a sexually transmitted disease. In fact, all that cytology is telling you when it is accurate is that there is a virus around. You could say now that screening is actually detecting sexually transmitted diseases, but we are seeing the psychological abnormalities rather than the DNA abnormalities.

The whole point about HPV testing is not only that it will be more efficient and cheaper, ultimately, but it will actually be a better test because it does not miss things. Half of the invasive cancers now are actually missed by cytology, but we would expect virtually none of those to be missed by HPV. If you go back and do archival smears on the ones that have been missed, they are all HPV-positive, even using an archival smear.

It is not just a question of changing thinking, although that clearly needs to take place. You are actually talking about the fundamental change of screening for what is causing the disease and it is important that you do not over-react. We know a great deal about the natural history and that, even in older women, most of these lesions regress. It is important not to over-react, just as it is important not to over-react to a borderline smear. If you just sensibly use what we know about the natural history, there is an enormous gain to be made, both in the quality of the programme and benefits to the women and in the costs.

Sasieni: Although women need to be educated about HPV, in many areas of medicine people have tests without really knowing what they are being tested for. This happens all the time: you give blood, and half a dozen tests are written down about what is going to happen. You are told that your tests were normal, but you are not given the individual test results. It is possible, although probably unlikely, that screening could happen in the same way. This is pretty much what happens in antenatal screening, where you have a quadruple test but you only receive one result – you have either tested positive or negative. You could, however, have a batch of tests, with a positive or negative result for each.

It is not necessarily the case that you have to tell women that they have a sexually transmitted disease – that would be stupid. Second, although in theory we would like to know about the natural history before introducing screening, that is some kind of ideal. It would have been ridiculous to say that we should not have had cervical screening for the last 20 or 30 years because we did not properly understand the natural history. In that time, thousands of lives have been saved by the screening programme. We understand far more and, of course, HPV infection is one of those things that we now understand about the natural history, and it happens right at the beginning.

Kieran Woodman's study[3] on HPV infection in teenagers is interesting, although it has very little relevance to screening because no one is saying that teenagers should be screened for HPV.

Prendiville: It is reasonable to assume that if HPV recognises the borderline cases, that is doing the same thing. However, if you use liquid-based cytology, the Edinburgh data suggest that the borderline cases come down to two or three percent, whereas if we are looking at women aged 25 years or 30 years old, the number of women with HPV would be fairly large compared to that, at 15–20%.

The arguments in favour of recognising women at risk of developing cancer by using HPV are compelling. I do not think that we should dismiss the genuine problem of identifying large numbers of women with a virus that is sexually transmitted – we should not ignore that, and we have to deal with it. If we are using HPV as a primary screening test, we need to develop a strategy for dealing with the real problem of telling a large number of women that they have an oncogenic or HPV infection. We should not say that. We should either offer to repeat the test and reassure the women that it has disappeared, or diminish the impact of it in some educational way. I do not quite know how we should do that, but we have to tackle that problem.

Deery: I have a question for Professor Herrington and Dr Cuzick. If you look at the HPV data according to the different ways in which you can assess the presence of HPV DNA, first of all you routinely find that the polymerase chain reaction (PCR) data for high-risk types, even when quite comprehensive, are measurably less than the return from signal amplification from high risk. That is the first point – that PCR appears to be less sensitive.

Cuzick: That is not true.

Deery: I will quote papers to you if you like. The latest paper in *JAMA* from Koutsky demonstrates that exactly.

My other question is why there is such variability, even though it is fairly impressive for sensitivity? Why is there such variability for high-grade disease within the available Hybrid Capture® data? The latest Koutsky paper suggests that it is 80–90% sensitive for CIN3 by comparison with liquid-based cytology, which is just over 60%, but that is quite different from some of the figures that you have presented (Chapter 10). If you look at the literature carefully, you can see that there is still a fairly broad spread of data apparently coming from the same test in relation to high-grade disease detection.

Herrington: The first point you made about PCR and Hybrid Capture II is untrue. It depends on who is doing the test and how experienced they are with the various modalities. If you are properly trained in Hybrid Capture II, and you have not done much PCR, then you would probably find your sensitivity with Hybrid Capture II is greater. The converse is also true. Atilla Lorincz demonstrates quite clearly that, if you are properly trained in Hybrid Capture II, you can achieve extremely good inter-laboratory agreement in terms of sensitivities.

With regard to the second point, which is that the sensitivity for the detection of high-grade disease varies according to who is doing the test, this comes back to the same thing. It depends on the level of training and the performance of a particular laboratory. When you look at carefully controlled laboratories that have been appropriately trained and done a good deal of this sort of work, the sensitivities are pretty much the same.

Cuzick: The HART study is a good example, where we have five different places across the UK and two different laboratories. The age-specific positivity of HPV is virtually identical across all of these, and the sensitivity is virtually identical across them. Many of the differences relate to the fact that you are actually dealing with different populations and often it is just the fact that the ages are different. If you look at younger populations, there will be much more transient infection and the positivity of HPV will be higher and the positive predictive value will be lower. However, the sensitivities are generally now all coming in at above 95%, in virtually all the modern studies with Hybrid Capture II.

Deery: The latest paper I quoted was is in *JAMA* in August.[4] But now we come to it: who should do Hybrid Capture II testing? When you are talking about implementing a screening test, who should do it? Do you need controls? Do you need quality assurance? Do you need a whole tranche of measures? Or does it not matter? At the moment, it is being sold as though it does not matter – whoever does it, does it.

Cuzick: You clearly need some quality control. It is rather less stringent. A laboratory needs to be trained and a panel of samples needs to be taken every year. It is really a fairly minor thing, but it needs to be done – any laboratory test needs some kind of quality control by external sources, regardless of how simple the test is.

Richart: Interlaboratory reproducibility for PCR is about 70%. For Hybrid Capture II it is about 98% and Papanicolaou smears are probably about 30%. For ASCUS and LSIL Papanicolaou smears, it is substantially less.

The data that were presented at the FDA included multiple studies involving about 45 000 women. As Dr Cuzick said, virtually all of the studies had the same results.[5]

McGoogan: In looking at strategies for using HPV testing, we must bear in mind that the peak detection rate for CIN3 currently is 25 to 30 years of age and the shift is tending to go downwards. We need to bear that in mind when looking at the strategies.

Shepherd: Professor Singer, how accurate is this new piece of equipment at looking at the endocervical canal? Are you able to angle your end probe to assess the lesions, which are probably the most difficult for us to detect – especially when we have borderline or inflammatory smears.

Singer: That has worried us from the very beginning. However, with most of the adenolesions, when you evert the end probe, you will find that 70–80% of the adenocarcinomas *in situ* – the ones that you are looking for – are visible in the lower part of the endocervix. As such, you can direct the probe to them. We angled it so that you can access that region.

Pushing it right up into the high endocervix is not possible with this. The new device that is being developed at the moment is like a cryoprobe, with a nozzle and then a shoulder that will detect lesions on the ectocervix. The nozzle will then get those endocervical ones. We have picked up most of the endocervical lesions with it.

Dr Tay, have you had similar experience in Singapore? Your results are identical.

Tay: We have not actually encountered any endocervical lesions high in the canal. But those adenocarcinomas that happen to be in the endocervical canal also extend quite far down, so there is no question of detecting it and also, with eversion of the cervix, which allows you to probe the lower end of the canal satisfactorily.

Tidy: All the studies to date have taken place in relatively high-prevalence settings. Are there any truly large studies of it in the screening situation? Belinson *et al.*[6] reported a study where one of these techniques was taken out into China and the specificity was 9%, having been 96% in the colposcopy clinic. Are there any really large studies to answer that question?

Singer: Belinson's study was conducted with one of the fluorescent techniques and not with TruScan‰ (Johnson & Johnson, Brunswick NJ, USA). We have taken it out to Brazil, where it has performed very well.

In the study I showed, about 500 women were volunteers who came through a screening programme. We are in the process of doing that and there are three large screening studies going on – one in San Diego, one in Barcelona and a major one in Italy. That is where it needs to be done, but you need large numbers of patients. In Singapore, there is also screening.

Tay: Yes, our population of 650 patients were purely screening – they were volunteers. We advertised for the women to come and they were screened with colposcopy at the end of the study.

References

1.   Davey DD, Austin M, Birdsong G, Buck HW, Cox JT, Darragh TM, *et al*. ASCCP Patient Management Guidelines, Pap test specimen adequacy and quality indicators. *Am J Clin Pathol* 2002;118:714–18.
2.   Kitchener HC, Patnick J, Vessey MP. LBC Pilot Studies using Human Papilloma Virus (HPV) Testing as Triage. London: NHS Cervical Screening Programme.
3.   Woodman CBJ, Collins S, Winter H, Bailey A, Ellis J, Prior P, *et al*. Natural history of cervical human papillomavirus infection in young women: a longitudinal cohort study. *Lancet* 2001;357:1831–6.
4.   Solomon D, Davey D, Kurman R, Moriarty A, O'Connor D, Prey M, *et al*. The 2001 Bethesda system: terminology for reporting results of cervical cytology. *JAMA* 2002;287:2114–19.
5.   Lorincz A, Richart RM. HPV DNA Testing as an adjunct to cytology in cervical screening programs. *Arch Pathol* (in press).
6.   Belinson J, Qiao YL, Pretorius R, Zhang WH, Elson P, Li L, *et al*. Shanxi Province Cervical Cancer Screening Study: A cross-sectional comparative trial of multiple techniques to detect cervical neoplasia. *Gynecol Oncol* 2001;83:439–44.

SECTION 4

NEW APPROACHES TO DETECTING LOWER GENITAL TRACT NEOPLASIA II

Chapter 13

The role of molecular markers in the detection of human papillomavirus-related lesions

Ralph M Richart

Introduction

Cervical cancer is the second leading cause of death from cancer among women worldwide, and in many developing countries it is the leading cause of death from cancer among women aged 35–45 years. It is preceded by an intraepithelial precursor stage at which the development of invasion can be prevented. Virtually all developed countries have initiated screening programmes using the Papanicolaou smear to detect these precursors (and invasive cancers). Most Papanicolaou smear screening programmes in Europe and Canada are 'organised', in a scheme through which healthcare authorities track women eligible for cervical cancer screening and, through invitations to be screened and incentives for screening provided to healthcare providers, the majority of women have a Papanicolaou smear either at or close to the intervals specified by the healthcare authorities.

In the USA, the screening programme is 'voluntary' but most of the eligible women in the population are screened nonetheless. The screening interval varies from an annual one in the USA to as long as three years in Europe and, in some countries, five years. The efficacy of a screening programme in reducing the incidence of and death rates from cervical cancer depends principally upon widespread population coverage but also, to a lesser degree, upon the screening interval and the age at which screening is initiated in each country. Nonetheless, the impact of cervical cancer screening has been well documented and has resulted in a striking decrease in the incidence of and deaths from cervical cancer in virtually all countries in which Papanicolaou smear programmes have been initiated. The contrast between cervical cancer incidence and death rates in screened versus unscreened populations is dramatic and lends further support to the contention that the programmes themselves are responsible for decreasing cervical cancer incidence and death rates.

The Papanicolaou smear test

Despite the enormous benefits that have accrued from Papanicolaou smear screening programmes, the Papanicolaou smear is a 50-year-old technology that relies upon the healthcare providers securing an adequate sample from the cervix and delivering that cellular sample to a slide that is then sent to a laboratory, screened by a cytotechnologist and diagnosed by a pathologist. It has been known since the advent of

Papanicolaou smear screening that the smear detects the majority of cervical cancers and precursors but that there is an unavoidable false negative fraction. It was not widely appreciated until recently, however, that the sensitivity of the Papanicolaou smear for high-grade cervical intraepithelial neoplasia (CIN) and invasive cancer is about 50–60% and its sensitivity for lower-grade lesions is even lower. The study by Fahey et al.[1] and the document published by the Agency for Health Care Policy and Research meta-analysis[2] brought the low sensitivity of the Papanicolaou smear into sharp focus and compelled investigators to re-examine the use of the conventional Papanicolaou smear in the detection of cervical cancer and its precursors. Alternative collection and specimen preparation techniques using liquid-based samples were developed in order to overcome some of the sampling problems associated with the conventional Papanicolaou smear. It has been accepted that liquid-based Papanicolaou smear samples have a higher sensitivity, a higher specificity and a lower unsatisfactory rate than conventional smears. It is estimated that the sensitivity of the ThinPrep® (Cytyc Corporation, Boxborough, MA) liquid-based cytology sample is about 85% for the detection of CIN3 or more and that it substantially increases the detection rate of low-grade squamous intraepithelial lesions(LSIL), high-grade squamous intraepithelial lesion (HSIL), invasive cancer and adenocarcinoma, at the same time as it decreases the unsatisfactory rate and the borderline or atypical squamous cell of undetermined significance (ASCUS) rate.[3,4] Even so, about 15% of cases of high-grade CIN and invasive cancers are missed on a single sample using liquid-based cytology.

Despite the relatively low sensitivity of the conventional Papanicolaou smear, cervical cancer can largely be prevented because the transit time from low-grade CIN to invasive cancer extends over years or decades, affording multiple opportunities to detect the cervical cancer precursor, provided that the Papanicolaou smear is repeated at regular intervals. The minority of women in whom the transit time to cancer is short may not have their CIN lesions detected even with periodic screening. These women are included in the 'interval cancer cases' that occur between regularly scheduled Papanicolaou smears and those women with interval cancers, as well as those in the health system who are not screened or who fail to present themselves to the health system for screening, make up the roster of women with undetected cancers, despite the widespread availability of screening. Because of these 'screening failures', it is widely recognised that there is a need both to include all women in the screening programme and to introduce a more sensitive test for cervical cancer and its precursors in order to prevent interval cancers.

The majority of women who are detected as having an abnormal Papanicolaou smear in the course of a screening programme are under 35 years old and have a diagnosis of ASCUS or LSIL. Papanicolaou smears are prepared from a sample that varies in its representation of the cervical lesion and Papanicolaou smear diagnoses represent only the least severe abnormality. A substantial proportion of patients with an LSIL Papanicolaou smear will, in fact, have a high-grade CIN lesion and even patients with an ASCUS Papanicolaou smear may have a high-grade lesion or even invasive cancer undiagnosed on the Papanicolaou smear.

Prior to the recognition that about 90% of patients with LSIL would clear the lesion spontaneously, most patients with low-grade CIN were treated to preclude its progression to a higher-grade lesion or even invasive carcinoma. According to the guidelines put forward by the Consensus Committee of the American Society for Colposcopy and Cervical Pathology,[5] patients with LSIL Papanicolaou smears should be colposcoped to rule out high-grade CIN or invasive cancer, after which the preferred method of management is prospective follow-up with human papillomavirus (HPV) DNA testing or a Papanicolaou smear. Treating patients with LSIL is an acceptable management approach.

There are, at present, no clinically useful markers for predicting which patients with an LSIL Papanicolaou smear will remit spontaneously and which will progress to a higher-grade lesion. Only through prospective follow-up and clinical observation is it possible to determine which patients are at risk of developing high-grade CIN or cancer. It would be useful to have a surrogate marker for progression so that patients with low-grade CIN lesions that are destined to progress could be identified early in the management process and treated appropriately. HPV causes cervical cancer and its precursors. More than 100 papillomaviruses have been identified, of which about 40 infect the male and female anogenital tract and about 15 confer oncogenic risk. When women are infected with HPV, the virus may remain latent and divide only when the cell divides. Alternatively, it may produce a productive viral infection in which viral replication occurs independently of cell division, or it may produce or develop into a true cancer precursor in which cell division is no longer under the control of the normal positive and negative feedback loops.

HPV is a DNA tumour virus that has eight genes or open reading frames. The six early genes encode for proteins that are important in the regulation of viral production, whereas the two late genes encode for the capsid protein that is wrapped around the double-stranded, circular DNA viral genome after it is synthesised. Two of the early genes (E1 and E2) encode for proteins that are important in regulating two of the other early genes (E6 and E7). The E6 and E7 encoded oncogenes produce proteins that are largely responsible for allowing the virus to replicate within the cell and also largely responsible for the virus's oncogenic properties. The HPV E6 gene product binds to the tumour-suppressor gene, p53, identifying it for ubiquitination and accelerated degradation. The HPV E7 encoded gene product complexes with the Rb tumour suppressor gene protein, leading to the upregulation of an E2F-like transcription factor that moves the normally quiescent cells in the suprabasal portion of the epithelium into the Gap 1 (G1) and synthesis (S) phases of the cell cycle. Largely because of the abrogation of the functions of the p53 and pRb proteins, the effect of an HPV infection on the cell is devastating. Multiple growth transcription factors are no longer held in check, the cells become immortalised, cell cycle checkpoints are disrupted, mutations are uncovered, p53's proofreading of the genome disappears, and aneuploidy and neoplasia result.

Markers

Numerous investigators have described markers[6] that are based on the known effects of HPV on the cell[7,8] and either observed or conjectural associations between specific nucleotides or proteins that are affected by the papillomavirus's disruption of the cell cycle. The intent of these studies is to identify markers that can be used either as an adjunct to or in place of the Papanicolaou smear for screening for cervical cancer or its precursors or to identify markers that predict the biology and natural history of established lesions such as LSIL.

Human papillomavirus DNA

Because it has been established that all cervical cancers and their precursors are caused by HPV, many investigators have looked to the detection of HPV DNA in cervical samples to identify women with an HPV infection or an HPV-induced neoplasm. The HPV DNA detection studies have included many assay systems, some with amplification and others without. Hybrid Capture® II (HCII) (Digene Corporation, Gaithersburg, MD, USA) is the most commonly used HPV DNA detection system and is the only commercially available US Food and Drug Agency (FDA)-approved system for HPV DNA testing. The company recently applied for FDA approval for the use of HCII adjunctively with the Papanicolaou smear, and summary data that were presented at the FDA hearing included prospective follow-up data on more than 40 000 women from eight centres.[9] The sensitivity of HCII adjunctively with a Papanicolaou smear exceeded that of a Papanicolaou smear alone for detecting CIN3 or more in all eight studies and was statistically significantly better in six of the eight studies. What is even more important from a screening perspective, the negative predictive value of HCII plus a Papanicolaou smear for CIN3 or more exceeded the Papanicolaou smear alone in all eight studies and was statistically significantly more sensitive in seven of the eight studies. HCII or other HPV DNA testing or typing assays does not predict prospectively which patients are at risk for progressing to neoplasia but, as the most important variable in distinguishing those patients at risk of progression from those patients whose lesions will remit spontaneously or remain quiescent is the persistent shedding of oncogenic-risk virus, HPV DNA testing can be used for prospective follow-up to monitor persistence or remission.

Ploidy measurements

It has been known for decades that the morphological atypia that is the hallmark of cervical dysplasia, SIL or CIN is a result of changes in ploidy. As a consequence of HPV infection and disruption of the cell cycle, HPV-infected nuclei become enlarged, hyperchromatic and atypical – features that are associated with heteroploidy. Although this feature of HPV infection is key to the cytological detection of HPV-related lesions – both cytologically and histologically – polyploidisation occurs in tissues other than the epithelium of the lower anogenital tract,[10] where it is also accompanied by nuclear enlargement, hyperchromasia and atypia. In studies dating back several decades,[11,12] it was reported that low-grade lesions were principally polyploid, that high-grade lesions were aneuploid and that aneuploidy was a good predictor of biological behaviour. The surrogate histological marker for polyploidy is the tripolar mitosis and the surrogate marker for aneuploidy is the highly atypical metaphase, particularly the three-group metaphase. Despite the high degree of correlation reported between ploidy level and subsequent clinical course, this marker was never widely used – perhaps because it is a complex, difficult and expensive procedure to measure ploidy in tissue sections. Ploidy analysis using flow cytometry in a fluid-based cytological sample does not provide the precision that can be achieved in histological sections.

HPV mRNA analysis

Because HPV E6, E7 open reading frames are unique and not found in the normal cell and because mRNA is internally amplified in the cell, the detection of HPV open reading frame E6, E7 encoded mRNA is a tempting target as a marker. Because successful viral replication depends upon the expression of the viral E6 and E7 early genes and the maintenance of the neoplastic state depends upon the continued expression of these genes, E6 and E7 transcriptional activity is always present in the HPV-infected cell. Furthermore, the pattern of gene expression varies with the severity of the lesion, with E6, E7 encoded transcripts being higher, in general, in high-grade than in low-grade lesions. Although most investigators have tested for mRNA using polymerase chain reaction from cells collected in a fluid-based system or using *in situ* hybridisation,[13] Patterson *et al.*[14] approached the problem using a modification of a previously described technique designed to detect HIV, which employs simultaneous immunofluorescence and ultrasensitive fluorescence *in situ* hybridisation in fluid-based cytology samples using the high through-put capabilities of flow cytometry. As with other putative markers, early studies of E6, E7 mRNA have had high sensitivity and good specificity for detecting cervical HPV-related lesions, but larger numbers of studied subjects are required to evaluate this system adequately.

Cell cycle proliferation markers

Proliferating cell nuclear antigen and Ki-67 have been extensively studied.[15-20] These antigens are recognised cell proliferation markers and appear to have some utility as an immunohistochemical stain in equivocal histological lesions. However, as they stain both proliferating cells and neoplastic cells, they may not prove useful as a screening marker or a predictor of biological behaviour.

Altered genes, proteins and other substances

Many immunohistochemical studies have been published in which genes and proteins have been examined for upregulation or downregulation for their use as a potential marker. These include HER2/neu,[20,21] CEA,[22] MN,[23,24] c-myc,[22] p53,[25] c-erb B-2,[26] various cyclins,[22,27-29] epidermal growth factor receptor,[30,31] as well as iron transferrin receptor proteins[31] and hypermethylation of p16.[32] Although there was a correlation between the presence of these potential markers and the presence of HPV-related lesions, the sensitivity and specificity of most of them were insufficient to be clinically useful, and there have been few follow-up studies since the initial publications.

p16[INK4A]

The detection of p16 overexpression as a specific marker for HPV-related lesions of the cervix has been described by Sano,[33] by Doeberitz[34] and Klaes *et al.*[35] p16 and other cyclin-dependent kinase inhibitors regulate the activity of cyclin-dependent kinase (CDK) 4 and CDK 6. In many cancers, p16 is inactivated and its gene product is not expressed. The consequence of the inactivation of p16 is enhanced activity of CDK 4 and CDK 6 and phosphorylation and inactivation of pRb. However, when pRb is directly inactivated by complexing with the HPV oncoprotein, E7, it can no longer function as a tumour suppressor protein. Since p16 expression is necessary for pRb's negative feedback control, reduced or lost pRb should lead to increased levels of p16 in HPV-related lesions.

Using antibodies to p16, Doeberitz[34] and Klaes *et al.*[35] reported a high degree of correlation between the immunohistochemical detection of p16 in tissue sections and the presence of oncogenic-risk HPV-induced CIN lesions. In their studies, all lesions graded at CIN2 or higher were p16 positive. Others, using different antibodies, have reported conflicting results, and Nuovo *et al.*[32] and Lin *et al.*[36] reported hypermethylation of p16 localised only to neoplastic cervical cells with loss of p16 protein expression.

Cdc6 and mini-chromosome maintenance proteins

Cdc6 proteins are components of the prereplication complex that is essential for the initiation of DNA synthesis.[37] Cdc6[38-41] is an unstable protein with a half-life of about five minutes. It is expressed just prior to the G1–S phase transition, and its abundance is downregulated by mitotic cyclins and CDKs and upregulated by CDK inhibitors. The abundance of Cdc6 declines after DNA synthesis is initiated and checkpoint controls are released, permitting the cell to enter mitosis. The protein is ubiquitinated and destroyed to prevent multiple rounds of DNA replication in a single cell cycle. Cdc6 must be newly synthesised after each replication cycle before a new synthetic cycle can begin.

Minichromosome maintenance (MCM) proteins are a group of related proteins that are also part of the complex that is required to initiate cell division. MCM proteins 2–7 are major components of the prereplication complex that 'licenses' chromatin for DNA replication. Although MCM proteins are abundant during all phases of the cell cycle, they are lost following exit from the cell cycle and must be resynthesised. Because high-grade CIN and invasive cancer cells functionally never leave the mitotic cycle due to the disruption of the normal control mechanisms for the conduct of cell division, both Cdc6 and MCM proteins are abundant and occupy all cellular compartments in neoplastic epithelia. In normal tissues, these proteins are restricted to the proliferative compartments, serving to distinguish between the two.

Williams et al.[42] and Freeman et al.[43] have studied antibodies to Cdc6 and MCM-encoded proteins as markers for cervical neoplasia and reported a high degree of sensitivity and specificity for the detection of CIN in both histological sections and Papanicolaou smears. Studies by others suggest that these markers may be useful in other neoplasms as well.[44,45]

Discussion

The complex processes that govern the conduct of the normal cell replication cycle are becoming better understood and the interrelationships between various genes and gene products have been clarified as well. Many markers have been examined for their potential use as either primary markers to be used in screening programmes for cervical neoplasia or as secondary markers to differentiate between patients with low-grade lesions who are likely to progress and those lesions that are likely to remit. Many of the markers that have been examined do not adequately distinguish between normal, reparative and inflammatory changes and HPV-related lesions. Although many investigators have reported a correlation between the presence of such markers and HPV-related lesions, there is neither sufficient specificity nor sufficient sensitivity to allow them to be used in a clinically useful way. Similarly, although there is both upregulation and downregulation of a number of cellular proteins associated with HPV infection or with disruption of the cell cycle caused by HPV infection, many of these changes are inconstant or are also found in benign proliferative or reparative conditions, thus potentially confounding their use for screening. More recent studies have concentrated on specific cell-cycle markers or on proteins that are uniquely and reproducibly disrupted following HPV infection or cervical neoplasia. Even these markers, however, are difficult to evaluate because of conflicting reports of their predictive value. Few, if any, of the molecular markers other than HPV DNA testing have been developed to the point that a standard test can be examined in a large number of women by several independent investigators. The published studies usually involve testing only small numbers of women and, although the studies show promise, a better evaluation of that promise will have to await further studies.

It is possible that there is no magic marker and that no single test will offer sufficient sensitivity and specificity by itself for it to be used for the myriad applications for which markers are needed. It may be that one or more screening tests may be used to identify a population at risk and that this population may require testing by one or more additional secondary markers to provide useful clinical information that can be used in screening programmes or for the study and prediction of natural history. The use of protein chips or gene expression chips containing multiple markers might be required to provide optimal clinical guidance.

References

1. Fahey MT, Irwig L, Macaskill P. Meta-analysis of Pap test accuracy. *Am J Epidemiol* 1995;141:680–89.
2. Agency for Health Care Policy and Research. *Evaluation of Cervical Cytology, Summary, Evidence Report/Technology Assessment, No. 5.* Rockville MD: AHCPR; 1999 [www.ahrq.gov/clinic/epcsums/cervsumm.htm].
3. Bernstein SJ, Sanchez-Ramos L, Ndubisi B. Liquid-based cervical cytologic smear study and conventional Papanicolaou smears: a metaanalysis of prospective studies comparing cytologic diagnosis and sample adequacy. *Am J Obstet Gynecol* 2001;185:308–17.
4. Ashfaq R, Gibbons D, Vella C, Saboorian MH, Iliya F. ThinPrep Pap test. Accuracy for glandular disease. *Acta Cytol* 1999, 43:81–5.
5. Wright TC Jr, Cox JT, Massad LS, Twiggs LB, Wilkinson EJ. 2001 consensus guidelines for the management of women with cervical cytological abnormalities. *JAMA* 2002;287:2120–9.
6. Whitfield ML, Sherlock G, Saldanha AJ, Murray JI, Ball CA, Alexander KE, *et al.* Identification of genes periodically expressed in their human cell cycle and their expression in tumors. *Molecular Biology of the Cell* 2002;13:1977–2000.
7. Clarke B, Chetty R. Cell cycle aberrations in the pathogenesis of squamous cell carcinoma of the uterine cervix. *Gynecol Oncol* 2001;82:238–46.
8. Southern SA, Herrington CS. Disruption of cell cycle control by human papillomaviruses with special reference to cervical carcinoma. *Int J Gynecol Cancer* 2000;10:263–74.
9. Lorincz A, Richart RM. Will HPV DNA testing replace the Pap? *Arch Pathol* (in press).
10. Wagner D, Richart RM. Polyploidy in the human endometrium with the Arias-Stella reaction. *Arch Pathol* 1968;101:200–5.
11. Wilbanks GD, Richart RM, Terner JY. DNA content of cervical intra-epithelial neoplasia studied by two-wavelength Feulgen cytophotometry. *Am J Obstet Gynecol* 1967;98:792–9.
12. Fu YS, Huang I, Beaudenon S, Ionesco M, Barrasso R, de Brux J, *et al.* Correlative study of human papillomavirus DNA, histopathology, and morphometry in cervical condyloma and intra-epithelial neoplasia. *Int J Gynecol Pathol* 1988;7:297–307.
13. Lamarcq L, Deeds J, Ginzinger D, Perry J, Padmanabha S, Smith-McCune K. Measurements of human papillomavirus transcripts by real time quantitative reverse transcription-polymerase chain reaction in samples collected for cervical cancer screening. *J Mol Diagn* 2002;4:97–102.
14. Patterson BK, Derbin D, Richart RM, Cox T, Pollina R, McCray N, *et al.* High throughput cervical cancer screening using intracellular HPV E6, E7 mRNA quantification by flow cytometry. Personal communication.
15. Cina SJ, Richardson MS, Austin RM, Kurman RJ. Immunohistochemical staining for Ki-67 antigen, carcinoembryonic antigen, and p53 in the differential diagnosis of glandular lesions of the cervix. *Mod Pathol* 1997;10:176–80.
16. al-Saleh W, Delvenne P, Greimers R, Fridman V, Doyen J, Boniver J. Assessment of Ki-67 antigen immunostaining in squamous intraepithelial lesions of the uterine cervix. Correlation with the histologic grade and human papillomavirus type. *Am J Clin Pathol* 1995;104:154–60.
17. Boon ME, Howard CF, Van Velzen D. PCNA independence of Ki-67 expression in HPV infection. *Cell Biol Int* 1993;17:1001–4.
18. Resnick M, Lester S, Tate JE, Sheets EE, Sparks C, Crum CP. Viral and histopathologic correlates of MN and MIB-1 expression in cervical intraepithelial neoplasia. *Hum Pathol* 1996;27:234–9.
19. Costa MJ. MN and Ki67 (MIB-1) in uterine cervix carcinoma: novel biomarkers with divergent utility. *Hum Pathol* 1996;27:217–19.
20. Bulten J, Vander Laak JAWM, Gemmink JH, Pahlplatz MMM, deWilde PCM, Hanselaar AGJM. MIB-1, a promising marker for the classification of cervical intra-epithelial neoplasia. *J Pathol* 1999;178:268–73.
21. Cirisano FD, Karlan BY. The role of the HER-2/neu oncogene in gynecologic cancers. *J Soc Gynecol Investig* 1996;3:99–105.
22. Dellas A, Schultheiss E, Leivas MR, Moch H, Torhorst J. Association of p27Kip1, cyclin E and c-

myc expression with progression and prognosis in HPV-positive cervical neoplasms. *Anticancer Res* 1998;18:3991–8.

23.   Liao SY, Brewer C, Zavada J, Pastorek J, Pastorekove S, Manetta A, *et al.* Identification of the MN antigen as a diagnostic biomarker of cervical intra-epithelial squamous and glandular neoplasia and cervical carcinomas. *Am J Pathol* 1994;145:598–609.

24.   Liao SY, Stanbridge EJ. Expression of MN/CA9 protein in Papanicolaou smears containing atypical glandular cells of undetermined significance is a diagnostic biomarker of cervical dysplasia and neoplasia. *Cancer* 2000;88:1108–21.

25.   Lie AK, Skarsvag S, Skomedal H, Haugen OA, Holm R. Expression of p53, MDM2, and p21 proteins in high-grade cervical intraepithelial neoplasia and relationship to human papillomavirus infection. *Int J Gynecol Pathol* 1999;18:5–11.

26.   Altavilla G, Castellan L, Wabersich J, Marchetti M, Onnis A. Prognostic significance of epidermal growth factor receptor (EGFR) and c-erbB-2 protein overexpression in adenocarcinoma of the uterine cervix. *Eur J Gynaecol Oncol* 1996;17:267–70.

27.   Nichols GE, Williams ME, Gaffey MJ, Stoler MH. Cyclin D1 gene expression in human cervical neoplasia. *Mod Pathol* 1996;9:418–25.

28.   Cho NH, Kim YT, Kim JW. Correlation between GI cyclins and HPV in the uterine cervix. *Int J Gynecol Pathol* 1997;16:339–47.

29.   Quade BJ, Park JJ, Crum CP, Sun D, Dutta A. *In vivo* cyclin E expression as a marker for early cervical neoplasia. *Mod Pathol* 1998;11:1238–46.

30.   Hale RJ, Buckley CH, Gullick WJ, Fox H, Williams J, Wilcox FL. Prognostic value of epidermal growth factor receptor expression in cervical carcinoma. *J Clin Pathol* 1993;46:149–53.

31.   Keesee SK, Domanik R, Patterson B. Fully automated proteomic detection of cervical dysplasia. *Anal Quant Cytol Histol* 2002;24:137–46.

32.   Nuovo GJ, Plaia TW, Belinsky SA, Baylin SB, Herman JG. *In situ* detection of the hypermethylation-induced inactivation of the p16 gene as an early event in oncogenesis. *Proc Natl Acad Sci USA* 1999;96:12754–9.

33.   Sano T, Oyama T, Kashiwabara K, Fukuda T, Nakajima T. Expression status of p16 protein is associated with human papillomavirus oncogenic potential in cervical and genital lesions. *Am J Pathol* 1998;153:1741–8.

34.   von Knebel Doeberitz M. New molecular tools for efficient screening of cervical cancer. *Dis Markers* 2001;17:123–8.

35.   Klaes R, Friedrich T, Spitkovsky D, Rodder R, Rudy W, Petry U, *et al.* Overexpression of $p16^{INK4A}$ as a specific marker for dysplastic and neoplastic epithelial cells of the cervix uteri. *Int J Cancer* 2001;92:276–84.

36.   Lin WM, Ashfaq R, Michalopulos EA, Maitra A, Gazdar AF, Muller CY. Molecular Papanicolaou tests in the twenty-first century: molecular analyses with fluid-based Papanicolaou technology. *Am J Obstet Gynecol* 2000;183:39–45.

37.   Newlon CS. Putting it all together: building a prereplicative complex. *Cell* 1997;91:717–20.

38.   Williams RS, Shohet RV, Stillman B. A human protein related to yeast Cdc6p. *Proc Natl Acad Sci USA* 1997;94:142–7.

39.   Yan Z, DeGregori J, Shohet R, Leone G, Stillman B, Nevins JR, *et al.* Cdc6 is regulated by E2F and is essential for DNA replication in mammalian cells. *Proc Natl Acad Sci USA* 1998, 95:3603–8.

40.   Weinreich M, Liang C, Stillman B. The Cdc6p nucleotide-binding motif is required for loading mcm proteins onto chromatin. *Proc Natl Acad Sci USA* 1999, 96:441–6.

41.   Fujita M, Yamada C, Goto H, Yokoyama N, Kuzushima K, Inagaki M, *et al.* Cell cycle regulation of human CDC6 protein: intracellular localization, interaction with the human MCM complex, and Cdc2 Kinase-mediated hyperphosphorylation. *J Biol Chem* 1999;274:25927–32.

42.   Williams GH, Romanowski P, Morris L, Madine M, Mills AD, Stoeber K, *et al.* Improved cervical smear assessment using antibodies against proteins that regulate DNA replication. *Proc Natl Acad Sci USA*1998;95:14932–7.

43.   Freeman A, Morris LS, Mills AD, Stoeber K, Laskey RA, Williams GH, *et al.* Minichromosome maintenance proteins as biological markers of dysplasia and malignancy. *Clin Cancer Res* 1999;5:2121–32.

44.   Alison MR, Hunt T, Forbes SJ. Minichromosome maintenance (MCM) proteins may be pre-cancer markers. *Gut* 2002;50:290–1.

45.   Going JJ, Keith WN, Neilson L, Stoeber K, Stuart RC, Williams GH. Aberrant expression of minichromosome maintenance proteins 2 and 5, and Ki-67 in dysplastic squamous oesophageal epithelium and Barrett's mucosa. *Gut* 2002;50:373–7.

Chapter 14

New approaches to colposcopy

Mahmood I Shafi

Introduction

Colposcopy is the examination of the cervix using a system that allows both magnification and illumination. It was first introduced in 1925 by Hans Hinselmann[1] and his objective was to detect cervical cancer at its earliest stage. He thought that with the colposcope it would be possible to detect cancer as a small ulcer or a small exophytic lesion. He soon realised that his suppositions were incorrect but nevertheless found it possible to detect changes in the cervical epithelium that fell outside the limits of normality. While colposcopy became widely practised in German-speaking and Latin American countries, it did not become popular in the English-speaking countries until the 1960s, about 20 years after the introduction of cervical cytology by Papanicolaou.[2] Its usage in the early years differs from its function today, where it is used primarily as a clinical method for the assessment of women with abnormal cervical cytology. In order to fully understand the functions of colposcopy, it is useful to have a working knowledge of cytology and histopathology (Figure 14.1).

Functions of colposcopy

All women with abnormal cervical cytology should be assessed with colposcopic examination. This allows identification of those women with a normal cervical

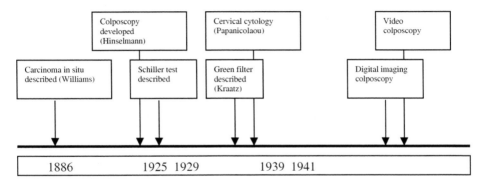

Figure 14.1 Timeline for colposcopy developments

transformation zone who are at minimal risk of cervical pathology. Where an abnormality is found, colposcopy is useful for the following purposes:

- identifying any malignant area that requires confirmation with a suitable biopsy
- recognising the cervical transformation zone
- identifying any premalignant change within the cervical transformation zone
- identifying the size and site of any abnormality
- taking biopsy of abnormal area for diagnostic purposes
- performing local treatment (excisional or ablative) for premalignant lesions
- follow-up of patients who have undergone previous treatment with a view to early recognition of residual/recurrent disease
- follow-up of patients who are managed conservatively with a surveillance programme in association with cervical cytology.

Diagnosis of invasive disease

One of the functions of colposcopic examination is to exclude malignant disease. Sometimes disease may present as obvious exophytic or ulcerative lesions. In other cases, diagnosis may be much harder and depend on the colposcopic features. Using extended (classical) colposcopy with saline gives the best assessment of the angioarchitecture, which is important if malignancy is suspected. Atypical vessels can be seen, particularly if a green filter is used at high magnification. With invasive disease, these vessels appear irregular with abruptly changing courses. The vessels are often of uneven calibre and are generally coarser than normal vessels.

While the hope is that early invasive lesions can be identified colposcopically, this is not always the case. Features associated with a higher likelihood of malignant change are large lesions with coarse changes of acetowhiteness, mosaicism and punctation. Other features to note are an irregular surface and lesions extending into the cervical canal, making full colposcopic assessment impossible. Even in those cases where disease is easily visualised, colposcopy is useful in delineating the extent of disease, particularly in terms of vaginal extension. This can influence subsequent treatment, taking into consideration the site and size of the lesion.

Diagnostic purposes

Neither cytology nor colposcopy are diagnostic. Using information on the cervical cytology report and the colposcopic findings, appropriate biopsy or treatment can be undertaken. These include the following:

- colposcopically directed punch biopsies
- excisional biopsies
- diathermy loop excision, large loop excision of transformation zone, loop electrodiathermy excision procedure
- laser excision
- knife cone biopsy
- wedge biopsy
- hysterectomy.

Whichever biopsy is used, it should be deep enough to establish the diagnosis, especially if invasive disease is suspected. Colposcopy should allow selection of the worst area to be biopsied so that significant disease is not missed. However, this is not reliable as there is considerable interobserver and intraobserver variability as to where the biopsy is taken from.[3]

Basic principles

Many types of colposcopy systems are available, but they all share certain principles. Colposcopy allows the distribution and type of abnormality to be assessed and plans can then be made for appropriate management. The colposcope is usually free standing but can be fixed to the ceiling or wall if desired. Major advances have occurred in the light source, fibre-optic cabling and refinement of the optical systems. The focal length varies from 200–300 mm, allowing the colposcopic examination to take place at a comfortable distance. Attachments can include teaching arms or video camera. A facility for a green filter allows better definition of blood vessels that appear black and prominent.[4]

Colposcopic examination can take place at a variety of magnifications, usually between six-fold and forty-fold. Three solutions are useful for the examination:

- saline – used to clean the cervix and to help in identification of abnormal vasculature

- acetic acid – 3% or 5%, used to stain epithelia. It is the pattern of this acetowhite change that forms the cornerstone of colposcopic impression. A number of parameters may be assessed, including the size of the lesion, degree of acetowhitening, the demarcation of abnormal/normal epithelia, presence of mosaic or punctation and abnormal surface structure

- Lugol's iodine (Schiller's test) – used to outline atypical epithelium, as this contains little or no glycogen and therefore will not take up the stain. Normal epithelium is glycogen-rich and will turn a dark brown colour on application of Lugol's iodine. Columnar epithelium also contains little or no glycogen and fails to take up the stain.

Colposcopic assessment continues to be a subjective assessment, and expertise is gained by a period of apprenticeship.[5] Many national colposcopy societies have introduced training programmes for colposcopy and there is now a greater emphasis on quality control. Several scoring systems have been devised for colposcopic assessment[6–8] but these have proved difficult to standardise, lack robustness when applied to the clinical situation and some remain to be validated in large prospective studies.[9]

New approaches

The new approaches to colposcopy are primarily related to the technology available for documentation, image viewing, storage and transmission. Some element of semiquantitation is feasible but not practical in a colposcopy setting.

Documentation

In the majority of clinics, line drawings are made to indicate the colposcopic abnormality. This is prone to misinterpretation over time, especially if different colposcopists make the drawings. Using the digital colposcopy format, it is technically easy to take an image of the cervix and compare this with another image taken at subsequent colposcopic examination. Digital imaging colposcopy systems have additional facilities that allow captions to be written on the images to help in documentation. With appropriate links, images can be imported from the histopathology and cytopathology, so that all appropriate information for the patient is collated. By linking the system to hospital computer record systems, routine patient information can be acquired and updated without additional input.

Digital imaging colposcopy

Digital colposcopy consists of digitally recording and processing the image using a charge couple device camera through an optical interface.[10-12] The system can interface with a network or modem, allowing remote consultation to take place with other colposcopists using conventional telephone lines. The charge couple device camera gives a high signal-to-noise ratio, excellent geometric stability, linear photometric response, a large dynamic range, high detective quantum efficiency, high spatial resolution and a high speed of data acquisition. Following digitisation, the image is displayed on a video monitor. The image can either be printed for a hard copy or it can be downloaded and stored on a computer. The system therefore allows real-time viewing, as well a facility for instant image capture. The image quality can be checked and further images taken if necessary. Areas of interest to the clinician can be enlarged and the image processed by introducing digital filters to accentuate differences in cervical morphology. The colposcopic detail can therefore be enhanced using these digital filters. Measurement facilities are available, allowing measurement and quantification of the colposcopic features such as intercapillary distance or lesion surface area. This aids basic and clinical research and can aid diagnostic accuracy by assessing the colposcopic parameters scientifically. It can also be used to assess any changes in the transformation zone, particularly in younger women where there is a desire for damage limitation, especially in those with low-grade abnormalities.

Multi-image viewing capacity is present, allowing comparison between colposcopic assessments taken chronologically or by comparison with reference images. A blink comparison in input and digital images allows serial assessments to take place for individual patients. The images can be stored on paperless filing systems but most colposcopy clinics prefer to have a hard copy for documentation purposes. The image can be stored either as a still picture or as a video of live colposcopy being undertaken. As the image is stored digitally, it can be transmitted anywhere down telephone lines, allowing the concept of telecolposcopy to be feasible (Figure 14.2).

The advantage of the digital colposcopy system is that it can facilitate clinical audit to take place and can be used for internal quality control. The system allows multicentre comparisons to be conducted, allowing collation of study material and colposcopic findings. It is ideal for natural history studies or for those patients with deferred treatment. In this latter case, the patient acts as her own control, allowing a conservative approach to younger women with low-grade lesions. The effect of interventions such as smoking cessation can also be assessed using these systems.

While statistical models can be developed to enhance diagnostic accuracy, these have limited potential in a clinical setting. Most of these models are converted into something simpler, allowing the clinician to devise scoring systems that are easily applicable and clinically useful.[8,12,13]

Of the clinical variables analysed in these studies, the referral status of cervical cytology and smoking were statistically significantly associated with prediction of

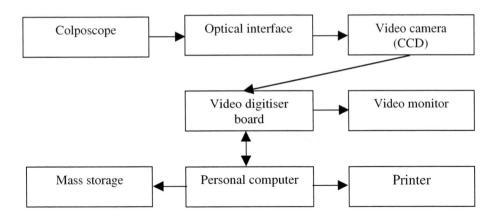

Figure 14.2 Schematic representation of digital imaging colposcopy; CCD = charge couple device

histological grade of abnormality. Age showed a trend, in that those with high-grade lesions tended to be older than those with low-grade lesions. Univariate analysis of the colposcopic features identified focality (annular versus unifocal/multifocal), surface pattern (irregular/intermediate versus smooth), degree of acetowhitening (marked/maximal versus slight), punctation/mosaic (coarse versus none/fine) and increasing surface area as predictors of worsening histological grade of the CIN. Other factors such as edge definition and edge regularity did not reach statistical significance in this analysis. Mathematical models can be constructed that predict histological grade, but these are difficult to use in practice. Using data from the analysis, a clinicocolposcopic index has been devised that is more practical to use within a clinical setting that is weighted to take into account the prognostic importance of index cytology and smoking status. Using this type of clinicocolposcopic index, a score can be derived for each individual patient, taking into account the important prognostic factors and also a weighting system applied to the variables. For each individual patient, a maximum score of 10 can be achieved. Those scoring 0–2 on this scale invariably have insignificant lesions. Those scoring 6–10 on this scale generally have high-grade disease present. In those scoring 3–5, the histological pattern is mixed with a tendency of the lesion to harbour CIN grade 1 or 2 (Table 14.1).

Table 14.1. Clinicocolposcopic index[8]

Variable	Score[a]		
	0	1	2
Index cytology	Low-grade	–	High-grade
Smoking status	No	–	Yes
Age	≤ 30 years	> 30 years	–
Acetowhitening	Slight	Marked	–
Surface area of lesion	≤ 1 cm² (small lesion)	> 1 cm² (large lesion)	–
Intercapillary distance	≤ 350 μm (fine or no mosaic/punctation)	> 350 μm (coarse mosaic/punctation)	–
Focality of lesion	Unifocal or multifocal	Annular	–
Surface pattern	Smooth	Irregular	–

[a] maximum score = 10

Videocolposcopy

Digital imaging systems are not portable and cannot be easily used in the community setting. However, the latest generation of portable video cameras allow digital capture and can easily be used in the primary-care setting. These have high resolution with autofocus facilities that are attached to a good light source and can be set to have the same focal length as a colposcope. Similar sort of magnifications to standard colposcopy can be attained.

Current devices feature a high degree of portability and can be mounted on a stand, allowing hands-free operation. These images can be viewed either as snapshot or video recordings, so that the assessment is the same as that undertaken using standard colposcopic techniques. The images can be viewed on a colour monitor or interfaced with a computer; the image or video can be captured by the computer. This can either be processed or archived as appropriate.[14] The system can be used by medical personnel, nurse colposcopists or practice nurses. Assessment of the images and video recordings can take place centrally with arrangements for suitable further management of the patient. An individual colposcopist can screen far more using this technology than with classical colposcopy or digital imaging colposcopy. The images can be sent down digital telephone lines, allowing remote colposcopic assessment to take place. This can be instantaneous or the video/images can be collated and assessed at appropriate time by the colposcopist.

Conclusions

Digital imaging technology has greatly aided visualisation, storage and transmission of images. The latest technology allows digital videocolposcopy to be undertaken and transmitted for remote consultations. The technology is useful for scientific studies and can allow a degree of quantification of a qualitative procedure. It can allow multicentre comparisons to take place, allowing sharing of data and colposcopic features. Using the currently available technology, remote colposcopic assessment is viable, depending upon the circumstances of the clinical situation.

References

1. Hinselmann H. Verbesserung der Inspektionsmöglichkeit von Vulva, Vagina und Portio. *Munch Med Wochenschr* 1925;77:1733.
2. Papanicolaou GN, Traut HF. The diagnostic value of vaginal smears in carcinoma of the uterus. *Am J Obstet Gynecol* 1941;42:193–206.
3. Buxton EJ, Luesley DM, Shafi MI, Rollason TP. Colposcopically directed punch biopsy: a potentially misleading investigation. *Br J Obstet Gynaecol* 1999;98: 1273–6.
4. Kraatz H. Farbfiltervorshaltung zur leichteren Erlernung der Kolposkopie. *Zentralbl Gynäkol* 1939;63:2307–9.
5. Etherington IJ, Luesley DM, Shafi MI, Dunn J, Hiller L, Jordan JA. Observer variability among colposcopists from the West Midlands region. *Br J Obstet Gynaecol* 1997;104:1380–84.
6. Reid R, Stanhope CR, Herschman BR, Crum CP, Agronow SJ. Genital warts and cervical cancer. IV. A colposcopic index for differentiating subclinical papillomaviral infection from cervical intraepithelial neoplasia. *Am J Obstet Gynecol* 1984;149:815–23.
7. Coppleson M, Pixley EC, Reid BL Colposcopy. *A Scientific and Practical Approach to the Cervix, Vagina and Vulva in Health and Disease*. Springfield, IL: Thomas; 1986.
8. Shafi MI, Nazeer S. Grading system for abnormal colposcopic findings. In: Bosze P, Luesley DM. *EAGC Colposcopy Handbook*. Budapest: Primed X Press; 2002.
9. Barasso R, Coupez F, Ionesco M, de Brux J. Human papillomaviruses and cervical intraepithelial neoplasia: the role of colposcopy. *Gynecol Oncol* 1987;27:197–207.

10.   Crisp WE, Craine BL, Craine EA. The computerized digital imaging colposcope: future directions. *Am J Obstet Gynecol* 1990;162:1491–8.
11.   Digital imaging colposcopy: basic concepts and applications. *Obstet Gynecol* 1993;82:869–73.
12.   Shafi MI, Dunn JA, Chenoy R, Buxton EJ, Williams C, Luesley DM. Digital imaging colposcopy, image analysis and quantification of the colposcopic image. *Br J Obstet Gynaecol* 1994;101:234–8.
13.   Shafi MI, Dunn J, Finn CB, Kehoe S, Buxton EJ, Jordan JA, *et al.* Characterisation of high and low grade cervical intraepithelial neoplasia. *Int J Gynecol Cancer* 1993;3:203–7.
14.   Etherington IJ, Luesley DM, Shafi MI, Dunn J, Hiller L, Jordan JA. Observer variability among colposcopists from the West Midlands region. *Br J Obstet Gynaecol* 1997;104:1380–84.

Chapter 15

The use of acetic acid in the diagnosis of cervical neoplasia

Allan B MacLean

Introduction

The number of cases of cervical cancer occurring in the world each year is close to half a million, with two-thirds of these women dying of their disease. The geographical areas with the most cases include Africa, Asia, Central and South America, where health spending is severely restricted and cervical cancer screening or early detection programmes do not exist.

Several studies have reported on the feasibility of visual inspection of the cervix.[1-4] Examination was performed in maternal or child health centres by medical or nursing professionals or by non-professionals trained to pass a speculum. Only 40–50% of cancers were accompanied by abnormal-looking cervices,[1] and only 29 cancers were found per 1000 high-risk women, i.e. with a suspicious-looking cervix with small growths or erosions that bled on touch.[2] Similar studies in Maharashtra[3] and Kerala,[4] India, divided appearances into low-threshold, for any cervical abnormality, and high-threshold, for one or more of the symptoms of bleeding on touch, suspicious growth or ulcer and a hard, irregular oedematous cervix. Of ten cancers, nine were detected within the low-threshold criteria but only six were if these were restricted to high-threshold criteria.[3] If moderate and severe dysplasia as well as cancer were included, the sensitivity of detection was 66% at low threshold, falling to 29% with high-threshold criteria; the respective specificities were 55% and 94%. The authors concluded that the test characteristics of visual inspection were not promising, with the sensitivity and specificity at low threshold being unsatisfactory and the sensitivity at high threshold being even lower.[4]

In an attempt to improve on this, the application of 3–5% acetic acid solution to the cervix was investigated by visual inspection with acetic acid (VIA). In an Indian study, 3000 women were examined by both VIA and cytology and those with abnormal cells were referred for colposcopy and biopsy.[5] VIA was positive in 298 cases (9.8%) and cytology in 307 (10.2%). Of the 51 cases of moderate or severe dysplasia, carcinoma *in situ* and invasive cancer that were identified, VIA detected 46 cases (90%) and cytology 44 (86%). VIA detected five lesions that were missed by cytology and cytology detected three lesions missed by VIA, while both techniques missed two lesions. Not only was the sensitivity of VIA better than visual inspection but the specificity was acceptable at 92%. The positive predictive value of VIA was17.0% and of cytology 17.2%. The authors concluded that the VIA merited further evaluation as a primary screening test in other low-resource settings. A similar study was conducted in Zimbabwe.[6] Women attending primary care clinics were recruited. In phase I, 8731 women were examined by VIA and cytology and those with abnormality referred for colposcopy and biopsy; VIA was positive in 20.2% of cases and cytology 14.6%. In phase II, 2203 women had VIA and cytology and all women were then seen for colposcopy. In this phase of the study, the VIA test-positive rate doubled to 40%; the possible reasons for this are included in the paper and include overcalling borderline appearances as abnormal to ensure that the nurse-midwives missed as few cases as possible. In phase II, the sensitivity of VIA compared with cytology for the detection of high-grade squamous intraepithelial lesions (HSILs) or invasive cancer was 77% versus 44%; the specificities were 64% and 91% and the positive predictive values 18.6% (VIA) and 33% (cytology). The authors concluded that the presence of sexually transmitted infection might have increased the false positive rates with VIA but that VIA was a readily available, potentially sustainable means of testing that, when coupled effectively with treatment, could reduce cervical cancer in populations with a high incidence.[6] The third group[7,8] with a large study using the technique of applying acetic acid, but calling it direct visual inspection (DVI), was based in Cape Town, South Africa. They compared DVI with cytology, HPV DNA testing and cervicography. Among 2944 women aged 35–65 years and living in Khayelitsha, DVI was positive in 18% and identified 67% of CIN2, CIN3 and invasive cancer. This sensitivity rate appeared to be similar to HPV DNA and cytology rates,[7] although, again, DVI, cytology and HPV DNA identified 24, 26 and 23 cases of HSIL or cancer per 1000 women tested, respectively, but classified 182, 71 and 137 women without disease as having abnormal results.[8] Once again, the low specificity of acetic acid application testing deters from wider use. However, understanding more about how acetic acid works on the cervix might improve on the above results.

The use of acetic acid for colposcopy

The original description of the 'Kolposkop' by Hinselmann includes his comment that 'Normally the examination is performed without immersion oil but sometimes it is advisable to use cedar oil for increased illumination'.[9] His aim was to identify 'dot-shaped' or 'pin-head size' carcinoma, which were usually impossible to discover clinically. During his later colposcopy experience, 2% acetic acid was used as a mucolytic,[10] but other effects were produced and the term 'leukoplakia' entered the colposcopic terminology.

It is recognised that, if 3–5% acetic acid is applied to an atypical transformation zone, after an interval of ten or so seconds the epithelium becomes white. The intensity of the effect and the rapidity with which it develops appear to be proportional to the degree of epithelial alteration, thus enabling an estimate of the histological abnormality to be made. This effect is transitory and, depending on the degree of epithelial alteration, may last no more than one minute or may persist for five or more minutes following the application of the acetic acid solution. Adjacent normal squamous epithelium does not change. Coppleson[11] explained these changes as being due either to an increased nuclear or cellular density, thickening of the epithelium, or an increased keratin covering. Stafl et al.[12] suggested that the changes occurred when the acetic acid drew out water from the cells, and that in the areas of high nuclear density the tissues then appeared white. Reid et al.[13] explained the altered tissue translucency as due to hypercellularity, increased nuclear density and DNA content, and the architectural disorganisation of the epithelium.

Acetic acid and acetowhite epithelium

Some years ago with Dr Ian More of the Department of Pathology, University of Glasgow, the author used transmission electron microscopy (TEM) to examine effects of the application *in vivo* of 5% acetic acid to normal and neoplastic cervical epithelium. TEM of the normal squamous epithelium showed intercellular and intracellular swelling and the appearance of cytoplasmic vacuoles of various sizes. The presence of intercellular fluid caused stretching and the attenuation of desmosomal junctions, with focal disruption (Figure 15.1). The surface cells are usually flattened, have shrunken pyknotic nuclei, a washed-out cytoplasm and residual glycogen (Figure 15.2). The cytoplasmic changes extend through the full thickness of the epithelium to the basement membrane and in some cases into the underlying stroma, with the fibroblasts showing dilatation of the cisterna of the rough endoplasmic reticulum. The size of the cytoplasmic vacuoles tends to be greater in the surface zone than in the deeper epithelium. The basal and parabasal cell nuclei showed more contrast than normal, with heterochromatin blocks situated close to the nuclear membrane (Figure 15.3).

Within the area of CIN, these changes extended into the epithelium but to a limited depth. The changes seen within CIN3 stopped in the mid-zone (middle third) of the epithelium (Figure 15.4). The surface zone of cells differed from normal squamous epithelium because many of the cells contained nuclei, with heterochromatin clumping as described for the basal cells of normal epithelium. Desmosomes are reduced (Figure 15.5). The deep zone showed no intranuclear changes, and cytoplasmic organelles including polyribosomes are clearly visible (Figure 15.6). The changes with CIN1 and CIN2 extended through the surface zone and into the middle and deep zones.

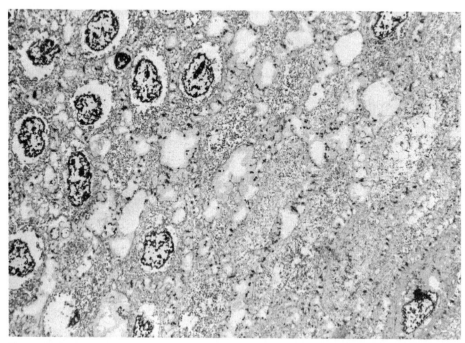

Figure 15.1 Low power transmission electron micrograph of normal cervical epithelium after the application of acetic acid

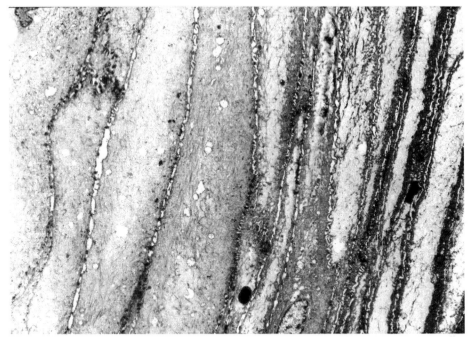

Figure 15.2 Transmission electron micrograph of surface layers of normal epithelium

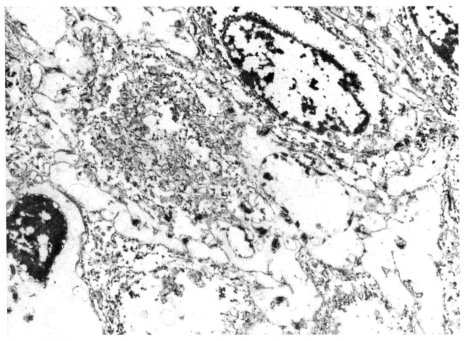

Figure 15.3 Transmission electron micrograph of deep layers of normal epithelium

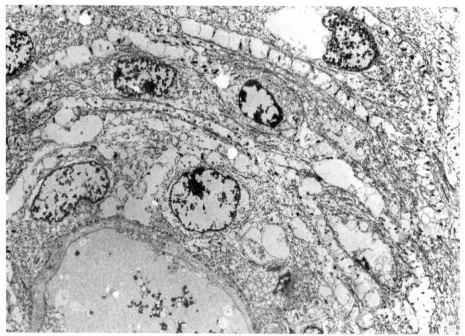

Figure 15.4 Transmission electron micrograph of mid-zone of cervical intraepithelial neoplasia grade 3

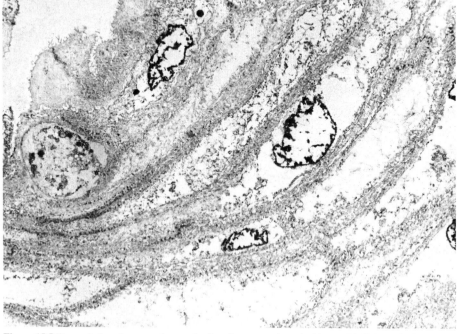

Figure 15.5 Transmission electron micrograph of surface zone of cervical intraepithelial neoplasia grade 3

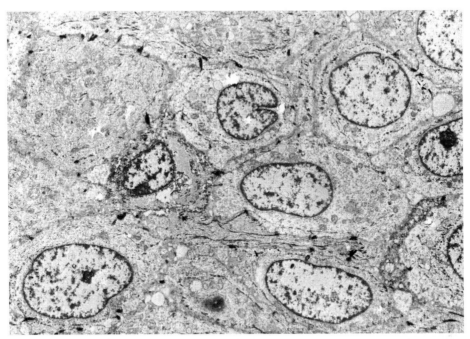

Figure 15.6 Transmission electron micrograph of deep zone of cervical intraepithelial neoplasia grade 3

If the cervix was biopsied 12 hours after application of acetic acid, there were features of reversal of the above changes, with recovery of the cytoplasm and desmosomes, and reduction in the perinuclear shrinkage compared with the appearances soon after acetic acid application.

Acetic acid is a carboxylic acid with a molecular weight of 60. Its concentrated form is known as glacial acetic acid and aqueous solutions of different concentrations will have different pH. Five percent acetic acid (0.8 molar) has a pH of 2.45, while a weaker solution such as 0.6% (0.1 molar) has a pH of 2.9.

The application of 0.1 molar solution to the atypical transformation zone of the cervix produces no effect at all, while 1% (0.16 molar) and 2% (0.3 molar) slowly produce a weak effect. The application of 3% (0.5 molar) or 5% solutions produce the effect recognised as acetowhite epithelium, while more concentrated solutions produce no greater effect but are more likely to produce discomfort and irritation for the woman. A 0.5 molar solution of sodium acetate does not produce any effect in the transformation zone. Inorganic acids such as phosphoric acid (0.5 molar solution; pH 1.83) and organic acids such as dicarboxylic lactic acid (0.5 molar solution; pH 2.35) or citric acid (0.5 molar solution; pH 2.1) have no effect on the cervix. The effect of acetic acid therefore is not due to the acetate ion or hydrogen ion concentration.

Other carboxylic acids, including formic acid (which has a characteristic smell of ants), propionic and butyric acids, and similar acids such as trichloroacetic, phenylacetic and isobutyric, have similar effects on the cervix. Valeric and caproic acids are less soluble and have unpleasant odours but also produce limited effects.

Placing tissue into water or aqueous solutions will dissolve many of the intracellular structures, to leave an empty cytoskeleton, unless the tissue is 'fixed'. This process preserves the structures (usually of protein but also of lipid, carbohydrate, glycoprotein or nucleoprotein nature) to make them optically dense so that they become visible on microscopy. No one fixative has the properties to enhance all structures, so often they consist of various mixtures, such as Zenker's, Flemming's, Hermann's, Mann's, Bouin's. Baker[14] subdivided fixatives into those of coagulant class, such as trichloroacetic acid, mercuric chloride, picric acid and chromic acid, which cause coagulation of cytoplasmic proteins to destroy or distort organelles and a non-coagulant class that include 5% acetic acid and 10% formalin. Non-coagulant fixatives crosslink protein molecules and convert the cytoplasm into an insoluble gel in which the organelles, e.g. mitochondria, are well preserved.

Acetic acid is included in fixative mixtures, e.g. Carnoy's acetic alcohol,[15] for preservation of chromosomes, to precipitate chromatin of interphase nuclei and for nucleoprotein determination.[15-18] The mechanisms by which acetic acid coagulates nucleic acids is obscure. It is a property of the undissociated acid and not the acetate ion,[17] explaining why the solution of sodium acetate did not produce any effect on the cervix. These properties are shared by the other carboxylic acids that are miscible with water and oil. Some of these differences are shown in Figure 15.7.

There have been observations that acetic acid did not preserve cytoplasmic inclusions; for example, Golgi, in 1898, did not include acetic acid in the fixative he used to demonstrate his 'apparatus'.[17] However, Baker showed that acetic acid at 5%, as included in Hermann's fluid, gives excellent mitochondrial preparations if the tissues are subsequently postosmicated (i.e. osmic acid added during the processing) and that Mann's fluid plus 5% acetic acid, again using postosmication, gave good preparations of the 'Golgi apparatus'. He also commented that there were differences in applying acetic acid to dead or living cells, where the effect was less 'destructive', for example of mitochondria.[17]

Acetic acid's contribution as a fixative is also to produce swelling and to counteract the shrinkage caused by other fixatives, such as of chloroplatinic acid in Hermann's solution. This swelling will produce artefactual shrinkage spaces in paraffin sections

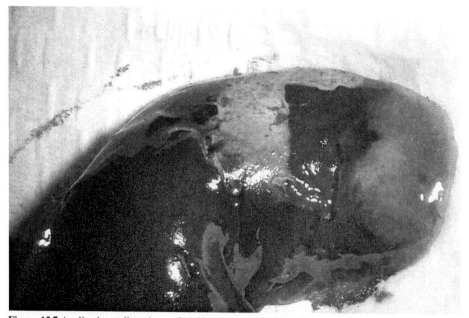

Figure 15.7 Application to liver tissue of trichloroacetic acid (left), saline (middle), acetic acid (right)

and on electron microscopy.[18,19] The third important property of acetic acid as a fixative is its speed of penetration into the tissue. In 1941, Medawar[20] performed experiments on the speed of penetration of various fixatives into tubes of plasma coagulum (believing that the homogeneous nature of the coagulum had the same sort of physiochemical organisation as living tissue) and demonstrated that acetic acid entered rapidly. Dempster[21] performed a similar study using blocks of liver tissue, and showed that acetic acid took approximately 15 minutes to penetrate 1 mm and osmic acid took 24 hours. It also seems likely that if tissue is not homogeneous the rate of penetration may not be linear. Furthermore, the penetration distance varies with fixative concentration.[22]

What happens when the acetic acid is applied to the cervix?

HSIL or CIN3 involve a surface epithelium that is several hundred microns (0.2 mm) thick. The nuclei will have extra nucleic acid[23,24] with aneuploidy or polyploidy. There will be additional nucleoprotein within the nucleus and cytoplasm. The application of acetic acid and its penetration into this epithelium will soon encounter undifferentiated, immature and neoplastic squamous cells. Nucleoprotein will be fixed or coagulated and the cells become opaque. Ordinarily, the epithelium will be transparent, allowing the visualisation of vessels in the stroma; the pink colour is due to this underlying vascularity. When the epithelium becomes opaque, the colour changes from pink to white because of the reflected light. The intensity of the white will be proportional to the amount of nucleoprotein precipitated and the degree of reflection of the light, i.e. the change of acetowhite epithelium appears faster with CIN3 than CIN1. Importantly, the changes will not be specific for neoplasia because increased nucleoprotein will be found during squamous metaplasia, healing and viral infection, which explains why acetowhite epithelium is found in these circumstances[13,25,26] and why false positives occur with VIA. If the epithelium is thin or eroded, or there is increased vascularity, the amount of nucleoprotein precipitation may not be sufficient to obscure the pink stroma and false negative VIA will occur. The effect of applying acetic acid to the cervix is clearly different from what happens to blocks of tissue. The cytoplasmic and nuclear changes must be reversible, as was shown in the TEM studies 12 hours after application or otherwise the epithelium would become necrotic and slough. Baker[14] has suggested that the effect of acetic acid is pH-dependent, and presumably when the pH rises the nucleoprotein recombines with its nucleic acid. Similarly, the swelling produced by the acetic acid is limited and, even if desmosomes are stretched, they remain secure and exfoliation does not occur.

Some of the changes seen on TEM may be artefactual because the tissue after exposure to acetic acid is placed into glutaraldehyde and osmium tetroxide before embedding in araldite, i.e. some of the intranuclear changes may be exaggerated. However, a study that used confocal microscopy to view cervical epithelium *in vitro* showed that the application of 6% acetic acid rapidly increased the backscattering from cell nuclei. Within seconds of application nuclei were imaged throughout the entire epithelium; the authors have suggested that the technology could be used in the future to assess nuclear/cytoplasmic ratio or nuclear deformity *in vivo*.[27]

Conclusions

Visual inspection of the cervix after the application of acetic acid (VIA/DVI) has been suggested as a screening test for cervical cancer, but it has limited sensitivity and low specificity. The appearance of the cervix after the application of acetic acid is due to the light reflected from the superficial layers of the epithelium; this is the effect of the carboxylic acid on nucleoprotein, which is increased in cervical neoplasia but also in viral infection, metaplasia and healing. The use of acetic acid to examine the cervix may have been by chance, and alternative or additional solutions should be considered to improve the diagnostic accuracy of this test.

References

1.   Sehgal A, Singh V, Bhambhani S, Luthra UK. Screening for cervical cancer by direct inspection. *Lancet* 1991;338:282.
2.   Singh V, Sehgal A, Luthra UK. Screening for cervical cancer by direct inspection. *BMJ* 1992;304:534–5.
3.   Nene BM, Deshpande S, Jayant K, Budukh AM, Dale PS, Deshpande DA, *et al.* Early detection of cervical cancer by visual inspection: a population–based study in rural India. *Int J Cancer* 1996;68:770–3.
4.   Wesley R, Sankaranarayanan R, Mathew B, Chandralekha B, Aysha Beegum A, Amma NS, *et al.* Evaluation of visual inspection as a screening test for cervical cancer. *Br J Cancer* 1997;75:436–40.
5.   Sankaranarayanan R, Wesley R, Somanathan T, Dhakad N, Shyamalakumary B, Amma NS, *et al.* Visual inspection of the uterine cervix after the application of acetic acid in the detection of cervical carcinoma and its precursors. *Cancer* 1998;83:2150–6.
6.   University of Zimbabwe/JHPIEGO cervical cancer project. Visual inspection with acetic acid for cervical cancer screening: test qualities in a primary-care setting. *Lancet* 1999;353:869–73.
7.   Denny L, Kuhn L, Pollack A, Wainwright H, Wright TC Jr. Evaluation of alternative methods of cervical cancer screening for resource-poor settings. *Cancer* 2000;89:826–33.
8.   Denny L, Kuhn L, Risi L, Richart RM, Pollack A, Lorincz A, *et al.* Two-stage cervical cancer screening: an alternative for resource-poor settings. *Am J Obstet Gynecol* 2000;183:383–8.
9.   Hinselmann H. Verbesserung der Inspektionsmöglichkeiten von Vulva, Vagina und Portio. *Munch Med Wochenschr* 1925;72:1733.
10.   Hinselmann H. Die Essigsaureprobe: ein Bestandteil der erweiterten Kolposkopie. *Dtsch Med Wochenschr* 1938;40.
11.   Coppleson M. Colposcopy, cervical carcinoma *in situ* and the gynaecologist. *J Obstet Gynaecol Br Cwlth* 1964;71:854–70.
12.   Stafl A, Friedrich EG, Mattingly RF. Detection of cervical neoplasia – reducing the risk of error. *Clin Obstet Gynecol* 1973;16:238–60.
13.   Reid R, Herschman BR, Crum CP, Fu YS, Braun L, Shah K, *et al.* Genital warts and cervical cancer. V. The tissue basis of colposcopic change. *Am J Obstet Gynecol* 1984;149:293–301.
14.   Baker JR. *Principles of Biological Microtechnique: A Study of Fixation and Dyeing.* London: Methuen; 1958.
15.   Merriam RW. Standard chemical fixations as a basis for quantitative investigations of substances other than deoxyribonucleic acid. *J Histochem Cytochem* 1958;6:43–51.
16.   Pearse AGE. *Histochemistry, Theoretical and Applied.* Vol. 1. 3rd ed. London: Churchill Livingstone; 1968.
17.   Baker JR. The effect of acetic acid on cytoplasmic inclusions. *Q J Microsc Sci* 1957;98:425–9.
18.   Kiernan JA. *Histological and Histochemical Methods. Theory and Practice.* 3rd ed. Oxford: Butterworth Heinemann; 1999.
19.   Sheehan DC, Hrapchak BB. *Theory and Practice of Histotechnology.* 2nd ed. London: Mosby; 1980.
20.   Medawar PB. The rate of penetration of fixatives. *J R Microsc Soc* 1941;61:46–57.
21.   Dempster WT. Rates of penetration of fixing fluids. *Am J Anat* 1960;106:59–72.
22.   Cafruny EJ. Studies on tissue fixation: the penetration of trichloracetic acid solutions into rat tissues. *J Histochem Cytochem* 1957;4:414–19.
23.   Mellors RC, Keane JF, Papanicolaou GN. Nucleic acid content of the squamous cancer cell. *Science* 1952;116:265–9.
24.   Von Bertalanffy L, Masin M, Masin F. A new and rapid method for diagnosis of vaginal and cervical cancer by fluorescence microscopy. *Cancer* 1958;11:873–87.
25.   Gottardi G, Gritti P, Marzi MM, Sideri M. Colposcopic findings in virgin and sexually active teenagers. *Obstet Gynecol* 1984;63:613–15.
26.   MacLean AB. Healing of cervical epithelium after laser treatment of cervical intra-epithelial neoplasia. *Br J Obstet Gynaecol* 1984;91:697–706.
27.   Collier T, Shen P, de Pradier B, Sung KB, Richards-Kortum R, Malpica A, *et al.* Near real time confocal microscopy of amelanotic tissue: dynamics of aceto-whitening enable nuclear segmentation. *Optics Express* 2000;6:40–8.

Chapter 16

New approaches to detecting lower genital tract neoplasia II

Discussion

Discussion following the papers by Professor Richart, Mr Shafi and Professor MacLean

Perrett: My question is directed at both Professor Richart and Professor Herrington and it concerns the cell cycle. I am an outsider in cervical disease but an insider in cancer generally. There has been much discussion of p16 but p15(ink4B) is also a very strong driver of the cell cycle. Have there been any studies on p15 in cervical disease and cervical intraepithelial neoplasia (CIN)?

Herrington: I do not know of any, and p16 has come up largely because of its relationship with pRb and E7. I do not think that the relationship, mechanistically, is as strong with p15. I am not aware of anything specific.

Richart: Nor am I.

Perrett: One of my interests is angiogenesis and there have been a number of papers (for instance, from Dobbs[1] and Guidi[2]) on the high expression of certain angiogenic stimulators in precancerous cervical lesions, such as CIN3, and the fact that they can also be picked up by enzyme-linked immunosorbent assays in serum. Have those markers been looked at – such as vascular endothelial growth factor?

Richart: Not to my knowledge.

Shepherd: I would like to ask Professor Richart what he and his US Food and Drug Administration (FDA) colleagues and US decision-makers – who I suspect are probably non-clinicians – will recommend to the male partners of all these women who are screened for human papillomavirus (HPV). A large number of the screened women in the USA and the UK are from differing ethnic backgrounds, where such a sensitive discussion may become medico-legally necessary, from what you have suggested. How will this be tackled?

Richart: We have been talking for the last 20 years about screening men and essentially we have finally decided to ignore them, for several reasons. First, it is very difficult to get them to attend. We established a colposcopy clinic for men at Columbia shortly after HPV was identified as an aetiological agent for CIN, but it was a semi-disaster because of non-attendance. Also, the penis is not highly amenable to colposcopy. Because it is a squamous epithelium, everything that affects any other squamous epithelium is also seen on the penis, and there are all sorts of lesions that might be condyloma but are not. Even the condylomas are extremely difficult to define both clinically and histologically.

Only 15–20% of male cancers are HPV-related, whereas most of the rest of them – as in the vulva – are related to irritation, uncircumcised status and other factors. We did not feel that we were shortchanging the men by not examining them and we did not think that they were at high risk of penile cancer because that disease is so rare.

The discussions about sexual transmissibility are important and everyone has wrestled with this issue. Nobody knows quite how to approach this. As in the UK, there have been many discussions on how to counsel patients, particularly those who are HPV DNA-positive and Papanicolaou smear-negative. This has come down to trying to de-emphasise the sexually transmitted aspects and emphasising that this is an extremely common virus that about 60–80% of women contract during their lifetime. I know that is a compromise but the issue is still being debated.

Education is essential. We have to get physicians to deal with HPV DNA-positive patients differently and get the patients to have a different understanding. Addressing both these problems is being required of Digene by the FDA.

Stanley: There are the antibodies that are used for the p16 and minichromosome maintenance (MCM) analyses. It is important to realise that those antibodies have been extraordinarily well characterised. There are actually several antibodies around these proteins but the MCMs, that particular antibody, has been specifically worked up for high sensitivity and specificity of detection of cells and cycle, not just for the cervix but also for prostate, for cells in urine, for cells in faeces from the colon.[3] This is a specific marker of dividing cells, which is one of its virtues.

It is similar with the p16 antibody – the MTM people have used that and characterised it very well. People should not rush out to the PharMingen catalogue and buy a few antibodies, come back and use them on their smears or biopsies, because you have to know about your reagents. You have to have them carefully characterised before you conduct the trials. That is why these two antibodies are showing such promise.

As a general comment, we have had a great deal of discussion about the difficulties of low-grade and high-grade lesions but, in fact, if you look at the cascade of things you can do, you can quite specifically get to a high-grade lesion. If you detect high-risk HPV and then show that there is an effect of that viral protein, i.e. an upregulation of p16, you are well placed to say that this person has a specific lesion. You can do all of this on one smear.

Herrington: I would just like to pick up on that point. I was involved in one of the MTM studies and two things struck me. One was how specific this positivity appeared to be for what seemed to be a persistent, high-risk HPV infection, be it low-grade or high-grade histologically.

The other, more striking, feature was that all of the immature lesions and the reactive lesions were absolutely negative. In diagnostic practice – not so much in screening – that is almost more important because the difficult lesions for us are these immature metaplastic ones, where we do not know whether they are immature or high-grade disease. That is where the MTM antibody will come in on biopsies at least.

I also have a question for Professor Richart about the E6, E7 RNA. Which types are you looking for? Supplementary to that, if you are looking at HPV 16, there are of course splice variants of E6, E7 RNA. Some of the splice variants do not encode full-length E6 protein and therefore are probably biologically less relevant.

Richart: We have not examined enough specimens to know whether this will be a problem.

Critchley: I have a question in response to what Professor Richart has told us about movements in the USA but I would perhaps address this to any of the clinical people working in the field. If the FDA accepts this Digene request and we see practice in the USA becoming HPV DNA screening accompanied by a smear, how will that influence and drive our practice in the UK, in terms of what patients then read about, find on the internet, ask for, or seek? That must inevitably have some impact on our practice, if a large developed country is using this as the gold standard.

Monaghan: One of the problems that we will have is that, in the USA, the FDA is extraordinarily powerful. Virtually everything they say is then taken by clinicians to be the way ahead, for a variety of reasons – whether it is good science, good practice, or gets them out of trouble with the lawyers.

We have to look at the differences here. Professor Richart, what is your penetration of cytology in the USA? What percentage of your population do you screen?

Richart: It is estimated at 93%.

Monaghan: No, the penetration of your population – what percentage are actually having smears on a regular basis? What is the population coverage?

Richart: I know it is an opportunistic programme but the last surveys in New York State showed that 93% of the people had had a Papanicolaou smear within the last five years.

Monaghan: That is interesting information, because it is a different perception of the data we have here. The problem here is that the decisions about how we practise, particularly at screening level, are mostly political ones. At the end of the day, whatever the National Institute for Clinical Excellence decides, we have to persuade politicians and the people providing local services to supply the money according to a whole raft of varying priorities to generate this. You are a great exponent of good practice but the day-to-day reality is that we will struggle to put these things in place, even with cogent arguments such as protection against lawsuits and best clinical practice. It will take a long time, even with a ten-year programme, mainly because we have to persuade politicians. This is the fundamental problem that we will have to work with.

This is why, when we make these recommendations, the sort of arguments that Professor Richart, Dr Cuzick and others have put forward should be at the forefront of our deliberations. We have to make sure that they are followed through in political terms. The modernisation agencies, with which I spend a great deal of time working at the moment, are interested in longer-term ways of improving care.

This brings me to what Dr McGoogan was saying. You may well find that, if we follow these recommendations, 80% of machines could be sitting idle. Or, conversely, you could be taking on the whole cytology load for the rest of England and Wales. We should therefore not rush to introduce new technology. We need to do some crystal-ball gazing and horizon-scanning to work out what will be best and cheapest in five, ten or fifteen years' time.

Richart: I feel very confident that, in the USA, we will be using HPV DNA screening soon, at least adjunctively. My bet would be that, within the next three to five years, we will move from adjunctive to primary screening. I am also reasonably confident that the automated screeners will enjoy a great deal of market penetration fairly quickly because we all have trouble recruiting cytotechnologists and would like to have a better screening mechanism. In fact, I am so confident in the utility of the automated screener that we plan to install one at Columbia in early to mid-2003.

Monaghan: The reality, however, is not all down to pounds, shillings and pence, or dollars. Much of this concerns changing mindsets. It will be fairly straightforward for us to get the clinicians but the obstructions in central government to changing mindsets are amazing. I have no idea where they are getting their advice from, but it is quite a struggle.

Sasieni: I find that the biggest opposition is in trying to evaluate any of these things within the screening programme. If HPV testing were introduced in the way in which it probably will be in the USA, it would be more expensive. People are very aware of the power of the NHS to buy cheaply. With liquid-based cytology, they have been in contact with both companies, asking what it would cost if they bought four million a year. However, if it is just a matter of an additional test, this means that you will be referring more women for colposcopy and, even if it is US$3 a time extra, that is US$3 a time extra for the four million tests that are done per year.

One of the key questions, as Dr Cuzick said, is whether five-yearly screening with both HPV and cytology is as good as three-yearly screening with cytology alone. Or is HPV alone, long-term, as good as cytology alone for looking at cancer incidence as opposed to CIN3 rates? Those questions require a large study, but there has been absolutely no support and, in fact, huge resistance to doing it within the cervical screening programme in England. Dr Cuzick is now trying to conduct a study in other countries because it is easier to obtain support in Italy and elsewhere in Europe than in England.

The Department of Health has set up a committee to look at new technologies and their possible five-year impact. They are looking at whether, if they put in place liquid-based cytology machines, these could all be made obsolete within a few years by HPV testing. There appears to be more resistance to HPV testing than to liquid-based cytology, possibly for the reason that Professor Shepherd has suggested about the impact on marital relationships. What if you had an HPV test that was negative three years ago, have been married to the same man for the last three years, and you then have a positive HPV test? We have not really had that situation because we have so far mostly just been doing one-off HPV testing, so that we can tell the woman that she has probably had this HPV since she was 17 years old without having known about it. However, if you have done a good test before, which was negative, and now it is positive, she may ask where she got it from.

Richart: We always fall back on latency, because we have no data on that at all.

Singer: You asked for a clinical response. We run a service in which we see about 2000 new patients a year. The problem that we will face is that there are moves afoot to demand that patients be sent to us with just one borderline smear. Even worse, if you find one koilocyte in a smear, the smear is now to be called low-grade. We are anticipating a 20% increase, with no obvious increase in money for it. No matter how much we show them that HPV is valuable – and we have been using it for five or six years now, as Mr Monaghan says, this is a political decision. At the end of it, when we hear about vaccination and we link the exciting bits with the vaccination to what is Professor Richart saying, we will be five to seven years behind what is currently available in other parts of the world. The Europeans are also ahead of us; we will be overtaken and shown to be still in the Ice Age.

Stanley: I would like to make a partial response to Professor Richart. He is being overoptimistic about the percentage decrease in price that can be obtained with an HPV test. Anything that has a basis of hybridisation will have a level below which you cannot go. It will not be as cheap as all that.

In the UK, there is always this intense negativity about any new development at all, which I find very difficult. There is tremendous capitalisation of basic research. We all beaver away, trying to work out molecular methods for this, that and the other. Here, we have a molecular basis for a disease. We can identify the agent and show that it is having an effect by looking at a molecular marker. We can look at its actual expression of genes in relatively simple terms – one, by a simple HPV test, and the other two by simple immunostaining – and yet everyone is discussing it as though it were something on the moon. This is here and now, and entirely feasible. If it is not done, as we have just heard, we will be years behind, and it will delay effective clinical practice.

Shafi: In response to what Professor Singer just said about the Ice Age, we are one of the few organised programmes to have had a major impact on cancer statistics.

Singer: Yes, but we are still staying there, and we are still living on that. You could argue that if it goes down seven percent, we will get down to zero, but I have seen 12 invasive cancers this year and it is therefore still out there.

Shafi: I know you have, Professor Singer, but for the last 14 years, the graphs that Dr Sasieni showed me were showing a considerable year-on-year decrease in cancer incidence and mortality. I appreciate that these are exciting developments and that we should embrace them but I would not like people to go away with the idea that the method employed has not had a major impact on cancer incidence and mortality. It is the organisation of the programme that has had that impact and the lessons that we have learned can also be applied to other countries – they also need to organise their screening programmes along the same lines, for very high coverage of the at-risk population.

Prendiville: I do not know what the precise incidence and mortality rates are for cervical cancer in the USA, but I understand that they have not changed substantially in the last ten years. The countries that have achieved the greatest reduction in incidence are those that have utilised cytology-based screening programmes – Finland and the UK. I do not for a moment suggest that this is the way we should go in the future, because that is not appropriate – we are at a different point in time now. If the UK is in the Ice Age at the moment, I am afraid that Ireland is even more primitive than that. We have not even started a cervical cytology programme yet.

Critchley: If you are to develop this telecolposcopy, how do you envisage running the panel of experts who will comment on the telephone-transmitted information?

Shafi: One of the systems we have developed in Birmingham is the use of videocolposcopy in a setting where women with minor abnormalities – either borderline or mild dyskaryosis – are video-imaged. That image is transmitted into the central colposcopy unit for assessment by one of the colposcopists. You can screen a far greater number of patients in your office, at your convenience, than you can if you refer all these patients to colposcopy clinics.

The other advantage is that it keeps patients out of the colposcopy clinic. One of my fears, especially where women with borderline or any dyskaryotic smear are being referred, is that this will inevitably lead to a much higher intervention rate for these women, with biopsies being taken and unnecessary treatments being undertaken for no benefit whatsoever.

Richart: Do you all use reflex HPV DNA testing for your borderline Papanicolaou smears?

Singer: No. It is used in private practice or research. If you have research funds or research programmes, then yes. But, as a national programme, as Dr Cuzick said, we have to wait until October 2003, although it has been known about and used for years. We use it outside the screening programme, if we are able to.

Sasieni: You have to have three borderlines before you go to colposcopy, or a borderline followed by something else. It changes the timescale, but it will not have that great an effect.

Richart: How many invasive cancers do you miss while you are waiting for the three?

Sasieni: Very, very few.

Deery: All organised programmes within Europe, and indeed Australia too in the state sectors, operate surveillance cytology. Low grades are triaged by repeat cytology. The benefit from those screening programmes is demonstrated by mortality incidence figures. If you pay for them in any country – Europe, Australia, Britain – you can get liquid-based cytology and HPV determinations. It is entirely likely that those commercial pressures, costs and considerations will determine what HPV testing and liquid-based cytology is available in our country.

Monaghan: Just to get a little perspective, last year we had a bonanza from the Chancellor of the Exchequer – £400 million extra, for the whole health service. We could have spent it all on radiation machines, not to get ahead but to play catch-up: that is just radiation machines, and nothing else.

If you then start to add in everything else that we need, you can just think of a number. That is the reality. The essential difference, Professor Richart, is that we still have a free service at the point of use for everybody. As you said, using simple methods, which can be mocked and laughed at, we have had one of the greatest changes in the incidence and death rates from cervical cancer of almost any country. All you have to do is to look just across the water to Denmark, to see what happens in a country that does not use screening – they have one of the highest incidence and death rates.

We are constantly compared with places like Iceland. I might remind you that Iceland has a population slightly smaller than Gateshead, where I live, and our screening rates and results are actually better than those of Iceland. Let us get this in perspective. We can also talk about the American indigenous population, which basically means the poor souls who cannot afford healthcare, and the results are not quite so hot there.

Tidy: Because of the difference in our borderline category compared with the Bethesda system, a large number of patients in the borderline category are HPV-positive. In the Bethesda system, if you have any evidence of koilocytosis with dyskaryosis, it is immediately classified as LSIL. We have a problem with reflex testing that matched what the ALTS (ASCUS–LSIL Triage Study) proved – that in LSILs it is a waste of time. Although the trials will show that reflex testing for borderline as currently defined would be a waste of time in this country, if we moved to the new British Society for Clinical Cytology terminology, where we move any evidence of koilocytosis into LSILs, then reflex testing in the new borderline category might be an improvement. However, I do not think it would work as it currently operates in England.

Singer: We have not so far mentioned the psychological problems engendered by the screening programme, and particularly HPV. I feel passionately that we do far more harm than good to these women. We traumatise them. It has been shown that, if a woman has a borderline smear, the psychological damage to her is the same as if she had had a high-grade smear. About 80% of these women are traumatised and we showed the first evidence of this 14 years ago. We have not even started to address the trauma that we inflict upon women coming to colposcopy and anyone who has had HPV. That is what I wanted HPV to come in for; it tears you up, when you use it in private practice and see how brilliantly it works, and yet you cannot use it in your NHS practice.

Jones: I have a very quick question: should we use 3% or 5% acetic acid?

MacLean: That is a good question, because there is a great deal of variation. If you use anything more than 5%, patients find it irritating and unacceptable. With 5%, various studies have been done in Africa,[4] showing that it is reasonably easy to make up, and reasonably stable, but I am not sure that there is any difference otherwise.

References

1. Dobbs SP, Hewett PW, Johnson IR, Carmichael J, Murray JC. Angiogenesis is associated with vascular endothelial growth factor expression in cervical intraepithelial neoplasia. *Br J Cancer* 1997;76:1410–15.
2. Guidi AJ, Abu-Jawdeh G, Berse B, Jackman RW, Tognazzi K, Dvorak HF, *et al.* Vascular permeability factor (vascular endothelial growth factor) expression and angiogenesis in cervical neoplasia. *J Natl Cancer Inst* 1995;87:1237–45.
3. Williams GH, Romanowski P, Morris L, Maduie M, Miks AD, Stoeber K, *et al.* Improved cervical smear assessment using antibodies against proteins that regulate DNA replication. *Proc Natl Acad Sci U S A* 1998;95:14932–7.
4. Niemand IC, Cronje HS, Botha JM. Physical properties of acetic acid vital in evaluation of the cervix for neoplastic changes. *Eur J Gynaecol Oncol* 2000;21:380–2.

SECTION 5

MANAGEMENT OF LOWER GENITAL TRACT NEOPLASIA I

Chapter 17

Should we ever treat lower-grade lesions?

Margaret E Cruickshank

Introduction

Cervical cytology is widely employed as a population-screening test to detect cervical intraepithelial neoplasia (CIN). The ultimate objective of screening is to reduce deaths from cervical cancer by detecting and treating preinvasive disease. High-grade CIN has a significant risk of progressing to invasive cancer[1] but the natural history of lower-grade abnormalities is less well understood. While the risk of progression to cancer appears to be low, data on the natural history of low-grade CIN are lacking, with most studies being based on women with abnormal smears and little evidence relating to women with low-grade disease.

The screening system used in the UK relies on cervical cytology for identification of a high-risk group of women who are referred on for further investigation by colposcopy and biopsy of any identified area of abnormality. Cytology showing severe dyskaryosis is a reliable indicator of underlying high-grade CIN[2] but, whereas severe dyskaryosis occurs in only 0.7% of reported smears, borderline and mild dyskaryosis occur in 6–8% of smears.[3] The lesser grades of abnormality represented by the 2.5% of smears in the UK show mild dyskaryosis with definite nuclear changes suggesting underlying low-grade CIN (CIN1), but there is a poor correlation between these mild cytological changes and the underlying histological changes in the cervical squamous epithelium. It is well documented that up to 40% of women with mild dyskaryosis have underlying CIN2–3 [4,5] and around 25–50% will have either no cervical pathology or human papillomavirus (HPV) changes only.[6,7]

The benefits of participating in screening should outweigh any consequent adverse effects. When abnormal smears were managed by cold-knife cone biopsy, surveillance was an attractive strategy. However, colposcopy offers a less invasive means of investigation. High-grade disease can be excluded and low-grade changes can be confirmed by punch biopsy, allowing these low-risk women the opportunity to regress under cytological surveillance and avoid unnecessary treatment. However, the lack of clinical evidence has meant that any benefits of treatment are unclear. Low-grade disease is most common in younger age-groups and is directly related to the high prevalence of HPV infection.[8] Although complications from a single excisional or ablative treatment are low, the persistence of HPV can result in repeated treatments for some women, which may place their reproductive and sexual health at risk.

In the UK, the current national guidelines for management of a single mildly dyskaryotic smear indicate that the smear should be repeated in six months' time and the woman should be referred for colposcopy if the abnormality persists.[9] These guidelines were produced on the basis of several published reports confirming the safety of surveillance, with concerns regarding the additional costs and dilution of resources if all women were referred for colposcopy. However, they have been revised and are now available for open consultation.[10] Women with a single mildly dyskaryotic smear should be referred for colposcopy. If we are to serve these women both efficiently and effectively, we need to understand who should be offered treatment and who can anticipate spontaneous regression. Clinical uncertainty is a product of the limitations of cytology and colposcopy and, indeed, targeted punch biopsy. The data available on the management of women with CIN1 are insufficient to advocate a single strategy and, while this demands further research, it should also prompt us to involve our patients in deciding on the best option for them.

Nevertheless, an efficient strategy for low-grade disease is necessary for our colposcopy services to cope with the anticipated increase in workload. With our current policy of surveillance, 70% of women with mild dyskaryosis ultimately come for colposcopy because of unresolved low-grade abnormalities, and the increase in workload from low-grade changes is predicted to be only 30%.[4] The problem will continue to challenge us until alternative strategies for secondary screening or treatment become available to cope with the large number of young women with minor abnormalities.

The diagnosis of lower-grade lesions

Cytology

Even in the hands of experts, cytology does not accurately reflect the underlying histology.[5,11,12] The sensitivity of cytology for separating CIN2 and CIN3 from CIN1 or viral changes has been reported as 41–52%[7,13,14] and cytology is more likely to miss small lesions.[15,16] A normal smear following one showing mild dyskaryosis may be falsely reassuring, as the false negative rate for repeat cytology has been reported as 24%[17] and the pre-existence of high-grade CIN cannot be excluded on the basis of cytology.

Colposcopy

A policy of avoiding treatment of low-grade lesions depends on being able to confidently exclude high-grade disease. The potential of colposcopy for characterising grades of CIN and for monitoring changes is limited by its subjective nature and its lack of both sensitivity and specificity in predicting the histological diagnosis. Colposcopic assessment is more sensitive than cytology in identifying high-grade lesions, but this is at the cost of reduced specificity.[13] This is probably due to the acetowhitening of the early immature stages of the metaplastic process and to viral change being mistaken for CIN. Small lesions tend to be classified as low-grade on colposcopy[16] and lesions within the endocervical canal may be missed. Colposcopic assessment and lesion surface area are both predictors of the histological grade of CIN.[11,16,17] However, these factors are not independent of each other and the colposcopist's opinion is influenced by knowledge of the referral cytology and the lesion size.[16] This has implications for the management of mildly abnormal smears, where the colposcopist may tend towards downgrading the severity of the underlying epithelial lesion.

Flat condylomas, a term that has been used to describe the colposcopic features of HPV infection, may coexist with CIN. There is a degree of overlap in the abnormal features seen colposcopically, which can suggest HPV infection or CIN and, histologically, features of both are often found in the same biopsy.[18] Colposcopy is not specific enough to distinguish between HPV changes and CIN. Features considered to be typical of HPV lesions, namely, surface roughness, satellite lesions and poor uptake of Lugol's iodine, were used. Vascular patterns also lack specificity, sensitivity and reproducibility. This supports the concept that HPV infection and CIN1 may both represent low-grade disease. Indeed, the recent Bethesda classification (cytol) suggests that koilocytic smears be regarded as representing low-grade disease. However, if vascular patterns normally associated with high-grade disease lack specificity and colposcopy tends to overcall, women with low-grade smears may be over-treated for a low-risk condition.

Colposcopically directed biopsy

To avoid over-treatment, initial assessment should include colposcopy, so that any abnormal features can be identified and punch biopsies taken under direct vision with at least two biopsies targeted at the most atypical area of any lesion seen. The results need to be considered along with the referral cytology and colposcopic findings. Punch biopsies are associated with both over-diagnosis and under-diagnosis,[19] with only a 54% concordance with the large loop excision of the transformation zone (LLETZ) specimen. There is a high level of inter-observer and intra-observer variability in diagnosing the grade of CIN.[20] Pathologists are able to distinguish high-grade lesions at a reasonable level from reactive change but have limited agreement in diagnosing low-grade lesions. There is a low positive predictive value for low-grade disease compared with CIN3. Over-interpretation is most likely in lesions where koilocytic changes are minimal or focal. The false positive rate of diagnosing HPV infection on routine histology is 75% and the positive predictive value of 56%.[21] Even when uniform and stringent histopathological criteria are applied to biopsy samples, over-diagnosis of HPV still occurs with a false positive rate of 34%. Thus, discrepancies arise both from the subjectivity in selecting the biopsy site and from the histopathologist's ability to interpret low-grade changes. However, the information obtained from biopsies is greater than the risks or disadvantages of unnecessary treatment.

Natural history studies

The rationale for cytological surveillance is to allow regression of minor abnormalities and viral disease, while using cytological examination to ensure that the woman does not progress to high-grade or invasive cancer. Older studies of the natural history of mild dysplasia have suggested a high regression rate of these abnormalities, although women with such changes were at significantly higher risk of developing CIN3 than women with a normal smear.[22] A critical review of such studies gave an overall regression rate of 57%, with a progression rate of 11% to CIN3.[23] A retrospective case–control study of a surveillance protocol with a median of seven years follow-up found that 46% of women on surveillance were subsequently referred for colposcopy because of persistent abnormalities.[24] In a retrospective study comparing the outcome for women with mild dyskaryosis attending either of two centres, one with a policy of surveillance and the other of early colposcopy, 33% of women on surveillance were referred for colposcopy.[25] At colposcopy following 24–32 months of surveillance, 12% of the women were found to have undetected CIN3. Two-thirds of these cases could have been detected by abnormal cytology on a further repeat smear. No women in the colposcopy group had CIN3 at the study colposcopy and 4% had CIN2. False negative rate of cytology was 33%, but surveillance was less costly than immediate colposcopy with a low-risk of missing CIN3 over time.

These surveillance studies are limited by the accuracy of cytology, so some women started on surveillance with either no disease or a high-grade lesion. In addition, the results from observational studies are limited by discrepancies in cytological and pathological reporting, clinical performance and adherence to clinical protocols.

In a prospective randomised trial,[4] 902 women with a single mild or moderate dyskaryotic smear were managed prospectively by immediate colposcopy and LLETZ or by increasing periods of surveillance with LLETZ at 6, 12 or 24 months. Although there was only a 15% regression rate of all women with mild dyskaryosis, this occurred principally in those women with CIN1 or HPV changes alone. This group of women has most to gain from surveillance. This trial also confirmed that cytological surveillance is safe, with 97% of women with underlying CIN3 being detected eventually by repeat cytology. In a trial by Shafi et al.,[6] 353 women with mild dyskaryosis or borderline nuclear changes and an adequate colposcopic examination were randomised to either immediate treatment by LLETZ or 24 months of cytological and colposcopic surveillance followed by LLETZ. The underlying rate of CIN3 (25%) in this study was the same in both the immediate colposcopy and the surveillance groups, indicating that high-grade lesions do not progress during the observation period but are present at the time of the initial abnormal smear. There were fewer low-grade lesions in the surveillance group (13% compared with 25% in the immediate treatment group) and a higher incidence of normal histology (20% compared with 0.6%) on completion of surveillance, again confirming that regression is confined to women with genuinely low-grade disease.

Default

These trials[4,6] indicate that a conservative approach allows resolution of low-grade CIN and koilocytic atypia, but both had default rates to surveillance of around 20% and the outcome for these women is unknown. In a four-and-a-half-year cytological surveillance study of women with borderline abnormalities or mild or moderate dyskaryosis,[26] 18% of women had had no further smears after their index smear and a further 22% who had at least one follow-up smear, subsequently defaulted. However, not all these women will be persistent defaulters and they may have attended outside the study areas; the main concern is unrecognised high-grade or invasive disease when women are assessed only by cytology.

Management following diagnosis of low-grade disease at colposcopy

Immediate referral to colposcopy allows triage to most appropriate management. Women with low-grade smear changes but normal colposcopy are at low risk, and can be reassured without waiting 12 months for two negative smears. Women with high-grade disease recognised on colposcopy or biopsy can be treated promptly. An Oxford study[27] reported on a colposcopy clinic protocol for the management of women with mildly abnormal smears. Women with negative colposcopy had repeat cytology; otherwise, biopsy was performed by punch or diathermy loop excision depending on the colposcopic findings. Fifty-six percent of women were discharged from their colposcopy clinic untreated after one year and only 40% had undergone treatment. To use such a protocol to prevent over-treatment is largely dependent on the expertise of the colposcopist in identifying correctly the underlying histology.

The clinical evidence presented so far relates to cytological abnormalities, although some data have been extrapolated from this to support conservative management of CIN1. It has been advocated that these women should be offered surveillance with the stipulation that they be treated if the lesions persist for two years or if the grade or size of lesion increases.[28] The limited data available support such a strategy. In a retrospective review of 30 women with biopsy-proven CIN1,[29] by six months of follow-up, 41% regressed to normal, 39% had persistent borderline or low-grade changes and 12% had high-grade disease identified. At 18 months of follow-up, 64% had resolved and 36% still had borderline or low-grade changes; no further cases of high-grade disease were found. In another retrospective study of 71 women with CIN1 or CIN2,[30] the median time to detecting high-grade disease was 10.5 months follow-up (range 6–62 months) and to regress to normal 23 months (12–89) months. The rate of progression of CIN1 was 36% but only 25% in HPV-negative lesions compared with 48% of HPV-positive lesions. A prospective cohort study[31] of 89 women with biopsy-proven CIN1 found a 75% resolution rate defined by two consecutive negative smears. The median time to resolution was nine months. This was a self-selected group in private practice, with 11 other women preferring immediate treatment. In a large retrospective analysis that reflects clinical practice (i.e., women referred with low-grade smears with high-grade disease excluded at colposcopy)[32] median duration of surveillance was 17 months, with 54% of women regressing to normal and 22% requiring treatment. Dyskaryosis on a repeat smear, the colposcopic opinion and cigarette smoking were all predictors of future treatment, cytology being the most significant factor. Although these data support a conservative approach, safety and effectiveness depend on patient compliance.

Psychological considerations

Women are known to have extremely high levels of anxiety prior to colposcopy[33] and they are as concerned about the procedure of colposcopy as the outcome. The degree of abnormality of the referral smear does not alter the degree of anxiety. Part of the problem is that many women are under-informed about their smear result and fear that they may have cancer. Anxiety appears to be most pronounced during the waiting period for the colposcopy appointment.

A case–control study comparing women undergoing surveillance for mild dyskaryosis with women referred for colposcopy found that the initial anxiety in women undergoing cytological surveillance is less than that of women referred for colposcopy but, following colposcopy, anxiety is rapidly resolved while elevated anxiety persists in women under surveillance.[34] A retrospective unmatched comparative study of 345 women with mild dyskaryosis[35] questioned women who had participated in an earlier study on the management of mild dyskaryosis.[25] The findings were similar, although the data were based on recollection of events 30 months previously. Women referred for colposcopy were more anxious and were more likely to think that they had cancer. However, women under surveillance had sustained anxiety, particularly in relation to waiting for smear results.

Part of the problem for women on surveillance is their understanding of the reason for conservative management. Women with pre-existing anxiety may be more anxious, regardless of which policy is adopted. Colposcopic and biopsy confirmation of low-risk disease may provide women with reassuring information before surveillance. However, interpretation of results from these studies is difficult to generalise because of the wide variation in study design and the different psychological tools used. Psychological and satisfaction measurements are needed from a randomised controlled trial, which would prevent potential bias from the many confounding variables.

Health economics

There are no economic data specifically related to the management of women with low-grade lesions. A decision analysis model has been used to compare the expected mortality and cost of alternative policies for low-grade smears.[36] The model is based on a number of assumptions about possible outcomes and uses results from previously published data to calculate probabilities. The use of cytological surveillance was not predicted to be financially cheaper, as 65% of women would eventually require colposcopy referral and an average of six additional smear tests would be required to save one colposcopy referral. A different method of mathematical modelling was used to compare surveillance with immediate colposcopy to measure their effect on the incidence of invasive cancer, number of smear tests and colposcopies.[37] The conclusion from this study was that immediate colposcopy would have only a minimal effect on the incidence of invasive cancer, reducing the number from 2.1 per 100 000 women per year to 2.0, at the expense of much additional colposcopy.

Mathematical modelling may fail to identify all the relevant service costs. A cost-effectiveness analysis was performed alongside the Aberdeen study on mild dyskaryosis.[38] A policy of immediate diagnosis and treatment at colposcopy increased the total costs but this was off set by a lower marginal cost-effectiveness ratio. Although the cost per woman was higher, as more cases of CIN3 were detected, the cost was lower for each case of CIN3 detected. The end result of immediate colposcopy is greater resource use. The health and economic cost implications of colposcopy with subsequent treatment of low-grade disease versus treatment-only for lesions unresolved after two years is not known.

Selection of high-risk women for treatment: use of HPV testing

The management of women with low-grade lesions would be rationalised if we could predict which lesions will persist or progress. Current conservative management depends on cytological or colposcopic surveillance to detect high-grade disease. CIN1 lesions positive for high-risk HPV types are significantly more likely to persist or progress[30] and the highest risk is for women who are persistently positive for high-risk HPV types.[39] Reflex HPV testing, where women found to have borderline or mild smears have a stored sample (taken at the time of the smear) tested for HPV, is currently being assessed in the HART (HPV in Addition to Routine Screening Trial) study and the National Health Service Cervical Screening Programme (NHSCSP) liquid-based cytology (LBC) HPV pilots in England. Referral to colposcopy or surveillance is determined by the HPV test result. The MRC TOMBOLA trial (Trial of Management of Borderline and Other Low-grade Abnormalities) includes a second randomisation of women seen for immediate colposcopy, so that women with low-grade lesions are managed either by LLETZ or cytological surveillance following confirmation of CIN1 on punch biopsy. This trial includes detailed psychological and health economic data and clinical outcome after three years follow-up. The LBC HPV pilots include information on anxiety and the acceptability of HPV testing. In the USA, the continuing ALTS trial (ASCUS LSIL Triage Study), which compares immediate colposcopy, cytological surveillance and HPV triage for women with low-grade smears, includes health economics. Data from all these studies will better inform clinicians on all the issues in the selective management of low-grade disease.

Alternative treatments

Women with low-grade lesions have essentially a viral (HPV) infection and the use of surgical procedures to destroy or remove the cellular changes that result from this viral infection seems paradoxical. Treatment directed at the infectious agent seems logical, although several uncontrolled and controlled observational studies on follow-up after treatment of CIN have shown that the elimination rate of HPV is high.[40–43] Imiquimod, a non-specific immune response modifier with antiviral activity, is licensed for the treatment of genital warts. Early clinical trials in Europe and USA for the treatment of low-grade cervical abnormalities have been stopped because of the high incidence of inflammatory effects on the vaginal mucosa. Other agents that can promote non-specific immune response, such as mistletoe derivatives and interferon, have also been used in treating HPV and CIN lesions but these have been limited by systemic adverse effects, inconvenience of administration and variable clinical response.

The alternative immunotherapies for low-grade cervical disease are the HPV vaccines. These may be prophylactic against HPV infection by producing an effective immune response at the site of infection or therapeutic vaccine to eliminate HPV infection of the basal cells of the cervical epithelium, limiting the duration of infection and the rate of re-infection. The aim of both prophylactic and therapeutic vaccines is to stimulate an adaptive immune response and produce an immune memory to HPV infection. Currently there are several phase I and II clinical trials, including phase I studies in virus-like particle (VLP) preparation vaccines for women with mild dyskaryosis (see also Chapter 20 for discussion of some HPV therapeutic vaccines in treating established CIN lesions). Data on the clinical efficacy of such vaccines are awaited. In relation to low-grade disease, where we can anticipate a high regression rate, this will require large cohorts of vaccinated women with long-term follow-up to identify accurately any benefit from vaccination itself. While data on high-grade lesions may be more immediately available, it may be some time before we can consider vaccination for low-grade disease.

Immune-suppressed women

Women either on long-term immunosuppressants or with chronic immunosuppression have a higher incidence of HPV infection, persistence of HPV infection and cervical disease. Low-grade abnormalities are common in HIV-infected women. However, there is no clinical evidence to suggest that these groups have accelerated progression of low-grade disease and, while care with cervical screening is essential and colposcopy may be of some additional benefit, they do not need to be treated for low-grade disease.[44] However, there is some evidence that severe HIV-related immunodeficiency increases the risk of CIN. There is a higher incidence of CIN in women with low CD4 cell count who are not receiving anti-retroviral therapy.[45] Anti-retroviral treatment may reduce this risk, probably by restoring or at least preserving immune function.

Conclusions

It is now widely accepted that low-grade cervical disease represents a viral infection and women are not at high risk of developing cancer. Low-grade lesions cannot be diagnosed by cytology alone, and colposcopy and histology results need to be considered together. Many of these lesions will regress within 9–24 months of detection with no clinical significance. Conservative management avoids over-treatment and at least 60% of lesions will regress by two years. However, some persist beyond two years and for these women, treatment is delayed. Low-grade disease is most common in women under the age of 30 years and while, in general, treatment should be avoided to allow regression, consideration must be given to women who wish to be treated. The psychological impact of low-grade lesions is significant and comparable to women with high-grade smears. The problem of default remains but initial assessment by colposcopy and biopsy should exclude women with prevalent high-grade disease from surveillance. Most women can be adequately managed by cytological follow-up and treatment need only be considered if either cytology or colposcopy suggest evidence of high-grade disease or if low-grade changes have not resolved by two years. HPV testing may be useful in identifying women who can avoid both unnecessary treatment and excessive surveillance. Data will be available in the next few years from large prospective studies (ALTS, TOMBOLA, NHSCSP LBC HPV pilots) on HPV testing, psychological effects and health economics of managing low-grade lesions.

References

1.   McIndoe WA, McLean MR, Jones RW, Mullins PR. The invasive potential of carcinoma *in situ* of the cervix. *Obstet Gynecol* 1984;64:451–8.
2.   Howells RE, O'Mahoney F, Tucker H, Millinship J, Jones PW, Redman CW. How can the incidence of negative specimens resulting from large loop excision of the cervical transformation zone (LLETZ) be reduced? An analysis of negative LLETZ specimens and development of a predictive model. *BJOG* 2000;107:1075–82.
3.   National Health Service Cervical Screening Programme. *Building On Experience: NHSCSP Annual Review.* Sheffield: NHSCSP; 2001.
4.   Flannelly G, Anderson D, Kitchener HC, Mann EMF, Campbell M, Fisher P, *et al.* Management of women with mild and moderate cervical dyskaryosis. *BMJ* 1994;308:1399–403.
5.   Walker EM, Dodgson J, Duncan I. Does mild atypia on a cervical smear warrant further investigation? *Lancet* 1986;ii:672–3.
6.   Shafi MI, Luesley DM, Jordan JA, Dunn JA, Rollason TP, Yates M. Randomised trial of immediate versus deferred treatment strategies for the management of minor cervical cytological abnormalities. *Br J Obstet Gynaecol* 1997;104:590–94.
7.   Soutter WP, Wisdom S, Brough AK, Monaghan JM. Should patients with mild atypia in a cervical smear be referred for colposcopy? *Br J Obstet Gynaecol* 1986;93:70–74.
8.   Schiffman MH, Bauer HM, Hoover RN, Glass AG, Cadell DM, Rush BB, *et al.* Epidemiologic evidence showing that human papillomavirus causes most cervical intra-epithelial neoplasia. *J Natl Cancer Inst* 1993;85:958–64.
9.   Duncan ID. *Guidelines for Clinical Practice and Programme Management.* 2nd ed. Publication No. 8. London: National Co-ordinating Network, NHS Cervical Screening Programme; 1997.
10.   British Society for Colposcopy and Cervical Pathology. Guidelines for clinical practice and programme management. [www.bsccp.org.uk/guidelines/g_index.html].
11.   Wetrich DW. An analysis of the factors involved in the colposcopic evaluation of 2194 patients with abnormal Papanicolaou smears. *Am J Obstet Gynecol* 1986;154:1339–49.
12.   Robertson JH, Woodend BE, Crozier EH, Hutchinson J. Risk of cervical cancer associated with mild dyskaryosis. *BMJ* 1988;287:18–21.
13.   Kierkegaard O, Byrjalsen C, Frandsen KH, Hansen KC, Frydenberg M. Diagnostic accuracy of cytology and colposcopy in cervical squamous intraepithelial lesions. *Acta Obstet Gynecol Scand* 1994;73:648–51.
14.   Reid R, Greenberg MD, Lorincz A, Jenson AB, Laverty CR, Husain M, *et al.* Should cervical cytology testing be augmented by cervicography or human papillomavirus deoxyribonucleic acid detection? *Am J Obstet Gynecol* 1991;164:1461–71.
15.   Giles JA, Hudson E, Crow J, Williams D, Walker P. Colposcopic assessment of the accuracy of cervical cytology screening. *BMJ* 1988;296:1099–102.
16.   Shafi MI, Dunn JA, Finn CB, Kehoe S, Buxton EJ, Jordon JA, *et al.* Characterisation of high and low grade cervical intra-epithelial neoplasia. *Int J Gynecol Cancer* 1993;3: 203–7.

17. Giles JA, Deery A, Crow J, Walker P. The accuracy of repeat cytology in women with mildly dyskaryotic smears. *Br J Obstet Gynaecol* 1989;96:1067–70.

18. Shafi MI, Dunn JA, Chenoy R, Buxton EJ, Williams C, Luesley DM. Digital imaging colposcopy, image analysis and quantification of the colposcopic image. *Br J Obstet Gynaecol* 1994;101:234–8.

19. Barrasso R, Coupez F, Ionesco M, de Brux J. Human papillomaviruses and cervical intra-epithelial neoplasia: the role of colposcopy. *Gynecol Oncol* 1986;27:197–207.

20. Buxton EJ, Luesley SM, Shafi MI, Rollason M. Colposcopically directed punch biopsies: a potentially misleading investigation. *Br J Obstet Gynaecol* 1991;98:1273–6.

21. Robertson AJ, Anderson JM, Swanson Beck J, Burnett RA, Howatson SR, Lee FD, *et al*. Observer variability in histopathological reporting of cervical biopsy specimens. *J Clin Pathol* 1989;42:231–8.

22. Abadi MA, Ho GYF, Burk RD, Romney SL, Kadish AS. Stringent criteria for histological diagnosis of koilocytosis fail to eliminate overdiagnosis of human papillomavirus infection and cervical intra-epithelial neoplasia grade 1. *Hum Pathol* 1998;29:54–9.

23. Nasiell K, Roger V, Nasiell M. Behavior of mild cervical dysplasia during long term follow-up. *Obstet Gynecol* 1986;67:665–9.

24. Ostor AG. Natural history of cervical neoplasia: a critical review. *Int J Gynecol Pathol* 1993;12:186–92.

25. Kirby AJ, Spiegelhalter DJ, Day NE, Fenton L, Swanson K, Mann EMF, *et al*. Conservative treatment of mild/moderate dyskaryosis: long-term outcome. *Lancet* 1992;339:828–31.

26. Jones MH, Jenkins D, Cuzick J, Wolfendale MR, Jones JJ, Balogun-Lynch C, *et al*. Mild cervical dyskaryosis: safety of cytological surveillance. *Lancet* 1992;339:1440–3.

27. Fletcher A, Metaxas N, Grubb C, Chamberlain J. Four and a half years follow up of women with dyskaryotic smears. *BMJ* 1990;301:641–4.

28. Merriman H, Charnock M, Gray W, Hallam N. Management of mild dyskaryosis. *BMJ* 1994;309:412–13.

29. Shafi MI, Luesley DM. Management of low grade lesions: follow-up or treat? *Baillieres Clin Obstet Gynaecol* 1995;9:121–31.

30. Heatley MK. The prognosis in cervical epithelial changes of uncertain significance is similar to that of cervical intra-epithelial neoplasia grade 1. *J Clin Pathol* 2001;54:474–5.

31. Hording U, Junge J, Rygaard C, Lundvall F. Management of low-grade CIN: follow-up or treatment? *Eur J Obstet Gynecol* 1995;62:49–52.

30. Falls RK. Spontaneous resolution rate of grade 1 cervical intra-epithelial neoplasia in a private practice population. *Am J Obstet Gynecol* 1999;181:278–82.

32. Teale G, Moffitt DD, Mann CH, Luesley DM. Management guidelines for women with normal colposcopy after low grade cervical abnormalities: population study. *BMJ* 2000;320:1693–6.

33. Marteau TM, Walker P, Giles J, Smail M. Anxieties in women undergoing colposcopy. *Br J Obstet Gynaecol* 1990;97:859–61.

34. Bell JS, Porter M, Kitchener HC, Fraser C, Fisher PM, Mann E. Psychological response to cervical screening. *Prev Med* 1995;24:610–16.

35. Jones MH, Singer A, Jenkins D. The mildly abnormal cervical smear: patient anxiety and choice of management. *J R Soc Med* 1996;89:257–60.

36. Johnson N, Sutton J, Thornton JG, Lilford RJ, Johnson VA, Peel KR. Decision analysis for best management of mildly dyskaryotic smear. *Lancet* 1993;342:91–5.

37. Sherlaw-Johnson C, Gallivan S, Jenkins D, Jones MH. Cytological screening and management of abnormalities in prevention of cervical cancer: an overview of stochastic modelling. *J Clin Pathol* 1994;47:430–35.

38. Flannelly G, Campbell MK, Meldrum P, Torgerson DJ, Templeton A, Kitchener HC. Immediate colposcopy or cytological surveillance for women with mild dyskaryosis: a cost effectiveness analysis. *J Public Health Med* 1997;19:419–23.

39. Kjaer SK, Van den Brule AJC, Paull G, Svare EI, Sherman ME, Thomsen BL, *et al*. Type specific persistence of high risk human papillomavirus (HPV) as indicator of high grade cervical squamous intra-epithelial lesions in young women: population based prospective follow up study. *BMJ* 2002;325:572–6.

40. Bistoletti P, Zellbi A, Moreno-Lopez J, Hjerpe A. Genital papillomavirus infection after treatment for cervical intra-epithelial neoplasia (CIN) III. *Cancer* 1998;62:2056–9.

41. Strand A, Wilander E, Zehbe I, Rylander E. High risk HPV persists after treatment of genital papillomavirus infection but not after treatment of cervical intra-epithelial neoplasia. *Acta Obstet Gynecol Scand* 1997;76:140–4.

42. Bollen LJM, Tjong-A-Hung SP, van der Velden J, Mol BWJ, Lammes FB, ten Kate FWJ, *et al*. Human papillomavirus DNA after treatment of cervical dysplasia. *Cancer* 1996;77:2538–43.

43. Cruickshank ME, Sharp L, Chambers G, Smart L, Murray G. Persistent infection with human papillomavirus following the successful treatment of high grade cervical intra-epithelial neoplasia. *BJOG* 2002;109:579–81.

44.   Cubie HA, Seagar AL, Beattie GJ, Monaghan S, Williams AR. A longitudinal study of HPV detection and cervical pathology in HIV infected women. *Sex Transm Infect* 2000;76:257–61.
45.   Delmas MC, Larsen C, van Benthem B, Hammers FF, Bergeron C, Poveda JD, *et al.* Cervical squamous intra-epithelial lesions in HIV-infected women: prevalence, incidence and regression. European Study Group on Natural History of HIV Infection in Women. *AIDS* 2000;14:1775–84.

Chapter 18

Excision of the transformation zone in the treatment of cervical intraepithelial neoplasia

Walter Prendiville

Introduction

The UK cervical screening programme has been a success. There were 2740 new cases of invasive cervical cancer in England and Wales in 1997. This is a 26% fall in incidence over the preceding five years with 9.3 cases per 100 000 women.[1] Even more importantly, the number of deaths from cervical cancer is falling by a rate of 7% per annum.

According to the Imperial Cancer Research Fund, cervical screening prevents between 1100 and 3900 cases of cervical cancer each year in the UK.[2] This is as much an organisational achievement as it is a medical or clinical triumph. Few nations of equivalent population have matched this reduction over such a short time. Sadly, in neighbouring Ireland the incidence rate of cervical cancer is now overtaking that of the UK. Ireland still has not established a national screening programme (Figure 18.1).

Cervical screening programmes are based upon the recognition of those women with an increased risk of developing cervical cancer. It is not the recognition of an abnormal smear which achieves the reduction of risk or affects the incidence or

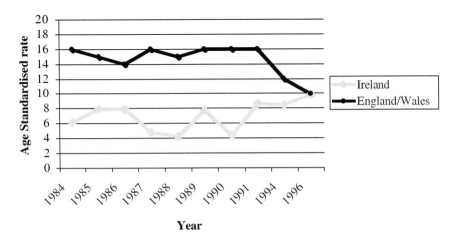

Figure 18.1. Incidence rates for cervical cancer over 20 years in two countries with (UK) and without (Ireland) a national cervical screening programme

Table 18.1. Choice of treatment modality for cervical intraepithelial neoplasia

Excisional	Destructive
Hysterectomy	Radical diathermy
Cone biopsy (variety of techniques)	Cryocautery
LLETZ	Cold (or thermal) coagulation
Laser excision	Laser ablation

mortality rates. Rather, it is the recognition and treatment of these cytological abnormalities which then affords the individual woman relative protection from cervical cancer. In the UK, this will usually mean excision of the transformation zone.

Colposcopic examination has several specific ambitions:

- to recognise the transformation zone

- to identify the most abnormal area within the transformation zone

- to rule out microinvasive disease

- to discriminate between high and low grade disease

- to facilitate treatment, where appropriate.

Perhaps the most important of these is to be able to rule out or recognise microinvasive disease. A number of authorities have attested to the difficulty of reliably so doing.[3–6] The most recent of these[6] found that colposcopy had only a 50% sensitivity (CI 40.1–59.04) in recognising early invasive disease where the ultimate diagnosis was made at conisation or hysterectomy. Furthermore, invasive disease does occasionally occur after destructive treatment[7] and after LLETZ.[8] Finally, unexpected invasive disease is revealed at large loop excision of the transformation zone (LLETZ) at an approximate rate of between one and five per 1000 cases.[9]

Etherington et al.[10] have undertaken an interesting study of pattern recognition in the mid-1990s. They circulated a selection of video clips of different case material to a number of trained colposcopists in the West Midlands. These revealed poor correlation between the different grades of cervical intraepithelial neoplasia (CIN). For CIN 1, kappa was 0.25, rising to 0.35 if the cytology report was revealed prior to diagnostic opinion.[10]

The treatment of CIN

The treatment of CIN must be as effective as possible but also be as minimally morbid as possible. There are two broad categories of treatment, excision or destruction of the transformation zone (Table 18.1).

Destructive techniques or ablative therapy

In terms of success rates, there are insignificant differences between the ablative methods. With the exception of radical diathermy, they may all be performed under local anaesthesia in an outpatient setting. Because of the difficulty of reliably recognising microinvasive disease and because of the concern about inadequately treating women, specific criteria must be satisfied before contemplating destructive therapy. These are as follows.

- The entire transformation zone must be fully visible.
- There must be no suspicion of invasive cancer.
- There must be no suspicion of glandular disease.
- There should be concurrence between cytology and histology.
- There should not have been previous treatment for CIN.

In practice, these criteria allow treatment of the great majority of cases of CIN referred for colposcopy.

Excision of the transformation zone

Hysterectomy

Hysterectomy represents over-treatment for CIN. The morbidity of hysterectomy is far greater than that associated with local excision of the transformation zone or ablative therapy. Also, on the rare occasion when unexpected microinvasive disease is revealed, a woman treated by hysterectomy may have been under-treated. Finally, if colposcopy has not been performed it is possible that untreated and potentially premalignant squamous epithelium may be left behind in the 4% of women with an 'original' or 'congenital' transformation zone. This is not to say that a woman with CIN may never be offered hysterectomy when there are other relative indications for it. It simply means that these women should first be colposcopically assessed.

Cold-knife cone biopsy

The term cone biopsy is not precise. Traditionally, a cone biopsy was a wide and deep excisional treatment, performed under general anaesthesia and using a number of haemostatic sutures. Large cone biopsies are associated with significant short- and long-term morbidity.[11–13] This includes perioperative, primary and secondary haemorrhage, pelvic infection and fertility-related morphological damage, specifically cervical stenosis. These larger cone biopsies predated the introduction of colposcopy and the realisation that the transformation zone could be completely visualised in the majority of cases of CIN. Cold-knife cone biopsy is still a popular method of treatment worldwide. It is still usually performed under general anaesthesia. Cold-knife cone biopsy is an effective treatment for CIN, with success rates in the 90–94% range.[14–16]

Laser cone biopsy

Laser cone biopsy became popular in the late 1970s and 1980s. It may sometimes be performed under local anaesthesia. By using a focused beam to cut and a defocused beam to coagulate any bleeding points, the use of haemostatic sutures may be avoided. A disadvantage of the technique is the possibility of burn artefactual damage, although many authors claim this to be rare after the initial learning curve. Success rates of over 90% are commonly reported.[14,15]

Electrosurgical excision of the transformation zone

The use of electrosurgery in order to resect cervical tissue was relatively brief. In 1938, Durel and Ratner described "planning excision of cervicitis" using a relatively thick wire (0.7 mm). The technique did not achieve widespread popularity. In 1953, Palmer, in France, used a finer wire to resect cervical tissue but reported a high failure rate. With the single exception of Rene Cartier's small loop, electrosurgical excision was almost universally replaced during the 1970s by destructive techniques. Rene Cartier used small square loops to resect biopsy strips of the transformation zone either for diagnostic reasons or in order to extirpate the entire transformation zone. He presented his findings at the World Colposcopy congress in London in 1981 and shortly afterwards Boulanger reported his series (1984).[17] LLETZ was developed in Bristol in the mid-1980s. The term LLETZ was coined in order to distinguish it from Cartier's small loop technique, from which it was developed. LLETZ uses larger loops with thin wire using an electrosurgical unit, which produces a constant low voltage and a blend mode of cutting with coagulation. It is performed under local anaesthesia in the great majority of cases and as an outpatient procedure. The procedure has been described in detail elsewhere.[18] It is now the most popular method of treatment for CIN in the UK.[19]

The efficacy of LLETZ was established in several short-term observational studies studies over the 1990s.[18,20,21] More recently, longer-term studies have reported effectiveness rates which compare favourably with the other excisional and ablative methods.[22-24] In Flannelly's 1997 study of 1000 women,[23] 317 were followed up for over four years. The residual dyskaryosis rate was 4.4% during the first 12 months.

Dobbs et al.[25] followed 394 women over ten years (mean 73 months) with an average of six smears per patient. The study had complete follow-up records for 343 patients and found that 4% had a proven histological 'recurrence' although, of course, it is not possible to know if these cases represent residual or new disease. Two patients had invasive disease, both stage 1a, and were treated by simple hysterectomy. In both cases incomplete excision had been recognised histologically at the time of LLETZ.

In Flannelly's 2001 report,[24] 3426 women were followed up after LLETZ for a mean of 35 months (9765 woman-years of follow up); 417 women (12.2%) had dyskaryotic smear at some time during follow up. Age and a histological report of incomplete excision were found to be independent risk factors for residual/recurrent disease such that cases could be categorised as follows:

1. age less than 50 years without margin involvement – 92% chance of normal smear

2. age 50 years or over with margin involvement – 57% chance of normal smear

3. age less than 50 years with margin involvement – 86% chance of normal smear.

The second group consitututes an especially high-risk category but comprises only 3% of women treated. It seems logical to consider retreating this group. Likewise, colposcopic and cytological monitoring of the lowest risk group (1) may be less intensive.

Comparative studies of therapeutic interventions for CIN

Despite the publication of a large number of randomised controlled trials comparing the different treatment modalities for CIN, a particular method has not yet supplanted all of the others and, at a global level, all of the available methods enjoy relative popularity. Reasons for this might include the local availability of specific equipment, historical preference in a particular unit and the lack of clear evidence in favour of one technique over another. Finally, until recently, most of the published trials were not sufficiently large to reveal clinically important differences.

Evidence from the Cochrane Database of Systematic Reviews

In many areas of clinical practice and in particular in obstetrics and gynaecology, formal meta-analytical reviews of published randomised controlled trials has been successfully used in order to closer approximate the truth about a particular intervention when individual trials have failed to convince. Such a review, examining treatment alternatives for CIN, has been published;[26] 28 individual trials were included for analysis. Not all were truly randomised controlled trials. Data were extracted from these publications by two of the reviewers independently. Seven different surgical treatment techniques were compared. The main result of the review was that no significant difference in success rates was apparent from these studies. The authors also concluded that LLETZ produced the most favourable specimens and was associated with least morbidity, although this opinion derives from one trial where randomisation was not assured.

Comparisons of ablative therapies

From the comparisons made among the ablative techniques, there are few clear messages. For those colposcopists still using cryocautery, the double-freeze technique is more successful than is the single-freeze technique. Laser therapy is more painful than cryocautery. Laser is associated with more postoperative bleeding then cryocautery. Laser is associated with fewer cases of unsatisfactory colposcopic examination at follow up than is cryocautery and, paradoxically, with more cases of cervical stenosis.

No method of ablation has a clearly better rate of success than any other, with the exception that cryocautery appears less successful than laser ablation for the treatment of high-grade CIN. This result was produced by the Cochrane reviewers stratifying the data from several individual studies.

Differences between excisional techniques

Laser cone versus cold-knife cone

This review revealed no difference in the incidence of residual disease between laser and knife conisation. Although the direction of effect was similar in both trials reporting on this outcome,[14,27] the confidence intervals crossed unity and therefore, statistically, no inference can be derived one way or the other (Figure 18.2). There was no difference in the rates of haemorrhage but laser was associated with significantly higher rates of satisfactory colposcopy (Figure 18.3) at follow up and with lower rates

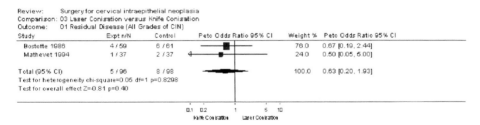

Figure 18.2. Comparison of outcome between laser and knife conisation (residual disease)

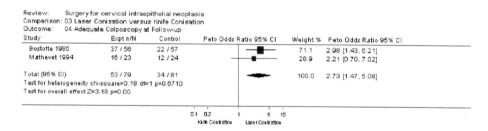

Figure 18.3. Comparison of outcome between laser and knife conisation (adequate postoperative colposcopy)

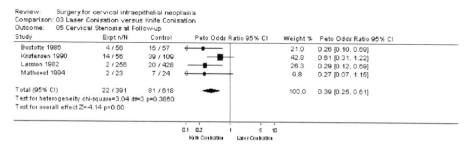

Figure 18.4. Comparison of outcome between laser and knife conisation (cervical stenosis)

of cervical stenosis (Figure 18.4). Not surprisingly, in the single trial which addressed the question of artefactual damage, this was evident in 14 of 35 patients treated by laser conisation and none in the cold-knife group.

Laser cone versus LLETZ

Three trials assessed residual disease.[27–29] The odds ratio in favour of LLETZ was 1.22 but again the 95% confidence intervals crossed unity, such that no inference can truly be drawn (Figure 18.5). LLETZ was shown to be far quicker than laser cone (Figure 18.6) and less painful (Figure 18.7). No difference was found for secondary haemorrhage and primary haemorrhage was not addressed in any of the studies evaluated. Laser conisation was associated with higher rates of significant artefactual damage (Figure 18.8). There was no apparent difference in either cervical stenosis or adequate colposcopy examination at follow up between the two methods of excision.

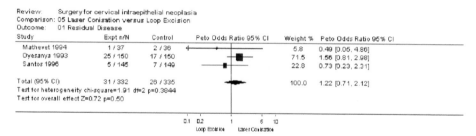

Figure 18.5. Comparison of outcome between laser conisation and knife excision (residual disease)

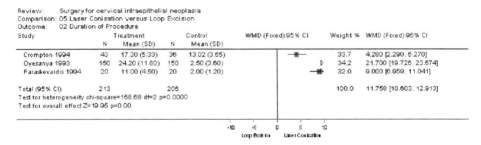

Figure 18.6. Comparison of outcome between laser conisation and loop excision (time of procedure in minutes)

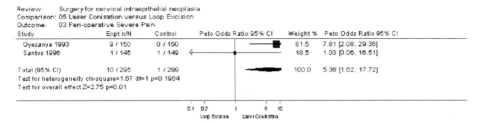

Figure 18.7. Comparison of outcome between laser conisation and loop excision (postoperative severe pain)

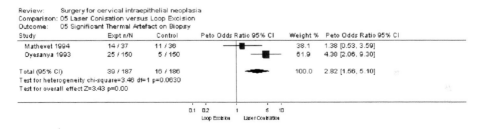

Figure 18.8. Comparison of outcome between laser conisation and knife excision (significant thermal artefact on biopsy specimen)

Cold knife versus LLETZ

Four trials included data concerning residual disease and there appeared to be a higher residual disease rate after LLETZ in these studies but the difference was only just significant, that is the confidence intervals reached but did not cross unity (Figure 18.9). There was no difference between the methods in terms of haemorrhage or cervical stenosis but LLETZ was associated with lower rates of unsatisfactory colposcopy at follow up although again the confidence intervals just crossed zero (Figure 18.10).

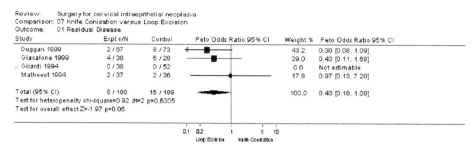

Review: Surgery for cervical intraepithelial neoplasia
Comparison: 07 Knife Conisation versus Loop Excision
Outcome: 01 Residual Disease

Figure 18.9. Comparison of knife conisation and loop excision (residual disease)

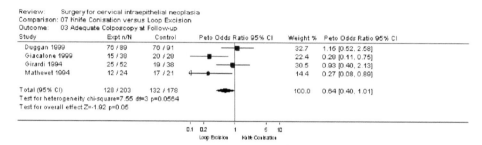

Review: Surgery for cervical intraepithelial neoplasia
Comparison: 07 Knife Conisation versus Loop Excision
Outcome: 03 Adequate Colposcopy at Follow-up

Figure 18.10. Comparison of knife conisation and loop excision (adequate postoperative colposcopy)

Differences between excisional and ablative techniques

Relatively few comparative studies have examined differences between ablative and destructive therapy. In the single published study of radical diathermy versus LLETZ, the only apparent difference was that radical diathermy was more painful. In a comparison of laser ablation versus laser conisation, no difference was revealed in terms of residual disease, perioperative bleeding or secondary haemorrhage. Laser ablation did appear to be associated with a higher rate of satisfactory examination at follow up but these data derive from one small trial.[30]

Laser ablation versus LLETZ

Three studies in the Cochrane meta-analysis compared these methods.[31–33] Subsequently, a fourth larger comparison was published.[34] No difference in residual disease nor in haemorrhage was evident in this later comparison but more women complained of pain during laser than at LLETZ (Figure 18.11).

What can be learned from the Cochrane review[26]?

The authors have gone to great pains to be as inclusive as possible. They examined and collated the data from 28 different studies. From the data presented, it could reasonably be argued that there is little difference between the methods in terms of success and that choice of method should depend upon other factors, for example morbidity, expense of technique, artefactual damage of the extirpated biopsy and ease of use.

There are several difficulties in deriving evidence from pooled data, even from

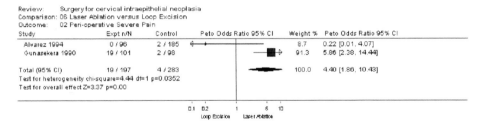

Review: Surgery for cervical intraepithelial neoplasia
Comparison: 06 Laser Ablation versus Loop Excision
Outcome: 02 Peri-operative Severe Pain

Study	Expt n/N	Control	Peto Odds Ratio 95% CI	Weight %	Peto Odds Ratio 95% CI
Alvarez 1994	0 / 96	2 / 185		8.7	0.22 [0.01, 4.07]
Gunasekera 1990	19 / 101	2 / 98		91.3	5.86 [2.38, 14.44]
Total (95% CI)	19 / 197	4 / 283		100.0	4.40 [1.86, 10.43]

Test for heterogeneity chi-square=4.44 df=1 p=0.0352
Test for overall effect Z=3.37 p=0.00

Figure 18.11. Comparison of laser ablation and loop excision (perioperative severe pain)

random or quasi-random trials. One problem is that of nomenclature. The meaning of the term cone biopsy is not universally agreed. For some authors any excision of the transformation zone equates to a cone biopsy. To others, a cone biopsy always means excision of part of the endocervical canal. We know that the morbidity of a traditional cone biopsy relates to the length of canal excised. It is logical to assume that a small cone biopsy will be associated with different success rates and morbidity risk than those associated with a large cone biopsy. While it is always possible to vary the length of cone excised using a knife or electrosurgical straight wire or laser beam, it is not possible to vary the extent of tissue excised using a standard LLETZ loop. It is, of course, possible to choose varying loop sizes and so achieve excision of any amount of endocervical tissue but the loop dimensions are not always detailed in publications of LLETZ. Indeed, in many of the larger LLETZ series[20,22,23] the data refer to routine office-based excisions of ectocervical transformation zones. These procedures will inevitably have different morbidity and success rates than for true cone biopsies, no matter which technique is chosen.

For example, in Mathevet et al.'s randomised controlled trial of conisation by knife, laser and LLETZ,[27] the LLETZ procedures were performed with loops whose height varied between 10 mm and 20 mm. When using a loop of only 10-mm length, it is not possible to produce a cone biopsy which would include a significant length of endocervical canal. It is not surprising that in this study the mean volume of cone tissue excised was 1.91 cm^3 for cone biopsy and 0.96 cm^3 for LLETZ. In truth, many of these LLETZ procedures were not cone biopsies but were LLETZ of ectocervical transformation zones. Again, in Girardi's study,[35] which is described as a randomised controlled trial, although allocation was by birth date, the mean weight of the LLETZ specimens was 2.6 g compared with 5.6 g for the knife cone biopsies.

Dey et al.[34] published a relatively large multicentre randomised controlled trial of LLETZ versus laser vaporisation. The authors appeared to take a neutral stance prior to commencing the study, believing that both methods were equally effective. They were critical of the previous randomised controlled trials of laser ablation versus LLETZ, arguing that in two of the studies included in the Cochrane review, the allocation could be considered non-random and in the other the inclusion criteria were broad (e.g. 50% of women allocated to laser did not have CIN). Other aspects of this trial[31] that give cause for concern include the fact that four times as many women with CIN3 were allocated to LLETZ than laser and that follow up was only for six months.

In Dey et al.'s study,[34] seven colposcopy clinics in the northwest of England were recruited to the study. Each centre was capable of providing laser or LLETZ as a routine method of treatment and 289 patients were randomly allocated to laser or LLETZ. The baseline patient characteristics and other outcomes support adequacy of randomisation and the follow-up period was longer than any other randomised controlled trial of similar design, at over six years. Women allocated to laser vaporisation were three times more likely to have a follow-up smear reported as moderated dyskaryosis or worse (≥ CIN2; high-grade squamous intraepithelial lesion) than women allocated to LLETZ (hazard ratio 3.01; 95% CI 1.27–7.12). The direction of effect was the same in all of the participating centres. There were no differences in morbidity outcome measures or in terms of birth rate or pregnancy outcome.

The authors of this study argue that the reason for lower rates of residual disease in the LLETZ arm may be due to greater depths of excision achieved with LLETZ compared with the depth of destruction achieved with laser.

Other advantages of excision over destruction

Apart from the apparent increased effectiveness shown in Dey et al.'s study,[34] there are other advantages of excision over destruction which might influence the choice of therapy for CIN today:

- invasive disease may be ruled out
- glandular disease may be revealed
- margins of excision may be assessed
- the degree of abnormality may be confirmed
- it allows self-audit of colposcopic expertise
- it accommodates every transformation zone type
- it allows selected patients to be treated at their first visit.

Over- and under-treatment of women with CIN

Over-treatment may occur in two circumstances. Firstly, when a transformation zone has been removed (or destroyed) without need; in other words, when histology reveals that there was not clinically important dysplasia present in the excised specimen. Secondly, when an excessive amount of normal tissue adjacent to the transformation zone has been removed.

Luesley et al.[36] have shown that, when a non-selective see-and-treat policy is adopted, the resultant normal histology rate is unacceptably high. At the Coombe Women's Hospital in Dublin,[37] where a selective see-and-treat policy prevails, it has been possible to keep the negative histology rate below 5% (Table 18.2). A selective

Table 18.2. Histological analysis of large loop excision of the transformation zone biopsies

	1993	1994	1995	1996	1997	1998	1999	2000	2001
Neoplasia not found	10	11	15	12	16	18	29	27	32
CIN1	83	59	35	36	56	65	68	159	139
CIN2	59	37	37	45	61	90	93	173	159
CIN3	109	110	117	155	189	255	224	187	192
Glandular neoplasia only	4	2	1	3	4	1	6[a]	1	4[a]
Microinvasion	6	3	4	4	1	11	3	4	2
Invasive neoplasia	5	11	7	7	3	5	4	3	4
Total	276	243	216	262	330	445	427	554	532

[a] These patients had a glandular abnormality; in each of them, there was an associated squamous abnormality (CIN); CIN = cervical intraepithelial neoplasia

see-and-treat policy simply means that women with a cytological and colposcopic suspicion of CIN2 or worse are offered treatment at their first visit routinely and women with low-grade lesions are not.

However, under-treatment is perhaps the greater sin. As one might expect, incomplete excision of the transformation zone is associated with a higher chance of there being residual disease.[22,38] The fact that incomplete excision does not usually result in residual disease is probably because of the combined effect of diathermy damage and the inflammatory response associated with the healing wound.

Also, just as incomplete excision at histology does not equate with residual disease at cytological and colposcopic follow up, so also is it true that residual disease may occur after apparent complete excision assessed by histology.[22,39,40] Finally, there are other important predictors of residual disease after LLETZ apart from histological incomplete excision. These include the patient's age and the severity of the disease.[24] However, in Dobbs et al.'s long-term follow-up study of patients treated by LLETZ, incomplete excision was an important predictor of residual disease.[25] Furthermore, it should be theoretically possible to completely excise the entire transformation zone by simply using bigger loops, although this would inevitably be at a cost of increased morbidity.[11,41]

Despite its obvious problems, incomplete excision is a common entity. In an as yet unpublished review by de Camargo et al. of papers reporting experience with cone biopsy, incomplete excision was reported in 20% of cases.[42] Although the range was quite wide, high rates were reported for all three modalities (Table 18.3).

Despite its obvious problems, incomplete excision is a common entity. The reported rates published range from 5% to 50% and relate to all methods of excision.[27,43]

Why does incomplete excision occur? Is it because the excision procedure has been too shallow for the particular transformation zone? Is it because colposcopists are incapable of reliably recognising the upper limit of the transformation zone? Is it that

Table 18.3. Incomplete excision in cone biopsy; involvement of margins

Series and reference	Date	Margins (% endocervical)	Method	Disease	Patients (n)
Cullimore et. al.[41]	1992	15.6[a]	Cold-knife	CIGN	51
Mathevet et. al.[27]	1994	14.0	Cold-knife	CIN, microinvasion	37
Jansen et al.	1994	22.0[a]	Cold-knife	CIN	316
Wolf et al.[40]	1996	43.0[a]	Cold-knife	CIGN, CIN	42
Monk et al.	1996	21.0	Cold-knife	CIN, microinvasion	369
Guerra et al.[43]	1996	5.4	Cold-knife	CIN, microinvasion	73
Gurgel et al.	1997	46.6 *	Cold-knife	Microinvasion	163
Partington et al.[30]	1998	18.0 *	Laser	CIN	50
Mor-Yosef et al.[45]	1990	20.0	Laser	–	550
Lopes et al.	1993	24.0	Laser	CIN, microinvasion	313
Mathevet et al.[27]	1994	51.0[b]	Laser	CIN, microinvasion	37
Andersen et al.	1994	6.6	Laser	CIN, CIGN	473
Guerra et al.[43]	1996	5.4	Laser	CIN, microinvasion	275
Mor-Yosef et al.[45]	1990	10.0	Loop diathermy	CIN3, microinvasion	50
Byrne et al.	1991	22.0	LLETZ	CIN, invasion	50
Montz et al.	1993	48.0[b]	LLETZ	CIN	25
Naumann et al.	1994	25.8[b]	LLETZ	CIN, microinvasion	120
Mathevet et al.[27]	1994	53.0[b]	LEEP	CIN	36
Felix et al.	1994	28.0	LEEP	CIN, microinvasion	57
Houghton et al.	1997	42.1[a]	LLETZ	CIGN	19

[a] not defined margin; [b] thermal artefact; CIN = cervical intraepithelial neoplasia; LEEP = loop electrosurgical excision procedure; LLETZ = large loop excision of the transformation zone

our pathologists are unable to recognise margin status because of artefactual damage? Or is it that we use inappropriate electrodes for different procedures?

The answer may be multifaceted. It is likely that performing excision of transformation zone using inappropriately sized electrodes is at least partly to blame. Also as referred to previously, the term cone biopsy means different things in different publications. In order that clarity prevails and that the results of treatment may be properly compared, a new classification system was proposed and accepted by the International Federation for Cervical Pathology and Colposcopy Nomenclature Committee in June 2001.[44] The system is designed with the twin ambitions of being simple and acceptable to practising colposcopists, as well as being able to accommodate every treatment circumstance that will arise in routine practice. It has three indices by which the transformation zone may be qualified. These are:

- the size of the ecto-cervical component of the transformation zone

- the position of the upper limit of the transformation zone

- the visibility of the upper limit of the transformation zone.

The three types of transformation can be distinguished as being completely ectocervical, fully visible with an endocervical component or not fully visible (Figure 18.12). By using these three variables it is possible to classify all transformation zones into three types. These are detailed in Table 18.4.

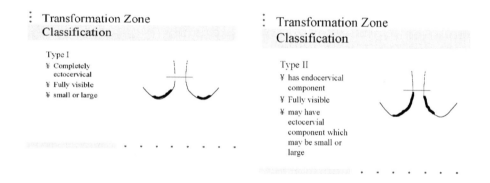

: Transformation Zone
   Classification

Type I
¥ Completely
  ectocervical
¥ Fully visible
¥ small or large

: Transformation Zone
   Classification

Type II
¥ has endocervical
  component
¥ Fully visible
¥ may have
  ectocervial
  component which
  may be small or
  large

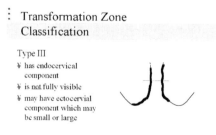

: Transformation Zone
   Classification

Type III
¥ has endocervical
  component
¥ is not fully visible
¥ may have ectocervial
  component which may
  be small or large

Figure 18.12. Classification of the transformation zone: digrammatic representation

Table 18.4. Classification of the transformation zone

	Size	Site	Visibility
Type I$_s$	Small	Completely ectocervical	Fully visible
Type I$_l$	Large	Completely ectocervical	Fully visible
Type 2$_0$	–	Totally endocervical	Fully visible
Type 2$_s$	Small	Partially endocervical	Fully visible
Type 2$_l$	Large	Partially endocervical	Fully visible
Type 3$_0$	–	Totally endocervical	Not fully visible
Type 3$_s$	Small	Partially endocervical	Not fully visible
Type 3$_l$	Large	Partially endocervical	Not fully visible

The qualification large or small refers purely to the ectocervical component of the transformation zone. Large here means that the transformation zone occupies more than half of the ectocervical epithelium.

These three different transformation zone types warrant an individualistic therapeutic approach. For example, it is entirely appropriate to use either an excisional or destructive method, provided the standard criteria are met, in order to successfully treat a large or small type-1 transformation zone, whereas it is entirely inappropriate to use a destructive method of treatment for any type-3 transformation zone.

Even if one uses an excisional technique for every circumstance, it is still necessary to modify the approach according to the type of transformation zone. If one uses diathermy excision as the routine treatment modality, the shape and size of the wire electrode needs to be modified according the transformation zone type. Table 18.5 details choices that may be considered appropriate for each type.

For the type-1 transformation zone, any treatment choice is likely to be successful and associated with low morbidity. For type-2 transformation zone, it may be possible to use a destructive method but an excisional method will offer greater security for the endocervical margin status. For any type-3 transformation zone, it is mandatory to use an excisional technique. The type-3 transformation zone has a high risk of incomplete excision. It is in this circumstance that it is wise to consider alternatives to the loop. Straight wire excision is such an alternative,[9] as is laser excision.[45]

Determining the optimum method of excision for the type-3 transformation zone will be revealed by appropriately designed randomised controlled trials. If the inclusion criteria in these studies contain only type 3, we will be likely to discover the optimum method of management for this difficult circumstance.

Table 18.5. Treatment choice versus transformation zone (TZ) type

TZ classification	Electrode choice	Alternative
Type 1 (small)	2 x 1.5-mm loop	Laser excision or any destructive procedure
Type 1 (large)	Wider loop or combination electrode[a]	Laser excision or any destructive procedure
Type 2 (small)	2 x 2-mm or larger loop or straight	Laser excision
Type 2 (large)	wire or combination electrode	
Type 3 (small)	Longer loop or straight wire or	Laser excision
Type 3 (large)	combination electrode	Cold-knife long cone

[a] Combination electrode treatment means excision of the central transformation zone with diathermy rollerball destruction of the peripheral ectocervical component

When to excise the transformation zone in women with CIN 2 – 3 (high-grade SIL)

'See-and-treat' is an attractive philosophy for many clinical scenarios in gynaecology. The opportunity of office hysteroscopy, endometrial biopsy and insertion of a progesterone-releasing intrauterine system is at once patient friendly and effective in the management of dysfunctional uterine bleeding. However, it is also clear that this approach might be inappropriate in the management of potential malignancy; for example, some ovarian cysts. For this reason, a number of colposcopists believe that the policy of see-and-treat should never be incorporated into the management of women with cytological abnormalities. However, it is only sensible to delay treatment of a condition by performing an investigation if the result is likely to affect the management.

Applying this logic to the management of women with a cytological suspicion of CIN3 lends convincing support to the philosophy of see-and-treat in certain defined and selected circumstances.

It would be wrong to treat every woman with a mildly abnormal smear because of the high rate of over-treatment. However, for a woman with an abnormal smear reporting severe dyskaryosis in whom a fully visible transformation zone reveals evidence of CIN3 to the examining colposcopist, there can be little benefit in delaying excisional treatment. A biopsy that supports the cytological and colposcopic suspicion of CIN3 will indicate treatment. On the other hand, a biopsy that reveals a lesser grade of abnormality would not persuade the reasonable colposcopist to withhold treatment in the presence of cytological and colposcopic evidence of CIN3. Table 18.2 illustrates how a selective see-and-treat policy is consistent with a low rate of excising normal epithelium.

There are other factors that influence a colposcopist's decision about when to treat. For example on occasions where the risk of follow up attendance default is high it may be prudent to treat at the first visit, even for mild cytological abnormalities.

References

1.   Office for National Statistics. Monitor Population & Health MB 1998/92.
2.   Sasieni PD, Cuzick J, Lynch-Farmery E. Estimating the efficacy of screening by auditing smear histories of women with and without cervical cancer. The National Co-ordinating Network for Cervical Screening Working Group. *Br J Cancer* 1996;73:1001–5.
3.   Benedet J, Nickerson K, White G. Laser therapy for cervical intraepithelial neoplasia. *Obstet Gynecol* 1981;57:188–91.
4.   Chappatte O, Byrne D, Raju K, Nayagam M, Kenney A. Histological differences between colposcopic-directed biopsy and loop excision of the transformation zone: a cause for concern. *Gynecol Oncol* 1991;43:46–50.
5.   Buxton EJ, Luesley DM, Shafi ML, Rollason M. Colposcopically directed punch biopsy: a potentially misleading investigation. *Br J Obstet Gynaecol* 1992;98:1273–6.
6.   Reiss, *et. al.* Validity of cytology and colposcopy-guided biopsy for the diagnosis of preclinical cervical carcinoma. *Rev Bras Ginecol Obstet* 1999;21(4):193–200.
7.   Anderson MC. The case in favour of large loop excision of the transformation zone for the treatment of cervical intra-epithelial neoplasia. In: Prendiville W, editor. *Large Loop Excision of the Transformation Zone: A Practical Guide to LLETZ*. London: Chapman and Hall Medical; 1993. p. 71–81.
8.   Shafi ML, Dunn JA, Buxton EJ, Finn CB, Jordan JA, Luesley DM. Abnormal cervical cytology following large loop excision of the transformation zone: a case controlled study. *Br J Obstet Gynaecol* 1993;100:145–8.
9.   Prendiville W. Large Loop Excision of the Transformation Zone. In: *Large Loop Excision of the Transformation Zone: A practical guide to LLETZ*. Prendiville W, editor. London: Chapman and Hall Medical; 1993. p. 35–57.

10. Etherington IJ, Luesley DM, Shafi MI, Dunn J, Hiller L, Jordan JA. Observer variability among colposcopists from the West Midlands region. *Br J Obstet Gynaecol* 1997;104:1380–4.

11. Luesley D, McCrum A, Terry P, Wade-Evans T. Complications of cone biopsy related to the dimensions of the cone and the influence of prior colposcopic assessment. *Br J Obstet Gynaecol* 1985;92–158.

12. Jordan J. Symposia on cervical neoplasia, excisional methods. *Colp Laser Surg* 1984;1:271.

13. Leiman G, Harrison N, Rubin A. Pregnancy following conisation of the cervix: complications related to cone biopsy. *Am J Obstet Gynecol* 1980;136:14–18.

14. Bostofte E, Berget A, Larsen J, Pedersen P, Rank F. Conisation by carbon dioxide laser or cold knife in the treatment of cervical intra-epithelial neoplasia. *Acta Obstet Gynecol Scand* 1986;65:199–202.

15. Tabor A, Berget A. Cold knife and laser conisation for cervical intra-epithelial neoplasia. *Obstet Gynecol* 1990;76:633–5.

16. Larson G. Conisation for preinvasive and invasive carcinoma. *Acta Obstet Gynecol Scand Suppl* 1983;114:1–40.

17. Boulanger JC, Vitse M, Lavallard C, Levet S, Deparis A. Comparative study of the treatment of cervical dysplasias with the CO_2 laser and electroresection with the diathermy loop. *Rev Fr Gynecol Obstet* 1984;79:797–803.

18. Prendiville W, Cullimore J, Norman S. Large loop excision of the transformation zone (LLETZ): a new method of management for women with cervical intra-epithelial neoplasia. *Br J Obstet Gynaecol* 1989;96:1054–60.

19. Kitchener HC, Cruickshank M, Farmery E. The 1993 British Society for Colposcopy and Cervical Pathology/National Co-ordinating Network United Kingdom Colposcopy Survery. *Br J Obstet Gynaecol* 1995;102:549–52.

20. Bigrigg MA, Coding BW, Pearson P, Read MO, Swinger GR. Colposcopic diagnosis and treatment of cervical dysplasia at a single visit. *Lancet* 1990;336:229–31.

21. Whiteley P, Oláh K. Treatment of cervical intra-epithelial neoplasia: experience with low voltage diathermy loop. *Am J Obstet Gynecol* 1990;162:1272.

22. Gardiel F, Barry Walsh C, Prendiville W, Clinch J. Turner MJ. Persistent intra-epithelial neoplasia after excision for cervical intra-epithelial neoplasia grade III. *Obstet Gynecol* 1997;89:419–22.

23. Flannelly G, Langham H, Jandial L, Mana E, Cambell M, Kitchener H. A study of treatment failures following large loop excision of the transformation zone for the treatment of cervical intra-epithelial neoplasia. *Br J Obstet Gynaecol* 1997;104:718–22.

24. Flannelly G, Bolger B, Fawzi H, De Lopes AB, Monaghan JM. Follow up after LLETZ: could schedules be modified according to risk of recurrence? *BJOG* 2001;108:1025–30.

25. Dobbs SP, Asmussen TM, Nunns D, Hollingworth J, Brown LJ, Ireland D. Does histological incomplete excision of cervical intra-epithelial neoplasia following large loop excision of transformation zone increase recurrence rates? A six year cytological follow up. *BJOG* 2000;107:1298–301.

26. Martin-Hirsch PL, Paraskevaidis E, Kitchener H. Surgery for cervical intra-epithelial neoplasia. *Cochrane Database Syst Rev* 2002; Issue 3.

27. Mathevet P, Dargent D, Roy M, Beau G. A randomised prospective study comparing three techniques of conisation: cold knife, laser, and LEEP. *Gynecol Oncol* 1994;54:175–9.

28. Oyesanya O, Amersinghe C, Manning E. Out patient excisional management of cervical Intra-epithelial neoplasia: a prospective randomized comparison between loop diathermy excision and laser excisional conisation. *Am J Obstet Gynecol* 1993;168:485–8.

29. Santos C, Galdos R, Alvarez M, Vberlarde C, Barriga O, Dyer R, *et al.* One-session management of cervical intraepithelial neoplasia. A solution for developing countries. *Gynecol Oncol* 1996;61:11–15.

30. Partington C, Turner M, Soutter W, Griffiths, Krausz T. Laser vaporization versus laser excision conisation in the treatment of cervical intra-epithelial neoplasia. *Obstet Gynecol* 1989;73:775–9.

31. Alvarez R, Helm W, Edwards P, Naumann W, Partridge E, Shingleton H, *et al.* Prospective randomised trial of LLETZ versus laser ablation in patients with cervical intra-epithelial neoplasia. *Gynecol Oncol* 1994;52:175–9.

32. Gunasekera C, Phipps J, Lewis B. Large loop excision of the transformation zone (LLETZ) compared to carbon dioxide treatment of CIN: a superior mode of treatment. *Br J Obstet Gynaecol* 1990;97:995–8.

33. Mitchell M, Tortolero-Luna G, Cook E, Whittaker L, Rhodes-Morris H, Silva E. A randomized clinical trial of cryotherapy, laser vaporization and loop electrosurgical excision for the treatment of squamous intra-epithelial lesions of the cervix. *Obstet Gynecol* 1998;92:737–44.

34. Dey P, Gibbs A, Arnold DF, Saleh N, Hirsch PJ, Woodman CBJ. Loop diathermy excision compared with cervical laser vaporisation fort the treatment of intra-epithelial neoplasia: a randomised controlled trial. *BJOG* 2002;109:381–5.

35. Girardi F, Pickel H, Joura EA, Breitenecker G, Gitsch G, Graf AH, *et al.* Guidelines for diagnosis and therapy of intraepithelial neoplasia and early invasive carcinoma of the female lower genital system

(cervix uteri, vagina, vulva) established by the AGK Colposcopy Work Group in the OGGG Austrian Society of Gynecology and Obstetrics. *Gynakol Geburtshilfliche Rundsch* 2001;41:197–200.

36.   Luesley DM, Cullimore J, Redman CW, Lawston FG, Emens JM, Rollason TP, *et al.* Loop diathermy excision of the cervical transformation zone in patients with abnormal cervical smears. *BMJ* 1990;300:1690–3.

37.   Coombe Women's Hospital. *Annual Report 2001.* Dublin; 2001.

38.   Shafi ML, Dunn JA, Finn CB, Kehoe S, Buxton EJ, Jordan JA, Luesley DM. Characterization of high- and low-grade cervical intra-epithelial neoplasia. *Int J Gynecol Cancer* 1993;3:203–7.

39.   Moore EJ, Fitzpatrick CC, Coughlan BM, McKenna PJ. Cone biopsy. A review of 112 cases. *Ir Med J* 1992;83:28–30.

40.   Wolf JK, Levenback C, Malpica A, Morris M, Burke T, Mitchell MF. Adenocarcinoma *in situ* of the cervix: significance of cone biopsy margins. *Obstet Gynecol* 1996;88:82–6.

41.   Cullimore JE, Luesley DM, Rollason TP, Byrne P, Buckley CH, Anderson M, *et al.* A prospective study of conization of the cervix in the management of cervical intra-epithelial glandular neoplasia (CIGN): a preliminary report. *Br J Obstet Gynaecol* 1992;99:314–18.

42.   De Camargo MJ, Prendiville W, Walker P. Diathermy cone Biopsy. A randomized controlled trial of two techniques (protocol, unpublished).

43.   Guerra B, Guida G, Falco P, Gabrielli S, Martinelli GN, Bovicelli L. Microcolposcopic topographic endocervical assessment before excisional treatment of cervical intraepithelial neoplasia. *Obstet Gynecol* 1996;88:77–81.

44.   Walker P, Dexeus S, De Palo TG, Barrasso R, Campion M, Girardi F, *et al.* International terminology of colposcopy: an updated report from the International Federation for Cervical pathology and Colposcopy. *Obstet Gynecol* 2003;101:175-7.

45.   Mor-Yosef S, Lopes A, Pearson S, Monaghan JM. Loop diathermy cone biopsy. *Obstet Gynecol* 1990;75:884–6.

Chapter 19

Antiviral vaccination for treating intraepithelial neoplasia

Alison Fiander and Stephen Man

Introduction

This chapter covers the use of antiviral vaccines in the treatment of intraepithelial neoplasia and does not, by definition, cover prophylactic vaccination, although this is an important approach that has been reviewed extensively elsewhere.[1] There is an addendum at the end of this chapter to update information on prophylactic vaccination. Additionally, the title focuses the scope of the chapter to intraepithelial neoplasia (pre-invasive disease) and therefore more limited reference is made to vaccine studies in invasive carcinoma.

Any part of the genital tract, including the anal canal, may be affected by intraepithelial neoplasia. The vagina and anus are particularly difficult to access, making assessment less reliable. Disease may be multifocal, multicentric (genital neoplasia syndrome) or sequential and tends to recur after ablation or surgical excision, presenting management difficulties. Lesions may be associated with distressing, unrelenting symptoms of pain, irritation or itching. In widespread disease, surgical excision can be mutilating and may have profound implications for body image and sexuality (Figures 19.1–19.3). The incidence of glandular neoplasia of the cervix appears to be increasing in younger women,[2] as does that of vulval intraepithelial neoplasia (VIN)[3] and anal intraepithelial neoplasia (AIN).[4] New strategies for the control and treatment of these diseases are therefore eagerly awaited.

Substantial progress has been made in the past decade in understanding host immune defence to human papillomavirus (HPV) infection[5] and in the development of candidate vaccines. This chapter describes animal models relevant to development of vaccines, the clinical trials undertaken so far, and challenges facing future development of therapeutic vaccines.

Background rationale to immunotherapy

Approximately 20 HPV types infect the lower genital tract, high-risk types being associated with intraepithelial neoplasia and cancer. The most common high-risk types are HPV16 and 18, although genotypes have been less well studied in VIN and AIN and may differ in immunocompromised individuals.

The rationale for immunotherapy of intraepithelial neoplasia is firmly based on the expression of HPV antigens that distinguish neoplastic from normal epithelia. The

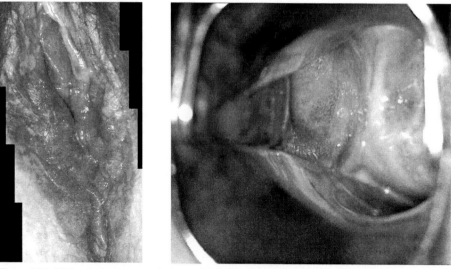

Figure 19.1 Widespread, symptomatic intraepithelial neoplasia grade 3 extending over (a) the vulva, perineum and an anterior anal skin tag and (b) the lower two-thirds of the vagina

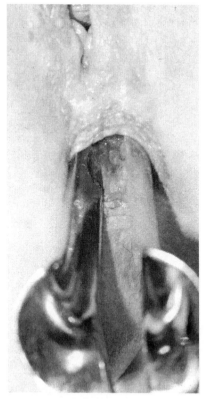

Figure 19.2 Multifocal, symptomatic intraepithelial neoplasia grade 3 extending perianally and involving the anal canal to the dentate line

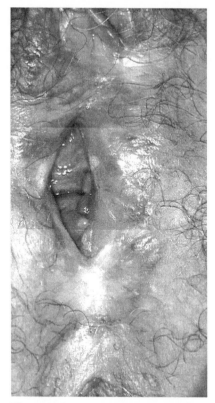

Figure 19.3 17-year history of widespread, symptomatic intraepithelial neoplasia grade 3 following multiple excisions, laser ablation and photodynamic therapy

Table 19.1. Antiviral vaccination in animal papillomavirus models

Virus/Model	Target Antigen /Vaccine	Outcome	Reference
BPV2	L1, L2 proteins	Protection and therapy	87
BPV4	E7 proteins	Protection and therapy	88
CRPV	E2 in lesions	T cell response, papilloma regression with CD8+ infiltration	84
CRPV	E6 + GM-CSF DNA	Protection and therapeutic responses	45
CRPV	E1, E2, E6, E7 Gene cocktail	DNA Protection	89
COPV	L1 VLP	Protection	90
COPV	L1 DNA vaccine	Protection	91
Murine	HPV16 E7 peptide	CD8 T cell response, protection against transplanted tumours	33
Murine	HPV16 E7 fused to glutathione-S-transferase	Protection against tumour challenge	92
Murine	HPV 16 E7 + fused BCG hsp 65	Immunogenicity, inhibition of tumour growth	39
Murine	Vaccinia virus +HPV16E7 fused to lysosome-associated membrane protein 1 (LAMP1)	Therapy of HPV 16 expressing lung metastases	93
Murine	Epitope string HPV 16 DNA (B, TH, CTL epitopes)	Therapy of HPV 16 expressing lung metastases	76,94
Murine	Alphavirus vector with HPV16 E7	Protection and therapy	95
Murine	Prime-boost: HPV16 E7 DNA + recombinant vaccinia virus	Enhanced immunogenicity	96
Murine	Prime-boost: HPV16 L2E6E7 fusion protein (TA-CIN) + recombinant vaccinia (TA-HPV)	Protection, prevention of tumour outgrowth in minimum residual disease	40
Murine	Recombinant Listeria with HPV 16 E7	Therapy of established tumours	25
Murine	Long peptides of HPV16 E7	Therapy of established tumours	77

BPV = bovine papillomavirus; COPV = canine oral papillomavirus; CRPV = cottontail rabbit papillomavirus

specific approaches adopted to date have been derived from animal models, together with knowledge of the natural history of HPV infection and the process of HPV carcinogenesis. A number of studies in animal models (Table 19.1) have demonstrated that therapeutic HPV vaccines can be effective in protection against tumour challenge or promoting disease regression, thereby establishing proof of concept.

For human disease it is possible to conceive two strategies for HPV related intraepithelial neoplasia: the first targeting low-grade disease or dysplasia, e.g. cervical intraepithelial neoplasia (CIN) grade 1, the second addressing high-grade disease, e.g. CIN 2–3, VIN3, etc. Determining which viral antigens are most appropriate to target results from knowledge of the viral life cycle.

In early disease, there is expression of multiple viral proteins dependent upon the differentiation state of the epithelial cell. The virus infects the basal cells of the epithelium and expresses the early proteins E1, E2 and E5. Expression of these proteins is abundant in the koilocytes found in low-grade CIN but expression is lost with disease progression. The E6 and E7 genes are expressed at very low levels in these cells, making them poor targets for therapy of low-grade disease. Several studies have shown that E2 is immunogenic to human T cells, marking it out as a potential target.[6–8]

As differentiation of the HPV infected epithelial cells proceeds, HPV gene expression changes to a 'late' pattern, with E4 and the viral capsid proteins (L1 and L2) being expressed. The L1 and L2 proteins have been targeted for antibody-mediated prophylactic responses[1] using virus-like particles (VLPs), and T cell responses against these proteins are readily detectable for both oncogenic[9] and non-oncogenic HPV types.[10,11]

A major problem with targeting low-grade disease is the fact that many lesions regress spontaneously and therefore large cohorts need to be vaccinated and followed up to assess the benefits of immunotherapy. This chapter therefore concentrates on high-grade disease, as this has been the initial area of attention for therapeutic vaccines.

In high-grade intraepithelial neoplasia, the E6 and E7 gene products are the clear targets, as expression of other viral gene products is largely lost and the persistence of E6 and E7 is required to maintain the transformed state.[12] Because of their applicability to cancer, most attention has been focused on these gene products, thus several vaccines based on HPV16 or HPV18 E6/E7 are currently being tested for safety, immunogenicity and clinical efficacy in phase I and II clinical trials. These use differing vaccine designs as described below. However, the inevitable bureaucratic delays in getting vaccines into clinical trials, together with the rapid developments in immunology and vaccinology, mean that these vaccines are already out of date. They are likely to be usurped by new therapeutic vaccines that are currently being studied in preclinical animal models (Table 19.1).

Types of vaccine

The induction of strong cell-mediated responses is an essential requirement for therapeutic vaccines. There has been an emphasis on CD8+ cytotoxic T lymphocytes (CTL) because of their demonstrable antiviral[13] and antitumour effector function.[14] However, induction and persistence of antiviral CD8+ CTL depends on CD4+ T helper cells.[15-17] The role of CD4+ T cells has been shown for HPV-associated warts, regression being associated with a CD4+ T cell response.[18] To date, vaccine development has focused on strategies designed to induce CD8+ T cell effectors, but it is likely that an optimal therapeutic immune response would include CTL and T helper responses.

Vaccines are composed of two components: an antigen-specific component to generate immunity specifically against HPV, and a non-specific component that delivers the antigen to the immune system in an appropriate form. In some cases, the delivery system can act as an adjuvant to boost the immune response against the specific antigen.

Recombinant viruses

Certain human viruses (not HPV) elicit extremely potent antibody and cell-mediated immune responses. Vaccinia virus was used globally in the eradication of smallpox and much is known about its clinical use.[19] The establishment of recombinant vaccinia virus technology[20] and other pragmatic reasons led to the use of this vector for the TA-HPV vaccine.[19] However there are safety concerns with the use of a live virus vector, particularly for use in premalignant disease. This has driven research into safer pox vectors including non-replicating attenuated vaccinia strains (MVA, NYVAC) and avian pox vectors,[21] although none of these has yet been used for HPV. Another virus that has been used widely in human vaccination is adenovirus and there are several prototypic HPV vaccines based on this vector.[22,23]

Table 19.2. Clinical trials of anti-human papillomavirus (HPV) vaccination for anogenital neoplasia

Vaccine	Patients	Response	Reference
Cervax16™ (HPV16 E6E7 protein with matrix adjuvant)	31 CIN1-3 LLETZ at 7 weeks	No clinical responses 12/20 T-helper response	97
Dendritic cells + tumour lysate	8 recurrent/advanced cervical cancer	2/8 HPV16 specific CTL 1/8 T-helper response 1 stable disease 6/12	50
E7 lipopeptide vaccine	12 advanced cervical cancer HLA-A2	E7 peptide specific CTL responses	35
E7 peptide with adjuvant E7 peptide with adjuvant and T helper epitope+lipid tail	10 high-grade CIN/VIN HPV16 + HLA A2 8 high-grade CIN/VIN HPV16 + HLA A2	3/18 complete response 6/18 partial response 10/16 E7 specific responses	62
Encapsulated plasmid DNA (ZYC101)	12 high-grade AIN	3/12 partial response 10/12 direct ELISPOT response	64
HPV16 E7 fusion protein + adjuvant	5 advanced cervical cancer	2/3 proliferative T-cell responses	38
HPV16 E7 peptides	15 HLA-A2 Recurrent/residual cervical cancer	2/15 stable disease >1yr	34
HspE7 (BCG hsp65+ HPV16 E7)	80 evaluable high-grade AIN	75% partial response at 6/12 95% response at 15/12 (51% PR, 44% CR)	61
TA-HPV	12 CIN3	3/12 HPV 18 specific CTL response	53
TA-HPV	18 VIN3	1/18 complete response 8/18 partial response 4 new ELISPOT responses	58
TA-HPV	12 VIN	1/12 complete clinical response 4/12 partial response 6 ELISPOT responses	59 60
TA-HPV	11 high-grade AGIN	No clinical responses	
TA-HPV recombinant vaccinia HPV16 &18 E6/E7	8 recurrent/advanced cervical cancer	HPV specific CTL in 1/3 1 patient disease free > 7 yr	51

AIN = anal intraepithelial neoplasia; CIN = cervical intraepithelial neoplasia; CTL = cytotoxic T lymphocytes; HLA = human leucocyte antigen; LLETZ = large loop excision of the transformation zone; VIN = vulval intraepithelial neoplasia

Recombinant bacteria

Bacteria, like viruses, are efficient at stimulating T cell responses. Certain bacterial toxins have been used as adjuvants in order to non-specifically boost immune responses, and others can deliver antigens efficiently into the major histocompatibility complex (MHC) class I antigen processing pathway.[24] HPV vaccine development in bacteria has largely focused on intracellular bacteria such as listeria,[25] salmonella[26] and bacillus Calmette-Guérin (BCG).[27] BCG has a well-established safety profile for human vaccine use.[25] Bacteria also have properties that facilitate mucosal delivery, allowing direct local application to mucosal lesions or use as oral or intranasal vaccines. Again, work has largely been done in animal models and there has been no clinical testing of bacteria-based vaccines.

Virus-like particles

An approach that has received much attention for prophylaxis of HPV infection has been the use of VLPs. These are recombinant HPV L1 and or L2 proteins that have been refolded to form structures with similarities to the intact virus particle.[28] There is the potential to use chimeric VLPs to combine prophylactic and therapeutic approaches. Immunogenicity and protection has been demonstrated in a murine model[29] and VLPs have been shown to generate human T cell responses *in vitro*.[9,30] However, no human trials have been performed to date with chimeric VLPs.

Proteins and peptides

CD8+ CTL recognise 9–11 amino acid peptides complexed to MHC class I molecules on the cell surface. Peptides themselves are likely to be poorly immunogenic, requiring adjuvant to promote sustained CD8+ T cell responses[31] and under some circumstances can have the unwanted effect of inducing tolerance.[31,32] Studies in mouse models using peptide vaccination have demonstrated protection against HPV expressing tumours[33] and led to a clinical trial in advanced cervical carcinoma.[34] (Table 19.2). No clinical responses or HPV-specific immune responses were seen in this trial, and it was suggested that the advanced stage of the cancer patients contributed to immunosuppression. By contrast, another study in advanced cancer patients using lipolated peptides was able to induce peptide specific responses[35] but no clinical response. A disadvantage of the peptide approach is that patients must express the appropriate human leucocyte antigen (HLA) molecule capable of binding the immunising peptide. Human studies have largely focused on HLA-A*0201 as it is the most frequently occurring allele.[36] However, this may exclude many patients for whom vaccination would be appropriate.

The need for patients of a particular HLA type can be circumvented by using full-length proteins to deliver all potential T cell epitopes to the immune system. Studies in mice have shown that CD8+ T cell responses can be generated against whole proteins (introduced artificially or from cells) by a phenomenon called 'cross priming', whereby proteins are transferred from phagocytic or apoptotic cells to dendritic cells.[37] The efficiency of this process can be increased by including either an adjuvant or by fusion to a carrier protein. Clinical testing of a glutathionine-S-transferase HPV16 E7 fusion protein in Algammulin adjuvant demonstrated CD4+ T helper and antibody responses but no CTL responses.[38] More recently, an HPV16 E7 protein fused to HSP65 from *Mycobacterium bovis* has shown to be efficacious in a murine model[39] and has started testing in HIV associated neoplasia. Another approach has been to fuse HPV16 E6/E7 to L2 (TA-CIN[40]) and this is also the subject of continuing clinical trials.

DNA vaccines

The use of "naked" DNA vaccines has great appeal based on simplicity, stability and cost.[41] Vaccination with DNA intramuscularly can generate protective CD8+ T cell responses in murine models. However, for high-risk HPVs, DNA immunisation may be problematic from the safety standpoint, as there will be concerns over potential host cell expression of oncogenes. This may be overcome by shuffling the DNA sequence[42,43] or by incorporating selected epitopes.[44] DNA vaccines produce weaker immune responses than those elicited by recombinant viral or bacterial vectors, but a major advantage of DNA vaccination is that a certain amount of 'tailoring' of vaccines can be done, e.g. adding cytokine genes[45] or molecules involved in antigen processing and presentation.[44]

Dendritic cells

Dendritic cells are potent antigen-presenting cells capable of direct activation of CD8+ T cells *in vitro* and *in vivo*.[46] Therefore dendritic cells could act as a delivery system and cellular adjuvant to the above approaches; however, this will require isolation and culture of dendritic cells from each patient. HPV-specific CTL responses have been generated using dendritic cells *in vitro*[47–49] but only a single human trial with dendritic cells in invasive cervical carcinoma has been carried out to date.[50] The labour-intensive nature of this approach may limit vaccination to small cohorts.

Clinical trials in high-grade intraepithelial neoplasia

Several of the early phase I and II clinical trials have been undertaken in invasive cervical cancer with later trials turning attention to high-grade intraepithelial neoplasia (Table 19.2). The first clinical trial in patients used TA-HPV (Xenova Research Ltd, Cambs.), a recombinant vaccinia virus encoding the HPV16 and 18, E6 and E7 open reading frames that has been extensively described.[19] Eight patients with recurrent or advanced cervical cancer received one dose by dermal scarification. Three patients developed an HPV-specific antibody response and one of three evaluable patients developed HPV-specific CTL response nine weeks following vaccination.[51] This patient has shown prolonged disease remission and is disease-free seven years later. A second dose of vaccine in this patient did not augment CTL responses (unpublished observations). The majority of women with late-stage disease appeared to be immunocompromised as judged by lymphocyte subset counts, delayed-type hypersensitivity responses to common recall antigens and T cell responses to influenza or allogeneic MHC.[52]

As a result of the observed immunocompromise, a further study was conducted among patient with preinvasive disease (CIN3) in order to further evaluate the safety and immunogenicity of TA-HPV. This group of patients was expected to have normal immunological function.

Adjuvant TA-HPV in CIN3: Cardiff

Twelve women with biopsy-proven CIN3 were vaccinated with two doses of TA-HPV two months apart, as an adjuvant to conventional excisional treatment. HPV18-specific CTL responses were detected in two women prior to vaccination and in a further three women after vaccination (25% response rate). No augmentation of HPV18-specific CTL responses was seen as a result of TA-HPV vaccination; either in those women with preexisting CTLs or in those who received the second vaccination.[53] One patient who failed to generate a response developed progressive disease. The assays used for CTL detection in this study, although successfully used in several patient studies,[54–56] were cumbersome to perform (14–21 day test) and relatively insensitive. Therefore a priority for future trials was the development of new immunology endpoint assays based on more sensitive methods.[57]

TA-HPV in VIN3: Manchester

Eighteen women with HPV16 positive VIN3 received one dose of TA-HPV and were followed up for 24 weeks.[58]

Lesion shrinkage was defined as a reduction in the longest lesion diameter of ≥ 50%. One patient had complete regression of all vulval lesions, histological resolution and viral clearance. Other responses were: symptom relief (9/14 patients); lesion shrinkage (8/18 patients); histological improvement (5/18 patients); HPV clearance (2/18 patients).

Six of 18 patients demonstrated enzyme-linked immunosorbent assay (ELISA) vaccinia immunoglobulin G (IgG) response prevaccination and all 18 demonstrated responses after vaccination (18/18 ELISA IgG and 17/18 interferon-gamma, IFN-γ, ELISPOT).

Systemic HPV responses were measured using IFN-γ ELISPOT to detect T cells recognising HLA-A2 restricted HPV16 E6 or E7 peptides. Five patients had HPV specific responses pre- and post-vaccination, one of which was a borderline response that was boosted following vaccination. In addition, there were borderline responses in three more patients following vaccination.

Six of the eight patients with measurable ELISPOT responses demonstrated improvement in the extent of the disease (lesion shrinkage with or without viral clearance). It was also noted that clinical responders had significantly more CD1a (Langerhans cells), CD4+ and CD8+ T cells in their vulval lesions prior to vaccination than those who did not respond, although the significance of this is unclear.

TA-HPV in high-grade AGIN: Cambridge

Twelve women with HPV16-positive high-grade anogenital intraepithelial neoplasia (AGIN) of up to 15 years duration received one dose of TA-HPV and were followed up for 24 weeks.[59] Five of the patients showed at least a 50% reduction in total lesion diameter, of whom one patient showed complete regression of her lesion. Overall, there was an average decrease in lesion size of 40%, with 83% of women showing some improvement. In contrast to the above study, there was less correlation between immunological and clinical responses (J Sterling, personal communication).

TA-HPV in high-grade AGIN and delayed conventional treatment: Cardiff

Eleven patients received a single dose of TA-HPV and delayed conventional treatment at 8–12 weeks for high-grade AGIN to assess initial clinical efficacy.[60] Initially, recruitment to this trial proved difficult, partly because of the ease and effectiveness of conventional treatment for CIN3. The study protocol was therefore extended to patients with other anogenital neoplasia for which alternative treatment options are less straightforward. Recruitment to this trial is now complete and immunological results are awaited.

Disappointingly, no striking clinical responses have occurred and neither histological improvement nor viral clearance. The Cardiff results differ from those seen in Manchester and Cambridge but may be explained by four patients having other HPV infections, besides HPV16 or HPV18, and 7 of 11 patients having cervical disease that was excised 8–12 weeks after vaccination. The delay in treatment may have been too short to see clinical improvement since complete responses took nine months or longer in Palefsky's study of vaccination for AIN.[61]

The above studies indicate that immunological and clinical responses are seen as a consequence of TA-HPV antiviral vaccination in patients with lower genital tract neoplasia, albeit at variable frequency thus far. The differing experience between research centres has not yet been explained but may reflect variation in patient cohorts. The inconsistent correlation between immunological and clinical response suggests either spontaneous regression of disease irrespective of a measured immune response or measurement of the wrong type of immune response (systemic versus local, Th1 response versus Th2 response, incomplete peptide panels for HPV, etc).

Multicentre prime-boost vaccination in high-grade AGIN

Recently, a prime boost strategy has been adopted by the three centres above using three doses of TA-CIN, a recombinant fusion protein (HPV16 L2E6E7) administered intramuscularly, followed by a single dose of TA-HPV by dermal scarification. Recruitment is completed and immunological and clinical results awaited.

Clinical evaluation compares the extent of disease over a 24-week period versus baseline status using histological, virological and visual assessments. The symptomatic extent of the anogenital disease has also been noted. Immunogenicity is being assessed by T cell proliferation, *in vitro* cytokine production, ELISPOT assays and continuing immunohistochemical evaluation of biopsies.

Peptide vaccine study in high-grade AGIN

Eighteen HPV16+ and HLA-A2+ women with high-grade AIN (16 CIN and 2 VIN) were treated with escalating doses of a peptide vaccine in incomplete Freund's adjuvant.[62] Patients received four immunisations of increasing doses of the vaccine each three weeks apart with definitive removal of dysplastic tissue three weeks after completing the protocol.

In this study, immune parameters were measured before and after vaccination. These included testing for CD8+ T cell responses, analysis of T cell markers associated with immunosuppression (CD3 ζ chain[63]), delayed-type hypersensitivity against the immunising peptide and immunohistochemistry to assess lesional infiltrate with CD4+, CD8+ and dendritic cells.

Clinically, the vaccine was well tolerated, with mild grade I/II toxicity only. Three patients cleared dysplasia by the end of the study. A further six patients had partial colposcopically measured regression of CIN greater than 50%. Clearance of HPV (detected by polymerase chain reaction) was seen in 12/18 patients by the end of immunisations, however, all biopsy samples were still positive by *in situ* RNA hybridisation after vaccination indicating that viral genetic material was still present within lesions. In general, the patients showed clear evidence of immune responses against the immunising peptide using *in vitro* assays (10/16), however no DTH was observed. Immunohistochemistry demonstrated an increased DC infiltrate in 6/6 patients tested consistent with an immune response after vaccination. By contrast CD3 ζ chain expression was decreased in 14/16 patients, a somewhat surprising finding in patients with CIN as opposed to advanced cancer.

This study does suggest immune responsiveness following immunisation in a significant proportion of patients and provides useful baseline data for future studies. However the clinical responses must be taken in the context that regression may occur in up to 30% of high grade AGIN spontaneously or following diagnostic biopsy.

Encapsulated plasmid DNA for HPV16+ high-grade AGIN

A phase I dose escalation study was performed in 12 patients with HPV16 plus high-grade AIN (2–3) in whom surgical management was not possible.[64] All recipients were HIV-negative and received four intramuscular injections of encapsulated plasmid DNA at three-weekly intervals. The plasmid encoded for multiple HLA-A2 restricted epitopes derived from the HPV16 E7 protein and was encapsulated in biodegradable polymer microparticles. Multiple doses of DNA were tested. Patients were assessed by HPV status, anal cytology, histology and direct IFN-γ ELISPOT assay for immunological responses. Results are shown in Table 19.3.

Table 19.3. Encapsulated plasmid DNA for HPV16+ high-grade anal intraepithelial neoplasia (reproduced with permission)[64]

Subject	DNA dose (μg)	Clinical response	ELISPOT response	HPV clearance
1	50	−	+	−
2	50	−	+	−
3	50	−	+	−
4	100	−	+	−
5	100	−	+	−
6	100	−	+	−
7	200	−	+	+
8	200	Partial	+	−
9	200	−	−	−
10	400	Partial	+	−
11	400	Partial	−	+
12	400	−	+	n/a

Adverse effects were minimal and transient. Three partial clinical responses were seen. Ten of twelve patients had direct IFN-γ ELISPOT responses (three of six possible epitopes studied). The authors noted the requirement for long-term follow up in order to determine duration of response in addition to the time lag for maximum clinical response.

Heat shock protein and HPV16 E7 fusion protein in high-grade AGIN

This study was presented at the 20th International HPV conference in Paris in 2002. Eighty-two HIV+ patients with high-grade AIN, of which 80 were evaluable, were vaccinated with three doses of 500 μg BCGhsp65 and HPV16E7 fusion protein (Stressgen Biotechnologies, Victoria, BC, Canada) subcutaneously. This was an open label study with six months of follow-up and included some patients who had previously been included in a placebo controlled double blind trial of hspE7 at a lower dose (3 x 100 μg), although this did not appear to affect the outcome of the present study. In addition, 57 patients agreed to long-term follow-up anoscopy and biopsy.

After six months there were no complete responses but a 75% partial response rate was seen with conversion from high-grade to low-grade AIN. Follow up to 15 months showed a 95% response rate (51% partial, 44% complete), some of the complete responses occurring by nine months. Of the complete responders one-third showed recurrence of low-grade AIN while two-thirds showed a durable response for up to two years. Elucidation of the full extent of responses and duration of response requires additional follow-up.

This study has been criticised for lack of a placebo control but it does appear that HspE7 has clinical activity in HIV+ patients with high-grade AIN and that responses may take some time to occur. Responses have not yet been correlated with other clinical indicators of immune or clinical status.

HPV16 E6/E7 fusion protein in CIN

This double blind placebo controlled trial was also presented at the 20th International HPV conference. Thirty-one patients with CIN1–3 (24 receiving vaccine and 7 placebo) received up to three doses fortnightly (20, 60, 200 μg) of E6/E7 fusion protein with an adjuvant saponin matrix (CerVax™; CSL, Parkville, VIC, Australia) followed by excisional treatment at week seven (one week after finishing vaccination protocol).

Ethical considerations did not allow for longer delay before treatment. In 12 of 20 given active vaccine a δ-interferon T-helper response was seen. No clinical responses were seen prior to conventional treatment but the delay prior to excision was too short to assess clinical efficacy.

Immunology of vaccine trials: what have we learnt?

Overall, the vaccine trials carried out to date have not reliably produced strong immune responses against HPV. These results must be considered disappointing, given that the design of the vaccines was geared to producing immune responses that were potentially therapeutic. Of course, this would not be of consequence if the same vaccines produced unequivocal clinical responses in every case. There are several non-mutually exclusive reasons to explain these observations.

Immunogenicity

The present generation of vaccines are simply not immunogenic enough. Responses have been weak and difficult to detect in comparison to the responses seen against viruses such as influenza or EBV. In the case of cancer patients, this may reflect immunosuppression, but in patients with pre-malignant disease, this is more likely to reflect the vaccine delivery system or the inherent nature of the antigen.

Vaccine dose

Dosage requirements for vaccines have been extrapolated from animal models, where the level of immunity is much higher, probably because most laboratory mice are kept under 'germ' free conditions. For the studies on vaccinia virus (TA-HPV) reviewed here, a dose of 2×10^6 plaque-forming units was given by intradermal scarification. This was based on experience from the smallpox campaign and successful vaccine 'take' can be seen assessed from cutaneous lesion formation and anti-vaccinia antibody detection. However, the actual specific dose of vaccine delivered was unknown and it is possible the dose used may be too low to induce strong cellular immunity in most patients. Some immunologists have argued that multiple large doses of vaccine are repeatedly required to stimulate the immune system for an optimal response.[65] For regulatory reasons it may be difficult to implement larger doses for vaccinia virus or other live vectors. However, increasing the dose may be particularly appropriate for peptides and soluble proteins with unknown biological stability *in vivo*.[65]

Vector

Viral vectors such as vaccinia virus have been shown to be extremely immunogenic. However, some have argued that prior exposure to vaccinia virus in individuals immunised for smallpox will limit HPV (or other antigen) specific responses.[21] This is also of concern for any vaccine based on adenoviruses, as many will have developed neutralising antibodies after natural infection with these common viruses. For vaccinia virus, prior immunity has not been a limiting factor in the trials carried out with TA-HPV to date, as the majority of the women immunised were too young to have received the smallpox vaccine. Furthermore, immune responses have been obtained in women who demonstrated detectable vaccinia antibodies.[50,51]

Antigen

It is possible that the structure (small size, lack of repeating structures) of HPV E6 and E7 proteins makes them poorly immunogenic. Vaccinia virus itself is highly immunogenic and it is possible that any anti-HPV responses will be swamped by anti-vaccinia responses.

Delivery

For ease of administration vaccines are given systemically, either intradermally (vaccinia) or intramuscularly (peptides). For mucosal pathogens such as HPV, vaccination at site of disease or mucosally may be of greater benefit.[66]

Detection (endpoint assays)

Detection of T cell responses has been revolutionised by development of more sensitive techniques capable of measuring antiviral responses directly from blood samples.[57] These include methods based on cytokine detection such as ELISPOT assay or intracellular cytokine staining, or detection of antigen-specific T cell responses using tetramers. However, even using these assays, immune responses after vaccination have still been relatively infrequent and low in magnitude. An important caveat in considering immune responses is that only responses in peripheral blood are being sampled. It is possible that this may not reflect the frequency of antigen specific T cells that have migrated to sites of disease.[67] Measurement of responses at sites of disease is possible[68] but technically difficult, especially in premalignant disease, where large biopsy samples are difficult to obtain. Another consideration for endpoint assays is the time interval between samples. For TA-HPV trials, four-weekly intervals were used, however it is possible that the responses could have been missed. Where responses have been seen (at week eight) they were transient and absent at intermediate time points.[51]

Challenges for therapeutic vaccination in lower genital tract neoplasia

The development of therapeutic vaccines for HPV-related neoplasia faces two main hurdles: improvement of vaccine immunogenicity and evaluating efficacy in clinical practice.

Vaccine dose

The issue of the optimum dose and frequency of vaccination for patients remains difficult. This can only really be resolved in the clinical trial setting. Several animal studies have suggested that a prime-boost approach using heterologous vaccines will be effective for antiviral vaccination.[69] Interestingly, vaccinia viruses or other pox viruses seem to be more effective at the boosting stage, rather than at the priming stage. Clinical trials using a prime-boost approach for HIV[69] and for HPV-associated lower genital tract neoplasia (see above) are currently in progress.

Vector design

There has been considerable progress in vector design, particularly in animal models where improved vectors have been more effective in eliciting immune responses that are either protective or therapeutic, for example, vectors containing signal sequences to improve MHC class I processing[44,70] or MHC class II processing.[71] Others have incorporated cytokines designed to promote inflammatory responses (GM-CSF)[72] or activate dendritic cells.[22]

One of the key developments in immunology relevant to vaccine design has been to link components of the innate immune response to specific adaptive immunity. Dendritic cells have proved to be key players in that they express receptors capable of interacting with proteins from pathogens.[46] These receptors trigger activation and maturation of dendritic cells for optimum antigen presentation. Other molecules that mediate their action through dendritic cells are heat shock proteins. These evolutionarily conserved proteins have been shown to be potent inducers of antitumour and antiviral immunity in animal models,[73] and capable of efficiently delivering antigens to dendritic cells. It is likely that incorporating dendritic cell-activating molecules into vectors will be a key feature of vaccine design. Another development has been the use of self-replicating *Alphavirus*-based vectors. These have been shown to be extremely potent, requiring very low doses to mediate protective or therapeutic effects in animal models.[74–76]

Direct vaccination using short (9–10 aa) peptides has largely fallen from grace due to a combination of theoretical concerns over tolerance induction[32] and disappointing clinical trials.[34] Recently, however, an approach based on vaccination using long peptides of HPV (25-30aa) has demonstrated promising results in animal models.[77] The authors suggest that the longer peptides are more easily taken up by dendritic cells and provide both helper and CTL responses. Other developments in vector design related to delivery will be discussed below.

Immune evasion and improving the antigen

HPVs are likely to use a variety of strategies to escape detection from the immune system. One escape mechanism that may have a direct effect on CTL recognition is the frequently observed downregulation of HLA class I molecules[78] in cervical carcinomas. Additional intracellular defects in HPV transformed cells may also limit the effectiveness of anti-HPV CTL.[79] Balanced against this, however, is the fact that there is never total HLA class I loss and that certain HPV epitopes can be presented on cervical carcinomas with severe antigen processing defects.[80]

The use of full-length proteins as immunogens may not efficiently generate dominant CTL responses against the appropriate epitopes.[81] This could be overcome by using fragments (15-30aa) of HPV E6/E7 for vaccination. A more labour-intensive approach would be to define multiple new peptide epitopes for HPV to cover all potential HLA combinations. The structure of these epitopes could be altered to improve binding to HLA class I molecules and modified epitopes included into a polyepitope vaccine construct. Using this approach vaccines could be tailored to certain combinations of HLA class I alleles or particular HPV types.

Delivery

The use of mucosal delivery of vaccines has improved the effectiveness of vaccines against HIV/SIV in animal models.[82] This route has been shown to be effective for prophylaxis in animal models but so far therapy has not been explored. Several studies have shown the benefit of infiltrating lymphocytes on papillomavirus lesion regression.[83,84] The trigger for this infiltration is not known but it may be possible to induce similar responses using direct intralesional vaccination.

An exciting prospect for vaccine delivery is via the gut mucosa. To this end several groups have been generating vaccines in yeast or potatoes, although it is not yet known whether such vaccines could generate therapeutic immune responses.

Logistics of therapeutic vaccine trials

Clinical trials of immunotherapy face several difficulties, not least the selection of suitable recipients for study. From a practical viewpoint it must be decided whether or not to HPV type prior to administration of immunotherapy. This will require HPV typing service laboratories rather than the current small-scale research HPV typing facilities. The aim of immunotherapy is to selectively increase and sustain the numbers of anti-HPV effector cells to eliminate HPV transformed neoplastic cells. The immunocompetence of the patient and the disease burden must be born in mind when selecting recipients for immunotherapeutic manipulation.

The majority of low-grade disease (80%) regresses spontaneously and large cohorts and long-term follow up are therefore required to assess efficacy of immunotherapeutic intervention. In addition, low-grade disease expresses different viral proteins to high-grade lesions: immunotherapy requiring to target alternative antigens. High-grade CIN is relatively common but conventional treatment is easy, cheap and effective, masking the benefits of adjuvant vaccination, which will again require large cohorts and long-term follow-up to assess an advantage for immunotherapy.

Conventional treatment of early cervical cancer results in 80–90% five-year survival and therefore immunotherapeutic intervention will require long-term follow-up. However, this group of patients may have the most to gain from immunotherapy while the disease burden is small, since recurrence is generally not curable. Late or recurrent cervical cancer is characterised by poor immunological status as evidenced by lymphopenia and tests of immune function[52] as well as prior immunosuppressive therapy, which mitigates immunotherapeutic intervention. In addition, late stage disease is genetically unstable and may have undergone further mutation to escape immunological control.

Genital neoplasia syndrome or VIN is difficult to manage, frequently multifocal and recurs following treatment and may therefore be an appropriate model by which to study the initial clinical efficacy of immunotherapy. The incidence of VIN and AIN appear to be increasing and the management of these conditions poses significant difficulties.

Trials require to be controlled in order to assess the benefits of immunotherapy since spontaneous regression or conventional therapies may achieve disease clearance. The induction of an immune response may prevent future recurrence and long-term follow up will be required to assess this. Another question to be addressed is the longevity of HPV specific memory following vaccination.

Assessment of immunological endpoints has been greatly improved by the development of more sensitive assays to detect antigen specific T cells. While these have been used to successfully detect responses against HPV peptides in some studies,[62,64] others have shown that the frequency of HPV specific T cells (even after vaccination) is very low and requires a period of *in vitro* stimulation.[80,85] Assays such as ELISPOT have the advantage over previously used assays in that they do not require large volumes of blood or the use of radioactivity. Nevertheless, they do not obviate the need to take repeated blood samples or to have good liquid nitrogen storage facilities.

A new technology that has considerable promise for vaccine trials is the cytokine bead array system.[86] This fluorescence-based assay allows simultaneous measurement of multiple cytokines, even in small fluid samples.[86] However, assessing cytokines produced by T cells still requires more cells than can be obtained from a biopsy. Thus there is a need to develop more sensitive assays capable of measuring immune responses at sites of disease.

Cost is a pertinent issue for the development of immunotherapy directed against anogenital neoplasia. DNA vaccines are the cheapest, easy to make and stable at room temperature, an important factor for field use in low resource settings. Considerable experience in the use and construction of recombinant viral vaccines means these too can be produced relatively cheaply. Short or long peptides and proteins are more expensive to produce at the required purity for clinical usage. This raises the question of who should fund immunotherapy studies, which impose considerable logistical and financial costs. There may be potential conflicts of interest if pharmaceutical companies fund trials, as well as a lack of equity in access to immunotherapeutic intervention for those living in developing countries, yet who bear the greatest burden in terms of HPV associated disease.

The future of therapeutic vaccines for HPV-related lower genital tract neoplasia

The first generation of HPV vaccines for therapy of HPV-related lower genital tract neoplasia have provided an important foundation for future testing. The safety of the approaches has been established and sporadic clinical and immunological responses have been obtained. At first sight this might suggest gloomy prospects but it is clear that future vaccines will benefit considerably from new developments in immunology. Disappointingly for clinicians, from current knowledge it is unlikely that a single-shot vaccine given in an outpatient clinic will be effective. However, a realistic scenario is administration of an initial dose in clinic followed by self-administration (by oral, nasal, vaginal, rectal routes) to boost or maintain the immune response. While this approach relies on antigen specific responses, it is possible that the optimum treatment will combine non-specific responses based on the innate immune response combined with strong systemic immunity against HPV. In this regard the application of immune modifiers such as cidofovir or imiquimod, combined with specific vaccination using current vaccines, is an avenue worthy of investigation.

Acknowledgements

The authors are grateful to Cancer Research UK who supported the two most recent Welsh trials of immunotherapy and acknowledge the tireless work of Dr Amanda Tristram as Clinical Research Fellow and Kelly Smith for laboratory studies.

References

1. Jansen K. HPV vaccines for protection against infection. In: Tindle RW, editor. *Vaccines for Human Papillomavirus Infection and Anogenital Disease*. Austin, TX: RG Landes Company, 1999: 33–8.
2. Townsend D. *Intraepithelial Neoplasia of the Vagina*. Edinburgh: Churchill Livingstone; 1991.
3. Ferenczy A. Intraepithelial neoplasia of the vulva. In: Coppleston M, editor. *Gynaecological Oncology*. 2nd ed. Edinburgh: Churchill Livingstone; 1992. p. 443–63.
4. Scholefield JH, Hickson WG, Smith JH, Rogers K, Sharp F. Anal intraepithelial neoplasia: part of a multifocal disease process. *Lancet* 1992;340:1271–3.
5. Stanley M. Immune responses to human papillomaviruses. In: Sterling J, Tyring S, editors. *Human papillomaviruses. Clinical and Scientific Advances*. London: Arnold; 2001. p. 38–49.
6. Bontkes HJ, de Gruijl TD, Bijl A, Verheijen RH, Meijer CJ, Scheper RJ, *et al.* Human papillomavirus type 16 E2-specific T-helper lymphocyte responses in patients with cervical intraepithelial neoplasia.

J Gen Virol 1999;80:2453–9.

7. Davidson EJ, Brown MD, Burt DJ, Parish JL, Gaston K, Kitchener HC, *et al.* Human T cell responses to HPV 16 E2 generated with monocyte-derived dendritic cells. *Int J Cancer* 2001;94:807–12.

8. Konya J, Eklund C, afGeijersstam V, Yuan F, Stuber G, Dillner J. Identification of a cytotoxic T lymphocyte epitope in the human papillomavirus type 16 E2 protein *J Gen Virol* 1997;78:2615–20.

9. Rudolf MP, Nieland JD, DaSilva DM, Velders MP, Muller M, Greenstone HL, *et al.* Induction of HPV16 capsid protein-specific human T cell responses by virus-like particles. *Biol Chem* 1999;380:335–40.

10. Steele JC, Roberts S, Rookes SM, Gallimore PH. Detection of CD4(+)- and CD8(+)-T-cell responses to human papillomavirus type 1 antigens expressed at various stages of the virus life cycle by using an enzyme-linked immunospot assay of gamma interferon release. *J Virol* 2002;76:6027–36.

11. Williams OM, Hart KW, Wang EC, Gelder CM. Analysis of CD4(+) T-cell responses to human papillomavirus (HPV) type 11 L1 in healthy adults reveals a high degree of responsiveness and cross-reactivity with other HPV types. *J Virol* 2002;76:7418–29.

12. Von Knebel-Doeberitz M, Rittmuller C, Zur Hausen H, Durst M. Inhibition of tumorigenicity of C4-1 cervical cancer cells in nude mice by HPV18 E6-E7 antisense RNA. *Int J Cancer* 1992;51:4706–11.

13. Zinkernagel RM. Immunology taught by viruses. *Science* 1996;271:173–8.

14. Boon T, Cerottini J-C, Van den Eynde B, van der Bruggen P, Van Pel A. Tumor antigens recognized by T lymphocytes. *Annu Rev Immunol* 1994;12:337–65.

15. Ridge JP, Di Rosa F, Matzinger P. A conditioned dendritic cell can be a temporal bridge between a CD4+ T- helper and a T-killer cell . *Nature* 1998;393:474–8.

16. Schoenberger SP, Toes RE, van der Voort EI, Offringa R, Melief CJ. T-cell help for cytotoxic T lymphocytes is mediated by CD40-CD40L interactions . *Nature* 1998;393:480–3.

17. Zajac AJ, Murali-Krishna K, Blattman JN, Ahmed R. Therapeutic vaccination against chronic viral infection: the importance of cooperation between CD4+ and CD8+ T cells. *Curr Opin Immunol* 1998;10:444–9.

18. Coleman N, Birley HDL, Renton AM, Hanna NF, Ryait BK, Byrne M, *et al.* Immunological events in regressing genital warts. *Am J Clin Pathol* 1994;102:768–74.

19. Borysiewicz L, Man S. Vaccinia based human papillomavirus vaccines in cervical cancer. In: Beverley P, Stern PL, Carroll M, editors. *Cancer Vaccines and Immunotherapy.* Cambridge: Cambridge University Press; 2000. p. 62–81.

20. Mackett M, Smith GL, Moss B. Vaccinia virus: a selectable eukaryotic cloning and expression vector. *Proc Natl Acad Sci U S A* 1982;79:7415–19.

21. Carroll M, Restifo N. Poxviruses as vectors for cancer immunotherapy. In: Beverley P, Stern PL, Carroll M, editors. *Cancer Vaccines and Immunotherapy.* Cambridge: Cambridge University Press; 2000. p. 47–61.

22. Tillman BW, Hayes TL, DeGruijl TD, Douglas JT, Curiel DT. Adenoviral vectors targeted to CD40 enhance the efficacy of dendritic cell-based vaccination against human papillomavirus 16-induced tumor cells in a murine model . *Cancer Res* 2000;60:5456–63.

23. He Z, Wlazlo AP, Kowalczyk DW, Cheng J, Xiang ZQ, Giles-Davis W, *et al.* Viral recombinant vaccines to the E6 and E7 antigens of HPV16. *Virology* 2000;270:146–61.

24. Mollenkopf H, Dietrich G, Kaufmann SH. Intracellular bacteria as targets and carriers for vaccination. *Biol Chem* 2001;382:521–32.

25. Gunn G, Zubair A, Peters C, Pan Z, Wu T, Paterson Y. Two *Listeria monocytogenes* vaccine vectors that express different molecular forms of human papilloma virus-16 E7 induce quantitatively different T cell immunity that correlates with their ability to induce regression of established tumours immortalised by HPV16. *J Immunol* 2001;167:6471–6479.

26. Londono LP, Chatfield S, Tindle RW, Herd K, Gao XM, Frazer I, *et al.* Immunisation of mice using *Salmonella typhimurium* expressing human papillomavirus type 16 E7 epitopes inserted into hepatitis B virus core antigen. *Vaccine* 1996;14:545–52.

27. Jabbar IA, Fernando GJ, Saunders N, Aldovini A, Young R, Malcolm K, *et al.* Immune responses induced by BCG recombinant for human papillomavirus L1 and E7 proteins. *Vaccine* 2000;18:2444–53.

28. Schiller JT, Lowy DR. Papillomavirus-like particles and HPV vaccine development. *Semin Cancer Biol* 1996;7:373–82.

29. Greenstone H, Nieland J, de Visser K, de Bruijn M, Kirnbauer R, Roden R, *et al.* Chimeric papillomavirus-like particles elicit anti-tumour immunity against the E7 oncoprotein in an HPV16 tumour model. *Proc Natl Acad Sci U S A* 1998;95:1800–5.

30. de Gruijl TD, Bontkes HJ, Walboomers JM, Coursaget P, Stukart MJ, Dupuy C, *et al.* Immune responses against human papillomavirus (HPV) type 16 virus-like particles in a cohort study of women with cervical intraepithelial neoplasia. I. Differential T-helper and IgG responses in relation to HPV infection and disease outcome. *J Gen Virol* 1999;80:399–408.

31. Aichele P, Brduschariem K, Zinkernagel RM, Hengartner H, Pircher H. T cell priming versus T cell

tolerance induced by synthetic peptides. *J Exp Med* 1995;182:261–6.

32. Toes REM, Offringa R, Blom RJJ, Melief CJM, Kast WM. Peptide vaccination can lead to enhanced tumor growth through specific t cell tolerance induction. *Proc Nat Acad Sci U S A* 1996;93:7855–60.

33. Feltkamp MCW, Vreugdenhil GR, Vierboom RPM, Ras E, Vanderburg SH, Terschegget J, *et al.* Cytotoxic T lymphocytes raised against a subdominant epitope offered as a synthetic peptide eradicate human papillomavirus type 16 induced tumors. *Eur J Immunol* 1995;25:2638–42.

34. Ressing ME, van Driel WJ, Brandt RM, Kenter GG, de Jong JH, Bauknecht T, *et al.* Detection of T helper responses, but not of human papillomavirus-specific cytotoxic T lymphocyte responses, after peptide vaccination of patients with cervical carcinoma. *J Immunother* 2000;23:255–66.

35. Steller MA, Gurski KJ, Murakami M, Daniel RW, Shah KV, Celis E, *et al.* Cell-mediated immunological responses in cervical and vaginal cancer patients immunized with a lipidated epitope of human papillomavirus type 16 E7. *Clin Cancer Res* 1998;4:2103–9.

36. Kast WM, Brandt RM, Sidney J, Drijfhout JW, Kubo RT, Grey HM, *et al.* Role of HLA-A motifs in identification of potential CTL epitopes in human papillomavirus type 16 E6 and E7 proteins. *J Immunol* 1994;152:3904–12.

37. Heath W, Carbone F. Cross-presentation, dendritic cells, tolerance and immunity. *Annu Rev Immunol* 2001;19:47–64.

38. Frazer I, Tindle R, Fernando G, Malcolm K, Herd KA, McFadyn S, *et al.* Safety and Immunogenicity of HPV16E7/Algammulin. In: Tindle RW, editor. *Vaccines for Human Papillomavirus Infection and Anogenital Disease.* Austin, TX: RG Landes Company; 1999.

39. Chu NR, Wu HB, Wu T, Boux LJ, Siegel MI, Mizzen LA. Immunotherapy of a human papillomavirus (HPV) type 16 E7-expressing tumour by administration of fusion protein comprising *Mycobacterium bovis* bacille Calmette-Guerin (BCG) hsp65 and HPV16 E7. *Clin Exp Immunol* 2000;121:216–25.

40. van der Burg SH, Kwappenberg KM, O'Neill T, Brandt RM, Melief C, Hickling J, *et al.* Pre-clinical safety and efficacy of TA-CIN, a recombinant HPV16 L2E6E7 fusion protein vaccine, in homologous and heterologous prime-boost regimens. *Vaccine* 2001;19:3652–60.

41. Liu MA. The immunologist's grail: vaccines that generate cellular immunity. *Proc Natl Acad Sci U S A* 1997;94:10496–8.

42. Osen W, Peiler T, Ohlschlager P, Caldeira S, Faath S, Michel N, *et al.* A DNA vaccine based on a shuffled E7 oncogene of the human papillomavirus type 16 (HPV 16) induces E7-specific cytotoxic T cells but lacks transforming activity. *Vaccine* 2001;19:4276–86.

43. Smahel M, Sima P, Ludvikova V, Vonka V. Modified HPV16 E7 Genes as DNA Vaccine against E7-Containing Oncogenic Cells. *Virology* 2001;281:231–8.

44. Velders M, Weijzen S, Eiben G, Elmishad A, Kloetzel P, Higgins T, *et al.* Defined flanking spacers and enhanced proteolysis is essential for eradication of established tumors by an epitope string DNA vaccine J. *J Immunol* 2001;166:5366–73.

45. Leachman S, Tigelaar R, Shlyankevich M, Slade M, Irwin M, Chang E, *et al.* Granulocyte-macrophage colony-stimulating factor priming plus papillomavirus E6 DNA vaccination: effects on papilloma formation and regression in the cottontail rabbit papillomavirus model. *J Virol* 2000;74:8700–8.

46. Banchereau J, Steinman RM. Dendritic cells and the control of immunity. *Nature* 1998;392:245–52.

47. Murakami M, Gurski KJ, Marincola FM, Ackland J, Steller MA. Induction of specific CD8+ T-lymphocyte responses using a human papillomavirus-16 E6/E7 fusion protein and autologous dendritic cells. *Cancer Res* 1999;59:1184–7.

48. Thornburg C, Boczkowski D, Gilboa E, Nair SK. Induction of cytotoxic T lymphocytes with dendritic cells transfected with human papillomavirus E6 and E7 RNA: implications for cervical cancer immunotherapy. *J Immunother* 2000;23:412–18.

49. Santin AD, Hermonat PL, Ravaggi A, Chiriva-Internati M, Zhan D, Pecorelli S, *et al.* Induction of human papillomavirus-specific CD4(+) and CD8(+) lymphocytes by E7-pulsed autologous dendritic cells in patients with human papillomavirus type 16- and 18-positive cervical cancer. *J Virol* 1999;73:5402–10.

50. Adams M, Borysiewicz L, Fiander A, Man S, Jasani B, Navabi H, *et al.* Clinical studies of human papilloma vaccines in pre-invasive and invasive cancer. *Vaccine* 2001;19:2549–56.

51. Borysiewicz LK, Fiander A, Nimako M, Man S, Wilkinson GWG, Westmoreland D, *et al.* A recombinant vaccinia virus encoding human papillomavirus type 16 and type 18, E6 and E7 proteins as immunotherapy for cervical cancer. *Lancet* 1996;347:1523–27.

52. Fiander AN, Adams M, Evans AS, Bennett AJ, Borysiewicz LK. Immunocompetent for immunotherapy? A study of the immunocompetence of cervical cancer patients. *Int J Gynecol Cancer* 1995;5:438–42.

53. Fiander A, Man S, Nimako M, Evans A, Adams M, Hickling J, *et al.* Clinical HPV vaccination programme utilising recombinant vaccinia virus encoding E6 and E7 proteins of HPV16 and 18. Paper presented at the 17th International Papillomavirus Conference, 9–15 January 1999, Charleston, USA.

54.   Nimako M, Fiander AN, Wilkinson GW, Borysiewicz LK, Man S. Human papillomavirus-specific cytotoxic T lymphocytes in patients with cervical intraepithelial neoplasia grade III. *Cancer Res* 1997;57:4855–61.

55.   Bontkes HJ, de Gruijl TD, van den Muysenberg AJ, Verheijen RH, Stukart MJ, Meijer CJ, *et al.* Human papillomavirus type 16 E6/E7-specific cytotoxic T lymphocytes in women with cervical neoplasia. *Int J Cancer* 2000;88:92–8.

56.   Kaufmann AM, Stern PL, Rankin EM, Sommer H, Nuessler V, Schneider A, *et al.* Safetry and immunogenicity of TA-HPV, a recombinant vaccinia virus expressing modified human papillomavirus 16 and HPV 18 E6 and E7 genes in women with progressive cervical cancer. *Clin Cancer Res* 2002;81:3676–85.

57.   McMichael A, O'Callaghan C. A new look at T cells. *J Exp Med* 1998;187:1367–71.

58.   Davidson E, Tomlinson A, Stern PL, Dobson J, Jack L, St. C. Roberts J, *et al.* A phase II trial to assess the safety, immunogenicity and efficacy of TA-HPV in patients with high grade vulval intraepithelial neoplasia (VIN). Poster/abstract presented at the 19th International Papillomavirus Conference, 1–7 September 2001, Brazil.

59.   Baldwin P, van Der Burg SH, Coleman N, Moseley R, Stanley M, Latimer J, *et al.* Vaccination for anogenital intraepithelial neoplasia with recombinant vaccinia virus expressing HPV16 and 18 E6 and E7. Poster/abstract presented at the 20th International Human Papillomavirus Conference, 4–9 October 2002, Paris.

60.   Tristram A, Man S, Smith K, Fiander A. Clinical effects of a vaccine (TA-HPV) in anogenital intraepithelial neoplasia. Poster/abstract presented at the 20th International Human Papillomavirus Conference, 4–9 October 2002, Paris.

61.   Palefsky J, Goldstone S, Neefe J. HSPE7 treatment of high-grade anal dysplasia: final results of an open-label trial and interim long-term follow-up. Paper presented at the 20th International Human Papillomavirus Conference, 4–9 October 2002, Paris.

62.   Muderspach L, Wilczynski S, Roman L, Bade L, Felix J, Small LA, *et al.* A phase I trial of a human papillomavirus (HPV) peptide vaccine for women with high-grade cervical and vulvar intraepithelial neoplasia who are HPV 16 positive. *Clin Cancer Res* 2000;6:3406–16.

63.   Kono K, Ressing ME, Brandt RMP, Melief CJM, Potkul RK, Andersson B, *et al.* Decreased expression of signal transducing zeta chain in peripheral T cells and natural killer cells in patients with cervical cancer. *Clin Cancer Res* 1996;2:1825–8.

64.   Klencke B, Matijevic M, Urban RG, Lathey JL, Hedley ML, Berry M, *et al.* Encapsulated plasmid DNA treatment for human papillomavirus 16- associated anal dysplasia: a Phase I study of ZYC101. *Clin Cancer Res* 2002;8:1028–37.

65.   Perez-Diez A, Spiess PJ, Restifo NP, Matzinger P, Marincola FM. Intensity of the vaccine-elicited immune response determines tumor clearance. *J Immunol* 2002;168:338–47.

66.   Gallichan WS, Rosenthal KL. Long-lived cytotoxic T lymphocyte memory in mucosal tissues after mucosal but not systemic immunization. *J Exp Med* 1996;184:1879–90.

67.   Evans EM, Man S, Evans AS, Borysiewicz LK. Infiltration of cervical cancer tissue with human papillomavirus- specific cytotoxic T-lymphocytes. *Cancer Res* 1997;57:2943–50.

68.   Passmore JA, Burch VC, Shephard EG, Marais DJ, Allan B, Kay P, *et al.* Single-cell cytokine analysis allows detection of cervical T-cell responses against human papillomavirus type 16 L1 in women infected with genital HPV. *J Med Virol* 2002;67:234–40.

69.   Hanke T. Vehicles for genetic vaccines against human immunodeficiency virus: induction of T cell-mediated immune responses. *Curr Mol Med* 2001;1:123–35.

70.   Brandsma JL. Animal models for HPV vaccine development. *Papillomavirus Reports* 1994;5:105–11.

71.   Wu TC, Guarnieri F, Stavely-O'Carroll KF, Viscidi RP, Levitsky HI, Hedrick L, *et al.* Engineering an intracellular pathway for major histocompatibility complex class II presentation of antigens. *Proc Natl Acad Sci U S A* 1995;92:11671–5.

72.   Chang YE, Laimins LA. Microarray analysis identifies interferon-inducible genes and Stat-1 as major transcriptional targets of human papillomavirus type 31. *J Virol* 2000;74:4174–82.

73.   Srivastava PK. Purification of heat shock protein-peptide complexes for use in vaccination against cancers and intracellular pathogens. *Methods* 1997;12:165–71.

74.   Restifo NP. The new vaccines building viruses that elicit antitumor immunity. *Curr Opin Immunol* 1996;8:658–63.

75.   Daemen T, Regts J, Holtrop M, Wilschut J. Immunization strategy against cervical cancer involving an alphavirus vector expressing high levels of a stable fusion protein of human papillomavirus 16 E6 and E7. *Gene Ther* 2002;9:85–94.

76.   Velders MP, McElhiney S, Cassetti MC, Eiben GL, Higgins T, Kovacs GR, *et al.* Eradication of established tumors by vaccination with Venezuelan equine encephalitis virus replicon particles delivering human papillomavirus 16 E7 RNA. *Cancer Res* 2001;61:7861–7.

77.   Zwaveling S, Ferreira Mota SC, Nouta J, Johnson M, Lipford GB, Offringa R, *et al.* Established

human papillomavirus type 16-expressing tumors are effectively eradicated following vaccination with long peptides. *J Immunol* 2002;169:350–8.

78. Connor ME, Stern PL. Loss of MHC class-I expression in cervical carcinomas. *Int J Cancer* 1990;46:1029–34.

79. Evans M, Borysiewicz L, Evans A, Rowe M, Jones M, Gileadi U, *et al.* Antigen processing defects in cervical carcinomas limit presentation of a HPV 16 E6 CTL epitope from human papillomavirus 16 E6. *J Immunol* 2001;167:5420–8.

80. Youde SJ, Dunbar PR, Evans EM, Fiander AN, Borysiewicz LK, Cerundolo V, *et al.* Use of fluorogenic histocompatibility leukocyte antigen-A*0201/HPV 16 E7 peptide complexes to isolate rare human cytotoxic T-lymphocyte- recognizing endogenous human papillomavirus antigens. *Cancer Res* 2000;60:365–71.

81. Palmowski MJ, Choi EM, Hermans IF, Gilbert SC, Chen JL, Gileadi U, *et al.* Competition between CTL narrows the immune response induced by prime- boost vaccination protocols. *J Immunol* 2002;168:4391–8.

82. Lehner T, Bergmeier LA, Panagiotidi C, Tao L, Brookes R, Klavinskis LS, *et al.* Induction of mucosal and systemic immunity to recombinant simian immunodeficiency viral protein. *Science* 1992;258:1365–9.

83. Coleman N, Stanley MA. Characterization and functional analysis of the expression of vascular adhesion molecules in human papillomavirus related disease of the cervix. *Cancer* 1994;74:884–92.

84. Selvakumar R, Schmitt A, Iftner T, Ahmed R, Wettstein FO. Regression of papillomas induced by cottontail rabbit papillomavirus is associated with infiltration of CD8+ cells and persistence of viral DNA after regression. *J Virol* 1997;71:5540–8.

85. van der Burg S, Ressing M, Kwappenberg K, de Jong A, Straathof K, de Jong J, *et al.* Natural T-helper immunity against human papillomavirus type 16 (HPV16) E7-derived peptide epitopes in patients with HPV16 positive cervical lesions: identification of three human leukocyte antigen class II restricted epitopes. *Int J Cancer* 2001;91:612–18.

86. Cook EB, Stahl JL, Lowe L, Chen R, Morgan E, Wilson J, *et al.* Simultaneous measurement of six cytokines in a single sample of human tears using microparticle-based flow cytometry: allergics vs. non- allergics. *J Immunol Methods* 2001;254:109–18.

87. Jarrett WF, Smith KT, O'Neil BW, Gaukroger JM, Chandrachud LM, Grindlay GJ, *et al.* Studies on vaccination against papillomaviruses: prophylactic and therapeutic vaccination with recombinant structural proteins. *Virology* 1991;184:33–42.

88. Campo MS. Towards vaccines against papillomavirus. In: Stern PL, Stanley MA, editors. *Human Papillomaviruses and Cervical Cancer*. Oxford: Oxford University Press; 1994. p. 177–91.

89. Han R, Cladel NM, Reed CA, Peng X, Christensen ND. Protection of rabbits from viral challenge by gene gun-based intracutaneous vaccination with a combination of cottontail rabbit papillomavirus E1, E2, E6, and E7 genes. *J Virol* 1999;73:7039–43.

90. Suzich JA, Ghim SJ, Palmer-Hill FJ, White WI, Tamura JK, Bell JA, *et al.* Systemic immunization with papillomavirus L1 protein completely prevents the development of viral mucosal papillomas. *Proc Natl Acad Sci U S A* 1995;92:11553–7.

91. Stanley MA, Moore RA, Nicholls PK, Santos EB, Thomsen L, Parry N, *et al.* Intraepithelial vaccination with COPV L1 DNA by particle-mediated DNA delivery protects against mucosal challenge with infectious COPV in beagle dogs. *Vaccine* 2001;19:2783–92.

92. Fernando GJ, Murray B, Zhou J, Frazer IH. Expression, purification and immunological characterization of the transforming protein E7, from cervical cancer-associated human papillomavirus type 16. *Clin Exp Immunol* 1999;115:397–403.

93. Ji H, Wang TL, Chen CH, Pai SI, Hung CF, Lin KY, *et al.* Targeting human papillomavirus type 16 E7 to the endosomal/lysosomal compartment enhances the antitumor immunity of DNA vaccines against murine human papillomavirus type 16 E7-expressing tumors. *Hum Gene Ther* 1999;10:2727–40.

94. Chen CH, Ji H, Suh KW, Choti MA, Pardoll DM, Wu TC. Gene gun-mediated DNA vaccination induces antitumor immunity against human papillomavirus type 16 E7-expressing murine tumor metastases in the liver and lungs. *Gene Ther* 1999;6:1972–81.

95. Cheng W, Hung C, Chai C, Hsu K, He L, Ling M, *et al.* Tumour-specific immunity and antiangiogenesis generated by a DNA vaccine encoding calreticulin linked to a tumour antigen. *J Clin Invest* 2001;108:669–78.

96. Chen C, Wang TL, Hung CF, Pardoll DM, Wu T. Boosting with recombinant vaccinia increases HPV16 E7-specific precursor frequencies of HPV16 E7-expressing DNA vaccines. *Vaccine* 2000;18:2015–22.

97. Frazer I, Quinn M, Nicklin J, Tan J, Perrin L, Ng P, *et al.* A randomised placebo controlled trial of immunotherapy for CIN. Paper presented at the 20th International Papillomavirus conference, 4–9 October 2002, Paris.

Chapter 20

Prophylactic vaccination

Margaret A Stanley

Substantial progress has been made in the past decade, both in understanding host defence to human papillomavirus (HPV) infection and in the development of vaccines to prevent and treat these infections. Prophylactic HPV vaccines are moving into late-stage clinical trials and therapeutic vaccines for the treatment of established HPV-induced disease are in phase I/II trials.

Humoral responses to papillomavirus infections

Papillomaviruses have an absolutely restricted host range, HPVs only infect humans, dog papillomaviruses only infect dogs, rabbit papillomaviruses only infect rabbits and so forth. Furthermore, they show an exquisite tissue tropism and only differentiated squamous epithelium will support the complete infectious cycle and the production of infectious particles. As a result, HPVs cannot be propagated in tissue culture, few virus particles can be isolated from lesions and significant amounts of purified virus have not been available for serological studies. The exceptions to this were natural infections in animals, dog, rabbit, cow and HPV-1 and HPV-11 in humans where adequate amounts of virus could be obtained. Serological studies using these papillomaviruses showed clearly that there were serum responses to viral capsid proteins in individuals who were or had been infected (reviewed in Stanley 2002[1]). In the animal models, seropositive individuals were resistant to subsequent viral challenge. The dominant humoral response was to determinants on the intact particle indicating that the generation of such responses would require correctly folded native protein.[2]

The major capsid protein, L1, of the papillomaviruses self-assembles into virus-like particles (VLPs) when expressed from eukaryotic expression vectors, including recombinant vaccinia, baculo- and Semliki Forest virus and yeast. These L1 VLPs lack the minor capsid protein L2 and viral DNA but are morphologically similar to virions. L1 VLPs closely approximate the antigenic characteristics of wild-type virions and have been used extensively in seroepidemiological studies revealing that type-specific antibody responses are common during and after infection with genital HPVs.

Prophylactic VLP vaccines

VLPs are clearly candidate immunogens for prophylactic vaccination and phase I vaccine studies with recombinant HPV L1 VLP vaccines have been reported.[3–6] Harro et al.[3] conducted a double-blind, placebo-controlled, dose escalation trial to evaluate the safety and immunogenicity of a baculovirus-expressed HPV 16 L1 VLP vaccine. Healthy adult volunteers were given the vaccine (at doses of 10 μg or 50 μg) or placebo with or without adjuvant (alum or MF59) by intramuscular injection at 0, 1 and 4 months. Serum antibody responses were measured with an HPV 16 L1 VLP-based enzyme-linked immunosorbent assay (ELISA). All VLP-immunised subjects, none of those given placebo, seroconverted and made anti-VLP antibody responses approximately 40-fold that identified in natural infections. Antibody responses were dose-dependent when vaccine was given without adjuvant or with MF59 but were dose-independent when administered with alum. The dominant antibody response was of the immunoglobulin G1 (IgG1) subclass and was shown to be neutralising by an HPV-16 pseudovirion-neutralising assay. The immunogenicity of an HPV-11 L1 VLP (yeast-derived) vaccine was evaluated in double blind, dose escalation (10, 20, 50 or 100 μg VLP) placebo-controlled trial in college women who tested negative for HPV-6/HPV-11 by polymerase chain reaction (PCR).[4] All vaccinees seroconverted with the generation of neutralising IgG as determined by the athymic mouse xenograft system. No individual in the placebo group seroconverted. In a phase I, blinded, placebo-controlled, randomised, dose escalation study of baculovirus expressed HPV-11 L1 VLPs healthy adult volunteers were given either vaccine at doses of 3, 9, 30 and 100 μg with alum, or alum alone without protein, by intramuscular injection at 0, 4 and 16 weeks. All vaccine doses induced a dramatic increase in serum antibody titres but a clear dose response was observed. The anti VLP antibodies induced were shown to be neutralising by using an in vitro reverse transcriptase PCR (RT-PCR)-based neutralisation assay[5] and virus titres declined by about $0.5_{\log10}$ between weeks 20 and 48 post vaccination. In this study, T cell responses were measured by lymphoproliferation and cytokine assays and interestingly some cross-reactivity to HPV-16 VLPs was observed. This suggests that T helper epitopes are conserved across serologically distinct genotypes and offers the tantalising possibility that a VLP vaccine against low-risk types might offer some protection against high-risk viruses.

Efficacy and duration of protection

Overall, the data from published phase I studies using HPV VLP vaccines including HPV-16/HPV-18 and/or HPV-6/HPV-11 L1 VLPs show that these vaccines are safe, well tolerated and highly immunogenic, inducing high levels of both binding and neutralising type antibodies. Phase II and phase III trials are in progress with these vaccines and in at least one of the phase III studies, vaccine efficacy will be measured as prevention of persistence of HPV DNA and prevention of development of both low- and high-grade cervical intraepithelial neoplasia (CIN). The key issues are whether the antibodies generated will be protective, how long the protection will last and to what extent they will be cross-protective against infection with other types. There is no information as yet on duration of protection and cross-reactivity but recent results from a double-blind, placebo-controlled, efficacy study of an HPV-16 L1 vaccine are very encouraging.[6] In this study, 2392 women aged 16–23 years were randomised to receive vaccine (three doses 40 μg yeast-derived VLP at 0, 3 and 6 months) or placebo. The primary endpoint was detection of persistent cervicovaginal HPV-16 infection (HPV-16 DNA detected at two consecutive visits). Of the 1533 HPV-16 naïve individuals followed for a median 17 months, HPV-16 DNA was detected in 0 vaccinees compared to 41 placebos, of whom nine had HPV-related CIN.

Conclusions

The data emerging from the HPV VLP vaccine trials are immensely encouraging but there are concerns relating more to social and economic issues rather than scientific ones. The major burden of malignant HPV-associated disease is in women in the developing world. Vaccines for these women must be cheap and easily delivered. VLP vaccines are likely to be expensive, require medical or paramedical personnel for delivery and cold storage to maintain stability. It is unlikely that they will be the optimal vaccine for the developing world but will be widely taken up in developed countries. Cheap and easily delivered alternatives are required. DNA vaccines may fill this niche but still have problems of delivery. Vaccines delivered directly to mucosal surfaces such as the oral or intranasal surface could be relatively inexpensive and this may be an area where HPV genes expressed in plants provide a cheap source. However, the reality of prophylactic vaccination via the mucosal route for HPV remains to be demonstrated.

References

1.   Stanley MA. Human papillomavirus vaccines. *Curr Opin Mol Ther* 2002;4:15–22.
2.   Steele JC, Gallimore PH. Humoral assays of human sera to disrupted and nondisrupted epitopes of human papillomavirus type 1. *Virology* 1990;174:388–98.
3.   Harro CD, Pang YY, Roden RB, Hildesheim A, Wang Z, Reynolds MJ, *et al*. Safety and immunogenicity trial in adult volunteers of a human papillomavirus 16 L1 virus-like particle vaccine. *J Natl Cancer Inst* 2001;93:284–92.
4.   Brown DR, Bryan JT, Schroeder JM, Robinson TS, Fife KH, Wheeler CM, *et al*. Neutralization of human papillomavirus type 11 (HPV-11) by serum from women vaccinated with yeast-derived HPV-11 virus-like particles: correlation with competitive radioimmunoassay titer. *J Infect Dis* 2001;184:1183–6.
5.   Evans TG, Bonnez W, Rose RC, Koenig S, Demeter L, Suzich JA, *et al*. A Phase 1 study of a recombinant viruslike particle vaccine against human papillomavirus type 11 in healthy adult volunteers. *J Infect Dis* 2001;183:1485–93.
6.   Koutsky LA, Ault KA, Wheeler CM, Brown DR, Barr E, Alvarez FB, Chiaccherini LM, *et al*. A controlled trial of human papillomavirus type 16 vaccine. *N Engl J Med* 2002;347:1645–51.

Chapter 21

Gene therapy in cervical cancer

Tay Sun-Kuie and Hui Kam-Mun

Introduction

Advances in DNA recombinant techniques and the understanding of the genetic basis of human diseases in the last few decades have laid a sound foundation for gene therapy as a new therapeutic approach to some hitherto incurable diseases. The concept of gene therapy is simple and involves the replacement of a defective or congenitally absent gene in a cell by a functional recombinant DNA. The classical example is illustrated by cystic fibrosis. The discovery of a gene controlling the transmembrane chloride channel responsible for the pathogenesis of cystic fibrosis in 1989 led to experimental gene therapy in animal models and clinical trials.[1–4] Although fewer than 0.5% of individuals have inherited diseases caused by single gene defects, the number of people affected by acquired genetic diseases, including cancer, is large. With the completion of the Human Genome Project in 2000, the accessible gene coding information of all the human genes widens the scope of gene therapy enormously.

Advantages and promises of gene therapy: hypothesis for clinical use

An efficient gene delivery system into the target cells is a prerequisite to gene therapy. Ideally, the gene must be replicated without loss of homology and expressed effectively in the target cells. Most importantly, gene therapy must be safe during the period of transfection and the lifetime of the patient.

Vectors

Both physical and virus-mediated methods have been developed for high-efficiency gene transfection of mammalian cells in the last decade. Physical methods include transfection by calcium phosphate precipitation,[5] electroporation,[6] microinjection,[7] liposome transfer[8] and receptor-mediated delivery.[9] The most commonly employed virus-mediated gene transfer systems are the retrovirus and adenovirus methods.[10–12]

Clinical application of retrovirus-mediated vectors is limited by two important factors: they can transduce only the dividing cells;[13] and their random integration into the host genome arouses fear of undesirable insertional mutations, especially when they involve tumour suppressor genes.[14] Physical methods of gene transfection by calcium phosphate precipitation, electroporation and microinjection are not suitable for *in vivo* application. Liposomal gene delivery system, on the other hand, appears to be an interesting method suitable for clinical application in humans. Liposomes are small

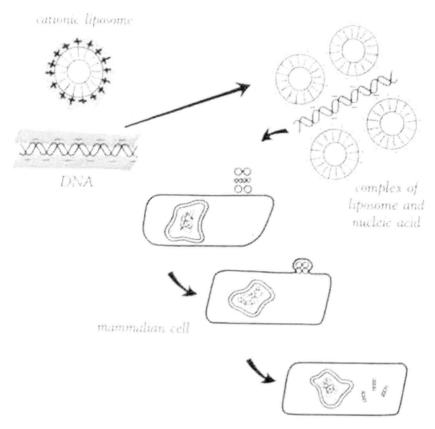

Figure 21.1. Schematic representation of mechanism of liposome-DNA complex transfection of mammalian cells

vesicles composed of one or more lipid layers. They are easy to prepare and administer, can be used to deliver any type of DNA or RNA (linear or supercoiled) of almost unlimited sizes and can transduce nondividing cells. Liposomes are nonimmunogenic and are degradable in the lungs and liver. The exact mechanism of the liposome-DNA complex transfer across the cell membrane is not fully understood but is believed to involve a direct endocytosis process (Figure 21.1). Nonetheless, they are highly efficient in *ex vivo* gene transfection in a number of human tumour cell lines. The transfection efficiency varies with different cell lines and different DNA employed. Human ovarian and cervical cancer cell lines are among those with the highest transfection rate.[15]

Expression of an inserted gene requires a promoter. It has been found that a promoter sequence of at least 600 base pairs of the immediate-early gene of human cytomegalovirus (CMV) contains consensus-binding sites of ubiquitous transcription factors SP1, cAMP response element binding protein, NF-kB factor and other transcription factors. The large number of protein transcription factors in CMV promoter-gene constructs confers the efficient expression of the gene in many different cell types.[16]

It is noteworthy that human gene therapy trials have confirmed that DC-chol cationic liposomes do not cause any toxicity in treated subjects.[17]

Clinical strategies for gene therapy in cancer

Current understanding of tumour biology in terms of cell proliferation, transformation and differentiation, and the host immune reactions to tumorigenesis, provides therapeutic strategies in gene therapy. Clinical trials have targeted the following candidate genes:

- replacement of defective genes for oncoprotein inhibitors or tumour-suppressor proteins: most notably, the *p53* gene[18]

- introduction of genes to inhibit activated oncogenes: antisense complementary oligonucleotides to inhibit expression of the most commonly occuring *ras, myc* and *fos* oncogenes[19]

- inhibition of tumour angiogenesis: applying suitable vectors to block the development of tumour vasculature[20]

- activation of the cellular immune response: gene vectors to deliver transcription factors for a large number of cytokines, growth factors, antigen presenting elements and other protein products to enhance the cellular immune response against tumour cells.[21] Others have experimented with peptide transcription units which produce protein fragments capable of binding to the major histocompatibility complex (MHC) type I protein to stimulate the T-cell dependent cellular immune response.[22]

- peptidomimetic inhibitors of oncoproteins: genes to produce domains of biologically active low molecular weight proteins to inhibit the key functional domains of cellular or viral oncoproteins.

Gene immunotherapy

Gene therapy of human cancers has demonstrated tumour regression in a small number of patients and has generated an intense interest among scientists and clinicians.[23] The significant clinical benefit of gene therapy, however, is yet to be proven. Practical difficulties limiting the success of gene therapy include:

- low efficiency of gene transfer to tumour or target cells *in vivo*

- low and unpredictable gene expression within the target cells

- short lifespan of gene expression within the target cells.

These problems are most critical in therapeutic approaches aimed to correct or replace genetic abnormalities or to inhibit activated oncogenes or viral oncogenes within the tumour cells, as the proportion of corrected cells is too small to have a clinical impact. One therapeutic strategy to circumvent the problems is to enhance tumour immunogeneity with a potent neo-antigen. Only a small number of tumour cells successfully transfected with the neo-antigen genes is needed to elicit a specific T-cell cytotoxic immune response to the tumour cells. Often, the immune stimulation by the neo-antigen may also provoke a nonspecific bystander immune response to the tumour cells, leading to tumour cell killing and clinical tumour regression. These characteristics of gene immunotherapy are demonstrated in animal studies.

In an AKR mouse model, injection of AKR36 leukaemia cell lines into the mouse resulted in a solid tumour formation. Intratumoral injection of H2-K^b–DC-chol-liposome complexes led to regression of the tumour.[24] The tumour regression has been

Table 21.1. Clinical features of nine patients in dose escalation study

Patient	Group	Dose	Primary tumour	Lesion treated	DNA type
1	1	8 µg DNA	NSCLC	Cutaneous metastasis	B13
2	1	8 µg DNA	NSCLC	Cutaneous metastasis	A2
3	1	8 µg DNA	NSCLC	Auxilliary lymph node	K^k
4	2	24 µg DNA	Melanoma	Cutaneous metastasis	B13
5	2	24 µg DNA	NSCLC	Auxilliary lymph node	A2
6	2	24 µg DNA	Melanoma	Inguinal lymph node	K^k
7	3	80 µg DNA	Breast carcinoma	Cutaneous metastasis	B13
8	3	80 µg DNA	Cervical carcinoma	Cervical lymph node	A2
9	3	80 µg DNA	Breast carcinoma	Auxilliary lymph node	K^k

NSCLC = non-small-cell lung cancer

shown to be mediated by CD3+ and CD3– T-cells.[25] When these mice were challenged with 'wild-type' AKR36 cell lines, no tumour developed as the mice had acquired immunity to the 'wild-type' AKR36 cells.[24] Plautz et al.[26] reported similar results with a slightly different mouse model.

The feasibility of gene immunotherapy with human leucocyte antigen (HLA) class I gene in cancer treatment was first demonstrated by Nabel et al.,[17] who injected HLA-B7-DC-chol-liposome complexes into metastatic melanoma. HLA-A2 and HLA-B13 were chosen as candidate genes for immunotherapy of gynaecological malignancies because of the high efficiency of expression of these genes in in vitro studies.[22] It would also be interesting to assess the feasibility of xenogeneic MHC DNA-liposome complex in immunotherapy for cancer.[24]

Gene immunotherapy using HLA-A2, HLA-B13 or xenogeneic H-2K^k

In a dose escalation study,[22] nine terminally ill cancer patients with systemic metastasis and who had exhausted all the available conventional therapies were recruited for the dose escalation and toxicity study (Table 21.1). The first three patients received 8 µg of either pHLA-A2, pHLA-B13– or H-2K^k-DC-chol/DOPE solution by intratumoural injection.

The patients were carefully monitored and no local or systemic adverse reactions, including haematological and serum biochemical assays for urea, electrolytes and liver enzymes, were observed. A second group of three patients was recruited and each of these received 24 µg of the respective DNA-liposome complexes. In the absence of any toxicity, a third group of patients was treated in the same manner, with the concentrations of the respective DNA escalated to 80 µg. Again, the safety of the liposome-DNA complexes was confirmed.

In another study, of the expression of exogenous DNA,[22] fine-needle aspiration biopsies of the treated lesions were analysed by reverse transcriptase-polymerase chain reaction technique for mRNA of the respective DNA injection at weekly interval for four weeks. mRNA for pHLA-A2 and –B13 were detectable one week after the injection and the gene expression lasted for the whole four weeks of the study. Semiquantitative assay showed that the expression level of HLA-A2 was three-fold higher than HLA-B13 (Figure 21.2). On the other hand, no mRNA was detected in patients treated with xenogeneic MHC DNA.

A phase I clinical trial using pHLA-A2, pHLA-B13 or xenogeneic H-2 K^k on terminal ovarian and cervical cancer patients, was conducted to assess biological response and toxicity.[22] The protocol is summarised below:

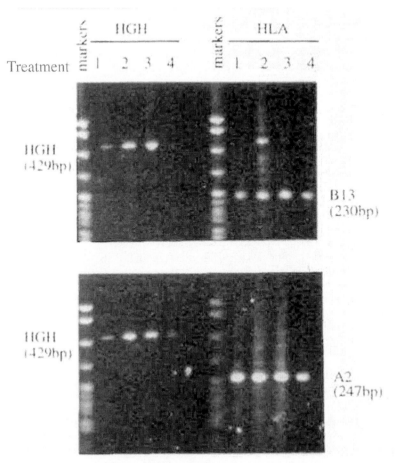

Figure 21.2. Semiquantitative assay of human leucocyte antigen (HLA)-A2 and HLA-B13 mRNA: the amount of polymerase chain reaction (PCR) products of HLA-A2 and HLA-B13 mRNA after each injection from patient no.1 were compared to the amount of human growth hormone (HGH)-specific PCR product using the same amount of mRNA; the gels obtained were then quantified and compared using the BioImage and Visage® system (MilliGen/Biioresearch, Ann Arbor, MI, USA)

The patient's vital signs and general conditions were monitored every 15 minutes for one hour. When the patient returned for subsequent injections, an interview on symptoms of any adverse reaction was conducted and a physical examination was performed. Venous blood was taken before each treatment for haematological, liver enzymes and measurement of tumour markers (if present). The surface dimensions of the tumour treated were measured before each treatment. Attention was also paid to any changes in the other untreated metastatic lesions on the same patients.

Two patients with squamous cell carcinoma of the cervix received pHLA-A2 treatment of metastatic cervical lymph nodes measuring 2.0 cm x 1.5 cm and 2.0 x 1.0 cm, respectively. One of these patients showed a complete resolution of the lymph node metastasis and the other showed an almost complete resolution of the lymph node. A third patient with squamous cell carcinoma of the cervix had a cervical lymph node of 2.0 cm x 1.5 cm received pHLA-B13 treatment. No response in the metastatic tumour was detected.

Table 21.2. Result of *in vitro* cytotoxic T-cell lysis (CTL) assay of lymphocytes obtained from the patient with complete regression of her cervical cancer

In vitro stimulator	E:T	Target CTL (% killing)	
		Autologous tumour cells	WT18
Unmodified autologous tumour cells	50:1	11	2
	25:1	12	0
	12.5:1	7	3
	6.25:1	4	2
HLA-A2 transfected autologous tumour cells	50:1	82	0
	25:1	39	0
	12.5:1	24	0
	6.25:1	15	0

E:T = effector T-cell to tumour cell ratio; HLA = human leucocyte antigen

Three patients with papillary serous adenocarcinoma of the ovary received pHLA-A2 treatment. Significant partial regression of the tumours was observed in a cervical lymph node of 2.0 cm x 1.5 cm and an abdominal wall tumour metastasis of 3.0 x 3.0 cm. The third patient with a large abdominal wall tumour of 6.0 cm x 6.0 cm did not demonstrate any regression of the tumour. Two ovarian cancer patients received pHLA-B13 treatment. The patient with a cervical lymph node of 2.0 cm x 3.0 cm showed a partial regression of the lymph node, while the other similarly treated patient with a 3.0 cm x 4.0 cm did not have a response. Two patients with papillary serous adenocarcinoma of the ovary received H-2 K^k to tumours of 1.5 cm x 1.0 cm and 6.0 cm x 6.0 cm on the anterior abdominal wall but did not show any significant tumour response.

Apart from a transient and mild degree of pain at the time of intratumoural injection of the DNA-liposome complex, no significant changes in the vital signs or evidence of immediate immunological reactions were observed. Similarly, no measurable changes in the investigations for serum urea and electrolytes, liver enzymes and haemotological parameters were detected after each weekly injection or at the completion of the treatment.

Successful culture of tumour cells *in vitro* throughout the study period was achieved in only one patient whose cervical cancer showed a complete tumour regression after HLA-A2 gene therapy. Lymphocytes were purified from 50 ml of peripheral blood of the patient. Cytotoxic T-cell lysis (CTL) assay with autologous lymphocytes and cultured tumour cells did not show any CTL activity at the effector T-cell to tumour cell ratio (E:T) of 100:1. However, in CTL assay with T-cells primed with HLA-A2 transfected autologous tumour cells *in vitro*, tumour cell lysis was observed in 82% of pHLA-A2-transfected autologous tumour cells compared with 11% killing of unmodified autologous tumour cells at an E:T ratio of 50:1 (Table 21.2). Cytotoxic killing was not observed when the primed T-cells were challenged with unrelated WT18 cell lines with homozygous HLA-A2 phenotype. The results confirmed the generation of HLA-A2 specific cytotoxic immune response in this patient.

Combined gene immunotherapy and radiotherapy in locally advanced cervical cancers

Cervical cancer is well suited for intratumoural gene immunotherapy, as the primary tumour is easily accessible for direct injection of DNA-liposome complexes and HLA-

A2 and HLA-B13 gene transfection and mRNA transcription can be achieved within a week. The usual time lapse between diagnosis of cancer and initiation of radiotherapy is an opportune period during which gene immunotherapy can be instituted. The biological response of the primary tumour to gene immunotherapy may be masked by the profound effect of radiotherapy. However, enhanced cytotoxic immune response may reduce the incidence of tumour recurrence locally and in distant sites. A pilot study (unpublished data) was conducted to test the feasibility of gene immunotherapy prior to radiotherapy (Table 21.3). Ten patients were recruited, eight with squamous cell carcinoma and two with adenocarcinoma. All the patients received four injections of HLA-liposome complexes at weekly intervals. Seven patients were given HLA-A2 and three were given HLA-B13. No adverse reactions were observed. No changes were detected in the dimensions of the tumours during the period under gene therapy, and all the patients received the standard external beam and intracavitary radiotherapy. Nine patients showed complete response to radiotherapy. One patient with stage 2B adenocarcinoma showed a partial regression of the tumour. With a median follow up of 46 months (range 18–60 months), two local recurrences of the tumours were detected and the partial responder died of progressive disease despite cytotoxic chemotherapy.

Future perspective

Gene immunotherapy is an attractive approach to enhance host anti-tumour immune response. Our approach with allogenic MHC DNA (HLA-A2 and HLA-B13) and liposome vectors is safe and has been shown to be able to elicit good anti-tumour activity in some cervical cancer patients. This approach of gene therapy overcomes the technical difficulty of low efficiency of tumour cell transfection with candidate genes *in vivo* since only a small proportion of tumour cell modification is sufficient to elicit the desired immune response.

Table 21.3. Protocol for feasibility study of combined gene immunotherapy and radiotherapy in locally advanced cervical cancer

Study process	Criteria and procedure
Elegibility	Histological diagnosis of cervical cancer
	FIGO stage II or greater
	HLA typing A2
	HIV negative
Recruitment	Informed consent
Gene therapy	Intratumoural injection of liposome HLA-A2 complexes
	Weekly injection for three weeks
	Assay for anti-tumour cytotoxic immune response
	Observe clinical tumour reponse
Standard radiotherapy	Standard external/brachy radiotherapy
	Assay for anti-tumour cytotoxic immune response
	Observe clinical tumour reponse
Follow-up	Four-monthly observation for three years
	Tumour response
	Relapse rate
	Treatment/relapse interval

HLA = human leucocyte antigen

A randomised controlled trial is warranted to investigate whether gene immunotherapy in combination with conventional therapy will prevent tumour relapse or metastasis.

References

1. Kerem B, Rommens JM, Buchanan JA, Markiewicz D, Cox TK, Chakravarti A, *et al.* Identification of the cystic fibrosis gene: genetic analysis. *Science* 1989;245:1073–80.
2. Berger HA, Anderson MP, Gregory RJ, Thompson S, Howard PW, Maurer RA, *et al.* Identification and regulation of the cystic fibrosis transmembrane conductance regulator-generated chloride channel. *J Clin Invest* 1991;88:1422–31.
3. Snouwaert JN, Brigman KK, Latour AM, Malouf NN, Boucher RC, Smithies O, *et al.* An animal model for cystic fibrosis made by gene targeting. *Science* 1992;257:1083–8.
4. Crystal RG, McElvaney NG, Rosenfeld MA, Chu CS, Mastrangeli A, Hay JG, *et al.* Administration of an adenovirus containing the human CFTR cDNA to the respiratory tract of individuals with cystic fibrosis. *Nat Genet* 1994;8:42–51.
5. Graham FL, Eb VD. A new technique for the assay of infectivity of human adenovirus 5 DNA. *Virology* 1973;52:456–67.
6. Shigeleawa K, Dower WJ. Electroporation of eukaryocytes and prokaryocytes: a general approach to the introduction of macromolecules into cells. *Biotechniques* 1988;6:742–51.
7. Capecchi M. High efficiency transformation by direct microinjection of DNA into cultured mammalian cells. *Cell* 1980;22:479–88.
8. Fraley R, Subramani S, Berg P, Papahadjopoulos D. Introduction of liposome-encapsulated SV40 DNA into cells. *J Biol Chem* 1980;255:10431–5.
9. Wu GY, Wilson JM, Shalaby F, Grossman M, Shafritz DA, Wu CH. Receptor-mediated gene delivery *in vivo*. Partial correction of genetic analbuminemia in Nagase rats. *J Biol Chem* 1991;266:14338–14342,.
10. Palmet TD, Hock WRA, Miller AD. Efficient retro-virus mediated transfer and expression of a human adenosine deaminase-deficient human. *Proc Natl Acad Sci U S A* 1987;84:1055–9.
11. Samulski RJ. Adeno-associated virus-based vectors for human gene therapy. In: Hui KM, editor. *Gene Therapy: From Laboratory to the Clinic.* Singapore: World Scientific; 1994. p. 232–71.
12. Hanania EG, Kavanagh J, Hortobagyi G, Giles RE, Champlin R, Deisseroth AB. Recent advances in the application of gene therapy to human disease. *Am J Med* 1995;99:537–52.
13. Salmons B, Gunzburg WH. Targeting of retroviral vectors for gene therapy. *Hum Gene Ther* 1993;4:129–41.
14. Temin HM. Safety considerations in somatic gene therapy of human diseases with retrovirus vectors *Hum Gene Ther* 1990;1:111–23.
15. Hui KM, Wee JLK, Oei AA, Koo WH, Ang PT, Tay SK. Immunotherapy of human cancers. *Ann Acad Med Singapore* 1996;25:113–19.
16. Gao X, Jaffurs D, Robbins PD, Huang L. A sustained, cytoplasmic transgene expression system delivered by cationic liposomes. *Biochem Biophys Res Commun* 1994;200:1201–6.
17. Nabel GJ, Nabel EG, Yang ZY, Fox BA, Plautz GE, Gao X, *et al.* Direct gene transfer with DNA-liposome complexes in melanoma: expression, biologic activity, and lack of toxicity in humans. *Proc Natl Acad Sci U S A* 1993;90:11307–11.
18. Kuball J, Wen SF, Leissner J, Atkins D, Meinhardt P, Quijano E, *et al.* Successful adenovirus-mediated wild-type p53 gene transfer in patients with bladder cancer by intravesical vector instillation. *J Clin Oncol* 2002;20:957–65.
19. Cunningham CC, Holmlund JT, Geary RS, Kwoh TJ, Dorr A, Johnston JF, *et al.* A Phase I trial of H-ras antisense oligonucleotide ISIS 2503 administered as a continuous intravenous infusion in patients with advanced carcinoma. *Cancer* 2001;92:1265–71.
20. Tanaka T, Manome Y, Wen P, Kufe DW, Fine HA. Viral vector-mediated transduction of a modified platelet factor 4 cDNA inhibits angiogenesis and tumour growth. *Nat Med* 1997;3:437–42.
21. Galanis E, Hersh EM, Stopeck AT, Gonzalez R, Burch P, Spier C, *et al.* Immunotherapy of advanced malignancy by direct gene transfer of an interleukin-2 DNA/DMRIE/DOPE lipid complex: phase I/II experience. *J Clin Oncol* 1999;17:3313–23.
22. Hui KM, Ang PT, Huang L, Tay SK. Phase I study of immunotherapy of cutaneous metastases of human carcinoma using allogeneic and xenogeneic MHC DNA-liposome complexes. *Gene Ther* 1997;4:783–90.
23. Gutierrez AA, Lemoine NR, Sikora K. Gene therapy for cancer. *Lancet* 1992;339:715–21.
24. Hui KM, Sim T, Foo TT, Oei AA. Tumour rejection mediated by transfection with allogeneic class I

histocompatibility gene. *J Immunol* 1989;143:3835–43.
25. Sabapathy TRK, Cheng Q, Hui KM. Characterisation of tumour-specific cytotoxic effector cells with a novel CD3-/thy-1+ phenotype. *Cell Immunol* 1995;166:141–53.
26. Plautz GE, Yang ZY, Wu BY, Gao X, Huang L, Nabel GJ. Immunotherapy of malignancy by *in vivo* gene transfer into tumours. *Proc Natl Acad Sci U S A* 1993;90:4645–4649.

Chapter 22

Management of lower genital tract neoplasia I

Discussion

Discussion following the paper by Dr Cruickshank

Wilkinson: In our consensus guidelines about a year ago, we looked at the issue of low-grade squamous intraepithelial lesions discovered on Papanicolaou testing. Because of the studies that you cited and the fact that many of these patients have high-grade lesions that are basically masked or they are not identifiable through the conventional methods of cytology, our recommendation was that the preferred approach for these patients would be to go to colposcopy first. The few exceptions to this would be patients who are very young, adolescent, or perhaps elderly, where an acceptable strategy might be cytology alone.

The issue really focuses on not missing the high-grade lesion in this subset of patients. What are your thoughts on that?

Cruickshank: What you are describing is the USA/UK divide. Your worry is missing high-grade lesions, while our worry is about over-treating women with low-grade disease. The recommended change to the UK guidelines is that women with low-grade smears will come to colposcopy after one smear. Studies are going on in the UK at the moment to see what will be the role of human papillomavirus (HPV) in triaging these women coming for colposcopy.

Our worry is that, once women come to colposcopy and we are happy that they do not have a high-grade lesion, what do we do with them then? We feel that there will be this avalanche of women coming into our clinics, and once we have excluded high-grade, what will we do with them?

The point about all these studies, although there are very different methodologies, is that most of them have about a 60% regression rate. Twenty percent had this high-grade disease, which was either unidentified or progressed. There is then still this 20% who you end up treating anyway, because they persist.

Wilkinson: In the guidelines, the consensus opinion was that they could be followed with cytology at 6–12 months, or simply have HPV testing at 12 months in that subset. If they still had HPV, then additional evaluation could be done, or if the cytology was abnormal – atypical squamous cell of undetermined significance (ASCUS) or worse – then additional evaluation would be done.

Monaghan: As a complement to that, I would like to record our experience, on which I would like to hear Dr Cruickshank's views. For the last almost three years now, we have been running a one-stop clinic, just for this group of patients, for the very reasons that have been identified.[1] They are women who are concerned. Many of them are not comfortable with surveillance. There is this degree of uncertainty, in that we know that about one-third of them may well have high-grade lesions.

In this one-stop clinic, six patients arrive at nine o'clock in the morning. They undergo colposcopy and biopsies are performed. The microwave technology in the pathology department allows us to produce a report by 11 o'clock that morning and the high-grade lesions can be treated there and then. They have had biopsy and we can go ahead and treat them. With the remainder, having performed colposcopy and biopsy, you can then send them away to comfortable and confident surveillance. This really does cut down the number of patients that we have to bring back to our review clinics and it cuts down that one-third of patients because we have treated them for their high-grade lesions.

We have also analysed the compliance and patient reaction to this, and we have found a very high compliance. You do not have a default rate, because you are treating the patients there and then. Patient satisfaction is very high. This is an alternative strategy.

Singer: Mr Monaghan, how many high-grade lesions do you think you missed by colposcopic biospy? We have heard that you are doing colposcopic biopsying, where the sensitivity is anywhere between 50% and 70%.

Monaghan: The consultant at my unit in Gateshead, who has been running this, is currently writing up this three-year experience. I cannot give you chapter and verse, but he has already presented the initial pilot to the British Society for Colposcopy and Cervical Pathology and also in Sunderland. It is a very low rate. Whether these are new lesions occurring during the surveillance period, or whether they have been missed, I think we are removing the 30-odd percent.

Singer: So you end up treating 30% of these who come to the clinic?

Monaghan: Yes, roughly one-third.

Singer: And these are borderline cases, as well as those with mild dyskaryosis in their smears?

Monaghan: We started off by including the inadequates, borderlines and mild dyskaryosis.

Deery: In 1988 we started a study to look at the safety of surveillance cytology and we recruited women with a previous history no longer than six months, with a previous mildly dyskaryotic smear – in our terminology. They were all admitted for colposcopy at approximately six months and about one-third of them had low-grade disease and another third had high-grade disease, while the remaining one-third had apparently regressed in the sense that they did not have a colposcopically visible lesion to biopsy.

Of over 200 patients, there were about 70 who actually had a low-grade cervical intraepithelial neoplasia grade 1 (CIN1) biopsy at the outgoing or final conclusional diagnosis from colposcopy. We were doing HPV testing at the same time and we were interested in looking at this group again, so we brought them back five years later. Every case of low-grade disease, of which there were about 29 out of the 79, that had progressed by five years – every single case – had actually progressed within 12 months.

The *Lancet* data published by Woodman *et al.* are very similar.[2] Every case of low-grade disease that progressed, associated with a high-risk virus, actually progressed by 18 months. I therefore want to ask : how do people square the idea of long-lived, low-grade disease with the knowledge that we have about the persistence of virus types? It does not make sense.

Stanley: I am not sure that I really understand this. You are basically saying that, if you have a low-grade lesion progressing to high-grade, how does this square with the persistence of virus?

Deery: There are supposedly some longitudinal studies published, with many low-grade lesions included, and they seem to continue for many years – 17 years, 18 years etc. Syrjanin has published 17-year data about the follow-up of low-grade lesions observed. How does that square with what we know about the resolution of virus infections?

Stanley: It is entirely consistent with what we know. The majority of virus infections are resolved in the sense that it is difficult to detect DNA but a proportion of them stay there as a persistent virus infection. This means that there is the constant shedding of virus. That is entirely consistent with what you have said.

Deery: But it does not seem to fit with the data that have been offered in publication about the resolution of virus infection and the lack of HPV evidence of it – non-oncogenic and oncogenic.

Stanley: I do not think that is right. These are presumably small numbers of people who persist with low-grade lesions from which virus can be recovered.

Deery: So are we expecting that high-risk viruses remain and surface in the midst of a high-grade lesion that has suddenly appeared seven years down the line? Is that the idea?

Stanley: No, you have a viral infection –a permissive viral infection – so that you are actually going through the full cycle and shedding virus. However, there must always be the probability of whatever genetic events there are occurring during that process. Therefore at any time, in theory, you could generate a high-grade lesion from that.

Deery: That appears to be the thesis, but we are told that the majority of HPV-16 and HPV-18 cases clear.

Stanley: Yes, they do.

Deery: Exactly, and if that is the case, are these other low-grade lesions, that turn into high-grade lesions some time down the line, something strange and unusual? Are they a minor population?

Stanley: They are not something unusual. If you have 100 women, let us say that 90 of them will clear, but ten of them will persist, with perhaps two of those progressing quickly to high-grade and a further unspecified number persisting for a long time. That is entirely consistent with the Syrjanen and Meijer story.[3,4]

Deery: Thank you. I just wanted to say something about the Flannelly paper.[5] This purported to follow low-grade lesions but, in fact, it followed low-grade and moderate dyskaryosis.

Cruickshank: I tried to make it clear that many of the historical data are not about lesions, but about smears and their unreliability. What we want to think about now is not smears. We have answered that question now and we are saying that patients are coming for colposcopy, and we now want to address low-grade lesions. But you are right, the Flannelly paper was mild and moderate and it is surprising to know that in 1989 we were wondering what to do with milds and moderates and now, today, we are thinking about what to do with borderlines.

Herrington: Related to this idea that persistent high-risk infection may lead to high-grade transformation many years down the line, this is just an issue of probability. You are looking at low-frequency events that, on a probability basis, in some women will happen quickly and in others will not. It is also an issue of the interaction between viral and host gene polymorphism and other factors such as smoking, so that you are looking at a multifactorial disorder based on probability. There will be a small number of people who will have high-risk infection for a long time and a low-grade lesion.

Discussion following the paper by Professor Prendiville

Wilkinson: I have a question about the type-3 lesions. When you used your larger LLETZ excision, you had persistent lesions up in the endocervix, I presume. Is there a place for a second loop excision of the apex of the first excision? In other words, what has been referred to by some as a 'Welsh hat' procedure? This would be a second loop, rather than using a larger loop to excise that.

Prendiville: The answer to that is not known because the randomised control has not been done. Personally, in the circumstances of doing a large or long cone biopsy, I do not like to dissect it with diathermy or anything else. When doing a large cone, I prefer to excise it as one piece, because that obtains better material for the pathologist, and there is less likely to be diathermy, laser or other artefactual damage.

The question is, how far up the canal do you go? Indeed, whether you are using laser or straight wire, the ambition should perhaps be to obtain a long cylinder, rather than a bigger and bigger cone. My own personal prejudice is that it is that a 'top hat' or an extra piece taken above the cone is less satisfactory than doing a slightly bigger one. Doing a slightly bigger or longer one with a straight wire or a laser is entirely feasible.

Jones: I liked the transformation zone classification. How did you define small and large?

Prendiville: Small and large pertains or relates only to the ectocervical component. Large is when it occupies more than half of the ectocervical epithelium.

Monaghan: I was going to ask the same. I also wanted to congratulate you on the beautiful demonstration of the natural history of a classification system. It starts off simple and then you move it on to the next committee and it becomes more complex, and by the time it gets to the third committee it is really complex.

Prendiville: If the cytologists are allowed to argue about nomenclature, surely we can too.

Discussion following the paper by Professor Fiander

Stanley: It is important for this group in that the endpoints for therapeutic vaccination of intraepithelial neoplasia may not be complete resolution of lesion – especially with these multifocal vulval and anal intraepithelial lesions. You have a mixture, with some areas that are recalcitrant to immune attack, because of immune evasion.

Part of the success of a therapeutic vaccine lies in whether it reduces lesion size. It then identifies those foci that must be dealt with by ablative therapy. The other positive point is that if you generate immune responses, then a question one hopes will be positively answered is that recurrence rates will be significantly reduced post-therapy.

Richart: Do we know what the effect of therapeutic vaccination will be on the patient who is HPV DNA positive, Papanicolaou smear-negative, with no colposcopically visible lesion? This would go a long way to solving one of the problems with primary HPV DNA screening, which is that patient who is positive with no lesion.

Stanley: We do not know but the expectation will be that you will generate strong immune responses, good immune memory, and you will not develop lesions.

Richart: Theoretically, it should be easier to eradicate the virus when there is a small copy number than when it is large.

MacLean: Professor Fiander, did none of the patients respond to vaccinia? I remember a situation some time ago where a patient was repeatedly vaccinated and there was no response, but it turned out that he had had smallpox as a child and therefore any attempt to vaccinate him did not work. I just wondered whether these people were vaccinia-naïve when you started.

Fiander: In the clinical trial where we did not see any clinical responses, they all responded to vaccinia. If you look at vaccinia antibodies, they all have an increase in their titres. So they do react, and they do seroconvert, or they show a memory secondary response to vaccinia. However, they are not then generating an HPV-specific response.

With regard to whether they are vaccinia-naïve or vaccinia-primed, in the first study in advanced cervical cancer patients, half of them were primed and half of them were naïve and it did not seem to make a difference. It did not correlate. This is possibly because they had been immunised against smallpox a number of years previously.

In the CIN trial, in which we gave them two doses of TA-HPV, a month apart, we were able to achieve clinical takes the second time, but it was much harder to get a clinical take and the lesions were much smaller. That was because they had been vaccinated with vaccinia twice, close together.

Adams: Where you had that slow resolution of anal intraepithelial neoplasia (AIN), was there any correlation between immune responses, be it ELISPOT or whatever, and the clinical effect?

Fiander: Professor Stanley might correct me here, but I do not think there was.

Stanley: No, and it is very interesting because in the majority of those patients the responses did not correlate with the HPV type either. Either there were cross-reactivities or they were non-specific.

Singer: I think you were saying that Palefsky had to wait about 9–12 months before he saw any response at all.[6]

Fiander: Yes, they saw no complete responses at six months and then, by 15 months, 41% had complete responses.

Singer: How do you tie that with reporting to an ethics committee?

Fiander: You probably have to choose your model. Vulval intraepithelial neoplasia (VIN) and AIN are perhaps more appropriately followed longer-term.

Singer: Because they are slower moving than cervix.

Tidy: Palefsky's studies are usually among men who are HIV-positive.[7] Is that study in HIV-positive men and does that have any bearing on this?

Fiander: I think that study was with men who were HIV-negative.[7]

Stanley: No, they were HIV-positive, so it is very difficult to interpret.

Critchley: If your objective ultimately with a vaccine might be to enhance an immunological response locally – and we heard from Professor Stanley that this may be one of the targets – how do you see future developments in directing your vaccine to the site where you want the response to be best facilitated?

Fiander: We need to explore two approaches. One is in administering the vaccine locally, either into the disease intralesionally or mucosally in the lower genital tract. The other possible strategy would be to use a topical adjuvant, and I am thinking of possibly a vaccination and something applied topically, such as imiquimod. Perhaps there would then be a TH_1-type response locally, which would help home in the immune response to the lesion that is diseased.

Discussion following Professor Stanley's supplementary paper

Adams: Can you remind us at what age patients would be vaccinated? Obviously, once infection has occurred and integration has occurred, then a prophylactic vaccine will not work.

Stanley: I will quote you what I think is happening, although it may well be that Professor Richart knows more than I do about the age range. My understanding is that the phase I and II trials were in women between the ages of 18 and 25 years. You have identified a clearly important issue: when will the vaccine be delivered and to which group of individuals? In other words, will we only vaccinate women or women and men? Will it be prepubertal girls, or will it be 15-year-olds? None of those issues has been adequately discussed and the logistics are ferocious.

Singer: In all these trials, I presume that the recipients were all antibody negative.

Stanley: In the NCI phase I trial, the recipients were antibody-negative.[8] In the phase I trials, I think they were all antibody-negative. In phase II trials, that was not the case – there were some individuals who were antibody-positive, and you could see that they stratified them. In the big phase III trial there is no question that many of the individuals would be antibody positive before receiving the vaccine. So far, in the small numbers they have, the evidence is that there is a booster effect of delivering vaccine.

Discussion following the paper by Dr Tay

Singer: Dr Tay, how did you get on with ethics – did you have problems there?

Tay: No, because we actually treated the patients while they were waiting for radiotherapy, so there was a time window of three weeks. This was sufficient time for us to administer immunotherapy, i.e. gene therapy. However, we obviously would not have enough time to observe whether there was any primary response to this gene therapy in the cervix, because the radiotherapy would very quickly cause tumour regression. Our objective was to see whether there was any alteration in the pattern of relapse. If there was an immune response to the antigen, there would probably be some memory T-cells, which should confer an immunity. That is what we saw in the animal models.

Singer: Do you think you will be given permission to look at earlier cases?

Tay: We have yet to challenge them, to see whether they would consider that ethical. For example, there are Wertheim hysterectomy patients.

Monaghan: In the study in preradiotherapy patients, were there not problems? You were basically looking at complications, because it was a phase II study. Surely, the complications would be compounded by the radiotherapy that the patient was then given. How do you separate the effects of the radiotherapy from the possible effects of your treatment?

Tay: Most of the gene transcription and expression is short-lived. If they do not actually produce any toxicity within the week following injection, then by the end of that week the gene is already no longer functional, so we do not expect to see any adverse effects. That is what we saw in the earlier study. Certainly, in this small group of patients that we looked into, there were no significant adverse effects.

Tidy: You have raised an interesting point. Many of the ethical issues are incredibly idiosyncratic to that particular committee. We have quite happily progressed protocols where we have not treated CIN3 for three months, on a drug trial, and yet another committee would say no, and that it must be treated. This means that, if you move from one ethics committee to another, you are at their whim. Translating research across international boundaries is limited by that.

Tay: That is generally true – it is up to the local community and the way they perceive the ethical issues. There are certainly many variations between different communities, even within the same country. Sometimes one ethical committee will say yes, while another says no.

References

1. Naik R, Abang-Mohammed K, Tjalma WA, Nordin A, de Barros Lopes A, Cross PA, et al. The feasibility of a one-stop colposcopy clinic in the management of women with low grade smear abnormalities: a prospective study. *Eur J Obstet Gynecol* 2001;98:205–8.
2. Woodman CB, Collins S, Winter H, Bailey A, Ellis J, Prior P, et al. Natural history of cervical human papillomavirus infection in young women: a longitudinal cohort study. *Lancet* 2001;357:1831–6.?
3. Kataja V, Syrjanen K, Mantyjarvi R, Vayrynen M, Syrjanen S, Saarikosi S, et al. Prospective follow-up of cervical HPV infections: life table analysis of histopathological, cytological and colposcopic data. *Eur J Epidemiol* 1989;5:1–7.
4. Remmink AJ, Walboomers JM, Helmerhorst TJ, Voorhorst FJ, Rozendaal L, Risse EK, et al. The presence of persistent high-risk HPV genotypes in dysplastic cervical lesions is associated with progressive disease: natural history up to 36 months. *Int J Cancer* 1995;61:306–11.
5. Flannelly G, Campbell MK, Meldrum P, Torgerson DJ, Templeton A, Kitchener HC. Immediate colposcopy or cytological surveillance for women with mild dyskaryosis: a cost effectiveness analysis. *J Public Health Med* 1997;19:419–23.
6. Palefsky J, Goldstone S, Neefe J. HSPE7 treatment of high-grade anal dysplasia: final results of an open-label trial and interim long-term follow-up. Paper presented at the 20th International Papillomavirus Conference, October 2002, Paris.
7. Palefsky JM, Holly EA, Hogeboom CJ, Ralston ML, DaCosta MM, Botts R, et al. Viral, immunologic and clinical parameters in the incidence and progression of anal squamous intraepithelial lesions in HIV-positive and HIV-negative homosexual men. *J Acquir Immune Defic Syndr Hum Retrovirol* 1998;17:314–17.
8. Harro CD, Pang YY, Roden RB, Hildesheim A, Wang Z, Reynolds MJ, et al. Safety and immunogenicity trial in adult volunteers of a human papillomavirus 16 L1 virus-like particle vaccine. *J Natl Cancer Inst* 2001;93:284–92.

SECTION 6

MANAGEMENT OF LOWER GENITAL TRACT NEOPLASIA II

Chapter 23

Diagnosis and management of cervical glandular intraepithelial neoplasia and early invasive lesions

Pat Soutter

Introduction

Adenocarcinoma *in situ* (AIS) of the cervix was first described in 1952.[1] The rate of AIS is said to be rising, especially in the past 15 years. Some have attributed this rise to the increase in use of oral contraceptives[2] and glandular abnormalities have been linked with infection by human papillomavirus type 18.[3] Many authors believe that AIS was previously under-diagnosed[4,5] and that, with greater awareness, subsequent figures merely reflect an increase in the rate of detection.[6] Nonetheless, AIS is found in only 1% of conisations.

Diagnosis

Glandular abnormalities are not readily detected by cytology.[7,8] However, a smear with abnormal glandular cells is a worrying finding, as invasive disease will be found in 40% and preinvasive lesions in a further 20–28%.[9,10] Even when the glandular changes are described as borderline (abnormal glandular cells of uncertain significance), invasion will be found in 4–16% and preinvasive disease in 17–40%.[9,11–13] In peri- and postmenopausal women, the invasive lesion may be endometrial in origin.

It is also not possible reliably to recognise AIS colposcopically. The net result is that 60% of cases of AIS are not suspected until after a cone biopsy has been performed.[14] Fortunately, AIS coexists with squamous cervical intraepithelial neoplasia (CIN) in two-thirds of cases so the colposcopist is alerted to the presence of an abnormality. Some 10% of women with AIS will have a coexisting invasive carcinoma that is not always glandular in type.[14]

Topography

Relatively little is known about the topography of AIS. Although AIS is located near the transformation zone in most women, this is not the case in 29%.[15] Multifocal lesions are found in 16%. These lesions may extend as far as 3 cm up the endocervical canal[16] but in women under 36 years they are usually less than 10 mm from the squamocolumnar junction.[17]

Investigation and diagnosis

A smear with abnormal glandular cells of uncertain significance (or borderline) is an indication for referral to colposcopy where the woman should be seen within four weeks if possible. If the glandular abnormality is more marked, the patient should be seen within two weeks as a suspected cancer.

If the patient is peri- or postmenopausal, it would be wise to investigate her endometrial cavity with the protocol used for postmenopausal bleeding. My own practice is to arrange a transvaginal ultrasound scan and perform a Pipelle sample of the endometrium only if the endometrium thickness is more than 5 mm.[18] Provided the instrument has been inserted satisfactorily into the uterine cavity, a histology report that no tissue was identified is regarded as negative. Curettage and hysteroscopy under general anaesthesia is reserved for those with thickened endometrium in whom a Pipelle could not be inserted or whose Pipelle result was worrying or who had other worrying clinical or ultrasound features.

Although colposcopy will not identify AIS, some 66% of women with AIS have coexisting CIN that can be recognised. Thus, colposcopy may be a useful investigation but negative findings in the face of a persistent or severe glandular abnormality in the smear should not dissuade the gynaecologist from performing a diagnostic conisation under colposcopic guidance. This should probably not be performed by large loop excision of the transformation zone (LLETZ) because of the inferior results reported by some (see below).

Treatment

Available data

There are no well-established guidelines for the treatment of AIS and only a small body of evidence exists at present on which such guidelines could be based. Treatment recommendations over the past 30 years have varied widely from observation following cone biopsy[19] to radical hysterectomy.[20] AIS commonly occurs in patients who are of childbearing age when conservative management may be advantageous but by the year 2000, the published data on the results of conisation were based on only 296 women, many of whom had been followed up for only a short time.[14] Since then the number reported has risen to 517 (Table 22.1). Some previous studies have referred only to recurrence of AIS and have not included cases of CIN in the recurrence rate. This seems to be a sophism given that many of these women had both AIS and CIN and that the women needed further treatment regardless of the histological phenotype of the lesion. Only one of these studies analysed the data with survival analysis to take into account the varying length of follow up.[14]

Hysterectomy

In spite of the emphasis on conservative treatment, about 42% of women with AIS were treated by some form of hysterectomy in two British series.[14,21] In the combined data, 9% of the women underwent a radical hysterectomy for invasive disease. Provided that invasive disease has been excluded, there are many women for whom 'simple' hysterectomy is the most appropriate treatment. With an endovaginal receiver coil, high resolution magnetic resonance imaging (MRI) can identify invasive cervical carcinomas as small as 200 cm^3.[22] With this technique, a negative MRI does not exclude

Table 22.1. Numbers of women treated conservatively by conisation and numbers who developed recurrent squamous or glandular cervical lesions; recurrences shown in brackets were invasive lesions (modified from Soutter et al. 2001[14])

Study	Year	Women treated conservatively (n)	Women with recurrent cervical pathology (invasion) (n)
Öster[4]	1984	4	0
Luesley[28]	1987	6	1
Hopkins[34]	1988	4	0
Andersen[5]	1989	23	0
Nicklin[17]	1991	9	2
Cullimore[19]	1992	43	1
Muntz [35] (updated by Shin[43])	1992 (2000)	18	0
Poynor[36]	1995	15	7 (2)
Im[37]	1995	3	1
Widrich[23] (updated by Kennedy[44])	1996 (2002)	34	6 (1)
Wolf[38]	1996	7	2 (1)
Denehy[39]	1997	19	1 (1)
Houghton[40]	1997	11	1
Maini[21]	1998	32	3 (2)
Azodi[41]	1999	12	2 (1)
Oster[42]	2000	56	0
Shin[43]	2000	95	4
Kennedy[44]	2002	61	9 (1)
Andersen[45]	2002	58	4
Soutter[14]	2001	59	4[a]
Total		517[b]	42 (8)[b]

[a] The 2001 paper[14] described three women with histological evidence of recurrence; the additional follow-up described in this chapter has identified one more; [b] These totals exclude women described by Widrich et al.[23] and Muntz et al.,[35] as both were updated by later publications

the presence of invasive disease but does reduce to negligible levels the risk of discovering at hysterectomy a cervical cancer whose treatment has been seriously compromised by this operation. If this technology is not available, the clinician and pathologist need to assess the risk of occult cancer in each case individually. A small cervix on clinical examination, close or involved margins at only one small discrete point, and a small volume of AIS all suggest a low risk of occult disease. However, in some cases it may be necessary to perform a second cone biopsy to exclude invasive disease before hysterectomy.

Conisation

Although LLETZ is now the most commonly used method of conisation for CIN, it is not the most suitable instrument for excising AIS, which is found so often within the endocervical canal. In 37 cases of AIS reported by Widrich et al.[23] cold-knife conisation resulted in 33% positive margins compared with 50% for LLETZ. Furthermore, among patients not undergoing hysterectomy as definitive treatment, recurrence was found in 29% of the women treated with loop excision compared with only 6% treated by cold-knife conisation, in spite of a much longer follow up in the latter group. I now prefer to use needle excision of the transformation zone (NETZ) in such women because of its greater flexibility, good haemostasis and the reduced risk of incomplete excision.[24]

Results of conisation

The 517 women reported to date had an 8.1% crude recurrence rate of histologically confirmed disease (Table 22.1). Invasive disease was found in 19% of these women at the time of recurrence.

With the advent of the web-browser-based software, Open-Exeter in 2002, it became possible to obtain from regional screening databases extended follow up information on the 59 women reported previously.[14] Thus far, with further information on 42 of these women, the median length of follow up has been increased from 78 to 203 weeks and the overall follow up from 6529 to 13 578 woman-weeks. One more patient with a histological recurrence of AIS has been identified. There was no further information about the remaining 17 women of whom 11 had moved to nine different health authorities to whose records we still do not have access, and five of whom have not responded to repeated invitations to attend for a smear.

With four histologically confirmed, recurrent squamous or glandular lesions among the 59 women managed conservatively, the crude recurrence rate in this study is somewhat less than those reported previously (Table 22.1). However, the results of the Kaplan–Meier survival analysis,[25] which takes account of the diminishing number of women under surveillance with increasing length of follow-up, suggest a recurrence rate by four years of 9.2% (SEM 4.8%) (Table 22.2). With only 30 women followed for four years and 19 for five years, it is not surprising that recurrences were not noted after this time. Given the well documented long-term risk of recurrence after treatment of CIN, it would not be surprising to find a similar situation with AIS.[26,27]

The rate of histological recurrence shows only part of the picture. In the current study[14] and in many previously reported, several women being managed conservatively developed cytological or colposcopic abnormalities and were advised correctly to undergo further surgery but no histological evidence of recurrent disease was identified. For example, in the study from Gateshead[21] only three women had histologically confirmed recurrence but additional treatment was required by a further eight of the 32 women followed conservatively. In the multicentre study coordinated from Birmingham,[28] six of the 43 women fell into this category. Thus, it seems appropriate to take these additional treatments into account when evaluating

Table 22.2. Kaplan–Meier survival analysis to calculate risk of recurrent disease and risk of further treatment to investigate suspected recurrence; summary data shown

Follow up (months)	At risk (*n*)	Further treatment			Histological recurrence		
		Recurrence	Censored	Kaplan–Meier survival function	Recurrence	Censored	Kaplan–Meier survival function
0–6	59	2	3	0.9646	1	4	0.9818
6–12	54	2	3	0.9268	2	3	0.9433
12–18	49	0	3		0	3	
18-24	46	0	1		0	1	
24–30	45	1	1	0.9062	0	2	
30–36	43	0	2		0	2	
36–42	41	0	6		0	6	
42–48	35	1	6	0.8760	1	6	0.9119
48–54	28	0	8		0	8	
54–60	20	0	1		0	1	

conservative management. The updated results of the London study[14] analysed with the method of Kaplan–Meier showed that 13.2% (SEM 5.6%) required further treatment by four years (Table 22.2). Four of these six cases required hysterectomy.

Conclusions

Women with AIS have a high risk of coexisting invasive disease. Some 30–40% will require a hysterectomy because of involved margins or invasion, or as elective treatment. Every effort must be made to exclude invasive disease before performing a 'simple' hysterectomy. When considering conservative treatment, the risk of recurrent disease and the difficulties in detecting recurrence need to be weighed against the issues surrounding future fertility. There is a place for conservative management but patients need to be carefully selected with clear margins on the cone biopsy and with no suspicion of invasion.

Those who choose conservative treatment must accept the need for careful follow up in a colposcopy clinic with failsafe procedures to minimise the risk of loss to follow up and to ensure optimum conditions for good smears taken with both spatula and endocervical brush.

All concerned must recognise that detecting recurrence may be difficult. Cytology is much less effective at identifying glandular abnormalities than squamous. The lesions themselves lie in the canal and may become buried during the healing process. Brush sampling of the lower endometrial cavity may complicate the cytological interpretation of glandular cell abnormalities after cone biopsy.

Young women have the most to gain from conservative treatment but some older women for whom hysterectomy might carry higher than usual risks might also be considered. For the rest, a simple hysterectomy is an effective treatment and may still be the most appropriate option for older women who do not wish to have more children provided that occult invasive disease has been excluded.

Early invasive adenocarcinoma of the cervix

'Microinvasive' adenocarcinoma of the cervix differs in several important ways from its squamous counterpart. There is no internationally recognised definition of microinvasive adenocarcinoma of the cervix. Measurement of the depth of invasion is difficult because of the lack of a clear baseline from which to measure. Indeed, it is often difficult to determine whether the lesion is truly invasive or remains intraepithelial. To overcome the problem of the uncertain baseline, some use tumour thickness. Others have suggested using estimates of the volume of the tumour based upon the measurements in a single plane multiplied by 1.5 times the largest measured depth or spread of invasion.[29] Others have not been able to reproduce these results and have suggested that depth of invasion was the most reliable prognostic parameter.[30] Many simply apply the FIGO definition of microinvasion in squamous lesions.

As a result of these difficulties, there may be substantial variability in interpretation between pathologists because it is so difficult to distinguish between AIS and early invasive disease. Indeed, many pathologists are reluctant to recognise microinvasive adenocarcinoma as an entity. In addition, there may be differences in prognosis between different histological subtypes.

Several factors have suggested that conservative therapy applicable to squamous microinvasion might not be appropriate for these glandular lesions. The several histological subtypes may have different prognoses. In addition to the difficulties in measuring depth of invasion, multicentric lesions are not uncommon and incomplete excision is frequent.[31]

Finally, this is a rare tumour about which little is known. The Surveillance, Epidemiology and End-Results (SEER) database in USA for 1988–97 recorded only 560 cases and meta-analysis of the published literature increased this total to 1170.[32]

Treatment of early invasive adenocarcinoma of the cervix

It was difficult to determine the surgical treatment performed in some of the studies identified in the meta-analysis but it seemed that, of the 1170 cases reported, approximately 520 were treated with radical hysterectomy, 389 with simple hysterectomy and only 96 were treated by conisation.[32] In the remainder, it was not possible to determine the operation performed. Lymph node metastases were found rarely. Among 531 who underwent pelvic lymphadenectomy or lymph node sampling, only 15 (2.8%) were found to have metastatic disease. Spread to the adnexa was not found in any of 155 women from whom the ovaries were removed.[33]

Results of treatment

The disease-free survival rate for all treatment methods combined was 98.7%.[32] None of the 96 women treated by conisation developed a recurrence but up to 10% also had radiotherapy or lymphadenectomy. Stage Ia2 patients did not have a significantly worse prognosis than Stage Ia1 but there was evidence that the women with more advanced disease had been treated more radically.

Conclusion

The prognosis for women with very small adenocarcinomas of the cervix is good when treated in the manner described in these publications. It would not be appropriate to extrapolate from these results to a conclusion that these women could be treated safely by conisation. It is quite clear that the clinicians involved have carefully selected the most appropriate treatment based upon clinical and histopathological parameters not fully represented in the FIGO staging.

It would seem that simple hysterectomy will be adequate treatment for most women. However, those with larger tumours or tumours that invade beyond 3 mm or who have other adverse prognostic features might be treated more safely with radical hysterectomy and pelvic lymphadenectomy. Cone biopsy may be adequate treatment for carefully selected young women only if the cone biopsy has been thoroughly sampled, and the margins are well clear of the tumour.[33]

References

1. Hepler TK, Dockerty MB, Randall LM. Primary adenocarcinoma of the cervix. *Am J Obstet Gynecol* 1952;63:800–80.
2. Ursin G, Peters RK, Henderson BE. Oral contraceptive use and adenocarcinoma of the cervix. *Lancet* 1994;344:1390–3.
3. Farnsworth A, Loverty C, Stoler MH. Human papillomavirus messenger RNA expression in adenocarcinoma *in situ* of the cervix. *Int J Gynecol Pathol* 1989;8:321–30.
4. Öster AG, Pagano R, Davoren RAM, Fortune DW, Chanen W, Rome R. Adenocarcinoma *in situ* of the cervix. *Int J Gynecol Pathol* 1984;3:179–90.
5. Andersen ES, Arffmann E. Adenocarcinoma *in situ* of the uterine cervix: a clinico-pathologic study of 36 cases. *Gynecol Oncol* 1989;35:1–7.

6. Boon ME, Baak JP, Kurver PJH. Adenocarcinoma *in situ* of the cervix: an underdiagnosed lesion. *Cancer* 1981;48:768–73.

7. Van Aspert-van Erp AJM, Bepvan't Hof-Grootenboer A, Brugal G, Vooijs GP. Endocervical columnar cell intraepithelial neoplasia: I. Discriminating cytomorphologic criteria. *Acta Cytol* 1995;39:1199–215.

8. Lee KR, Manna EA, St John T. Atypical endocervical glandular cells: accuracy of cytological diagnosis. *Diagn Cytopathol* 1995;13:202–8.

9. Cullimore J, Scurr J. The abnormal glandular smear: cytologic prediction, colposcopic correlation and clinical management. *J Obstet Gynaecol* 2000;20:403–7.

10. Leeson SC, Inglis TCM, Salman WD. A study to determine the underlying reason for abnormal glandular cytology and the formulation of a management protocol. *Cytopathology* 1997;8:20–6.

11. Mohammed DKA, Lavie O, Lopes A de B, Cross P, Monaghan JM. A clinical review of borderline glandular cells on cervical cytology. *BJOG* 2000;107;605–9.

12. Zweizig S, Noller K, Reale F, Collis, Resseguie L. Neoplasia associated with atypical glandular cells of undetermined significance on cervical cytology. *Gynecol Oncol* 1997;65:314–18.

13. Kennedy AW, Salmieri SS, Wirth SL, Biscotti CV, Tuason LJ, Travarca MJ. Results of the clinical evaluation of atypical glandular cells of undetermined significant (AGCUS) detected on cervical cytology screening. *Gynecol Oncol* 1996;63:14–18.

14. Soutter WP, Haidopoulos D, Gornall RJ, McIndoe GA, Fox J, Mason WP, *et al.* Is conservative treatment for adenocarcinoma *in situ* of the cervix safe? *BJOG* 2001;108:1184–9.

15. Colgan TJ, Lickrish GM. The topography and invasive potential of cervical adenocarcinoma *in situ* with and without associated squamous dysplasia. *Gynecol Oncol* 1990;36:246–9.

16. Bertrand M, Lickrish GM, Colgan TJ. The anatomic distribution of cervical adenocarcinoma *in situ*; implications for treatment. *Am J Obstet Gynecol* 1987;157:21–5.

17. Nicklin JL, Wright RG, Bell JR, Samaratunga H, Cox NC, Ward BG. A clinicopathological study of adenocarcinoma *in situ* of cervix. The influence of cervical HPV infection and other factors, and the role of conservative surgery. *Aust N Z J Obstet Gynecol* 1991;2:179–83.

18. Smith-Bindman R, Kerlikowske K, Feldstein VA, Subak L, Scheidler J, Segal M, *et al.* Endovaginal ultrasound to exclude endometrial cancer and other endometrial abnormalities. *JAMA* 1998;280:1510–17.

19. Cullimore JE, Luesley DM, Rollason TP, Byrne P, Buckley CH, Anderson M, *et al.* A prospective study of conisation of the cervix in the management of cervical intraepithelial glandular neoplasia (CIGN). A preliminary report. *Br J Obstet Gynaecol* 1992;99:314–18.

20. Weisbrot IM, Stabinsky C, Davis AM. Adenocarcinoma *in situ* of the uterine cervix. *Cancer* 1972;29:1179–87.

21. Maini M, Lavie O, Comerci G, Cross PA, Bolger B, Lopes A, *et al.* The management and follow up of patients with high-grade cervical glandular intraepithelial neoplasia. *Int J Gynecol Cancer* 1998;8:287–91.

22. deSouza NM, McIndoe GAJ, Soutter WP, Krausz T, Chui M, Hughes C, *et al.* Value of magnetic resonance imaging with an endovaginal receiver coil in the preoperative assessment of Stage I and IIa cervical neoplasia. *Br J Obstet Gynaecol* 1998;105:500–7.

23. Widrich T, Alexander D, Kennedy W. Adenocarcinoma *in situ* of the cervix: management and outcome. *Gynecol Oncol* 1996;61:304–8.

24. Basu PS, D'Arcy T, McIndoe A, Soutter WP. Is needle diathermy excision of the transformation zone a better treatment for cervical intraepithelial neoplasia than large loop excision? *Lancet* 1999;353:1852–3.

25. Kaplan EL, Meier P. Nonparametric estimation from incomplete observations. *J Am Stat Assoc* 1958;53:457–81.

26. Soutter WP, de Barros Lopes A, Fletcher A, Monaghan JM, Duncan ID, Paraskevaidis E, *et al.* Invasive cervical cancer after conservative therapy for cervical intraepithelial neoplasia. *Lancet* 1997;349:978–80.

27. Chew GK, Jandial L, Paraskevaidis E, Kitchener HC. Pattern of CIN recurrence following laser ablation treatment: long-term follow-up *Int J Gynecol Cancer* 1999;9:487–90.

28. Luesley DM, Jordan JA, Woodman CBJ, Watson N, Williams DR, Waddell C. A retrospective review of adenocarcinoma *in situ* and glandular atypia of the uterine cervix. *Br J Obstet Gynaecol* 1987;94:699–703.

29. Kaspar HG, Dinh TV, Doherty MG, Hannigan EV, Kumar D. Clinical implications of tumor volume measurement in stage I adenocarcinoma of the cervix. *Obstet Gynecol* 1993;81:296–300.

30. Kaku T, Kumura T, Sakai K, Amada S, Kobayashi H, Shigematsu T, *et al.* Early adenocarcinoma of the uterine cervix. *Gynecol Oncol* 1997;65:281–7.

31. Ostor A, Rome R, Quinn M. Microinvasive adenocarcinoma of the cervix: a clinicopathological study of 77 women. *Obstet Gynecol* 1997;89:88–93.

32. Smith HO, Qualls CR, Romero AA, Webb JC, Dorin MH, Pallida LA, *et al.* Is there a difference in

survival for IA1 and IA2 adenocarcinoma of the uterine cervix? *Gynecol Oncol* 2002;85:229–41.

33. Ostor AG. Early invasive adenocarcinoma of the uterine cervix. *Int J Gynecol Pathol* 2000;19:29–38.

34. Hopkins MP, Roberts JA, Schmidt RW. Cervical adenocarcinoma *in situ*. *Obstet Gynecol* 1988;71:842–4.

35. Muntz HG, Bell DA, Lage JM, Felman S, Rice LW. Adenocarcinoma *in situ* of uterine cervix. *Obstet Gynecol* 1992;80:935–9.

36. Poynor EA, Barakat RR, Hoskins WJ. Management and follow-up of patients with adenocarcinoma *in situ* of the uterine cervix. *Gynecol Oncol* 1995;57:158–64.

37. Im DD, Duska LD, Rosenhein NB. Adequacy of conization margins in adenocarcinoma *in situ* of the cervix as a predictor of residual disease. *Gynecol Oncol* 1995;59:179–82.

38. Wolf JK, Levenback C, Malpica A, Morris M, Burke T, Mitchell MF. Adenocarcinoma *in situ* of the cervix: significance of cone biopsy margins. *Obstet Gynecol* 1996;88:82–6.

39. Denehy TR, Cregori CA, Breen LJ: Endocervical curettage, cone margins and residual adenocarcinoma *in situ* of cervix. *Obstet Gynecol* 1997;90:1–6.

40. Houghton SJ, Schafi MI, Rollason TP, Luesley DM. Is loop excision adequate primary management of adenocarcinoma *in situ* of the cervix? *Br J Obstet Gynaecol* 1997;104:325–9.

41. Azodi M, Chambers SK, Rutherford TJ, Kohorn EI, Schwartz PE, Chambers JT. Adenocarcinoma *in situ* of the cervix: management and outcome. *Gynecol Oncol* 1999;73:348–53.

42. Öster AG, Duncan A, Quinn M, Rome R. Adenocarcinoma *in situ* of the uterine cervix: an experience with 100 cases. *Gynecol Oncol* 2000;79:207–10.

43. Shin CH, Schorge JO, Lee KR, Sheets EE. Conservative management of adenocarcinoma *in situ* of the cervix. *Gynecol Oncol* 2000;79:6–10.

44. Kennedy AW, Biscotti CV. Further study of the management of cervical adenocarcinoma *in situ* *Gynecol Oncol* 2002;86:361–4.

45. Andersen ES, Nielsen K. Adenocarcinoma *in situ* of the cervix: a prospective study of conisation as definitive treatment *Gynecol Oncol* 2002;86:365–9.

Chapter 24

Pathology of vulval cancer and precancers

Edward J Wilkinson

Vulval intraepithelial neoplasia

Squamous vulval intraepithelial neoplasia (VIN) is a proliferative epithelial neoplastic process involving vulval squamous keratinocytes and characterised by abnormal squamous epithelial maturation with nuclear enlargement and atypia. Terms that have been applied to these findings include vulval dysplasia of mild, moderate, or a severe degree, carcinoma *in situ*, bowenoid papulosis, Bowen's disease, erythroplasia of Queyrat and VIN.[1-3] VIN is increasing in incidence in contrast to vulval invasive squamous carcinoma.[4-6]

General features

Women with VIN may vary in age from early adolescents to the elderly.[4] Some patients with VIN are asymptomatic but most patients experience symptoms, with vulval pruritus being the most common. On physical examination, VIN lesions may be of various colours and one patient may have multiple lesions that are of different colour. Approximately 50% of patients with VIN have lesions that are white to grey in colour. These lesions are typically acetowhite with the application of acetic acid (3%). Approximately 25% of cases have pigmented lesions, which may vary in appearance from pale brown to dark brown to black in colour. Pigmented lesions tend to be seen in areas of vulval skin rather than mucous membranes. Vulval epithelial lesions may also be red in colour and these account for the remaining approximately 25% of cases. Such lesions are typically encountered in the mucosa of the vulval vestibule. VIN lesions are usually macular in character with irregular outlines, although papular lesions and papillary lesions may also be observed.

In approximately 70% of cases the VIN lesions are multifocal, the remaining 30% being solitary lesions.[2,7-9] Approximately one-third of the patients with VIN have perianal lesions in addition to the lesions involving the vulva.

Microscopic features

VIN is an epithelial disorder involving a disorderly growth of keratinocytes and characterised by a lack of cellular maturation within the epithelium, associated with nuclear atypia including nuclear pleomorphism, hyperchromasia, coarse nuclear chromatin and radial dispersion of the chromatin toward the nuclear membrane. Mitotic figures are commonly observed above the basement membrane, and include V-shaped, dispersed and other abnormal figures. Abnormalities are confined to the area above the basement membrane of the epithelium. However, VIN lesions have intraepithelial radial growth and that can involve the epithelium of skin appendages. Skin appendage involvement by VIN is observed in slightly less than 25% of cases. Depending upon the location of the skin appendages, the VIN may extend as deeply as 2.7 mm, this depth observed primarily in hair-bearing areas.[10] The epithelium involved by VIN is typically thickened and has been measured from 0.10 mm to 0.90 mm (mean 0.52 mm) in thickness.[11] VIN lesions may be associated with marked hyperkeratosis and parakeratosis with epithelial dyskeratosis and prominent small keratinocytes with orangophilic cytoplasm, termed 'corp ronds', that represent aggregates of tonofilaments within these abnormal keratinocytes.

Histopathological types of VIN are recognised and these include basaloid (bowenoid), warty (condylomatous), differentiated (simplex), and pagetoid types. Basaloid VIN lesions are composed of cells that are atypical, with cellular features resembling basal keratinocytes. The cells have enlarged hyperchromatic nuclei with minimal cytoplasm and indistinct cell membranes. The abnormal cells have little or no maturation within the epithelium. The surface epithelial cells may demonstrate perinuclear clearing that is characteristic of koilocytosis. Some parakeratosis and hyperkeratosis may be seen but it is usually not prominent. The nuclear chromatin features with lack of maturation have microscopic features reminiscent of carcinoma *in situ* grade 3 (CIN3) of the cervix. Basaloid VIN is considered, in this chapter, to encompass those lesions described as bowenoid VIN when used to describe histopathological features. The term bowenoid papulosis is commonly used, especially by dermatologists.[12] Bowenoid papulosis refers clinically to multiple pigmented papules, which are described primarily in younger women and often associated with pregnancy. Spontaneous regression of these lesions is recognised and, in one series, represented the only clinical VIN subset that regressed spontaneously.[13] Microscopic features of lesions described as bowenoid papulosis have cellular features of VIN. These lesions lack cellular maturation, with the cells resembling basal cells, as in basaloid VIN. In some cases the degree of nuclear pleomorphism, nuclear chromatin abnormalities and abnormal mitoses, is less pronounced. Nuclear chromatin changes may be relatively bland in appearance. As with other basaloid VIN lesions, these lesions usually have associated human papillomavirus-16 (HPV-16), are DNA aneuploid, and can be associated with invasive squamous cell carcinoma.

VIN of warty type has some microscopic features resembling typical vulval condyloma, with prominent hyperkeratosis, parakeratosis and an irregular verrucoid surface. The keratinocytes tend to mature somewhat toward the surface and have atypical nuclei with nuclear pleomorphism, hyperchromasia and coarse nuclear chromatin. Abnormal mitotic figures are usually present. Near the surface koilocytotic changes may be seen with the atypical nuclei having perinuclear cytoplasmic halos. Some multinucleated keratinocytes are usually present.[14,15]

VIN of the differentiated (simplex) type is often associated with vulval lichen sclerosus and, unlike basaloid and warty VIN lesions, is not typically associated with HPV.[14–16] VIN of differentiated type was first described by Able in 1965.[16] Women with the differentiated VIN are typically older when they present, as compared with women with basaloid or warty types of VIN.[15] This lesion is characterised by epithelium that has relatively normal superficial maturation. However, there is nuclear atypia with some nuclear pleomorphism. The nuclei have prominent nucleoli and chromatin clearing with radial dispersion of chromatin toward the nuclear membrane. These cells however, have a moderate amount of eosinophilic cytoplasm similar to benign epithelial hyperplastic changes. Hyperkeratosis is usually present. The characteristic important distinction is that the basal and parabasal epithelial cells have increased eosinophilic cytoplasm with the most prominent nuclear abnormalities in the basal and parabasal areas. In the basal areas keratin pearl formation may occur, with dyskeratotic cells. The findings are often associated with adjacent vulval lichen sclerosus and may be associated with squamous cell carcinoma of the usual keratinising squamous cell type.[14–18]

Pagetoid VIN is extremely rare. Unlike other VIN lesions, in pagetoid VIN the abnormal keratinocytes are clustered or occur as single cells throughout the thickness of epithelium of otherwise normal appearance. In this respect, the lesion resembles Paget's disease or melanoma *in situ*, with a 'pagetoid' pattern of growth.[19] There are insufficient cases of this variant to characterise the clinical features or the association with papillomavirus.

The inter-observer reproducibility of knowledgeable pathologists being able to histopathologically distinguish basaloid, warty and differentiated types of VIN has been shown to be fair (κ 0.31–0.43).[20] Warty and basaloid VIN types may be seen together in a single patient, and occasionally even in a single VIN lesion.

Histopathological grading

The World Health Organization (WHO) has accepted three grades of VIN:

- VIN1: mild dysplasia

- VIN2: moderate dysplasia

- VIN3: severe dysplasia/carcinoma *in situ*.[22]

This terminology follows the recommendations of the International Society for the Study of Vulvovaginal Disease (ISSVD) and the International Society of Gynecological Pathologists. These organisations, however, did not include the dysplasia/carcinoma *in situ* terminology in the classification, although WHO retained this terminology to be consistent with the cervical terminology of WHO.[2,21] With this classification VIN1 is defined as loss of epithelial maturation with abnormal keratinocytes and nuclear abnormalities of the lower one-third of the epithelium, with otherwise normal appearing maturation to the surface. VIN1 lesions are considered as equivalent to flat condyloma acuminatum of the vulva. In most studies of VIN, VIN1 lesions are extremely rare and, if they are described, they are usually associated with or adjacent to VIN2 or VIN3 lesions. VIN2 lesions lack epithelial maturation extending to the mid to lower two-thirds of the epithelium. This loss of cellular maturation is associated with mitotic figures being identified in the areas of epithelial abnormality, and these mitotic figures are usually atypical. The epithelial nuclear abnormalities are as described in the basaloid and warty types of VIN as described above. There may be a prominent superficial granular layer with hyperkeratosis. The grading system does not include the measurement of the keratin layer in determining if the lower two-thirds of the epithelium. VIN2 lesions are often associated with VIN3 lesions.

VIN3 has lack of epithelial maturation beyond the lower two-thirds of the epithelium, with nuclear abnormalities and mitotic activity seen in the upper one-third of the epithelium. The vast majority of basaloid and warty-type VIN lesions are VIN3 lesions as defined.

A study comparing the pathologist's ability to consistently discriminate between VIN2 and VIN3 lesions demonstrated that the consistency of discrimination is poor.[23]

Differentiated (simplex) type is, by definition, classified as VIN3 by WHO.[21] There has been significant debate addressing the terminology of VIN, with continuing efforts to apply the Bethesda cytological terminology to VIN. This system would employ the terms VIN 'low grade' for VIN1 and VIN 'high grade' for VIN2 or VIN3. This change in terminology would be in keeping with changes occurring in cervical pathology as referenced in some major articles relating to management of cervical squamous lesions.[23] The ISSVD Committee on Terminology has made the recommendation that the term VIN1 should be eliminated and that such cases should be called condyloma acuminatum. Cases having morphologic features of VIN2 or VIN3 should be classified as VIN without a numerical grading.[24] The ISSVD further proposes that VIN lesions can be histopathologically categorised as either differentiated, referring to the differentiated (simplex) form or VIN, undifferentiated, referring to basaloid or warty, as well as other classifiable or nonclassifiable types of VIN.

This proposal has not been reviewed by the International Society of Gynecological Pathologists, nor has it been considered by WHO. It is recognised that many pathologists never use the term VIN1, rather reporting such lesions as flat condyloma acuminatum.[3]

Immunohistochemical studies of VIN have demonstrated both high and low molecular weight keratins in most VIN lesions.[25] Studies on immunohistochemical markers for cell proliferation, such as MIB-1 (Ki-67) have demonstrated cell proliferation throughout most of the epithelial thickness in these lesions. Such proliferation is also seen in vulval squamous cell carcinoma.[26] VIN of the differentiated type does express p53 in basal cells in most cases;[16] p53 is also expressed in squamous carcinoma associated with the differentiated type of VIN. Molecular studies for HPV in VIN have demonstrated that, with the exception of the differentiated type VIN, HPV is identified associated with most VIN lesions. The most commonly encountered HPV type is HPV type 16.[14,15,17,27] In a study of 12 cases of differentiated VIN, HPV was identified in the VIN lesion in one of 12 patients.[16]

Differential diagnosis

The recognition of associated squamous cell carcinoma with VIN is essential for proper therapy.[28] VIN must be distinguished from other intraepithelial neoplastic process. Melanoma *in situ*, including superficial spreading malignant melanoma, vulval Paget's disease and pagetoid urothelial intraepithelial neoplasia (PUIN) may clinically or microscopically resemble VIN and can be distinguished by immunohistochemical studies. VIN and Paget's disease are not immunoreactive for melanoma-related antigens including Melan-A, HMB-45, or S-100. VIN lesions are also not immunoreactive for cutaneous Paget's disease-related immunohistochemical markers including carcinoembryonic antigen (CEA) and gross cystic disease fluid protein-15 (GCDFP-15).[29,30]

Other lesions to be distinguished include basal-cell carcinoma, condyloma acuminatum following topical podophyllin application and multinucleated squamous atypia of the vulva.[3,5,31,32]

Clinical behaviour and treatment issues

Most women with VIN are treated by local excision of one or more lesions for both diagnostic and therapeutic reasons. Multiple lesions, once a diagnosis is established, may be treated by additional excisions or local laser ablation or topical medications including topical 5-fluorouracil, bi- or trichloroacetic acid or other acceptable treatment. Long-term follow-up studies are rare. In a retrospective study of five women with VIN3 who were biopsied but not otherwise treated, four of the five subsequently presented with invasive squamous carcinoma of the vulva.[34] All four of these carcinomas were associated with HPV-16.

Patients presenting with VIN may have associated superficially or frankly invasive squamous cell carcinoma associated with the VIN. This is reported in 10% or more of cases of clinically typical VIN.[5,28] These associated squamous cell carcinomas are found only when excision of the VIN lesion is performed and histopathological study of the lesion made. Superficially invasive squamous carcinoma accounts for approximately 50–75% of invasive cases identified and the remainder are frankly invasive squamous carcinoma. It is also recognised that VIN is found adjacent to superficially invasive carcinoma of the vulva in the surgical specimen in approximately 70% of cases. In women with frankly invasive squamous cell carcinoma, VIN is found adjacent to the tumour in approximately 20% of cases.[17,34–37] Studies on the treatment of women with VIN treated by local excision are few. However, in a study of patients treated with local excision and who had margins free of VIN, the recurrence rate was 6%. In those patients with VIN extending to a surgical margin, recurrence or persistence of VIN was observed in 20% of the cases.[7] It is also recognised that because of the frequency of monoclonal focal lesions of VIN, it is generally reasonable to assess each lesion and biopsy more than one such lesion because there can be substantial microscopic variation from lesion to lesion in a given patient.[38] It is recognised that approximately 30% of the women with VIN will have cervical or vaginal intraepithelial neoplasia either at the same time as the identification of their cervical lesions or at some other time.

Studies have been reported that VIN lesions that are pigmented papular lesions may regress with observation.[39] Some of these cases have been observed in pregnant women and the lesions regressed postpartum.[13,40] The lesions that have been described appear to fill the criteria of what has been clinically called 'reversible vulval atypia' or 'bowenoid papulosis'.[39,40]

Squamous cell carcinoma of the vulva

Superficially invasive squamous cell carcinoma (FIGO stage 1A: American Joint Commission on Cancer (AJCC) stage T1a, N0, M0).[41]

Definitions

Squamous cell carcinoma of the vulva is an invasive tumour of keratinocytic origin. The vast majority of invasive tumours of the vulva are in this category and arise from the overlying epithelium or epithelial skin appendages. For purposes of discussion, squamous carcinomas can be placed into two categories. First, those that are superficially invasive and, second, those that are deeper than superficially invasive. Superficially invasive carcinoma of the vulva is defined as a squamous carcinoma with a depth of invasion of 1 mm or less and a tumour diameter of 2 cm or less, with clinically negative regional nodes.[42] This staging was first proposed by the ISSVD in 1994 and was referred to as ISSVD stage 1A.[43] The understanding of the definition of 'depth of invasion' is key to this staging system. The depth being measured – the depth of tumour invasion into the dermis or submucosa – is measured from the epithelial–dermal junction of the adjacent most superficial normal dermal papilla to the deepest point of invasion. This measurement is distinguished from the 'thickness of the tumour', a measurement defined as the measurement of the tumour from the surface of the tumour, or the bottom of the granular layer if a keratinised layer is present, to the deepest point of invasion (FIGO stage 1A; AJCC stage T1a, N0, M0).[2,34,41–45] The measurements of depth of invasion and thickness of the tumour can usually be readily made in superficially invasive vulval tumours that are completely excised. When the entire tumour cannot be mounted on a single glass slide, measurement may be somewhat more difficult. In the staging rules, the presence or absence of vascular space involvement associated with stage 1A vulval tumours does not change the stage, provided that the vascular invasion does not exceed 1 mm in depth of invasion and is contiguous with the primary tumour site.

Clinical features

Superficially invasive vulval carcinoma is commonly associated with VIN. However, no specific findings of lesions that are clinically consistent with VIN could be identified to reliably distinguish VIN lesions associated with superficially invasive squamous cell carcinoma.[28]

Histopathological findings

Superficially invasive carcinoma arising in VIN can be identified histopathologically through observation of a number of diagnostic findings. There is a loss of the orderly palisade of orientation of the basal cells seen in typical VIN lesions. The invasive focal tumour has tumour cells within the dermis beneath the apparent basement membrane, identified at the epithelial dermal junction. Solitary or small groups of neoplastic squamous cells may be seen in the dermis at the site of invasion. The neoplastic invasive squamous cells usually have prominent eosinophilic cytoplasm, in contrast to the adjacent intraepithelial neoplastic cells comprising the VIN lesion. The nuclei of the invasive squamous neoplastic cells are also often associated with nuclear enlargement, nuclear chromatin clearing, radial dispersion of the chromatin and prominent nucleoli. In some cases, small dyskeratotic cells and keratin pearls may be present within the focus of invasion. In the adjacent dermis there is often associated oedema or fibrosis with a desmoplastic-like response usually associated with a localised chronic inflammatory cell reaction.[45] Immunohistochemical studies are generally not useful in determining whether or not a focal area is invasive. However, laminin has been demonstrated to be continuous in the basement membrane in VIN but discontinuous in areas of invasive squamous carcinoma.[46] Histopathological features that contribute to understanding the character of a superficially invasive carcinoma are of value to include within the pathology report, as reported by the College of American Pathologists.[42] These findings include the measurements of the thickness and the depth of invasion of the tumour. The method of measurement of the depth of invasion and thickness should also be reported when applicable. The presence or absence of capillary-like space (vascular space) involvement by tumour should be noted. The maximum diameter of the tumour may include both the measurement made on the excised specimen as well as the diameter as measured clinically. It is important to note that adjacent vulval intraepithelial neoplasia should not be included in the measurement of the diameter of the invasive tumour.

Clinical behaviour

There is essentially no regional lymph node metastasis associated with a solitary stage 1A superficially invasive vulval squamous cell carcinoma.[36,45,47] The usual treatment is total excision of the lesion (partial deep vulvectomy) with a 1–3-cm margin of resection without inguinal–femoral lymph node dissection.[3,47–49]

Vulval squamous cell carcinoma

Carcinoma of the vulva accounts for approximately 3–8% of tumours of the female genital tract. Squamous cell carcinomas make up the vast majority of these cases. The incidence of vulval squamous cell carcinoma is estimated in the USA to be 1.5 per hundred thousand women per year. Tumour incidence does increase with age. The mean age of presentation has been reported between 60 and 75 years of age.[50] Vulval squamous cell carcinoma however, has been reported in a 12-year-old.[51]

Additional risk factors that have been recognised include genital granulomatous inflammatory disease, immunodeficiency and vulval condyloma acuminatum. Cigarette smoking and long-standing lichen sclerosus are also independent risk factors.[4] Other factors such as the number of lifelong sexual partners and poor perineal hygiene have also been reported. Type A blood type also appears to have a significantly higher association with vulval squamous cell carcinoma related to lichen sclerosus, as compared with other blood types, although this association is not seen in women with vulval squamous cell carcinoma related to VIN.[52] Immunosuppression, including that related to renal transplantation, is recognised as an associated risk.[53] Women with Fanconi's anaemia have a recognised risk of vulval and other mucosal carcinomas.[54]

Women with vulval lichen sclerosus have a risk of vulval squamous carcinoma, the carcinoma typically arising within the vulval lichen sclerosus. In these patients, the lifetime risk may be as high as 21%.[3,55] In a study of women with lichen sclerosus, 9% were found to have VIN while under observation and 21% were found with vulval squamous cell carcinoma. The mean time between the diagnosis of lichen sclerosus and vulval carcinoma was four years, the time interval ranging from one to 23 years.[55]

Studies examining epithelial changes adjacent to invasive squamous cell carcinoma of the vulva from total vulvectomy or partial vulvectomy specimens have demonstrated the frequency of adjacent lichen sclerosus ranging from 15% to 40%, although higher estimates have been made.[37] VIN is also recognised as a precursor to vulval squamous cell carcinoma. There is some correlation between the histopathological type of VIN and the histological type of invasive carcinoma, with correlation between basaloid squamous carcinoma and basaloid VIN, condylomatous (warty) squamous carcinoma and warty VIN, and differentiated VIN and keratinising squamous carcinoma.[15]

Clinical and pathological findings of invasive vulval squamous cell carcinoma

Invasive squamous cell carcinomas of the vulva may have a variety of clinical and gross appearances. The tumours may be ulcerated, form a discrete nodule, present as an exophytic mass or have a papillomatous warty appearance. Although most squamous cell carcinomas are solitary lesions, multifocal squamous carcinoma is observed in approximately 10% of cases.[37] The majority of squamous cell carcinomas are found on the labia minora or majora, with the tumour often being located in the transition area from the vulval vestibular non-keratinised epithelium to the keratinised epithelium of the labia. The clitoris is involved as the primary site in up to 15% of cases.[48]

Microscopic features of vulval squamous cell carcinoma

There are a number of histopathological types of vulval squamous carcinoma that have been reported, including:

- squamous cell carcinoma of the usual type

- basaloid carcinoma (formally referred to as cloacogenic carcinoma)
- warty (condylomatous) carcinoma
- spindle cell carcinoma
- acantholytic squamous cell carcinoma
- lymphoepithelial-like carcinoma
- squamous cell carcinoma with tumour giant cells
- verrucous carcinoma

Squamous cell carcinomas of the usual type may be keratinising or non-keratinising. When keratinisation is present, keratin pearls and/or dyskeratotic squamous cells may be seen. Non-keratinising squamous cell carcinomas of the usual type do not show significant areas of keratinisation. Squamous carcinomas that are associated with lichen sclerosus are usually of a keratinising type and approximately half of those tumours express p53, as does the associated differentiated VIN if present.[16]

Grading of the usual type squamous cell carcinomas has been undertaken by a number of organisations. A grading system that has been suggested is as follows. Grade 1 tumours have no undifferentiated cells. Grade 2 tumours have undifferentiated cells but they comprise less than half the tumour. Grade 3 tumours have undifferentiated cells comprising half or more of the tumour.[3] The American Joint Committee on Cancer (AJCC) suggests the following grading system: GX being grade not assessed, G1 being well differentiated, G2 moderately differentiated, G3 partially differentiated, G4 undifferentiated.[41]

Basaloid squamous carcinomas show little differentiation. Tumour cells grow in cords and clusters and often have a hyalinised adjacent dermis. Basaloid squamous cell carcinomas are commonly associated with basaloid VIN lesions, and both are associated with HPV-16.

Warty (condylomatous) carcinoma typically has a keratotic papillomatous surface and may demonstrate prominent intracellular bridges and dermal vascular growth that supports the papillomatous surface epithelium. The tumour infiltrates the dermis and forms irregular cell groupings that have squamous pearls in their centre. There is prominent nuclear pleomorphism; hyperchromasia and multinucleated keratinocytes are common. Approximately 75% of these cases have adjacent warty or basaloid VIN. These tumours are most commonly associated with warty type VIN and are predominately associated with HPV-16.[15,56,57]

Squamous cell carcinoma with tumour giant cells

Squamous cell carcinoma with tumour giant cells is a variant of squamous cell carcinoma, characterised by large multinucleated tumour cells often with prominent eosinophilic cytoplasm. These tumours often lack keratin pearl formation or dyskeratosis and their cellular features may histologically resemble malignant melanoma. There is typically no adjacent in situ melanoma and these tumours are not immunoreactive for markers for melanoma including HMB-45, S-100 and Melan-A.[3]

Spindle cell carcinoma

Spindle cell tumours are remarkable both for the spindle cell features of the neoplastic squamous cells and the adjacent supporting dermis that also often has spindle shaped cells.[58] These tumours may have tumour giant cells and resemble sarcoma; however;

both the spindle cells and giant cells are all immunoreactive for cytokeratin.[59] These tumours are immunoreactive for cytokeratin and this distinguishes them from most spindle celled mesenchymal tumours.

Acantholytic squamous cell carcinoma (adenoid squamous cell carcinoma)

This carcinoma is characterised by pseudo-glandular areas that are formed by central cellular acantholysis.[60] The gland-like structures have lining composed of a single layer of squamous cells. Within the lumens of these gland-like spaces, the acantholytic squamous cells are seen as single cells and as small groups of squamous cells. The acantholytic cells do contain glycogen that can be identified by periodic acid Schiff reagent and digested with diastase however, they do not contain mucin. They do have a hyaluronic acid content.

Lymphoepithelioma-like carcinoma

These tumours are uncommon but, when seen, are usually found in older women and have not been demonstrated to be associated with Epstein–Barr virus in this site. The tumour is composed of malignant squamous cells intermixed with a prominently lymphocytic infiltrate. The malignant squamous cells may be in clusters or may be as single cells surrounded by the intense lymphocytic infiltration. When first encountered these tumours may resemble inflammatory conditions or lymphoma. Immunohistochemical studies for cytokeratin demonstrate the immunoreactive neoplastic squamous cells intermixed with the inflammatory cells. The epithelial cells do not react with lymphocytic markers, as do the adjacent lymphocytes. Lymphocytic markers such as lymphocyte common antigen (LCA/CD-45) may be of use.

Verrucous carcinoma

Verrucous carcinoma of the vulva has a unique clinical appearance, often presenting as a marked verrucoid exophytic mass that may resemble vulval condyloma acuminatum. Giant condyloma of Bushke–Lowenstein is now considered a verrucous carcinoma. The pattern of invasion is also unique, in that these tumours have a pushing border-forming prominent acanthosis-like epithelial downgrowth, with bulbous enlargement of the involved epithelium and compressed dermis deep and adjacent to the bulbous epithelial growth.[61] This diagnosis should be made only when the findings are characteristic. If intermixed with typical squamous carcinoma or associated with typical invasive features of squamous carcinoma the tumour should not be classified as a verrucous carcinoma. Verrucous carcinomas may be markedly hyperkeratotic. Microscopic features demonstrate prominent acanthosis with a bulbous and pushing tumour dermal interface. This tumour does not have a distinctly infiltrative pattern of growth. An additional important feature is that the tumour cells are extremely well differentiated with minimal pleomorphism. If significant atypia is present it will be at the tumour dermal interface. Mitotic figures may be seen at the interface and these are usually normal in appearance. The tumour cells have prominent cytoplasm and the nuclei tend to be uniform without significant pleomorphism. Prominent hyperkeratosis is usually present. At the tumour–dermal interface there is usually a chronic inflammatory cell infiltrate. Verrucous carcinomas have been associated predominately with HPV-6 or variants of type 6, unlike squamous carcinomas of the basaloid or warty types, which are typically associated with HPV-16.[15,57,62] In some cases, a verrucous carcinoma may be adjacent to squamous cell carcinoma or condyloma acuminatum.[63]

Verrucous carcinomas are typically DNA diploid, unlike the usual squamous cell carcinoma that is typically DNA aneuploid.

Basal cell carcinoma

Basal cell carcinoma of the vulva is a relatively uncommon tumour and accounts for approximately 5–7% of all vulval carcinomas.[64] These tumours occur predominately in older women, with a mean age of presentation of 70–76 years of age. In addition, these tumours are most common on the labia majora. Associated Paget's disease has been observed in one case.[65]

On clinical and gross examination, basal cell carcinomas are typically firm to hard on palpation and are typically well circumscribed. These tumours may be raised and nodular or ulcerated. Vulval basal cell carcinomas are usually under 2 cm in diameter but they may be up to 10 cm in diameter. It is estimated that approximately 50% of basal cell carcinomas of vulval are of the infiltrative type.

On microscopic examination, basal cell carcinomas of the vulva are similar to those seen on the skin and other sites, having relatively small cells with hyperchromatic nuclei. Some nuclear pleomorphism may be noted. The neoplastic basal cells may grow in groups or form typically rounded groups of cells forming well-circumscribed dermal masses. The peripheral cells within these groups have a palisaded growth pattern. Squamous differentiation can occur in some basal cell tumours and these tumours should still be classified as basal cell carcinoma. The adjacent dermis may be markedly fibrotic and hyalinised. Basal cell carcinomas may express BerEP4, distinguishing them from squamous cell carcinoma.[66] Basal cell carcinomas may be mixed with squamous cell carcinoma and in such cases should be classified as mixed carcinoma. These tumours, unlike the usual basal cell carcinoma, have aggressive behaviour like squamous cell carcinoma.

Local excision (partial deep vulvectomy) is the usual treatment of basal cell carcinoma of the vulva. Recurrence has been reported in up to 20% of the cases.[64] Metastasis to regional lymph nodes is infrequent.[64,67] The overall prognosis is excellent.

Vulval Paget's disease and Paget-like lesions

Vulval Paget's disease has been recognised to be a heterogeneous group of intraepithelial neoplastic processes that may be of cutaneous or non-cutaneous origin. A classification has been proposed by Wilkinson and Brown:[29]

- Paget's disease of primary cutaneous origin:
  - as a primary intraepithelial neoplasm
  - as an intraepithelial neoplasm with invasion
  - as a manifestation of underlying adenocarcinoma of skin appendage or vulval glandular origin

- Paget's disease of noncutaneous origin:
  - secondary to anorectal adenocarcinoma
  - secondary to urothelial neoplasia
    - as a manifestation of intraepithelial urothelial neoplasia (PUIN)
    - as a manifestation of urothelial carcinoma
  - as a manifestation of other noncutaneous carcinoma: (endocervical adenocarcinoma, endometrial adenocarcinoma, ovarian carcinoma, etc.)

Clinical features

Paget's disease of cutaneous and non-cutaneous origin may have similar appearances on vulval skin or mucosa. In all cases, the skin or squamous mucosa involved by Paget's disease usually has a pink to red erythematous appearance. In some cases, the entire involved skin or mucosa is entirely erythematous. In other cases, within the areas of erythematous epithelium small patches of white appearing epithelium can be identified. Paget's disease may resemble a typical erythematous dermatitis and delay in diagnosis may occur if biopsies of the lesion are not performed.

Although most cases of Paget's disease are localised, the disease can be extensive and involve most of the vulval and perianal areas, as well as the vaginal mucosa. It can extend to and involve the medial aspects of the thighs as well as the buttocks.

In the clinical setting some differences can sometimes be identified in localised cases to assist in distinguishing these entities. If the Paget's disease primarily involves the labium majora and does not extend into the vestibule or perianal areas, it is most probably a primary cutaneous Paget's lesion. If the Paget's disease primarily involves the periurethral area or extensively involves the vulval vestibule, it may be of urothelial origin (PUIN). If the Paget's disease primarily involves the perianal areas it may be of anorectal origin.

Paget's disease of any origin is relatively uncommon, accounting for 2% or less of all vulval tumours.[29,68] Paget's disease of cutaneous origin presenting as an intraepithelial neoplasm is the most common type. Cutaneous vulval Paget's disease is observed primarily in older white postmenopausal women. It has been described in younger women and in one remarkable report of a 24-year-old black woman with vulval Paget's disease.[69]

Paget's disease as an intraepithelial neoplasm with associated invasion of the Paget cells is a relatively uncommon finding and has been observed in approximately 10% of reported Paget's disease.[70,71]

Paget's disease can be a manifestation of underlying adenocarcinoma of skin appendage or vulval glandular origin. These cases are probably the most rare of the cutaneous vulval Paget's disease group. Such findings have been reported associated with adenocarcinoma of the Bartholin gland.[72]

Microscopic features

Vulval cutaneous Paget's disease is most commonly an intraepithelial neoplasm when identified. However, the Paget cells can involve the adjacent skin appendages, which should not be interpreted as invasion provided the cells remain intraepithelial. Paget cells within the epithelium form groups that are often in the basal or parabasal areas. In addition, single cells and small groups of cells are often found in the mid and upper epithelium. In some cases the Paget cells form small glandular acini within the epithelium. Paget cells are typically larger than basal or parabasal keratinocytes and have distinctively paler cytoplasm. Cytoplasm from Paget cells may appear vacuolated and signet ring cells may be seen in some cases. The nuclei of the Paget cells are typically larger than the nuclei of the adjacent keratinocytes in all levels of the epithelium. They usually have a slightly granular to coarse chromatin with prominent nuclei. Mitotic figures may be seen in Paget cells and when found are often unrelated to their location within the epithelium.

In the skin or mucosa involving cutaneous Paget's disease, invasion of the dermis by Paget cells may occur. Invasion is characterised as single and clustered Paget cells within the superficial dermis beyond the basement membrane of the overlying epithelium.[70,71] Invasion may be associated with a chronic inflammatory cell response. A search for such areas of invasion when examining skin or mucosa excised for Paget's disease should also include a search for underlying associated skin appendage or vulval glandular adenocarcinoma. Invasion by intraepithelial cutaneous Paget's disease is identified in 10–20% of patients with typical clinical cutaneous Paget's disease.

Clinical behaviour

Women with vulval Paget's disease often have a history of being treated with topical medications for various clinically interpreted dermatoses without recognising the Paget's disease. Biopsy is appropriate for pathological and definitive diagnosis. For treatment, and to exclude underlying invasive Paget's disease or associated cutaneous adenocarcinoma, these patients require excision of the visible Paget's lesion (partial deep vulvectomy) with 1–3 cm grossly clinically free margins of resection. There is evidence to support not using frozen section for margin assessment in vulval Paget's disease, provided that the excision has clinically visible normal skin at the margins.[68] The recurrence rate of vulval Paget's disease with or without involved margins, and determined microscopically, is approximately the same.[68] It is recognised that Paget cells can be identified in skin with clinically normal appearance remote from skin involved with cutaneous Paget's disease.[73] Should the patient have a local recurrence, or recurrence of Paget's disease at another site, this can be treated with local excision or more conservative management. Surgical margins of clinically normal skin or mucosa of 1–3 cm is considered sufficient. Should invasive tumour be identified in the excised Paget's lesion, more extended surgery can be performed, including partial deep vulvectomy with ipsilateral inguinal–femoral lymphadenectomy.[47]

Paget's disease secondary to rectal or anal adenocarcinoma

Patients with vulval Paget's disease presenting as a manifestation of anorectal adenocarcinoma have vulval involvement secondary to contiguous extension of the Paget's disease from the perianal area to the vulva. Clinically this anorectal variant of Paget's disease may be recognised by perianal localisation in the early phase of the disease. For such patients, prognosis is highly dependent upon the recognition and the extent of the associated anal or rectal adenocarcinoma. Complete evaluation of the patient's anal and rectal areas is appropriate in such cases, in addition to examination of vulva, vagina and cervix. In such patients, excision of the cutaneous Paget's disease may not be the treatment of choice, given the fact that the anal/rectal lesion is present. The therapeutic decision must be based on the clinical findings and judgement of the physician.

Microscopic features of Paget's disease of anorectal origin may be initially indistinguishable from Paget's disease of cutaneous origin. These cases, however, can be distinguished by pathologic assessment. Immunohistochemical studies can be of value in distinguishing these.[29,74]

Paget-like disease secondary to urothelial neoplasia

PUIN is an epithelial neoplastic presentation on the vulval vestibule and/or vulva of a neoplastic process arising in the urothelium of the bladder or the urethra. It may be related to intraepithelial or invasive bladder or urethral epithelial carcinoma. Cases of PUIN are relatively uncommon. The Paget's disease may be confined to the periurethral mucosa of the vulval vestibule or may involve much of the vulval vestibule and extend to the labia minora and majora. Evaluation of the urethra and bladder, as well as the vulva, vagina and cervix, is essential to determine the origin of the identified Paget's disease.

Histopathological features of PUIN are similar to the microscopic features of Paget's disease of cutaneous or rectal origin. However, the Paget cells of urothelial origin typically do not form signet-ring-type cells. In addition, the cells usually are as large or larger than adjacent keratinocytes and usually lack prominent nuclei. Cytological findings demonstrate cells that are those of high-grade urothelial neoplasia, having large hyperchromatic nuclei with nuclear pleomorphism, coarse chromatin and small or absent nucleoli. These cells can be identified by scraping the involved vulval epithelium and may be seen in vaginal cytological samples when the vagina is involved.[30,75,76]

These three recognised variants of cutaneous and noncutaneous vulval Paget's disease and Paget-like lesions can be distinguished employing immunohistochemical methods. Vulval cutaneous Paget's disease of cutaneous origin typically expresses CEA, GCDFP-15 and cytokeratin-7, and may express cytokeratin-20. Paget's disease of anorectal origin expresses cytokeratin-20 and CEA but does not express cytokeratin-7 or GCDFP-15. PUIN usually expresses cytokeratin-7 and may express cytokeratin-20 but does not express CEA or GCDFP-15. These lesions also typically express uroplakin-III.[29,30]

Other intraepithelial lesions

Other intraepithelial neoplasms encountered in the vulval skin that are not cutaneous or necessarily epithelial in origin include vulval melanoma *in situ*, clear cell papulosis and bowenoid reticulosis. These lesions typically do not have clinical characteristics of vulval Paget's or Paget-like disease. Microscopically, they may resemble vulval Paget's disease. Immunohistochemical studies are of great value in that melanomas typically express MELAN-A, HMB45, S-100 but lack expression of cytokeratins, CEA or uroplakin-III.

Clear cell papulosis is a localised proliferation of Toker cells that are Paget-like cells. This lesion typically occurs in children and involves the skin of the lower abdomen. This lesion has also been described in males in the lower genital tract.[77] Toker cells are typically tadpole or caudate shaped, unlike typical Paget's cells. They do, however, have immunohistochemical findings similar to cutaneous Paget's cells and the relationship between these two entities has still to be resolved.

Bowenoid reticulosis is a recognised lymphoproliferative neoplastic process that is intraepithelial but can be distinguished using appropriate lymphocytic markers. These cells do not express typical markers of Paget's disease such as CEA, cytokeratins or those described in non-cutaneous Paget's disease.

Proliferative epithelial changes associated with vulval Paget's disease

It is recognised that patients with vulval Paget's disease of cutaneous or rectal type may have associated fibroepitheliomatous-like hyperplastic changes including squamous cell hyperplasia or papillary hyperplasia. Such changes have been observed associated with vulval Paget's disease in approximately 30% of typical cutaneous vulval Paget's disease and in approximately 90% of cases with perianal Paget's disease.[78] In addition, approximately 10% of patients with vulval cutaneous Paget's disease may have associated VIN or squamous carcinoma of the vulva.[78]

Additional vulval tumours

The many types of malignant tumours of the vulva include malignant melanoma, Merkel cell tumour and adenocarcinomas of various origins including those of mammary-like gland origin. Bartholin's gland carcinomas are not included in this discussion, nor are tumours that arise in sweat glands or other rare adenocarcinomas arising from Skene's glands and other sites. There are also soft tissue malignant tumours that may arise in the vulva, including leiomyosarcoma. Discussion of these tumours is beyond the scope of this chapter but they are reviewed in other reference works.[3]

References

1.   Ridley CM, Frankman O, Jones ISC, Pincus S, Wilkinson EJ. New nomenclature for vulvar disease: International Society for the Study of Vulvar Disease. *Hum Pathol* 1989;20:495–6.
2.   Wilkinson EJ, Kneale B, Lynch PJ. Report of the ISSVD Terminology Committee. Proceedings of the VIII World Congress, Stockholm, Sweden. *J Reprod Med* 1986;31:973–4.
3.   Wilkinson EJ. Premalignant and malignant tumors of the vulva. In: Kurman RJ, editor. *Blaustein's Pathology of the Female Genital Tract*. 5th ed. New York: Springer-Verlag; 2002. p. 99–149.
4.   Brinton LA, Nasca PC, Mallin K, Baptiste MS, Wilbanks GD, Richart RM. Case–control study of cancer of the vulva. *Obstet Gynecol* 1990;75:859–66.
5.   Colgan TJ. Vulvar intra-epithelial neoplasia: a synopsis of recent developments. *J Lower Genital Tract Dis* 1998;2:31–6.
6.   Sturgeon SR, Brinton LA, Devesa SS, Kurman RJ. *In situ* and invasive vulvar cancer incidence trends (1973–1987). *Am J Obstet Gynecol* 1992;166:1482–5.
7.   Friedrich EG Jr, Wilkinson EJ, Fu YS. Carcinoma *in situ* of the vulva: a continuing challenge. *Am J Obstet Gynecol* 1980;136:830–43.
8.   Crum CP, Liskow A, Petras P, Keng WC, Frick HC II. Vulvar intra-epithelial neoplasia (severe atypia and carcinoma *in situ*). A clinicopathologic analysis of 41 cases. *Cancer* 1984;54:1429–34.
9.   Patterson JW, Kao GF, Graham JH, Helwig EB. Bowenoid papulosis. A clinical pathologic study with ultrastructural observations. *Cancer* 1986;57:823–36.
10. Shatz P, Bergeron C, Wilkinson EJ, Arseneau J, Ferenczy A. Vulvar intraepithelial neoplasia and skin appendage involvement. *Obstet Gynecol* 1989;74:769–74.
11. Benedet JL, Wilson PS, Matisic J. Epidermal thickness and skin appendage involvement in vulvar intra-epithelial neoplasia. *J Reprod Med* 1991;36:608–12.
12. Wade TR, Kopf AW, Ackerman AB. Bowenoid papulosis of the genitalia. *Arch Dermatol* 1979;115:306–8.
13. Jones RW, Rowan DM. Spontaneous regression of vulvar intraepithelial neoplasia 2–3. *Obstet Gynecol* 2000;96:470–2.
14. Park JS, Jones RW, McLean MR, Currie JL, Woodruff JD, Shah KV, et al. Possible etiologic heterogeneity of vulvar intra-epithelial neoplasia. A correlation of pathologic characteristics with human papillomavirus detection by *in situ* hybridization and polymerase chain reaction. *Cancer* 1991;67:1599–607.
15. Toki T, Kurman RJ, Park JS, Kessis T, Daniel RW, Shah KV. Probable nonpapillomavirus etiology of squamous cell carcinoma of the vulva in older women: a clinicopathologic study using *in situ*. *Int J Gynecol Pathol* 1991;10:107–25.
16. Yang B, Hart WR. Vulvar intra-epithelial neoplasia of the simplex (differentiated) type: a clinicopathologic study including analysis of HPV and p53 expression. *Am J Surg Pathol* 2000;24:429–441.
17. Leibowitch M, Neill S, Pelisse M, et al. The epithelial changes associated with squamous cell carcinoma of the vulva: a review of the clinical, histological and viral findings in 78 women. *Br J Obstet Gynaecol* 1990;97:1135–1139.
18. Wilkinson EJ. Normal histology and nomenclature of the vulva, and malignant neoplasms, including VIN. *Dermatol Clin* 1992;10:283–96.
19. Raju RR, Goldblum JR, Hart WR. Pagetoid squamous cell carcinoma in situ (Pagetoid Bowen's disease) of the external genitalia. *Int J Gynecol Pathol* 2003 (in press).
20. Trimble CL, Diener-West M, Wilkinson EJ, Zaino RJ, Kurman RJ, Shah KV. Reproducibility of the histopathological classification of vulvar squamous carcinoma and intra-epithelial neoplasia. *J Lower*

Genital Tract Dis 1999;3:98–103.

21. Scully RE, Bonfiglio TA, Kurman RJ, Silverberg SG, Wilkinson EJ, in collaboration with pathologists in 10 countries. *Histological Typing of Female Genital Tract Tumours. World Health Organization International Histological Typing Classification of Tumours.* New York: Springer-Verlag; 1994.

22. Preti M, Mezzetti M, Robertson C, Sideri M. Inter-observer variation in histopathological diagnosis and grading of vulvar intra-epithelial neoplasia: results of an European collaborative study. *BJOG* 2000;107:594–9.

23. Wright TW, Cox JT, Massad LS, Twiggs LB, Wilkinson EJ. 2001 Consensus guidelines for the management of women with cervical cytological abnormalities. *JAMA* 2002;287:2120–9.

24. Sideri M, Haefner H, Heller D, Neill S, Preti M, Scurry J, Wilkinson EJ, Jones RW. Squamous vulvar intra-epithelial neoplasia. Modified Terminology. ISSVD Vulvar Oncology Subcommittee. International Society of Vulvovaginal Disease classification of Vulvar Intra-epithelial Neoplasia. 2003 (in press).

25. Esquius J, Brisigotti M, Matias-Guiu X, Prat J. Keratin expression in normal vulva, non-neoplastic epithelial disorders, vulvar intra-epithelial neoplasia, and invasive squamous cell. *Int J Gynecol Pathol* 1991;10:341–55.

26. van Hoeven KH, Kovatich AJ. Immunohistochemical staining for proliferating cell nuclear antigen, BCL2, and Ki-67 in vulvar tissues. *Int J Gynecol Pathol* 1996;15:10–16.

27. Crum CP, Braun LA, Shah KV, Fu YS, Levine RU, Fenoglio CM, *et al.* Vulvar intra-epithelial neoplasia. Correlation of nuclear DNA content and the presence of a human papilloma virus (HPV) structural antigen. *Cancer* 1982;49:468–71.

28. Chafe W, Richards A, Morgan L, Wilkinson E. Unrecognized invasive carcinoma in vulvar intra-epithelial neoplasia (VIN). *Gynecol Oncol* 1988;31:154–62.

29. Wilkinson EJ, Brown HM. Vulvar Paget disease of urothelial origin: a report of three cases and a proposed classification of vulvar Paget's disease. *Hum Pathol* 2002;33:549–54.

30. Brown HM, Wilkinson EJ. Uroplakin-III to distinguish vulvar Paget's disease secondary to urothelial carcinoma. *Hum Pathol* 2002;33:545–8.

31. McLachlin CM, Kozakewich H, Craighill M, O'Connell B, Crum CP. Histologic correlates of vulvar human papillomavirus infection in children and young adults. *Am J Surg Pathol* 1994;18:728–35.

32. Wade TR, Ackerman AN. The effects of resin of podophyllin on condyloma acuminatum. *Am J Dermatopathol* 1984;6:109–22.

33. Jones RW, McLean MR. Carcinoma *in situ* of the vulva: a review of 31 treated and 5 untreated cases. *Obstet Gynecol* 1986;68:499–503.

34. Dvoretsky PM, Bonfiglio TA, Helmkamp BF, Ramsey G, Chuang C, Beecham JB. The pathology of superficially invasive, thin vulvar squamous cell carcinoma. *Int J Gynecol Pathol* 1984;3:331–42.

35. Ross MJ, Ehrmann RL. Histologic prognosticators in stage I squamous cell carcinoma of the vulva. *Obstet Gynecol* 1987;70:774–84.

36. Zaino RJ, Husseinzadeh N, Nahhas W, Mortel R. Epithelial alterations in proximity to invasive carcinoma of the vulva. *Int J Gynecol Pathol* 1982;1:173–84.

37. Zaino RJ. Carcinoma of the vulva, urethra and Bartholin's gland. In: Wilkinson EJ, editor. *Pathology of the Vulva and Vagina, 1. Contemporary Issues in Surgical Pathology.* New York: Churchill Livingstone; 1987. p. 119–54.

38. Wilkinson EJ, Friedrich EG Jr, Fu YS. Multicentric nature of vulvar carcinoma *in situ. Obstet Gynecol* 1981;58:69–74.

39. Wade TR, Kopf AW, Ackerman AB. Bowenoid papulosis of the genitalia. *Arch Dermatol* 1979;115:306–8.

40. Friedrich EG Jr. Reversible vulvar atypia. A case report. *Obstet Gynecol* 1972;39:173–81.

41. American Joint Commission on Cancer. *Cancer Staging Manual.* 6th edition. Philadelphia, PA: Lippincott Raven; 2002.

42. Wilkinson, EJ: Protocol for the examination of specimens from patients with carcinomas and malignant melanomas of the vulva: a basis for checklists. Cancer Committee of the American College of Pathologists. *Arch Pathol Lab Med* 2000;124:51–6.

43. Kneale BL. Microinvasive Cancer of the Vulva: Report of the International Society for the Study of Vulvar Disease Task Force, VIIth Congress. *J Reprod Med* 1984;29:454–456.

44. Wilkinson EJ, Rico MJ, Pierson KK. Microinvasive carcinoma of the vulva. *Int J Gynecol Pathol* 1982;1:29–39.

45. Wilkinson EJ. Premalignant and malignant tumors of the vulva. In: Kurman RJ, editor. *Blaustein's Pathology of the Female Genital Tract.* 5th ed. New York: Springer-Verlag; 2002. p. 99–149.

46. Ehrmann RL, Dwyer IM, Yavner BA, Hancock WW. An immunoperoxidase study of laminin and type IV collagen distribution in carcinoma of the cervix and vulva. *Obstet Gynecol* 1988;72:257–62.

47. Burke TA, Eifel PJ, McGuire P, *et al.* The vulva. In: Hoskins WJ, Perez CA, Young RC, editors. *Principles and Practice of Gynecologic Oncology.* 3rd ed. Philadelphia, PA: Lippincott-Raven; 2000. p. 717–53.

48. Hacker NF, Berek JS, Lagasse LD, Nieberg RK, Leuchter RS. Individualization of treatment for stage I squamous cell vulvar carcinoma. *Obstet Gynecol* 1984;63:155–62.

49. Micheletti L, Preti M, Zola P, Zanotto Valentino MC, Bocci C, Bogliatto F. A proposed glossary of terminology related to the surgical treatment of vulvar carcinoma. *Cancer* 1998;83:1369–75.

50. Hacker NF, van-der-Velden J. Conservative management of early vulvar cancer. *Cancer Suppl* 1993;71:1673.

51. Rabah R, Farmer D. Squamous cell carcinoma of the vulva in a child. *J Lower Genital Tract Disease* 1999;:204–6.

52. Rolfe KJ, Nieto JJ, Reid WMN, Perrett CW, MacLean AB. Is There a Link Between Vulvar Cancer and Blood Group? *Eur J Gynaecol Oncol* 2002;23:111–12.

53. Caterson RJ, Furber J, Murray J, McCarthy W, Mahony JF, Sheil AG. Carcinoma of the vulva in two young renal allograft recipients. *Transplant Proc* 1984;16:559–61.

54. Wilkinson EJ, Morgan LS, Friedrich EG Jr. Association of Franconi's anemia and squamous-cell carcinoma of the lower female genital tract with condyloma acuminatum. *J Reprod Med* 1984;29:447–447.

55. Carlson JA, Ambros R, Malfetano J, Ross J, Grabowski R, Lamb P, *et al*. Vulvar lichen sclerosus and squamous cell carcinoma: a cohort, case control, and investigational study with historical perspective; implications for chronic inflammation and sclerosis in the development of neoplasia. *Hum Pathol* 1998;29:932–48.

56. Downey GO, Okagaki T, Ostrow RS, Clark BA, Twiggs LB, Faras AJ. Condylomatous carcinoma of the vulva with special reference to human papillomavirus DNA. *Obstet Gynecol* 1988;72:68–72.

57. Okagaki T, Clark BA, Zachow KR, Twiggs LB, Ostrow RS, Pass F, *et al*. Presence of human papillomavirus in verrucous carcinoma (Ackerman) of the vagina. Immunocytochemical, ultrastructural, and DNA hybridization studies. *Arch Pathol Lab Med* 1984;108:567–70.

58. Steeper TA, Piscioli F, Rosai J. Squamous cell carcinoma with sarcoma-like stroma of the female genital tract. *Cancer* 1983;52:890–8.

59. Santeusanio G, Schiaroli S, Anemona L, Sesti F, Valli E, Piccione E, *et al*. Carcinoma of the vulva with sarcomatoid features: a case report with immunohistochemical study. *Gynecol Oncol* 1991;40:160–3.

60. Lasser A, Cornog JL, Morris JM. Adenoid squamous cell carcinoma of the vulva. *Cancer* 1974;33:224–7.

61. Brisigotti M, Moreno A, Murcia C, Matias-Guiu X, Prat J. Verrucous carcinoma of the vulva: a clinicopathologic and immunohistochemical study of five cases. *Int J Gynecol Pathol* 1989;8:1–7.

62. Rando RF, Sedlacek TV, Hunt J, Jenson AB, Kurman RJ, Lancaster WD. Verrucous carcinoma of the vulva associated with an unusual type 6 human papilloma virus. *Obstet Gynecol* 1986;67:70–5S.

63. Dinh TV, Powell LC Jr, Hannigan EV, Yang HL, Wirt DP, Yandell RB. Simultaneously occurring condylomata acuminata, carcinoma *in situ* and verrucous carcinoma of the vulva and carcinoma *in situ* of the cervix in a young woman. *J Reprod Med* 1988;33:510–13.

64. Feakins RM, Lowe DG. Basal cell carcinoma of the vulva: a clinicopathologic study of 45 cases. *Int J Gynecol Pathol* 1997;16:319–24.

65. Ishizawa T, Mitsuhashi Y, Sugiki H, Hashimoto H, Kondo S. Basal cell carcinoma within vulvar Paget's disease. *Dermatology* 1998;197:388–90.

66. Tellechea O, Reis JP, Domingues JC, Baptista AP. Monoclonal antibody Ber EP4 distinguishes basal-cell carcinoma from squamous-cell carcinoma of the skin. *Am J Dermatopathol* 1993;15:452–3.

67. Benedet JL, Miller DM, Ehlen TG, Bertrand MA. Basal cell carcinoma of the vulva: clinical features and treatment results in 28 patients. *Obstet Gynecol* 1997;90:765–8.

68. Fishman DA, Chambers SK, Schwartz PE, Kohorn EI, Chambers JT. Extramammary Paget's disease of the vulva. *Gynecol Oncol* 1995;56:266–70.

69. Stapleton JJ. Extramammary Paget's disease of the vulva in a young black woman. *J Reprod Med* 1984;29:444–6.

70. Hart WR, Millman JB. Progression of intra-epithelial Paget's disease of the vulva to invasive carcinoma. *Cancer* 1977;40:2333–7.

71. Lee SC, Roth LM, Ehlich C, Hall JA. Extramammary Paget's disease of the vulva. A clinicopathologic study of 13 cases. *Cancer* 1977;39:2540–9.

72. Wheelock JB, Goplerud DR, Dunn LJ, Oates JF 3rd. Primary carcinoma of the Bartholin gland: a report of ten cases. *Obstet Gynecol* 1984;63:820–4.

73. Gunn RA, Gallager HS. Vulvar Paget's disease: a topographic study. *Cancer* 1980;46:590–4.

74. Nowak MA, Guerriere-Kovach P, Pathan A, Campbell TE, Deppisch LM. Perianal Paget's disease: distinguishing primary and secondary lesions using immunohistochemical studies including gross cystic disease fluid protein-15 and cytokeratin 20 expression. *Arch Pathol Lab Med* 1998;122:1077–81.

75. Hendsch SA, Glover SD, Otis CN, Donovan JT. Atypical glandular cells of underdetermined significance from extramammary Paget's of the bladder. *Obstet Gynecol* 2002;99:912–914.

76. Malik S, Wilkinson EJ: Pseudopagets disease of the vulva: a case report. *J Lower Genital Tract Dis* 1999;3:201–3.
77. Chen YH, Wong TW, Lee JY. Depigmented genital extramammary Paget's disease: a possible histogenetic link to Toker's clear cells and clear cell papulosis. *J Cutan Pathol* 2001;28:105–8.
78. Brainard JA, Hart WR, Proliferative epidermal lesions associated with anogenital Paget's disease. *Am J Surg Pathol* 2000;24:543–52.

Chapter 25

The molecular biology of lichen sclerosus and the development of cancer

Christopher W Perrett

Lichen sclerosus

Lichen sclerosus, a non-neoplastic epithelial disorder of the vulva, is an inflammatory dermatosis whose aetiology remains unknown, although there have been several theories proposed, e.g. immunological,[1] hormonal,[2] enzymatic,[3] infectious,[4] familial[5] and the itch–scratch hypothesis.[6] The histological appearance is of hyperkeratosis, which is often thicker than the underlying epidermis, loss of rete ridges and vacuolar degeneration of the basal layer. The most striking changes are found in the dermis, which becomes oedematous and homogenised in early lesions and hyalinised and sclerotic later. The dermal superficial vascular plexus is pushed deeper and there is a mononuclear cell infiltrate, which can be dense and extensive or sparse and patchy in well-established lesions. The infiltrate is typically situated below the oedematous or hyalinised zone.[7]

There is an association between lichen sclerosus and squamous cell carcinoma of the vulva (SCC), with an estimated 4.5% of women (n = 140/3093 cases) with lichen sclerosus progressing to cancer.[8] The average time of the precursor lichen sclerosus progressing to SCC was ten years in reported cases, although the mean age of onset of lichen sclerosus is generally 20 years younger than that of SCC.[8,9] Histological studies have found lichen sclerosus in proximity to SCC with a frequency of 45% (n = 980/2159 cases, range 2–100%).[8] In identifying the molecular pathways involved in the malignant progression of lichen sclerosus, an analysis of such histologically 'adjacent' lichen sclerosus lesions (SCC/LS), compared with lichen sclerosus not apparently associated with malignancy ('lichen sclerosus alone'), is valuable. Multiple SCC can also arise against a general background of lichen sclerosus.[8,10] The research team at the Department of Obstetrics and Gynaecology, Royal Free and University College Medical School (RFUCMS) examined a patient who presented with multiple and recurrent SCC against a background of lichen sclerosus over a period of 29 years.[11]

The medical treatment preferred at present for lichen sclerosus is topical corticosteroids, with many authors confirming their effectiveness in both symptom control and improvements in clinical and histological appearance of the disease.[12–14] However, persistence of symptoms and resistance to treatment have also been well documented.[8,15,16] Research has indicated that the use of topical corticosteroids in certain lichen sclerosus patients does not prevent the development of vulval cancer itself.[10,11]

Squamous cell carcinoma of the vulva

SCC has an estimated incidence of 1.8 per 100 000[17] rising to 20 per 100 000 after the age of 75 years.[18] It accounts for approximately 4% of all gynaecological malignancies and less than 1% of all cancers in women.[19]

SCC appears to have two separate aetiologies.[20,21] When the disease occurs in younger women it is often associated with human papillomavirus (HPV) infection and is histologically basaloid or warty in appearance. Such SCCs are often multifocal and have a recognised precursor lesion of undifferentiated vulval intraepithelial neoplasia (VIN). The majority of SCCs occur in older women, however, and are rarely associated with HPV; they are described histologically as keratinising. These SCCs do not have an established premalignant lesion, although, as described above, there is an association with lichen sclerosus. Successful management of SCC depends on early diagnosis, as lesions with a depth of less than 1 mm have a good prognosis.[22] It is therefore essential to be able to recognise changes that may indicate premalignancy and to be able to discriminate between those patients who are at a high risk of SCC and those who are not.

Tumour growth and progression

In order to identify the steps involved in the potential malignant progression of lichen sclerosus it is necessary to understand the molecular pathology of epithelial cancer itself. Carcinogenesis is a multistage process.[23] It can be observed both histologically and at the molecular level, although molecular changes can frequently precede any recognisable morphological change. As the normal epithelium progresses towards malignancy, abnormal cell proliferation, clonal expansion and local invasion of the underlying mesenchyme occur. The initial event in this process is DNA damage in the stem cell population, affecting both oncogenes and tumour suppressor genes. In the vulva, this stem cell population is in the basal layer of the epidermis. Growth factors and hormones may then promote division and de-differentiation of such abnormal cells. As tumour invasion occurs proteolytic enzymes, produced by the adjacent stroma, and tumour cell motility factors become important. Tumours can also produce a range of proteins (angiogenic factors) that stimulate the growth of blood and lymph vessels into the growing mass and allow metastasis to occur. The molecular events underlying the progression of SCC are important in indicating new markers of both prognosis and diagnosis in this disease as well as identifying the changes involved in malignant progression.

Inherited susceptibility to vulval cancer

Dominant and recessive inheritance

A small proportion of solid tumours exhibit a pattern of dominantly inherited susceptibility. An analysis of such pedigrees has led to the identification of tumour suppressor genes.[24] In such familial tumours a genetic change (mutation) in one allele of the tumour suppressor gene is already inherited through the germ line and loss of the second allele results in tumour formation in the affected tissue; this is Knudson's 'two-hit' hypothesis. Examples of tumour suppressor genes involved in such inherited cancer syndromes include *P53* (in the Li Fraumeni syndrome), *RB1* (in retinoblastoma) and the DNA mismatch repair genes *MSH2* and *MLH1* (in hereditary non-polyposis colon cancer, HNPCC). Because short DNA (CA) repeat sequences are particularly vulnerable to mismatch repair damage, they are often observed as microsatellite instability in HNPCC. Microsatellite instability is now also a frequent finding in a wide variety of sporadic tumours.

Equally rare are recessively inherited cancer syndromes involving DNA repair deficiencies. These include xeroderma pigmentosum and Fanconi's anaemia. This latter disease has particular relevance to vulval cancer, since the Fanconi anaemia genes predispose to tumours of the oropharyngeal system and lower genital tract, including SCC.[25,26] To date, there have been no studies examining the Fanconi anaemia gene complex in SCC or adjacent, potentially premalignant, lesions, such as lichen sclerosus.

Systemic inheritance

As well as the classic inherited tumour syndromes described above, there are other pedigrees where the inheritance is not so clear-cut. This may be because the penetrance of the predisposing single gene is relatively low or the diseases are due to multiple genes contributing in a coordinated manner. Genes involved in this type of inheritance include those involved in the immune response.

The major human histocompatibility (human leucocyte antigen) system regulates two main sets of cell surface determinants involved in interactions between lymphocytes and other cells in the control of the immune response. The HLA system is highly polymorphic and this polymorphism affects the ability of individuals with a specific 'HLA type' to respond to different immune stimuli. There are three classical HLA class I genes (HLA-A, B, C) and three classical HLA class II groups of genes (HLA-DR, DQ, DP). Individuals are heterozygous at their HLA locus, and the genes are co-dominantly expressed. HLA differences have been shown to be associated with several autoimmune or immune-related diseases, e.g. rheumatoid arthritis.[27] A number of associations between HLA and different cancers has also been suggested, e.g. Hodgkin's disease.[28]

In terms of vulval pathology, there is an association between lichen sclerosus and autoimmunity.[1] Other work has shown that the immunogenetic profile, in particular the HLA-DQ7, DQ8 or DQ9 cell surface determinants, may affect lichen sclerosus expression with regard to site and extent of disease.[29] Unpublished work by RFUCMS has shown that the HLA-B27 phenotype has a higher frequency, compared with controls, in patients who have a histological diagnosis of SCC with adjacent lichen sclerosus, and HLA-B38 has a higher frequency in lichen sclerosus alone, compared with controls. These data suggest that HLA type, in particular HLA-B27, may be involved in the malignant progression of lichen sclerosus. To date, however, the role of other modulatory genes close to the HLA locus and interacting with it, e.g. tumour necrosis factor-alpha (TNFα), has yet to be elucidated.

Work by RFUCSM has also identified a link between blood group antigen expression and vulval disease.[30] The four basic blood groups are A, B, AB and O. The ABO antigens are reaction products catalysed by glycosyltransferases in a co-dominant fashion. Specific cancers have shown a preponderance towards certain blood groups, e.g. ovarian cancer and blood group A.[31] In our work we examined 39 SCCs (29 with histologically associated lichen sclerosus) and 56 patients with lichen sclerosus alone. Significant increases (compared with the control population) were noted in blood group A for both SCC/LS patients and those with lichen sclerosus alone.[30] Such differences may be due to diminished immunological surveillance.[32]

Since both HLA type and blood group may predispose patients to SCC/LS and lichen sclerosus alone, a detailed analysis using a combination of such markers would be valuable.

Oncogenes and tumour suppressor genes

The abnormalities that are involved in carcinogenesis are often the products of oncogenes and tumour suppressor genes and, frequently, interactions between these two types of genes is essential for malignancy.[33]

Oncogenes

Proto-oncogenes are found in normal cells and encode proteins involved in normal cellular function. However, if these genes are altered (e.g. by mutation, deletion or amplification) they become oncogenes and this can lead to increased proliferation as part of the stepwise progression to the development of cancer.

Tumour suppressor genes

Tumour suppressor genes encode proteins that inhibit cell proliferation; they were originally identified by an analysis of familial cancers. Loss of one allele of a tumour suppressor gene is not usually enough to cause a malignant change; loss of the second allele is also required. In familial cancers, one of the genetic changes (mutation) is already present and the second allele can be then lost by a variety of means, including chromosomal loss or deletion. In sporadic tumours, two such genetic 'hits' are required at the tumour suppressor gene locus. When loss of function of the tumour suppressor gene occurs by chromosomal loss or deletion it can be detected by loss of heterozygosity analysis. Indeed, loss of heterozygosity has frequently been used to identify the chromosomal location of potential tumour suppressor genes in the human and other genomes.[34]

Loss of heterozygosity depends upon differences in the lengths of amplified DNA sequences between the two alleles of the gene. The alleles of most genes frequently differ in changes in microsatellite lengths. Individuals who have two different alleles at the gene locus in histologically normal vulval tissue or blood are heterozygous, and two bands can be detected on molecular analysis. In tumour tissue from the same donor, however, if the tumour suppressor gene has undergone a deletion or chromosomal loss, there is loss of one of the bands (loss of heterozygosity). At the protein level, such genetic changes (e.g. at *RB1*) often result in loss of protein product (i.e. 'abnormal' protein expression). Loss of heterozygosity also has an important role to play in 'clonality analysis'. Thus, if the same allele loss is detected in both a potentially pre-malignant lesion and the histologically adjacent tumour (e.g. SCC/LS), this suggests that there has been a cellular progression from one lesion to the other. Other methods applicable to clonality analysis include X-chromosome inactivation and mutational studies.

P53

P53, the 'guardian of the genome', is a well-characterised tumour suppressor gene that codes for the p53 protein. In normal mammalian cells in response to DNA damage, *P53* is activated and this results in programmed cell death (apoptosis) or cell cycle arrest, to allow such damage to be repaired.[35] Loss of normal (wild type) p53 function can be produced by mutation (mutant type p53) and/or deletion (detected by loss of heterozygosity). Alternatively, the formation of complexes with cellular and viral oncoproteins (e.g. Mdm-2 and HPV E6) will inhibit p53 function. Inactivation of p53 by such mechanisms will inhibit apoptosis/cell cycle arrest and allow damaged DNA to be passed to daughter cells, potentially leading to malignancy.

The majority of the mutations found in *P53* have been located in exons 5–8. *P53* mutations are the most frequent genetic changes in human cancers and the spectrum of mutations can indicate tumour aetiology and molecular pathogenesis.[35] Such mutations can be detected by direct sequencing of the *P53* gene or, alternatively, by immunohistochemical analysis of the p53 protein. Most mutations in *P53* lengthen the half-life of the protein, allowing detection on frozen or paraffin-embedded histological sections or cytological smears. Since *P53* is a tumour suppressor gene, two genetic hits are generally required for loss of function. In a wide variety of sporadic cancers, both mutation and loss of heterozygosity are found at the *P53* locus.[35] Like loss of heterozygosity, *P53* mutations can be used in clonality analysis of tumours and adjacent lesions. Thus, if a tumour is from the same clone of cells as the adjacent lesion, the identical *P53* mutation will be found in both tissues.

The cell cycle

The cell cycle is a highly organised process that ensures that there is complete and accurate replication of the cell prior to division. It is composed of four main phases: G1 and G2 (the gap phases), the mitosis phase (M) and the DNA synthesis phase (S). The cycle is controlled by a series of checkpoints and all human cancers analysed to date show abnormalities in the G1/S checkpoint.[36] Such checkpoint abnormalities can lead to increased cellular proliferation. Ki67, a protein expressed throughout the cell cycle, is a valuable marker of such proliferation and has been used in tumour prognostic and diagnostic studies.

Key regulators of cell cycle progression are the cyclin dependent kinase (cdk) proteins, whose kinase activity is dependent on their association with cyclins. Important in such cell cycle regulation at the G1/S transition is the interaction of the oncoprotein cyclin D1 and cdk4, the complex of which phosphorylates the retinoblastoma protein (pRb), a key step in the progression through G1. Amplification of the cyclin D1 gene or overexpression of the cyclin D1 protein can shorten the G1/S transition and lead to the abnormal proliferation found in tumours.[37] A further group of proteins involved in control of the cell cycle are the cyclin dependent kinase inhibitors (cdki). These include the tumour suppressor protein p21[WAF1/CIP1], which is activated by p53 and inhibits cyclinD1/cdk4 function. If wt p53 is activated by cell damage, p21[WAF1/CIP1] levels are increased and the G1/S transition is inhibited. Loss of p21[WAF1/CIP1] function by gene deletion can be detected by reduced levels of protein expression.

Apoptosis

Apoptosis provides a mechanism whereby cells are removed in a regulated manner. It is a 'programmed' cell death as it is driven from within the cell. There is a family of apoptotic genes that encode endogenous cellular proteins that form hetero- and homodimers important in apoptosis. The Bcl-2 oncoprotein suppresses cell death and is downregulated by p53. On the other hand, the Bax protein accelerates programmed cell death and is upregulated by p53. It is the ratio of the levels of these two proteins which determines whether the cell will survive, leading to potentially abnormal proliferation, or undergo apoptosis; a reduction of Bax is often equivalent to elevated levels of Bcl-2.

Clonality analysis in vulval disease

Epithelial tumours are generally monoclonal, i.e. they are derived by cell division from a single cell. Until recently, clonality studies were performed using X-chromosome inactivation analysis. This depends on the fact that, in females, roughly half of the cells have the maternal X chromosome active, whereas in the other half it is the paternal X chromosome that remains operative; this occurs during early embryonic development. Thus, a female who is heterozygous for the two alleles of a gene on the X chromosome represents a mosaic of cells, half of which express one allele and the other half the other allele. However, a clonal tumour in such a female will not be a mosaic, i.e. all the cells will be derived from a single cell which had a specific allele inactivation pattern and will result in a single band on gel analysis. Although powerful, X-chromosome inactivation analysis has certain drawbacks[24] and is now frequently being complemented by mutation, microsatellite instability and loss of heterozygosity analysis.

In vulval disease, clonality analysis would be a powerful method of identifying which lesions had progressed to cancer. To date, studies have shown that SCC, like other epithelial tumours, is monoclonal,[38,39] although a similar analysis of the adjacent lesions, including a limited number of SCC/LS lesions, was conflicting.[38,39] These earlier studies were extended by our own unpublished data, where a combination of *P53* mutational studies, p53 immunohistochemistry and loss of heterozygosity was applied in a clonality analysis of a series of SCC and SCC/LS samples. These techniques identified 42% of lichen sclerosus lesions which shared the same molecular clonal profile as the adjacent SCC (unpublished data). A more detailed analysis, using further loss of heterozygosity/ microsatellite instability markers will further increase the power of this technique and pinpoint those lichen sclerosus lesions which share the same exact genetic profile as the adjacent SCC, thus generating powerful markers in the malignant progression of lichen sclerosus.

The molecular pathology of lichen sclerosus and the effect of treatment

There have been many molecular studies examining the pathogenesis of lichen sclerosus, several focusing on the structural profile of the disease.[40,41] However, there has been little work examining the malignant progression of lichen sclerosus. Furthermore, details on the treatment of patients and its effect on such progression remain sparse. The RFUCSM team examined the effect of lichen sclerosus treatment on tumorigenic markers. By analysing such markers in both treated and untreated lichen sclerosus patients, and comparing the results with SCC/LS and SCC, an initial molecular map of the malignant progression of lichen sclerosus could be constructed. We examined cell cycle/apoptotic protein expression in lichen sclerosus patients divided into those who had used topical corticosteroids within the last month (treated group), those who had not used them in the last month (untreated group) and a group including both sets of these patients, together with those whose treatment was unknown (combined group). Fifty-three percent of the treated group showed overexpression of p53 compared with 19% of the untreated group and 36% of the combined group; significance was demonstrated between treated and untreated groups (unpublished data).[42] The treated group also showed significantly higher Ki67 proliferation rates compared with the untreated group, although no other cell cycle and apoptotic markers showed any significant change. These data are backed up by clinical and histopathological studies which have shown that, although treatment of lichen sclerosus with topical corticosteroids frequently results in improvement of symptoms, patients on topical corticosteroid treatment can still progress to cancer.[10,11] The molecular progression of such lesions appears to involve cell cycle regulation by p53. To date, however, it is not known if the p53 overexpression found in this work is due to overexpression of wild-type or mutant-type p53. Furthermore, the mechanisms underlying the regulation of such p53 expression by topical corticosteroids is currently unknown and requires further study.

Oncogene analysis in vulval cancer and lichen sclerosus

To date, apart from specific apoptotic and cell cycle oncogenes described later, there have been few studies examining the role of oncogenes in SCC and lichen sclerosus. The oncogenes *EGFR*, *RAS* and *MYC* have been studied in SCC, but no changes were found compared with normal tissue.[43,44] This is important work which needs to be extended to other oncogenes, also with an analysis of adjacent lesions.

Cell cycle and apoptotic analysis of vulval cancer and adjacent lichen sclerosus lesions

An analysis of SCC and SCC/LS provides a valuable model in the malignant progression of lichen sclerosus. Such an analysis also generates potential markers of prognosis in SCC.

P53

Several groups have examined p53 expression in SCC,[45,46] However, few have examined adjacent lesions. In our work (unpublished data) we analysed patients with SCC and those with SCC/LS and compared the results to control vulval tissue. Sixty-nine percent of the SCCs demonstrated p53 overexpression compared with 52% of adjacent lichen sclerosus, with no expression in the control tissue.[47] This compared with 36% of lichen sclerosus lesions alone. Such p53 overexpression can represent a number of mechanisms, including expression of wild-type or mutant-type p53 and inactivation by other oncoproteins (e.g. Mdm-2). However, since our work (unpublished data) showed that Mdm-2 was not overexpressed in any of the lesions studied, and p53 expression correlated with high cellular proliferation rates, as measured by Ki67, the work suggested that inactivation of the *P53* gene by mutation or loss of heterozygosity may be found in such lesions. Mutation, microsatellite instability and loss of heterozygosity *P53* analysis was therefore performed on SCC and SCC/LS.

As also found by other authors,[48,49] *P53* mutations in our unpublished study were found in exons 5, 6 and 7 of the gene but the predominant mutation, found in 67% of SCCs and 47% of adjacent lichen sclerosus lesions, was a nonsense mutation at codon 136, exon 5 (Gln→stop).[50] Since this mutation appears to be relatively frequent in SCC and SCC/LS, it opens up the possibility of molecular scanning for potential malignancy using *P53* chip technology. Sixty-six percent of p53-positive SCCs and 20% of p53-positive adjacent lichen sclerosus lesions showed mutations in the *P53* gene, indicating that, although mutant-type p53 is involved in the pathogenesis of such lichen sclerosus lesions, wild-type p53 can also be expressed in a proportion of cases. This was also implied by the finding of p21[WAF1/CIP1] in such p53-positive lesions. Loss of heterozygosity and microsatellite instability at *P53* were rare, however. At other loci, SCC and adjacent lichen sclerosus have been shown to demonstrate loss of heterozygosity and microsatellite instability at chromosomal locations 3p, 10q and 22q (unpublished data).[51–53] Such genetic instability is generally rare in premalignant lesions, although lichen sclerosus lesions have been shown to be aneuploid.[8]

An analysis of the *P53* mutation profile also provides an insight into the potential aetiology of these vulval diseases. The majority of *P53* mutations identified in SCC are transitions at CpG sites. These are generally believed to be caused by endogenous processes, possibly involving inflammatory free radical damage in response to scratching.

Cyclin D1 and *RB1*

In our unpublished work, SCC and SCC/LS were examined for cyclin D1 and *RB1* changes.[54] Although SCCs and SCC/LS showed abnormal expression of cyclin D1 and pRb, similar changes were also found in control vulval tissue. Loss of heterozygosity and microsatellite instability at the *RB1* locus was found to be a rare event.

Apoptotic proteins

Unpublished work by the RFUCSM research team has indicated that apoptotic proteins are involved in the formation of SCC, although it appears to be loss of Bax expression rather than increased regulation of Bcl-2.

Prognostic and diagnostic significance

The prognostic and diagnostic significance of p53 expression in SCC has been examined in other studies showing associations with tumour grade;[45] this was also confirmed in the work of the RFUCSM research team. It has also been shown that abnormal pRb and cyclin D1 expression correlate with tumour grade, depth of invasion and disease-free survival.[54]

In a separate study, we examined the usefulness of molecular marker expression as a potential predictor of SCC onset or recurrence.[11] The RFUCSM research team examined a patient who was first diagnosed with lichen sclerosus and then subsequently developed SCC lesions over a period of 29 years. She was treated with surgery and topical corticosteroids over this time. In a preliminary molecular analysis, a combined p53/Ki67/loss of heterozygosity scoring system identified lichen sclerosus lesions which had a high risk of malignant progression. This type of work will be valuable in identifying areas of lichen sclerosus that should be scrutinised for close follow-up and potential excision.

Tumour promotion and de-differentiation

Hormones and growth factors have been implicated as tumour promoters in a number of cancers, including gynaecological tumours.[55] To date, however, there have been few studies examining such effects in lichen sclerosus and SCC. Both the normal vulva and SCC express very low levels of oestrogen and progesterone receptors, although androgen receptors are found.[56–58] Since stimulatory growth factors also have an important role to play in mitogenesis[55] they may have significance in the malignant progression of lichen sclerosus. TGFα levels are high in SCC and correlate with metastasis, although levels of other growth factors such as epidermal growth factor (EGF) and fibroblast growth factor (FGF) are low.[44]

Proteolytic enzymes and tumour cell motility factors

There have been limited studies examining proteolytic enzymes and cell adhesion molecule expression in SCC and adjacent lesions. One study found that the molecule CD44, involved in cell-matrix interactions, was a predictor of tumour aggressiveness, but other tumour markers (e.g. E-cadherin) did not show any such correlations.[44]

Angiogenesis

Angiogenesis is the stimulation of new blood vessel growth. Without angiogenesis, tumour expansion cannot proceed beyond 1–2 mm, as tumour proliferation is severely limited by nutrient supply to, and waste removal from, the tumour. However, angiogenesis can also have a role to play in premalignant lesions, e.g. those of the cervix.[59] Vascularisation is also required for tumour cells to spread into the circulation. A number of angiogenic stimulators have now been identified in tumours and stroma, they include vascular endothelial growth factor (VEGF) and platelet-derived endothelial cell growth factor/thymidine phosphorylase (PD-ECGF/TP). Both growth factors are frequently overexpressed in solid tumours. Angiogenesis can also be measured by an immunohistochemical analysis of the number of vessels in a tumour (microvessel density). Studies on microvessel density and angiogenic growth-factor expression have been performed in SCC and SCC/LS.

Thus, in SCC, a combination of high microvessel density and VEGF tissue levels indicates significantly poorer overall survival[60] and such a relationship with survival can also be found in higher preoperative serum VEGF concentrations.[61] We have found that VEGF is highly expressed in SCC but is not found in lichen sclerosus adjacent to SCC, lichen sclerosus alone or normal vulval tissue.[62,63] On the other hand, PD-ECGF/TP was expressed in all the lesions tested, including normal vulva. Unlike VIN, VEGF and PD-ECGF/TP are not valuable markers of malignant progression in lichen sclerosus [62] and the molecular events underlying blood vessel formation in this disease, and its malignant progression, remain to be elucidated.

Conclusions and future prospects

Although there is a recognised association between lichen sclerosus and SCC, the molecular events leading to potential malignant progression still remain to be fully identified. Work from the RFUCSM research team and others has identified several key areas that are important in this analysis and will provide valuable sources for future research.

Thus, the role of the Fanconi anaemia gene complex in SCC and lichen sclerosus remains to be evaluated, as does more detailed work investigating associations with HLA, blood group and immunomodulatory genes, such as TNFα.

In SCC/LS, a detailed analysis using a combination of loss of heterozygosity and microsatellite instability markers may specifically identify those lichen sclerosus lesions which share the same genetic profile as SCC, thus generating powerful genetic markers in the malignant progression of lichen sclerosus. Further work in this field needs to involve oncogenes. In terms of tumour suppressor genes, the *P53* mutation profile has indicated a hot spot nonsense mutation at codon 136, exon 5, which is frequent in SCC and SCC/LS and opens up the potential of gene scanning to identify high-risk cases. Retrospective work by the RFUCSM research team in a patient with multiple and recurrent SCC lesions has also shown that a combination of p53 and Ki67 expression, together with loss of heterozygosity analysis, will be valuable in identifying areas of lichen sclerosus which should be scrutinised for close follow-up and potential excision.

Corticosteroid treatment of lichen sclerosus results in increased cell cycle protein expression, particular p53 expression. It is not yet known if this is due to *P53* mutations or overexpression of wild-type p53 and the mechanisms underlying such regulation need to be elucidated.

Finally, the molecular mechanisms important in growth stimulation and de-differentiation of SCC may provide new molecular markers of lichen sclerosus malignant progression; androgen may be important in this respect.

Acknowledgements

I would like to express my thanks to my (now former) PhD student, Kerstin Rolfe, who provided a large amount of the published and unpublished data representing the work of the RFUCSM research group's work in this field; this has constituted her PhD thesis. In addition, one of my current students, Lan Fong Wong Te Fong, provided some of the data on angiogenesis in vulval disease.

References

1. Meyrick Thomas RH, Ridley CM, McGibbon DH, Black MM. Lichen sclerosus et atrophicus and autoimmunity: a study of 350 women. *Br J Dermatol* 1998;118:41–6.
2. Friedrich EG, Kalra PS. Serum levels of sex hormones in vulva lichen sclerosus and the effect of topical testosterone. *N Engl J Med* 1984;310:488–91.
3. Godeau G, Frances C, Hornebeck W, Brechemier D, Robert L. Isolation and partial characterization of an elastase-type protease in human vulva fibroblasts: its possible involvement in vulvar elastic tissue destruction of patients with lichen sclerosus et atrophicus. *J Invest Dermatol* 1982;78:270–5.
4. Cantwell AR. Histologic observations of pleomorphic, variably acid-fast bacteria in scleroderma, morphea and lichen sclerosus et atrophicus. *Int J Dermatol* 1984;23:45–52.
5. Sahn EE, Bluestein EL, Oliva S. Familial lichen sclerosus et atrophicus in childhood. *Pediatr Dermatol* 1994;11:160–3.
6. Scurry J. Does lichen sclerosus play a central role in the pathogenesis of human papillomavirus negative vulvar squamous cell carcinoma? The itch-scratch-lichen sclerosus hypothesis. *Int J Gynecol Cancer* 1999;9:89–97.
7. Goolamali SK, Goolamali SI. Lichen sclerosus. *J Obstet Gynaecol* 1997;17:5–12.
8. Carlson JA, Ambros R, Malfetano J, Ross J, Grabowski R, Lamb P, *et al.* Vulvar lichen sclerosus and squamous cell carcinoma: a cohort, case control and investigational study with historical perspective; implications for chronic inflammation and sclerosis in the development of neoplasia. *Hum Pathol* 1998;29:932–48.
9. Wallace HJ. Lichen sclerosus et atrophicus. *Trans St John's Hosp Dermatol Soc* 1971;57:9–30.
10. Carli P, Cattaneo A, De Magnis A, Biggeri A, Taddei G, Giannotti B. Squamous cell carcinoma arising in vulval lichen sclerosus: a longitudinal cohort study. *Eur J Cancer Prev* 1995;4:491–5.
11. Rolfe KJ, Eva LJ, MacLean AB, Crow JC, Perrett CW, Reid WMN. Cell cycle proteins as molecular markers of malignant change in vulvar lichen sclerosus. *Int J Gynecol Cancer* 2001;11:113–18.
12. Dalziel KL, Millard PR, Wojnarowska F. The treatment of vulval lichen sclerosus with a very potent topical steroid (clobetasol propionate 0.05%) cream. *Br J Dermatol* 1991;124:461–4.
13. Bracco GL, Carli P, Sonni L, Maestrini G, De Marco A, Taddei GL, *et al.* Clinical and histologic effects of topical treatments of vulval lichen sclerosus. A critical evaluation. *J Reprod Med* 1993;38:37–40.

14. Carli P, Bracco G, Taddei G, Sonni L, De Marco A, Maestrini G, *et al.* Vulvar lichen sclerosus: immunohistologic evaluation before and after therapy. *J Reprod Med* 1994;39:110–14.

15. Elchalal U, Gilead L, Vardy DA, Ben-shachar I, Anteby SO, Schenker JG. Treatments of vulvar lichen sclerosus in the elderly: an update. *Obstet Gynecol Surv* 1995;50:155–62.

16. Meffert JJ, Davis BM, Grimwood RE. Lichen sclerosus. *J Am Acad Dermatol* 1995;32:393–416.

17. Silverberg E. Statistical and epidemiological information on gynecologic cancer. *CA Cancer J Clin* 1980;30:9.

18. Crum CP. Carcinoma of the vulva: epidemiology and pathogenesis. *Obstet Gynecol* 1992;79:448–54.

19. Parker SL, Tong T, Bolden S, Wingo PA. Cancer Statistics, 1997. *CA Cancer J Clin* 1997;47:5–27.

20. Kurman RJ, Toki T, Schiffman MH. Basaloid and warty carcinomas of the vulva. Distinctive types of squamous cell carcinoma frequently associated with human papillomaviruses. *Am J Surg Pathol* 1993;17:133–45.

21. Trimble CL, Hildesheim A, Brinton LA, Shah KV, Kurman RJ. Heterogeneous etiology of squamous carcinoma of the vulva. *Obstet Gynecol* 1996;87:59–64.

22. Wilkinson EJ, Rico MJ, Pierson KK. Microinvasive carcinoma of the vulva. *Int J Gynecol Pathol* 1982;1:29–39.

23. Franks LM, Teichs NM. *Introduction to the Cellular and Molecular Biology of Cancer.* 3rd ed. Oxford: OUP; 1997.

24. Wasan HS, Bodmer WF. Inherited susceptibility to cancer. In: Franks LM, and Teich NM, editors. *Introduction to the Cellular and Molecular Biology of Cancer.* 3rd ed. Oxford: OUP; 1997. p. 60–91.

25. Kennedy AW, Hart W. Multiple squamous-cell carcinomas in Fanconi's anemia. *Cancer* 1982;50:811–14.

26. de Winter JP, van der Weel L, de Groot J, Stone S, Waisfisz Q, Arwert F, *et al.* The Fanconi anemia protein FANCF forms a nuclear complex with FANCA, FANCC and FANCG. *Hum Mol Genet* 2000;9:2665–74.

27. Gregersen PK, Silver J, Winchester RJ. The shared epitope hypothesis: an approach to understanding the molecular genetics of susceptibility to rheumatoid arthritis. *Arthritis Rheum* 1987;30:1205–13.

28. Amiel JL. Study of the leukocyte phenotypes in Hodgkin's disease. In: Curtoni ES, Mattiuz PL, Tos RM, editors. *Histocompatibility Testing.* Copenhagen: Munksgaard; 1967. p. 79–81.

29. Marren P, Yell J, Charnock FM, Bunce M, Welsh K, Wojnarowska F. The association between lichen sclerosus and antigens of the HLA system. *Br J Dermatol* 1995;132:197–203.

30. Rolfe KJ, Nieto JJ, Reid WMN, Perrett CW, MacLean AB. Is there a link between vulval cancer and blood group? *Eur J Gynaecol Oncol* 2002;23:111–12.

31. Henderson J, Seagrott V, Goldacre M. Ovarian cancer and ABO blood groups. *J Epidemiol Commun Health* 1993;47:287–9.

32. Smith DF, Prieto PA. Forssmann antigen. In: Roitt IM, Delves PH, editors. *Encyclopaedia of Immunology,* Volume 2. London: Academic Press; 1992. p. 591–92.

33. Kemp CJ, Burns PA, Brown K, Nagase H, Balmain A. Transgenic approaches to the analysis of ras and p53 function in carcinogenesis. *Cold Spring Harbor Symp Quant Biol* 1994;59:427–34.

34. Lander ES, Linton LM, Birren B, Nusbaum C, Zody MC, Baldwin J, *et al.* Initial sequence and analysis of the human genome. *Nature* 2001;409:860–921.

35. Ryan KM, Philips AC, Vousden KH. Regulation and function of the p53 tumour suppressor protein. *Curr Opin Biol* 2001;13:327–32.

36. Clurman BE, Roberts JM. Cell cycle and cancer. *J Natl Cancer Inst* 1995;87:1499–505.

37. Gillett C, Fantl V, Smith R, Fisher C, Bartek J, Dickson C, *et al.* Amplification and overexpression of cyclin D1 in breast cancer detected by immunohistochemical staining. *Cancer Res* 1994;54:1812–17.

38. Kim YT, Thomas NF, Kessis TD, Wilkinson EJ, Hedrick L, Cho KR. P53 mutations and clonality in vulvar carcinomas and squamous hyperplasias: Evidence suggesting that squamous hyperplasias do not serve as direct precursors of human papillomavirus-negative vulvar carcinomas. *Hum Pathol* 1996;27:389–95.

39. Tate JE, Mutter GL, Boynton KA, Crum CP. Monoclonal origin of vulvar intra-epithelial neoplasia and some vulvar hyperplasias. *Am J Pathol* 1997;150:315–22.

40. Mihara Y, Mihara M, Hagari Y, Shimao S. Lichen sclerosus et atrophicus. A histological, immunohistochemical and electron microscopic study. *Arch Dermatol Res* 1994;286:434–42.

41. Marren P, Dean D, Charnock M, Wojnarowska F. The basement membrane zone in lichen sclerosus: an immunohistochemical study. *Br J Dermatol* 1997;136:508–14.

42. Rolfe KJ, Crow JC, Reid WMN, Benjamin E, MacLean AB, Perrett CW. The effect of topical steroids on Ki67 and p53 expression in vulval lichen sclerosus. *Br J Dermatol* 2002;147:503–8.

43. Tate JE, Mutter GL, Prasad C J, Berkowitz R, Goodman H, Crum CP. Analysis of HPV-positive and -negative vulvar carcinomas for alterations in c-myc, Ha-, Ki-, and N-ras genes. *Gynecol Oncol* 1994;53:78–83.

44. Ambros RA, Kallakury BVS, Malfetano JH, Mihm MC Jr. Cytokine, cell adhesion receptor, and tumor suppressor gene expression in vulvar squamous carcinoma: Correlation with prominent

fibromyxoid stromal response. *Int J Gynecol Pathol* 1996;15:320–5.

45.   McConnell DT, Miller ID, Parkin DE, Murray GI. p53 protein expression in a population based series of primary vulval squamous cell carcinoma and immediate field change. *Gyecol Oncol* 1997;67:284–6.

46.   Scheistroen M, Tropé C, Pettersen EO, Nesland JM. p53 protein expression in squamous cell carcinoma of the vulva. *Cancer* 1999;85:1133–8.

47.   Rolfe KJ, Crow JC, Benjamin E, Reid WMN, MacLean AB, Perrett CW. Abnormalities in the G1/S cell cycle checkpoint in vulval cancer. *Br J Obstet Gynaecol* 2000;107:817.

48.   Lee YY, Wilczynski SP, Chumakov A, Chih D, Koeffler HP. Carcinoma of the vulva: HPV and p53 mutations. *Oncogene* 1994;9:1655–9.

49.   Milde-Langosch K, Albrecht K, Joram S, Schlechte H, Giessing M, Loning T. Presence and persistence of HPV infection and p53 mutation in cancer of the cervix uteri and vulva. *Int J Cancer* 1995;63:639–45.

50.   Rolfe KJ, Crow JC, Reid WMN, MacLean AB, Perrett CW. Is vulval lichen sclerosus a pre-malignant lesion? Proceedings of the British Gynaecological Cancer Society, 2001 p. 21.

51.   Lin MC, Mutter GL, Trivijisilp P, Boynton KA, Sun D, Crum CP. Patterns of allelic loss (LOH) in vulvar squamous carcinomas and adjacent non-invasive epithelia. *Am J Pathol* 1998;152:1313–18.

52.   Flowers LC, Wistuba II, Scurry J, Muller CY, Ashfaq R, Miller DS, *et al.* Genetic changes during the multistage pathogenesis of human papillomavirus positive and negative vulvar carcinomas. *J Soc Gynecol Invest* 1999;6:213–21.

53.   Pinto AP, Lin MC, Sheets EE, Muto MG, Sun D, Crum CP. Allelic imbalance in lichen sclerosus, hyperplasia, and intra-epithelial neoplasia of the vulva. *Gynecol Oncol* 2000;77:171–6.

54.   Rolfe KJ, Crow JC, Benjamin E, Reid WMN, MacLean AB, Perrett CW. Cyclin D1 and retinoblastoma protein in vulvar cancer and adjacent lesions. *Int J Gynecol Cancer* 2001;11:381–6.

55.   Perrett CW. The molecular biology of hormone-dependent gynaecological cancers. In: O'Brien PMS, MacLean AB, editors. *Hormones and Cancer*. London: RCOG Press; 1999. p. 32–41.

56.   MacLean AB, Nicol LA, Hodgins MB. Immunohistochemical localization of estrogen receptors in the vulva and vagina. *J Reprod Med* 1990;35:1015–16.

57.   Mosny DS, Brito F, Bender HG. Immunohistochemical investigations of estrogen receptors in normal and neoplastic squamous epithelium of the vulva. *J Reprod Med* 1990;35:1005–7.

58.   Hodgins MB, Spike RC, Mackie RM, MacLean AB. An immunohistochemical study of androgen, oestrogen and progesterone receptors in the vulva and vagina. *Br J Obstet Gynaecol* 1998;105:216–22.

59.   Dobbs SP, Hewett PW, Johansen IR, Carmichael J, Murray JC. Angiogenesis is associated with VEGF expression in cervical intra-epithelial neoplasia. *Br J Cancer* 1997;76:1410–15.

60.   Obermair A, Kohlberger P, Bancher-Todesca D, Tempfer C, Sliutz G, Leodolter S, *et al.* Influence of microvessel density and vascular permeability factor/vascular endothelial growth factor expression on prognosis in vulvar cancer. *Gynecol Oncol* 1996;63:204–9.

61.   Hefler L, Tempfer C, Obermair A, Frischmuth K, Sliutz G, Reinthaller A, *et al.* Serum concentrations of vascular endothelial growth factor in vulvar cancer. *Clin Cancer Res* 1999;5:2806–9.

62.   MacLean AB, Reid WMN, Rolfe KJ, Gammell SJ, Pugh HEJ, Gatter K C, *et al.* Role of angiogenesis in benign, premalignant and malignant vulvar lesions. *J Reprod Med* 2000;45:609–12.

63.   Wong Te Fong LF, Rolfe KJ, Crow JC, Reid WMN, MacLean AB, Perrett CW. Vascular endothelial growth factor (VEGF) and platelet-derived endothelial cell growth factor/thymidine phosphorylase (PD-ECGF/TP) as potential markers in the malignant progression of vulval intra-epithelial neoplasia (VIN) and lichen sclerosus to vulval cancer. *J Obstet Gynaecol* 2000;20:559.

Chapter 26

Treatment of vulval intraepithelial neoplasia

Ronald W Jones

Two doyens of vulval disease, Woodruff and Friedrich, both refer to carcinoma *in situ* of the vulva as a challenge.[1,2] These observations remain pertinent today. No optimal method of managing all cases of vulval intraepithelial neoplasia (VIN) exists. Many factors are responsible, including the heterogeneous nature of the condition and the large field effect created by the human papillomavirus (HPV). Management strategies need to take into account the symptoms, potential for cancer, unnecessary mutilation and psychosexual dysfunction. The management of the two broad groups of squamous VIN – the more common HPV-related (warty/basaloid) VIN and HPV-negative differentiated VIN – need to be considered separately because of their differing clinical features, histopathology and natural history. This chapter principally addresses the management of the more common HPV-related warty/basaloid VIN.

The importance of VIN and the rationale for its treatment relate to its associated symptoms and the potential for progression to invasive carcinoma.[3] Differences in opinion with respect to the nature of VIN and the desire to avoid unnecessary or potentially mutilating surgery have influenced attitudes towards management.[4,5] For example, some would argue that asymptomatic VIN does not require treatment.[6] However, in the absence of controlled studies assessing the outcome of treatment versus observation of asymptomatic VIN and in the knowledge of the relatively short transit time to invasion and the increasing frequency of VIN-related vulval cancer in younger women, such a policy has obvious ethical implications (with the exception of those cases where specific clinical features point to spontaneous regression, see Chapter 7).

The heterogeneous nature of the disorder requires individualised management. Factors that need to be taken into account when planning treatment include the exclusion of early invasive carcinoma, the patient's age, sexual history, the site and extent of the lesion and the potential for psychosexual dysfunction.[7] Treatment should be as conservative as possible, with the avoidance of potential vulval mutilation. Management should ideally be carried out by clinicians experienced in the treatment of lower genital tract neoplasia.

A magnifying instrument such as a colposcope is a necessary adjunct to the examination and treatment procedure. The application of 5% acetic acid for five minutes prior to the examination may enhance the appearance of non-keratinised (e.g. red) lesions. However, caution is required with this technique, which may create local discomfort and enhance clinically unimportant (HPV) change.[8] Many experienced vulvologists have ceased using acetic acid routinely. The toluidine blue test is no longer recommended because of its lack of specificity. Photography and/or accurate documentation of VIN lesions is of assistance, particularly when there is extensive or recurrent disease.

Pretreatment biopsies should be performed of the most significant lesions under local anaesthetic. Large lesions may require multiple "mapping" biopsies. Excision is mandatory if there is any suspicion of invasion. Ideally, a gynaecological pathologist should examine the material. Occult invasive carcinoma has been reported in 18–22% of excised specimens in women in whom a pretreatment biopsy has reported VIN alone.[9–11]

With the exception of those women with the specific clinical features where spontaneous regression might be anticipated, treatment should be considered for all women with a histological diagnosis of VIN3. VIN1 is a histological finding, usually representing HPV effect or reactive change and does not require treatment. VIN2 is an uncommon histological diagnosis and decisions on treatment need to be individualised.

Treatment options

Observation

Spontaneous regression occurs in a well-defined clinical setting.[12] Thirty-two of 370 (9%) of cases of VIN2 and VIN3 on the National Women's Hospital (New Zealand) dataset underwent spontaneous regression. The majority of cases occurred in non-European women under 30 years and regression typically occurred in the first year. The lesions were characteristically small, multifocal, pigmented papules and sited in the perineum, posterior labia minora and interlabial sulci. No recurrences have been recorded in this group. Young women with these characteristics should be managed expectantly. While the literature predominantly portrays this condition (sometimes termed Bowenoid papulosis) as a benign condition, caution is necessary because there are reports of such cases progressing to invasion, including in very young women.[13]

Excisional techniques

Local excision

This is the most universally applicable method of treatment and should be the only option where the possibility of invasion exists. Most high-grade VIN lesions have a sharp transition (both clinically and histologically) with adjacent normal skin and there is no advantage in performing "wide" excisional techniques. Generally, a 5-mm margin should suffice. The use of a magnifying instrument, e.g. a colposcope, facilitates examination of the lesion and its margins. Excision is the method of choice for small unifocal lesions. The excision should be superficial, allowing preservation of the subcutaneous tissue.

Skinning vulvectomy

This technique, involving the use of split skin grafts, was introduced in the 1960s and offered the opportunity of excising wide areas of multifocal VIN. A significant convalescence is required and recurrence rates (which do not appear to relate to surgical margins) remain high.[14]

Simple vulvectomy

This unnecessary and mutilating procedure was commonly employed until 30 years ago. Rarely, it may be an option in an elderly woman with an extensive lesion(s).

Other surgical therapies

These include cryotherapy, diathermy, loop excision and ultrasonic aspiration.[15–17]

Carbon dioxide laser

The role of laser vaporisation techniques continues to stimulate debate. If the studies referred to above demonstrating occult invasion in approximately 20% of cases of VIN are indeed representative, there can be no case for ablative therapy.[9–11] However, in the absence of controlled studies and in the knowledge of the heterogeneity of VIN, an empirical approach to the use of ablative laser techniques will continue. Reid has described the principles and technique in detail and has stressed that "it is a safe and efficient procedure in the hands of expert physicians, but should not be attempted by those who are less experienced".[18,19] Exclusion of invasion must be the priority of the laser ablative surgeon. This involves thorough preoperative vulvoscopy and mapping biopsies by an experienced clinician. Laser vaporisation is best suited to young women with extensive multifocal disease and where preservation of vulval appearance is a priority. A detailed knowledge of the anatomy of the vulval skin and its appendages is imperative. The technique is best employed in non-hairy skin where VIN usually does not extend deeper than 1 mm. VIN in hairy skin is best excised because the involved skin appendages can extend 3 mm into the dermis. Sideri *et al.*[20] noted that, while laser vaporisation produced good cosmetic results, laser excision revealed unrecognised early invasion in 12% of cases. Significant rates of recurrence are reported following laser vaporisation.[21] To some extent this should be expected and may relate more to the nature of the cases treated by laser (often extensive multifocal disease), the presence of occult VIN in residual skin appendages and the extensive HPV reservoir. There is a place for combined surgical excision and laser vaporisation.[22]

Medical therapies

A variety of medical therapies has been employed to treat VIN. The majority are novel and have not become standard therapy. These include topical dinitrochlorobenzene, topical and intradermal bleomycin, interferon and peptide vaccine.[23–26] There are conflicting reports on the efficacy of photodynamic therapies.[27,28] The major concern with any form of medical treatment is of unrecognised invasive cancer. Spirtos noted that 9% of patients initially entered into the interferon study were found to have invasive cancer.[25] Five of twelve women treated with bleomycin progressed to invasive disease.[24] Attempts to treat VIN with topical 5-fluorouracil have largely been abandoned. Sillman reviewed the use of 5-fluorouracil in VIN and recorded remissions in 34% and failures in 59%.[29]

Imiquimod

This immune response modifying agent, which is effective against genital warts, has theoretical advantages and has been shown to be effective in some VIN lesions. To date, small series with limited follow up have reported worthwhile rates of regression of VIN following imiquimod application.[30,31] In the series reported by Jayne and Kaufman, however, 2/13 cases of invasion occurred in fields of regressing VIN.[32] The place of imiquimod in the treatment of VIN can only be assessed when the results of properly controlled studies with long-term follow-up are published.

Recurrences

VIN is a disease of viral origin affecting a wide field and it is unrealistic to expect that the standard methods of treatment today – excision and laser – will provide a permanent cure in the majority of patients. Most studies report recurrences in the order of 30%. Life-table analysis by Herod et al.[21] demonstrated the risk of recurrence in surgically treated patients to be in the order of 55%, with a low risk after four years of follow up. Buscema et al.[33] found no differences in recurrence rates between wide local excision (30%) and simple vulvectomy (32%). Rettenmaier et al. report recurrence rates of 27% after skinning vulvectomy.[14]

Surgical principles would suggest that the status of surgical margins should provide some indication of potential future recurrences. Surprisingly, the evidence is conflicting. While Rettenmaier et al.[14] found no relationship between surgical margins and recurrences, Modesitt et al.[10] established that the recurrence rate was three times higher when surgical margins were positive. Recurrences do not appear to relate to smoking behaviour.[34] A large Norwegian study failed to demonstrate a relationship between positive surgical margins of VIN and future invasive vulval cancer.[35] Eight of sixteen women who developed invasive vulval cancer had negative resection margins at the time of primary surgery for VIN. The risk of recurrent VIN is significantly higher in women with multifocal VIN compared with unifocal VIN.[34] While many recurrences reflect persistent disease, new disease in a 'field of risk' is to be expected.

The future

Management strategies need to be directed at the primary aetiological agent, HPV. This might be achieved with preventive vaccination. Alternatively, therapy needs to be directed at preventing the tissue effects of the virus.[26]

Differentiated (simplex) VIN

In its pure form it is a relatively uncommon condition. It is seen most frequently in older women in association with HPV negative keratinising carcinomas or in association with lichen sclerosus and/or squamous hyperplasia. It may have a relatively brief intraepithelial phase before progressing to invasion. There are no diagnostic clinical features. However, persistent hyperplasia should alert the clinician to the possibility of differentiated VIN. A short trial of a potent topical steroid might initially be considered in this situation. Unless such lesions resolve quickly, they should be excised.[36]

References

1.   Woodruff JD, Julian C, Puray T, Mermut S, Katayama P. The contemporary challenge of carcinoma in situ of the vulva. Am J Obstet Gynecol 1973;115:677–86.
2.   Friedrich EG, Wilkinson EJ, Fu YS. Carcinoma in situ of the vulva: a continuing challenge. Am J Obstet Gynecol 1980;136:830–42.
3.   Jones RW, Rowan DM. Vulvar intra-epithelial neoplasia III: a clinical study of the outcome in 113 cases with relation to the later development of invasive vulvar carcinoma. Obstet Gynecol 1994;84:741–5.
4.   Van Beurden M, Van Der Vange N, Ten Kate FJW, De Craen AJM, Schilthuis MS, Lammes FB. Restricted surgical management of vulvar intra-epithelial neoplasia 3: focus on exclusion of invasion and relief of symptoms. Int J Gynecol Cancer 1998;8:73–7.

5.   Jones RW. Management of VIN 3. *Int J Gynecol Cancer* 1998;8:509–10.

6.   Kagle MJ, Ansink A. Vulval intra-epithelial neoplasia: presentation and management. In: *Cancer and Precancer of the Vulva*. Luesley DM, editor. London: Arnold; 2000. p. 86–96.

7.   Thuesen B, Andreasson B, Bock JE. Sexual function and somatopsychic reactions after local excision of vulvar intra-epithelial neoplasia. *Acta Obstet Gynecol Scand* 1992;71:126–8.

8.   Stefanon B, De Palo G. Is vulvoscopy a reliable diagnostic technique for high grade vulvar intra-epithelial neoplasia? *Eur J Gynaecol Oncol* 1997;18:211.

9.   Chafe W, Richards A, Morgan L, Wilkinson E. Unrecognized invasive carcinoma in vulvar intra-epithelial neoplasia. *Gynecol Oncol* 1988;31:154–62.

10.   Modesitt SC, Waters AB, Walton L, Fowler WC, Van Le L. Vulvar intra-epithelial neoplasia III: occult cancer and the impact of margin status on recurrence. *Obstet Gynecol* 1998;92:962–6.

11.   Husseinzadeh N, Recinto C. Frequency of invasive cancer in surgically excised vulvar lesions with intra-epithelial neoplasia (VIN 3). *Gynecol Oncol* 1999;73:119–20.

12.   Jones RW, Rowan DM. Spontaneous regression of vulvar intra-epithelial neoplasia 2–3. *Obstet Gynecol* 2000;96:470–2.

13.   Planner RS, Andersen HE, Hobbs JB, Williams RA, Fogarty LF, Hudson PJ. Multifocal invasive carcinoma of the vulva in a 25 year old women with Bowenoid papulosis. *Aust N Z J Obstet Gynaecol* 1987;27:291–5.

14.   Rettenmaier MA, Berman ML, DiSaia PJ. Skinning vulvectomy for the treatment of multifocal vulvar intra-epithelial neoplasia. *Obstet Gynecol* 1987;69:247–50.

15.   Forney JP, Morrow CP, Dowsend DE, DiSaia PJ. Management of carcinoma *in situ* of the vulva. *Am J Obstet Gynecol* 1977;127:801–6.

16.   Bloss JD. The use of electrosurgical techniques in the management of premalignant disease of the vulva, vagina and cervix: an excisional rather than ablative approach. *Am J Obstet Gynecol* 1993;169:1081–5.

17.   Rader JS, Leake JF, Dillon MB, Rosenshein NB. Ultrasonic surgical aspiration in the treatment of vulvar disease. *Obstet Gynecol* 1991;77:573–6.

18.   Reid R, Elfont EA, Zirkin RM, Fuller TA. Superficial laser vulvectomy. II. The anatomic and biophysical principles permitting accurate control over the depth of dermal destruction with the carbon dioxide laser. *Am J Obstet Gynecol* 1985;152:261–71.

19.   Reid R. Superficial laser vulvectomy. III. A technique for appendage-conserving ablation of refractory condylomas and vulvar intra-epithelial neoplasia. *Am J Obstet Gynecol* 1985;152:504–9.

20.   Sideri M, Spinaci L, Spolti N, Schettino F. Evaluation of CO_2 laser excision or vaporization for the treatment of vulvar intra-epithelial neoplasia. *Gynecol Oncol* 1999;75:277–81.

21.   Herod JJO, Shafi MI, Rollason TP, Jordan JA, Luesley DM. Vulvar intra-epithelial neoplasia: a long term follow up of treated and untreated women. *Br J Obstet Gynaecol* 1996;103:446–52.

22.   Bornstein J, Kaufman RH. Combination of surgical excision and carbon dioxide laser vaporization for multifocal vulvar intra-epithelial neoplasia. *Obstet Gynecol* 1988;158:459–64.

23.   Foster DC, Woodruff JD. The use of dinitrochlorobenzene in the treatment of vulvar carcinoma *in situ*. *Gynecol Oncol* 1981;11:330–9.

24.   Roberts JA, Watring WG, Lagasse LD. Treatment of vulvar intra-epithelial neoplasia (VIN) with local bleomycin. *Cancer Clin Trials* 1980;3:351–4.

25.   Spirtos NM, Smith LH, Teng NNH. Prospective randomized trial of topical α-interferon (α-interferon gels) for the treatment of vulvar intra-epithelial neoplasia III. *Gynecol Oncol* 1990;37:34–8.

26.   Muderspach L, Wilczynski S, Roman L, Bade L, Felix J, Small LA *et al*. A phase I trial of a human papillomavirus (HPV) peptide vaccine for women with high-grade cervical and vulvar intra-epithelial neoplasia who are HPV 16 positive. *Clin Cancer Res* 2000;6:3406.

27.   Hillemanns P, Untch M, Dannecker C, Baumgartner R, Stepp H, Diebold J. *et al*. Photodynamic therapy of vulvar intra-epithelial neoplasia using 5-aminolevulinic acid. *Int J Cancer* 2000;**85**:649–53.

28.   Fehr MK, Hornung R, Schwarz VA, Simeon R, Haller U, Wyss P. Photodynamic therapy of vulvar intra-epithelial neoplasia III using topically applied 5-aminolevulinic acid. *Gynecol Oncol* 2001;80:62–6.

29.   Sillman FH, Sedlis A, Boyce JG. A review of lower genital tract neoplasia and the use of topical 5-fluorouracil. *Obstet Gynecol Surv* 1985;50:190–220.

30.   Davis G, Wentworth J, Richard J. Self-administered topical imiquimod treatment of vulvar intra-epithelial neoplasia. A report of four cases. *J Reprod Med* 2000;45:619–23.

31.   Todd RW, Etherington IJ, Luesley DM. The effects of 5% imiquimod cream on high-grade vulval intra-epithelial neoplasia. *Gynecol Oncol* 2002;85:67–70.

32.   Jayne CJ, Kaufman RH. Treatment of vulvar intra-epithelial neoplasia 2/3 with imiquimod. *J Reprod Med* 2002;47:395–8.

33.   Buscema J, Woodruff JD, Parmley TH. Carcinoma *in situ* of the vulva. *Obstet Gynecol* 1980;55:225–30.

34.   Küppers V, Stiller M, Somville T, Bender HG. Risk factors for recurrent VIN. Role of multifocality and grade of disease. *J Reprod Med* 1997;42:140–4.

35.   Iversen T, Tretli S. Intra-epithelial and invasive squamous cell neoplasia of the vulva; Trends in incidence, recurrence, and survival rate in Norway. *Obstet Gynecol* 1998;91:969–72.

36.   Hart WR. Vulvar intra-epithelial neoplasia: Historical aspects and current status. *Int J Gynecol Pathol* 2001;20:16–30.

Chapter 27

Management of lower genital tract neoplasia II

Discussion

Discussion following Mr Soutter's paper

Shepherd: Mr Soutter, can you comment on the role of dilatation and curettage when carrying out a conservative or diagnostic conisation in this situation? Might that have helped to prevent your 'horror story' of the recurrence of what I assume was an endocervical carcinoma, not uterine corpus, in the patient you mentioned?

Soutter: There are many horror stories of different sorts, from all kinds of different centres. If we are looking at someone who already has a histological diagnosis of an adenocarcinoma, or a small invasive adenocarcinoma on the cervix, then a curettage of the uterus is as useful as endocervical curettage is in any context – and, in my book, that is not very useful at all.

Shepherd: How will you guarantee that you have sampled right up to the isthmus, at the very top of the endocervical canal, unless you are actually certain that you are removing the whole of the endocervical canal? Unless you are doing a hysterectomy, there is no other way you can do that.

Soutter: These patients present with abnormal glandular cells in their smear, so you do a large cone biopsy. If the lesion is completely excised, with good margins, what more can you do? If you perform an endocervical curettage, or a curettage of the endometrial cavity, you do not obtain very good material.

Shepherd: You commented that an extraordinarily large number, about 40–50%, have involved margins.

Soutter: Yes, but in those circumstances you will not go on and say that conservative therapy is satisfactory. Do you see what I mean? I personally would not use a negative curettage as a means of saying that there was nothing in the canal or the uterus, in a patient whose endocervical margins were involved. It depends how you intend to use that information.

Monaghan: I would agree that this is a bizarre and fickle disease. Two of my own longest term recurrences at 13 and 15 years were in women who actually had adenocarcinoma *in situ* diagnosed initially.

   Could I come back to the thorny question of the skip lesions and multifocal disease, because this bedevils us endlessly. There was a slight inconsistency in what you were saying in that you reported what you thought was a high multifocal rate and yet, if you have a margin that is clear, you are comfortable with conservative care. There is a discrepancy there. My own practice is to be very conservative in these things.

When Isabella Maini studied our series, she found that so long as there was a clear margin, the risk of invasive disease was nil thereafter – and these were long-term reviews.[1] We had some new disease in terms of abnormal smears, but we had the same problem as you report in that, when we came to reassess them, we did not find lesions. As you know, the abnormal glandular cell is a problem, pathologically. How do you square this circle?

Soutter: First, it seems more likely that skip lesions, or lesions high up the canal, are more common in older women – the group for whom one would advocate cone biopsy least readily.

The second point is that one man's clear margins are another man's uncertain and involved margins. Once again, this is one of the most difficult aspects of this whole business. In your study, clear margins meant clear margins, which meant no disease. You could, however, pick up three of four other studies where clear margins were still associated with recurrent adenocarcinoma *in situ*, or with adenocarcinoma *in situ* found in hysterectomies performed shortly thereafter. Whether this is real disease or not, or whether it is an artefact – we all know all the problems.

It boils down to the fact that we are trying to give advice for workers out in the field. Pathologists out in the field perhaps do not have the sort of resources to invest in very detailed histological examination of these cone biopsies. They therefore say that the margins are clear when more careful scrutiny would show that they were not. That is the sort of problem we face.

Prendiville: I know you used the microcolpohysteroscope many years ago. Is it of any value in this situation?

Soutter: No, none at all.

Deery: The Östör review, if I am right, was a peer review of collected cases.[2] He made the comment that the multicentricity of the disease, looking at microinvasive disease, did not appear to require long cylindrical cones. This was from his review mainly of hysterectomy specimens, but there was also a proportion of about 20 cones.

Soutter: I have to say that I read that as a throwaway remark, for which I did not see the justification. I do not really know what he meant by that.

Tidy: al-Nafussi, in his study, reported that.[3] If you have 3 mm of disease-free margin, the chance of finding a lesion higher up in the canal is almost zero?

Soutter: One of the huge problems with this is that you have someone who says that, and you can pick up another two papers that will contradict it. It boils down first of all how many patients they are actually talking about – many of the studies are small. Secondly, how carefully have the cone biopsies been examined? The other point about the al-Nafussi study is the recurrence rate: they talk only about glandular recurrences but ignore the squamous recurrences, which are a very important component of this.[3] They have said that they have no recurrences, or one or two, but in fact they had quite a number of squamous recurrences.

Shafi: One of the take-home messages from the BSCCP-sponsored study that was reported by John Cullimore was that all of these patients should have central pathological review.[4] In that group of patients, which was quite a large number, about one in ten had early invasive disease; in those patients where the originating pathology department thought it was just pre-invasive disease. In a further one in ten patients there was no actual disease present, again where preinvasive disease was first suspected. One of the key take-home messages therefore had to be that there should be some kind of central pathology review in the gynaecological pathology department.

Soutter: Yes, that is a good principle for uncommon conditions. The difficulty that reviewing pathologists always have is that all they get is the slides that have been cut from the blocks that were taken. I would imagine that most pathologists however, if they wanted to review it, would want to cut the blocks themselves. There is an argument for letting the pathologists have the cone biopsy to cut up themselves, to make their own preparation from their own material, if it was known in advance that this patient might have adenocarcinoma *in situ*. You would then have very different results.

Jones: Are you able to make a clear statement with respect to skip lesions?

Soutter: No.

Singer: Professor Richart, is the American experience in the way of managing these different? Mr Soutter's study was essentially a review of UK centres.

Richart: Speaking personally first, I do not know how to make the diagnosis of microinvasive cancer of the endocervix. I do not know where the basal lamina is and I do not know where to measure from. I do not know what depth constitutes microinvasion. We do not have the same data for endocervical microinvasion that we have for the lesions in the squamous epithelium. In all other respects, we manage patients in the same way as you do. The adenocarcinoma *in situs* are treated with conisation, for the most part, if the patient is young and wants children, or by simple hysterectomy if they have completed child-bearing.

Singer: What about the follow-up of these patients after treatment? Is there a role for human papillomavirus (HPV) DNA testing?

Richart: There is no adequate evidence yet. At the American Society for Colposcopy and Cervicopathology Consensus meeting[5] there was the anticipation that with more data, HPV DNA will be useful in following these patients. We will be able to use HPV DNA testing to determine who, at least, has persistent disease, and we will probably have a much earlier march on who has recurrent disease, using HPV DNA testing.

MacLean: For the patient who presents with an AGUS (atypical glandular cells of uncertain significance) smear, the management could include an excisional procedure and then curettage of both the canal and body of the uterus. Mr Soutter made a response that you would not include curettage but I feel that part of the management of those patients has to have some kind of sampling above your excision. Would you like to comment on that?

Soutter: Thank you for giving me the chance to clarify that. I was starting from the standpoint that we were not looking at someone with an abnormal smear, but at someone with a histological diagnosis. My personal management of women with abnormal glandular cells, whether it is AGUS or malignant glandular cells, is that in young women we do a cone biopsy but we do not curette or look at the endometrial cavity because it is so unlikely that they will have an endometrial cancer. However, we would curette the cavity in older women because, by that stage, the likelihood of them having endometrial cancer as an explanation for their abnormal smear is starting to arise. Personally, I do not think that curettage of the endocervix or the endometrial cavity is a helpful means of determining the distribution of adenocarcinoma of the cervix.

Discussion following Dr Wilkinson's paper

MacLean: Dr Wilkinson, one of the problems among pathologists in the UK is that there is a great deal of inconsistency in the reporting of vulval lesions. They still use terms like 'vulval dystrophy'. It would be useful to advocate using the terminology you presented. I realise that the terminology for vulval intraepithelial neoplasia (VIN) is continuing to evolve and, as you demonstrated, it may just come back to VIN-'blank'. It would be nice to have a statement that we could include in our recommendations, both for that and also the minimum data required for a description of invasive vulval cancer.

Wilkinson: The American Registry of Pathology has spent a great deal of energy on that. This is the third version of the fascicle that was addressed in rather great detail. There are also the standard textbooks of pathology, to which I have contributed a few chapters, as in Blaustein's current fifth edition of *The Pathology of the Female Genital Tract*, which discusses that in detail.[6] I would think that most practising pathologists would be familiar with those reference texts and it might be worth pointing those things out to them.

Shafi: Dr Wilkinson, with regard to differentiated and undifferentiated VIN, what does that mean clinically to the gynaecologist in long-term outcome?

Wilkinson: The term 'undifferentiated VIN' is something that the International Society for the Study of Vulvovaginal Disease has proposed, but it is not a usable term currently. The term 'differentiated VIN' is used among pathologists. Those lesions have some distinctive morphological features but they also tend to express p53 and they are treacherous lesions. They are often associated with carcinoma and commonly associated with lichen sclerosus. A differentiated VIN has a very important connotation for clinical care and the management of the patient.

   With the other types of vulval intraepithelial neoplasia, the morphologic types, I do not know whether there is much differentiation as far as their behaviour is concerned. They are aneuploid lesions, HPV containing, mostly HPV-16, and they predominate in younger women.

Deery: As Dr Shafi said, the minimum dataset exists. It is very like the dataset that we saw and in fact it is minimal.

Jones: It was very useful when Dr Wilkinson stated what wide excision meant, i.e., a 1-cm margin. From a clinical perspective, where you see the edge of a VIN lesion, does that correlate with the microscopic lesion underneath?

Wilkinson: In my experience, it does. It is a discrete margin, usually. Most of the time, you can see those, but sometimes in some patients, especially when they involve the clitoral area and so on, it is not clear where the edge might be when you are doing the excision. Having a visible margin makes sense and this is something that Neville Hacker proposed many years ago.[7] This is good practice.

Tidy: We undertook a small study, looking at excision margins, assessing where the margin was and then going outside, and then taking multiple biopsies.[8] This does not really predict. There is normal-looking skin with VIN histologically present, and that might explain why the recurrence rate and the persistence rate is so high, because, macroscopically, you just cannot be sure where the margin is. The larger the margin you have, the better it is, but it is not quite so straightforward.

Singer: We looked many years ago at colposcopy in aiding the assessment of the morphological limits but it was not of much help. The only aid was the irregularity of the surface, the presence of hyperkeratosis; most of the time, however, the finding of acetowhite epithelium was also not of much help.

Monaghan: We have become concerned about this problem of margins in both invasive cancer and VIN, but they are actually different. In invasive cancer, there is no doubt that a margin of 2 cm really cuts down the local risk of tumour recurrence, but you are dealing there with unifocal disease, mostly in older patients.

The problem with VIN is that you are mostly managing young women with multifocal disease. It is not only multifocal as you look at it, but it is multifocal in a temporal fashion as well. This means that, as you roll forward in time, you are not really having recurrences of your original disease, but new disease all the time. This also accounts for why, in Dr Jones's studies, you are looking at recurrent VIN and invasive cancers occurring far ahead in time. You have this broad field defect, which just goes rolling on and on. Although, aesthetically, it is good to have a clear margin, I do not think you should beat yourself too hard about recurrences.

Wilkinson: That is an excellent point. In fact, I have tried to use the words 'recurrence' and 're-occurrence', although perhaps that does not make it as clear as necessary. However, there is no question in the vulva that new tumours can arise outside the primary site. I do not know whether it is really reasonable to call those 'recurrent' because they are new tumours in the same field, although they are not the same tumour. Those VIN lesions, which are often precursors, are clonally different and you could probably do studies to discriminate tumours when they occur.

Monaghan: When I was appointed to the Northern Gynaecological Oncology Centre, Gateshead, I inherited many years of experience of handling large numbers of vulval tumours and I then added 28 more years of experience to that. We have patients that Stanley Way looked after, who are still coming back now with new tumours. They just keep coming, and coming and coming. You have patients that you just keep chipping away at, they are a 'no discharge' group so far as I am concerned, because you do not discharge them.

Richart: Because this is such a difficult disease to treat, with a high re-occurrence rate, this is a perfect group on which to try a therapeutic vaccine. Because the recurrence rates are high and occur fairly quickly, results should be available fairly quickly.

Stanley: Could I just reinforce that? This is something that I have been saying for several years now. If you are going to look at therapeutic vaccines, then direct it against the oncogenic HPVs. Cervical intraepithelial neoplasia (CIN) is not the disease in which to do it. The diseases to do it in are anal (AIN) and vulval intraepithelial neoplasia (VIN). First of all, there are no serious ethical problems, because there is no satisfactory management for the majority of cases and, secondly, you can observe what is going on, which is extremely important. Thirdly, for the reasons I mentioned earlier, one has to be sensible about the endpoints here. There may not be complete resolution of lesions because, as has been very elegantly stated, there is a temporal event here. There are early and late lesions, and some lesions will be invasive. Hopefully, if you can clear the field of infection, you ought then to be able to deal with the neoplasia, the cancer, as oncologists.

Discussions following Dr Perrett's and Mr Jones' papers

Jones: Could I take Dr Perrett slightly to task? He made the observation that the progression rate for VIN and lichen sclerosus were the same. It is really important to stress that, as far as we can see, untreated VIN in older women always progresses untreated. You said that 96% of women with lichen sclerosus do not progress. Those are two ends of the spectrum and it is very important that we convey that message.

Perrett: That is very true. I was thinking specifically of treated VIN, rather than untreated. Nevertheless, that is a very important point.

Singer: Just as an anecdotal aside, at the Whittington Hospital, London, we had the late Dr Marjorie Ridley with us for many years. We follow just about 120 of her patients, most of whom are under treatment. We have about one woman every one to two years developing vulval cancer, literally in front of our eyes.

Jones: On the point of the malignant potential of lichen sclerosus, it is a matter of semantics. Should we talk about lichen sclerosus as being a premalignant condition on the vulva? As a clinician, I also see vulval cancers arising in a background of lichen planus, lichen simplex chronicus – conditions where there is continued, proliferative activity in the vulval skin, as is occurring in lichen sclerosus. The reason why lichen sclerosus is seen so commonly adjacent to vulval cancers is simply because it is a common disorder.

Singer: Professor Richart taught me many years ago that it is not the lichen sclerosus that causes the cancer, but the company that lichen sclerosus keeps. In other words, the vulval skin adjacent to the lichen sclerosus is bad company.

MacLean: I agree with Dr Jones that a precancer or premalignancy probably defies definition. I am sure that the pathologists would say that we do not fulfil their criteria in terms of neoplastic change prior to invasion.

For clinicians looking after lichen sclerosus, somehow we have to give it a label. There is a series of conditions arising in lichen planus and lichen simplex. However, the majority of patients coming through a vulval clinic do not have an increased risk of developing vulval cancer. There is nevertheless a cohort of women with lichen sclerosus plus hyperplasia, plus differentiated VIN, who are part of a spectrum where there is an increased risk. Gynaecologists and dermatologists and genitourinary medicine physicians managing these vulval clinics have to earmark these patients for increased surveillance, because they are at risk. I agree that 'premalignant' or 'precancer' are not the right terms, but I am not sure what alternative there is.

Jones: Would it be possible to say just that they are 'associated with'? Could I make one further comment? Potent topical corticosteroids have revolutionised the management of women with lichen sclerosus, but I still believe that there is a place for surgery for the woman with persistent hyperplasia that does not resolve. It is so often under these lesions that you find differentiated VIN, which is a premalignant condition. It is only by excising this that you know. I believe that surgery still has some role in the management of lichen sclerosus, although this message has not quite got through.

Monaghan: You are absolutely right, but I was a little concerned that you were still producing a great deal of smoke in your system. Why not use your laser as an excisional tool?

Jones: I do, and I do not.

Monaghan: I find it a little anomalous that you have said three or four times that excision is the gold standard and yet you use CO_2 laser vaporisation. In fact, I actually find that excision is faster than vaporisation, because you are not taking out so much tissue.

Jones: The only thing is that, if you are excising, you do not achieve the same result cosmetically with large areas. One of the reasons is that these are young women who want a good cosmetic result and once you start excising very wide areas ...

Monaghan: I believe the 20% underlying cancer problem.

Singer: This leads us on further into the treatment. If a young woman has multifocal disease, how do you treat it? Do you do local excisions? What do you do – especially if it is getting down towards the perineum and the anus? Do you use the CO_2 laser for skinning excision, as Mr Monaghan and many of us do?

Jones: I use both excision and/or vaporisation.

Singer: Do you leave islands of normal skin in between?

Jones: Yes.

Monaghan: I am happier to excise the multiple lesions and just keep on excising. The point you made about warning the patient that it will need multiple treatment is very important. Many people arrive expecting to have a single treatment, but you have to impress on them that they will be seeing a great deal of you, and you of them, over the years.

Could I make a final point about immunocompromise? I have used a broad term because I recognise that there are people here with more skills about immunology than I have. We have a big renal transplant programme locally and we have had five patients who have undergone renal transplant who have had long-term, multifocal disease affecting cervix, vagina, vulva and anus.

There have been two peculiar cases, referred to me by Professor Singer, of women with granulocytopenia. He referred a lady with widespread vulval disease and, on the second page of the referral, he said, by the way, that she had a white count of 0.8, or something like that. Interestingly, we managed both those patients, because they had infection problems, with granulocyte cell stimulating factor. I just wondered whether anyone else had used this as a boost while treating patients, because it certainly gets them through the management and the recovery phase quite well.

Tidy: I agree with you about the older patient, where the solitary lesion is suspicious for cancer. However, our experience with large field effects in young women with VIN and AIN is that they are at incredibly high risk of occult invasive disease. They worry me more. We have become a little more aggressive in excising it all, and we do find small microinvasive cancers, which were perhaps suggested there on vulvoscopy. I am concerned about large field effects and the same basis that the large field effect on CIN is associated with invasive disease too. We are semi-aggressive on that and I would not like to ablate them because of that.

My second point is more educational in nature. There is increasing use of immunosuppressive therapy by physicians for conditions such as systemic lupus erythematosus and myasthenia gravis. The immunologists now describe all these immunodeficiency syndromes. In particular, I have a clinical suspicion that azathioprine is a major problem in HPV-related VIN. We should perhaps make clinicians aware that the expanding use of immunosuppressive agents in general medicine could make VIN a problem in some of their patients.

Singer: While on that subject, in one of the recommendations we must mention smoking again in relation to the vulva. There are a number of papers showing regression of lesions as you cut out the smoking, and we have found that with a few patients.

Shepherd: Those comments about multifocal disease are very true and I am quite surprised that you are not more concerned about this younger group too. We are seeing an increasing number of younger women, under the age of 30 years, who either have extensive multifocal disease or who have quite extensive invasive cancer. That is the feel of what we have been saying, and picking up on what Mr Tidy has said, I agree with you.

There is the question of observing these and assuming that these 30-year olds will all regress but I think the danger is as bad for these women as it is for the untreated older woman who will inevitably progress. The message here, loud and clear, is that VIN is a considerably more aggressive disease than we have hitherto accepted. We have always said that only four to five percent will progress in time, but those four to five percent are those that are treated. It is the untreated and unreferred younger patients who are at considerably higher risk of going on, and they have to be treated aggressively, watched and followed up in the long term.

Jones: I agree entirely with that. However, there is a subset of women with those brown papules just a few millimetres in diameter, the so-called Bowenoid papulosis, which histologically is VIN3, and they would all disappear.

Shepherd: They are a different disease process.

Jones: Yes, exactly.

Stanley: Could I make a plea for some collaborative research here? First of all, no centre has sufficient patients to investigate on its own. We need some basic information. There are some quite interesting signals coming out from the small trials we have had so far. Firstly, we need to know what HPV types are in there. Secondly, preliminary studies on small numbers are striking. There really appears to be an association between a specific HLA-DQ haplotype, and these patients with HPV-16-positive VIN. This needs to be sorted out and it can only be done by collaboration and by people pooling their information and patients. I make that plea, because I think this is a priority.

Singer: Professor MacLean, you were chairman of the British Vulval Society: are they involved in this at all? Are they in charge of multicentre studies and so on?

MacLean: There are various collaborating centres but it is certainly not as defined as perhaps Professor Stanley would like. We will probably have to encourage people to come together because, as you say, these lesions are few and far between. Looking at HLA types, one of the difficulties is that people use different techniques, so that to do this there clearly has to be a centre that will be defined and will do the HLA testing consistently. There has to be the appropriate funding, but there are opportunities in this country for people to work together, to apply for funding and to take this forward. If this study group is one of the stimuli to do that, then well done.

Stanley: That is absolutely right. I am suggesting that there is a collaborative group that will identify centres to do the laboratory research and do it to controlled standards and quality. HLA haplotyping, in particular, is not a trivial exercise and the selection of populations for control has to be done very carefully. There are people who are very good at that in Britain, so I am suggesting that there should be an organisation so that the very best data can be obtained from the material you have.

References

1.   Maini M, Lavie O, Comerci G, Cross A, Bolger B, Lopes A, *et al.* The management and follow up of patients with high grade cervical glandular intraepithelial neoplasia *Int J Gynecol Cancer* 1998;8:287–91.

2.   Östör AG, Duncan A, Quinn M, Rome R. Adenocarcinoma *in situ* of the uterine cervix: an experience with 100 cases. *Gynecol Oncol* 2000;79:207–10.

3.   Kurian K, al-Nafussi A. Relation of cervical glandular intraepithelial neoplasia to microinvasive and invasive adenocarcinoma of the uterine cervix: a study of 121 cases. *J Clin Pathol* 1999;52:112–17.

4.   Cullimore JE, Luesley DM, Rollason TP, Byrne P, Buckley CH, Anderson M *et al*. A prospective study of conisation of the cervix in the management of adenocarcinoma-in-situ and glandular atypia of the cervix. *Br J Obstet Gynaecol* 1992;99:314–18.

5.   American Society for Colposcopy and Cervicopathology Consensus meeting [www.asccp.org/consensus/about.shtml].

6.   Wilkinson EJ, Xie DL. Benign diseases of the vulva; Premalignant and malignant tumors of the vulva. In: Kurman RJ, editor. *Blaustein's Pathology of the Female Genital Tract*. 5th ed. NY: Springer Verlag; 2002. p. 37–98, 99–149.

7.   Hacker NF, van der Velden J. Conservative management of early vulvar cancer. *Cancer* 1993;71(4 Suppl):1673–7.

8.   Tidy JA, Smith JH. Can we reliably excise VIN and AIN? Paper presented at 10th World Congress of Cervical Pathology and Colposcopy, Buenos Aires, November 1999.

SECTION 7

MANAGEMENT OF LOWER GENITAL TRACT NEOPLASIA III

Chapter 27

Surgical management of cervical cancer

John H Shepherd

Cancer of the cervix has been recognised as a disease entity since the days of Hippocrates. Traditional treatment involved surgical excision, as well as cauterisation. In more modern times, Wertheim's radical abdominal hysterectomy has been the standard treatment for an invasive cervical cancer and more advanced disease has been treated by radiotherapy. In the past, combination radical surgery and radiotherapy was standard, but the morbidity of this combined approach has led to a more selective individualisation of treatment. As a result, only a small number of patients require both modalities and these will have an accepted increased morbidity from the consequences of a combined radical approach. More recently, combination chemotherapy has proved to be more successful than radiotherapy alone.

In the 1890s, William Halstead described the surgical principles for the management of solid cancer tumours. Although originally for breast cancer, these were soon applied to the cervix and Wertheim adhered to these principles when describing his radical hysterectomy. These consisted of a wide surgical excision of the primary tumour, i.e. the cervix and surrounding tissue, which included the uterus, parametrium, the upper vagina and paracolpos. In his original procedure, Wertheim only removed suspect, enlarged bulky lymph nodes. Subsequently, Meigs added his bilateral pelvic lymphadenectomy to the Wertheim procedure, so that the Wertheim–Meigs procedure become the gold standard for surgical management of early cervical cancer. This procedure was promoted in both Europe and the USA. Prominent and eminent pelvic surgeons such as Victor Bonney and John Howkins established their reputations in the UK in the middle of the last century with this procedure for the surgical treatment of stage 1b and early stage 2a and 2b carcinoma of the cervix.

With the recognition that cervical cancer could be more superficially invasive, whether recognised or occult, it was realised that cone biopsy for certain cases of superficially invasive disease was adequate treatment. Once recognised as a separate entity, FIGO stage 1a could therefore perfectly adequately be managed in a more conservative way. Accepting that the incidence of lymph node metastases for a microinvasive or superficially invasive cancer, stage 1a, is less than 5% meant that a pelvic node dissection was unnecessary. Cone biopsy was initially carried out as a diagnostic procedure but, with the advent of colposcopy and, more frequently, diagnosed intraepithelial carcinoma (carcinoma *in situ* or cervical intraepithelial neoplasia), more conservative methods of local ablation or excision became accepted. It is, therefore, now adequate for such superficially invasive tumours to be locally excised by a conisation procedure. Provided that clear margins are obtained and that there are no other adverse prognostic factors such as lymphovascular space involvement, conservative follow-up is sufficient.

With poor prognostic superficially invasive tumours, such as those to a depth of more than 3 mm, i.e. stage 1a2, the question has to be raised as to whether hysterectomy and, indeed, pelvic node dissection are necessary. The instance of nodal metastases will still be less than 5% and it may therefore be argued that the risks of the procedure outweigh the potential benefits. It therefore becomes important to review carefully all superficially invasive tumours and assess prognostic factors. With an increasing instance or risk of lymph node metastases, pelvic node dissection will be necessary and on occasions cone biopsy or hysterectomy with pelvic node dissection may be advocated. This in itself will adhere to Halstead's principles of surgical oncology. Drawing up hard-and-fast rules and guidelines for this stage of disease is not straightforward, as other factors need to be taken into account, including the age of the patient and her fertility wishes. Individualisation of patient care, with stage 1a2, is therefore crucially important with a truly multidisciplinary team approach to the decision regarding her management.

A more radical approach, however, is required when dealing with a truly invasive carcinoma, i.e. stage 1b and above. It is generally accepted that a tumour with a depth greater than 5 mm and a diameter of more than 7 mm will require a traditional radical surgical approach or, alternatively, whole pelvic radiotherapy. It is also accepted that stage 1b1 tumours, i.e. less than 4 cm in diameter, should initially be treated by radical surgery. If there is obvious pelvic node involvement, it could be argued that primary radiotherapy should be undertaken but, even so, many authorities may prefer the surgical approach in order to remove the primary tumour and resect bulky lymph nodes if found unexpectedly at surgery. The risk of lymph node metastases for stage 1b tumours will be in the region of 16–18%. Provided that preoperative assessment with either computed tomography scans or magnetic resonance imaging (MRI) do not show enlarged nodes, then most of these patients will undergo surgery. In the future there will be more accurate assessment of lymph node status, either by sentinel node assessment using radioactive isotopes or fluorescein dyes to predict nodal metastases. Iron oxide particles, such as sinerem, followed by MRI scans are proving to be accurate in their prediction of nodal disease.[1] If there is undisputed positive nodal spread, many authorities would advocate avoiding surgery and treating with primary radiotherapy. This would apply to the larger tumours, i.e. stage 1b2, measuring more than 4 cm in diameter, although if there is no obvious lymph node spread, the case for radical hysterectomy with adequate wide resection margins is still sound. Treatment with combination chemoradiotherapy has significantly improved the prognosis and survival of patients over and above treatment by radiotherapy alone, but as yet this has not been compared to an adequate study with radical surgery. The long-term morbidity of radiotherapy for both young and old is significant and this needs to be weighed up against the disadvantages of a radical surgical procedure and potential morbidity with regard to hospital stay and possible surgical complications. Overall, however, the adverse effects and consequences of radical combined treatment still outweigh those of single modality treatment alone.

Extensive surgical resection

The extent of parametrial and paracervical resection will depend upon the size of the tumour. Many authorities have questioned the need for excision of the whole parametrium.[2] There does appear to be little point in excessive resection of normal tissue when there is a low instance of lymphovascular or lymph node spread. Now it is accepted that metastases to lymph nodes occur by embolisation rather than permeation, obtaining a clear margin may mean that only 1–2 cm of clearance of a tumour is necessary rather than a more extensive excision with more extensive margins. This is a principle that has been applied to other solid tumours, including carcinoma of the breast and colon. More radical excision has not resulted in improvement with survival or outcome. This subject has been debated with the questioning of how important removal of parametrium at surgery is, with such cases of carcinoma of the cervix.[3] By choosing patients with smaller tumours, i.e. those less than 2 cm (in Covens's study[3] less than 3 cm) it is possible to identify a lower-risk group who could be treated surgically by a lesser resection, i.e. modified radical hysterectomy, in order to reduce morbidity and then identify higher-risk prognostic variables to indicate which patients should be treated by additional postoperative radiation therapy. While accepting that the presence of lymph node metastases is a poor prognostic finding, other studies have shown that a larger tumour diameter, deep stromal invasion and lymphatic space involvement are also unfavourable characteristics. Careful selection will reduce the need for combined treatment. It is accepted that there is a significant bladder and bowel dysfunction in approximately 10% of women treated with radical hysterectomy. However, with a lesser surgical procedure, bladder voiding dysfunction and other morbidity is halved when compared with a standard radical hysterectomy.[4]

Current treatment, therefore, must emphasise the need for maintaining good survival while at the same time decreasing the morbidity of treatment. Combination treatment inevitably will increase this morbidity, not only in the terms of bladder and bowel function but also lymphoedema and effects on vaginal function. A lesser surgical procedure such as a modified or type 2 radical hysterectomy for early stage cancer after appropriate preoperative assessment will have similar overall survival results.[5]

Fertility-sparing surgery

In discussion of the need for parametrial and paracervical resection, the concept of conservation of the uterine corpus must be carefully considered. There is little question that the principles of wide surgical resection of a tumour with adequate clear margins and simultaneous assessment and removal of potential lymph node metastases must be adhered to, although there is still scope for preservation of normal adjacent tissue. This concept has been applied to breast cancer with a significant reduction in the need for mastectomy with a resulting conservation of normal breast tissue and inevitable cosmetic and psychological benefits. The same principles may be applied to cervical cancer. As screening programmes become more effective and early-stage disease is detected, there will be a need for women who wish to preserve their fertility, and who may have postponed childbearing for professional and social reasons, to adopt a more conservative approach to the management of an early stage cervical cancer. With more precise assessment using MRI and lymph node imaging, it should be possible to predict those patients who have disease confined to the cervix in its lower portion. These women may be suitable for more conservative but locally radical excision in the form of trachelectomy with upper colpectomy and paracervical excision as opposed to a full radical hysterectomy.

Radical trachelectomy has now become an accepted surgical modality for a highly selected group of young patients wishing to conserve their fertility.[6] Laparoscopic pelvic lymphadenectomy is carried out simultaneously and, if patients are warned that the final histopathological features may be unfavourable, then either surgical completion of a radical hysterectomy procedure or postoperative radiotherapy may be required. By careful selection, however, a cohort of patients has shown that fertility may be preserved and that childbearing following resection of the cervix is possible. The risks of the procedure are inevitably premature labour with spontaneous premature rupture of the membranes due to a chorioamnionitis and ascending infection. The absence of a cervix removes the protective cervical mucus plug. However, mid-trimester abortion may be prevented or at least reduced by the insertion of an isthmic cerclage at the time of the trachelectomy. The obstetric and neonatal consequences, however, of the procedure necessitate very careful antenatal monitoring and delivery in a unit able to monitor and manage premature birth. Delivery by classical caesarean section is necessary, as the cervix has been removed up to and including the isthmus and, therefore, a lateral or transverse incision into the lower segment may result in severing the uterine arteries and extension of the incision into the parametria. A low vertical incision, therefore, after trachelectomy is advisable in order to avoid such complications. To date, approximately 300 such cases have been performed with delivery of over 50 babies, all by caesarean section.

Careful selection of patients for trachelectomy has resulted in a low recurrence rate, but these have been recorded at any time between six months and seven years following the procedure. Careful follow-up is therefore needed not just for five years but for a continuing length of time and it may be that late recurrences indicate another primary tumour manifesting as opposed to a true recurrence. Nevertheless, the question must be raised as to whether if hysterectomy had been carried out in the first place, central recurrence or further occurrence of disease could have been avoided; hence the need for careful scrutiny and reporting following such management.

It is envisaged, therefore, that in the future there will be an increasing need for fertility-sparing surgery. Tumour bulk and volume will be predicted more accurately by MRI assessment. Prognostic factors will determine the likelihood of lymph node metastases. Studies assessing lymphangiogenesis[7] and therefore the likelihood of lymph node spread will predict a high-risk group of patients who may require lymph node dissection or not be eligible for a more conservative approach. Such studies will in future enable surgeons to decide which patients may be treated by an adequate wide local excision of whatever primary is involved and follow high-risk patients with adjunctive treatment, be it chemotherapy or radiotherapy. For the cervix, chemoradiotherapy will be appropriate. While combination modality treatment does have a higher morbidity, careful selection with the reduction of surgical resection will on an individual basis result in better patient care and hopefully improve results while reducing morbidity. It is only by such individualisation that tailored treatment may be decided upon.

References

1.   Rockall AG, Barbar SA, Sohaib SA, Singh N, Jeyarajah A, Shepherd JH, Reznik RH. Diagnostic performance of ultrasmall particles of iron oxide (USPIO) in lymph node assessment in gynae malignancy. Abstract. Society of Gynecological Oncology, New Orleans, February 2003.
2.   Hagen B, Shepherd JH, Jacobs IJ. Parametrial resection for invasive cervical cancer. *Int J Gynecol Cancer* 2000;10:1–6.
3.   Covens A, Rosen B, Murphy J, Laframboise S, De Petrillo AD, Lichrish G, *et al.* How important is removal of the parametrium at surgery for carcinoma of the cervix? *Obstet Gynecol Surv* 2002;5:285–6.
4.   Landoni F, Maneo A, Cormio G, Perego P, Milani R, Caruso O, *et al.* Class II versus class III radical hysterectomy in stage Ib-IIa cervical cancer: a prospective randomised study. *Gynecol Oncol* 2001;80:3–12.
5.   Michalas S, Rodolakis A, Voulgaris Z, Vlachos G, Giannakoulis N, Diakomanolis E. Management of early-stage cervical carcinoma by modified (type II) radical hysterectomy. *Gynecol Oncol* 2002;85:415–522.

6.   Shepherd J H, Mould T, Oram DH. Radical trachelectomy in early stage carcinoma of the cervix: outcome as judged by recurrence and fertility rates. *Br J Obstet Gynecol* 2001;108:882–5.
7.   Van Trappen PO, Gyselman VG, Lowe DG, Ryan A, Oram DH, Bosze P, *et al*. Molecular quantification and mapping of lymph-node micrometastases in cervical cancer. *Lancet* 2001;357:15–20.

Chapter 29

Surgical management of invasive vulval carcinoma

John Monaghan

Introduction

Vulval carcinoma is rare, representing 4–6% of genital cancers. It is a condition mainly affecting the elderly, the average age of presentation being in the late seventh decade. However, the age range is wide and in younger women there appears to be a clearer association with vulval intraepithelial neoplasia (VIN).

Indeed, it is highly likely that there are two distinct conditions: the condition affecting the younger patients (less than forty-five years of age) being clearly associated with a precancerous element, often multifocal and often recurring at intervals. The disease affecting older patients appears to be unifocal, not always preceded by VIN, but more commonly associated with lichen sclerosus.

Historical surgical treatment

We have had clear indications as to the surgical management of vulval carcinoma for almost a century. Basset, working in Paris in 1914,[1] outlined the importance of the metastases to the groin and of removing the lymphatic ray connecting the primary tumour on the vulva with the primary lymph node site in the groin. Basset also outlined, mainly working on cadavers, the value of the *en bloc* dissection of the vulval tumour, together with the lymphatic ray and the groin nodes.

Bonney, in the late 1920s, also developed the radical vulvectomy and groin node dissection,[2] but it was Stoekel,[3] working first in Munich and then in Berlin, who demonstrated the need for individualisation of surgical treatment. In Stoekel's monograph published in 1930, he outlined every known variation of surgical treatment, many of which have later been rediscovered by other experts around the world.

Stanley Way,[4] working in Gateshead in the 1940s, reconfirmed the importance of the lymphatic drainage of the vulva and also outlined his ultra-radical vulvectomy, which he combined with groin node dissection and pelvic node dissection, markedly improving the survival data for these patients.

The significant downside of these large procedures was the enormous morbidity associated with them: major wound breakdowns resulting in prolonged periods of hospitalisation, and although recovery with good nursing was a normal consequence the morbidity was quite unacceptable. During the 1960s, a resurrection of separate groin incisions was developed. It became clear quickly as these procedures gained in popularity over the next 20 years that separate incisions should be reserved for those patients who had relatively small tumours, those patients who had no clinical evidence of metastases to the groin and for those patients who showed no evidence of lymphatic stasis.[5]

Technique of the vulval incision

The incisions in the groin and on the vulva have been many and various. As more conservative individualised care has developed it has become clear that the most important element in the vulva incision is to achieve an adequate margin. This margin has been better and better defined and it is now generally accepted that a margin of 1–2 cm around the tumour will, for the vast majority of patients, give complete local control.[6] As far as the groin node dissections are concerned, it is essential to remove not only the superficial nodes which tend to be widespread with a variable anatomy, but also the more constant deep groin nodes, the inguinofemoral nodes, which tend to be clustered around the fossa ovale close to the passage of the saphenous vein into the femoral vein.

Laterality

It has also become clear with time that it is not necessary to perform bilateral groin node dissections in all patients. We now understand that where a tumour can be identified as a truly lateral tumour (and the author's definition of laterality is a tumour lying between a line drawn horizontally across the urethra and a line drawn horizontally across the fourchette) this lateral tumour can be safely dealt with by an ipsilateral groin node dissection.

However, where it is found that the ipsilateral node contains metastases it is essential to then dissect at a separate procedure the contralateral lymph nodes.

Probably the most important development in recent times is that there have been improvements in our ability to identify lymph node metastases. There is no doubt that one of the major elements of mutilation and long-term morbidity that occurs in association with the surgical management of vulval carcinoma is that of chronic lymphoedema. The incidence of lymphoedema has been variably reported as 13–60%.[7,8] However, more recent data using plethysmographic techniques measuring the volume of the legs has demonstrated that in almost 100% of patients there will be a significant change in leg volume following routine groin lymphadenectomy. Therefore there has been a major effort to try to reduce the impact of groin node dissection while at the same time understanding the failure to adequately treat groin node metastases will inevitably result in the death of a patient.

The great value of groin node dissection lies in the ability of this technique, not only to remove obvious clearly identifiable metastases to the nodes, but also to remove micrometastases which have a potential at a later date to develop into a recurrence, resulting in an extraordinarily difficult clinical situation from which the patient rarely recovers.

In the past, a number of studies have been carried out to attempt to identify pre-operatively the presence or absence of groin node metastases. We know from very large series that the overall incidence of groin node metastases is approximately 30%. In small tumours this figure will drop to as low as 10%. Therefore, by definition, a significant majority of patients will be receiving a debilitating therapy without any real advantages.

Preoperative identification of lymphatic spread and nodal involvement

The techniques that have been used in the past for identification of groin node metastases have been somewhat simplistic and limited in their capacity to identify involved nodes.

Palpation

This method of assessment is notoriously inaccurate, with error rates of between 13% and 39%.[7,9]

Computerised tomography

This noninvasive technique has now been eliminated as a technique for identification of groin nodes, mainly due to the high false positive and false negative rate due to an unacceptably high limit of resolution.

Magnetic resonance imaging

This technique, once more a noninvasive process, has been extensively investigated but remains unacceptable, in that it generates far too high a false negative rate, which would result almost inevitably in the death of a patient. Continuing investigations and assessment as the technology improves, however, are being maintained.

Ultrasound

The use of ultrasound, together with fine-needle aspiration, has been demonstrated to be of value. Modifications in size and pattern of nodal morphometry can be demonstrated and, in some hands, high but not yet acceptable levels of specificity can be achieved. This technique, however, is not yet safe enough to be brought into general use.

Lymphangiography

Many individual clinicians have demonstrated a great usefulness of this technique. A difficulty with it is that it is operator dependent and, although in one centre, high degrees of resolution may be achieved, in others, this technique is not readily transferable to all patients.

Sentinel node assessment

In 1979, Phillip DiSaia[10] advocated the identification of a sentinel node on the medial side of the superficial nodes of the groin, which he stated would give an indicator as to the presence or absence of metastases in the remaining nodes in the groin. This technique did not establish, mainly due to the significant difficulties in identification of this sentinel node.

In the 1990s, Levenback reinvestigated the use of vital blue dyes, which markedly improved the ease of identification of the sentinel node.[11] These positive results encouraged further investigation, including the use of technetium scanning using a neo probe. Although the vital blue dye was of value it was not constant and not always could the dye be identified in a node or lymphatics. However, the use of scanning with a Neoprobe device has demonstrated high sensitivities and specificities with, in recent publications from Italy and Amsterdam,[11-14] 100% accuracy in identifying positive and negative lymph nodes. This technique is now being widely piloted and it is beginning to appear that we may have a technique that will allow us to dispense with groin node dissections in a majority of patients.

Technique of surgery

The techniques of surgery for vulval carcinoma are relatively simple. However, an individual's experience would be limited without centralisation of service. Vulval carcinoma should now be managed entirely within the ambit of a cancer centre, resulting in a relatively small number of individuals building the surgical skills required to deal effectively with this cancer. The use of extended therapies such as anovulvectomy and exenteration, which may be required from time to time, also confirms the need for centralisation. The role of the multidisciplinary team in the development of therapies for recurrence including the use of plastic surgery skills, radiotherapy and chemotherapy skills confirm the need for this cancer to be managed in a multidisciplinary environment.

Conclusions

For the immediate future it is clear that the primary management of carcinoma of the vulva will remain surgical.

The importance of preoperative identification of groin node metastases using sentinel node techniques will allow a marked reduction in morbidity associated with the disease by dispensing with groin node dissections in a significant number of patients.

The long-term care of vulval cancer patients, with their marked propensity for recurrence, should be performed within a multidisciplinary team setting.

The high cure rates associated with modern management of vulval carcinoma must be maintained and any new therapies developed must be well piloted, although it is almost impossible to perform surgical trials in such a rare tumour prior to their introduction into standard practice.

References

1. Basset A. Traitement chirurgical opératoire de l'épithelioma primitif du clitoris. *Rev Chir* 1912;46:546–70.
2. Berkeley C, Bonney V. *A Textbook of Gynaecological* Surgery. 3rd ed. London: Cassell; 1935.
3. Stoekel W. Zur Therapie des Vulvakarzinoma. *Zentralbl Gynakol* 1930;1:47–71.
4. Way S. *Malignant Disease of the Vulva*. Edinburgh: Churchill Livingstone; 1982.
5. Hacker NF, Leuchter RS, Berek JS, Castaldo TW, Lagasse LD. Radical vulvectomy and bilateral inguinal lymphadenectomy through separate groin incisions. *Obstet Gynecol* 1981;58:574–9.
6. Heaps JM, Fu YS, Montz FJ, Hacker NF, Berek JS. Surgical pathologic variables predictive of local recurrence in squamous cell carcinoma of the vulva. *Gynecol Oncol* 1990;38:309–14.
7. Monaghan JM, Hammond IG. Pelvic node dissection in the treatment of vulval cancer- is it necessary? *Br J Obstet Gynaecol* 1984;91:270–4.
8. Cavanagh D, Roberts WS, Bryson SCP, Marsden D, Ingram JM, Anderson WR. Changing trends in the surgical management of invasive carcinoma of the vulva. *Surg Gynecol Obstet* 1986;162:164–8.
9.. Benedet JL, Turko M, Fairey RN, Boyes DA Squamous cell carcinoma of the vulva: results of treatment, 1938–1976. *Am J Obstet Gynecol* 1979;134:102–7.

10.   DiSaia PJ, Creasman WT, Rich WM. An alternative approach to early cancer of the vulva. *Am J Obstet Gynecol* 1979;133:825–32.

11.   Levenback C, Burke TW, Gershenson D, Morris M, Malpica A, Ross MI. Intraoperative lymphatic mapping for vulvar cancer. *Obstet Gynecol* 1994;84:163–7.

12.   DeCesare SL, Fiorica JV, Roberts WS, Reintgen D, Arango H, Hoffman MS, *et al.* A pilot study utilizing intraoperative lymphoscintigraphy for identification of the sentinel nodes in vulvar cancer. *Gynecol Oncol* 1997;66:425–8.

13.   Terada KY, Coel MN, Ko P, Wong JH. Combined use of intraoperative lymphatic mapping and lymphoscintigraphy in the management of squamous cell cancer of the vulva. *Gynecol Oncol* 1998;70:65–9.

14.   de Hullu JA, Hollema H, Piers DA, Verheigen R, van Diest PJ, Mounts MJ, *et al.* Sentinel lymph node procedure is highly accurate in squamous cell carcinoma of the vulva. *J Clin Oncol* 2000;18:2811–16.

Chapter 30

Chemoradiation of cervical and vulval cancer: review of clinical evidence and treatment recommendations

Malcolm Adams and Carol Louise Hanna

Introduction and background

Invasive cervical cancer is the second most common cause of female cancer death worldwide.[1] For many years the standard curative treatment for invasive cervical cancer has been radical surgery for early disease and radical radiotherapy for advanced disease (FIGO stages 2b to 4a). Typically, radical radiotherapy is given as a combination of external beam treatment and brachytherapy. For radical radiotherapy the treatment outcome is dependent upon the total treatment time and the radiation dose to point A.[2-5] Preferably, overall treatment time should be limited to eight weeks[2-4] and the dose to point A should lie between 85–90 Gy for advanced cancer patients.[5] Another important factor which may influence treatment results is the haemoglobin level during radiation treatment.[6]

Several chemotherapy agents including cisplatin[7] and 5-fluorouracil[8] have been shown to act as radiosensitisers *in vitro*. In addition, cisplatin has been shown to be the most effective cytotoxic agent for the treatment of metastatic disease.[9] Therefore, in theory, the addition of chemotherapy to radical radiotherapy could potentially increase local tumour control and decrease distant relapse. A previous systematic review and meta-analysis failed to show a benefit to adding chemotherapy in the neoadjuvant setting, despite clear evidence that chemotherapy induced primary tumour regression.[10] In contrast, the use of concurrent cisplatin and radiotherapy yielded significant survival benefits in five randomised trials reported in 1999 (Table 30.1).[11-15] Consequently, in the same year, the US National Cancer Institute issued a clinical alert, which stated that "strong consideration be given to the incorporation of concurrent cisplatin-based chemotherapy with radiation therapy in women who require radiation therapy for treatment of cervical cancer". However, these five trials formed only a subset of published chemoradiation data and a subsequent National Cancer Institute of Canada trial demonstrated no survival advantage for concurrent platinum based chemoradiation in stage 1b to 4a cervical cancer patients (Table 30.1).[16] These conflicting data plus a number of small randomised controlled trials (RCTs) with insufficient statistical power provided a rationale for a systematic review and meta-analysis.[17-18]

With regard to vulval cancer, concurrent chemoradiation has also been employed in the management of selected patients. Non-randomised phase II studies in locally

Table 30.1. Six key platinum-based randomised clinical trials of chemoradiation in cervical cancer

Trial	Reference	FIGO stage	Patients (*n*)	Chemoradiation regimen	Three-year survival (%)
SWOG 879	Peters et al.[11]	1a2–2a post-surgery	127	XRT+PF	87
			116	XRT	77
GOG 123	Keys et al.[12]	1b2 (> 4 cm)	183	XRT+IC+P+S	83
			186	XRT+IC+S	74
GOG 8	Whitney et al.[13]	2b–4a	177	XRT+IC+PF	67
			191	XRT+IC+HU	57
RTOG 9001	Morris et al.[14]	2b–4a	195	XRT+IC+PF	75
			193	XRT+IC	63
GOG 120	Rose et al.[15]	2b–4a	176	XRT+IC+P	65
			173	XRT+IC+PFHU	65
			177	XRT+IC+HU	47
NCIC CTG CX.2	Pearcey et al.[16]	1b (> 5cm)–4a	183	XRT+IC+P	69
			186	XRT+IC	66

F= 5-fluorouracil; GOG = Gynecologic Oncology Group; HU= hydroxyurea; IC= intracavitary brachytherapy; NCIC CTG = National Cancer Institute of Canada Clinical Trials Group; P = cisplatin; RTOG = Radiotherapy Oncology Group; S= surgery; SWOG = South west Oncology Group; XRT= external radiotherapy

advanced disease report its role prior to surgery as neoadjuvant therapy[19–22] or as an option for primary treatment in patients with inoperable disease.[23–28]

Radical chemoradiation in cervical cancer

The evidence from randomised controlled trials

Considerable interest worldwide has focused on the five randomised phase III trials[11–15] which have shown a significant survival advantage for cisplatin-based therapy given concurrently with radiation therapy. The patient populations in these studies included women with FIGO stages 1b2–4a cervical cancer treated with primary radiation therapy and women with FIGO stages 1–2a disease found to have poor prognostic factors (metastatic disease in pelvic lymph nodes, parametrial disease or positive surgical margins) at time of primary surgery. Although these five trials[11–15] varied in terms of FIGO stage of disease, dose of radiation and treatment schedule of cisplatin and radiation, they all demonstrated a significant survival benefit for this combined approach. Overall, the risk of death from cervical cancer was decreased by 30% to 50% by concurrent chemoradiation. Consequently, based on these results, significant expert opinion felt that strong consideration should be given to concurrent cisplatin-based chemotherapy in addition to radiation therapy in all women who require radiation therapy for treatment of cervical cancer.[30] Subsequently, however, in 2000, a further study of concurrent cisplatin and pelvic radiotherapy in locally advanced cervical cancer reported no significant survival advantage for chemoradiation.[16] The suggested explanations for these conflicting data have included inadequate radiation dose in the control arm[29] and inadequate maintenance of haemoglobin during chemoradiation.[18] In addition, the platinum-based chemoradiation trials represented only a subset of the literature on chemoradiation in cervical cancer. Other clinical trials had been reported using other cytotoxic agents in combination with radiation.[32–38] Meta-analysis of available studies offered a means of pooling survival rates from a wider range of RCTs to evaluate the roles of both platinum-based and non-platinum-based concurrent chemoradiotherapy in cervical cancer.

Meta-analyses of chemoradiation trials

Two meta-analyses have been published (a meta-analysis performed by the Cochrane Collaboration, which included both platinum- and non-platinum-based chemotherapy[17]) and a Canadian meta-analysis of platinum-based chemoradiation.[18] Both meta-analyses have made a significant contribution to understanding the value of concurrent chemoradiation in cervical cancer and need to be considered in detail.

Patients included in the meta-analyses

The Cochrane meta-analysis[17] identified 17 published[11–16,31–40] and two unpublished randomised trials comprising 12 platinum-based and seven non-platinum-based trials, which together included 4580 patients. The Canadian meta-analysis[18] identified eight platinum-based randomised RCTs of 2251 patients with reported survival data;[11–16,39,41] this included the five positive platinum-based trials,[11–15] the negative National Cancer Institute of Canada (NCIC) study[16] and two further clinical trials.[39,41]

Methods and endpoints

In the Cochrane analysis,[17] overall survival and progression-free survival were considered the primary outcomes and hazard ratio was considered the most appropriate measure for time-to-event meta-analysis. Sufficient data were available from 11 of the trials to estimate the hazard ratio for overall survival and 13 trials to estimate the hazard ratio for progression-free survival. In many reports included in the Cochrane analysis, the overall local and distant recurrence was presented, rather than a time-to-event analysis. Consequently an odds ratio was calculated taking no account of time to recurrence. It was noted that only nine studies reported acute toxicity in detail. Consequently, toxicity data had to be grouped as a single odds ratio for each site, e.g. haematological, genitourinary, dermatological or neurological. Late toxicity was described in detail in only three studies and could only be reviewed qualitatively.

In the Canadian analysis,[18] mortality data were pooled and expressed as a risk ratio for death with 95% confidence limits. A risk ratio less than one indicated the experimental arm (cisplatin-based chemoradiation) gave improved survival compared with the control treatment. The eight trials analysed were divided into six containing patients with locally advanced disease and two containing patients with high-risk early disease. The high-risk early disease group consisted of one trial with patients with stage 1b tumours greater than 4 cm and the other had adverse pathological features following surgery, namely parametrial invasion, positive surgical margins and positive pelvic nodes. The rates of local recurrence were available in seven of the studies and in six trials the distant metastatic rate was available. Data on acute adverse effects were available from seven of the studies. Late toxicity was infrequently described and was reported in only four of the eight studies in the Canadian analysis.[18]

Results: survival

In the Cochrane meta-analysis,[17] it was possible to obtain sufficient data from 11 trials to estimate the hazard ratio of survival. A hazard ratio across all trials of 0.71 (95% CI 0.63–0.81; $P < 0.0001$) was demonstrated, representing a highly significant survival benefit for chemoradiation: a 29% reduction in the risk of death. The absolute improvement in survival was 12% (95% CI 8–16) from 40% to 52%. There was evidence of a greater survival benefit in the trials using platinum-based chemotherapy (HR 0.70; 95% CI 0.61–0.80; $P < 0.0001$) as compared with trials with non-platinum chemoradiation (HR 0.81; 95% CI 0.56–1.16, P 0.20). Further analysis suggested that the effect was greater in trials with a higher proportion of early stage patients, although there was heterogeneity in the trials of more advanced patients.

Pooled survival rates from the eight RCTs in the Canadian analysis[18] also demonstrated a highly statistically significant advantage in favour of cisplatin chemoradiation, with a relative risk of death of 0.74 (95% CI 0.64–0.86). The absolute reduction in the risk of death was 11%. The pooled relative risk of death among the six trials that included locally advanced disease was 0.78 (95% CI 0.67–0.90). The pooled relative risk for the two trials, including high-risk early disease, also showed significant survival benefit for cisplatin-based chemoradiation at 0.56 (95% CI 0.41–0.77).

Thus, both meta-analyses indicated a survival benefit for cervical cancer although the effect appeared to be more marked for patients with early (stage 1 and 2) disease with high-risk features.

Data from 13 trials in the Cochrane analysis were also available for calculation of hazard ratio for progression-free survival. The results strongly favoured chemoradiation. (HR 0.61; 95% CI 0.55–0.68), which translated into an improvement in progression-free survival of 16% from 47% to 63%.

Results: local and distant recurrence

The Cochrane analysis reported that the rate of local recurrence, based on 12 trials, was significantly reduced by chemoradiation (OR 0.61; 95% CI 0.51–0.73; $P < 0.0001$). Distant recurrence data were also available from 12 trials and demonstrated a clear reduction of distant metastases with chemoradiation (OR 0.57; 95% CI 0.46–0.77; $P < 0.0001$). This reduction in distant recurrence was also observed separately in the platinum (OR 0.60; 95% CI 0.46–0.77; $P < 0.0001$) and non-platinum groups (OR 0.52; 95% CI 0.35–0.76; $P < 0.0008$).

The Canadian analysis also noted that chemoradiation produced a trend towards improved local control in six out of seven trials and there was a trend for improvement in distant metastasis rates in six studies. The Cochrane analysis suggested that the sheer magnitude of the reduction in distant metastases was likely to be the consequence of cytotoxic chemotherapy acting systemically as well as improving local control.

Results: toxicity

In the Cochrane analysis, acute toxicity was noted in detail in only eight published and one unpublished trial. Acute haematological toxicity and gastrointestinal toxicity was observed to be greater in the chemoradiation group. Leucopenia grade 3 and 4 was 16% versus 8% and for thrombocytopenia 1.55 versus 0.2% in the chemoradiation arms versus the radiation-only groups, respectively. Similarly, grade 3 and 4 gastrointestinal toxicity was greater in the combined arm. The Canadian analysis also noted increased acute haematological and gastrointestinal toxicity.

Late toxicity was recorded in only three studies in the Cochrane analysis, with no evidence of differences in bladder and gastrointestinal toxicity. However, there were seven toxic deaths in the published papers, one in the control group, five in the experimental group and one in a patient who declined chemotherapy.

Only four out of eight trials reported on late complications in the Canadian analysis but there was no observed increase in late morbidity. In fact, in one trial,[16] a lower rate of late complications was observed when cisplatin was added to radiotherapy than radiotherapy alone (6% versus 12%).

Conclusions from the meta-analyses

While it has been argued that suboptimal radiation in the control arm could be the explanation for the superior results of chemoradiation, there is little evidence to support this. The point-A dose in most of the cisplatin-based trials was of the order of 80–90 Gy. Lukka et al.[18] noted a benefit for the use of cisplatin-based chemotherapy even with standard doses of radiotherapy in the Radiotherapy Oncology Group trial.[14] Nevertheless, acute toxicity is increased with chemoradiation, which may lead to harmful prolongation of treatment time. The potential harmful effect has been estimated to be approximately a loss of 1% for every day treatment is prolonged past seven weeks.[4] Anaemia has long been thought to be an adverse prognostic factor in patients receiving radical radiotherapy for advanced cervical cancer[6] and has been suggested as an explanation of the lack of improvement in survival observed with chemoradiation in the NCIC trial. Therefore, maintenance of haemoglobin may be an important consideration in patients receiving chemoradiation.[42]

The data on late morbidity for chemoradiation remain sparse and it is too early to determine its effect on late toxicity. More information is needed on this key parameter. However, there is now sufficient evidence from the two meta-analyses to conclude that chemoradiation significantly improves overall survival in locally advanced cervical cancer with a greater effect in early high-risk disease. Weekly cisplatin 40 mg/m^2 appears to be less toxic than a combination of cisplatin and 5-fluorouracil[15] and is probably the best recommendation at present. However, further studies are required to determine the optimum chemoradiation regimen and to clearly quantify late toxicity for the management of this disease.

Vulval cancer

The standard treatment for vulval carcinoma is surgery. For small node-negative tumours, the overall survival is 90% at five years. Survival and local control falls with increasing stage and the number of nodal metastases.[43–44] The survival for larger lesions, with three or more unilateral or two or more bilateral nodes, falls to only 29% at five years.[44] Primary tumours that involve the anus, rectum, rectovaginal septum, proximal urethra or bladder are uncommon but pose a particular problem because primary surgical clearance requires exenteration and radical vulvectomy, which may be associated with significant mortality and morbidity. Radiotherapy was traditionally regarded as having a limited role in the radical treatment of vulval cancer because severe radiation reactions are common. However, in the 1980s, several investigators[45–48] reported promising results for preoperative radiotherapy followed by limited surgical resection or, in some cases, primary radiotherapy alone. These reports suggested that preoperative radiation doses of 45–55 Gy could produce a good response permitting subsequent organ-sparing surgery without loss of local control. For example, Hacker et al.,[46] in a small series of patients with T3 and T4 tumours, found preoperative radiotherapy at a dose of 44–54 Gy to result in no residual tumour in the vulvectomy specimen and five of eight patients were without evidence of disease at 15 months' to ten years' follow up. Perez[47] reported local control in ten of 13 patients with T3 or T4 tumours with primary radiation doses of 50–70 Gy. Thus, these early studies suggest that radical radiotherapy may play an important role in selected patients with vulval cancer. Preoperative radiotherapy is a feasible treatment option to reduce the extent of surgery in stage 3 or 4 disease and could be successfully used alone as a curative treatment in patients medically unfit for surgery. In addition, a Gynecologic Oncology

Group RCT[49] found that survival and local control was improved when radiation was used postoperatively in those patients with positive lymph nodes.

The subsequent investigation of concurrent chemoradiotherapy in vulval cancer followed from the promising results seen in anal cancer.[50–51] In this disease, the addition of concurrent chemotherapy to radical radiation has improved local control and disease-free survival and few patients require surgery for dermal or sphincter toxic effects.[50–51] The *in vitro* data mentioned earlier supporting the radiosensitising properties of drugs such as 5-fluorouracil and cisplatin[7–8] may be relevant to vulval cancer. Theoretically, these drugs may be used in conjunction with radiation to improve local and distant control compared with a higher dose of radiation.

Disappointing results have been reported for preoperative combination chemotherapy alone. Benedetti Panici *et al.*[52] treated 21 patients with FIGO stage 4a vulval squamous carcinoma with three cycles of cisplatin (100 mg/m^2 day one), bleomycin (15 mg days one and eight) and methotrexate (300 mg/m^2 day eight). Only 10% of patients had a partial response in the primary, although 67% had a complete or partial response in nodal metastases. Relapse occurred in 68% of operated patients within 3–17 months. The three-year survival was only 24% and was influenced by stage, pathological down-staging and nodal involvement. The authors concluded that there was no substantial benefit from the addition of preoperative chemotherapy without concurrent radiotherapy.

Clinical evidence supporting the concurrent addition of chemotherapy to radiation in vulval cancer to date is confined to non-randomised phase II studies. In these studies it has been used preoperatively in advanced disease to down-stage and reduce the extent of surgery and as a primary treatment for advanced disease when the disease is inoperable or in patients medically unfit for surgery.

Preoperative chemoradiation (Table 30.2)

Moore *et al.*[19] assessed the feasibility of reducing the extent of radical surgery required for primary T3 and T4 tumours. They treated 73 FIGO stage 3 and 4 patients prospectively with cisplatin /5-fluorouracil-based chemoradiation followed by surgical excision of the residual primary tumour with bilateral inguinal and femoral lymph node dissection. The radiation fraction size was kept to 1.7 Gy per day delivered with anterior and posterior fields to a total tumour dose of 47.6 Gy. Most patients (71 of 73; 97%) completed chemoradiation and 33 of 71 (46.5%) had no visible cancer after completing treatment. Of the remaining 38, five had positive resection margins following surgery and four received further treatment. Toxicity was considered to be acceptable, with acute cutaneous effects and surgical wound complications being the most common effects. Using this strategy of preoperative split-course twice-daily chemoradiation, 69 out of 71 (97.2%) had resectable disease and it was possible to retain urinary and bowel continence in 68 out of 71 patients; 54.9% remained disease free at a median follow up of 50 months. The group concluded that preoperative chemoradiation was a feasible treatment option in advanced vulval cancer and may avert the need for exenterative surgery in the majority of patients.

In contrast, disappointing survival despite an objective response rate of 75% was reported by Scheistroen and Trope,[20] with a combination of bleomycin plus a lower radiation dose of 30–45 Gy. Only four of 20 patients with primary disease went on to surgery and none of the patients with recurrent disease. The median survival for the patients with primary disease was only eight months. The authors found no evidence of benefit for preoperative chemoradiation and suggested that increased radiation dose and more aggressive surgery may improve results.

Table 30.2. Preoperative chemoradiation phase II studies

Reference	Date	Patients (n)	Chemoradiation/radiation treatment	Clinical response	Outcome, Resectability/DF survival	Morbidity, urinary and GI continence, severe toxicity
Moore et al.[19]	1993	73 primary T3/T4 (50 N0/N1: 23 N2/N3)	2 cycles P+F split with concomitant twice daily RT 47.6 Gy	CCR = 46.5% (53.5% gross residual disease)	2.8% non-resectable disease; 54.9% DF survival at 50 months	Mild acute toxicity: 3/71 loss of urinary/GI continence
Landoni et al.[21]	1996	41 primary; 23 T2, 17 T3; 1 T4; (32 N+); 17 relapse; (7 N+)	Two cycles F 750 m² for 5 days and mitomycin C 15 mg bolus with RT (54 Gy)	Vulval: CCR = 31% CR +PR =80% Inguinal nodes: CCR=33% CR+PR =79%	72% had surgery; 62% alive at 34 months; 2/16 not having surgery alive	Early severe toxicity in 3 patients and 1 treatment death
Lupi et al.[22]	1996	24 primary: 1 T1, 2 T2, 17 T3, 4 T4 (24 N+); 7 relapse	Two cycles F 750 m² for 5 days and mitomycin C 15 mg bolus prior to radical surgery (36 Gy)	Primary: CR+PR = 22/24 (92%) Recurrent: CR+PR = 7/7	68% recurrence-free at 34 months	Post operative morbidity 65%; mortality rate 13.8%
Scheistroen et al.[20]	1993	20 primary; 22 recurrent	Bleomycin 180 mg with 30–45 Gy concurrent RT	Primary: CR+PR =15/20, 75% CR = 25% Recurrent: CR+PR = 13/22, 59%	Median survival 8 months	Acceptable toxicity

CCR = clinical complete response; CR = complete response; DF = Disease-free; F= 5-fluorouracil; P = cisplatin; PR = partial response; RT = radiotherapy

Two groups have studied preoperative chemoradiation with 5-fluorouracil and mitomycin (Table 30.2).[21,22] Lupi[22] reported that 22 of 24 patients (92 %) with primary disease and seven of seven (100%) with recurrent disease had an objective response, using a split radiation course of 54 Gy to the vulva and 36 Gy to the inguinal nodes. However, postoperative morbidity and mortality were high at 65% and 13.8%, respectively. At a median follow up of 34 months, 68% were recurrence free. They concluded that preoperative chemoradiation might have a role if morbidity could be reduced. Landoni et al.[21] reported an objective response rate of 80%, with evidence of pathological complete response in 31% with a split radiation dose of 54 Gy. Severe early toxicity was seen in three patients and one patient had a treatment-related death. The authors felt treatment provided good local control, with acceptable toxicity, but that further follow up was required to determine long-term outcome.

While these data suggest that chemoradiation can down-stage advanced vulval cancers and thereby reduce the need for aggressive surgery in selected patients, the approach remains investigational.

Preoperative chemoradiation conclusions

To date, there is no proven survival benefit for preoperative chemoradiation and there is a potential for severe morbidity in these patients. Ideally, such treatment needs to be performed by a specialist team in the context of a clinical trial. The optimum regimen has not yet been described. Suggested options include a radiation dose of up to 55 Gy with concomitant single agent cisplatin, cisplatin with 5-fluorouracil[19] or single agent 5-fluorouracil[19] in conjunction with expert surgery. To date follow up is too short and the number of patients too small to allow detailed analysis of patterns of failure and survival. These phase II trials will contribute to the design of future controlled trials to evaluate this approach.

Primary chemoradiation

The role of primary chemoradiation in the treatment of vulval cancer is also unclear and has yet to be studied in RCTs. Several phase II trials[23-28,53] have reported small numbers of patients with advanced vulval cancer unable to tolerate radical surgery, using a variety of primary chemoradiation regimens (Table 30.3). Most studies have used chemotherapy combinations of cisplatin, 5-fluorouracil and mitomycin C with concurrent radiation doses of 40–50 Gy. Such studies have reported a high response rate with complete responses in 50–67% and a crude three-year survival rate of 47–84%.

Berek[23] reported a complete response rate of 67% in a group of 12 patients with FIGO stage 3 and 4 disease. Cisplatin was administered in a dose of 50 mg/m^2 on days one and two or as 100 mg/m^2 on day 1. The 5-fluorouracil was administered as an intravenous infusion of 1000 mg/m^2 for four to five days and chemotherapy was repeated on day 28. Concurrent external radiation to a dose of 44–54 Gy was administered to the primary tumour plus inguinal and iliac regions to a level below the common iliac nodes. On completion of chemoradiation, radical surgery was performed in four patients. The treatment was reported as being well tolerated and 10 of 12 patients have remained disease free with a follow up of 7–60 months. Similar response rates have been reported in other clinical studies[24,25,27,28,53] using cisplatin plus 5-fluorouracil chemoradiation, with radiation doses of 40–50 Gy to the pelvis and slightly higher doses to the vulva and groin. Cunningham et al.[25] reported only one recurrence in ten patients with a complete response with a follow up of 7–81 months.

Table 30.3. Primary chemoradiation studies

Reference	Date	Patients (n)	Treatment	Clinical response	Outcome	Toxicity
Berek et al.[23]	1991	12 FIGO stage 3/4	P + F; RT 44–54 Gy	CR=67%; CR+PR=92%	10/12 patients disease-free follow up 7-60 months	Grade 3 desquamation 2 patients; 1 DVT
Eifel et al.[24]	1995	12 FIGO Stage 3/4	P + F; RT 40–50 Gy	PR=92%	6/12 disease-free at 17–30 months	Well tolerated minimal haematological toxicity, no treatment delays
Cunningham et al.[25]	1997	14 FIGO stage 3/4	P + F RT 45–50 Gy	CR= 64%; CR+PR =92%	CR: 1/10 recurrence at 7-81 months; PR: all dead	Treatment delays in 5 patients; 1 DVT; 1 colonic stricture
Koh et al.[26]	1995	20 FIGO stage 3/4	P + F or mitomycin C; RT 30–54 Gy	CR= 50%; PR =40%	49% disease-free at 5 years	Well tolerated major toxicity radiation vulvitis
Russell et al.[27]	1992	25 FIGO stage 2-4	F ± F; RT 44–54 Gy	Primary CR=89%; Recurrent CR =57%	14/25 disease-free at 24 months	Well tolerated
Wahlen et al.[28]	1995	19 AJCC stage 2-4	F + +mitomycin C; RT 45–50 Gy	CR=53%; PR=37%	Local control in 14/19; 4/5 failures rendered disease-free with surgery	Well tolerated

AJCC = American Joint Committee on Cancer; CCR = clinical complete response; CR = complete response; DVT = deep vein thrombosis; F= 5-fluorouracil; P = cisplatin; PR = partial response; RT = radiotherapy

They concluded that surgical resection was not necessary in patients with a clinical complete response. Russell et al.[27] noted that the complete response rate in their series was higher in previously untreated patients (16 of 18; 89%) compared with those with recurrent disease (four of seven; 57%).

Han et al.[53] have analysed the impact of chemoradiation or radiation alone in 54 patients with locally advanced vulval cancer. Fourteen patients were treated with primary concurrent chemoradiation, 12 with primary radiation, six with adjuvant chemoradiation and 22 with adjuvant radiation therapy. Chemotherapy consisted of infusions of 5-fluorouracil and either cisplatin or mitomycin C at the discretion of the physician. Radiation was given with chemotherapy to a dose of 45–46 Gy to the pelvis, vulva and inguinal regions, with a boost to all gross disease. Those patients treated with radiation alone were treated with 40–50 Gy in the first phase with a boost to 60 Gy to gross disease. They found that there was a statistically significant increase in relapse-free and overall survival in those patients treated with primary chemoradiation compared with primary radiation alone. However, this was not a randomised study.

Primary chemoradiation conclusions

From these small, phase II randomised studies, it appears that primary chemoradiation is a therapeutic option to be considered in those deemed unsuitable for surgery. The optimum regimen has yet to be defined and should be the subject of future controlled clinical trials. However, caution is warranted in designing aggressive treatment regimens for patients with vulval cancer, who are often elderly with concurrent medical problems. These patients need to be treated in expert specialised multidisciplinary teams with experience of this disease.

References

1.   Ferlay J Bray F, Pisani P, Parkin DM. GLOBOCAN 2000: *Cancer Incidence, Mortality and Prevalence Worldwide, Version 1.0.* IARC CancerBase No. 5. Lyon, IARC Press, 2001 [http://www-dep.iarc.fr/dataava/infodata.htm].
2.   Lanciano R, PajakT, Martz K, Hanks GE. The influence of treatment time on outcome for squamous cell cancer of the uterine cervix treated with radiation. A patterns of-care study. *Int J Radiat Oncol Biol Phys* 25:391–7.
3.   Girinsky T, Rey A, Roche B Haie C, Gerbaulet A, Randrianarivello H. Overall treatment time in advanced cervical cancer, a critical parameter in treatment outcome. *Int J Radiat Oncol Biol Phys* 1993;27:1051–6.
4.   Perez C, Grigsby PW, Castro-Vita H, Lockett MA. Carcinoma of the uterine cervix. I. Impact of prolongation of overall treatment time and timing of brachytherapy on outcome of radiation therapy. *Int J Radiat Oncol Biol Phys* 1995;32:1275–88.
5.   Eifel P, Thomas WW Jr, Smith TL Morris M, Oswald MJ. The relationship between brachytherapy dose and outcome in patients with bulky endocervical tumors treated with radiation alone. *Int J Radiat Oncol Biol Phys* 1994;28:113–18.
6.   Bush RS. The significance of anemia in clinical radiation therapy. *Int J Radiat Oncol Biol Phys* 1986;12:2047–50.
7.   Dewit L. Combined treatment of radiation and cisdiamino dichloroplatinum (II): a review of experimental and clinical data. *Int J Radiat Oncol Biol Phys* 1987;13:403–26.
8.   Byfield J. 5-Fluorouracil radiation sensitization. *Invest New Drugs* 1989;7,111–16.
9.   Omura GA. Chemotherapy for stage IV B or recurrent cancer of the uterine cervix. *J Natl Cancer Inst* 1996;21:123–6.
10.   Tierney JF, Stewart LA, Parmar MKB. Can the published data tell us about the effectiveness of neoadjuvant chemotherapy for locally advance cancer of the cervix? *Eur J Cancer* 1999;35:406–9.
11.   Peters WA, Liu PY, Barrett RJ Gordon W, Stock R, Berek F, *et al.* Concurrent chemotherapy and pelvic radiation therapy compared with pelvic radiation alone as adjuvant therapy after radical surgery in high-risk early stage cancer of the cervix. *J Clin Oncol* 2000;18:1606–13.

12. Keys HM, Bundy BN, Stehman FB. Cisplatin, radiation and adjuvant hysterectomy compared with radiation and adjuvant hysterectomy for bulky stage 1B cervical cancer. *N Engl J Med* 1999;340:1154–61.

13. Whitney CW, Sauser W, Bundy BN, Malfetano JH, Hannigan EV, Fowler JR WC, *et al*. Randomised comparison of fluorouracil plus cisplatin versus hydroxyurea as an adjunct to radiation therapy in stage 2b /4a in carcinoma of the cervix with negative lymph nodes: a Gynecologic Oncology and South West oncology group study. *J Clin Oncol* 1999;17:1339–48.

14. Morris M, Eifel P, Lu J, Grigsby PW, Levenback C, Stevens RE, *et al*. Pelvic radiation with concurrent chemotherapy compared with pelvic and para-aortic radiation for high-risk cervical cancer. *N Engl J Med* 1999;340:1137–43.

15. Rose PG, Bundy BN, Watkins EB, Thigpen JT, Deppe G, Maiman MA, *et al*. Concurrent cisplatin –based radiotherapy and chemotherapy for locally advanced cervical cancer. *N Engl J Med* 1999;340:1144–53.

16. Pearcey RG, Brudage MD, Drouin P, Jeffrey J, Johnston D, Lukka H, *et al*. A clinical trial comparing concurrent cisplatin and radiation therapy versus radiation alone for locally advanced squamous cell carcinoma of the cervix carried out by the National Cancer Institute of Canada clinical trials group. *Proceedings of the Annual Meeting of the American Society of Clinical Oncologists* 2000;19:378a.

17. Green JA, Kirwan JM, Tierney JF, Symonds P, Fresco L, Williams C, *et al*. Survival and recurrence after concomitant chemotherapy and radiotherapy for cancer of the uterine cervix; a systematic review and meta-analysis. *Lancet* 2001;358:781–6.

18. Lukka H, Hirte H, Fyles A, Thomas G, Elit L, Johnston M, *et al*. Concurrent cisplatin-based chemotherapy plus radiotherapy for cervical cancer: a meta-analysis. *Clin Oncol* 2003;14:203–12.

19. Moore DH, Thomas GM, Montana GS, Saxer A, Gallup DG, Olt G. Pre-operative chemoradiation for advanced vulvar cancer: a phase II study of the Gynecologic Oncology Group. *Int Radiat Oncol Biol Phys* 1998;42: 79–85.

20. Scheistroen M, Trope K. Combined bleomycin and irradiation in pre-operative treatment of advanced squamous cell carcinoma of the vulva. *Acta Oncol* 1993;32:657–61.

21. Landoni F, Maneo A, Zanetta G, Colombo A, Nava S, Placa, *et al*. Concurrent pre-operative chemotherapy with 5 fluorouracil and Mitomycin C and radiotherapy (FUMIR) followed by limited surgery in locally advanced recurrent vulvar carcinoma. *Gynecol Oncol* 1996;61:321–7.

22. Lupi G, Raspagliesi F, Zucali R, Fontanelli R, Palanini D, Kenda R, *et al*. Combined pre-operative chemoradiotherapy followed by radical surgery in locally advanced vulvar cancer. A pilot study. *Cancer* 1996;77:1472–8.

23. Berek JS, Heaps JM, Fu YS, Juilard GJ, Hacker NF. Concurrent cisplatin and 5-fluorouracil chemotherapy and radiation therapy for advanced-stage squamous cell carcinoma of the vulva. *Gynecol Oncol* 1991;42:197–201.

24. Eifel PJ, Morris M, Burke TW, Levenback C, Gershenson DM. Prolonged continuous infusion cisplatin and 5-fluorouracil with radiation for locally advanced carcinoma of the vulva. *Gynecol Oncol* 1995;59:51–6.

25. Cunningham MJ, Goyer RP, Gibbons SK, Kredenster DC, Malfetano JH, Keys H. Primary radiation, cisplatin and 5-fluorouracil for advanced squamous carcinoma of the vulva. *Gynecol Oncol* 1997;9:258–61.

26. Koh WJ, Wallace HJ, Greer BE, Cain J, Stelzer KJ, Russell KJ, *et al*. Concurrent radiation therapy and chemotherapy in the treatment of primary squamous cell carcinoma of the vulva. *Cancer* 1995;75:258–61.

27. Russell AH, Mesic JB, Scudder SA, Rosenberg PJ, Smith LH, Kinney WK, *et al*. Synchronous radiation and cytotoxic chemotherapy for locally advanced or recurrent squamous cancer of the vulva. *Gynecol Oncol* 1992;47:14–20.

28. Whalen SA, Slater JD, Wagner RJ, Wang WA, Keeney ED, Hocko JM, *et al*. Concurrent radiation therapy and chemotherapy in the treatment of primary squamous cell carcinoma of the vulva. *Cancer* 1995;75:2289–94.

29. Thomas GM. Improved treatment for cervical cancer: concurrent chemotherapy and radiotherapy. *N Engl J Med* 1999;340:1198–9.

30. Pearcey RG, Mohamed IG, Hanson J. Treatment of high-risk cervical cancer. *N Engl J Med* 1992;341:695–6.

31. Wong LC, Ngan ANY, Cheung ANY, Cheng DKL, Ng TY, *et al*. Chemoradiation and adjuvant chemotherapy in cervical cancer. *J Clin Oncol* 1999;17:2055–60.

32. Roberts KB, Urdaneta N, Vera R, Vera A, Gutierrez, Ott S, *et al*. Interim results of a randomised trial of mitomycin C as an adjunct to radical radiotherapy in the treatment of locally advanced squamous cell carcinoma of the cervix. *Int J Cancer* 2000;90:206–23.

33. Thomas GM, Dembo A, Ackerman I, Franssen E, Balogh J, Fyles A, *et al*. A randomised trial of standard versus partially hyperfractionated radiation with or without concurrent 5-fluorouracil in locally advanced cervical cancer. *Gynecol Oncol* 1998;69:137–45.

34. Fernandez DJ, Vidyasagar MS, Rao S, Rao KK, Shenoy A, Kasturi DP. Synchronous 5-fluorouracil, mitomycin-C, and radiation therapy in the treatment of locally advanced carcinoma of the cervix. Radiotherapy and Oncology: Association of Radiation Oncologists of India 16th Annual Meeting and Roentgen Centenary Celebration, 2–4 February 1995. p. 97–103.

35. Hernandez JRA, Sanchez RH, Canfield FM Orozco AF. Cancer cervico uterino. Etapa clinical III. Tratamiento combinaod de radioterpia y quimioterpia [Cervico- uterino cancer. Clinical stage III. Combined treatment with radiotherapy and chemotherapy]. *Ginecol Obstet Mex* 1991;59:238–42.

36. Hongwei C, Junjie F, Mingzhong L. The effect of randomised trial of hyperthermo radiochemotherapy for carcinoma of the cervix. *Chinese Journal of Oncology* 1997;24:249–51.

37. Lorvidhaya V, Tonusin A, Sukhomya W, Changiwit W, Nimmolrat A. Induction chemotherapy and irradiation in advanced carcinoma of the cervix. *Gan To Kagaku Ryoho* 1995;22 Suppl 3:244–51.

38. Singh P, Dharmalingham SK, Tan MK, Tan CK. Chemotherapy–radiotherapy combination in the treatment of carcinoma of the cervix. *Southeast Asian J Trop Med Public Health* 1985;16:665–8.

39. Tseng C-J, Chang C-T, Lai C-H, Oong Y-K, Hong J-H, Tang SG, *et al.* A randomised trial of concurrent chemoradiotherapy versus radiotherapy in advanced carcinoma of the uterine cervix. *Gynecol Oncol* 1997;66:52–8.

40. Lira Puerto V, De LA, Huerta R, Cortes H, Fernandez A, Silva A, *et al.* Cisplatin (CDDP) plus radiotherapy (RT) vs. radiotherapy alone in locally advanced cervical cancer. Proceedings of the Annual Meeting of the American Society of Clinical Oncology. 1990;9:Abstract 633.

41. Wong LC, Choo YC, Choy D, Sham JST, Ma HK. Long term follow up of potentiation of chemotherapy by cis-platinum in advanced cervical cancer. *Gynecol Oncol* 1989;35:159–63.

42. Symmonds EM. Chemoradiation: The new gold standard for non-surgical treatment of cervical cancer. *Clin Oncol* 2002;14:201–2.

43. Podratz KC, Symmonds RE, Taylor WF. Carcinoma of the vulva: analysis of treatment failures. *Am J Obstet Gynecol* 1982;143:340–51.

44. Homesley HD, Bundy BN, Sedlis A, Yordan E, Berek JS, Jahshan A, *et al.* Assessment of current International Federation of Gynaecology and Obstetrics staging of vulvar carcinoma relative to prognostic factors for survival (a Gynecologic Oncology Group study). *Am J Obstet Gynecol* 1991;164:997–1004.

45. Boronow RC. Combined therapy as an alternative to exenteration for locally advanced vulvo-vaginal cancer: rationale and results. *Cancer* 1982;49:1085–91.

46. Hacker NF, Berek JS, Juillard JF, Lagasse LD. Pre-operative radiation therapy for locally advanced vulvar cancer. *Cancer* 54:2056–61.

47. Perez CA, Grigsby PW, Galakatos A, Swanson R, Camel HM, Kao MS, Lockett MA. Radiation therapy in management of carcinoma of the vulva with emphasis on conservation therapy. *Cancer* 1993;71:3707–16.

48. Thomas GM, Dembo AJ, Bryson SC, Osborne R, DePetrillo AD. Changing concepts in the management of vulvar cancer. *Gynecol Oncol* 1991;42:9–21.

49. Homesley HD, Bundy BN, Sedlis A, Yordan E, Berek JS, Jahshan A, *et al.* Prognostic factors for groin dissection node metastasis in squamous cell carcinoma of the vulva (a Gynecologic Oncology Group study). *Gynecol Oncol* 1993;49:279–83.

50. Cummings B, Keane T, Thomas G, Harward A, Rider W. Results and toxicity of the treatment of anal carcinoma by radiation therapy and chemotherapy. *Cancer* 1989;54:2062–8.

51. UKCCR Anal Cancer Trial Working Party. Epidermoid anal cancer: results from the UKCCR randomised trial of radiotherapy alone versus radiotherapy, 5-fluorouracil, and mitomycin. *Lancet* 1996;348:1049–54.

52. Bendetti Panici P, Greggi S, Scambia G, Salerno G, Mancuso S. Cisplatin, bleomycin and methotrexate pre-operative chemotherapy in locally advanced vulvar carcinoma. *Gynecol Oncol* 1993;50:49–53.

53. Han SC, Kim DH, Kacinski BM. Addition of 5-fluorouracil and mitomycin-C or 5- fluorouracil and cisplatin to radiation therapy decreases the local relapse rate and improves cause specific survival in patients with vulva cancer. Proceedings of 41ˢᵗ American Society for Therapeutic Radiation Oncology. *Int J Radiat Oncol* 1999;45 Supplement:208–9.

Chapter 31

Management of lower genital tract neoplasia III

Discussion

Discussion following Professor Shepherd's paper

Wilkinson: Mr Monaghan, the sentinel lymph node technique in the USA seems to be spearheaded, primarily, by the breast surgeons, while the gynaecological surgeons seem remarkably reluctant to take on sentinel lymph node sampling. Is this something that is coming? I remember when Iverson first presented some of his classic work on lymph node drainage in the pelvis, using similar techniques, this seemed to have a great deal of promise but somehow it never caught on.[1]

Monaghan: The difficulty has been in getting a sure-fire, comfortable system that we knew would work every single time. Although the Vital Blue dyes looked very promising, we rapidly came up against circumstances where they just did not quite work or you could not get a good node. Knowing the disastrous effects of leaving tumour behind in the groin nodes, everyone was very reluctant to rush headlong into using a technique where there was a risk, even though small, of leaving those metastases.

   We are much more comfortable with the Neoprobe device, and it just seems to work. It is interesting, however, that the idea of the sentinel node has to be modified occasionally, because it is sometimes sentinel nodes. In Nicoletta Colombo's series,[2] their biggest number was three different nodes, all very close together, with technetium in them. We have had two nodes sitting right next to each other. You have to be prepared to take a good block around there, re-check that you have all the technetium in the sample you have taken out and that there is nothing left behind. If there is even the suggestion of anything left behind, you have to go back and take a little more out.

   The difference in impact of the surgery is just phenomenal. We are keen not to perform extensive surgery on elderly ladies. The sentinel node actually allows us to extend our surgical treatment into patients where we are really uncomfortable about the impact of big surgery.

Shepherd: We have taken a different approach to the question of nodal dissection. As Mr Monaghan mentioned, we have done a good deal of work using ultrasound for the groins in vulval cancer and we have built up quite a large experience of fine needle aspiration with a view to conservative management in negative cases, and so on.

   With regard to the cervix, we have also been looking more closely at the value of magnetic resonance imaging (MRI). I mentioned iron oxide particles and imaging and, in particular, the Sinerem® (Guerbet, Aulnay-sous-Bois, France) study that we are doing at St Bartholomew's and the Royal Marsden Hospitals, London.. We are looking at the uptake of these particles in patients prospectively when they are undergoing a node dissection and the correlation is extremely good. We have taken this approach to try to avoid node dissection, as one would have to do with sentinel nodes in these patients. We are very happy with the way this particular study is going.

We see it as a way of avoiding surgery altogether in these patients, with very careful imaging assessment. We may have to lend you a machine to get up North, Mr Monaghan, but you have to have the right driver for the machine and that is what is so important. It is the interpretation of that particular assessment. The way forward will be with better imaging, using adjunctive modalities and new techniques.

MacLean: My experience has been as Mr Monaghan describes, but using the plastic surgeons who use this technique for the management of melanomas, particularly when the melanoma may go to almost any set of nodes – axillary, inguinofemoral and so on. Their experience in being able to identify a sentinel node and dissect it makes the management of melanoma much easier. In my limited experience with vulval disease, the hand-held gamma camera enables you to find and dissect the sentinel node; once that is removed the rest of the groin contents should be negative for radio signal. In one patient the sentinel node contained tumour but the rest of the groin nodes were negative. With experience, it will be possible to limit the extent of surgery and thereby reduce the risk of lymphoedema. I can see that this is the way to go.

Shepherd: The difference there, though, is that those patients will have to undergo surgery, and one is trying to dictate therefore the extent of the radicality for melanoma surgery. To a certain extent, that applies to vulval cancers. Cervical cancer is a very different situation and we are making a big decision between either a radical surgical approach or a tailored surgical approach, or chemoradiotherapy. That is the difference. We are trying to reduce the morbidity of combined treatments and we are all striving to do that in our attempts to avoid radical surgery and radical radiotherapy combined, as far as possible.

Monaghan: Professor Shepherd, I was delighted to see that you began by reducing the radicality in the parametrium. Could I try to persuade you to stop doing radical trachelectomies and simply just amputate the cervix? I really do not see the need for that. It is a lovely dissection and, from a surgeon's point of view it is a delight to do, but the dissection of the paracervical tissues is really quite unnecessary in these small tumours.

Shepherd: That will be proved to be correct but we have to get there in a stepwise fashion. We took this approach because we cannot suddenly go to doing just a cone biopsy. The reason why this operation has not caught on in America is quite obvious, because they are terrified of the first failure and therefore the lawsuit. We are able to show, however, that by looking at these recurrences (and the pattern of our recurrences mirrors the pattern that has occurred in Canada and in France) we will come to the stage where we will be able to do less in the way of parametrial resection.

You must understand, nevertheless, that to obtain ethical committee approval, let alone the agreement of our colleagues, it has to be stepwise. It is not so long ago that I stood up in the College here and was accused, by a Fellow of this College, of being tantamount to being a murderer for not carrying out ultraradical surgery in a small volume cancer. We have to convince the population at large in a stepwise fashion, but I agree that we will get there, and we will select patients out.

Monaghan: The important data that you really must start to include are the survival data. What you have concentrated on a great deal, obviously, is the fertility problem and the need to generate babies. I was just doing some crude mathematics and your recurrence rates are extraordinarily low and your survivals are extremely high, as you would expect in small tumours. It is important to start including survival data, since you now have a great deal of long-term review, just to show where this very limited surgery fits in to the spectrum of care.

Shafi: I would like to elaborate on that. I was going to ask, is radical trachelectomy too radical, particularly taking into account the imaging modalities that we have now in being able to assess patients far better than we have traditionally been able to do, with very good MRI? Also, there is the potential use of hysteroscopy too, at the time of surgery, to assess whether there is any endocervical involvement of disease too.

If a large part of the canal is involved, or if the magnetic resonance imaging (MRI) shows a considerable amount of disease there, then we should not really be doing a trachelectomy in those patients. For that subset of patients who are suitable for a radical trachelectomy, I really do agree that this is too radical a procedure. You can tailor your surgery to take away far less of the tissue, going back again to Halsted's principles of good, clear margins.

Shepherd: Yes, we are much more comfortable now with the MRI. Certainly, this group of 60-odd that we have has been in conjunction with the development of MRI. MRI is better at staging than I am, and I have to admit that, whether by formal staging, even though we often carry it out. MRI is also better at measuring the length of the canal, right up to the isthmus, because we believe firmly that we should take that tissue out for the adenocarcinomas, although there is now a place for conserving possibly an upper centimetre or so of the endocervix for squamous cell lesion at the lower end. It is far better at measuring that than we are. We have hysteroscoped all these patients and I have to say that MRI is better at it than I am.

Singer: At the last Study Group 20 years ago, we agonised about microinvasive carcinoma. Indeed, the impetus for the review of the staging came from here.[3]

Where do we go as far as recommendations are concerned, in respect of microinvasive Ia1 and Ia2. First of all there is the role, if there is a role, of MRI here – and then where do we go? Is a cone, a radical cone, good enough? Is it a trachelectomy, plus or minus lymphadenectomy? What will the recommendations be? I ask this because stage Ia1 is still in the preserve of the cancer unit. The 'experienced gynaecologist' does not have to send on to the cancer centre, but it is when it is a Ib1 that he will refer it on. Many of them will be looking for recommendations from here.

Monaghan: The recommendation that we are making currently for the units is that the primary surgery will be performed in the unit, which is essentially to make a diagnosis. What we want is for all pathology to be reviewed in the centre.

Singer: Certainly Ia2.

Monaghan: Ia1; with all invasive cancers now, we are saying they should refer the lot as a specimen. This has been a development of the guidelines that we wrote three or four years ago, when we felt that the management of the Ia1 cases would be entirely within the unit. We are now finding that the pathologists in the unit often feel more comfortable if they can have central review and central measurement, and then we can confirm management. As far as Ia1 is concerned, we are looking at a zero risk of nodal metastases, so we are comfortable with a cone biopsy with a loop cone and, as long as the margins are free, we can leave it. If the margins are not free, you have an obligation to repeat the cone and you must do another one. Although we have published on cytological review of these, we are much more comfortable in repeating the cones with an incomplete margin.

Ia2 presents us with problems, because we have a node metastasis rate of somewhere between three and five percent – some people make it higher, others make it lower, but the average is around three to five per cent. In these cases we have an obligation to use a node assessment method. This may be sophisticated MRI or, in our hands, it would be a laparoscopic surgical approach to the lymph nodes while, in other places, they may well be using sentinel node technology. Assessment of the nodes in those cases is mandatory.

As far as the central disease is concerned, we are now much more comfortable with very limited surgery for Ia2s. The cone biopsy with a margin is adequate; you will cure the patients.

Singer: With a lymphadenectomy?

Monaghan: With a lymphadenectomy. As long as you have a reasonable margin, you do not need to do much more. For the older patient, a simple hysterectomy may be the appropriate procedure. For the younger patient, you have fertility-sparing opportunities. It is interesting that Professor Shepherd says that you have only one microinvasive tumour in your radical trachelectomy, which is absolutely correct. We should not be doing radical trachelectomies for Ia2 cases. With the early Ib1 cases, we have opportunities for very limited central surgery, again with lymphadenectomy, or lymph node assessment. We are becoming much more conservative.

There are two areas in which we have problems. First, what is the position, frequency and importance of the paracervical node? At first, Professor Eric Burghardt produced his results many years ago, showing parametrial/paracervical nodes spreading right the way across the parametrium. These were almost certainly lymphatic aggregates, they were not nodes. He selected sections where he purported to show these things but I think this has been demonstrated not to be correct. However, you will have 1–3% of patients with paracervical nodes. How do we assess that node? Can your MRI do it? This is where the radical trachelectomy is useful because, if you have paracervical nodes, you will automatically identify them and take them out, because that is where you are dissecting. With that little caveat of the paracervical node, which can be a problem, and be a first staging post, I would be very conservative with central disease management. Professor Shepherd, how do you feel?

Shepherd: Yes, that is correct. In answer to your question about the FIGO staging and recommendations, I can certainly remember that you began the great debate that then occurred and continued from the east and the west side of the USA and affected the FIGO reclassification and nomenclature exactly.

Tidy: You were talking about changing radicality and you have focused on the known poor prognostic factors and perhaps new molecular ones. Is there any evidence that making your surgery any more radical with poor prognostic factors makes any difference? Or should they be the people who are put into adjuvant trials in terms of either gene therapy, vaccination or chemotherapy?

Shepherd: That is absolutely right. What we are looking at here is the change in approach of avoiding surgery altogether. It is these new methods that will avoid that, because these patients will have to have some form of chemoradiotherapy at the moment and they would be the ideal patients to be included in some prospective study, having as adjunctive therapy either gene therapy or vaccination. I foresee that we will be using prognostic factors to reduce the indication for surgery in many patients, in fact. Having said that, there will be a significant number of patients. At the other end of the spectrum, the elderly form a group of patients who should be having surgery and not chemoradiotherapy, because that is pretty morbid for elderly patients. The previous assumption that young, fit women have surgery while older women should have radiotherapy is now no longer correct. The morbidity in the older age group for many of these women is not small and they should be having short, sharp operations, tailored, depending on their prognostic factors, rather than suffering from the long-term consequences, as opposed to complications, of radiotherapy. The emphasis for the place of surgery and the selection of surgery is changing.

Discussions following Mr Monaghan's paper

Cruickshank: You are right in that micrometastasis is a significant prognostic factor for recurrence. Did any of the imaging techniques detect micrometastasis or are the sentinel nodes tested for micrometastasis.

Monaghan: In one of the studies in the Netherlands, which Anka Ansinck is coordinating,[3] they are using cytokeratin assessment of nodes and doing this as part of that study. We have the technology to do this, but the difficulty is in just getting the pathologists up and running to do this.

Our nervousness with sentinel nodes is in not really understanding the real importance of micrometastases in the generality of inguinal nodes. If you go back to where we were in the 1940s and 1950s and do just radical vulvectomies, you have a 40–45% overall survival rate for cancer of the vulva. If you do groin node dissections, that figure rises to about 75%. What we do not understand is why that makes such a difference when the difference is not actually reflected in the number of positive nodes that you pick up. It must be micrometastases that you are identifying or removing with your nodes.

Our nervousness with sentinel nodes comes from whether we can be absolutely sure, by saying that one or two nodes are negative, that there is nothing else anywhere else. The real difficulty is that, if there are groin metastases, the patients die, basically. They are extraordinarily difficult to treat. It is a major leap. I have the same nervousness that Professor Shepherd has with moving down from radical trachelectomy. We must not compromise cure in a move towards conservativism. This is difficult. Centralising the services will, however, help enormously by stopping the occasionalists and pulling the work together, getting the high-quality pathologist as part of your teams, where you can explore these issues on a regular basis. In the longer term, this will improve the situation. But then again, I have been wedded to centralisation for 28 years.

Herrington: There is a problem with the definition of micrometastasis because the presence of cytokeratin-positive or epithelial cells in a lymph node does not equal metastasis. They could simply be passing through and be destined to die off. We should therefore be cautious about using ancillary molecular or immunohistochemical techniques to pick these things up when we do not actually know what they mean. You have demonstrated quite nicely that extranodal invasion, or extracapsular rupture in a lymph node, is a clear prognostic indicator, but that is a metastasis that has demonstrated its ability to infiltrate beyond the node, so that you have a clear biological indicator there. These studies that are trying to look at cytokeratins are really trying to run before they can walk.

Monaghan: That is absolutely right. The corollary at the other end is that the tiny peripheral sinus embolus has the same prognosis as a node-negative patient. It is a matter of knowing how the thing will perform. Nowhere in cancer do we have very good measures of tumour cell performance. We do not know which will actually implant, which will grow and which will die off. We know that there are millions of cancer cells wandering around the body and virtually all of them just disappear.

Tidy: As a general comment for everyone interested in vulval disease, I wonder whether it is the time to look at a different staging strategy, because the disease is changing. We are seeing younger women coming through, with small foci of invasion, which may be 2 mm deep, but only 2 mm wide. We have the concept of volume disease in the cervix, so is it not time to look at volume in the vulva as a prognostic marker? Do you do a groin node dissection on a patient with a 2 mm by 2 mm lesion? Or do you not, and just hope that they have good prognostic disease? I do not think there are any volume data out there in vulval disease, so far as I am aware.

Wilkinson: That is a very good issue. I looked at that a number of years ago in a paper that I published in the *International Journal of Gynaecological Pathology.*[5] It appears that with tumour volume in the vulva, the threshold for node metastases is lower than in the cervix. In the cervix, it is probably around 500 cubic millimetres or less, while in the vulva it is probably around 300 cubic millimetres maximum. This needs to be looked at, because stage I encompasses that group. We are all agreed that the VIN component should not be included in the measurement of the tumour, so when you look at those tumours they are often very small. On the other hand, they are often multifoci in a single VIN lesion, just like in CIN lesions where you will see multiple foci of invasion sometimes.

Discussion following Dr Adams' paper

Adams: Could I just make a comment, following what Professor Shepherd said about the elderly patient. I find this really quite difficult because, if you have a 70- or 80-year-old lady, should you give her chemoradiation? We try not to be ageist, but there is no doubt that elderly patients do not tolerate their treatment as well. They tend to run into problems with bone marrow suppression, so that you end up prolonging the treatment. Sometimes, I feel that we would be better off treating these patients surgically, if they are operable but I am not quite sure which ones are the best to treat in this setting.

Shepherd: Our experience, when we looked at that study, and published it seven or eight years ago, and used this in 36 patients with advanced vulval cancer, aiming to avoid exenteration and avoid a stoma, the elderly patients tolerated this badly.[6] Their brisk desquamation of the perineum was pretty morbid and I have to say that many of these women stayed in hospital for four to six weeks. We only had one patient who I had to divert to have a colostomy because of a very brisk reaction. Having said that, if they got through it, our data showed a 36% complete response rate and that still holds out now. We are still seeing patients coming back to the clinic who have had that treatment and have done well. However, when the morbidity is there, it is pretty awful and they hate it. So, if it is surgically resectable, we should cut it out.

Adams: I am sorry, but I meant that in the context of cervical cancer. Obviously, on vulval cancer I would agree with you entirely. However, where we are increasingly using chemoradiotherapy as a standard treatment in groups of cervical cancer patients, it is difficult to know which ones should have just straight radiation or perhaps go to surgery. Age is not the factor *per se*, but this is a difficult group to assess.

Monaghan: Dr Adams, you have talked about exenteration. To get things into perspective, in my personal series of vulval cases which, before I retired stood at 711,

I did three exenterations, that is all. I am not sure, therefore, how many I would have avoided by using chemoradiation. This is a very surgically orientated series and leaves big holes, which we fill in. The patients do well. For the old ladies, I can remember that the average age in this series was 69 years, so this is not a young person's disease by and large, even though we have a lot of young people, a large number are very elderly. A 98-year-old, three years afterwards, wrote to me to say that she was bored with coming to the follow-up clinics and refused to come back again at 101 years, so I let her off.

Remember, we are also doing surgery under what is effectively local anaesthetic, because we are using spinals and epidurals. These patients are wide awake while you are operating on them and their recovery is amazingly quick. As Professor Shepherd says, the instant relief of symptomatology really is a great benefit. The downside to chemoradiation, and radiation prior to that, is the uncertainty. Although all the series, from Dick Boronow's series[7] onwards, give good long-term clearance, you cannot pick them. To have one-third of your patients with a good response and a long-term survival, whereas with surgery you can have 100% with a good response, leaves you in rather a dilemma.

Shafi: Just to highlight the situation with chemoradiotherapy coming in for locally advanced disease and our surgery for early stage disease becoming less and less radical, what do we do with that cohort of patients in whom we have traditionally performed radical hysterectomy? Some of these patients are ending up with a radical hysterectomy and, if they are node-positive, moving on to chemoradiotherapy. You are then having three radical treatments in that one individual patient. My concern is that the morbidity associated with that is not just an additive, but it is multiplicative, and they end up with a great deal of morbidity.

Should we in fact be moving to a phase where we conserve either cervical amputation or trachelectomy for the early lesions, but for those lesions where you are considering a radical procedure, they should actually initially assess the nodes either laparoscopically or extra-peritoneally? Those patients who are node-positive should then proceed to chemoradiotherapy without the surgery, because surgery will not add anything to the outcome for that group of patients.

Adams: That is certainly an interesting approach. We are always reluctant to combine the two radical treatments because, inevitably, there is an increased morbidity, as you have said. Quite honestly, I think that is an interesting approach. We are probably talking about a small group of Ib1 cases, with perhaps 3 cm of tumour, and you do a nodal assessment. If that is feasible, then I would welcome it.

Shepherd: The preoperative assessment of the nodes and the bulk of the tumour, as we are all leaning towards, is absolutely vital. As an aside, I would say that one positive node at a radical hysterectomy would not necessarily mean that these patients needed to have radiotherapy, and especially not chemoradiotherapy. We would look at that node very carefully if it was totally replaced, and if there was extracapsular spread and so on. However, with just one node, which may be just a small focus, we would sit with that.

If we had patients who we found at a radical hysterectomy had positive nodes unexpectedly, then the big debate would be whether we should continue with that surgery or not, should we abandon the surgery? In our department, where there are four of us, it is interesting that we are split so that two of us will continue with the radical surgery and take the bulky nodes out and do the resection, while the other two will not. Needless to say, it is the senior two who will carry on, do it and remove the nodes and then give the patient radiotherapy or chemoradiotherapy, while the younger two, who we have trained, have decided not to follow those lines.

There is evidence to show that removing bulky nodes is of benefit. I must say that this is an area (whether you take the uterus out or not, and I still believe that we should remove the primary tumour under those circumstances) where there may be a place in the future for removing bulky nodes before you irradiate them in a simple debulking sort of way.

Shafi: It is not the bulky nodes situation that I am concerned about, but it is all patients with Stage Ib1 tumours who we consider for radical surgery, radical hysterectomy. About 15% of those will have pelvic disease and it is a question of picking out those 15% and trying to limit your morbidity for those patients. Should we assess all of these patients prior to their radical hysterectomy, with the use of, say, laparoscopic lymphadenectomy? If they are node-positive, your surgery will not add anything to their management and they should be going on the chemoradiotherapy.

Shepherd: The answer is yes. We are trying to avoid unnecessary lymphadenectomy in the other 85%, because we over-treat a huge number of patients, either by node dissection or by parametrectomy. What we must try to do (and we are looking at the scientists) is to find ways of doing that in ways which, at the moment, are just not available. We are getting there. As we have said, we are doing better imaging, and the other approach is laparoscopic surgery. We are taking a non-surgical approach, because I want to avoid the morbidity of surgery.

Monaghan: We have actually come through something similar in the past. In the early 1980s I performed about 160 paraortic node dissections extraperitoneally, in the same way that the urologists approach the ureter, in order to define when we needed to do para-aortic node dissections. We were able to say very clearly where we had certain volumes of tumour that, below that, there was absolutely zero risk of paraortic node dissection and, as a consequence, para-aortic node dissection was taken out. This was at the time when a great deal of discussion was going on about removing the nodes, stop, irradiate the patient. I agree with Professor Shepherd that that completely prohibited. You are getting the worst of all worlds because you are operating on the patient and you are irradiating them, and you are doing some ineffectively, and you are leaving tumour behind.

We need better assessment. As you say, 1% of stage Ib1 tumours will be node-positive. Not all of those will need adjunctive radiotherapy. If we can assess them better, and I do not have quite the love affair with scanning that Professor Shepherd has, but whatever method we use, if we can categorise those patients before we get to surgery, we will be doing them a favour. The real crunch is not the 15% with the positive nodes, but the 80-odd percent with the negative nodes – and can we really leave those nodes behind? That is what we are trying to do with the vulva, and that is what we are trying to do with the breast. This would have a really big impact: not worrying about how radical you are going to be, but working out how conservative you can be in the other direction. That would be a step in the right direction.

Deery: We have not really discussed glandular disease at all in the cervix. Is there a strategically different approach to early stages of glandular disease, surgically and so forth?

Shepherd: We have briefly mentioned this. As far as fertility-sparing surgery is concerned, we started by excluding, with our ethical committee's approval, glandular tumours. I now think that, as far as removing the whole cervix is concerned, it is more appropriate for glandular tumours because it takes care of the worry about the skip lesions and the upper end of the endocervical canal. As long as we can image and know that the tumour is confined to the endocervix, and does not involve the lower segment of the uterus and has expanded and extended up there, then as long as you remove the whole of the cervix, whether or not by radical trachelectomy, the advantage of radical trachelectomy under these circumstances is that you know that you are removing the whole of the cervix. With a cone biopsy you are not removing the whole of the cervix, however much you think you are doing a long, thin, radical cone, you are not removing the whole cervix. There is a place for it in the glandular tumours. We can be more conservative with the squamous tumours if we can image and know where that primary cancer has been situated. So yes, it is as applicable, if not more so.

Jones: My most satisfied vulval cancer patient was a very young woman with a stage Ib cancer of the clitoris. She refused to have surgery but had curative radiotherapy, so there is a role for radiotherapy in specific circumstances. She absolutely refused surgery but opted for radiotherapy, and she was cured.

References

1.   Iversen T, Aas M. Lymph drainage from the vulva. *Gynecol Oncol* 1983;16:179–89.
2.   Colombo N. Personal communication.
3.   Jordan JA, Sharp F, Singer A, editors. *Pre-clinical Neoplasia of the Cervix. Proceedings of the Ninth RCOG Study Group*. London: RCOG Press; 1981.
4.   Ansinck A. Personal communication.
5.   Wilkinson EJ, Rico JM, Pierson KK. Microinvasive carcinoma of the vulva. *Int J Gynecol Pathol* 1982;1:29–39.
6.   Sebag-Montefiore DJ, McLean C, Arnott SJ, Blake P, Van Dam P, Hudson CN, *et al*. Treatment of advanced carcinoma of the vulva with chemoradiation – can exenterative surgery be avoided? *Int J Gynecol Cancer* 1994;4:150–5.
7.   Boronow RC, Hickman BT, Reagan MT, Smith RA, Steadham RE. Combined therapy as an alternative to exenteration for locally advanced vulvovaginal cancer. II. Results, complications, and dosimetric and surgical considerations. *Am J Clin Oncol* 1987;10:171–81.

SECTION 8

MANAGEMENT OF LOWER GENITAL TRACT NEOPLASIA IV

Chapter 32

Management of vaginal intraepithelial neoplasia and invasive vaginal cancer

Pat Soutter

Introduction

This chapter describes the management of these rare conditions. The squamous intraepithelial neoplasias are reported to have an incidence of about 0.2 per 100 000 woman years[1] while the rate for all invasive tumours is about 0.7 per 100 000.[2] A fuller description of the epidemiology, aetiology and pathology may be found in more general textbooks of gynaecology.

Vaginal intraepithelial neoplasia

Vaginal intraepithelial neoplasia (VAIN) is divided into grades 1–3. Vaginal epithelium does not normally have crypts so the epithelial abnormality remains superficial until invasion occurs. The exception to this follows surgery (usually hysterectomy) when abnormal epithelium can be buried below the suture line or in suture tracks. In 67% of cases, VAIN is a vaginal extension of CIN.[3] More than 78% of cases involve the upper vagina and 61% are multifocal.[1]

In most cases VAIN is diagnosed colposcopically during the investigation of an abnormal smear. However, it may not be recognised until after a hysterectomy has been performed. When this happens, abnormal epithelium is likely to be buried behind the sutures used to close the vault. Consequently, a portion of the lesion will remain invisible and non-evaluable. In such cases, 28% will prove to have unexpected invasive disease.[4] Untreated or inadequately treated VAIN may progress to frank invasive cancer.[5,6]

Colposcopy of the vagina

Colposcopy of the vagina is more difficult than the cervix, partly because of the greater area of epithelium to be examined, partly because the surface of the vaginal epithelium is irregular and partly because it is difficult to view the vaginal walls at right angles. The blades of the speculum will obscure the view of the vagina unless rotated or partly withdrawn. If the patient has had a hysterectomy it is difficult to see into the angles of the vagina and impossible to visualise epithelium that lies above the suture line or vaginal adhesions. The colposcopic features of VAIN are similar to those of CIN except that mosaic is seen less often.

Management

Uterus in situ

In many cases, what appears to be an area of VAIN spreading off the cervix on to the adjacent vaginal walls is no more than a congenital transformation zone. Such a lesion does not require treatment. Multiple biopsies are required to determine the diagnosis and are best taken under general anaesthesia. This also allows a better view of the vaginal epithelium. The temptation to treat these lesions under the same anaesthetic without waiting for the histology should be resisted.

The histology must be reported by a pathologist with experience in this field because the implications of treatment are considerable for some of the women. If the pathology confirms VAIN2–3, these lesions may be treated with superficial ablation or excision. In practice, excision is only appropriate for sexually active women who still have a uterus *in situ* if the lesion is small or confined to the vaginal skin adjacent to the cervix.

Post-hysterectomy

Following hysterectomy, women should not be treated by ablative therapy because of the risk of disease being buried behind the suture line at the vault and the high risk of invasion.[4] A possible exception is the unusual case where the lesion is well away from the suture line. In the author's experience, a vaginal colpectomy allows a satisfactory excision with less morbidity and a more rapid recovery than an abdominal operation. Radiotherapy is a highly effective alternative.

Treatment modalities

The management of VAIN after hysterectomy in a young woman is likely to be surgical. If the lesion is extensive, prior laser therapy may be helpful in reducing the extent of disease. In older patients with associated medical conditions that increase the risks of anaesthesia and surgery, and especially when access is difficult, surgery offers few additional benefits but carries a potential for greater morbidity. Radiotherapy is therefore likely to be the treatment of choice. Whatever the circumstances it would be sensible for such patients to be evaluated and treated by those with experience of this unusual but troublesome condition.

5-fluorouracil

In the only controlled trial of this cytotoxic drug in this condition, 5-fluorouracil was worse than placebo in the treatment of vaginal HPV.[7] Early reports of treatment of VAIN with this agent were encouraging with only 20% recurrence rates.[8] However, the length of follow up was short. More recent studies describe recurrence rates of 59%.[1] This cannot be recommended.

Carbon dioxide laser

Excellent results have been reported by some authors, with 10–20% recurrence rates.[9–11] However, many of the women in these series required several treatments and the follow up was often quite short. Failure rates of 38–57% have been reported by others[1,5,12,13] and reports of invasive disease in post-hysterectomy patients treated with the laser illustrates the dangers of overlooking disease buried above the suture line.[5] Provided invasive disease has been excluded, laser vaporisation is a satisfactory way of treating

VAIN in women who have not undergone previous surgery. Thus, although the laser may be useful in reducing the size of a large lesion or in treating women who have not had a hysterectomy and who have multifocal disease, it should not be used as the sole method of treatment in VAIN of the vaginal vault following hysterectomy.

Partial or total vaginectomy

Partial colpectomy is the longest established treatment. The vaginal route is preferred because it is usually easier with less morbidity but it can prove to be extremely taxing in patients with a narrow introitus and no laxity of the vaginal vault. Surgery is the only effective option available to patients previously treated with radiotherapy and is the treatment of choice for women who are post-hysterectomy. The reported recurrence rate is 0–5%.[1,4,12]

Where the lesion involves a large area of the vagina there may be a place for laser vaporisation to reduce the size of the lesion. The entire lesion is vaporised under general anaesthesia and, some months later when the effect of the laser treatment can be assessed, the vault of the vagina is excised. When this approach is unsuccessful and in older patients, total vaginectomy or radiotherapy is required.

Radiotherapy

There can be no doubt that intracavitary radiotherapy is a highly effective treatment for VAIN.[14,15] The two major concerns about this form of therapy are the possibility of radiation-induced cancer and the effects it may have upon coital function. Radiation-induced second cancer in the vaginal vault may occur but it is probably an extraordinarily rare event.[16,17] Brachytherapy to the vault of the vagina is unlikely to cause major coital problems if the patient and her spouse are encouraged to resume normal sexual relations as soon as possible.[15] Where the area of disease is more extensive, no method of therapy is likely to be free of the risk of inducing sexual dysfunction.

Cancer of the vagina

The great majority (92%) of primary vaginal cancers are squamous. Clear-cell adenocarcinomas, malignant melanomas, embryonal rhabdomyosarcomas and endodermal sinus tumours are the most common of the small number of other tumours seen rarely in the vagina. These are not discussed here.

There is little firm evidence of aetiological agents. The irritation caused by procidentia and vaginal pessaries has been suggested but this is an infrequent association. A field effect in the lower genital tract has been suggested by the observation of multicentric neoplasia involving cervix, vagina and vulva and both immunosuppression and infection with HPV have been suggested.

The aetiological role of radiotherapy is hard to determine but is no longer simply a theoretical question in view of the proposal that preinvasive disease of the vaginal vault after hysterectomy should be treated by radiotherapy.[15] Three small case series have raised a concern that women less than 40 years old, treated with radiotherapy for cervical cancer, may be at a high risk of subsequently developing vaginal cancer 10–40 years later.[16,17] However, two large studies with 3239 and 25 995 women, respectively, showed no evidence that vaginal cancer is induced by radiotherapy.[18,19]

For some time, the prevalence of clear-cell adenocarcinoma of the vagina was

Table 31.1. FIGO Staging of vaginal cancers

Stage	Description
I	Carcinoma is limited to the vaginal wall
II	Carcinoma has involved the subvaginal tissue but has not extended to the pelvic wall
III	Carcinoma has extended to the pelvic wall
IVa	Carcinoma invades the bladder or rectal mucosa or has spread by direct extension beyond the true pelvis or any combination of these
IVb	Spread to distant organs beyond the true pelvis

thought to be increased by intrauterine exposure to diethylstilboestrol. With the accrual of more information the risks now seem to be low and to lie between 0.1 and 1.0 per 1000.[20,21]

Natural history

Although the upper vagina is the most common site for invasive disease, about 25–30% is confined to the lower vagina, usually the anterior wall.[22–24] Squamous vaginal cancer spreads initially by local invasion. Lymphatic spread occurs by tumour embolisation to the pelvic nodes from the upper vagina and to both pelvic and inguinal nodes from the lower vagina.[23] Haematogenous spread is unusual.

Clinical staging

The FIGO clinical staging is shown in Table 31.1.

Diagnosis and assessment

Before making a diagnosis of primary vaginal cancer, the following criteria must be satisfied:

- the primary site of growth must be in the vagina
- the uterine cervix must not be involved
- there must be no clinical evidence that the vaginal tumour is metastatic disease.[25]

The most common presenting symptom is vaginal bleeding (53–65%), with vaginal discharge (11–16%) and pelvic pain (4–11%) being less common. The rate of detection of asymptomatic cancer with vaginal cytology varies greatly (10–42%) depending on the patient population studied. Most of the disease thus detected is at an early stage.

A careful examination under anaesthesia is the most important part of the pretreatment assessment of invasive cancer of the vagina. Colposcopy will identify coexisting VAIN and help to determine the extent of a small lesion. A combined vaginal and rectal examination will help to detect extravaginal spread. Cystoscopy and proctosigmoidoscopy are indicated if anterior or posterior spread is suspected. A generous, full-thickness biopsy is essential for adequate histological evaluation. A chest X-ray and an intravenous pyelogram are the only radiological investigations required routinely. Magnetic resonance imaging using an intravaginal receiver coil is undoubtedly the most accurate way to visualise the size and extent of the lesion.

Treatment

The treatment of vaginal cancer requires considerable individualisation. The choice of appropriate treatment depends upon the stage of disease, the volume of the tumour, the woman's general health and her age.[26] Many of these women are elderly and frail and in many centres more than half are treated with radiotherapy. However, surgery gives excellent results in stage I and small volume stage II disease.[26] Larger volume tumours and tumours in the medically compromised are often better managed by radiotherapy. Bulky stage II tumours and stage III–IV tumours may be treated by radiotherapy or chemoradiotherapy. Women with stage IVa disease that is limited to the central pelvis and without evidence of metastases should be considered for exenteration.

Surgery

A stage I or small volume stage II lesion in the upper vagina can be adequately treated by radical hysterectomy (if the uterus is still present), radical vaginectomy and pelvic lymphadenectomy.[26] If the tumour is located in the lower vagina and close to the introitus, a relatively narrow vulvectomy will often be required to achieve local clearance. In addition, groin node dissection should be performed rather than the pelvic lymphadenectomy. This approach gives five-year survival rates of 77–91%. Exenteration is required for more advanced lesions and carries the problems of stomata. Surgery may be used successfully in women who have had prior pelvic radiotherapy.[16]

Radiotherapy

Early cases, stage I–IIa, may be treated entirely with interstitial therapy with iridium-192. This is afterloaded into three concentric rings of stainless-steel guide needles located by a specially designed template.[27] The objective is to achieve a tumour dose of 70–80 Gy in two fractions, each over 72 hours, two weeks apart. This approach seems to give better results than intravaginal radiotherapy.[28] Cases with parametrial involvement receive teletherapy to the pelvis as for carcinoma of the cervix, with a tumour dose of 45 Gy followed by interstitial or intracavitary therapy to a total dose of 70–75 Gy. The field may be extended to include the groins if the tumour involves the lower half of the vagina.

As with the treatment of vulval carcinoma, the severe complications of radiation have become much less common as a result of modern treatment methods and more sophisticated linear accelerators. Vaginal stenosis may occur and is more likely when advanced tumours are treated.[29] There has been a reduction in the instance of vaginal stenosis from 25–32% to 10–15%, although it is obviously a problem for sexually active patients. Mucosal ulceration, either immediate or delayed, can be a distressing complication but conservative therapy, sometimes aided by grafts, is usually effective. Approximately 10% of patients develop a fistula or other serious complication.[22,24,28,29] and these are almost invariably associated with teletherapy for advanced disease. Vesicovaginal and rectovaginal fistulae and small bowel complications are especially frequent if previously irradiated patients are treated with radiotherapy.

The five-year survival figures described range widely from 42% to 91% for stage I disease and from 2% to 70% for stage II.[26] This is partly because many series report on small numbers of women treated with a variety of techniques over a long period of time. The results of a review of data published between 1980 and 2000 are shown in Table 31.2.

Table 31.2 Vaginal cancer five-year survival rates

Stage	Primary radiotherapy (%)	Primary surgery (%)
I	68	77
II	48	52
III	34	44
IV	19	14

Conclusions

Invasive vaginal cancer is a rare tumour more often seen in association with an antecedent cervical malignancy. Radiotherapy is the main treatment method for women with larger tumours but surgery gives excellent results in appropriately selected patients. Individualisation of treatment regimens and multidisciplinary care is essential for the best results.

References

1. Dodge JA, Eltabbakh GH, Mount SL, Walker RP, Morgan A. Clinical features and risk of recurrence among patients with vaginal intraepithelial neoplasia. *Gynecol Oncol* 2001;83:363–9.
2. National Statistics. *Cancer Statistics Registrations in 1995–97.* MB1 No. 28. London: HMSO; 2001.
3. Nwambeni N J, Monaghan JM. Vaginal epithelial abnormalities in patients with CIN: clinical and pathological features and management. *Br J Obstet Gynaecol* 1991;98:25–9.
4. Ireland D, Monaghan JM. The management of the patient with abnormal vaginal vault cytology following hysterectomy. *Br J Obstet Gynaecol* 1988;95:973–5.
5. Woodman CBJ, Jordan JA, Wade-Evans T. The management of vaginal intraepithelial neoplasia after hysterectomy. *Br J Obstet Gynaecol* 1984;91:707–11.
6. Aho M, Vesterinen E, Meyer B, Purola E, Paavonen J. Natural history of vaginal intraepithelial neoplasia. *Cancer* 1991;68:195–7.
7. Holmes MM, Weaver SH 2nd, Vermillion ST. A randomized, double-blind, placebo-controlled trial of 5-fluorouracil for the treatment of cervicovaginal human papillomavirus. *Obstet Gynecol* 1999;7:186–9.
8. Petrilli ES, Townsend DE, Morrow CP, Nakao CY. Vaginal intraepithelial neoplasia: biological aspects and treatment with topical 5-fluorouracil and the carbon dioxide laser. *Am J Obstet Gynecol* 1980;138:321–8.
9. Townsend DE, Levine RU, Crum CP, Richart RM. Treatment of vaginal carcinoma *in situ* with the carbon dioxide laser. *Am J Obstet Gynecol* 1982;143:565–8.
10. Jobson VW, Homesley HD. Treatment of vaginal intraepithelial neoplasia with the carbon dioxide laser. *Obstet Gynecol* 1983;62:90–3.
11. Campagnutta E, Parin A, De Piero G, Giorda G, Gallo A, Scarabelli C. Treatment of vaginal intraepithelial neoplasia (VAIN) with the carbon dioxide laser. *Clin Exp Obstet Gynecol* 1999;26:127–30.
12. Lenehan PM, Meffe F, Lickrish GM. Vaginal intraepithelial neoplasia: biologic aspects and management. *Obstet Gynecol* 1986;68:333–7.
13. Hoffman MS, Roberts WS, LaPolla J, Fiorica JP, Cavanagh D. Laser vaporization of grade 3 vaginal intraepithelial neoplasia. *Am J Obstet Gynecol* 1991;165:1342–4.
14. Hernandez-Linares W, Puthawala A, Nolan JF, Jernstrom PH, Morrow CP. Carcinoma *in situ* of the vagina: past and present management *Obstet Gynecol* 1980;56:356–60.
15. Woodman CBJ, Mould JJ, Jordan JA. Radiotherapy in the management of vaginal intraepithelial neoplasia after hysterectomy. *Br J Obstet Gynaecol* 1988;95:976–9.
16. Barrie JR, Brunschwig A. Late second cancers of the cervix after apparent successful initial radiation therapy. *Am J Roentgenol Ther Nucl Med* 1970;109:109–12.
17. Futoran RJ, Nolan JF. Stage I carcinoma of the uterine cervix in patients under 40 years of age. *Am J Obstet Gynecol* 1976;125:790–7.
18. Choo YC, Anderson DG. Neoplasms of the vagina following cervical carcinoma. *Gynecol Oncol* 1982;14:125–32.

19.   Boice JD Jr, Day NE, Andersen A, Brinton LA, Brown R, Choi NW, *et al.* Second cancers following treatment for cervical cancer. An international collaboration among cancer registries. *J Natl Cancer Inst* 1985;74:955–5.
20.   Coppleson M. The DES story. *Med J Aust* 1984;141:487–9.
21.   Herbst AL. Behavior of estrogen-associated female genital tract cancer and its relation to neoplasia following intrauterine exposure to diethylstilbestrol (DES). *Gynecol Oncol* 2000;76:147–56.
22.   Pride GL, Schultz AE, Chuprevich TW, Buchler DA. Primary invasive squamous carcinoma of the vagina. *Obstet Gynecol* 1979;53:218–25.
23.   Monaghan JM. Management of vaginal carcinoma. In: Shepherd JH, Monaghan JM, editors. *Clinical Gynaecological Oncology*. London: Blackwell; 1985. p. 154–66.
24.   Gallup DG, Talledo OE, Shah KJ, Hayes C. Invasive squamous cell carcinoma of the vagina: a 14-year study. *Obstet Gynecol* 1987;69:782–5.
25.   Beller U, Sideri M, Maisonneuve P, Benedet JL, Heintz APM, Ngan HYS, *et al.* Carcinoma of the vagina. 24th Annual Report of the Results of Treatment in Gynaecological Cancer. *J Epidemiol Biostat* 2001;6:141–52.
26.   Tjalma WAA, Monaghan JM, de Barros Lopes A, Naik R, Nordin AJ, Weyler JJ. The role of surgery in invasive squamous carcinoma of the vagina. *Gynecol Oncol* 2001;81:360–5.
27.   Branson AN, Dunn P, Kam KC, Lambert HE. A device for interstitial therapy of low pelvic tumours – the Hammersmith Perineal Hedgehog. *Br J Radiol*1985;58:537–42.
28.   Eddy GL, Marks RD Jr, Miller MC III, Underwood PB Jr. Primary invasive vaginal carcinoma. *Am J Obstet Gynecol* 1991;165:292–8.
29.   Puthawala A, Syed AMN, Nalick R, McNamara C, DiSaia PJ. Integrated external and interstitial radiation therapy for primary carcinoma of the vagina. *Obstet Gynecol* 1983;62:367–72.

Chapter 33

Management of perianal intraepithelial and invasive neoplasia

John Tidy

Introduction

Perianal neoplasia is a rare condition and may be managed by a diverse group of medical specialists. Most cases will be seen by surgeons and gynaecologists but genitourinary physicians and dermatologists will also encounter the disease. The approach to management has evolved by drawing parallels with the aetiology of other genital neoplasia such as cervical intraepithelial neoplasia (CIN) and vulval intraepithelial neoplasia (VIN). The diagnostic criteria and the treatment of perianal intraepithelial neoplasia are broadly based on those for CIN and VIN.[1]

The malignant potential of perianal intraepithelial neoplasia remains unclear. It is recognised that squamous anal cancers are associated with intraepithelial neoplasia, often coexisting, and patients have been reported to progress from intraepithelial neoplasia to cancer. However, the true risk of progression may never be fully quantified due to the inherent ethical problems in observational studies.[2]

The treatment of invasive disease is by chemoradiotherapy in most cases to allow preservation of anal function.

Epidemiology

The true incidence of this disease is difficult to establish, given the differences in terminology. Some authors separate Bowen's disease of the perianal region from anal intraepithelial neoplasia (AIN). This distinction is more common in surgical texts, while most gynaecologists prefer the use of the term AIN rather than Bowen's disease. This probably reflects the gynaecological concept of a field-change effect of the anogenital tract. As such, the differences in terminology are arbitrary and not helpful to understanding the disease process or treatment.

Histologically, Bowen's disease and AIN are similar and share features with VIN and CIN. These include loss of epithelial cell maturation and cytological abnormalities including hyperchromasia, pleomorphism, cell crowding and abnormal mitoses. AIN can be graded following the same criteria for CIN. There are no specific histopathological features that allow AIN to be separated from VIN. The pathologist can reliably report the presence of intraepithelial neoplasia but requires the surgeon to inform them of the anatomical site of the biopsy. Without strict criteria for where VIN ends and AIN begins there remains the possibility of error in assessing the incidence of AIN.

Anal cancer is rare and it affects women more frequently than men, the ratio is 3:2. The number of registered cases in the UK has been static over the years 1995–97 with approximately 600 new cases per year.[3] The increased incidence of invasive squamous cancer in women may reflect the higher incidence of perianal intraepithelial neoplasia (66–79%) when compared with men. The disease usually presents in the fifth decade of life and there is frequently a past history of other genital neoplasia, CIN being the most common.[4,5]

Aetiology

Human papillomavirus

Many of the aetiological factors related to the development of cervical and vulval neoplasia are shared with perianal neoplasia and probably reflect a common pathway for development. Human papillomavirus type 16 (HPV-16) has been found in 56–80% of cases of squamous cell carcinoma of the anus and AIN, with an increased incidence reported in AIN3 compared with AIN1.[6-8] The incidence of HPV in rectal adenocarcinoma is 0%.[9] There is also evidence of increased p53 expression in high-grade AIN and anal cancers, irrespective of the presence of HPV infection. Elements that work down stream of p53 in the cell cycle such as p21 and p27 may be altered in anal cancers and the presence of p21 expression may be an indicator of good prognosis.[10]

The timing of acquisition of HPV infection is unclear but it is likely to be in keeping with other genital neoplasia, which appears to be soon after the onset of sexual activity.[11] In a large case cohort study from Norway and Finland the serum from 760 000 individuals was examined for the presence of antibodies to HPV-16 and HPV-18. There was a three-fold increased relative risk for developing anal and perianal cancer if HPV-16 antibodies were present and 4.4-fold increased risk for the presence of HPV-18 antibodies. The persistence of seropositivity may be important because the highest risk for developing cancer was in the subgroup of individuals who were seropositive over the age of 45 years.[12]

Variant forms of HPV-16 may be linked to an increased risk of developing both intraepithelial and invasive neoplasia of the cervix. In a prevalence study based in Costa Rica,[13] variants of HPV-16, with DNA sequence changes in the noncoding region of HPV-16, were associated with increased incidence of high-grade intraepithelial lesions and invasive cancer. Variant forms of HPV-16 have been linked to the development of anal neoplasia. Two studies found an increased risk (3.2–3.4) associated with non prototype HPV-16 strains.[14,15] In one study, the non prototype HPV-16 most commonly associated with anal neoplasia contained sequence variations within the E6 protein.[15]

The expression of cadherin, cytokeratins and p53 appear to be different between cancers of the anal margin and anal canal. These findings suggest that while both cancers represent variants of squamous differentiation the histological origins of these cancers are distinct.[16]

Immunosuppression

There is an increased risk, about 5–6%, of developing neoplastic changes after transplantation and this may be due to suppression of the T cell response consequent to use of immunosuppressive agents.[17,18] Renal transplant patients were found to have an increased incidence of AIN (24%).[8] Immunosuppressive therapy is now used in autoimmune conditions such as systemic lupus erythematosus, myasthenia gravis and inflammatory bowel disease, as these groups of patients may be at greater risk of developing AIN.

HIV infection

HIV infection is associated with an increased risk of developing AIN but it is unclear if there is an increased risk of anal cancer. Two small studies reported a 60-fold increased risk of developing and then dying from anal cancer in HIV-infected individuals.[19,20] The incidence of anal cancer has increased in Denmark three-fold in women and 1.5-fold in men since 1957.[21] However, most of this increase occurred before the recognition of HIV and AIDS. Further case–control studies of single men in San Francisco reported increased incidence of Kaposi sarcoma and non-Hodgkin's lymphoma but no increase in the incidence of anal cancer.[22,23]

Holly *et al.* reported the prevalence of anal squamous intraepithelial lesions in 317 women. The presence of high-grade lesion was 6% in women who were HIV positive and 2% in women who were HIV negative. In the HIV-positive group, 28% had some abnormality, whether abnormal anal cytology or biopsy-proven disease. The presence of abnormal anal cytology was associated with receptive anal intercourse, the detection of HIV RNA, low CD4 count, anal HPV DNA and abnormal anal cervical cytology.[24]

The presence of low-grade lesions in women who are HIV positive may be clinically more important than low-grade lesion in those who are HIV-negative. In one study, 62% of low-grade lesions in men who were HIV positive progressed to high-grade lesions within two years.[25] It has been proposed that men who are HIV-positive should be screened with anal cytology to reduce the risk of anal cancer.[26] It is currently unclear if this should apply to women who are HIV positive.

Diagnosis

Cytology

Exfoliative anal cytology may be a potential screening test for AIN and help in the follow up of treated patients. Although causing some discomfort it is less invasive than anal colposcopy. Cells from the anal canal are best collected using a robust brush device and the slide and sample are prepared and stained as for conventional cervical cytology, the Papanicolaou technique. Interpretation of anal cytology requires training but reliable criteria have been established using a three-tier grading system to describe anal dyskaryosis.[27] Anal cytology has a sensitivity of 50–75% but has a trend to underestimate the histological grade of any identified lesion.[28,29]

Clinical presentation

Pruritus and soreness are the most common symptoms reported by women presenting with perianal intraepithelial neoplasia. However, asymptomatic presentation may occur with abnormal changes to the perianal skin being noted at gynaecological examination or during pregnancy. Occasionally, AIN is reported when apparently normal skin tags are excised. The reason why women are symptomatic is unclear but it may be the result of local inflammation association with the intraepithelial neoplasia leading to altered cytokine expression affecting local nerve sensation. The diagnosis of intraepithelial neoplasia is usually suspected when there is alteration of the perianal skin. There is thickening of the skin compared with the adjacent skin and there are changes in skin colour. The alterations in skin colouration may be whitening, due to hyperkeratosis, there may be increased pigmentation creating dark black/blue lesions or red erythematous lesions.

Nonpathological changes in the pigmentation of the perianal region can occur. These pigmented changes are not thickened and often have a symmetrical distribution.

At the time of diagnosis the full extent of the lesion must be assessed. Acetic acid and toluidine blue adds little to the clinical examination of perianal disease. Lesions that encroach on the anal verge may enter the anal canal, which is best assessed using a Graham Anderson proctoscope. To visualise the entire circumference of anal canal the proctoscope, which has a 45-degree oblique end, is rotated as it is withdrawn. Proctoscopy does not have to be undertaken if the perianal disease does not encroach onto the anal verge in most cases. There is a low incidence of AIN within the anal canal in the absence of any perianal disease. However, the exception to this may be women who are HIV positive, particularly if they practice anal intercourse.

The recognition of AIN within the anal canal is based on the features associated with CIN. There is a transformation zone between the squamous epithelium of the lower anal canal and the columnar epithelium of the upper anal canal. The perianal skin is keratinised, hair bearing squamous epithelium. The keratinisation is lost within the lower anal canal and the epithelium thins. It now has the features of a squamous mucosal epithelium. The anal canal is fully visualised, after which 5% acetic acid is applied. AIN lesions will become acetowhite, using a similar grading system to that for CIN, high-grade and low-grade lesions can be recognised. The positive predictive value to detect high-grade AIN, based on the colposcopic features associated with high-grade CIN, is reported as 49%. Low-grade AIN can be separated from high-grade AIN by using the colposcopic features for CIN.[30] Biopsies should be taken from any abnormal areas consistent with high grade AIN. Lesions not involving the anal canal are best biopsied using a dermatological skin punch under local anaesthesia. If the lesion is large and there is significant extension to the anal canal then multiple biopsies to map the extent of the lesion are required and are best performed under local regional or general anaesthesia. Lesions within the anal canal can be biopsied using biopsy forceps such as mini Tischler.

Recognition of early invasive disease

The risk of invasive disease being present, but unrecognised clinically, is directly related to the extent of the intraepithelial neoplasia lesion, i.e. the larger the field change of intraepithelial neoplasia, the higher the risk of early invasive disease. This observation presents a difficult clinical situation since larger lesions are more difficult to manage and surgical excision of these lesions is associated with higher morbidity. The morbidity may be acute occurring at the time of the excision or delayed because of alteration of the appearance of the anogenital region or from anal dysfunction.

The following features are associated with the presence of early invasive disease and, if present, should give cause for concern: excessive thickening of the skin, particularly in association with fissuring or early ulceration; the presence of atypical blood vessels. These patterns are similar to those seen in the cervix, including abnormal branching patterns and bizarre vessels such as tadpoles or hairpin vessels. Visualisation of these features often requires high-power magnification with a colposcope, videocolposcope or operating microscope.

Management

Low-grade intraepithelial lesions

AIN1 and AIN2 are considered low-grade lesions but they do have the potential to progress. Because of the morbidity associated with any treatment conservative management is justifiable.[31] Patients should be seen every six months for examination, including anal colposcopy if any lesion enters the anal canal. However, a more aggressive approach may be necessary in patients who are HIV positive, who may have a greater chance of disease progression. Early treatment of low-grade lesions, particularly if they are small, may prevent high-grade disease from developing and offer a procedure of lower morbidity.

High-grade intraepithelial lesions

The management of this condition has evolved significantly over the past decade. Surgery has been the mainstay of treatment and the potential for development of invasive disease resulted in many patients undergoing extensive surgery for this condition. However, the consequences of this extensive surgery have resulted in a high level of morbidity in women undergoing treatment and so a more conservative approach has been adopted.

Extensive surgery to the anal region will result in faecal incontinence or anal stricture formation. The risk of these conditions increases with the percentage of the anal skin excised but becomes significant once more than 40% of the anal skin is removed. While the most severe morbidity is linked to excision or damage to the anal sphincter, it is clear that the removal of the perianal epithelium and subcutaneous fat is linked to the development of mild morbidity such as incontinence of flatus.

Marchesa et al.[5] reported a retrospective series of 47 patients treated for AIN. One patient had clinically unrecognised invasive disease at presentation. Twenty were treated by local excision or laser ablation; the recurrence rate after local excision was 53.3% and 80% after laser ablation. Wide local excision was performed in 26 cases where extensive preoperative mapping biopsies followed by intraoperative frozen sections were used to achieve a 1-cm disease-free margin. The recurrence rate was 23.1%. The mean time to recurrence was similar in all groups (38–41 months) but patients in the group treated conservatively were more likely to have multiple recurrences. Three of the patients treated conservatively subsequently developed invasive disease; none of the patients treated more radically developed invasive disease.[5] A review of 19 patients treated over a 25-year period with local excision and reconstruction reported a local recurrence rate of 31% at five years.[4] Five patients had unrecognised invasive disease at the time of resection.

The departments of gynaecology and surgery in Sheffield have acquired considerable expertise over many years in the management of perianal intraepithelial neoplasia. Initially the treatment offered was to excise all the affected perianal tissue. If greater than 50% of the anal verge had to be removed then the area was reconstructed using a split-thickness skin graft applied following the creation of a temporary colostomy. To avoid the morbidity associated with the formation and then reversal of the colostomy, this procedure was then superseded by the use of a rectal pull-through to replace the use of split thickness skin grafts. In this procedure, the anal and perianal skin was removed and the rectum above the lesion pulled through the anal sphincter and sutured to the perianal skin. This procedure generally did not require a temporary colostomy and so was associated with a lower morbidity rate. However Brown et al.,[2] in reviewing the patients treated in Sheffield, found a significant morbidity related to all forms of surgical treatment. Between 1989 and 1996, 34 women with identified high-grade perianal intraepithelial neoplasia underwent local excision of all macroscopically abnormal disease. The resulting defect was either left open, closed primarily or skin grafted. In 19 cases, despite the surgical intention of complete excision, there was evidence of disease at the excision margins and 12 of these women developed high-grade recurrent disease within one year of surgery. Of the 15 women who had their disease completely excised, only two recurred at six and 32 months after surgery. At the time of surgery, 15 patients had lesions measuring less than 1 cm in diameter and all underwent local excision with primary closure. Eight of these women had positive resection margins and six subsequently developed further disease. Of the seven women with negative resection margins, only one developed further disease. Nineteen women had lesions measuring greater than 1cm in diameter and of these, ten had lesions that occupied greater than 50% of the anal verge. These women were treated with attempted complete excision of the disease and the defect either closed by skin grafting or closed primarily with a rectal pull-through; 50% had positive margins and two developed further disease. Of five cases with negative resection margins, one woman developed further disease. In the nine cases where less than 50% of the anal verge was involved, excision was performed. Six had positive resection margins and, of these, four developed further disease. In three cases with negative resection margins there was no evidence of further disease. These operations were associated with significant acute morbidity, not only at the time of initial surgery but also associated with reanastomosis at the closure of the colostomy. Long-term morbidity has been high in those patients who have undergone surgery for lesions greater than 1 cm. One patient who underwent excision for a lesion less than 50% of the circumference of the anal verge subsequently developed faecal incontinence and required a permanent colostomy. Two of the ten patients who had extensive lesions excised developed faecal incontinence requiring the use of pads. A further two patients developed anal stenosis, one of whom required a permanent colostomy.[2]

Chang *et al.* reported a prospective study of 37 men treated for high grade AIN with a strategy of incisional biopsy of the lesion with cautery to the entire lesion. All treatment was directed using an operating microscope. If the lesion involved the entire circumference of the anus the treatment was staged to prevent injury to the anal sphincter. The treatment was well tolerated with no evidence of anal dysfunction. None of the eight HIV negative men developed any recurrence compared with 23 of 29 HIV positive men, the mean time to recurrence was 12 months.[32]

If ablative treatments are considered then the depth of tissue destruction must be at least 2.2 mm below the basement membrane to ensure eradication of disease extending into skin appendages such as sweat glands and hair follicles.[33] Unless an ablative technique can guarantee this depth of destruction then surgical excision should be the treatment of choice.

Treatment of invasive disease

Surgical excision of perianal or anal cancer required the removal of the anus with permanent colostomy formation. Five-year survival is 40–70%.[34] Radiation has the potential to cure anal cancer and thus potentially avoid a permanent colostomy. Three randomised clinical trials have examined the use of chemotherapy in addition to radiotherapy. The UK Coordinating Committee on Cancer Research trial randomised 585 patients to either radical radiotherapy alone or with 5-fluorouracil and mitomycin.[35] The European Organisation for Research and Treatment of Cancer trial randomised 110 patients to the same treatments although the chemotherapy regimen differed slightly.[36] There was a significant improvement in local disease control (61% versus 39%) and a lower rate of permanent colostomy. There was no improvement in overall survival but it has been proposed that the use of abdominoperineal resection as a salvage treatment for locally recurrent disease may account for the lack of difference in the overall survival rates.

The role of mitomycin has been evaluated in a randomised controlled trial of 310 patients.[37] The addition of 5-fluorouracil to mitomycin resulted in an improvement in disease free survival (67% versus 50%) and a lower locoregional recurrence rate (17% versus 36%) but there was no improvement in overall survival (67% versus 65%).[37]

Cisplatin is a recognised chemosensitiser and is used in the treatment of cervical cancer in addition to radiotherapy. Two small trials of cisplatin, 5-fluorouracil and radiotherapy have provided encouraging results with overall survival rates of 84–97%.[38,39] This combination of treatment is being investigated by a large randomised trial in the USA.

Persistent or recurrent disease

Disease persisting after chemoradiotherapy is treated by abdominoperineal resection. Recurrent disease can be managed by local excision or abdominoperineal resection and the five-year survival rate is 45–58%.[40,41]

References

1. Scholefield JH, Sonnex C, Talbot IC, Palmer JG, Whatrup C, Mindel A, *et al*. Anal and cervical intraepithelial neoplasia: possible parallel. *Lancet* 1989;ii:765–9.
2. Brown SR, Skinner P, Tidy J, Smith JH, Sharp F and Hosie KB. Outcome after surgical resection for high-grade anal intraepithelial neoplasia (Bowen's disease). *Br J Surg* 1999;86:1063–6.
3. Office for National Statistics. *Cancer Statistics Registrations: Registrations of Cancer Diagnosed in 1995–1997, England and Wales.* Series MB1, no. 28.London: ONS; 2001.
4. Sarmiento JM, Wolff BG, Burgart IJ, Frizelle FA, Ilstrup DM. Perianal Bowen's disease: associated tumours, human papillomavirus, surgery and other controversies. *Dis Colon Rectum* 1997;40:912–18.
5. Marchesa P, Fazio VW, Oliart S, Goldblum JR, Lavery IC. Perianal Bowen's disease: a clinicopathologic study of 47 patients. *Dis Colon Rectum* 1997;40:1286–93.
6. Scholefield JH, Hickson WGE, Smith JHF, Rodgers K, Sharp F. Anal intraepithelial neoplasia: part of a multifocal disease process. *Lancet* 1992;340:1271–3.
7. Ogunbiyi OA, Scholefield JH, Robertson G, Smith JHF, Sharp F, Rodgers K. Anal human papillomavirus infection and squamous neoplasia in patients with invasive vulvar cancer. *Obstet Gynecol* 1994;83:212–16.
8. Ogunbiyi OA, Scholefield JH, Raftery AT, Smith JH, Duffy S, Sharp F, *et al*. Prevalence of anal human papillomavirus infection and intraepithelial neoplasia in renal allograft recipients. *Br J Surg* 1994;8:365–7.
9. Frisch M, Glimelius B, van den Brule AJ, Wohlfahrt J, Meijer CJ, Walboomers JM, *et al*. Sexually transmitted infection as a cause of anal cancer. *N Engl J Med* 1997;337:1350–8.
10. Holm R, Skovlund E, Skomedal H, Florenes VA, Tanum G. Reduced expression of p21 WAF1 is an indicator of malignant behaviour in anal carcinomas. *Histopathology* 2001;39:43–9.
11. Woodman CB, Collins S, Winter H, Bailey A, Ellis J, Prior P, *et al*. Natural history of cervical human papillomavirus infection in young women: a longitudinal cohort study. *Lancet* 2001;357:1831–6.
12. Bjorge T, Engeland A, Luostarinen T, Mork J, Gislefoss RE, Jellum E, *et al*. Human papillomavirus infection as a risk factor for anal and perianal skin cancer in a prospective study. *Br J Cancer* 2002;87:61–4.
13. Hildesheim A, Schiffman M, Bromley C, Wacholder S, Herrero R, Rodriguez A, *et al*. Human papillomavirus type 16 variants and risk of cervical cancer. *J Natl Cancer Inst* 2001;93:315–18.
14. Xi LF, Critchlow CW, Wheeler CM, Koutsky LA, Galloway DA, Kuypers J, *et al*. Risk of anal carcinoma *in situ* in relation to human papillomavirus type 16 variants. *Cancer Res* 1998;58:3839–44.
15. Da Costa MM, Hogeboom CJ, Holly EA, Palesky JM. Increased risk of high grade anal neoplasia associated with a human papillomavirus type 16 E6 sequence variant. *J Infect Dis* 2002;185:1229–37.
16. Behrendt GC, Hansmann ML. Carcinomas of the anal canal and anal margin differ in their expression of cadherin, cytokeratins and p53. *Virchows Arch* 2001;439:782–6.
17. Porreco R, Penn I, Droegemueller W, Greer B, Makowski E. Gynecologic malignancies in immunosuppressed organ homograft recipients. *Obstet Gynecol* 1975;45:359–64.
18. Penn I. Cancer is a complication of severe immunosuppression. *Surg Gynecol Obstet* 1986;162:603–10.
19. Selik RM, Rabkin CS. Cancer death rates associated with human immunodeficiency virus infection in the United States. *J Natl Cancer Inst* 1998;90:1300–2.

20. Melbye M, Cote TR, Kessler L, Gail M, Biggar RJ. High incidence of anal cancer among AIDS patients. *Lancet* 1994;343:636–9.
21. Frisch M, Melbye M, Moller H. Trends in incidence of anal cancer in Denmark. *BMJ* 1993;306:419–22.
22. Harnley ME, Swan SH, Holly EA, Kelter A, Padian N. Temporal trends in the incidence of non-Hodgkin's lymphoma and selected malignancies in a population with a high incidence of acquired immunodeficiency syndrome. *Am J Epidemiol* 1988;128:261–7.
23. Rabkin CS, Yellin F. Cancer incidence in a population with a high prevalence of infection with human immunodeficiency virus type 1. *J Natl Cancer Inst* 1994;86:1711–16.
24. Holly EA, Ralston ML, Darragh TM, Greenblatt RM, Jay N, Palefsky JM. Prevalence and risk factors for anal squamous intraepithelial lesions in women. *J Natl Cancer Inst* 2001;93:843–9.
25. Palefsky JM, Holly EA, Hogeboom CJ, Ralston ML, DaCosta MM, Botts R, *et al.* Viral, immunologic and clinical parameters in the incidence and progression of anal squamous intraepithelial lesions in HIV-positive and HIV-negative homosexual men. *J Acquir Immune Defic Syndr Hum Retrovirol* 1998;17:314–17.
26. Goldie SJ, Kuntz KM, Weinstein MC, Freedberg KA, Welton ML, Palefsky JM. The clinical effectiveness and cost-effectiveness of screening for anal squamous intraepithelial lesions in homosexual and bisexual HIV positive men. *JAMA* 1999;281:1822–9.
27. Scholefield JH, Johnson J. Guidelines for anal cytology – to make cytological diagnosis and follow up much more reliable. *Cytopathology* 1998;9:15–22.
28. Northfelt DW, Swift PS, Palefsky JM. Anal neoplasia. Pathogenesis, diagnosis and management. *Hematol Oncol Clin North Am* 1996;10:1177–87.
29. Palefsky JM. Anal human papillomavirus infection and anal cancer in HIV-positive individuals: an emerging problem. *AIDS* 1994;8:283–95.
30. Jay N, Berry JM, Hogeboom CJ, Holly EA, Darragh TM, Palefsky JM. Colposcopic appearance of anal squamous intraepithelial lesions. *Dis Colon Rectum* 1997;40:919–28.
31. Scholefield JH. Anal intraepithelial neoplasia. *Br J Surg* 1999;86:1363–4.
32. Chang GJ, Berry JM, Jay N, Palefsky JM, Welton ML. Surgical treatment of high grade anal squamous intraepithelial lesions. *Dis Colon Rectum* 2002;45:453–8.
33. Skinner PP, Ogunbiyi OA, Scholefield JH, Start RD, Smith JH, Sharp F, *et al.* Skin appendage involvement in anal intraepithelial neoplasia. *Br J Surg* 1997;84:675–8.
34. Ryan DP, Compton CC, Mayer RJ. Carcinoma of the anal canal. *N Engl J Med* 2000;342:792–800.
35. UK Coordinating Committee on Cancer Research. UKCCR: Epidermoid anal cancer: results from the UKCCR randomised trial of radiotherapy alone versus radiotherapy, 5-fluorouracil, and mitomycin. UKCCR Anal Cancer Trial Working Party. *Lancet* 1996;348:1049–54.
36. Flam M, John M, Pajak TF, Petrelli N, Myerson R, Doggett S, *et al.* Role of mitomycin in combination with fluorouracil and radiotherapy, and of salvage chemoradiation in the definitive nonsurgical treatment of epidermoid carcinoma of the anal canal: results of a phase III randomised intergroup study. *J Clin Oncol* 1996;14:2527–39.
37. Bartelink H, Roelofsen F, Eschwege F, Rougier P, Bosset JF, Gonzalez DG, *et al.* Concomitant radiotherapy and chemotherapy is superior to radiotherapy alone in the treatment of locally advanced anal cancer: results of a phase III randomised trial of the European Organisation for Research and Treatment of Cancer Radiotherapy and Gastrointestinal Cooperative Groups. *J Clin Oncol* 1997;15:2040–9.
38. Doci R, Zucali R, La Monica G, Meroni E, Kenda R, Eboli M, *et al.* Primary chemoradiation therapy with fluorouracil and cisplatin for cancer of the anus: results in 35 consecutive patients. *J Clin Oncol* 1996;14:3115–21.
39. Gerard JP, Ayzac L, Hun D, Romestaing P, Coquard R, Ardiet JM, *et al.* Treatment of anal canal carcinoma with high dose radiation therapy and concomitant fluorouracil-cisplatium: long term results in 95 patients. *Radiother Oncol* 1998;46:249–56.
40. Pocard M, Tiret E, Nugent K, Dehni N, Parc R. Results of salvage abdomino-perineal resection for anal cancer after radiotherapy. *Dis Colon Rectum* 1998;41:1488–93.
41. Allal AS, Laurencet FM, Reymond MA, Kurtz JM, Marti MC. Effectiveness of surgical salvage therapy for patients with locally uncontrolled anal carcinoma after sphincter-conserving treatment. *Cancer* 1999;86:405–9.

Chapter 34

Management of lower genital tract neoplasia IV

Discussion

Discussion following Mr Soutter's paper

Adams: One of the problems about interstitial radiotherapy is competence or experience. The vast majority of radiation oncologists see very few of them and, more and more, we find that we just do not have any experience with implants. This is happening with tongue implants too. This facility should be available on a supra-regional basis, but I would not like to do the occasional one myself.

Shepherd: That is absolutely right. There are very few centres that have these after-loading techniques of either high-dose or low-dose; this is really a very specialised area. Perhaps I could just make one comment, on a slight disagreement with Mr Soutter. Following the discussion we had following Dr Adams' paper (Chapter 31), I am not sure that elderly women should be excluded from the benefits of surgery yet again, and given radiotherapy. With regard to vaginal intraepithelial neoplasia (VAIN), for example, one of the most important things to someone who you think has VAIN, be it on a smear or a proven biopsy, is to exclude invasive cancer. It is extremely important in their treatment to get the diagnosis right.

Mr Paul Curtis was a registrar with us at Bart's and we wrote up a series of these cases,[1] including young and old women, showing how entirely feasible doing an upper partial colpectomy from the vaginal route is. Sure, it can be hazardous following previous surgery, but it is crucially important. It is also very important after previous radiotherapy, when the patient cannot or should not have more radiotherapy, and the morbidity may therefore be less to approach this surgically. It is very important to make the correct diagnosis.

Let me follow that up with a question to you. We have been discussing the role of human papillomavirus (HPV) and so on. In patients who have been treated for cervical cancer, be it by radiotherapy or by surgery, we have a dilemma in knowing how to follow these patients up. A certain number of them will come back with abnormal smears because, traditionally, we are always doing smears, suggesting that they may have some form of intraepithelial neoplasia. That, of course, then leads to a necessary or perhaps unnecessary, but an inevitable, series of investigations. Can you advise us? How should we follow up patients who have been treated previously? Should we be taking smears? Should we be doing HPV studies on them? Can we pick out at-risk patients for follow-up, whether it is for recurrence or for further field change?

Soutter: First, let me comment about the old women/young women issue. I should have prefaced my remarks about old women by saying that the definition of an old woman is entirely subjective and seems to be proportional to one's own age. I agree with you, absolutely, and I will modify what I say about age because, like you, I have treated many elderly women with this for a whole variety of different reasons. 'Old' really means old and unfit, very unfit. Talking about follow-up, do you mean the follow-up of patients with VAIN or vaginal cancer?

Shepherd: I really meant patients who had been treated for either cervical or vaginal cancer, either surgically or by radiotherapy, who will then have an abnormal smear.

Soutter: Your guess is as good as mine. If HPV could help clearly to differentiate those who have recurrent disease, then that would be marvellous. I have to say that I take a slightly nihilistic view about following up patients who have had primary treatment for carcinoma of the cervix, because such a small proportion of them have salvageable disease if it recurs. I fully agree that there is a small cohort whom we can salvage, and there is a small cohort who develop VAIN and we should look for these. However, in the process, we very often pick up women with recurrent disease, for whom we can do nothing, and I do not feel that we are doing them a favour in finding the disease at this stage when it is untreatable. That is just a purely personal view. The short answer to what you are saying about how to follow them up is that I have no idea.

Deery: There have been suggestions that, if you still have a high-risk HPV-type present, then you almost certainly have disease in the margins.

Shafi: There are published data on this, which support not doing any vaginal vault cytology in those women who have been treated for invasive disease of the cervix. Vaginal vault cytology should be reserved for those patients who have had a hysterectomy for pre-invasive disease, and you are looking for an extension of that pre-invasive disease onto the vagina.

Coming back to the excision side of things for VAIN in those patients who have had a hysterectomy, this is really one of the few places that CO_2 laser therapy has an exceptionally good role, because you can excise the lesions very precisely and comfortably. Upper colpectomy is not an easy operation, as everyone would agree. It is one of the least favourite operations for most gynaecological oncologists, either abdominally or vaginally. If you can eliminate the lesion with a CO_2 laser, that certainly is the preferred tool in my hands. It does not really matter what tool you use, but it is the excision of that area in its entirety that is really important.

Tidy: I would echo Mr Shafi's point. We looked at our follow-up for vault smears with about 3500 smears from 200 patients and found that in fact we did the patients more harm by investigating the abnormal smear and we did not detect any recurrences. We have therefore abandoned routine vault cytology as a result of that because it just does not help – it hinders in many respects.

Jones: The practical point about upper vaginectomy is that, if you lift the epithelium off with some fluid, whether it is local or not, that absolutely revolutionises it and a difficult procedure becomes much easier.

Singer: I hate to be anecdotal, but 15 years ago I had a woman who was then 72 or 73 years old, referred because she had had a hysterectomy 20 years previously. She was inadvertently called for a smear by her general practitioner and was found to have severe dyskaryosis. The hysterectomy, as far as we know, was not for cervical intraepithelial neoplasia (CIN). She had a patch of abnormal epithelium right at the vault, the type that Mr Jones has just described. We injected the vault with large amounts of saline, so that the abnormal tissue appeared on top of the little hillock, and then virtually undertook a cone biopsy of the vault, taking a wide excision around the abnormal tissue. They were then just left or sutured up. It was VAIN3, query complete, query not. We debated as to what should be done further and said that we could either give her radiotherapy or we could take out the whole of the vagina (vaginectomy). She opted to be followed up. Miss Betty Mansell saw her twice a year. Then, about four or five months ago, she noticed a small sinus opening up in the vault. It was opened up with some Des Jardins forceps, and she put in a Pipelle sampler but could not get any more than fragments of tissue showing dysplastic epithelium. The woman went to Australia to visit her family and then came back a few months later. We opened this sinus under anaesthetic and obviously she had a small carcinoma in that sinus. She has done very well for 15 years, she is now in her eighties and has had a brilliant quality of life, not withstanding the very minor treatment that she opted for at that time.

Jones: You did not mention imiquimod in the treatment of VAIN.

Soutter: You are referring to the letter from Diakomanolis in the *New England Journal of Medicine*.[2] I have a feeling that this is 5-fluorouracil all over again.

Jones: Can you tell me why VAIN is so much less common than VIN? Is there any reason for that?

Soutter: I cannot tell you why.

Fiander: In terms of topical therapy for VAIN, we are actually looking at the use of cidofovir in Cardiff, which appears quite promising. We are undertaking a pilot study at the moment but have not yet published the work. Cidofovir is useful for women who have multifocal vaginal disease that you cannot excise because it is too large an area. It is an antiviral that is used in HIV-positive patients for cytomegalovirus infection, but you can have it made up as a topical preparation and apply it directly to the lesion.

Singer: Does it have the same effect as imiquimod?

Fiander: No, not really, it seems to be an antiviral, antitumour effect. It induces apoptosis.

MacLean: Mr Soutter, in the discussion about the cytological follow-up of cervical cancer treated patients, what about the follow up looking for VAIN in those patients who have had hysterectomies for CIN? There was a comment from Ian Duncan about how long these patients should be followed up, recognising that some of them develop their disease more than two years after their primary treatment. Could you comment on how frequently they should be followed up after hysterectomy for CIN, and for how many years?

Soutter: Dr Sasieni and I have completed, but not yet written up, a meta-analysis of long-term follow-up of women treated for CIN. Some of those data relate to women treated with hysterectomy. The striking feature about the hysterectomy data is that the risk of subsequently developing invasive disease appears to remain at the same level for as long as there are data to follow it up. There is no obvious reduction with time in the risk of developing invasive cancer. The same is true of patients who have had their cervix treated with conservative therapies. This is because, very largely, the rate of invasion is related not to the primary treatment but rather to the efficacy of the programme for detecting recurrent intraepithelial disease.

MacLean: Mr Jones, I know about your experience with the late Bill McIndoe's publication.[3] Some of those VAIN patients had a long disease course before invasion was recognised.

Jones: Yes, decades.

Shafi: One of the prerequisites of a screening programme is that the condition has to be common. VAIN and vaginal cancer are not common disorders and would not satisfy the prerequisites of a screening programme for that.

Shepherd: But we are not talking about a screening programme here. We are talking about patients who have been treated by hysterectomy for CIN3, and who then appear still to have a risk of developing invasive cancer. Surely a certain percentage of them must still be at risk for developing field-change VAIN. What I do not understand is why patients who have already had an invasive cancer are not still at the same risk of developing significant precancer or further cancer, be it field change, or reoccurrence or whatever. Surely, those patients who have been treated by chemoradiotherapy must be more at risk because they have been immunocompromised. I cannot quite see the logic of why they are not at similar, if not greater, risk.

Shafi: I take on board the data from Mr Soutter that the recurrence, or reoccurrence, can occur well out from initial management. Women who have had a hysterectomy for CIN, which has been completely excised, and they have negative vaginal vault cytology after that, have very little chance, I would imagine, of having recurrent disease in the upper vagina. You are then screening for VAIN and vaginal cancer, and I contend that it is not a common condition for us to go out and screen for.

Singer: But not only vagina, but vulva as well, as we will hear from Mr Tidy in a moment. It is a field change, all the way down. These cases need to be followed. If we have done a hysterectomy, of which there are very few these days for CIN, because it is usually recurrence, they are the ones that you do not want to come back. They need to be seen, certainly at yearly follow-ups, and also the vulva as well.

Shafi: For life?

Singer: Yes, this is follow-up, not screening.

Shepherd: That certainly seems to be the message from Mr Jones's data on the vulva. That is a new change for us and we would really need to have pretty good grounds for not doing it for the vagina as well.

Discussion following Mr Tidy's paper

Perrett: Mr Tidy, you answered my question towards the end of your paper, but my impression is that there are no pathological studies looking at adjacent lesions to anal cancer. The only molecular studies, including the p21/p53 data you mentioned, show adjacent normal epithelium to anal cancer. In other words, anal cancer can come from normal epithelium potentially, as well as from AIN3.

Tidy: That is true. There is the scratch–itch cycle around the anus, so that patients will develop non-HPV-related anal cancer. So there is another pathway and it is not all HPV-related AIN.

Critchley: I had the same question as to whether it was always related to HPV and whether patients who were HPV-negative could develop AIN.

Jones: It seems to me that there may be AIN involving the transformation zone in the anal canal, and AIN on a so-called native squamous epithelium distal to that. Could you comment about two possible lesions? Gabriele Medley, the cytopathologist who has an interest in this, tells me that the histopathology of the transformation zone in the anal canal is identical to that in the cervix. We might therefore expect a slightly different natural history to the transformation zone-type of AIN compared with the native squamous epithelium more distally. Could you comment on that, please?

Tidy: You are right, there are two different diseases, given the same label. In Palevsky's study, a large proportion of these are AIN of the transition zone, whereas the majority of ours are perianal disease that goes into the canal.[4] When the initial studies were done, everyone had anoscopy and, from that, we were able to prove that the actual incidence of AIN in the transformation zone, in the absence of perianal disease in our population, was so low that it did not warrant investigation. However, if you have a population of men with a high incidence of HIV and receptive anal intercourse, then you find a different disease that may involve the transformation zone more than the women we have been looking at.

MacLean: Mr Jones, I agree with you. There has been a series of reports. In Friedrich's series of 50 cases of VIN,[5] the one cancer was in a 21-year-old immune-suppressed patient and her disease was arising from that transition zone. You showed a case in an immune-suppressed patient.

Mr Tidy, you commented on the need to proctoscope these patients, but I just wonder whether there is not a group of women who are immune-suppressed, who do not necessarily have a lesion, and continuity with a lesion coming across the perineum, but who may have changes within that transition zone that put them at greater risk. There are also a great many women who are immune-suppressed for all sorts of reasons. To have to examine them all would be taxing on colposcopy services. However, do you think that we should perhaps make a recommendation as to whether immune-suppressed or renal transplant patients should also be included for proctoscopy?

Tidy: No, but we need to educate our physician colleagues who put patients on these drugs that this is a problem that can occur. If someone starts reporting vulval irritation or perianal itching, they should be examined. I do not think that there is high enough incidence to warrant proctoscopy but it would be more a matter of education for those physicians who put patients on immunosuppressants.

Fiander: I would just like to take you up on that last point. If a quarter of renal transplant patients are going to develop AIN, should we not be screening them? Similarly, should we not be undertaking colposcopy on them? Ninety-five percent of renal transplant patients have a problem with controlling HPV infection within five years of their transplant, so should we not screen them? This is an at-risk group.

Tidy: Proposed new guidelines suggest that all patients who are being considered for dialysis and then possible transplantation should have a screening colposcopy to establish their disease status at that time. We would like to go back and look at our renal transplant patients to see what has happened to them; it may be an artificially high level. You will know that, when you have an interest in an area, you seem to be able to find a high incidence and then someone else looks at it and finds that the incidence is only two percent. I would therefore not say, based on one series, that you could recommend that everyone ought to undergo anoscopy. We are reassured that, if they do not have perianal disease, then you do not need to look in their anus. It would be nice for someone else to do it on a different population and see what they came up with.

MacLean: Dr Deery was shaking his head and Dr McGoogan was nodding hers. Is that because of the differences in using liquid-based cytology? What about the role of cytological assessment, rather than having to resort to colposcopy? You do not believe that, Dr Deery?

Deery: The experience I have had at the Royal Free Hospital, London, is that I was involved in the colposcopy of renal transplant patients. I had completely enough of multifocal lower genital tract intraepithelial neoplasia on the clinical details, and specimens from all over the place. Of course, they are full of HPV and interesting things, and you can have a stab at predicting them and so on, but it is an excellent opportunity to look at an alternative technology.

MacLean: Were your smears taken with a spatula or a Cervex® broom?

Deery: Both ways: with broom, spatulas and taken into fluid sometimes, broken off into fluid, vortexed and so on, because we like liquid-based cytology.

MacLean: I have a slide that you prepared for me of some spindle cells taken from a perianal scrape.

Deery: Yes, from a high-grade case. I agree with what Mr Tidy said earlier that, so long as you are picking up high-grade disease and you are hawkish about it (and you do have to be hawkish about it and get used to the experience) otherwise you will have faint cytology which under-estimates the disease and so on. The specimens are difficult because anal area specimens do not 'come away', they are in skin, with a great deal of differentiation, and they do not separate easily, even with quite vigorous scrapes.

MacLean: Would you be able to characterise on the cytology whether or not the lesion had become invasive?

Deery: Cytology for invasive disease is about probabilities. If you have ulceration and polymorpholeukocytes, then you might make a prediction. However, if you look very carefully at those predictions, you will only get it right – even with very good interpretation – in 60–75% of cases.

McGoogan: About ten years ago we did routine anal cytology on all of our HIV-positive homosexual males, but we have virtually abandoned that now. We have been guilty in this discussion of talking about immunosuppressed patients as though they are all the same, but their disease condition and their state of health is much more important in deciding who is likely to progress and who is not. The UK and Californian experiences are extremely different in that. We have many patients in Edinburgh with high-grade AIN that we are just following, and they are the ones who get anal cytology. Anal cytology is difficult and has a high inadequate rate. It is unpleasant for the patient, and so it is not the best way to do it. It is certainly not a good screening test and you cannot, with confidence, predict when something is about to become invasive, or has just become invasive. That really is a clinical decision on your patient. However, it is probably more correlated with the state of health of the patient than with an actual histological lesion.

References

1. Curtis P, Shepherd JH, Lowe DG, Jobling T. The role of partial colpectomy in the management of persistent vaginal neoplasia after primary treatment. *Br J Obstet Gynaecol* 1992;99:587–9.
2. Diakomanolis E, Haidopoulos D, Stefanidis K. Treatment of high-grade vaginal intraepithelial neoplasia with imiquimod cream. *NEJM* 2002;347:374.
3. McIndoe WA, McLean MR, Jones RW, Mullins PR. The invasive potential of carcinoma *in situ* of the cervix. *Obstet Gynecol* 1984;64:451–8.
4. Chang GJ, Berry JM, Jay N, Palefsky JM, Welton ML. Surgical treatment of high grade anal squamous intraepithelial lesions. *Dis Colon Rectum* 2002;45:453–8.
5. Friedrich EG, Wilkinson EJ, Fu YS. Carcinoma *in situ* of the vulva: a continuing challenge. *Am J Obstet Gynecol* 1980;136:830–43.

SECTION 9

RECOMMENDATIONS

Chapter 35

Recommendations arising from the 44th Study Group: Lower Genital Tract Neoplasia

Recommendations fall into three categories:

1. Recommendations for **clinical practice** (principally aimed at Fellows and Members of the Royal College of Obstetricians and Gynaecologists) based upon research evidence (where available) and the consensus view of the Group. The clinical practice recommendations have been graded from 'A' to 'C' according to the strength of evidence on which each is based (Table 35.1). The scheme for the grading of recommendations is based on the system adopted by both the NHS Executive and the Scottish Intercollegiate Guidelines Network.

2. Recommendations for **future research** in those clinical areas where the Group identified a need for further evidence on which to base practice.

3. Recommendations relating to **health education** and **health policy**.

Recommendations for clinical practice

Cervical neoplasia

1. Both conventional and liquid-based smear samples are best taken with either a single ectocervical broom or a combination of spatula and endocervical brush. (Grade A)

2. Excisional methods to treat cervical intraepithelial neoplasia grade 2 (CIN2 and CIN3) are superior to destructive methods. The resultant histology reduces the risk of inappropriate treatment of occult carcinoma. (Grade B)

3. Loop excision and laser excision of the transformation zone appear to be equally effective, but loop excision has advantages of cost, short duration of treatment and less pain. (Grade A)

4. Conisation, i.e. laser, knife or loop, appears to be adequate management for cervical glandular intraepithelial neoplasia providing the cone margins are clear, there is no pathological suspicion of invasion and long-term follow-up is agreed. (Grade C)

5. Older patients with atypical glandular cells of uncertain significance (AGUS) must be considered for possible lesions higher in the genital tract. (Grade C)

6.   Microinvasive cervical glandular neoplasia is not an accepted definition; management of apparent early invasive adenocarcinoma of the cervix requires careful histological review and assessment by a gynaecological oncologist. (Grade C)

7.   Individualisation of patient care with a multidisciplinary review should be undertaken for all patients with invasive cervical cancer. (Grade C)

8.   Surgery for cervical cancer may be considered as an option for old and young alike. (Grade C)

9.   Young women with early-stage cervical cancer desirous of fertility should be considered for locally radical fertility-sparing surgery. (Grade C)

10.   Expert imaging of the cervix, e.g. with magnetic resonance imaging, is essential before deciding on treatment of early cervical cancer. (Grade C)

11.   A number of women with disease resistant to standard treatment may be suitable for ultra-radical surgery. Quality-of-life issues and reconstruction of pelvic structures should be considered. (Grade C)

12.   All patients with high-risk or advanced (stage Ib2 or greater) cervical cancer should be considered for chemoradiation. (Grade C)

13.   Participation of patients with cervical cancer in clinical trials to determine optimal regimen for chemoradiation is desirable. (Grade C)

Vaginal neoplasia

14.   Treatment by excision is the preferred option for vaginal intraepithelial neoplasia grade 3 (VAIN3), especially if the uterus has been removed previously. (Grade C)

15.   5-fluorouracil has no place in the management of vaginal intraepithelial neoplasia. (Grade C)

Vulval neoplasia

16.   Examination of the vulva is a significant part of the physical examination of adult women. Clinically abnormal vulval skin requires a biopsy and histopathological examination for appropriate diagnosis and clinical management. (Grade C)

17.   Untreated vulval intraepithelial neoplasia (VIN) has a significant invasive potential. The increasing frequency of VIN in young women has been associated with an increased incidence of VIN-related cancer. While most VIN-related cancers occur in the first decade following diagnosis and treatment, later cases occur and therefore the patients need long-term follow up. (Grade C)

18.   Long-term follow-up of patients with lichen sclerosus is required because a small proportion will develop vulval cancer. The risk is increased where there is clinical or histological evidence of hyperplastic changes. (Grade C)

19.   The radicality of the vulval excision must now be individualised according to the extent of the cancer (and not the adjacent epithelial changes). (Grade C)

20.   Sentinel node identification may allow management to reduce the morbidity of lymphadenectomy without increasing the risk of groin node recurrence. (Grade C)

21. Patients with vulval cancer who are not suitable for radical surgery because of poor medical condition or advanced local disease should be considered for chemoradiation by an expert multidisciplinary team. (Grade C)

Anal neoplasia

22. If vulval or perianal intraepithelial neoplasia extends to within 1.5 cm of the anus, the anal canal should be examined for anal intraepithelial neoplasia (AIN). (Grade C)

23. The morbidity following the treatment of high-grade AIN is significant. Surgery may be required for symptoms and to exclude invasion, but otherwise observation is thought to be appropriate. (Grade C)

24. Chemoradiation is the treatment of choice for anal carcinoma. (Grade C)

General

25. Issues of patient consent and management of women who test positive for human papillomavirus (HPV) must be considered before performing HPV testing. (Grade C)

Recommendations for research

1. The combination of high-risk HPV DNA testing and cytology offers a greater than 99% negative predictive value. Both adjunctive HPV DNA testing and primary HPV DNA testing may offer significant benefits to a cervical neoplasia screening programme.

2. Other markers, such as HPV RNA and the use of chip technology, should also be evaluated.

3. Further assessment of p16 and minichromosome maintenance proteins as markers of cervical neoplasia should be carried out.

4. Further research is required to understand how keratinocytes with HPV genomic material escape immune surveillance, and how immune response to such altered keratinocytes can be enhanced.

5. The results of several studies on the contribution of HPV testing to cervical screening for borderline or mildly dyskaryotic changes are awaited before definitive recommendations can be made to guide UK practice.

6. HPV testing may be useful in avoiding both unnecessary treatment and prolonged surveillance. Data will be available in the next few years from large prospective studies (ALTS, TOMBOLA, HART, LBC, HPV pilots) on HPV testing, psychological effects and health economies.

7. Liquid-based cytology preparation systems differ in their technology and methodology used. New liquid-based cytology systems require technical and qualitative evaluations before implementation with the National Health Service Cervical Screening Programme. These should include an assessment of the equipment, risk assessments, professionally led evaluation of the end product and also of the utility and limitations as a common platform for new technologies such as HPV testing and automated scanners. Criteria should be developed and

published for these evaluations as soon as possible.

8. The techniques of visual inspection with acetic acid (VIA) and opticoelectric devices need further evaluation.

9. Research should be encouraged into whether solutions of fixatives other than acetic acid might provide better definition of cervical neoplasia.

10. The use of video colposcopy in various clinical settings should be studied.

11. There is a need for an appropriately designed trial on which method to use to treat type III transformation zones, i.e. when the endocervical lesion is not colposcopically visible in its entirety.

12. The Study Group recognises the need to undertake further studies of therapeutic immunotherapy and recommends that these be evaluated in patients with (HPV-16+) high-grade VIN and AIN (high-grade anogenital neoplasia, AGIN) as the preferred model.

13. Consideration should be given to the use of intralesional or mucosally delivered vaccines and the possibility of administering a topical adjuvant in the management of lower genital tract neoplasia.

14. Collaborations between centres are to be encouraged in order to recruit sufficient numbers of patients for treatment within an appropriate time frame. This could include clinical, immunological and genetic collaborations.

15. Incorporation of immunotherapy into surgical or chemoradiation treatment protocols should be considered for invasive cervical carcinoma.

16. Funding is required to support trials of therapeutic immunotherapy and consideration given to support of a coordinating body.

17. Gene immunotherapy with HLA-A2 or HLA-B13 is safe and has demonstrated interesting biological response in cervical and ovarian cancer. Further research in randomised control trials to assess benefits in local and distant recurrence and survival when used in conventional modality of therapy is recommended.

18. Further research is desirable to understand what molecular pathological inheritance factors increase the risk of lichen sclerosus progressing to cancer.

19. Participation of patients with cervical cancer in clinical trails to determine optimal regimen for chemoradiation is desirable.

Recommendations for health policy and education

1. HPV infection is extremely common and approximately 80% of sexually active women in the UK will be infected with HPV at some point before the age of 30 years.

2. Although HPV infection is required for the development of cervical cancer, fewer than 10% of those with persisting infection would develop cervical cancer even if they were never treated.

3. Progression to invasive cancer is extremely rare within ten years of HPV infection and in most cases could be prevented by treatment of early precancerous stages.

4. The presence of oncogenic high risk HPV DNA is, at present, the best molecular

marker for assessing the risk of cervical neoplasia.

5. Cell-cycle control proteins show significant promise as markers of oncogenic HPV infection.

6. Women need clear and up-to-date information about the significance of HPV. In association with this Study Group, patient information sheets should be designed and made available.

7. National cytology societies should seek convergence for the descriptions and terms adopted within current cytological terminologies.

8. Subject to cost considerations, liquid-based cytology should be implemented as the routine screening test because it provides a better sample for cytology assessment, thereby reducing the rate of unsatisfactory smears, and also because it provides a common platform to which other new technologies can be added.

9. Different collection devices and methods are required for liquid-based cytology systems. Training of all smear takers is important in the optimal use of sampling devices in order to obtain samples of appropriate quality for cervical screening.

10. Numerous historical studies describe something of the natural history of lower genital tract precancers. It is no longer ethical to postpone any treatment indefinitely, so studies of the natural history are no longer possible.

11. VIA and opticoelectrical devices may have an advantage of almost instant clinical diagnosis.

12. It appears that VIA/direct visual inspection may contribute to cervical cancer screening but false negatives will mean missed diagnosis and false positives will lead to either over-treatment or the need for further triage.

13. Early results in respect of one of the opticoelectrical devices shows results comparable with cytology, i.e. 70% sensitivity in detection of high-grade cervical disease. When combined with cytology, the sensitivity is in excess of 90%.

14. All individuals undertaking colposcopy should have completed or be undertaking the British Society for Colposcopy and Cervical Pathology/RCOG certification for colposcopy.

15. Colposcopic index usage improves the diagnostic accuracy. There may be the potential to include other parameters such as HPV test results (if known) in these indices.

16. Colposcopists should understand why acetowhite epithelium does not always represent cervical neoplasia.

17. Low-grade lesions cannot be identified on cytology alone. Cytology, colposcopy and histology of targeted biopsies all have limitations and should be considered together in managing low grade lesions.

18. Conservative management avoids over treatment and 60–70% of low-grade intraepithelial lesions will regress spontaneously within 10–23 months.

19. The psychological impact of cervical disease is significant and is not related to the degree of abnormality.

20. Because of the difficulties in interpreting cervical glandular pathology, referral for review by a gynaecological cancer centre pathologist is recommended.

21. Vulval Paget's disease is usually of cutaneous origin but may be a manifestation of urothelial or anorectal neoplasia. Histopathological study and clinical assessment can distinguish these.

22. VIN has a significant invasive potential.

23. A VIN lesion may be associated with invasive squamous cell carcinoma. Biopsy and histopathological evaluation of representative lesions is required for diagnosis and evaluation of possible invasion.

24. Invasive vulval carcinoma requires management by clinicians skilled and experienced in the management of such cases. For proper clinical and pathological staging it is necessary to measure tumour diameter, thickness, depth of invasion and status of the inguinofemoral lymph nodes. The term 'microinvasion' is not recommended in referring to superficially invasive vulval carcinomas. International Federation of Obstetrics and Gynaecology (FIGO) staging is recommended in all cases.

25. The contribution of the gynaecologist to managing vulval disease must be encouraged by providing further educational meetings.

26. Delays in the management of vulval cancer still occur because of patient delay and clinician misdiagnosis of suspicious vulval lesions.

27. The term AIN is preferred to Bowen's disease.

Index